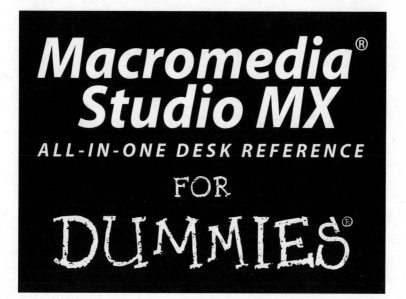

Macromedia® Studio MX
ALL-IN-ONE DESK REFERENCE
FOR
DUMMIES®

by Damon Dean, Andy Cowitt, Ellen Finkelstein, Doug Sahlin, and Camille McCue

WILEY

Wiley Publishing, Inc.

Macromedia® Studio MX All-in-One Desk Reference For Dummies®

Published by
Wiley Publishing, Inc.
909 Third Avenue
New York, NY 10022
www.wiley.com

Copyright © 2003 by Wiley Publishing, Inc., Indianapolis, Indiana

Published by Wiley Publishing, Inc., Indianapolis, Indiana

Published simultaneously in Canada

For general information on our other products and services or to obtain technical support, please contact our Customer Care Department within the U.S. at 800-762-2974, outside the U.S. at 317-572-3993, or fax 317-572-4002.

Wiley also publishes its books in a variety of electronic formats. Some content that appears in print may not be available in electronic books.

Library of Congress Control Number: 2002114769

ISBN: 0-7645-1799-6

Manufactured in the United States of America

10 9 8 7 6 5 4 3 2 1

1Q/RS/QS/QT/IN

About the Authors

Damon Dean has been working in Internet technologies and development for nearly a decade as an Editor, Producer, and Developer. As a Development Editor for Sybex, Damon was responsible for developing both the multimedia and computer game book lines. After developing those properties into profitable units, he moved on to Postlinear Entertainment, where he produced and designed online multiplayer computer games for publishers such as Sega and MGM. Three years later, Damon took his software development skills and moved into Web development. As a founding member of 415 Productions, Damon worked with several large companies, including Credit Suisse, Robert Mondavi, HP, and BART. His application design and development resume includes architecting and building Content Management Systems, Extranets, corporate Intranets, and enterprise CRMs. After four years at 415, Damon moved on in the summer of 2001 to be the Internet Services Director at a private foundation in Oakland, CA.

Damon has written several books dating back to 1996. His first book, *A Pocket Tour of Multimedia on the Internet* (Sybex), was eventually translated into five languages. In 1997, Damon began a relationship with Wiley Publishing (formerly IDG Books) and has written several books for them, including *Web Channel Development For Dummies, FrontPage 2000 For Dummies Quick Reference, Act! 2000 For Dummies Quick Reference* (coauthor), and most recently, *Cascading Style Sheets For Dummies*.

Andy Cowitt is a Senior Integrator for 415, Inc., a Web development firm in San Francisco. Having been at 415 since the company started, Andy has worked on Web sites and multimedia applications for Apple, Oracle, Macromedia, the San Francisco Symphony, KQED, and Beaulieu Vineyards, among others. He's been using Macromedia's Web development products since each of them arrived on the scene. In his spare time, Andy has been known to write, sing, and play guitar for his pop band, The Pinecones. He lives in Oakland with illustrator Michael Wertz and their dog, Olive.

Ellen Finkelstein has written numerous best-selling computer books on AutoCAD, PowerPoint, and Flash. She writes articles for several Web sites and is also a content consultant for Web sites and presentations. Her *AutoCAD 2002 Bible* is in its third edition, and her *Macromedia Flash MX For Dummies* is in its second edition. She writes at home so that she can take the bread out of the oven on time.

Doug Sahlin is an author, graphic designer, and Web site designer living in Central Florida. He is the author of ten books on computer graphics and Web design including *Fireworks 4 For Dummies, Macromedia Flash MX ActionScript For Dummies,* and *Flash MX ActionScript for Designers*. His articles and tutorials have appeared in national publications and have been featured at Web sites devoted to graphics and Web designs. While he's busy writing, Doug's steadfast companion and social secretary, Niki the Cat, occupies a small sliver of sunlight beside the computer. When he's not busy writing, Doug designs Web sites for his clients. When he manages to find a spare moment away from the computer, Doug enjoys photography, music, or curling up with a good book.

Dedications

Damon Dean: For Chris, Gatsby, and China

Andy Cowitt: For Michael Wertz and Olive

Ellen Finkelstein: To MMY, for giving me the knowledge of how to live Enlightenment in daily life.

Doug Sahlin: Dedicated to the memory of George Harrison, the quiet Beatle. All things must pass, but your music lives on forever.

Authors' Acknowledgments

Damon Dean and Andy Cowitt: As with any book, there's a big cast of characters that help to bring it all together. First and foremost, we'd like to acknowledge the patient, thoughtful work of editors: Project Editor Kala Schrager, Copy Editor Jean Rogers, and Technical Editors Jen DeHaan, Danilo Celic, and Ron Rockwell. Additionally, we'd like to thank Acquisitions Editor Steve Hayes, who, for some reason, keeps asking us to come back and write books. I guess we miss our deadlines better than the other guys.

Damon would like to thank Craig Ziegler, Vincent James, Eric Schmidt, and Daniel Hai, all of whom work at the California HealthCare Foundation, for their support while writing this book. In addition, Damon would like to thank his friends and family, who consistently put up with his crankiness as this book got closer and closer to being completed, specifically Chris Jennings, Ryan Clifford, Matthew Allington, and of course, his parents, John Dean and Kathy Dean. He'd also like to thank his grandmother . . . just because.

Andy says thanks to Grace and everyone else at 415, past and present, with special thanks to Bethel Kusz and Damon Dean.

Ellen Finkelstein: I'd like to thank Damon Dean, who took overall responsibility for the book and made it all hang together. Jen DeHaan was an expert technical editor and she added precision and some great ideas to the book. Kala Schrager, the Project Editor, kept us all in line and tracked innumerable chapters and figures. You did a great job, Kala! Personally, I'd like to thank my husband, Evan, and kids, Yeshayah and Eliyah, who helped out around the house and had patience while I was writing.

Doug Sahlin: This project was a great deal of fun thanks to the well-oiled team at Wiley Publishing. Thanks to Acquisitions Editor Steve Hayes for making my participation in this project possible. Kudos to fellow music lover and Joni Mitchell fan, Project Editor Kala Schrager, for making this an enjoyable and relatively pain-free process. Thanks to the lovely and talented literary agent extraordinaire, Margot Maley Hutchinson, a talented woman who has a remarkable way of turning lemons into lemonade. Thanks to my friends in the graphic design community for moral and technical support. As always, thanks to my friends, mentors, and family, especially you, Karen and Ted. And thanks to my dear mother, Inez, a kind woman with a strong guiding hand, the wind in my sails when I was young man. Your kindness, spirit, and wonderful smile live on forever in my memory.

Publisher's Acknowledgments

We're proud of this book; please send us your comments through our online registration form located at www.dummies.com/register/.

Some of the people who helped bring this book to market include the following:

Acquisitions, Editorial, and Media Development

Project Editor: Kala Schrager

Acquisitions Editor: Steve Hayes

Copy Editor: Jean Rogers

Technical Editors: Jen DeHaan, Danilo Celic, Ron Rockwell

Editorial Manager: Kevin Kirschner

Editorial Assistant: Amanda Foxworth

Cartoons: Rich Tennant, www.the5thwave.com

Production

Project Coordinator: Erin Smith

Layout and Graphics: Amanda Carter, Joyce Haughey, Stephanie D. Jumper, Kristin McMullan, Tiffany Muth, Jeremey Unger

Proofreaders: Laura L. Bowman, Tyler Connoley, John Greenough, Andy Hollandbeck, Susan Moritz, Charles Spencer

Indexer: Anne Leach

Publishing and Editorial for Technology Dummies

    Richard Swadley, Vice President and Executive Group Publisher

    Andy Cummings, Vice President and Publisher

    Mary C. Corder, Editorial Director

Publishing for Consumer Dummies

    Diane Graves Steele, Vice President and Publisher

    Joyce Pepple, Acquisitions Director

Composition Services

    Gerry Fahey, Vice President of Production Services

    Debbie Stailey, Director of Composition Services

Contents at a Glance

Table of Contents

Introduction

Macromedia has always been known as a leading-edge design company. Since it introduced Director more than a decade ago, Macromedia has shrewdly developed products (like Fireworks and Dreamweaver) and acquired products (such as Flash and FreeHand) geared toward turning artists into developers. With its acquisition of Allaire, Macromedia added a powerful technology platform to its suite of design-oriented products. Macromedia Studio MX represents the natural evolution and integration of the Macromedia products into a single set of Web development tools. The result? We've worked in Web development since its inception, and we can honestly say that there's never been a product that is as user friendly, powerful, and complete as Macromedia Studio MX.

About This Book

Macromedia Studio MX All-in-One Desk Reference For Dummies (we know, it's a mouthful) is designed to be a hands-on, easy-to-understand guide to the features in all the Macromedia Studio MX products. The no-nonsense approach is designed to help you begin to build Web sites by covering the basics in a clear and concise fashion. The way we see it, you've got things to do, and reading a book, even a clever one, takes up valuable time. The faster we can help you do something or answer a question, the better.

How to Use This Book

You can use this book in a few different ways:

✦ **As a reference:** If you already have a Web site and use Macromedia Studio MX, this book can be a handy refresher for that thing you couldn't quite remember how to do. Whether it's exporting graphics to Macromedia Flash MX from FreeHand 10, or the right syntax for a query in ColdFusion MX, use this book to fill in those gaps that we all have . . . especially as you get older.

✦ **To guide you through building a Web site:** Several authors have contributed to the creation of this book. All of us have a wealth of experience in the process of building Web sites. In this book, we've tried to impart as much of our collective knowledge about the processes and pitfalls of building Web sites using these tools as we can.

✦ **To learn about the tools:** In this All-in-One Desk Reference, each mini-book has at most 150 pages to cover a product or topic, which means that we get right to the point and make the topics covered easy to understand. We believe that this approach makes learning these products easier.

Three Presumptuous Assumptions

Before you dive in to the book, we thought we should give you some advance warning of our expectations. We know, you're the audience, so we shouldn't be presuming anything! But, just so you know where we're coming from, here are our three basic assumptions about you, the reader:

✦ **You're in a hurry.** Frankly, if you wanted a more in-depth book, you'd have picked up a regular *For Dummies* book on one or all of these products. Hence the no-nonsense, get it done, and keep on moving approach you're gonna see inside this book.

✦ **You know something about Web development.** This isn't a book where we're going to spend a lot of time talking about HTML and how it works. So you won't find a chapter anywhere in this book entitled "What the Internet Is and How It Works."

✦ **You'll experiment on your own.** The approach here is to give you quick, useful examples of how things work across all these products. In some cases, the examples can be fairly sophisticated. In most cases, though, it's the basics. Our hope is that you'll take those basic examples and build your own, more complex ones on top of that, according to the complexity of your site.

Macintosh versus Windows

Macromedia Studio MX is both a Windows and a Macintosh product. In this book, you see us use the Windows commands, and the figures are all from either showing Windows 2000 or Windows XP. The reason we chose to use the Windows version is because the ColdFusion MX Developer Edition is included on the Windows version, but not the Macintosh version of the product. If you are using Macromedia Studio MX on the Mac, you can still do everything in Book VI if you're using ColdFusion MX at your place of business or if your Internet Service Provider (ISP) supports ColdFusion MX.

In general, you can convert between Windows (PC) and Macintosh key commands by using the following equivalencies:

✦ The Crtl key on a PC is equivalent to the Cmd (⌘) key on a Mac.

✦ The Alt key on a PC is equivalent to the Option key on a Mac.

✦ The Enter key on a PC is equivalent to the Return key on a Mac.

How This Book Is Organized

Like all the All-in-One Desk References, this book's chapters are organized into minibooks. Most of the minibooks revolve around products, but two are geared toward the Web development process. The following sections describe each minibook in more detail.

Book 1: An Introduction to Building Web Sites

Before we jump into the products in the Macromedia Studio MX suite, we want to frame the conversation around how Web sites get built: things to consider, organizing yourself, and so on. This minibook walks you through how to figure out what it is you're really building, and how you should go about preparing to build it.

Book 11: Dreamweaver MX

Dreamweaver MX is the crux of any Web development effort with Macromedia Studio MX, so naturally, this is a good place to start. In this minibook, you get a hands-on look at how you can use Dreamweaver MX to create and manage your Web sites, whether they're more design oriented (with Macromedia Flash MX) or technology driven (with ColdFusion MX).

Book 111: Fireworks MX

Whereas Dreamweaver MX is the tool that helps you manage your Web site, Fireworks MX is designed to spur your creative vision. This minibook shows you how to use the variety of tools in this impressive program to bring the look and feel of your site to life. It also shows you how to use Fireworks MX in conjunction with the other Macromedia Studio MX products (such as Macromedia Flash MX) effectively.

Book 1V: FreeHand 10

This is the minibook for the true illustrators. Whether the final product is a Flash-based or a traditional HTML-based site, FreeHand 10 gives designers the tools they need to create compelling imagery. In this minibook, you find out how to turn your ideas into working graphical art to be used in a variety of Web applications.

Book V: Macromedia Flash MX

Macromedia Flash MX is probably the most exciting of the Macromedia products. Macromedia Flash MX delivers animation, sound, and interactivity to the Web like no other product ever has. If you've ever wanted to find out how to use this tool to add some new zeal to your Web site, then this is the minibook for you!

Book VI: ColdFusion MX

ColdFusion MX is the newest addition to the Macromedia family, and perhaps it's the most important. ColdFusion, left for dead by many in the industry, now appears well poised to lead mainstream Web development into the dynamic content arena. In this minibook, you too can find out just how easy it is to use ColdFusion MX to create dynamic Web sites.

Book VII: Bringing It All Together

In this minibook, we introduce you to a man named Earl, and his online business, Earl's Bowlateria. From start to finish, we follow the development of Earl's Web site by using each of the Macromedia Studio MX products to create and manage this product-focused business site.

Icons Used in This Book

Along the way, when there's something of interest to point out, we toss in one of the icons you see in the left margins. When you see one, slow down for a moment to check it out to see what's up!

If there's a way to make something easier, or a more commonly accepted way of doing something, we tell you about it. This is the icon to look for!

When we really want to reinforce something, we throw in a Remember icon.

Pitfall ahead! That's what this icon is all about. If something could cause trouble, we let you know.

Because we love technology, you have to forgive us for geeking out every now and then. When we do, though, we let you know with this icon.

This icon highlights new features in the Macromedia Studio MX suite of products.

Where to Go from Here

If you've read this far, then you may actually be a candidate for reading this book cover to cover! From here, we suggest you dive right in to whatever section you're most interested in. Remember, all these minibooks are self-contained and don't require you to read the others. So have at it. It's buffet time, and your plate needs a fillin' up!

Macromedia has also released a new version of the Studio MX suite called Macromedia Studio MX Plus. This package includes Macromedia Contribute, which is a new product that allows you to easily update and publish content to existing Web sites even if you don't know HTML. To find out more about Macromedia Contribute, check out Chapter 1 of *Macromedia Contribute For Dummies,* by Janine Warner (Wiley Publishing) by going to www.dummies.com/extras and clicking on the link for Macromedia Studio MX All-in-One Desk Reference For Dummies.

Book I

An Introduction to Building Web Sites

The 5th Wave   By Rich Tennant

"Sometimes I feel behind the times. I asked my 11 year old to build a Web site for my business, and he said he would, only after he finishes the one he's building for his ant farm."

Contents at a Glance

Chapter 1: Why Build a Web Site?

In This Chapter

✔ Exploring the reasons that Web sites get built

✔ Finding your place on the Web

✔ Understanding what drives people to the Web

✔ Investigating common types of Web sites

✔ Getting ready to build a Web site

So you want to build a Web site? Well, congratulations! If you're reading this book, then you've probably already purchased a copy of Macromedia Studio MX, and you're ready to dive right in. Macromedia Studio MX is a fantastic tool that enables you to create a wide array of content and graphics to deploy on a Web site that is dynamic and easy to maintain.

But software isn't all you need in order to create a fantastic site. It also takes creativity, a good eye, a well-thought-out plan, and some serious soul searching about why you want to undertake this endeavor in the first place. This chapter offers some insight into how sites get built, why they are created, and who they are aimed at. So grab your pen and paper and get ready to jot down your own ideas about the great site that you want to build.

Understanding Why People Build Web Sites

In the early days of the Internet, all Web sites generally looked the same and served similar functions. Back then, an average Web site could be described as a big online book with linked pages. In short, in its infancy, the Internet was not all that interesting graphically and was severely lacking in interactive sophistication.

All that has changed. Today's Internet is a dynamic amalgam of text, graphics, interactive tools, commerce, and communication. If you are a part of a business, an association, the government, or an academic institution, chances are a Web site supports some or all of the mission of the group. But not every venture requires a Web site, which naturally leads to the question, "Why built a Web site?" Most organizations and individuals establish a presence on the Internet for one or more of the following reasons:

✦ To sell a product or service directly online, as shown in Figure 1-1

✦ To provide information or tools

✦ To provide an extension of or support for products and services

✦ To find other organizations or people to work in a particular area of interest

✦ To introduce and promote an organization and its mission

✦ To remain competitive with other organizations that are already on the Internet

✦ To promote community development by bringing groups of people together around ideas, people, or causes, either online or in person

✦ To share artwork, writing, or photographs

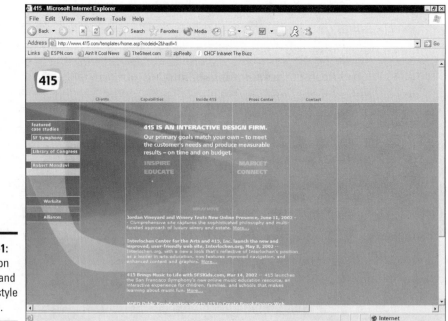

Figure 1-1:
A common product and service style Web site.

Finding Your Place on the Web

Before you begin to think about the kind of site you're going to build (either for yourself or for your organization), you should consider each of the following questions carefully. Doing so can help you target your site to an appropriate audience and prepare yourself for the work ahead.

✦ **Consider your content:**

- What is the content going to be on your site? Is it unique?

- How often will you be updating this content?

- Are there any other sites that already do what you want to do? If so, how will you differentiate your site?

Consider the early explosion of sites during the dot-com boom. At one point, more than five pet sites were all trying to hock their wares to users. Only one survived, and that was because it was a traditional retailer first. Market saturation is a sure way to spell doom for your venture, so be sure to check out the competition first!

✦ **Select a format and interface:**

- What are the variety of formats that your content will be delivered in?

- What are the technical requirements needed to view your content? Will users need a video or audio player or plug-in? For example, Macromedia Flash MX requires a plug-in to show animation.

✦ **Know your audience:**

- What audience or audiences are you trying to reach with this content?

- Do they need or want it?

- Is there any other place they can get this content already?

- What are the demographics and technical capabilities of this audience?

- If your site has more than one audience, are there differences between them and do they need the content delivered differently? If so, you will want to take advantage of ColdFusion MX's dynamic scripting language to deliver different content to different audiences.

✦ **Manage your workload:**

- How much time and effort are you willing to give in order to support this site?

- Are other people working on the site with you?

- Who's going to create the graphical design for the site? Of course, if it's you, you've got powerful tools at your disposal with Macromedia Studio MX.

- Are there any deadlines you need to keep in mind when developing your site?

These questions have no right or wrong answers. Instead, they're designed to help you formulate an idea of where you're going when you're building a site. Frankly, if you're building a personal site, then these questions are moot to some degree because you can build whatever you want and it may not matter whether someone else can read it or see it. Of course, if you're thinking about selling your new products on the Web, then these questions can be critical to your overall business success, not just your Web site's success. For example, if you find that a number of other sites have similar products or a similar focus to what you had in mind for your site, you may consider not building a site at all or changing the focus of the products you are selling.

What Drives People to the Web

What kinds of services, you may be wondering, are people looking for on the Internet? Six years ago, the Internet was largely a research medium, meaning that people would hit the Internet to try to find information about something fairly academic or obscure. This is not surprising, given that universities were the first groups to start putting their content online.

Today, the number of reasons people head to the Internet has grown dramatically, and includes the following:

- ✦ To research, compare, and purchase products
- ✦ To find and interact with other people (business colleagues, friends, romantic interests)
- ✦ To get daily news and information requirements delivered in real time
- ✦ To search for and find information about any topic or organization of interest
- ✦ To deliver and promote their own messages and products to others on the Web
- ✦ To watch or listen to events, online and otherwise, delivered in a variety of audio and video formats
- ✦ To educate themselves via online classes and enrollment in universities
- ✦ To play games and entertain themselves
- ✦ To complete all sorts of personal and professional tasks that can now be done securely online, such online banking, personal finance, investing, tax submission, travel, donating, and procurement

These items run the gamut of professional and personal, and they cross demographic lines. What is common among most online users, though, is that they begin their online usage with a focused purpose, and that focus then bleeds over into surfing for things that interest them throughout the Web.

Choosing the Right Type of Web Site

For all its diversity in content, the Internet really doesn't have that many different types of Web sites. Why do so many Web sites look alike? The main reason is that people want their sites to be easy to use, free (or close to it), and similar to other sites they've seen or experienced. This has resulted in the emergence of some standard types of Web sites. A number of components for these sites can be found in ColdFusion MX as well. Where applicable, we've noted it in the list below. The most common types of sites include:

✦ **The Product Site:** The most common type of site. Generally, the site offers some basic information about a company, its products, staff members, perhaps a product demo, and a way to contact the organization to get more information. An example of this kind of site would be www.symantec.com.

✦ **The Commerce Site:** A storefront on the Internet. Whether it's a single company that carries just their products or a retailer that sells a wide array of products, these sites are geared towards purchasing products and offering accessories to complement those products. An example of this kind of site would be www.macys.com. ColdFusion MX offers tools that can help you to easily add these kinds of functions to your site.

✦ **The Portal Site:** A site that aggregates content from a wide variety of sources. Portal sites tend to be rich in content and links but short on graphics. The idea is to provide users with a launching pad to other destinations on the Internet, though in recent years, many of these portals are adding features to try to keep their users on their site. An example of this kind of site is www.yahoo.com. ColdFusion MX includes robust search capabilities that enable you to have more content-rich sites that are easily indexed and searched.

✦ **The News Site:** A site that, in general, mirrors an offline counterpart, such as ABC News. These sites provide a lot of the same information as their offline counterparts through the use of text, video, audio, and graphics, and also provide services geared towards the online audience, such as chat sessions, newsletters, and personalized content. An example of this kind of site would be www.cnn.com. ColdFusion MX includes tools for adding chat to your site as well.

✦ **The Application Site:** A type of site that offers perhaps the greatest diversity of all the sites. Application sites are geared towards a specific purpose, such as banking, investing, automobile purchasing, travel planning, photo galleries, event planning, or online greetings. Some of the commonalities among these sites include user accounts, password protection, and the widespread use of e-mail campaigns to try to keep users coming back. Examples of this kind of site include `www.egreetings.com`, `www.imotors.com`, and `www.bankofamerica.com`.

✦ **The Personal Site:** Personal sites also offer a great deal of variety in their design and function. Personal sites usually include some of the designer's work, opinions, and rants; links to other sites; and pictures. An example of this kind of site would be `www.loungeboy.com`.

Macromedia Studio MX: Your Ally in Development

After you've answered a number of the questions above, you may be wondering how you're going to build your grand Web site. Well, don't fret. With Macromedia Studio MX, you have the most complete, user-friendly, and popular development suite on the market. Even though professionals use these products all the time, Macromedia Studio MX is truly designed for the first-time Web developer. With an array of tutorials, wizards, and interfaces that keep you as distant from the code as you want to be, Macromedia Studio MX makes the Herculean task of building powerful Web applications seem like just another project.

The goal with Macromedia Studio MX is to help you, the developer, build compelling and powerful Web sites in the shortest amount of time, while simultaneously helping you alleviate cost and resource issues common to Web development. Macromedia Studio MX includes several tools to help make this happen:

✦ **Dreamweaver MX:** The premier tool for easily building Web pages. In this latest version, it has been combined with ColdFusion to make developing dynamic Web applications much easier.

✦ **Fireworks MX:** A leading tool for the graphical development of a site. Fireworks MX helps you design the look and feel of your site, as well as prepare the graphics for inclusion in an HTML or CFML file.

✦ **Macromedia Flash MX:** The world's most popular tool for adding animation and sound to Web sites. Macromedia Flash MX will truly change the way any site works.

   ✦ **FreeHand 10:** The Web developer's best friend for creating illustrations
      for Fireworks MX and Macromedia Flash MX.

   ✦ **ColdFusion MX:** Give yourself the powerful tools to add databases,
      e-mail servers, and other dynamic elements to your site. ColdFusion MX
      allows you to take control of one of the most powerful — but also easy
      to learn — scripting languages for the development of compelling Web
      applications.

Before You Start: Things to Know

Hopefully, all this information hasn't scared you into dropping this book and
deciding to open a lemonade stand instead. This last section is just a quick
check of some things you should be aware of before you jump into this
venture called Web development:

   ✦ **Plan ahead.** Building a Web site always takes longer than you think, so
      give yourself more time than you originally planned for!

   ✦ **Get organized.** Remember to categorize your content and use those
      categories as the initial architecture for your site when you're doing the
      user interface design.

   ✦ **Always do the user interface design before the graphics design.** The
      user interface design specifies how your site will work, while the graphical
      design is the look and feel. If you do the graphics before the architecture is
      done, you'll likely end up redoing a lot of your design after you've figured
      out how your site is going to work.

   ✦ **Not all browsers are the same.** Internet Explorer and Netscape
      Navigator are the two most common browsers, and in recent versions,
      they've adopted the same standards. But there are still quirky differ-
      ences between the two browsers, and you have to check your work on
      both browsers.

   ✦ **Not all platforms are the same.** If only they were! Explorer and Navigator
      work slightly differently on the Mac, in Windows, and in Unix. If you're
      developing on the PC, find a friend or a graphic designer with a Mac and
      check your work on her system as well. Dreamweaver MX also includes
      some tools to help you verify whether your site will work the way you
      hope it does on a variety of platforms.

   ✦ **It's okay to steal.** That one may sound weird. But if you see something
      you like on a site — rollovers are a good example — it's okay to view the
      source code and use it in your site, as long as you give credit where
      credit is due. If the code is copyrighted, be sure you can reuse it before
      plopping it in your site.

✦ **Lots of stuff can be had for free.** The Web is filled with geeks like us who have made all sorts of crazy applications, like chat engines, bulletin boards, and even wholesale applications. A lot of them can be had for free or something close to it. This is where sites like www.google.com and www.download.com can be your friend.

✦ **Old content equals a dead site.** You have to be prepared to update your site on a semi-regular basis. When content is stale, people will notice, and they will stop coming.

✦ **If you build it, tell someone.** It's one thing to build a site. Site-search spiders will eventually find you, but if you really want to be seen, then you really need to promote yourself. When you're done building, remember, you're not done promoting.

✦ **Don't be afraid to ask.** Building sites is fun, or at least it's supposed to be. But it can be especially frustrating if you can't figure out how to do something. Well, here's a secret: Developers like to talk about what they do. So if you're stuck, try finding a user group or searching the Web for an answer to your question. Someone may have come across the problem before, and if they haven't, then there are plenty of resources for asking. Macromedia is also very good about supporting these kinds of groups, so you can always check out its Web site at www.macromedia.com for listings of developer resources.

Chapter 2: Developing Web Content

*O*ne of the things you find out when you do Web development for a living is that the Internet is all about repetition. No matter how many sites you build, the discussion always begins with "So, what's the content gonna be for this site?" Usually, the response is something vaguely resembling a blank stare. Companies, organizations, and individuals usually come to the conclusion that they need a Web site long before they've thought about what should be on that site.

Some basic rules of content development are common to all Web sites. This chapter gives you the basics to consider as you're doing perhaps the most important part of building your Web site: contemplating, designing, and creating your content.

Developing Content: A Four-Step Process

Developing your content strategy can be the best part of building a Web site because it's the one time you can sit around a table with your fellow colleagues (or your trusty pet, if you're building a personal site) and truly be creative about the kinds of things you want on your Web site. When you're in the throes of development, you may find yourself uttering: "Remember when we thought this was a good idea!"

Content development follows a fairly structured course in the modern world of Web design. It usually includes the following four basic steps:

1. Brainstorm the types of information that you want to include on your Web site.

2. Put that information into categories that make sense for the type of Web site you're building and the way you want users to interact with the site.

3. Gather and create the content for the site.

4. Prepare your content for the Web.

A great temptation is to just start building a site the moment something cool comes along, be it an idea, a graphic, or even words. The reason to do all this planning before even cracking any HTML code in Dreamweaver MX or generating any graphics in Fireworks MX is to make sure that you don't get too far down the path of development and suddenly find yourself backed into a corner, trying to put content where it doesn't really belong.

Choosing and Organizing Content

You may be wondering just what, exactly, is considered content. Here's a little content quiz consisting of three simple yes or no questions:

1. Is a mailing list sign-up form, as shown in Figure 2-1, considered content?

2. Is a downloadable file considered content?

3. Is a picture of a product, or even of you, considered content?

The answer to all these questions is yes. In practical terms, every single thing you put on a Web site is considered content.

Figure 2-1:
A mailing list sign-up form.

Classifying common types of Web content

The fact that everything is content doesn't really help you get your site organized. Thankfully, while anything can be content, things tend to show up on Web sites in some pretty common formats.

As you begin to think about what you want to put on your Web site, you should also consider the different forms that you want that content to take. To give you a kick-start, Table 2-1 includes the most common forms of content and the data that makes up that content.

Table 2-1	Common Types of Web Site Content
Content Type	*Data Commonly Associated with This Type of Content*
Graphics	GIF and JPEG files
Documents	Word, Excel, PowerPoint, and Adobe Acrobat (PDF) files
Text	HTML text
Audio	WAV, AIFF, MP3, Real Audio, and Windows Media files
Video	QuickTime, Real Video, Windows Video
Plug-Ins	Flash animations, QuickTime VR, IPIX, and other tools that allow users to view video and graphic content beyond what basic HTML can support
Forms	Elements within HTML designed to either submit information or used to return targeted content back to a user's browser

Categorizing your content

In addition to organizing your content by its file type, assigning meaningful categories to your content makes developing your site infinitely easier. You can categorize your content in any way that makes logical sense for the site you're building, and in nearly every case, you can categorize your content more than one way, so don't worry about limiting yourself to just one method.

The following list includes some of the most common ways to categorize content:

✦ **Organizing by concept:** This varies from site to site, but this method entails organizing your site by the major thematic elements, as defined by the content that you're going to be putting up. An example of this is organizing a company site around the various products it offers.

✦ **Classifying by function:** *Functions* are things you can do on a site, and functions can serve as organizing principles for your site. For example, the content of a financial services site may be categorized around a series of investing and banking tools. That financial services company may also choose to categorize its content both by the tools on the site (functions) *and* by the various products it offers (concepts), which demonstrates that there's more than one way to slice content.

✦ **Categorizing by logical steps:** Some sites dispense with the notion of concepts or functions altogether and focus on tasks that get something done. Online auto sites, for example, like to walk visitors through a series of steps to find the car they're looking for, offering related content at appropriate points along the way.

✦ **Sorting by topics or keywords:** Sites with a diverse array of content tend to offer users a couple of ways of getting at information. Keywords (topics) are a common way to associate content with more than one area of interest. For example, a music store may organize its site by concepts such as instruments, sheet music, and accessories, *and* sort the content by topics such as pianos, drums, guitars, amplifiers, and flutes, to name just a few.

✦ **Arranging hierarchically:** This method of categorization assumes that some content elements are more important than others, which is reflected in how the content is displayed on the site. Hierarchy is often used in conjunction with another categorization scheme. To go back to the banking example for a moment, imagine that you've got your portfolio online. Usually, your portfolio is organized by concept or function, as well as by hierarchy. The portfolio is given more prominence than the other products the bank sells, because the folks at the bank know that the content in the portfolio is more important to the user.

✦ **Grouping by type:** As noted in the previous section, content type is the other major way to categorize content. On a number of media sites, such as the ABC News site (www.abcnews.com), you can easily find all the video content in a single location, in addition to being able to get your news by feature area.

Creating Content for the Web

If you've got the right tools, creating content for the Web is a breeze. And because you've got a copy of Macromedia Studio MX, you've already got a host of tools that can help you create all sorts of content for your site. To recap, here is a list of some of the content you can create with Macromedia Studio MX:

✦ **Fireworks MX:** Create quality photo-realistic graphics that can be used in Dreamweaver MX or Macromedia Flash MX.

✦ **Dreamweaver MX:** Create pages from basic HTML to complete database driven applications, as well as use the publishing tools to help you maintain your site.

✦ **FreeHand 10:** Make illustrations that can be used to create the look and feel of your Web site or your Flash movie.

✦ **Macromedia Flash MX:** Create animations that bring your site to life.

✦ **ColdFusion MX:** Create dynamic, database-driven applications.

In addition to these tools, you'll find that other non-Macromedia software tools can be essential to generating and managing content (this is about all you're going to hear from us on these tools in this book):

✦ **Microsoft Word:** Word is the most common word processor in the world for a reason. When you're creating text for Web sites, there's still no better tool out there than Word for quickly and easily creating text.

✦ **Adobe Acrobat:** The Acrobat PDF format has become the downloadable document format of choice in the Web world. If you're going to develop large, text-heavy documents for the Web, then investing in the full version of Adobe Acrobat is worth the money. PDF files ensure that your documents will always have the same look and feel, regardless of what browser or platform users may have. Offering PDF files for download will also make your users happy because they only need to download the free Adobe Acrobat Reader to read your PDF documents.

✦ **Microsoft Excel:** As a spreadsheet, Excel can serve two very useful purposes. It can help you manage your content by providing you with a nice tool to manage your categorized data. With Excel, you can also save data in CSV format, which is the most common data format for importing into a database. So, for example, if you are providing your users with a list of the names and addresses of your association, then you might consider providing the information in CSV format, so that users can import those addresses into their own address book.

✦ **Microsoft Access (or equivalent):** Access is a database. If you create an e-commerce site, you'll find that your product data is best kept in a database, rather than in plain text. Access is the most commonly available database (though not necessarily the most robust), and is easily compatible with ColdFusion MX.

Prepping Content for the Web

When preparing your content for delivery to the Web, here are a few handy tips to keep in mind:

✦ **Have a plan:** If you haven't gone through the process of content development outlined previously in this chapter, your content is likely to be disorganized. Be sure you have an overview of your content, as well as an outline that shows all the various formats that your content will take and how you're choosing to categorize it.

✦ **Choose the right format:** Take a long hard look at your content. Are you using the right format for certain types of content? Are your graphics in acceptable formats, such as GIF and JPEG? Are your downloadable items in PDF format? Be sure you're using the commonly accepted Web file formats, and if you're not, be sure to create some text to explain why you're not using standard formats.

✦ **Be consistent:** The Web relies on developers being at least somewhat consistent. So if you have a product data sheet available in PDF format, make sure that your other documents are in PDF format. Similarly, try to stick to the same audio and video formats. That way, when people get to your site, they'll know what to expect, and they're not likely to get frustrated.

✦ **Make your content more easily digestible:** One last thing to keep in mind: Just because you've written the Great American Novel and you want to put it on the Web doesn't mean that you should just put the whole thing up in one huge piece. The Web is made to deliver content in small chunks, and the best sites give viewers the facts first, and then let people delve deeper at their leisure. Remember, people are busy, and they may just need the quick facts. For you as the developer, this means creating highlights, summaries, thumbnails, or charts that provide an introduction or an overview to your core content.

Chapter 3: Choosing the Right Tools for the Job

In This Chapter

✔ Developing a Web site with Dreamweaver MX

✔ Using Fireworks MX for design

✔ Creating illustrations with FreeHand 10

✔ Animating with Macromedia Flash MX

✔ Using ColdFusion MX to add dynamic content

You've probably heard that old saying, "A craftsman never blames his tools." Nowhere is that saying more appropriate than with Macromedia Studio MX. With five incredibly powerful tools at your fingertips, you can create compelling and dynamic sites in no time flat.

Of course, even though a craftsman never blames his (or her) tools, a craftsman does need to know which tools to use for a given job, and sometimes, in the world of Web development, that's not always so clear. This chapter is designed to clarify this issue by highlighting the do's and don'ts of each of the Macromedia Studio MX products.

If you're already familiar with the products in Macromedia Studio MX, then just take a gander at the following section and then head right to Book I, Chapter 4.

Before You Begin: Where Not to Use Macromedia Studio MX

Although you certainly can use Macromedia Studio MX for every bit of your site development, some things are better done outside the tool suite:

+ **Content development and management:** This is the process of developing the written content for the site, as well as managing the collection and status of each piece of content on the site. Products like Microsoft Word, WordPerfect, Microsoft Excel, and Microsoft Access are more appropriate tools for this job.

+ **Project management:** This is the process of managing the steps of the project from start to finish, as well as where and how to allocate resources to the project. You may want to use Macromedia Sitespring, Microsoft Project, or Microsoft Excel to manage your project.

Using Dreamweaver MX for Web Development

No matter how graphic intensive or dynamic you want your site to be, you'll always come back to the fact that you have to build your Web site with something. In Macromedia Studio MX, Dreamweaver MX is the Web development workhorse. You can use Dreamweaver MX, shown in Figure 3-1, for a host of practical Web development tasks:

+ Create and edit HTML or ColdFusion Markup Language code.

+ Create "Sites" — a confusing Dreamweaver MX term that means a place either locally on your computer or on a remote server where you keep all the content for your Web site. When your content is in a Dreamweaver Site, you can set up page templates and run various reports on your site content.

+ Upload all your Web pages from your local computer to a Web server on the Internet that houses your site.

+ Set up connections between your Web site and a database to make the site dynamic.

+ Preview your work using Macromedia's Preview in Browser tools before you publish it on the Web.

+ Review code for errors and badly formed code.

The best way to think of Dreamweaver MX is as the glue that binds your site together. Other Macromedia products like Macromedia Flash MX and Fireworks MX help to add flair and pizzazz to your site, but to actually include the files that these applications produce in your site requires the HTML and publishing tools that only Dreamweaver MX offers.

Ultimately, most of your content ends up in an HTML or CFM (ColdFusion MX) page, so if you don't have Microsoft Word or WordPerfect, Dreamweaver MX can also be used to create content as you would in a word processing program.

Figure 3-1:
Dream-
weaver MX
is used for
many Web
development
tasks.

Designing with Fireworks MX

Fireworks MX is easily the most versatile of all the tools in Macromedia
Studio MX. As shown in Figure 3-2, Fireworks MX is primarily geared
towards creating the graphical design of your site. With Fireworks MX, you
can accomplish the following tasks:

✦ Create graphical elements that make up the look and feel of your site by
using the Fireworks MX text and editing tools.

✦ Apply filters that create photo-quality effects for the imagery in your site.

✦ Manipulate text to be used in graphical elements.

✦ Use layers to manage the depth and positioning of elements on the
screen during your graphics development.

✦ Work with slices and the Web layer to cut up your designs in preparation for integration into HTML using Dreamweaver MX.

✦ Use tools to optimize the size and color of images on your site.

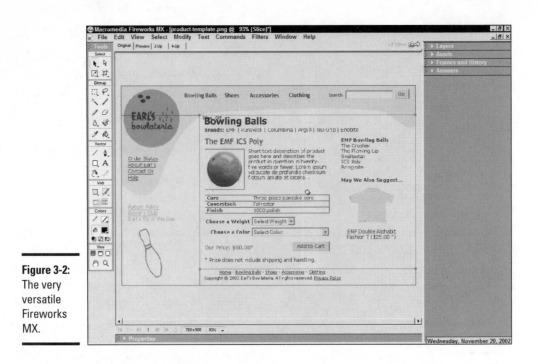

Figure 3-2:
The very versatile Fireworks MX.

These are just the core elements of Fireworks MX. In addition to being a powerful graphics development tool, Fireworks MX also incorporates elements of FreeHand 10, Dreamweaver MX, and even Macromedia Flash MX, providing you with additional functionality, such as the following:

✦ Creating vector images that can be used in Macromedia Flash MX animations.

✦ Creating basic animations and publishing your layered images as a Flash movie.

✦ Creating image rollovers that are common to most sites nowadays using the scripting language JavaScript.

✦ Generating the HTML to accompany your sliced images. Within the Web layer in Fireworks MX, you can divide an image into multiple pieces, each of which is called a *slice*. (See Book III, Chapter 6 for more information about slices.)

All told, you can use Fireworks MX for a variety of development tasks.

Illustrating with FreeHand 10

At first glance, with the flexibility of Fireworks MX, you may think that FreeHand 10 is the odd man out in Macromedia Studio MX. Not true! Although many of the tools are identical to those you find in Fireworks MX, FreeHand 10 offers illustrators and Macromedia Flash MX developers a greater degree of control and integration in their work.

Some of things that distinguish FreeHand 10, which is shown in Figure 3-3, from Fireworks MX include the following:

✦ A wider array of line art creation and manipulation tools

✦ Greater control of styles

✦ Better color management tools

✦ Increased integration with Macromedia Flash MX

✦ More import and export options

Figure 3-3:
FreeHand 10
in action.

These distinctions may seem a bit subtle, and to some degree, they are. However, when you get down to the nuts and bolts of building Macromedia Flash MX animations, for example, you'll see that FreeHand 10 provides nearly seamless integration with the product, offering you a more diverse palette for developing compelling animations.

Creating Animation with Macromedia Flash MX

After you've got a few Web sites under your belt, you may find that HTML and graphics get boring after a fashion. Sure, they're necessary, but soon you'll begin to wonder what else you can do to add some pop to your sites. That's where Macromedia Flash MX comes in. Macromedia Flash MX enables you to add animation, sound, and interactivity to your site.

This is accomplished through the use of the downloadable Flash plug-in that users can automatically get when they visit your site. Macromedia Flash MX, shown in Figure 3-4, can radically change the way in which your site works. Macromedia Flash MX allows you to create a more compelling user experience. Gone are the boundaries created by HTML and limited graphics. Although you still need help from the other Macromedia Studio MX products, you can think of Macromedia Flash MX as an entirely new development platform for building your site.

Figure 3-4:
Macromedia
Flash MX
changes the
way you
think about
a site.

Creating a Dynamic Site with ColdFusion MX

Static HTML only gets you so far with Web development. After you've built that first-generation site, you may soon find that your Web site development needs have grown and you require more out of your development tools. What do we mean by more? Well, imagine you want to do any of the following:

+ Customize the content of a site based on how a visitor got there.

+ Personalize the site by letting users choose their own content.

+ Open a store on the Internet with a host of product information contained in databases.

+ Create interactivity in your site through the use of forms.

All these items go beyond what Dreamweaver MX or Macromedia Flash MX can provide as development tools. After you hit this proverbial Web development wall, it's time to turn to ColdFusion MX, which provides the following tools:

+ A custom scripting language that enables you to query databases, create and test variables, and extend the functionality of your site through the use of specific ColdFusion tags and functions. For more information about ColdFusion MX's scripting language, be sure to check out Book VI.

+ An application server (a program on a computer that serves a specific function) that reads the custom scripting language and turns it into HTML that people can see in their browser.

+ An administrative component that enables you to configure all the different elements of your site, such as databases, virtual directories, log files that capture site tracking information, and e-mail features.

Chapter 4: Best Practices for Web Development

In This Chapter

✔ **Understanding the basic steps of development**

✔ **Setting your site requirements**

✔ **Ensuring a smooth Web site build**

✔ **Testing your site**

✔ **Involving the right people at the right time**

*T*he late-night, caffeine-fueled, build-it-as-you-go model of Web development was fine when the industry was just getting started. However, Web development today is a more standard practice and is subject to repeatable processes, just like other areas of software development. The result of the growing maturity in the industry is a set of "best practices" for Web development. Think of a *best practice* as an industry-accepted, commonly agreed upon way of performing a task or set of tasks.

Certainly, you can still build a Web site in more than one way. Best practices are designed just to give you some guidance in the following areas:

✦ Ensuring that the site is easy to build and easier to maintain

✦ Helping you avoid doing unnecessary work on a site

✦ Confirming that your Web site is built according to industry standards

✦ Making certain that you have the right people involved in the site development at the right time

Each of the sections of this chapter deals with a common aspect of Web development and provides you with the key points for making that part of the development run smoothly.

You should be aware that these tips and suggestions are not absolutes. Every site is a bit different, but you can use this chapter as a checklist guide for the kinds of things you *can* do. Your site may require more or less attention depending on your requirements.

Additionally, this chapter is limited to the general best practices for developing sites. Each of chapters within Book II through Book VI covers the best way to perform operations with each of the individual Macromedia Studio MX products.

Following the Best Path of Development

The early days of Web sites saw a wide variety of methods and approaches to development, but today most common types of Web sites follow an accepted path from start to finish. Building a Web site takes six basic steps. The details within each step can be specific to the type of site you're building — product site, e-commerce site, and so on — but the basic steps remain the same.

Step one: Develop a site concept

Before you can build a site, you've got to have a mission and purpose for it. This process involves asking yourself and your colleagues a number of questions about who you're trying to reach and why. Book I, Chapter 1 includes more information on this process.

Step two: Define your requirements

After you've decided what your site is all about, you need to come up with some basic requirements for the site. *Requirements* are the minimum number of things that the site must conform to. These requirements break out along the following categories:

✦ **Feature requirements:** The basic set of site features and what those features need to accomplish.

✦ **Technical requirements:** The minimum technical specifications for the site. Table 4-1 includes the common technical requirements for Web sites.

✦ **Design requirements:** The aesthetic and accessibility requirements for the site. Design requirements may include things like using the proper corporate colors, and accessibility requirements generally include things like adding a text-only version of a site so that it can be read by text readers.

Table 4-1	Common Technical Requirements for Web Sites
Requirement	*Best Practice Option*
Screen resolution	800 x 600 pixels
Minimum browser support	Netscape Navigator 4.7 and Internet Explorer 4.0
Use of Web safe colors	No longer required, as almost all monitors can display 16-bit color

Requirement	Best Practice Option
Minimum connection speed to design site for	56 kilobits per second (Kbps)
File extensions	Should still conform to the standard "dot and three characters" (`.htm`, `.cfm`, `.asp`, `.jsp`) where possible
Style sheets (Yes or No)	Yes
Dynamic HTML (Yes or No)	No, unless the site is designed to work with Internet Explorer only
Database of choice	Microsoft SQL Server

Step three: Generate content

During this step, you work to generate the various types of content that will make up the content of your site. Book I, Chapter 2 covers the details of generating content for Web sites.

Step four: Design the site

This design step covers four different aspects of design, and in general, they follow this sequence:

1. **Complete the feature design.**

   In the second step of Web site development, you set out the require-ments for features on the site. Here, you get down to the nitty-gritty and design exactly how those features will work. For example, if you want to collect mailing list information, you need to articulate precisely how the information is captured, what kind of response is sent to a user, and where that information goes.

2. **Work through the user interface design.**

   The user interface design is the way the site works, minus the aesthet-ics. It includes the composition of pages, the structure and look of the content, and it applies the logic of the feature design above.

3. **Consider the graphics design.**

   After the feature and user interface design are complete, your site is ready for the aesthetics. You may want to create graphics for logos, icons, navigation, sidebars, backgrounds, and other site elements.

4. **Complete the technical design of the site.**

   Truth be told, you can do the technical design after you complete the user interface design, but usually it ends up being the last design step. You must design the technical components that enable all the features of the site to be realized.

Step five: Build the site

After you've completed the design step, you're ready to start building the site. This includes generating all the code, supporting databases, generating HTML, and posting content. Building the site can take weeks, and you should keep a number of basic rules of development in mind when building your site. Here are the most critical ones:

✦ **Work internally.** Don't do all your development work on the site for everyone to see. Be sure to work on the site either internally (on your corporate network or your personal machine) or on a different URL than the final address. This way you can make all the mistakes you like and the real world isn't likely to see them.

✦ **Go wide, then deep.** A good strategy is to always build the structure of the site first, including the navigation, and then fill it in with the content within individual sections. Figure 4-1 shows the navigational structure of a typical site.

✦ **Centralize your images.** Centralizing your images makes finding images and generating the proper code that much easier. The norm is to include all images in a folder called images at the root level of your site.

Figure 4-1: The typical inverted L shape of a site's navigation.

Primary and secondary navigation

✦ **Whenever possible, use relative paths.** Using a *relative path* simply means that your links to external files — HTML files, images, PDFs, and so on — are relative to the location of the file you're currently working on. This makes changing links and moving things around in folders that much easier.

✦ **Keep filenames simple.** Always keep your filenames in lowercase letters, and don't include spaces in filenames, folder names, or URLs. This ensures that no matter what type of Web server your site is hosted on — Windows, Macintosh, or Unix — the files can be read by any Web browser.

✦ **Use folders to segment your content.** This provides your site with a structure that makes finding and managing your content and code easier.

✦ **Always comment your code.** Commenting code is a common software development practice. As you're writing your code, you add comments next to major features and functions so that someone else can understand your work if you're not there to explain it to them. If the code is logically laid out with comments, managing it is much easier. Figure 4-2 shows what commented code looks like in Dreamweaver MX.

Figure 4-2:
Always
comment
your code!

✦ **Do everything you can to protect your applications.** Hacking is serious business, and the last thing you want to have happen is for your site to be compromised. Here are just some of the things you can do to ensure that your site is designed with security in mind:

- Always use digital certificates when sending users private information over the Internet. A *digital certificate* is a secure, encrypted digital key that ensures that only your Web browser and the server that issued the key can see the data being transmitted back and forth. You can learn more about certificates at www.verisign.com.

- If you're doing e-commerce, don't use Microsoft Access. Access isn't nearly as secure as Microsoft's SQL Server.

- Never query a database directly for a user's private information such as username, password, or credit card numbers. With SQL, you can use stored procedures to query a database and mask the code from potential hackers. While stored procedures are outside the scope of this book, you can read more about them in Anthony T. Mann's *Microsoft SQL Server 2000 For Dummies,* published by Wiley Publishing, Inc.

- Always try to build your applications in three tiers. A three-tiered application, the concept of which is shown in Figure 4-3, ensures that the business logic for your site is separate from your display code and your database logic. This is both more secure, and it makes changing components of your Web application easier because of the modular nature of a three-tiered application.

  In the three-tiered model, the Web browser can only talk to an intermediary application or object (sometimes called a COM object) and can only pass a finite set of variables to this intermediary. In turn, the intermediary negotiates with the data layer to retrieve only the specified information, which it passes back to the display layer. This ensures that the end user can't directly connect to the data layer.

✦ **Set up a mechanism for sharing files.** When you're working on the same files with more than one person, set up a convention for sharing the files, so as to avoid overwriting each other's work. Dreamweaver MX comes with some source control tools which help in this process, but you shouldn't rely just on the product. You should have an agreed upon procedure for working on the same files.

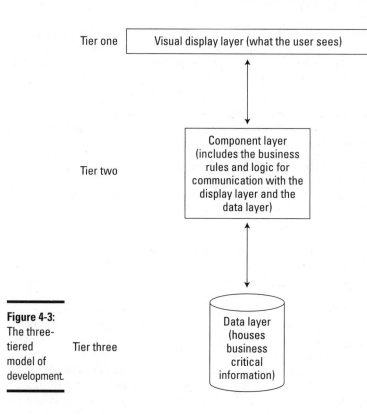

Tier one — Visual display layer (what the user sees)

Tier two — Component layer (includes the business rules and logic for communication with the display layer and the data layer)

Figure 4-3:
The three-tiered model of development.

Tier three — Data layer (houses business critical information)

Step six: Test and deploy your site

Before you can launch your site, you need to test it. Although test plans vary depending upon the sophistication of the site, here are four good things you should do when testing your site:

✦ **Check your site on multiple browsers.** Testing your site on various current and previous versions of browsers ensures that it works for the largest possible number of users. You should also check on different platforms as well (PC and Mac at the least).

You can get old versions of the Netscape browser at `wp.netscape.com/download/archive.html?cp=dowarc` and old versions of Internet Explorer at `www.oldversion.com/msie.shtml`.

✦ **Try your site with different Web connections of varying download speeds.** If you're building your site at work, you may have a very fast Internet connection. Try a 56 Kbps connection to see how well your site loads at that speed. If pages load within a few seconds, then your site is in good shape.

✦ **Test all of your forms and features.** Walk through each form, again preferably on multiple browsers and operating systems, to ensure that all your tools and forms work properly.

✦ **Enlist your friends and colleagues as site testers.** The more people who look at your site, the better. You're probably too close to the site by the time you've finished it anyway, and fresh eyes can see things you can't. Also, other people are likely to give you good feedback on structure and ease-of-use.

After you've finished testing your site, which in generally takes at least a week, you should give yourself at least another week to fix any problems you've found during the testing phase.

When you're ready to roll out your site, a good idea is to do a soft launch first. A *soft launch* is when you launch a site but don't really tell anyone about it. People who already know something about you or may be looking for your site will start to check it out and may provide you with some additional feedback. But you won't be faced with a big barrage of people, and you'll have a chance to troubleshoot anything you may have overlooked in making the jump from working on a site internally and having a site out there live for the real world.

Getting the Right People at the Right Time

If you're building a site on your own, then you are always the right person at the right time. In most cases, however, you're building a site with a group of people. Some of these people are site builders, and others are around to approve content and give general direction. Keeping all the parts moving smoothly can be tricky. The following sections help you get the right people on board at the right time.

Building a team

Just how big is this project you're working on? How much money do you have to spend? When do you need it done? The answers to these three questions let you know just how big of a team you may need to build to complete your site. If you plan to assemble an internal team to build your site, these are the roles that you absolutely need:

✦ **Producer:** Perhaps this is you. The producer manages all the resources of the project, internal and external. This means keeping the master budget and schedule, and providing all the resources with their tasks and deadlines. Largely overlooked, the producer is the conduit that keeps the project moving from start to finish.

✦ **Programmer:** Programmers come in all shapes and sizes. Some can only do HTML, while others are adept at building all sorts of software applications. If you've got a smaller project, you should only need one engineer, but if your project is larger, you should consider having an integrator for lower-level HTML coding and a senior programmer for more complex coding tasks.

✦ **Designers:** Again, if you're building a smaller site, you can probably get away with a designer who does both user interface design and graphical design. Alternatively, as the producer, you're probably also qualified to handle the user interface duties as well as the feature design role. The larger the site, the more you'd want to look at separate specialists for user interface and graphical design.

✦ **Content Specialists:** Generating content is always overlooked in building a team. Whether you have a contract writer or someone internal to your organization who is good at collecting and synthesizing data, it's always a good idea to have someone around dedicated to developing content for the site.

✦ **Quality Assurance:** Someone's gotta test the site, and as we mention previously, you're probably not the ideal person to do it. The best testers are meticulous, accountant-types who like to poke and prod at things and find holes. A lot of times, this function can be contracted out.

✦ **Approvers:** Unless you're building the site for yourself, then you're probably accountable to someone. Those would be your approvers, and yes, they're an essential part of the team, because ultimately, they are the ones who give you the yea or nay on whether your site gets up on the Internet!

If you were to contract out these resources through a single firm, or through a variety of independent contractors, you'd still be looking for each of these skill sets. The method of employment doesn't really matter, though it's worth noting that it's generally cheaper to contract the resources yourself. Firms, on the other hand, offer turn-key solutions that you don't generally get when you build an internal team.

Involving the right people at the right time

Knowing when to get people involved can be tricky. Ideally, you'd want everyone there all the time, but that can get expensive, so you want to get people on board at the right time for the right tasks. Table 4-2 includes many of the key milestones in a Web development project and who you really need to have involved during those parts of the process.

Table 4-2	When to Involve People in the Web Development Process
Key Milestone	*Who's Involved*
Site conceptualization	Everyone
Requirements gathering	Producer, Designers, Programmers, Approvers
Generating Content	Producer, Content Specialists, User Interface Designers, and occasionally Graphics Designers and Programmers
Feature Design	Producer, User Interface Designer, Programmer
User Interface Design	Producer, User Interface Designer
Graphic Design	Producer, Graphic Designer, Programmer, Approvers
Build Phase	Everyone
Test and Deploy	Producer, QA, Programmers, Approvers, and occasionally Designers

Book II

Dreamweaver MX

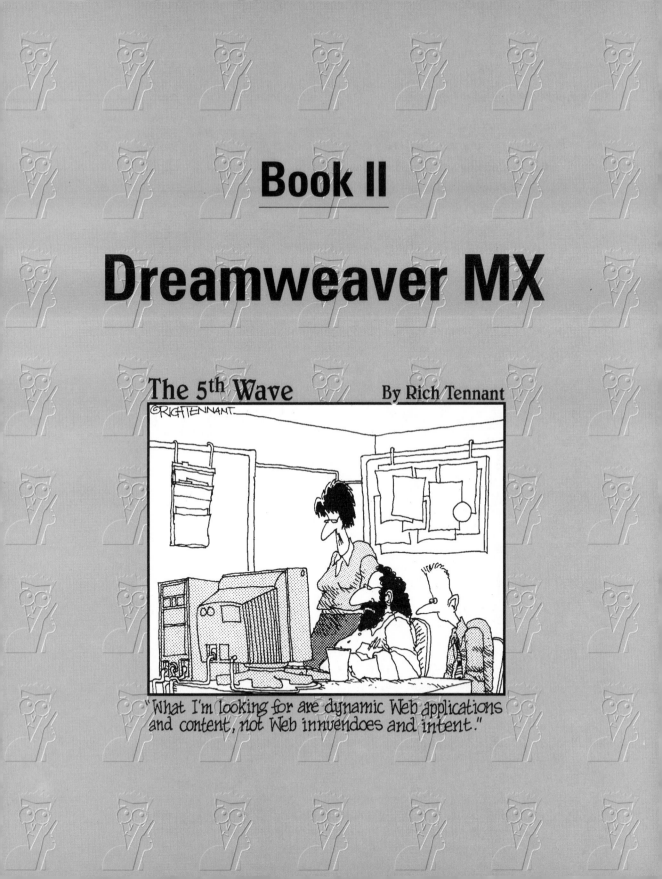

The 5th Wave   By Rich Tennant

"What I'm looking for are dynamic Web applications and content, not Web innuendoes and intent."

Contents at a Glance

Chapter 1: Introduction to Dreamweaver MX

In This Chapter

✔ **Discovering the power of Dreamweaver MX**

✔ **Getting familiar with the Document window**

✔ **Choosing between Standard and Layout views**

✔ **Examining a site with the Site window**

✔ **Exploring toolbar buttons**

✔ **Using panels and property inspectors**

✔ **Finding out how to get help**

*I*f you're looking for a Web design tool that's both easy enough for beginners *and* sophisticated enough for Web design gurus, you've come to the right place. Dreamweaver MX from Macromedia is a powerful program that enables you to create almost any type of Web page. This chapter covers the Dreamweaver MX basics and introduces you to some of the program's essential tools.

Dreamweaver MX is the industry standard for Web site design and production. Whether you're interested in creating a site for fun, such as an online photo album or a site devoted to one of your hobbies, or for business, such as an online store, Dreamweaver MX's flexible interface provides simultaneous graphical and HTML editing. In other words, using Dreamweaver MX, you can not only lay out pages like an artist, but you can fine-tune the associated code like a programmer. Additionally, Dreamweaver MX's built-in FTP features let you upload your site to the Web in a snap, so that you can share your masterpieces with the world.

Exploring the New Dreamweaver MX Interface

In early 2001, Macromedia and the Allaire Corporation announced that they were merging and keeping the Macromedia name. Allaire's flagship products, Homesite and ColdFusion, were considered by many to have the best overall developer-friendly interface for building Web sites. Macromedia's Dreamweaver MX, known industry wide to have a great development interface for nondevelopers, was viewed as quite cumbersome and frustrating to use if you were a Web programmer or a more advanced developer. To give you some idea of how different the interfaces were, Figure 1-1 shows both the old Dreamweaver interface and the old ColdFusion interface.

For a year and a half, Homesite and ColdFusion Studio lived side by side with Dreamweaver. With Dreamweaver MX, Macromedia has finally integrated the two interfaces into one single, powerful product. If you're happy with the way Dreamweaver used to work, and you have no overwhelming desire to see the new Dreamweaver MX interface, don't worry, you've got options.

Selecting an interface on start-up

When you start Dreamweaver MX for the first time, you're asked to choose the way you want your workspace set up, as shown in Figure 1-2. You have two options:

✦ **Dreamweaver MX Workspace:** The new interface that combines Dreamweaver and Homesite/ColdFusion Studio into a single product.

✦ **Dreamweaver 4 Workspace:** The familiar interface that you're accustomed to seeing with Dreamweaver. It's not precisely the same, but it's darn close.

To take full advantage of all that Macromedia Studio MX has to offer, you're better off choosing the Dreamweaver MX workspace. In these authors' humble opinions, it's an easier workspace to orient yourself in and you can easily find the tasks you want to complete.

Changing your interface

Suppose you pick the Dreamweaver MX interface, and you decide that we're kooks and that the Dreamweaver 4 interface is infinitely better. You can easily switch back by following these steps:

1. **Choose Edit⇨Preferences from the main menu, or simply press Ctrl+U.**

The Preferences dialog box appears, as shown in Figure 1-3.

2. **Select General from the Category area.**

3. **Click the Change Workspace button.**

This brings up the same Workspace Setup dialog box that you saw when you launched the product for the first time.

4. **Select the interface that you want to use.**

You can also choose to have the new MX interface without the Homesite interface by deselecting the Homesite/Coder-Style option.

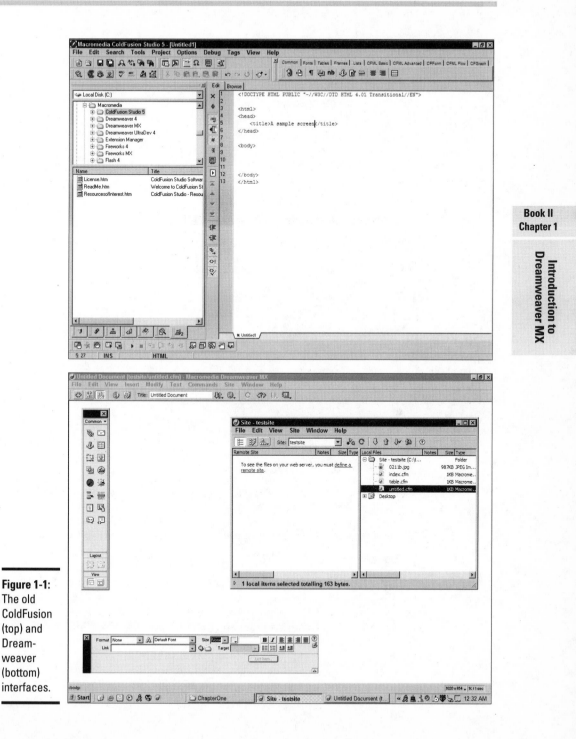

Figure 1-1:
The old
ColdFusion
(top) and
Dream-
weaver
(bottom)
interfaces.

Figure 1-2:
Please
choose a
workspace.

Figure 1-3:
The
Preferences
dialog box.

5. **Click OK to change the interface.**

A dialog box appears, saying that your changes will take effect the next time you start Dreamweaver MX.

You can read more about using the Homesite coding-style in Book VI.

Introducing the Document Window

Your primary workspace in Dreamweaver MX is the Document window, which appears automatically when you start Dreamweaver MX. In the

Document window, you construct your individual Web pages using panels, inspectors, and dialog boxes to format your work. The three primary views in Dreamweaver MX are as follows:

✦ **Design view:** The graphical view of your document, as shown in Figure 1-4. The Design view is also the default view.

✦ **Code view:** This view shows the underlying code of your document. You can select this view by choosing View⇨Code from the main menu.

✦ **Design and Code view:** As you may expect, this is a split screen view that includes both the Design and Code windows. You can select this view by choosing View⇨Code and Design from the main menu.

When you have several documents open in a site, you can select which document you want to work on by clicking the document's name at the bottom of the Dreamweaver MX document window. You can also click the Site tab in the Files panel to work on an entire site.

Figure 1-4:
The default
Design
view.

Choosing between Standard and Layout Views

You can work with content in your Document window using either the Standard view or the Layout view. If you've used a previous version of Dreamweaver, you'll recognize the Standard view as the familiar — and only — graphical view in which you lay out pages in the Document window. These two views are only available when using the Design or the Code and Design views, and provide you with different methods of placing content on your page.

The Layout view was introduced in Dreamweaver 4 and has been carried through to all the various workspace options in Dreamweaver MX. It is specifically geared towards helping you design your Web page using tables. In the Dreamweaver 4 workspace, you find the Layout view in the Objects panel, along the left side of the screen. In the Dreamweaver MX workspace, you can find the Layout view by clicking the Layout tab along the top of the Document window in the Index panel.

The advantage of the Layout view over the Standard view is that it provides a simpler interface for drawing and editing tables and table cells. Two special tools are available only when working in Layout view: the Draw Layout Cell button and the Draw Layout Table button. A table created with the Draw Layout Table tool is shown in Figure 1-5. Both of these tools can help you quickly and easily generate tables or table cells in Dreamweaver MX, and are described in more detail in Book II, Chapter 2.

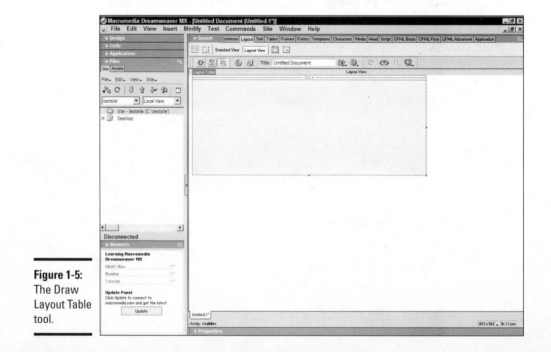

Figure 1-5:
The Draw Layout Table tool.

Examining Your Site with the Site Window

Dreamweaver MX offers Web developers the opportunity to work on individual files that make up a Web site, as well as manage their entire Web site, all through the Dreamweaver interface. This concept is called, not surprisingly, a *Site;* to avoid confusion, we call them *Dreamweaver Sites.* Dreamweaver Sites can include the following elements:

✦ HTML, CFM, ASP, and other files that make up the code of the site

✦ Graphics, such as GIF and JPEG files

✦ Documents, such as PDF files and DOC files

Dreamweaver Sites are handled a little differently, depending upon which workspace (Dreamweaver MX or Dreamweaver 4) you've selected. If you're in the Dreamweaver MX workspace, Dreamweaver Sites are initially viewable within the Files panel (open the Files panel by pressing F8). In the Dreamweaver 4 version of the product, Dreamweaver Sites are their own floating window, as shown in Figure 1-6.

**Book II
Chapter 1**

**Introduction to
Dreamweaver MX**

Figure 1-6:
The Site
window in
the Dream-
weaver 4
workspace.

In either case, the Web site management tools that are available to Dreamweaver Sites are designed to give you total control over the way in which your Web site is built and then maintained from your local computer. They key features of the Dreamweaver Site tools include:

✦ Asset management tools that help you manage all the files that make up your site. These tools, for example, keep track of all your files and the links between files. Anytime you move a file, these tools will change the related links in other files.

✦ Basic source control to ensure that files don't get overwritten. These tools lock files so that when you're working on a particular file, others on your team can't edit that same file.

✦ Publishing tools that allow you to use FTP to upload the content from your site locally to the remote server where the site is housed.

✦ Utilities that create site maps, check links, check the HTML code, and run reports on who's been working on what.

Dreamweaver Sites are covered in more detail in Book II, Chapter 3.

Exploring Toolbar Buttons

Dreamweaver MX provides you with a number of useful view buttons (shown in Figure 1-7 and Figure 1-8) that you can use to see different views of your site. You can easily switch among views to examine your site in different ways. Each Dreamweaver MX view offers specialized menus and tools to help you perform your work in that view. Certain views are available for an individual document or page, whereas other views are available for the entire site. At any time while you work, you can choose to preview your site in target Web browsers, which enables you to see your site from the user's perspective.

Figure 1-7 shows the following site-related view buttons:

✦ **Connect to Remote Host button:** Connects your local computer and your Web host, allowing you to transfer files between the two computers.

✦ **Refresh button:** Refreshes the files in the site.

✦ **Get File(s) button:** Downloads (retrieves) documents and files from the host.

✦ **Put File(s) button:** Uploads (sends) documents and files to the host.

✦ **Check Out button:** Locks files for editing by a single individual.

✦ **Check In button:** Replaces files on the server and makes them available for editing by unlocking them.

✦ **Expand/Collapse button:** Makes the Site tab full-screen with remote and local files side-by-side.

Figure 1-8 shows the following documented-related view buttons:

✦ **Code View button:** Enables you to view the HTML page code full-screen.

✦ **Code and Design View button:** Allows you to view the HTML page code and the Document window at the same time.

✦ **Design View button:** Enables you to view the Document window full-screen.

✦ **Server Debug button:** Runs the page through the server in the workspace window rather than in the browser.

✦ **Live Data View button:** Allows you to test your dynamic content in the workspace window rather than in the browser.

✦ **File Management button:** Click and then select Get to retrieve files from the Web site host or select Put to send files to the host.

✦ **Preview/Debug in Browser button:** Click and select to preview or debug in IE or Navigator.

✦ **Refresh button:** Reloads your page.

✦ **Reference button:** Click to open the Reference panel for CSS, HTML, and JavaScript assistance.

✦ **Code Navigation button:** Allows you to set breakpoints in your code to stop the program from executing its code. Used for debugging applications.

✦ **View Options button:** Click to select tools (such as Visual Aids and the Ruler) to assist you in viewing your site.

Figure 1-7:
Site-related
view
buttons.

Connect to Remote Host
Get File(s)
Check Out
Expand / Collapse
Refresh
Check In
Put File(s)

Figure 1-8:
Documented-
related view
buttons.

Design View
Preview/Debug in Browser
Code
View
Live Data View
Reference
Server Debug
Refresh
View Options
File
Management
Code and Design View
Code Navigation

Some of the these items appear differently and in slightly different locations, depending upon which workspace option you've chosen for Dreamweaver MX.

Using Panels and Property Inspectors

You can use Dreamweaver MX panels and Property inspectors to enter details about all aspects of your Web site. These interfaces offer areas where you can add and format page features, set up navigation and behaviors, and manage the workflow of building your site.

Understanding the role of panels

A *panel* typically provides information about all instances of a particular page feature. For example, the Layers panel lists information about all the layers on the current page. One panel you may find very helpful is the Insert panel, which enables you to add features, such as images, tables, and media, to your pages without accessing menus. You see an example of the Insert panel, as well as its Dreamweaver 4 counterpart, the Objects panel, in Figure 1-9. These panels actually combine several panels into one. To work with a different panel, you simply click the tab selector located at the top of the Insert panel to select a new panel. If you're using the Object panel from the Dreamweaver 4 workspace, you can click the Panel selector at the top of the Object panel and select one of the panels from the drop-down list.

Figure 1-9:
The Insert and Object panels.

Working with the Property inspector

The Property inspector is unique to the individual document object it represents and contains details on attributes of the object. For example, selecting text on a page opens the Text Property inspector, where you can format the text size, font, color, link, and other information. To make certain that the Property inspector is shown below the Document window, choose Window⇨Properties from the main menu. You see an example of a Text Property inspector in Figure 1-10.

Figure 1-10:
The Text
Property
inspector.

**Book II
Chapter 1**

Introduction to
Dreamweaver MX

TIP

The Property inspector has a small down arrow in the lower-right corner, called an Expander button. Click the button to enlarge the Property inspector to view additional formatting options. In an expanded Property inspector, click the small up arrow in the lower-right corner to collapse the inspector.

Getting Help

Dreamweaver MX offers a variety of tools to help you find the answer to virtually any question you have about the program. The Help tools provide basic information for beginners as well as advanced references detailing HTML and JavaScript code.

You can get help by clicking the Help button — the small question mark — in the top-right corner of some panels. Similarly, you can open the drop-down list in the top-right corner of any panel and select Help from the list.

You can also access help using the Help menu located on the main menu. Just choose Help and then select one of the following options:

✦ **Using Dreamweaver MX:** Provides definitions and itemized steps in performing routine Dreamweaver MX tasks. It contains Help Contents, Index, and Search categories.

✦ **Reference:** Opens a panel offering a dictionary-style reference on CSS, HTML, Accessibility requirements, Sitespring tags, and JavaScript. You can also access the Reference panel by clicking the Reference button in the Document window.

✦ **Dreamweaver Exchange, Dreamweaver Support Center, and Macromedia Online Forums:** Connects you to the Web, where you can find constantly updated information on working with Dreamweaver MX, answers to Frequently Asked Questions, and program extensions. You can also join a developer's forum where you can chat with other Dreamweaver MX users to get (and give) help.

✦ **Extending Dreamweaver MX:** Provides assistance in performing more advanced Dreamweaver MX tasks, especially tasks involving the integration of adjunct programs, such as Macromedia Flash MX, with Dreamweaver MX. This help option contains nitty-gritty information about application programming interfaces (APIs) — specific software interfaces that allow you to integrate Dreamweaver MX with databases, the C and Java programming languages, and much more.

Chapter 2: Creating Basic Web Pages

In This Chapter

- ✔ **Customizing what you see in the Document window**
- ✔ **Establishing page properties**
- ✔ **Entering text and line breaks**
- ✔ **Manipulating images**
- ✔ **Working with links and anchors**
- ✔ **Working with tables**

*T*he most significant (and, fortunately, the easiest) process in building a Web site is creating the individual pages that convey the site's content. Even if you plan on creating an ultra-hip site chock full of animation and interactive forms, the vast majority of your site-building efforts are spent constructing basic Web pages comprised of words and images. This chapter shows you how to set up, color, and name individual Web pages. You also discover how to add basic elements, such as text, graphics, and tables, to your pages.

Setting Your Ruler and Grid Options

Dreamweaver MX offers you complete control over how you work in the Document window by providing two guide tools — rulers and a grid — to help you accurately lay out your work. You can customize a variety of guide tool attributes, such as ruler increments and grid snapping, to suit your personal preferences and speed Web page development.

Here's a brief look at all your options with rulers and grids:

✦ **Turning rulers on and off:** Using rulers — both horizontal and vertical — in the Document window can help you measure and position page elements. Toggle the rulers on and off by choosing View⇨Rulers⇨Show from the main menu or by pressing Ctrl+Alt+R.

✦ **Moving and resetting the origin:** By default, the origin, or (0,0) coordinate, of a Dreamweaver MX ruler is set to the upper-left corner of the Document window. You can reposition it to any coordinate in the Document window by clicking the origin cross hairs and dragging them to new coordinates, which can be useful if you want to use the rulers to position elements of a table whose upper-left corner doesn't sit at (0,0) in the Document window. Reset the origin to its default position by choosing View⇨Rulers⇨Reset Origin from the main menu.

✦ **Changing ruler measurement units:** You can change the ruler's measuring increment by choosing View⇨Rulers from the main menu and then choosing Pixels, Inches, or Centimeters from the drop-down list.

✦ **Viewing the grid:** Dreamweaver MX provides a Document window grid that can assist you in visually positioning and aligning page elements. You can toggle the grid on and off by choosing View⇨Grid⇨Show Grid from the main menu. The grid is shown in Figure 2-1.

✦ **Activating and deactivating grid snapping:** The Document window grid offers a snapping feature that causes a page element to automatically align precisely with the snap-to points you define, which can be useful when you draw, resize, or move a layer (see Book II, Chapter 5 for the skinny on layers). You can toggle grid snapping on and off by choosing View⇨Grid⇨Snap to Grid from the main menu.

Figure 2-1:
The grid
is on.

Adjusting page size

When you design Web pages, you must consider how your target audiences will view them. People looking at your page may view it at any number of screen resolutions from 640 x 480 to 1024 x 768 or beyond. Your audience may even view your pages using WebTV, with a resolution of 544 x 376. Because pages appear differently at different resolutions, Dreamweaver MX offers you the ability to build your pages for a variety of monitor resolutions. The higher the resolution, the larger the workspace in your Document window.

If you want to size your pages, you must be in the Design workspace, and your Document window can't be maximized in the integrated workspace. To size your pages, click the Window Size Indicator in the middle of the status bar (which, in turn, is located along the very bottom of the Document window) and select a standard size — for example, 640 x 480 — from the drop-down list. (The Selecting Edit Sizes option on the drop-down list allows you to specify any height and width dimensions you want.)

 You can adjust how the grid appears in the Document window through the Grid Settings dialog box. To do so, open the Grid Settings dialog box by choosing View⇨Grid⇨Edit Grid from the main menu and change any (or all) of the attributes that appear. When you finish, click the Apply button to view the effect of your changes. Click OK to accept the changes and close the dialog box.

Establishing Page Properties

The Page Properties dialog box provides you with control over how several key page properties appear, including the title of the page, page background color, link colors, and page margins. Selections apply only to the current page, not to the entire site. Open a Page Properties dialog box similar to the one you see in Figure 2-2 by choosing Modify⇨Page Properties from the main menu or by pressing Ctrl+J. Then make changes to any of the following:

Figure 2-2:
The Page
Properties
dialog box.

✦ **Title:** Enter a page title in the text field. This title appears in the title bar area of the window both during construction in Dreamweaver MX and when the page is viewed in a Web browser.

✦ **Background Image:** Click the Browse button to locate the image file that you want to appear as the Document window background. If the image is smaller than the available background area, the image is *tiled* (repeated in a checkerboard fashion, like floor tiles) to fill the background.

✦ **Background, Text, Links, Visited Links, and Active Links:** Click the Color box next to each property and pick a color from the Web safe color palette that appears, or enter a hexadecimal color code directly in any Color Code text field. You can also customize your own colors by selecting the color wheel and entering either RGB values or Hue, Saturation, and Luminosity values, as shown in Figure 2-3. For more information about using colors for the Web, see Book III, Chapter 2. Book III, Chapter 3 includes information on how to use the color picker to select colors in both Dreamweaver MX and Fireworks MX.

✦ **Left Margin and Top Margin:** Enter a number (in pixels) in these text fields to set up margins that affect how your page appears in Microsoft Internet Explorer. Enter a whole number for the number of pixels of buffer space you want between the left and top edges of your document and the content of the document.

✦ **Margin Width and Margin Height:** Enter a number (in pixels) in these text fields to set up margins that affect how your page appears in Netscape Navigator. Enter a whole number for the number of pixels of buffer space you want between the left and top edges of your document and the content of the document.

✦ **Document Encoding:** Choose a language for character encoding of text on your page. For example, if you want to create Web pages capable of displaying text in Korean, you can choose Korean (EUC-KR); if you want to display text in English, choose Western (Latin1). Click the Reload button to display the page with the changed encoding.

✦ **Tracing Image:** Click the Browse button to locate the image file you want to use as a guide for laying out your Web page in the Document window. This feature is handy for developers who prefer to mock up a portion of their Web page design in a graphics program and then recreate that design in their Web pages. Tracing images appear in Dreamweaver MX only as a pattern to help guide you in creating an actual Web page; the tracing images never appear on the finished Web page.

✦ **Image Transparency:** Drag the slider to adjust the visibility level of the tracing image. At 0 percent, the tracing image is invisible; at 100 percent, the image is completely opaque.

**Book II
Chapter 2**

**Creating Basic
Web Pages**

Figure 2-3:
The color
picker.

Click the Apply button to view the effect of any property you change. Click OK to accept your changes and close the Page Properties dialog box.

Even if you choose to use a background image, select a complementary background color — the color shows while the background image is downloading.

Working with Text

As we mention in Book II, Chapter 1, Dreamweaver MX has three different design views: Design, Code, and Code and Design. The following sections apply when you're working in the Design view or Code and Design view of Dreamweaver MX. In these views, you can enter and manipulate text on a Web page in Dreamweaver MX by using similar procedures to those you use when working with a word-processing document.

Adding, editing, and deleting text

To enter text on a page, click in the Document window and begin typing. Your mouse pointer appears as a blinking cursor that moves along with the text you enter. When you reach the end of a line, the text automatically wraps to the next line. Dreamweaver MX automatically adds the associated code for your new text in the HTML for the page.

To delete text from a page, in the Document window, select the item that you want to delete and press Backspace or Delete on your keyboard.

You can also modify how text appears on a page by editing its font, size, color, alignment, and other attributes. To modify text in the Document window, click and drag to select the text you want to modify. Doing this opens the Text Property inspector, as shown in Figure 2-4. (If the Text Property inspector does not appear, choose Window➪Properties from the main menu to open it.) In the Text Property inspector, modify any of the following properties:

Figure 2-4:
The Text
Property
inspector.

Figure 2-4:
The Text
Property
inspector.

✦ **Format:** From the first drop-down list, select a default text style. Heading 1 is the largest style and Heading 6 is the smallest, but none of the headings correlates with a specific pixel size. Select Paragraph for the basic body text of your pages. Select Preformatted if you want spaces, tabs, and new lines in a paragraph to show up in a browser (ordinarily, when you add multiple spaces in a row or tabs to your HTML — this is particularly obvious in the Dreamweaver MX document's Code view — they appear as single spaces).

✦ **Font:** Select a font face from the drop-down list. Browsers show your text formatted as the first font in your selection that resides on the user's computer. Choosing Edit Font List allows you to add additional fonts you may have installed on your computer to the font face drop-down list.

✦ **Size:** Select a font size from the drop-down list. The options include none (choosing this option displays text in the default size 3), 1 through 7 (smallest to largest, respectively), +1 through +7, and -1 through -7. Choosing a font size of -2 displays text 2 font sizes smaller than the previously specified font size. Alternatively, choosing a font size of +2 displays text 2 font sizes larger than the previously specified font size.

✦ **Color:** Click the color box and select a text color from the Web safe color palette that appears. Alternatively, you may enter a hexadecimal color code directly in any color code text field. (To set the default text color for a page, check out the "Establishing Page Properties" section, earlier in this chapter.)

✦ **Bold or Italic:** Click the Bold button to make your selected text appear in bold. Click the Italic button to italicize your selected text. You can click either button or both.

✦ **Alignment:** Click an alignment button to align your text. Choices are Left, Center, Right and Justify.

✦ **Link:** Type a URL in this field to transform text into a hypertext link. You can also use the Point to File tool to link to a file. To link to a file using this tool, just follow these steps:

   1. **Open the Files panel by choosing Window⇨Site or by simply pressing the F8 key.**

   2. **Open the Explorer to the folder location that includes the file you want to link to by selecting the collapsing menu squares.**

3. **Click and hold the Point to File icon in the Properties window.**

4. **Drag the pointer to the file you want to link to and release the mouse button when the pointer is over the file.**

   When you're dragging the icon, a line appears from the origin point to your cursor, as shown in Figure 2-5.

   After you let go of the mouse button, the link to the file appears in the Link text field. If you select the Link drop-down list, it shows you your recent links as well.

✦ **Target:** From the drop-down list, select one of the following:

   • _blank: Opens the link in a new window.

   • _parent: Opens the link in the parent of the currently opened window. If the window with the link in it is not in a frame, the linked page opens in the same window as the link. If the link is in a frame, the linked window will open in the parent frame or in the parent window of the frame with the link. See Book II, Chapter 4 for more information about frames.

   • _self: Opens the link in the currently opened window; this is the default target.

   • _top: Opens the link in the top-level window, replacing frames, if any.

**Book II
Chapter 2**

**Creating Basic
Web Pages**

Figure 2-5:
The line helps you see which file you're choosing.

✦ **List:** Click the Unordered List icon next to the Target field to transform text into an unordered (bulleted) list; click the Ordered List icon to transform text into an ordered (numbered) list.

✦ **Placement:** Click the Text Outdent icon you find next to the Ordered List icon to outdent (decrease the indent) the selected text; click the Text Indent icon to indent the selected text.

Inserting a line break

When you want to start a new line in a word-processing program, you press the Enter key. If you press Enter in Dreamweaver MX, you create a paragraph break, which starts a new paragraph, creating a blank space between paragraphs. If you want to start a new line directly under another line of text and without the big space between lines, you need to insert a line break. In Dreamweaver MX, you create a line break by choosing Insert⇨Special Characters⇨Line Break from the main menu or by pressing Shift+Enter. Alternatively, you may click the Insert Line Break button from the Characters tab in the Insert panel. If the panel doesn't show, open it by choosing Window⇨Insert from the main menu. Dreamweaver MX places the cursor at the start of the next line and creates the line break HTML code for the page.

Manipulating Images

Aside from entering text, manipulating images on a Web page is probably the most common Dreamweaver MX function you perform. You can add or delete an image and modify its properties to create an aesthetically pleasing layout that effectively conveys the information you want to deliver to the user.

To see how to place an image on the background of your page, check out the "Establishing Page Properties" section, earlier in this chapter.

Inserting an image

To insert an image on a page, follow these steps:

1. **Choose Insert⇨Image from the main menu.**

   Alternatively, you can click the Insert Image button on the Common tab, which is part of the Insert panel. If the panel doesn't show, open it by choosing Window⇨Insert from the main menu.

2. **In the Select Image Source dialog box (shown in Figure 2-6), click the image you want to insert.**

   If the image is outside the folder that holds your HTML document, click the arrow tab beside the Look In text field and browse to select the file you want.

Figure 2-6:
Select an
image.

3. **Click OK to insert the image.**

   Note: Every image you want to include on a Web page must reside
   within the root folder of the current site (typically, you should have
   your HTML files in the site root folder — the master folder that holds
   everything on your site — and all your images in an images folder that's
   also in the site's root folder). If you attempt to insert an image from
   another location, Dreamweaver MX asks whether you want to copy the
   image to the current site root folder. Click Yes. In the Copy File As dialog
   box, you can enter a new name for the image in the File Name text field,
   or you can accept the current name and click the Save button.

Always be sure you have saved your HTML file at least once before you
insert an image into it. If your file isn't saved, Dreamweaver MX won't know
where to place the image in relation to the file. After you've saved the file in
a particular folder, the location is known and Dreamweaver MX can include
the correct relative location of the image.

Put a check in the Preview Images check box at the bottom of the Select
Image Source dialog box to view a thumbnail image before you select it for
insertion. The preview area also tells you the size of the image and the
expected download time.

Deleting or moving an image

To delete an image from a page, click the image in the Document window
and press the Delete key on your keyboard.

If you want to move the image from one place on the page to another, you
can click the image in the Document window, press Ctrl+X to cut the image,
click the spot on the page where you want to move the image and press
Ctrl+V to paste the image. You can also move an image, by clicking and
dragging it to a new location.

Modifying an image

You can modify how an image appears on a page by editing its size and alignment, adding a border, and changing other attributes.

To modify an image, click the image in the Document window to select it. If the Image Property inspector does not appear, choose Window⇨Properties from the main menu to open it.

To see all the options the Image Property inspector offers, click the down arrow in the bottom right-hand corner of the Image Property inspector. (Clicking the up arrow displays fewer options.)

You can do any of the following things to modify an image:

✦ **Resize the image:** Click and drag a sizing handle to change the dimensions of the image. To resize the image maintaining the same proportions, hold down the Shift key as you drag a sizing handle. You can also resize the image by typing new pixel dimensions in the W and H text fields in the Image Property inspector. If you want to resize the image and have it look good, you're better off resizing the image in Fireworks MX. See Book II, Chapter 8 for information on how to make Fireworks MX your primary image editor.

✦ **Align the image:** In the Image Property inspector, click an alignment button to position the image on the page (or within a cell if the image is located in a table cell). Alignment button choices consist of Left, Center, and Right. To align an image with special word wrapping, select one of the alignment options, which are detailed in Table 2-1, from the Align drop-down list that appears when you position your image near a bunch of text.

✦ **Add a border to the image:** In the Image Property inspector, enter a number in the Border text field to add a border of that thickness to the image. Border thickness is measured in pixels.

✦ **Pad an image with spaces:** In the Image Property inspector, enter a number in pixels in the V Space (V for vertical) text field for the space you want to appear between the top and bottom of the image and other page elements; then enter a number in pixels in the H Space (H for horizontal) text field for the space you want to appear between the image and page elements on either side of the image.

✦ **Make the image a link:** In the Image Property inspector, enter a URL in the Link text field.

✦ **Specify alternative text for the image:** In the Image Property inspector, enter alternative text in the Alt text field. (Specifying alternative text ensures that when viewers' browsers don't — or can't — display the image, some meaningful text appears instead.)

✦ **Name the image:** In the Image Property inspector, enter a name in the text field next to the thumbnail image. (Naming an image is important if you want to refer to that image using a scripting language, such as JavaScript.)

✦ **Edit the image:** In the Image Property inspector, click the Edit button.

Dreamweaver MX doesn't enable you to edit images directly. Instead, clicking the Edit button opens an image-editing program that's installed on your computer. To specify a new image-editing program, choose Edit➪Preferences from the main menu. In the Preferences dialog box, choose File Types/Editors from the Category menu. Choose an image extension (.gif, .jpg, or .png) from the Extensions menu. Then choose a program from the Editors menu and click the Make Primary button. Fireworks MX is your default primary image editor if you installed Macromedia Studio MX. If there are no choices in the Editors menu, click the add (+) button to open the Select External Editor dialog box so you can browse to the editor on your computer. You can add a new image editor by clicking the add (+) button. Click OK to apply your changes and close the dialog box.

✦ **Change the image file:** In the Image Property inspector, enter a different filename in the Src text field (or click the file icon to browse for image files).

✦ **Add an image map:** In Dreamweaver MX, you can add multiple hotspots to images to create an image map. In the bottom left of the Image Property inspector, you see an arrow pointer and some image tools (a rectangle, circle, and free form image creator). With these tools, you can create hotspots on your .jpg or .gif images, and specify the following for each hotspot:

   • The link location for the hotspot

   • The target window for the link

   • The alternate text for the hotspot

Table 2-1	Aligning an Image in Relation to Text
Alignment Option	*Effect on Image and Text Wrapping*
Browser Default	Same as Bottom alignment
Baseline	Same as Bottom alignment
Top	Aligns the image top with the highest other inline element
Middle	Aligns the image middle with the text baseline
Bottom	Aligns the image bottom with the text baseline
Text Top	Aligns the image top with the text top
Absolute Middle	Aligns the image middle with the text middle

(continued)

Table 2-1 *(continued)*

Alignment Option	Effect on Image and Text Wrapping
Absolute Bottom	Aligns the image bottom with the bottom of the text descenders
Left	Aligns the image flush left
Right	Aligns the image flush right

Working with Links

Linking your page to other Web pages enables you to direct visitors to related content on the Web. To insert a link, you must specify an image or some text to serve as the link; you must also specify the link location to which you want to send your visitors. The link can go to a page within your site or to a page elsewhere on the Web.

Inserting a link

To insert a link on a page, follow these steps:

1. **Select the text or image you want to make into a link.**

   Doing so opens the Property inspector for your text or image. If the Property inspector does not appear, choose Window⇨Properties from the main menu to open it.

2. **In the Link area of the Property inspector, enter the destination URL of the link (text or image) that you created in Step 1.**

   The URL you specify can be any valid URL, for example, a Web page within your own site (somePage.html), a page on the Web (http://www.someSite.com/somePage.html), or even an e-mail address (mailto:somebody@somewhere.com).

   Alternatively, you may click the File Folder icon you see in the Property inspector to display the Select File dialog box. After you browse your computer using the Select File dialog box and select a file, click OK to make that file the target of a link.

 To create an e-mail link quickly, click anywhere in your document and choose Insert⇨E-mail Link from the main menu. Specifying the same value for the Text and E-mail fields that appear allows folks who haven't configured their Web browsers to handle e-mail automatically to see the e-mail address on the page. Then, they can copy and paste the e-mail address information into their e-mail program of choice.

Deleting a link

To delete a link from text or an image, without deleting the text or image itself, follow these steps:

1. **Select the text or image you want to remove the link from.**

The Property inspector for your text or image opens. If the Property inspector doesn't appear, choose Window⇨Properties from the main menu to open it.

2. **In the Property inspector, delete the URL from the Link text field.**

Note that if you delete a linked image or linked text from a page, the link gets deleted along with the text or image.

Using named anchors

When you want to create a navigational link that connects users not only to a page, but also to a specific location on the page, you need to create a *named anchor.* Named anchors are frequently used for jumping to exact positions within a large block of text so that users don't have to scroll through sentence after sentence to find the information they need. Setting up named anchors is especially useful when creating links from a directory or a table of contents to the content it presents.

Inserting a named anchor

Place an anchor anywhere on your Web page as follows:

1. **In the Document window, click at the position you want to insert the named anchor.**

2. **Click the Named Anchor button on the Common tab of the Insert panel or choose Insert⇨Named Anchor from the main menu.**

The Named Anchor dialog box appears, as in shown in Figure 2-7.

3. **Type a name in the Anchor Name text field.**

4. **Click OK.**

Book II
Chapter 2

Creating Basic
Web Pages

Figure 2-7:
The Named
Anchor
dialog box.

It's a good idea to insert the named anchor tag slightly above the actual position where you want the link to target. Doing so gives your targeted content a little padding on top. Otherwise, the top of your image or your first line of text appears flush with the top of the browser window.

Linking to a named anchor

To link to a named anchor, follow the procedure outlined in the "Inserting a link" section, earlier in this chapter, with the following modifications:

✦ **Linking to a named anchor on the current page:** In the Link text field of the Property inspector, type a pound sign (#) followed by the anchor name.

✦ **Linking to a named anchor on a different page:** In the Link text field of the Property inspector, type the page's URL followed by a pound sign and then the anchor name.

Be sure not to include any spaces in the names of anchors. These may not be read by the various Web browsers.

Working with Tables

Adding a table to a Web page can help you lay out page elements more easily in the Document window. Tables consist of as many holding areas, or *cells,* as you want, and you can place virtually any Web element, such as text or an image, into a cell. Cells are organized horizontally into *rows* and vertically into *columns.* Dreamweaver MX provides you with complete control over the size, position, color, and other attributes of your table. And you can edit these attributes at any time via the Table Property inspector.

Inserting a table

To add a table, choose Insert⇨Table from the main menu to open the Insert Table dialog box, as shown in Figure 2-8. Alternatively, you may click the Insert Table button on the Tables tab within the Insert panel. Enter the following information in the Insert Table dialog box:

✦ **Rows:** Enter a number in the text field for the number of rows in the table.

✦ **Columns:** Enter a number in the text field for the number of columns in the table.

✦ **Cell padding:** Enter a number in the text field specifying how many pixels of padding you want between the inside edge of a cell and its contents.

✦ **Cell spacing:** Enter a number in the text field specifying how many pixels you want separating cells.

✦ **Width:** To create a table whose width varies depending on the width of the browser window, select Percent from the drop-down list and then enter a number (1–100) in the text field for the percent of page width you want the entire table to occupy. To create a table with a fixed width, select Pixels from the drop-down list and enter a number of pixels for the width of the entire table.

✦ **Border:** Enter a number in the text field for the width of the table borders in pixels. Entering 0 causes the borders to disappear.

Figure 2-8:
Fill out the Insert Table dialog box to create a table.

Book II Chapter 2

Creating Basic Web Pages

After you've entered all this information, click OK to insert the table. An empty table is shown in Figure 2-9. To enter data into the table, just click on an individual cell and enter the content you want in that cell.

Figure 2-9:
Your first table!

Deleting a table

To delete a table from a page, click the border of the table to select it and then press the Backspace or Delete key. Dreamweaver MX removes the table from your page and deletes the associated code in the HTML for the page. Naturally, everything that was in the table is also deleted from the page.

Using layout tables

The use of tables is central to building great Web pages. What happens, though, when you want to put an image right smack in the middle of a page, or when you want to have one column of information along the right side of the page, and a square text block at the bottom of the page? You can nest tables, which is to build new tables inside of cells of other tables. This is the tried and true method for a lot of developers, but creating nested tables is complicated and not at all fun, especially with complex pages.

Thankfully, Dreamweaver MX offers an easy way to work with complex tables called layout tables. With a layout table, you tell Dreamweaver MX where you want to put something on the screen, and the program generates all the required table work to make it happen.

To create a layout table, just follow these steps:

1. **From the Document window, click the Layout tab in the Insert panel.**

2. **Click Layout view to switch to it from Standard view.**

3. **Select the Draw Layout Table tool.**

4. **Click and drag the cross hair to create the layout table of your choice.**

   A light green table appears, as shown in Figure 2-10, with the dimensions you gave it.

5. **To create individual cells within that table, click the Draw Layout Cell tool and draw a cell anywhere within the table.**

   If you create a layout cell outside a layout table, Dreamweaver MX will create both the cell and the table to support it. Note that you cannot draw a new cell that overlaps an existing cell in the table.

If you create a layout cell, you can immediately edit the cell you created. However, if you create a layout table, you either have to switch back to Standard view to edit the single cell of that table or create a layout cell within the table before you can edit the table.

Figure 2-10:
Drawing a
layout table.

Storing Information in Table Cells

After you insert a table on a page, you can add or delete elements, such as
text and images, in the table cells:

 ✦ **Adding an image to a cell:** To add an image to a table cell, click to position the cursor in a table cell and choose Insert➪Image from the main
   menu. Browse and select an image you want to add to the cell and then
   click OK. (For more information on inserting images, flip to the
   "Inserting an image" section, earlier in this chapter.)

 ✦ **Adding text to a cell:** To add text to a table cell, click to position the
   cursor in a table cell and type the text you want placed inside the cell.

 ✦ **Deleting an image from a cell:** To delete an image from a table cell,
   select the image and press Backspace or Delete.

 ✦ **Deleting text from a cell:** To delete text from a table cell, select the text
   and press Backspace or Delete.

Chapter 3: Creating and Using Dreamweaver Sites

In This Chapter

✔ **Defining a site in Dreamweaver MX**

✔ **Creating sites**

✔ **Setting up remote connections**

✔ **Exploring advanced settings**

✔ **Publishing your site**

✔ **Maintaining your site**

✔ **Using source control**

Dreamweaver MX can be used to create a variety of different kinds of Web pages. During the course of building a Web site, you'll find that you add pages, graphics, links, and all sorts of related information into a single location to be posted eventually to a Web server on the Internet. After your site is complete, you'll probably want to make updates and fixes. Heck, you may even be making more than one site at the same time!

To help facilitate management of your Web site (or sites), Dreamweaver MX offers a suite of site management tools. These tools are collectively called a *Dreamweaver Site*. Catchy, isn't it? This chapter explores how these tools can be used to help make the management of your Web site easier.

Defining a Site in Dreamweaver MX

Figure 3-1 shows a typical relationship between where you build your Web site (your desktop) and where the site actually lives on the Internet (a Web server). Sites in Dreamweaver MX are meant to facilitate getting all the correct information from your desktop to the Web server and generally make the Web page creation process easier. Specifically, a Dreamweaver Site enables you to do the following:

✦ Seamlessly move files back and forth between your local machine and your Web server

✦ Keep all your site files in a single location

✦ Generate pages for your site based on templates that you create

✦ Run reports on the pages in your site to check links, page load, and other key functions

✦ Use source- and version-control to manage who works on what files and when they do it, which can prevent team members from accidentally overwriting each other's work when building or maintaining a site collaboratively

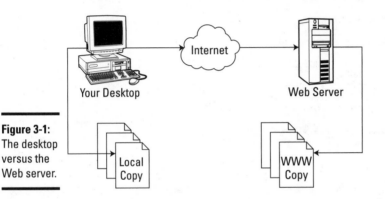

Figure 3-1:
The desktop
versus the
Web server.

Creating Your First Site

Dreamweaver MX likes you to use its sites. In fact, every time you save a file or insert a graphic into a page that's not already saved to a site, the product asks you if you want to create a site or add the file to an existing site. Now that's determination!

You can create a site in Dreamweaver MX manually or by using a wizard, as the following sections describe.

Creating a site manually

This section shows you how to create a Dreamweaver Site manually. The following steps walk you through inputting the minimum amount of information that you need to input to create your site. However, you can choose from a number of other options, and they are covered in the "Using Advanced Site Options" section, later in this chapter.

To create a basic site manually, follow these steps:

1. **Make sure the Files panel is open by choosing Window⇨Site from the main menu.**

Alternatively, you can also just press F8.

2. **Choose Site⇨New Site from the main menu.**

The Site Definition dialog box, shown in Figure 3-2, appears.

Figure 3-2:
Defining
your site.

3. **Set the options for your site by filling out each of the following pieces of information:**

- **Site Name:** Choose a name that you can remember easily and that applies to the function of the site.

- **Local Root Folder:** This is the location on your hard drive where you want to store the files that make up your site. Again, you should title the folder something intuitive and easy to remember. If you want to browse for a folder, just click the folder icon to the right of the text field.

- **Refresh Local File List Automatically:** Dreamweaver MX defaults to having this option checked. When this option is selected, Dreamweaver MX refreshes the list of files in the your site every time you copy a file into the site.

- **Default Images Folder:** This is the standard directory for images used on your site. Dreamweaver MX adds images here when you copy image files into your site. A good practice is to name this folder `images` (if your site is going to be hosted on a UNIX-based server, you need to be consistent about using upper- and lower-case letters in filenames and links to those files from your site). Again, if you want to browse for the directory, just click the folder icon next to the text field.

- **HTTP Address:** This is the URL of your Web site. Dreamweaver MX uses this to verify that links in your site are working properly.

- **Enable Cache:** Selecting this option speeds up Dreamweaver MX's site management tools and is required for the Assets panel to work. See your documentation for information about using the Assets panel.

4. **Click OK to create the site.**

Dreamweaver MX creates a folder for your site if it doesn't exist on your hard drive, but it doesn't create the images directory within that folder. Thus, it's always a good idea to create your folders on the hard drive first, and then create your site.

Creating a site using a wizard

You may think that using a wizard to create a site is easier, which is true if you're creating a complex site. However, if you're creating a simple site, the manual route is the way to go.

To use the wizard, follow these steps:

1. **Choose Site⇨New Site from the main menu.**

   The Site Definition dialog box appears (refer to Figure 3-2).

2. **Click the Basic tab.**

   The first page of the wizard, shown in Figure 3-3, appears.

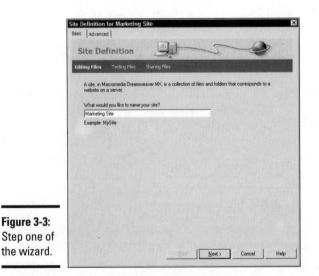

Figure 3-3:
Step one of
the wizard.

3. **Enter a name for your site and then click Next.**

   The Editing Files, Part 2 page of the wizard appears.

4. **If your site is going to be dynamic, choose a server technology to process Web pages before they're sent to the user, and then click Next.**

   Dreamweaver MX provides you with several server options, including ASP, JSP, and PHP; this is Macromedia Studio MX, so naturally you find that ColdFusion MX is one of the options. You can select a technology by selecting the Yes radio button and selecting your Web serving technology from the drop-down list.

5. **Choose how you want to edit your files, and then click Next.**

   If you have selected to use a server technology on the Editing Files, Part 2 page, on the Editing Files, Part 3 page you get the Dynamic options shown in Table 3-1; if not, you get the Static options. Click the radio button next to the option you want to choose.

Table 3-1	Site Editing Options		
Option	*Description*	*Dynamic Option*	*Static Option*
Edit and test locally	Allows you to edit your files and test them locally using ColdFusion MX as your Web server.	Yes	No
Edit locally, then upload to remote testing server (Edit local copies on your machine, then upload to server when ready)	In this mode, you edit the files on your computer, and then manually upload them using Dreamweaver MX's FTP tools to move the files to a remote server.	Yes	Yes
Edit directly on (remote testing) server using local network	This option allows you to edit files directly on a volume on your internal network.	Yes	Yes
Edit directly on (remote testing) server using FTP or RDS	With this option, Dreamweaver MX puts and retrieves files on a remote server using FTP or Remote Development Services (RDS, a connection method used in conjunction with ColdFusion MX). These are the most dangerous methods of editing. We recommend against them.	Yes	Yes

6. **Configure your testing environment.**

   Based on the testing methodology you chose, you are asked to configure your testing environment. Here are the various options:

• **Edit and Test Locally:** For this method, you are asked to provide the local URL for testing. Usually, this is `http://localhost/folder`, where `folder` is the name of the root folder of your site.

In order to ensure that this method works properly, always make sure that you create your site within the directory for `http://localhost` on your hard drive. For most Windows 2000 or XP computers, this location is `C:\inetpub\wwwroot\` by default.

• **Edit Locally, Then Upload to Remote Testing Server:** If you've selected this route, you are asked to select a method of connecting to the remote location for your site. Your options are Local/Network, FTP, RDS (Remote Development Services, used in conjunction with ColdFusion MX), and the always popular, "I'll set this up later." Figure 3-4 shows the local/network option.

Figure 3-4:
Connecting using your local network.

• **Edit Directly on (Remote Testing) Server Using Local Network:** If you've chosen this option, then you are asked for the URL of the remote server so that Dreamweaver MX knows where to look to test your site.

• **Edit Directly on (Remote Testing) Server Using FTP or RDS:** This option looks remarkably similar to Edit Locally and Test Remote. You need to provide all the data required for local/network, FTP, or RDS (Remote Development Services) to connect to a remote server, including things like your username and password. You can choose to skip this step and set up the connection later. Figure 3-5 shows the FTP requirements that are requested. See the following section for more information on FTP and RDS setup.

Figure 3-5:
FTP
requirements
for editing
remotely.

7. **Configure your file sharing options and click Next.**

   Dreamweaver MX includes options for source control, which you can use to prevent team members from overwriting each others' work when collaborating. You can choose to enable it here by selecting the Yes radio button. File sharing is discussed in more detail in the section, "Using Source Control," later in this chapter.

8. **Review your settings and click Done to set up your site.**

   The Site Definition window closes. Click Done to close the Edit Sites dialog box.

Setting Up a Remote Connection

After you create your site, either by using the wizard or by setting it up manually, it's a good idea to get connected to the place where the remote version of your site (the one users will access via the World Wide Web) will live. Dreamweaver MX can connect to a remote server in a variety of ways. The route you choose depends largely on how you plan to build and maintain your site. You have essentially three different scenarios, as follows:

✦ **Creating and testing your site solely on your own computer:** For example, this may be the case if you're building your site for someone else, say a client. Here the remote server is your computer — not all that remote!

✦ **Creating your site on your computer, but testing it somewhere else:** This is the most common situation. Dreamweaver MX has three different delivery options for this scenario: FTP, Remote Development Services (RDS), and local network connection.

✦ **Creating and testing your site on a remote machine:** In this case, the options are the same as in the previous bullet. The only difference is that when you're editing, you're editing files directly on the remote location, leaving nothing on your local machine.

In many cases, your remote location is at an externally hosted Internet Service Provider (ISP). If you've got an account set up with an ISP, make sure to get the following information, which is required for Dreamweaver MX to set up a connection to your remote Web server:

✦ An IP address or a URL to be used when posting your files

✦ A folder on the remote server where you are supposed to keep your site files

✦ A username for your account

✦ A password for your account

To set up a remote connection, follow these steps:

1. **Choose Site⇨Edit Sites to bring up the Edit Sites dialog box, shown in Figure 3-6.**

Figure 3-6:
The Edit
Sites dialog
box.

2. **Select your site and then click the Edit button.**

The Site Definition dialog box appears.

3. **From the Category list on the Advanced tab, select Remote Info.**

Along the right side of the dialog box, the Local Info is replaced with the Remote Info. If you haven't set up a connection previously, all you see is the Access drop-down list.

4. **Select an option from the Access drop-down list.**

   You can choose from several Access options in this list, including:

   - **FTP:** The industry standard File Transfer Protocol.
   - **Local/Network:** A location on your local (meaning office, home office, and so on) network.
   - **RDS:** ColdFusion MX's Remote Development Services allows secure remote access to files within a ColdFusion MX application server.
   - **SourceSafe Database:** SourceSafe is Microsoft's version control application. With Dreamweaver MX, you can integrate SourceSafe and use it for your version control.
   - **WebDAV:** This stands for Web-based Distributed Authoring and Versioning. Like SourceSafe, it's a standard for version control and is used with Web servers like Apache Web Server and Microsoft's IIS.

5. **Fill out the appropriate information for the connection type you selected.**

   Leave the source control settings alone for the moment, which are described in the "Using Source Control" section, later in this chapter. The following list describes the information needed for each connection type:

   - **FTP:** In addition to the four items we note at the beginning of this section (host, folder, username, and password), you also need to check the Passive FTP check box if you plan to use Passive FTP (which is unlikely). If there's a firewall you need to work through, you can click the Firewall Settings button to set the Firewall preferences in the pop-up window, as shown in Figure 3-7. Check the Use SSH Encrypted Secure Login check box if you want to use encrypted secure logins (again, not likely). After you've added the necessary settings, you're able to connect to your ISP.

     If you select Automatically Upload Files to Server on Save, Dreamweaver MX will automatically make a connection to the remote server and upload your file each time you save it.

     Select the Enable File Check In and Check Out option if you're working in a collaborative environment and you want to ensure that other team members can't work on a file at the same time you're working on it.

   - **Local/Network:** Here, you only need to specify the location of the remote folder on the network, which you can enter manually or by clicking the folder icon to browse the network for the folder location. You can also check the Refresh check box if you'd like the list of files on your site to be automatically refreshed when a new file is added.

Figure 3-7:
Setting your
firewall
preferences.

- **RDS:** With RDS, after you select it from the drop-down list, you need to click the Settings button next to the list to configure the RDS connection, as shown in Figure 3-8. To configure RDS, you need a host name (IP address or URL), port number (the default is 80), the directory of the site on the host, a username, and a password. If you don't want the password saved, then deselect the Save check box.

Figure 3-8:
The
Configure
RDS Server
dialog box.

- **SourceSafe:** Like RDS, with SourceSafe you have to select the Settings button next to the drop-down list. Then you specify the location of the SourceSafe Database Path (a path to an .ini file, usually on a network volume), the name of the project, a username, and a password. If you don't want the password saved, then deselect the Save check box.

- **WebDAV:** With WebDAV you must also click the Settings button next to the drop-down list to configure the connection. You need the URL of the connection, a username, a password, and an e-mail address. If you don't want the password saved, then deselect the Save check box.

6. **Click OK to put the changes into effect.**

Using Advanced Site Options

If you used the wizard to create your site, you may have been struck by the array of questions asked. That's because you can configure a number of advanced settings with Dreamweaver MX. Most of them you're not likely to need, but just in case, we describe them in the following sections. All these options can be accessed by selecting the name of the item in the Category field of the Site Definition dialog box (refer to Figure 3-2).

Testing your server

Select Testing Server from the Category list on the Advanced tab of the Site Definition dialog box to access this area. If you're building a dynamic site, you need to have a Web server running that can process the pages and render them as HTML. (For more on how this is accomplished, see Book VI, Chapter 3.) To specify a Web serving technology, do the following:

1. **Select a Web server from the Server Model drop-down list, as shown in Figure 3-9.**

You have several options here, but if you're working within the Macromedia model, your most likely selection is going to be ColdFusion MX.

Book II
Chapter 3

Creating and Using
Dreamweaver Sites

Figure 3-9:
Choosing a
Web server.

2. **Choose the kinds of pages that will be in the site.**

   Dreamweaver MX needs to know if you're just going to be using Dreamweaver MX files, or Dreamweaver UltraDev files as well (UltraDev is a Web application tool whose capabilities have been absorbed into Dreamweaver MX). If this is a new site, then select Dreamweaver MX Pages Only from the This Site Contains drop-down list. If you're updating an older site that was built in Dreamweaver UltraDev, then select Both Versions.

3. **Select an Access type.**

   You can choose from either FTP or Local/Network. Choosing either will provide additional fields for you to fill out, as specified for each Access type in the "Setting Up a Remote Connection" section, earlier in this chapter. Choose None if you don't want to use a testing server.

4. **Click OK to save your settings.**

Cloaking

Cloaking is a handy and appropriately named feature in Dreamweaver Sites. When enabled, cloaking allows you to hide different file types or folders from Dreamweaver MX's site tools. This can be especially helpful if you keep your raw asset files (your source Fireworks PNGs, Flash FLAs, and so on) in the same directory as the site itself, but you don't want the files uploaded or downloaded, included in reports, or otherwise touched by various Dreamweaver MX operations. To engage this feature, select the Enable Cloaking check box, as well as the Cloak Files Ending With check box, and add the file extensions for the file types you want to mask. See the online Help files for more details.

Using Design Notes

Design Notes aren't really necessary unless you're working on your site collaboratively in Dreamweaver MX with other people. Then, they can be especially helpful. For example, you can use Design Notes to let others know the status of a given file. To engage Design Notes, simply select the Maintain Design Notes check box. If you want to move the notes to the server when the site is published, so other team members can access them, select the Upload Design Notes For Sharing check box.

Setting up a site map

If you select Site Map Layout, you can set up the specifics of how you'd like your site's Site Map to look. You can specify the following:

✦ The home page for the site map, which can be different from the home page (index.htm) of the site

✦ The number and width of the columns of the map

✦ The labels for the site map icons

✦ Whether or not to display items marked hidden

✦ Whether or not to display dependent files

Selecting columns for the File View

For the File View, shown in Figure 3-10, you have six built-in columns to choose from: Name, Notes, Size, Type, Modified, and Checked Out By. However, you can also add and remove your own columns by clicking the (+) and (–) buttons, respectively. For a column you create, you can also specify the following:

✦ The column name

✦ The column's Design Note association, if its contents relate to a specific Design Note

✦ The text alignment for the column

✦ The option to show or not show the column in the File View (*Note:* The Name column cannot be hidden or moved.)

✦ Whether or not to share the column so other workers on the site can see it (*Note:* You must have Maintain Design Notes checked to share a column.)

Book II
Chapter 3

Creating and Using
Dreamweaver Sites

Figure 3-10:
The File
View.

Publishing Your Site

After you've set up a remote site in a Dreamweaver MX Site, publishing your site is a snap. To publish your site to a remote server, just follow these steps:

1. **Make sure the Files panel is open by choosing Window⇨Site or by pressing F8.**

2. **On the Sites tab, click Expand/Collapse to switch to File View mode.**

   This brings up the same File View shown in Figure 3-10.

3. **If you haven't connected to the remote server since you launched Dreamweaver MX most recently, click the Connection button at the left of the Site tab of the Files panel to establish a connection with the remote server.**

4. **Click the Site Files button along the top left of the screen to show both the remote and local site files.**

   The resulting side-by-side view is shown in Figure 3-11.

Figure 3-11:
Remote and local sites.

5. **To copy files from the Local to Remote servers, or vice versa, simply click and drag the elements from local to remote, or vice versa.**

   Alternatively, select a file and click the Put button (upward pointing blue arrow) to copy a file from the local server to the remote server or the Get button (downward pointing green arrow) to copy a file from the remote server to the local server.

If you ever want to see what's going on behind the scenes when you're copying those files, just choose View⇨Site FTP Log from the Site tab within the Files panel. The Results panel appears/expands and shows you the remote connections being set and all the commands for the files being sent.

Maintaining Your Site

After your site is built, you want to make sure that it's running at peak efficiency. To help in this effort, Dreamweaver MX offers some valuable tools that can help you keep on top of the wide array of items that go into keeping your site running smoothly. The two basic types of tools, reports and link checkers, are described in detail in the following sections.

Running reports

Reports encapsulate information about various aspects of your site at the time the reports are run, giving you a snapshot of things, such as which files on your site are currently being worked on by different team members, whether all the images on a selected page have Alt tags, and more. To run a report in Dreamweaver MX, just follow these steps:

1. **Choose Site⇨Reports from the main menu.**

   The Reports dialog box, shown in Figure 3-12, appears.

2. **Choose what you want to run the report against.**

   You can choose to run a report on the currently selected document, the entire site, or a folder within the site. Make your selection by selecting one of these options from the Report On drop-down list.

3. **Select the reports you want to run by selecting the check box next to their names.**

Figure 3-12:
The Reports
dialog box.

You can run eight possible reports, across two categories:

- **Checked Out By:** This report tells you what files in source control are currently being used by different members of the team. If you want the report to show only which files are currently checked out by a particular team member, click the Report Settings button at the bottom of the dialog box while the report is selected and add an individual's name to the text input field in the Checked Out By dialog box that pops up.

- **Design Notes:** This report prints out all the Design Notes associated with files on the site. To filter your results via the Design Notes dialog box, shown in Figure 3-13, click the Report Settings button while the Design Notes report is selected.

Figure 3-13:
Filtering
results.

- **Combinable Nested Font Tags:** This report details locations in the code where overlapping Font tags could be merged. For example, if you change the size of a block of text, your code might contain something like this:

```
<FONT face="Arial"><FONT size="2">Some
    text.</FONT></FONT>
```

When it could and should be

```
<FONT face="Arial" size="2">Some text.</FONT>
```

Book II
Chapter 3

Creating and Using
Dreamweaver Sites

- **Accessibility:** If you run this report, the site files are scanned to find places where the code is not ADA (Americans with Disabilities Act) compliant. For more information about accessibility, browse to the W3C Web Accessibility Initiative pages at `www.w3.org/WAI/Resources/`.

- **Missing Alt Text:** This report looks for images to make sure they have Alt tags (see the section on modifying an image in Book II, Chapter 2 for a little info on Alt text).

- **Redundant Nested Tags:** This report searches the code for locations where extra tags can be eliminated.

- **Removable Empty Tags:** If you're working in Design mode and moving lots of things around, sometimes the underlying code can be left with lingering, empty tags. This tool finds those empty tags.

- **Untitled Documents:** This report searches for pages that may have a filename but don't have a title.

4. **Click OK to run the reports.**

   The results appear in the Site Reports tab of the Results panel, as shown in Figure 3-14.

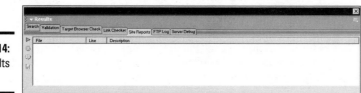

Figure 3-14:
The Results
panel.

Checking links

In addition to the reports that help to clean your code, Dreamweaver MX can also check the links on your site. To run this report, choose Site➪Check Links Sitewide from the Site tab of the Files panel or press Ctrl+F8 to run the site link checker. You see the results in the Link Checker tab in the Results panel. The report shows you broken links, external links, and orphaned files.

Using Source Control

Source control allows team members to check out a document in your site, thereby locking it and making it uneditable by others until the team member who checked it out checks it back in again. This process is intended to ensure that files don't get overwritten accidentally and that data doesn't get lost during the development process.

In most large-scale software development projects, where you've got multi-tudes of people working on a single code-base, source control is critical. If your site requires that more than three people work on the same pages and code, you should consider taking advantage of this feature in Dreamweaver MX.

To set up source control, do the following:

1. **Choose Site⇨Edit Sites, select your site, and then select Edit to open the Site definition dialog box.**

2. **Click Remote Info from the Advanced tab.**

3. **Set your source control options at the bottom of the screen.**

   You have several options here, including the following:

   • Enable file check in and check out by selecting the check box with that name

   • Check out files automatically when you open a document within the site

   • Provide your name and e-mail address for site reporting and informational purposes

   You must have selected an Access option on the Remote Info screen before you can get the Check In/Check Out options to show up at the bottom of the page. See the "Setting Up a Remote Connection" section, earlier in this chapter, for more information about Access options.

4. **Click OK to save your settings.**

To work with a file after you've enabled source control, right-click on the file from the Files panel and select one of the following options:

✦ **Get:** Retrieves the most recent version of the file and copies it locally.

✦ **Check Out:** Makes your local version the only editable version of a document and ensures that others can't open and save the file.

✦ **Put:** Copies the local version of your file to the remote location.

✦ **Check In:** Puts your local version of the file on the server and unlocks it so that others can check it out and work on it if need be.

Chapter 4: Punching Up Your Pages with Forms and Frames

In This Chapter

↙ Incorporating forms into your Web page

↙ Structuring your pages with frames

Two of the more popular Web page features, forms and frames, are also two of the most advanced features. You use them in your Web pages to serve the following functions:

✦ **Forms:** Enable you to gather information and feedback from the users who visit your Web pages. *Forms* can consist of text fields, buttons, check boxes, radio buttons, and drop-down lists, which enable the user to enter information or to choose among options you present.

✦ **Frames:** Enable you to construct sophisticated navigational schemes for your Web site. *Frames* are actually separate Web pages that are partitioned off so that two or more can be displayed in the same browser window at the same time. For example, one frame may be a navigational page consisting of a list of links to other pages; that frame remains in place in its portion of the browser window even when the user clicks a link to display a different Web page in the other frame.

In this chapter, you see how to work with these powerful features in Dreamweaver MX.

Incorporating Forms into Web Pages

Forms on the Web serve the same purpose as the paper-based forms you fill out — they provide a structured format for gathering specific information. The difference is that Web-based forms usually require less time for keyboard-savvy users to fill out (and using Web-based forms also saves a few trees otherwise destined for a paper mill).

Dreamweaver MX offers you a number of handy tools for creating Web-based forms that you can easily include on your Web pages. You can incorporate everything from text fields to radio buttons, and you can create surveys, gather user data, and conduct e-commerce.

Creating Web-based forms requires two steps:

1. Creating the form that users see and interact with, which we demonstrate how to do using Dreamweaver MX in this chapter.

2. Creating the processing program that accepts and processes form input, which we cover in more detail in Book VI, Chapter 4.

Adding a form

Before you can insert specific form objects, such as check boxes, on your Web page, you must first add a form to the page so that the appropriate code is written to the HTML page code.

To add a form to a page, click in the Document window where you want to add the form and choose Insert⇨Form from the main menu or click the Form button from the Forms tab on the Insert panel. (If the Insert panel is not open, choose Window⇨Insert from the main menu to open the panel.)

Dreamweaver MX adds the form to the page as indicated by the red dashed lines and also adds the associated form tag to your HTML page code, as shown in Figure 4-1. You can now insert form objects inside the red dashed lines of the form.

Figure 4-1:
The dashed line means you've created a form!

If you attempt to add a form object without first adding a form, a dialog box appears, asking whether you want to add a form tag. Click Yes to add both the form tag and the object to your page.

Specifying form properties

A form has five properties that you can set using the Form Property inspector: Form Name, Action, Method, Enctype, and Target. Click the form to open the Form Property inspector. (If the Property inspector does not appear, open it by choosing Window⇨Properties from the main menu.) Then specify the following properties:

✦ **Form Name:** Enter an alphanumeric name in the empty text field. The advantage of naming your form is that you can use the name to reference the form in a scripting language that you use to retrieve, store, and manipulate the form data.

✦ **Action:** Enter the URL of the application document/file that processes the form data. Alternatively, you can browse to the location by clicking the folder and making a selection in the Select File dialog box.

You can select the following three common actions:

- Enter the URL of a ColdFusion MX page that evaluates the form after it's been submitted. The URL generally resembles the following:

  `http://www.server.com/form.cfm`

- Enter the JavaScript program that runs after the user submits the form. The action appears as follows:

  `javascript:function()`

  Here, `function` refers to the name of your form-handling function.

- Enter a `mailto:` address where the form data goes after the user clicks Submit. A `mailto:` address appears similar to the following:

  `mailto:gruntworker@formhandling.com`

✦ **Method:** Select a method from the drop-down list for how the form data passes to the processing entity that you specified in the Action field. Choices are Default, GET, and POST. (Default and GET are the same.) GET sends the form data by appending it to the URL that the Action specifies. POST sends the form data as a separate entity. GET limits the amount of data that can pass along, but POST does not.

In other words, if you were to choose GET, the URL sent to the server might look something like `http://www.server.com/coldfusionpage.cfm&bowlingballcolor=blue`, with the form data stuck onto the end. If you were to choose POST instead, the URL would just look something like `http://www.server.com/coldfusionpage.cfm`.

Most of the time, whether you choose GET or POST doesn't really make a difference. However, there are times when you may want to choose one over the other. For example, for security purposes, you may not want information, such as a credit card number, ever being shown in a browser's history. And if the user might choose to bookmark the URL, whether or not to have all of the form data appear could affect your decision. If the form data included secure user information (such as the credit card example), then you probably wouldn't want to have the form data appear. However, if the form data included search criteria, the user might want to bookmark the URL complete with the search parameters.

Data received at the specified `mailto:` address is not formatted for easy reading: It appears as strings of code with the form data embedded within it. This may depend on the encoding option, which we are about to discuss.

✦ **Enctype:** This is an optional attribute. For enctype, your choices are `application/x-www-form-urlencoded` (the default), and multi-part/form-data. `application/x-www-form-urlencoded` replaces all blank characters in the text with a plus sign (+), and other non-printing characters with symbols and numbers. This is often necessary for the server to interpret the information it is receiving — for example, when you've used the GET method, the browser would not be able to process a URL with blank spaces in it. Multipart/form-data does not do this conversion, but instead transfers the information as a compound MIME document. Multipart/form-data is the method that must be used if you are using an `<INPUT TYPE="file">` element in the form. Instead of either of these two options, you can type in text/plain, which will also send the data unencoded; however, this is not a W3C standard.

✦ **Target:** This is also an optional attribute. If you do not specify a target, the server will assume that you want any information that is sent back to the browser (the URL of the response page, for example) sent to the same window or frame that your original form is in. If you wish the form submission's results to appear in a different frame or window, you must specify the name of the target window in this attribute.

Labeling form objects

Dreamweaver MX enables you to provide descriptors for form objects and provide the user with directions about how to complete the information requested for each option. To add descriptors to form objects, simply position your cursor in the form and begin typing. Then insert the form object you want.

Using text fields

Text fields are blank text boxes that you can insert in your form to hold alphanumeric information that the user types. You can set up a text field to hold a single line of text, multiple lines of text, or a password, as follows:

✦ **Single line:** Provides space for the user to enter a single word or short phrase of text.

✦ **Multi line:** Provides space for the user to enter a longer string of text. Appropriate for a comment box.

✦ **Password:** Provides space for the user to enter a password. An asterisk appears in the text field for each character that the user types.

To add a text field, do the following:

1. **In the Document window, click where you want to add the text field and choose Insert⊏⟩Form Objects⊏⟩Text Field from the main menu, or click the Insert Text Field button on the Form tab from the Insert panel.**

If the Insert panel is not open, choose Window⊏⟩Insert from the main menu to open the panel.

Dreamweaver MX adds a text field to your form, and a Text Field Property inspector appears. If the Text Field Property inspector does not appear, choose Window⊏⟩Properties from the main menu to open the inspector.

2. **Fill in the following fields of the Text Field Property inspector to define the parameters of the text field:**

• **Text Field name:** Enter a name in the empty field. The field is referenced by this name in the HTML page code.

• **Char Width:** Enter a whole number for the approximate visible width of the field. (The width is approximate because text characters in your form are displayed differently according to users' browser settings.)

• **Max Chars:** (Applies to Single line and Password fields only.) Enter a whole number to indicate the maximum number of characters that the user can enter in the field. Max Chars can be different from Char Width.

• **Num Lines:** (Applies to Multi line fields only.) This specifies the height, in lines, of the form element, and may be affected by the setting for Wrap (see below).

• **Type:** Select a radio button for Single line, Multi line, or Password.

• **Init Val:** (Optional) Enter an alphanumeric word or phrase that occupies the text field when the user first encounters the field. Users can enter their own information over the Init Val.

• **Wrap:** (Applies to Multi line fields only.) Select an option for text wrapping from the drop-down list. Options consist of Default, Off, Virtual, or Physical. Default and Off are the same and do not wrap text until the user presses the Enter key. The Virtual option wraps text on the user's screen but not when the form is submitted. The Physical option wraps text both on the user's screen and when the form is submitted.

Setting up buttons

After a user enters data into a form, the user must then perform some sort of task to transmit the data from his or her computer to another computer that can process the information. Dreamweaver MX offers you three buttons to use to activate your form: Reset, Submit, and None:

✦ **Reset:** After the user clicks this button, it erases all data entered into the form, allowing the user to reenter data into a fresh, clean form.

✦ **Submit:** After the user clicks this button, the form data scoots off to another computer based on the specified action. (You see how to set the action of a form in the "Specifying form properties" section, earlier in this chapter.)

✦ **None:** After the user clicks this button, it executes the programming function that the Web designer assigned to it.

To insert a button, do the following:

1. **Click where you want to add the button in the Document window and choose Insert⇨Form Objects⇨Button from the main menu, or click Insert Button on the Form tab in the Insert panel.**

   If the Insert panel is not open, choose Window⇨Insert from the main menu to open the panel.

   Dreamweaver MX adds a button to your form. The Button Property inspector should also be visible. If the Button Property inspector does not appear, choose Window⇨Properties from the main menu to open the inspector.

2. **Fill in the following fields of the Button Property inspector to define the parameters of the button:**

   • **Button name:** Enter a name in the empty text field. This name identifies the button in the HTML code.

   • **Label:** Enter the text that you want to appear on the button.

   • **Action:** Select a radio button to indicate the function of the button. Choices consist of Reset form, Submit form, and None.

You can create a graphical Submit button — a button created from a small image — by choosing Insert⇨Form Objects⇨Image Field from the main menu or by clicking the Insert Image Field button on the Form Objects panel. Then browse to the image file in your site or type the path to and name of the image file directly into the File Name field. When you finish, click OK to create the graphical Submit button.

Adding other form elements

In addition to the text fields and buttons, you can add a variety of form elements that help your users give you information. Figure 4-2 shows some of the useful form elements you can add to your forms. To insert any of the elements you see in Figure 4-2, follow these steps:

1. **Position your cursor in the area of the Document window where you want to add the element.**

2. **Click the appropriate button on the Form Object panel from the Insert panel (see Figure 4-2), or choose Insert⇨Form Objects⇨Desired Form Element from the main menu.**

    If the Insert panel is not open, choose Window⇨Insert from the main menu to open the panel.

    Dreamweaver MX adds the element to your form, and the appropriate inspector appears. (If the appropriate inspector does not appear, open it by choosing Windows⇨Properties from the main menu.)

3. **Fill in the fields of the inspector.**

    If you're adding a radio group, jump menu, or image, a dialog box will pop up and ask you for additional information. Fill in your choices for each of these.

4. **Click OK to apply your selections and close the dialog box.**

Figure 4-2:
Form
elements.

Structuring Pages with Frames

Frames are divisions of a Web page that enable you to load information independently into distinct regions of the browser window. Frames are useful if you want to display certain information on-screen while changing other information. You frequently see three-frame pages on the Web — the top frame shows the site's title graphic, the left frame shows the navigation bar, and the large body frame changes to show the content that you select.

A special HTML page called a *frameset* defines the structure and formatting of frames on your Web page. As you work with frames, be aware that you must always save the frameset page to lay out the size, position, and borders of your frames, along with the content that you want to display in each frame.

Adding frames

You can add a frame to a frameless Document window or to an existing frame within the Document window. Adding a frame to an existing frame divides the existing frame into two or more regions.

To add a frame, click the Document window or existing frame in the area where you want to add the frame. Choose Insert⇨Frames and select an option from the drop-down list, which is detailed in Table 4-1.

Table 4-1	Options for Creating Frames
Frame Option	*What It Does*
Left	Creates a vertical frame down the left side
Right	Creates a vertical frame down the right side
Top	Creates a horizontal frame across the top
Bottom	Creates a horizontal frame across the bottom
Bottom and Nested Left	Splits the page in two — top and bottom — and creates a left frame in the top frame
Bottom and Nested Right	Splits the page in two — top and bottom — and creates a right frame in the top frame
Left and Nested Bottom	Splits the page in two — right and left — and creates a bottom frame in the right frame
Right and Nested Bottom	Splits the page in two — right and left — and creates a bottom frame in the left frame

Frame Option	What It Does
Top and Bottom	Creates three frames
Left and Nested Top	Splits the page in two — right and left — creates a top frame in the right frame
Right and Nested Top	Splits the page in two — right and left — and creates a top frame in the left frame
Top and Nested Left	Splits the page in two — top and bottom — and creates a left frame in the bottom frame
Top and Nested Right	Splits the page in two — top and bottom — and creates a right frame in the bottom frame

You can also add a frame by clicking the button on the Frames tab in the Insert panel corresponding to the frame type you want to create. The light-blue frame in each button represents where the content of the existing frame is placed after you add the new frame.

A third method of adding a frame is to drag the outer border of the current frame, or Alt+click in the inner border. You can then follow the steps in the next section to modify this new frame.

Modifying frames

You use the Frame Property inspector to select the source page that appears in a frame. You also use the Frame Property inspector to format the appearance of an individual frame. To modify a frame, follow these steps:

1. **Open the Frames panel by choosing Window⇨Others⇨Frames from the main menu.**

   Note: You can't simply click a frame to open its associated Frame Property inspector. If you click a frame, you're actually clicking the source page that resides in the frame — a process identical to clicking in the Document window for that page. To select a specific frame, press the Alt key and then click in the frame. You see the Frame Property inspector for an individual frame, as shown in Figure 4-3.

2. **In the Frames panel, click the frame that you want to modify the attributes of.**

   A Frame Property inspector appears for the selected frame. If the inspector doesn't appear, open it by choosing Window⇨Properties from the main menu.

Figure 4-3:
Individual
frames.

3. **In the Frame Property inspector, enter a name for your frame in the Frame Name text field.**

   This name is the name by which the frame is referenced in the Frames panel, target drop-down lists, and the HTML page code. The frame name must start with a letter, and you should not use hyphens, spaces, or periods. You should also avoid using JavaScript-reserved names, such as `top`. Although these words and symbols may be accepted, if you are using any scripting (JavaScript, VBScript) to manipulate your frames, the results may be inconsistent or wrong. It's a good idea to get into the habit of avoiding these words and characters. Word separation can be indicated by capitalization, and underscore characters can also be used.

4. **In the Src text field, enter the name of the source page whose content you intend to display in the frame.**

   Alternatively, you can click the Src folder and browse to select the source page.

5. **Select a scrolling option for your selected frame from the Scroll drop-down list. The options are as follows:**

   • **Yes:** Adds scroll bars to the frame, whether they're needed or not.

   • **No:** Doesn't add scroll bars to the frame, even if a scroll bar is needed to display the entire frame.

- **Auto:** Places one or more scroll bars in the frame if the frame contents exceed the frame boundaries.

- **Default:** Places one or more scroll bars in the frame, depending on the user's browser settings.

6. **Select the No Resize check box if you don't want the user to be able to resize the frame.**

   If you do want the user to be able to resize the frame, leave the check box deselected.

7. **Format the frame border appearance by selecting a choice from the Borders drop-down list box:**

   - **Yes:** Creates a three-dimensional look for the borders. (This doesn't work in all browsers.)

   - **No:** Creates a single-color flat look for the borders.

   - **Default:** Enables the user's browser to set how borders appear.

8. **Select a border color for the frame by clicking the Border Color swatch and selecting a color from the Color palette that appears.**

   Alternatively, you can enter a hexadecimal color code in the Border Color text field. (This doesn't work in all browsers.)

9. **Enter a number in pixels in the Margin Width and the Margin Height text fields.**

   Margin Width specifies the horizontal standoff space between the frame content and the frame border. Margin Height specifies the vertical standoff space between the frame content and the frame border. This is in addition to any values that the page called into the frame already has assigned.

Deleting frames

To delete a frame, select the frame border and drag it to the edge of the parent frame or to the edge of the Document window — whichever is closer. If you only have two frames on the page, this action will result in a frameset with only one page in it.

Saving frames

Saving a frame means that you're saving the HTML page from which the source content of the frame originates. To save a frame, follow these steps:

1. **Select the frame by clicking in it.**

2. **Choose File⇨Save Frame from the main menu.**

3. **On the first save, enter a name in the File Name text field of the Save As dialog box that appears and click the Save button.**

   Future saves require that you complete only Steps 1 and 2.

Saving framesets

Saving a frameset means saving the layout of frame positions, frame names, and border formatting on a page. Keep in mind that you must save individual frames to save the content contained in those frames. To save a frameset, follow these steps:

1. **Select the frameset by clicking one of its borders.**

2. **Choose File⇨Save Frameset from the main menu.**

   Note: This will not work if the frameset is nested.

3. **On the first save, enter a name in the File Name text field of the Save As dialog box that appears and click Save.**

   Future saves require that you complete only Steps 1 and 2.

If you have made changes to individual frames — not just the frameset — since your last save, Dreamweaver MX asks if you want to save individual frames. Make sure that you do so.

Setting no-frames content

Text-based browsers and many older browsers frequently don't support frames and can't correctly display pages that you create by using frames.

To help ensure that the maximum number of users can view your page correctly, Dreamweaver MX offers you a method for building *no-frames* pages as companions to your frame-enabled pages. To create a no-frames page for your current frameset, follow these steps:

1. **Choose Modify⇨Frameset⇨Edit NoFrames Content from the main menu.**

   A blank, NoFrames Content page appears in the Document window and replaces your frame-enabled page, as shown in Figure 4-4.

2. **On the NoFrames Content page, insert the content that you want to appear in NoFrames browsers.**

   This content can include text, images, and other page elements.

3. **Return to your frame-enabled page by choosing Modify⇨ Frameset⇨Edit NoFrames Content from the main menu.**

Figure 4-4:
An
alternative
NoFrames
page.

Targeting content

You can set up a two-frame frameset in which you use the left frame for navigation and the main frame to display any link that the user clicks in the navigation frame. You need to set up only the link to target the main frame as the location where you want the selected HTML page to open.

Set up a target by following these steps:

1. **Select the text or image that you want to act as a link.**

Doing so opens the associated Property inspector. If the inspector doesn't appear, open it by choosing Windows➪Properties from the main menu.

2. **In the Link field, enter the name of the HTML source page that will appear in the frame.**

Alternatively, you can click the Link folder and browse to select the source page.

3. **From the Target drop-down menu, select the target frame where the link is to appear.**

All available targets are listed in the menu. These targets include the names of all frames that you set up and also the following system-wide targets:

- _blank: Opens a new browser window and shows the link in that window. The current window remains open.

- _parent: Opens the link in a window that replaces the frameset containing the current page.

- _self: Opens the link in the current frame. The linked page replaces the page in the current frame. If you want the link to open in the current frame, you can select _self or you can leave the Target area in the Property inspector empty.

- _top: Opens the link in a window that replaces the outermost frameset of the current page. (Same as _parent, unless you're using nested framesets.)

Chapter 5: Laying Out Pages with Layers

In This Chapter

✔ **Adding, selecting, and deleting a layer**

✔ **Placing objects in a layer**

✔ **Including a background image or color in a layer**

✔ **Naming a layer**

✔ **Nesting layers**

✔ **Aligning layers**

✔ **Changing the visibility of a layer**

✔ **Layering layers: Setting the z-index**

✔ **Moving and resizing a layer**

*T*o precisely lay out the content of your Web page, you can use tables (see Book II, Chapter 2), or you can use the latest and greatest layout aid: layers. You can think of layers in Dreamweaver MX as separate pieces of paper that you fill with content (images, text, and so on) and shuffle, stack, position, and overlap until your Web page looks exactly the way you want. Dreamweaver MX layers use a now common companion to HTML called Cascading Style Sheets in order to place your content anywhere on the screen. However, you should be aware that Cascading Style Sheets are only supported in Internet Explorer and Netscape Navigator versions above 4.0. For more information about Cascading Style Sheets, check out *Cascading Style Sheets For Dummies* by Damon Dean (published by Wiley Publishing, Inc.).

Before you begin working with layers, you should first have the Layers panel open. To do this, choose Window⇨Others⇨Layers, or if you're in hurry, simply press F2.

Adding a Layer

Adding a layer to the workspace of your Document window, shown in Figure 5-1, can be done using one of the following two methods:

✦ **Choose Insert⇨Layer.** If there is nothing on the page already, as in this case, a new layer appears in the upper-left corner of your Document window.

✦ **Click the Draw Layer button from the Common tab in the Insert panel.** (If the Insert panel is not visible, open it by choosing Window⇨ Insert from the main menu.) Position the cross hair cursor anywhere in your Document window and click and drag until the layer obtains the dimensions you want. Release the mouse button.

For each layer you draw, Dreamweaver MX places a layer marker in the upper-left corner of the Document window. For Cascading Style Sheet (CSS) layers, which are applicable to both Internet Explorer and Netscape Navigator, the marker appears as the letter C in a yellow box. When invisible elements, such as these layer markers, are added to a page, the design view in Dreamweaver MX usually renders the page a little differently than a browser, so be sure to check how your work looks in an actual browser.

Figure 5-1:
Your first
layer!

Selecting a Layer

Selecting a layer enables you to identify which layer you want to affect when executing a layer operation, such as moving or naming the layer. Use any of the following methods to select a layer:

✦ In the Document window, click on the boundary of the layer.

✦ In the Document window, click on the layer handle — the square enclosing a small grid located at the top-left corner of the layer.

✦ In the Document window, click on the layer marker that appears as the letter C in a yellow box.

✦ In the Document window, press the Shift key and click anywhere inside the layer.

✦ In the Layers panel, click the name of the layer.

✦ Click the layer's HTML tag in the tag selector of the Document window status bar. The HTML tag will look something like this:

```
<div#Layername>
```

Selection handles appear on the boundary of the layer to indicate that you have selected it.

Deleting a Layer

Deleting a layer removes the layer, the layer's contents, and the layer marker from the Document window. To delete a layer, select the layer and press the Delete or Backspace key.

Don't delete a layer if you want to remove it from one page and add it to another. Instead, cut the layer by choosing Edit⇨Cut from the main menu. Open the page where you want to add the layer and choose Edit⇨Paste.

Placing Objects in a Layer

To add an object to a layer, click inside the layer and follow the normal procedure for adding the object. For instance, add text to a layer by clicking inside the layer and typing text; add other objects to a layer by clicking inside the layer and choosing Insert from the main menu.

Including a Background Image or Color in a Layer

By default, an unnested layer does not have a color or background image, and will just display what lies beneath it. (A nested child layer has the same color or background image as its parent. For more about nested layers, see the section, "Nesting Layers," later in this chapter.)

You can change the background of any layer by including a background image or color in the layer by following these steps:

1. **Select the layer where you want to change the background.**

   If the Layer Property inspector does not appear, open it by choosing Window⇨Properties.

2. **In the Layer Property inspector, change one of the following:**

   - **Bg Image:** Click the folder to the right of the text field and browse to select a background image from the Select Image Source dialog box that appears. Click the Select button to accept your image choice and close the dialog box. The path to and name of the background image appear in the Bg Image field, and the image is added to the background of the layer. Figure 5-2 shows a layer with a background image.

   - **Bg Color:** Click the color box (the little gray box with an arrow on it) and select a color from the color palette that appears. Alternatively, you can enter a hexadecimal number for a color in the Bg Color box. The new color appears in the background of the selected layer.

Figure 5-2: An image added to a background.

Naming a Layer

The first layer you add to a page is automatically named Layer1; the second layer you add is named Layer2; and so on. You can change these default number names to other names that help you more easily distinguish layers when working with HTML and examining layers with the Layer Property inspector or Layers panel.

To name a layer using the Layers panel, follow these steps:

1. **Select the layer to open the Layers panel.**

   If the Layers panel does not appear, open it by choosing Window⇨ Others⇨Layers from the main menu.

2. **Double-click the Name column for the layer whose name you want to change.**

   The current name is selected.

3. **Enter a new name for the layer.**

Get in the habit of appropriately naming your layers as soon as you create them. The name *BlueprintImageMap* helps you remember a layer's content much better than *Layer15*. Remember that layer names cannot contain spaces.

Nesting Layers

A *nested* layer is a layer that has all of its HTML code lying within another layer. The nested layer is often referred to as a *child* layer, whereas the layer on which it depends is called the *parent* layer. A child layer can be drawn completely inside its parent (as shown in Figure 5-3), in an intersecting arrangement with its parent, or completely unattached to its parent, depending on the effect you want to achieve. A nested layer inherits the same visibility of its parent and moves with the parent when the parent layer is repositioned in the Document window. Some versions of Netscape have issues with nested layers, so try to avoid using them if there is a simpler way to accomplish the same thing.

Enabling nesting

To create nested layers in the Document window, you must first enable nesting. To do so, follow these steps:

1. **Choose Edit⇨Preferences to open the Preferences dialog box.**

2. **In the Preferences dialog box, choose Layers in the category area.**

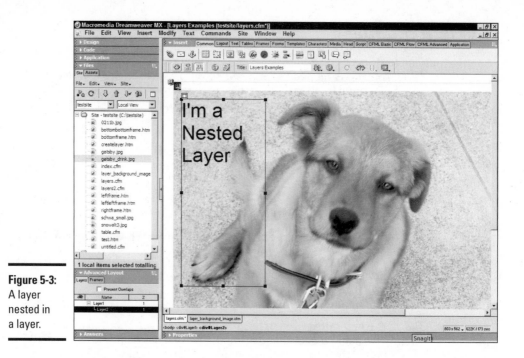

Figure 5-3:
A layer
nested in
a layer.

3. **Select the Nesting check box.**

4. **Click OK to close the Preferences dialog box.**

5. **In the Document window, choose Window⇨Layers to open the Layers panel.**

6. **In the Layers panel, make sure that the Prevent Overlaps option is deselected.**

Creating a new nested layer

Use either of these methods to draw a nested layer:

✦ Click inside an existing layer and choose Insert⇨Layer.

✦ Click the Draw Layer button from the Common Objects panel and drag your mouse onto the parent layer.

Either method causes a child layer of default size to appear inside the parent layer. If the dimensions of the parent layer are smaller than the dimensions of the child layer, the child layer will exceed the boundaries of the parent.

Nesting an existing layer

To change the nesting of an existing layer, follow these steps:

1. **Open the Layers panel by choosing Window⇨Layers.**

2. **In the Layers panel, press and hold the Ctrl key while using the mouse to click and drag the intended child layer on top of its new parent.**

   The child is in the correct position when you see a box appear around its intended parent layer.

3. **Release the mouse button.**

   The new child-parent relationship is shown in the Layers panel.

Dreamweaver MX draws the new child layer and updates the associated code for changed layer-nesting in the HTML source code for your page.

Collapsing or expanding your view in the Layers panel

You can change how you view the names of nested layers in the Layers panel by collapsing or expanding your view:

+ **To collapse your view:** Click the minus sign (–) in front of a parent layer. Names of nested child layers for that parent are hidden.

+ **To expand your view:** Click the plus sign (+) in front of a parent layer. Names of nested child layers for that parent appear.

Aligning Layers

Aligning layers with each other can help you precisely lay out visual content in the Document window. You can align the top, left side, right side, or bottom of layers.

To align layers, select the layers you want to align by pressing and holding the Shift key and then clicking each layer in the Document window. Choose Modify⇨Align and choose one of the following options from the submenu:

+ **Left:** Assigns the x-coordinate of the last selected layer to all selected layers.

+ **Right:** Aligns the right side of all selected layers with the right side of the last selected layer.

+ **Top:** Assigns the y-coordinate of the last selected layer to all selected layers.

✦ **Bottom:** Aligns the bottom of all selected layers with the bottom of the last selected layer.

✦ **Make Same Width:** Gives all the layers the same width as the last selected layer.

✦ **Make Same Height:** Gives all the layers the same height as the last selected layer.

Changing the Visibility of a Layer

You can specify whether a layer is visible or hidden when a Web page *loads* — first appears in the user's browser window — and as a result of specific actions by the user. Visibility can change as many times as you want. Visibility options consist of the following:

✦ **Default:** The layer's initial visibility is the default setting, which is visible. To edit layer default settings, choose Edit⇔Preferences from the main menu, and the Preferences dialog box (see Figure 5-4) appears to display the layer default settings that you can change.

Figure 5-4: Setting your default preferences for layers.

✦ **Inherit:** For a nested layer, the layer's initial visibility is the same as the visibility of its parent. For an unnested layer, selecting the inherit option causes the layer to appear as visible.

✦ **Visible:** The layer's initial visibility setting is visible.

✦ **Hidden:** The layer's initial visibility is hidden.

You can use either the Layer Property inspector or the Layers panel to set layer visibility. By setting layer visibility, you can create scripts that cause images to appear (or disappear) in response to user interaction. For example, you can create an image of a widget that appears on a Web page after a user clicks a link marked, <u>Click here to see our top-of-the-line widget!</u>

To set the initial visibility of a layer via the Layer Property inspector, select the layer in the Document window to open the Layer Property inspector. If the inspector does not appear, open it by choosing Window⇨Properties from the main menu. Click the down arrow on the Visibility list box and choose a visibility option from the drop-down list.

Layering Layers: Setting the Z-index

The *z-index* of a layer indicates the layer's position in a stack of multiple layers. Z-indices are useful when you have a handful of layers — some containing transparent portions, some of different sizes — stacked one on top of the other. Changing the z-index of your layers lets you "shuffle" the layers — much as you shuffle a deck of cards — to create interesting visual effects.

Z-indices are measured in whole numbers and do not have to be consecutive — for instance, you can have three layers with z-indices of 1, 3, and 7, respectively. The layer with the largest z-index sits on top of the layer stack, and the layer with the smallest z-index sits on the bottom of the layer stack. Layers with larger z-indices obscure those with smaller z-indices. You can change the z-index of a layer in either the Layer Property inspector or the Layers panel.

To assign the z-index of a layer by using the Layer Property inspector, follow these steps:

1. **Select the layer to open the Layer Property inspector.**

If the Layer Property inspector does not appear, open it by choosing Window⇨Properties from the main menu.

2. **Enter a new number in the Z-Index field of the Layer Property inspector.**

To assign the z-index of a layer using the Layers panel, follow these steps:

1. **Select the layer to open the Layers panel.**

   If the Layers panel doesn't appear, open it by choosing Window⇨Others⇨ Layers from the main menu.

2. **Click the Z column for the layer whose z-index you want to change.**

   The current z-index is selected.

3. **Enter a new z-index for the layer.**

   The new number appears in the Z column for the selected layer.

To assign relative z-indices to layers by reordering layers in the Layers panel, follow these steps:

1. **Open the Layers panel by choosing Window⇨Others⇨Layers from the main menu.**

   The Layers panel lists layers in order of descending z-index. Nested layers are listed in descending order within their parent layer.

2. **Click the name of a layer for which you want to change the z-index.**

3. **Drag the layer name into a new list position and release the mouse button.**

   As you drag, the selected layer is indicated by a thick line.

Figure 5-5 shows the effect of changing a z-index. In the top image, the z-index of the text is higher than the image. As a result, the text is on top. Conversely, in the bottom image, the image has the higher z-index value, and as a result, it's on top of the text. Dreamweaver MX reorders the list in the Layers panel and renumbers layer z-indices to reflect your change. Also, Dreamweaver MX updates the associated code for the layers' z-indices in the HTML source code for your page.

Because you don't have to number the z-index of layers consecutively, consider leaving gaps between indices, in case you later want to add new layers into the middle of the stack. For instance, use only even numbers for your indices so that you can easily sandwich a layer with an odd-numbered z-index in between.

Figure 5-5:
The effect of
changing
z-indices.

Moving a Layer

You may want to move a layer to a place in another location in the
Document window or to a position relative to the grid or to other objects.

To move a layer, select the layer in the Document window and then reposition
your selection by using one of the following three methods:

✦ Click and drag the layer to a new location and release the mouse button.

✦ Press the arrow keys you find on the numeric keypad on your keyboard
to nudge the layer up, down, left, or right one pixel at a time.

✦ In the Layer Property inspector, enter a new value in the T (top) and
L (left) fields to indicate the pixel coordinates of the layer's top-left corner.

When moving layers, you can choose to enable or prevent layer overlap, depending on how you want the final image montage to appear. You enable or prevent layer overlap by selecting or deselecting the Prevent Overlaps check box in the Layers panel.

Resizing a Layer

Resizing a layer means changing its height and width dimensions. To resize a layer, select the layer and perform one of the following tasks:

✦ Click and drag a selection handle — one of the large dots on the layer boundary — until the layer obtains the dimensions you desire.

✦ In the Layer Property inspector, enter a new width in pixels at the W field and a new height in pixels at the H field. If the Layer Property inspector does not appear, open it by choosing Window⇨Properties.

You can change the height and width dimensions of multiple layers at the same time as follows:

1. **Press and hold the Shift key while selecting each layer you want to resize.**

   If the Multiple Layers Property inspector does not appear, open it by choosing Window⇨Properties.

2. **In the Multiple Layers Property inspector, enter a new width in pixels in the W field and a new height in pixels in the H field.**

Chapter 6: Using ColdFusion MX in Dreamweaver MX

In This Chapter

✔ Exploring how ColdFusion MX is integrated into Dreamweaver MX

✔ Using the Tag Editor and the Insert panel

✔ Viewing database connections

✔ Using the Bindings tabs to get dynamic data

✔ Taking a brief look at server behaviors and components

*O*ne of the biggest changes in Macromedia Studio MX is the integration of ColdFusion MX into Dreamweaver MX. For years, the two products have had a symbiotic relationship, and as a result, their integration has been an exceptionally smooth one. Dreamweaver was always better than ColdFusion as a graphical HTML editor. ColdFusion and its sister product, Macromedia HomeSite, were the better choices for the HTML editor who preferred a coder-friendly interface. This chapter provides the lowdown on the new features in Dreamweaver MX that bring ColdFusion MX to life.

This chapter only covers the ColdFusion features now available in Dreamweaver MX. For a complete run-down of ColdFusion MX and how it works, check out Book VI.

Understanding the Integration of ColdFusion MX and Dreamweaver MX

Before the MX version, Dreamweaver was largely geared toward the basics of HTML editing, such as creating and editing tables, graphics placement, text editing, and some basic site management tools. With the integration of ColdFusion MX, the product has become immediately more robust with a host of features that can make your site more dynamic.

Before Dreamweaver MX arrived, ColdFusion was made up of three components:

✦ A Web-based application server that read HTML and ColdFusion code and generated HTML for a browser to view.

✦ A scripting language that enabled users to perform a number of dynamic functions like querying databases, and personalizing Web pages based on user input.

✦ A stand-alone development tool (ColdFusion Studio) that was used to create ColdFusion code and manage some parts of the application server.

With the introduction of Dreamweaver MX, ColdFusion Studio was simply integrated into the new Dreamweaver MX interface. This resulted in a single product that incorporates both the WYSIWYG (What You See Is What You Get) interface that Dreamweaver users are accustomed to and the more developer-friendly ColdFusion Studio code environment. The other elements of ColdFusion have remained largely the same with the introduction of Macromedia Studio MX.

Remnants of ColdFusion Studio are littered throughout Dreamweaver MX, and although the new style and look of Dreamweaver MX will be familiar to users of previous versions of ColdFusion and Dreamweaver, it does take some time to get familiar with this new interface.

In Dreamweaver MX, you can find ColdFusion features in the following areas:

✦ **Code view:** Select the Code view by choosing View⮑Code. This is the development view that is more traditionally associated with ColdFusion Studio. Figure 6-1 shows both the view from the ColdFusion Studio 5 and the new Code view. You can see that a lot of the physical features look the same.

✦ **Insert panel:** Take another look at Figure 6-1, paying particular attention to the tabs in both products. Previous versions of Dreamweaver didn't have these tabs; this is a convention adopted from ColdFusion. You can see a number of ColdFusion-specific elements in the tabs in Dreamweaver MX, notably the Script, CFML Basic, CFML Flow, CFML Advanced, and Application tabs.

If your Dreamweaver Site is not configured to use ColdFusion MX as the testing server, these tabs may not show up. To use ColdFusion MX as the testing server for your Site, choose Site⮑Edit Sites, then select your Site and click Edit. In the Category column, select Testing Server and then finally, select ColdFusion from the Server Model drop-down list.

Figure 6-1:
Separated
at birth?

Book II
Chapter 6

Using ColdFusion MX
in Dreamweaver MX

✦ **Application panel:** To bring up the Application panel, choose Window and then any of the following: Database, Bindings, Server Behaviors, or Components. This brings up the Application panel with the appropriate tab selected. Within the Application panel, you can configure databases, set up links to your remote site, and create ColdFusion components.

✦ **Code panel:** The Code panel, not to be confused with the Code view, provides some valuable reference information about your code. (The Code panel is shown in Figure 6-2.) You can bring up the panel by choosing Tag Inspector, Snippets, or Reference from the Window menu:

   • **Tag Inspector tab:** The Tag Inspector tab reviews the quality of your HTML and CFML code.

   • **Snippets tab:** In the Snippets tab, you can create reusable chunks of code.

   • **Reference tab:** The Reference tab gives you access to O'Reilly's HTML reference guide.

Figure 6-2:
The Code
panel.

Using Features on the Insert Panel

The Insert panel houses a number of ColdFusion MX features, and using those ColdFusion MX features is pretty straightforward. Almost all the features include a Help button to explain to you precisely what the feature does.

To insert a ColdFusion MX feature, you follow these steps:

1. Select the tab in the Insert panel for the element you want to insert.

You can choose from five ColdFusion tabs: Script, CFML (ColdFusion Markup Language) Basic, CFML Flow, CFML Advanced, and Application. The other tabs are for regular Dreamweaver MX features.

2. Click the icon of the feature you want to insert.

This brings up a dialog box with all the parameters for that feature. Figure 6-3 shows a dialog box for a Cfquery tag (with Cfquery, you can retrieve information from a database). Not all features will bring up a dialog box, as is the case with Cfquery. For more information on how to use all these features, check out Book VI.

If you move your mouse over an icon and keep it there, the name of the feature will appear over the icon, allowing you to see what function that icon serves.

Book II
Chapter 6

Using ColdFusion MX in Dreamweaver MX

Figure 6-3:
The Cfquery dialog box.

3. Enter all the pertinent information in the dialog box for the element that you selected in Step 2.

Again, the information you must enter varies, depending on which tags or elements you selected.

4. Click OK to insert the element.

Figures 6-4 through 6-8 show all the ColdFusion MX elements that you have access to through the Insert panel. For a more detailed explanation of how to use these elements in your site, check out Book VI.

Figure 6-4 shows the Script tab of the Insert panel in Dreamweaver MX, which allows you to access the following ColdFusion MX features:

◆ **Script:** Provides an interface for adding JavaScript and VBScript

◆ **Noscript:** Specifies the content to display when scripting is not enabled on a browser

◆ **Server-Side Include:** Selects an include file

Server-Side Include

Script

Figure 6-4:
The Script
tab of the
Insert panel.

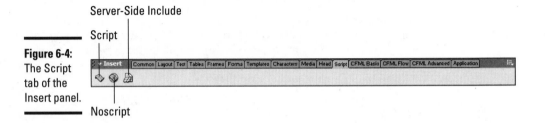

Noscript

Figure 6-5 shows the CFML Basic tab of the Insert panel in Dreamweaver MX, which allows you to access the following ColdFusion features (a lot of these are ColdFusion Markup Language tags, which are discussed in more detail in Book VI, Chapter 3):

◆ **Server variable:** Creates server variables

◆ **cfquery:** Creates a <CFQUERY> tag

◆ **cfoutput:** Creates a <CFOUTPUT> tag

◆ **cfinsert:** Creates a <CFINSERT> tag

◆ **cfupdate:** Creates a <CFUPDATE> tag

◆ **cfinclude:** Creates a <CFINCLUDE> tag

◆ **cflocation:** Creates a <CFLOCATION> tag

◆ **cfset:** Sets the value of a variable

◆ **cfparam:** Creates a parameter

◆ **Comment:** Creates the comment arrows

◆ **Surround with #:** Surrounds the selected text with # signs

◆ **cfscript:** Creates a <CFSCRIPT> tag into which you can put ColdFusion Script

Figure 6-5:
The CFML Basic tab of the Insert panel.

**Book II
Chapter 6**

Using ColdFusion MX
in Dreamweaver MX

Figure 6-6 shows the CFML Flow tab of the Insert panel in Dreamweaver MX, which allows you to access the following ColdFusion MX features:

✦ **cftry:** Creates a `<CFTRY>` tag

✦ **cfcatch:** Creates a `<CFCATCH>` tag

✦ **cfthrow:** Creates a `<CFTHROW>` tag

✦ **cflock:** Creates a `<CFLOCK>` tag

✦ **cfswitch:** Creates a `<CFSWITCH>` tag

✦ **cfcase:** Creates a `<CFCASE>` tag

✦ **cfdefaultcase:** Creates a `<CFDEFAULTCASE>` tag

✦ **cfif:** Creates a `<CFIF>` tag

✦ **cfelse:** Creates a `<CFELSE>` tag

✦ **cfelseif:** Creates a `<CFELSEIF>` tag

✦ **cfloop:** Creates a `<CFLOOP>` tag

✦ **cfbreak:** Creates a `<CFBREAK>` tag

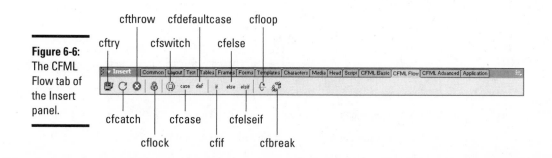

Figure 6-6:
The CFML Flow tab of the Insert panel.

Figure 6-7 shows the CFML Advanced tab of the Insert panel in Dreamweaver MX, which allows you to access the following ColdFusion MX features:

+ **cfcookie:** Enables you to specify the parameters of creating a cookie

+ **cfcontent:** Enables you to specify how to create a content tag

+ **cfheader:** Enables you to specify the parameters of creating a header

+ **ColdFusion Page Encoding:** Sets your page encoding information

+ **cfapplication:** Enables you to specify your application parameters

+ **cferror:** Specifies error information

+ **cfdirectory:** Allows you to work with directories (create, delete, list, and so on)

+ **cffile:** Enables you to work with files (create, append, write, and so on)

+ **cfmail:** Specifies how to send mail through ColdFusion MX

+ **cfpop:** Specifies how to send messages through a POP server

+ **cfhttp:** Specifies how to make an HTTP request

+ **cfhttpparam:** Specifies how to set parameters for an HTTP request

+ **cfldap:** Specifies how you can access an LDAP store

+ **cfftp:** Specifies how to make an FTP request

+ **cfsearch:** Builds you an interface to Verity to make searches

+ **cfindex:** Builds you an interface to index a Verity search collection

+ **cfmodule:** Allows you to specify a module

+ **cfobject:** Enables you to call a component

+ **cfchart:** Specifies how to use ColdFusion MX's charting features

+ **More Tags:** Brings up the Tag Chooser dialog box

Figure 6-7:
The CFML
Advanced
tab of the
Insert panel.

cfcookie   cfapplication   cfmail   cfldap   cfmodule

cfheader   cfdirectory   cfhttp   cfsearch   cfchart

cfcontent   cferror   cffile   cfpop   cfftp   cfobject

ColdFusion Page Encoding   cfhttpparam   cfindex   More Tags

Figure 6-8 shows the Application tab of the Insert panel in Dreamweaver MX, which allows you to access the following ColdFusion features:

✦ **Recordset:** Allows you to connect to a database and retrieve data from that database. It creates the <CFQUERY> tag for you

✦ **Repeated Region:** Enables you to create a repeated region

✦ **Dynamic Table:** Specifies a dynamic table

✦ **Dynamic Text:** Specifies some dynamic text

✦ **Recordset Navigation Bar:** Creates a dynamic navigation bar for a recordset

✦ **Recordset Navigation Status:** Tells you where you are in the collection of your recordset

✦ **Master Detail Page Set:** Creates a master detail page

✦ **Record Insertion Form:** Creates a form to insert a database record

✦ **Record Update Form:** Creates a form to update a database record

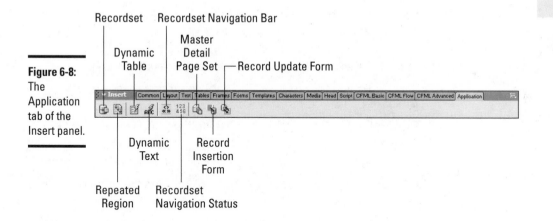

Figure 6-8:
The Application tab of the Insert panel.

Editing a Tag

After you've inserted a tag into your ColdFusion code, you may need to edit that tag. You can edit the code directly, or you can use the Tag Editor, which provides a cleaner way to see all the parameters for your tag. (**Note:** Not all tags have this option. If you don't see Edit Tag in Step 3, then you know the tag you're working with doesn't support this feature.) To use the Tag Editor, follow these steps:

1. **Switch to the Code view by choosing View⇨Code.**

2. **Place your cursor anywhere in the tag you want to edit.**

3. **Right-click and choose Edit Tag from the contextual menu.**

   The Edit Tag dialog box appears.

4. **Change the value in the dialog box, and then click OK to update the tag.**

   The value will change, depending on which tag you're editing.

Getting Data from a Database

You can set up a database connection using the ColdFusion Administrator, as described in Book VI, Chapter 6. Using the Dreamweaver MX interface, however, you can look directly into a database to see the tables and columns that make up a database when you're in Code view. More importantly, you can then easily add those tables and columns to your ColdFusion code simply by dragging them onto the screen:

1. **Open the Database tab in the Application panel by choosing Window⇨Database.**

   You see a list of the databases on your testing server. For this example, we use the CompanyInfo database, one of the sample databases that comes with ColdFusion MX.

2. **Click the plus (+) button next to the CompanyInfo database.**

   This shows you the views, tables, and stored procedures for the database.

3. **Expand the Employee table by clicking the plus (+) button next to the table.**

   All the columns in the table should now be visible, as shown in Figure 6-9.

4. **Click and drag the LastName column from the panel onto the work area.**

   You see that this adds the column name to the work area.

For the feature described in the previous steps to work, you need to have an active Testing Server configured, and you need to know the Remote Data Services password for your testing server. Check out Book VI, Chapter 2 for more information.

Figure 6-9:
The
Employee
table.

Now, by itself, this doesn't really accomplish a whole lot. All you've really
done is drag a column name onto your work area. To really see it in action,
try adding the code text to your page, in between the <BODY> tags:

```
<CFQUERY name="DatabaseTest" datasource="CompanyInfo">
select LastName from Employee
</CFQUERY>

<CFOUTPUT query="DatabaseTest">
#lastname#<BR>
</CFOUTPUT>
```

Now, press the F12 key to preview the page in a Web browser, and you see a
whole list of last names, as shown in Figure 6-10. If you'd like, try adding
some other fields in the code between `select` and `from`, making sure that
the fields are all separated by commas. If you then add the field name to
`cfoutput`, surrounded by pound signs (#), you see those fields displayed
as well. For more information on accessing data from a database using
ColdFusion MX, check out Book VI, Chapter 3.

Figure 6-10:
Getting last
names from
a database.

Using the Bindings Tab

The Bindings tab of the Application panel provides another interface to data sources, and for someone unaccustomed to working with ColdFusion MX, it is an easy way to begin to understand CFML. *Binding,* in the Dreamweaver MX vernacular, is just a link between the page and some other datasource that provides data to the page. With this interface, you can build the same query we used in the example in the previous section, "Getting Data from a Database," as follows:

1. **Press Ctrl+N and then select Dynamic Page and ColdFusion before clicking the Create button.**

   This creates a new ColdFusion document.

2. **Save the document into a site that has a remote server configured to see the sample ColdFusion MX databases.**

3. **Switch to the Bindings tab by choosing Window⇨Bindings.**

4. **Click the plus (+) button and select Recordset (Query) from the drop-down list.**

   The Recordset dialog box, shown in Figure 6-11, appears.

**Book II
Chapter 6**

**Using ColdFusion MX
in Dreamweaver MX**

Figure 6-11:
The
Recordset
dialog box.

5. **Name the Recordset** DatabaseTest.

6. **Select CompanyInfo from the Data Source drop-down list.**

   You may also need to input the username and password for the testing
   server as well. If you configured the remote testing server, then you
   should know the username and password. If not, then you may need to
   check with your organization's database administrator.

7. **Select the Employee table from the Table drop-down list.**

8. **Select the radio button labeled Selected from the Columns option,
   and choose LastName from the scroll list (it will show up when you
   select the radio button).**

9. **Leave the Filter and Sort fields empty.**

   These two tools, which you should try as you get more comfortable
   with using the Bindings tab, allow you to further refine and sort the data
   from the Employee table.

10. **Click OK to add the Binding.**

    Dreamweaver MX adds a new record in the Bindings tab and the follow-
    ing code to the Code view, as shown in Figure 6-12:

    ```
    <CFQUERY name="DatabaseTest" datasource="CompanyInfo">
    SELECT LastName FROM Employee
    </CFQUERY>
    ```

    This code tells the server to get all the last names from the Employee
    table in the CompanyInfo database. When the page is read, this query
    retrieves the data and makes it available to be output.

Figure 6-12:
Your first
Binding!

11. To make the last names output when the page is loaded, click and drag the LastName lightning bolt icon from the Bindings tab on the Application panel to the Document window.

Dreamweaver MX creates the following code and adds it to your workspace:

```
<CFOUTPUT query="DatabaseTest">
#DatabaseTest.LastName#
</CFOUTPUT>
```

This tells ColdFusion MX to display the LastNames (all of them) when the page is loaded.

12. Press F12 to preview the page.

When the page loads, you'll notice that the names are output one right after another without anything in between them. You can add a line break (`<BR>`) or a comma after `#DatabaseTest.LastName#`, and ColdFusion MX will add the comma or line break after every record.

Queries are only one kind of Binding that Dreamweaver MX supports. You can see all the others when you click the plus (+) button on the Bindings tab. As you become more familiar with ColdFusion MX, you'll no doubt want to use some of these other kinds of Bindings.

Introducing Server Behaviors and Components

The Server Behavior and Components tabs in the Application panel are similar in both design and concept to the Bindings panel. The following sections cover them only cursorily, because to take full effect of these tools, you need an advanced working knowledge of ColdFusion MX and code development.

Understanding server behaviors

Server behaviors are code elements that make a request to the ColdFusion Server and receive some sort of data in return. If that sounds similar to the preceding Bindings example, it is! You can do that Recordset example from the earlier section, "Using the Bindings Tab," in the Server Behaviors tab. However, a number of more advanced server behaviors are beyond simple queries that you can do from this tab. Table 6-1 describes each of the server behaviors that Dreamweaver MX offers.

Table 6-1	Server Behaviors
Name	*Function*
Recordset	Makes a query to a data source
Stored Procedure	Passes information to a Stored Procedure
CFParam	Builds a `<CFPARAM>` tag
Repeat Region	Allows you to create a repeated region
Recordset Paging	Creates forward, backward, first, and last links for a recordset
Show Region	Shows a region of content based on preset conditions
Display Record Count	Displays the record count for a recordset
Dynamic Text	Displays dynamic text based on a query
Insert Record	Inserts a record through a form
Update Record	Updates a record through a form
Delete Record	Deletes a record through a form
Dynamic Form Elements	Creates form elements based on a corresponding query and recordset
User Authentication	Creates all the code necessary to add user authentication to a site

Considering components

Components are reusable bits of ColdFusion code that can be used throughout your Dreamweaver Site. Dreamweaver MX comes with a number of example components to show you how they work. In practical terms, though, you create your own components based on the needs of your site.

Suppose that you're building a site that sells boxes online, and you have a tool that calculates the volume of the various types of boxes that you sell. Because it's used globally by the site, this tool shouldn't be repeated in every single ColdFusion MX page. Instead, it should be in an area where all pages can access it and just pass along the value obtained by performing a calculation. If you built it as a component, this calculator could be accessed anywhere, and if there are ever any changes to the tool (say you changed from cubic feet to cubic meters), you'd only need to make the change once, instead of many times.

The Components tab provides developers with a framework for building these kinds of tools. From this tab, you can specify the following for a new component:

✦ General information about the component (such as its name and where it's located)

✦ Properties of the component (queries, arrays, strings, and so on)

✦ The functions associated with the component

✦ The arguments (data) the component will accept from another page or form

Chapter 7: Advanced Web Page Design Techniques

In This Chapter

✔ Adding a link to an image

✔ Creating clickable hotspots

✔ Adding Flash text rollovers

✔ Adding Flash button rollovers

✔ Adding graphic rollovers

✔ Setting up a navigation bar

✔ Adding audio and video to your pages

✔ Creating animation

In previous chapters of Book II, we focus on providing a good working knowledge of Dreamweaver MX. Now we need to spend some time looking at the more advanced uses of Dreamweaver MX in Web development. In this chapter, we show you how to make images a bit more striking and how you can bring some other multimedia elements to life.

Creating Clickable Image Maps

You can designate certain areas of an image as *hotspots* — active areas that a user can click to open a link to another Web page or activate some other behavior. Hotspots can be shaped like rectangles, circles, or polygons (irregular objects). The coordinates of the hotspots are grouped into chunks of HTML code called *image maps*.

Creating a hotspot

Check out Figure 7-1. It shows a typical navigation bar for a site as a single JPEG image. The following procedure shows you how to create an image map for part of that image by adding hotspots:

Figure 7-1:
A typical
JPEG
navigation
image.

1. **Select the image that you want to add a hotspot to.**

The Image Property inspector appears. If the bottom half of the Image Property inspector is not visible, click the Expander button, which is the down arrow in the bottom-right corner.

2. **In the Map area of the Image Property inspector, click the Hotspot button for the shape you want to draw.**

You can choose from a rectangle, a circle, and a polygon. Your mouse pointer becomes a cross hair cursor when you move it over the image.

3. **Draw the hotspot according to the shape you select:**

- **Circle or rectangle:** Click your cross hair cursor on the image and drag to create a hotspot. Release the mouse button when your hotspot reaches your desired dimensions. The area you draw is highlighted light blue, and the Hotspot Property inspector appears.

- **Polygon:** Click your cross hair cursor on the image once for each point. Click the Arrow tool in the Image Property inspector to close the shape. The area you draw is highlighted light blue, and the Hotspot Property inspector appears.

4. **In the Hotspot Property inspector, supply the following information:**

   - **Map:** Enter a unique name for the image map.

   - **Link:** Enter a URL or the name of an HTML file you want to open when the user clicks the hotspot. Alternatively, you can click the folder and browse to select the link from your files.
     Note: Completing this field is optional. Instead, you may choose to attach a behavior to the hotspot.

   - **Behaviors:** To attach a behavior other than a link to the hotspot, open the Behaviors panel by choosing Window⇨Behaviors from the main menu. Then click the add (+) button in the Behaviors panel, which opens a pop-up menu of available behaviors, including Check Plugin, Play Sound, Popup Message, Preload Images, and many others. Choose a behavior from the pop-up menu, complete the information in the dialog box that appears for your selected behavior, and click OK.

   - **Target:** Complete this field if you entered a link in the Link field and want the link to open in a window or frame other than the one you're linking from. Click the arrow and select from the drop-down list a target window where you want your selected link to appear. You can select from the following choices: _blank (opens the link in a new window), _parent (opens the link in the parent of the currently opened window; if the currently opened window was opened from another frame, the link will open in that frame), _self (the default; opens the link in the currently opened window; not selecting a Target produces the same effect), and _top (opens the link in the top-level window, replacing frames, if any). If you have created frames, you can also select a frame name from this list. (See Book II, Chapter 4 for more information about frames.)

   - **Alt:** Enter the text you want to show when the user moves the mouse pointer over the hotspot. Alt text also makes information about the hotspot accessible to vision-impaired users.

Modifying a hotspot

If you need to change the size or shape of a hotspot after you've created it, or you need to change the link, target, or Alt information for the hotspot, use the following procedure to edit the hotspot:

1. **On an image in the Document window, click the hotspot you want to modify.**

   The Hotspot Property inspector appears. If the inspector does not appear, open it by choosing Window⇨Properties from the main menu.

2. **Edit the Link, Target, or Alt information you want to change in the Hotspot Property inspector.**

3. **If you want to reshape or resize the hotspot, select the Arrow tool in the Hotspot Property inspector, and then click on any handle of the selected hotspot and drag the handle to a new location.**

4. **If you want to reposition the hotspot, select the Arrow tool in the Hotspot Property inspector, and then click anywhere within the hotspot and drag to a new location.**

5. **You can delete a hotspot by selecting it and pressing the Delete key on your keyboard.**

Adding Flash Text Rollovers

A *text rollover* is text that changes color when users move their mouse pointer over it. (One color appears to "roll over" to the next color.) One way to create text rollovers in Dreamweaver MX is by adding *Flash text* to your pages, as described in the following section.

Flash text (and Flash buttons) are so called because Dreamweaver MX implements these features using the same code that Macromedia Flash MX (the animation program included in the Macromedia Studio MX suite) uses.

Adding Flash text

To add hyperlinked Flash text that changes color when users roll their mouse over it, follow these steps:

1. **Click in the Document window where you want to add Flash text.**

2. **Choose Insert⇨Interactive Images⇨Flash Text.**

3. **In the Insert Flash Text dialog box, shown in Figure 7-2, select a font from the Font drop-down list.**

Figure 7-2:
Choose how
you want
the text to
appear in
the Insert
Flash Text
dialog box.

4. **Enter a point size for your text in the Size text field.**

5. **If you want, you can also format the text.**

   You can click the Bold button and/or Italics button. You can also click an alignment button. Alignment choices are Left, Center, and Right.

6. **Select a Color (initial color) and a Rollover Color (color the text changes to when users move their mouse pointer over it) by clicking the color swatch in each area and selecting a color from the color palette that appears.**

7. **Enter your text in the Text field. Select the Show Font option if you want to view the characters in the Text field in your selected font.**

8. **In the Link field, enter a URL or the name of the page you want to appear when the user clicks the Flash text.**

   Alternatively, you can click the Browse button to select a page from your files.

9. **In the Target area, click the arrow and select from the drop-down list a target window where the linked page will appear.**

   If you have created frames, you can select a frame name from this list, or you can select from the following choices:

   - _blank: Opens the link in a new window.

   - _parent: Opens the link in the parent of the currently opened window.

   - _self: Opens the link in the currently opened window; this is the default. Leaving the Target area empty produces the same result.

   - _top: Opens the link in the top-level window, replacing frames, if any.

10. **Select a Background color by clicking the Bg Color swatch and selecting a color from the color palette that appears, or type in a hexadecimal number.**

    Your Flash text appears over the background color you choose.

11. **Enter a name for your Flash text component in the Save As field or click the Browse button to select a name from your files.**

    You must save Flash text with an .swf extension.

12. **Click OK to create your Flash text and close the dialog box.**

To preview the rollover effect of your Flash text, select the text in the Document window to open the Flash Text Property inspector. In the Property inspector, click the Play button to view your Flash text as it will appear in the browser window. Click the Stop button when you're done.

Changing Flash text

You can change an existing Flash text object by simply double-clicking the object in the Document window. Doing so opens the Insert Flash Text dialog box, where you can change various attributes of the object as we describe in the previous section.

Adding Flash Button Rollovers

Buttons that change appearance when users move their mouse pointer over them — called *button rollovers* — are so popular that Dreamweaver MX gives you a way to create them quickly and easily as Flash movies. To learn about how to create button rollovers using images and behaviors instead of Flash button rollovers, see the "Inserting Image Rollovers" section, later in this chapter. (Book III, Chapter 5 describes how to make rollovers in Fireworks MX using images and behaviors.)

Adding a Flash button

To add a Flash button, follow these steps:

1. **Click in the Document window in which you want to add a Flash button.**

2. **Choose Insert⇨Interactive Images⇨Flash Button to open the Insert Flash Button dialog box, as shown in Figure 7-3.**

Figure 7-3:
Add an interactive button with the Insert Flash Button dialog box.

3. **In the Insert Flash Button dialog box, scroll through the button selections in the Style list to select a style.**

You can preview the style in the Sample area of the dialog box — just point to the sample with your mouse to see the Flash button in action.

You can get new Flash buttons on the Macromedia Dreamweaver MX Web site by clicking the Get More Styles button in the Insert Flash Button dialog box. A Web page on Macromedia's site opens in your browser. Select "Flash media" from the Browse Extensions drop-down list. On the Flash media page that opens, click the <u>Additional Flash Button Styles</u> link. The Additional Flash Button Styles Extension page loads in your browser. From that page you can download the new buttons.

4. **If your selected button has a placeholder for text, enter the text that you want to appear on the button in the Button Text area.**

5. **Select a font for your Flash button text from the Font drop-down list.**

6. **Enter a point size for your text in the Size field.**

7. **In the Link field, enter a URL or the name for the page that you want to appear when the user clicks the Flash button.**

Alternatively, you can click the Browse button to select a page from your files.

8. **In the Target area, click the down arrow and select from the drop-down list a target window where the linked page will appear.**

If you have created frames, you can select a frame name from this list, or you can select from the following choices:

- `_blank`: Opens the link in a new window.

- `_parent`: Opens the link in the parent of the currently opened window.

- `_self`: Opens the link in the currently opened window; this is the default. Leaving the Target area empty produces the same result.

- `_top`: Opens the link in the top-level window, replacing frames, if any.

9. **Select a Background color by clicking the Bg Color swatch and selecting a color from the color palette that appears.**

Alternatively, you can enter a hexadecimal color code in the Bg Color field.

Your Flash button displays with the background color you select.

10. **Enter a name for your Flash button in the Save As field or click the Browse button to select a name from your files.**

The Flash button filename requires an `.swf` extension. Dreamweaver MX will add the extension automatically if you don't enter it.

11. **Click OK to create your Flash button and close the dialog box.**

To see what a Flash button looks like in action, select the button in the Document window to open the Flash Button Property inspector. In the Property inspector, click the Play button to view your Flash button as it appears in the browser window. Click the Stop button when you finish.

Changing a Flash button

To change an existing Flash button object, simply double-click the object in the Document window. Doing so opens the Insert Flash Button dialog box, where you can change your button as we describe in the previous section.

Inserting Image Rollovers

An *image rollover* (often just referred to as a *rollover*) is a behavior that changes an image whenever users move their mouse pointer over the image. Rollovers add interactivity to a Web page by helping users to see what parts of the page are links to other Web pages.

A rollover is actually two images — one for normal display on a page (the original image) and one that is slightly modified for display when the image is rolled over (the rollover image). You can modify an image by changing the color or position, adding a glow or a shadow, or you can add another graphic — such as a dog changing from sleeping to wide-awake. For a rollover to work best, the normal and rollover states of the image should share the same width and height.

As with all images, you can't create the original image or the rollover image directly in Dreamweaver MX; you must use an image-editing program, such as Fireworks MX.

Insert a rollover by following these steps:

1. **Click inside the Document window where you want to insert the image rollover.**

2. **Click the Rollover Image button from the Common tab on the Insert panel to open the Insert Rollover Image dialog box, which is shown in Figure 7-4.**

Figure 7-4:
Creating an
image
rollover.

Insert Rollover Image

Image Name: PressOne

Original Image: PressOne.gif   Browse...

Rollover Image: PressOff.gif   Browse...

☑ Preload Rollover Image

Alternate Text:

When Clicked, Go To URL: http://www.mysite.com/press/index.cfm   Browse...

OK
Cancel
Help

3. **In the Insert Rollover Image dialog box, enter a unique name for the rollover in the Image Name field, making sure there are no spaces in the name.**

The rollover is referred to by this name in the HTML page code. Keep in mind that this rollover name refers to the combined original image/rollover image pair.

4. **Enter the name of the original image file in the Original Image field or click the Browse button to select an image from your files.**

The original image appears on the page when the user's mouse pointer is *not* over the image.

5. **Enter the name of the rollover image file in the Rollover Image field or click the Browse button to select an image from your files.**

The rollover image appears on the page when the user's mouse pointer *is* over the image.

6. **Select the Preload Rollover Image check box.**

This feature makes the rollover action appear without delay to users as they move the mouse pointer over the original image.

7. **If you want users to go to another page when they click the rollover image, enter a URL of the page you want them to go to in the When Clicked, Go To URL text field.**

Alternatively, you can click the Browse button to select a page from your files.

8. **Click OK to accept your choices and close the dialog box.**

To check the rollover, preview your page in a browser by choosing File↪ Preview in Browser or by clicking the Preview in Browser button and using your mouse to point to the original image. You can also press F12 to preview in the default preview browser. If you haven't set a default preview browser, you will have to do so. See your documentation for details.

Setting Up a Navigation Bar

A *navigation bar* is a group of buttons that users can access to move throughout your Web site. Buttons within a navigation bar may present users with options, such as moving backwards, moving forwards, returning to the home page, or jumping to specific pages within the site.

Each button in a navigation bar possesses properties similar to a rollover in that the button *changes state* — or appears differently — based on where the user is positioning the mouse pointer. However, a navigation bar button can possess as many as four different states:

✦ **Up:** The original state of the button

✦ **Over:** How the button appears when a user moves their mouse pointer over it

✦ **Down:** How the button appears as a user is clicking it

✦ **Over While Down:** How the button appears when the user moves their mouse pointer over it after clicking it and arriving on the page it represents

A navigation bar differs from individual rollovers in that clicking a navigation bar button in the Down state causes all other buttons in the bar to revert to the Up state.

To create a navigation bar, just follow these steps:

1. **Select the Navigation Bar button from the Common tab in the Insert panel or choose Insert⇨Interactive Images⇨Navigation Bar.**

Whichever method you choose, the Insert Navigation Bar dialog box appears, as shown in Figure 7-5.

2. **In the Insert Navigation Bar dialog box, enter a name for the first button in the Element Name field.**

The new button appears in the Nav Bar Elements field. Don't use spaces in the naming of any of these elements.

3. **For each state of the button — Up Image, Over Image, Down Image, and Over While Down Image — enter the name of the image file that you want to use in the associated field.**

Alternatively, you can click the Browse button for each field and select an image from your files. You must supply the Up Image. All other states are optional and can be left blank.

You don't need to use all four navigation bar button states — creating only Up and Down works just fine.

Figure 7-5:
From the Insert Navigation Bar dialog box, you can create an entire navigation bar.

4. **In the When Clicked, Go To URL text field, enter a URL or the name for the page you want to appear when the user clicks the navigation bar button.**

   Alternatively, you can click the Browse button to select a page from your files.

5. **From the drop-down list, select a target window where you want the linked page to appear.**

   If you aren't using frames, the only option is to use the Main window.

6. **Click the Add Item (+) button to add another navigation bar button.**

   Repeat Steps 2 through 5 to format the new button.

   Note: You can remove any button already created by clicking its name in the Nav Bar Elements field and clicking the Remove Item (–) button. You can also reorder the sequence of the buttons as they will appear on the page by clicking a button name in the Nav Bar Elements field and clicking the up or down arrow button.

7. **In the Options area, select the Preload Images check box if you want the rollover effects to appear without delay as soon as the page loads.**

8. **To set the current button to appear in the Down state when the user first sees the navigation bar (which you might do to indicate the current page is the one represented by the button), select the Show "Down Image" Initially check box in the Options area.**

   The Over While Down state works in combination with this option.

9. **Select Horizontally or Vertically from the Insert drop-down list to position the navigation bar horizontally or vertically.**

10. **To set up the button images in a table format, select the Use Tables check box.**

11. **Click OK to accept your choices and close the dialog box.**

To check the navigation bar, you must preview your page in a browser. Choose File⇨Preview in Browser or click the Preview in Browser button and use your mouse to point to the buttons.

To change elements of an existing navigation bar, choose Modify⇨ Navigation Bar from the main menu. The Modify Navigation Bar dialog box is nearly identical to the Insert Navigation Bar dialog box shown in Figure 7-5, except that you can no longer change the orientation of the bar or access the Use Tables check box.

Adding Audio and Video to Your Pages

You have two basic options, which are described in detail in the following sections, for adding downloadable audio and video to your Web pages:

✦ **Embedding:** You can embed an audio or video file to display a playback console on a Web page that users can use to play, rewind, and fast-forward the media file. (You can also embed an audio file and make it invisible to create a background audio effect.)

Users must have an appropriate plug-in installed on their machines to play the embedded audio or video file. To ensure maximum compatibility, you may wish to use SWFs to present audio and video.

✦ **Linking:** You link to an audio or video file to give users the choice of whether or not to view that media file.

Keep in mind that most audio and video files are large — large enough that many folks impatiently click the Stop button on their browsers before a Web page chock-full of audio or video effects has a chance to finish loading. Keep the following basic rules in mind to help you use audio and video effectively in your Web pages:

✦ Use audio and video only when plain text just won't do.

✦ Keep your audio and video clips as short (and corresponding file sizes as small) as possible.

Embedding an audio or video clip

You can embed an audio or video file by following these steps:

1. **In the Document window, click the location in your page where you want to add an embedded audio or video file.**

2. **Click the Plugin button on the Media tab of the Insert panel or choose Insert⇨Media⇨Plugin.**

The Select File dialog box, shown in Figure 7-6, appears.

Figure 7-6:
Select a
media file to
import.

3. **In the File Name field in the Select File dialog box, enter the path or browse to the audio or video file that you want to embed and click OK.**

If the file is outside your current root directory, Dreamweaver MX asks whether you want to copy the file to your site's root directory. Click Yes.

4. **In the Plugin Property inspector, size the Plugin placeholder to any dimensions you prefer.**

You can either enter a width and height in the W and H text fields in the Plugin Property inspector, or you can drag a handle on the placeholder to manually resize.

Test in all your target browsers (the browsers your users are likely to view your site with) to ensure that users can view all the audio playback controls or video area and controls.

You can click the Play button in the Plugin Property inspector to play your media file without previewing your page in a browser.

Embedding background music

Embedding *background music* (music that plays automatically after the user opens a page) in your page can be controversial because users may be unpleasantly surprised by audio when they are expecting silence, and because users have no way to turn off the music from within the browser. If you don't need to worry about such things, follow these steps to embed background music:

1. **In the Document window, click the location in your page where you want to add an embedded audio file.**

   This should be an out-of-the-way location, like the bottom of your page, so the embedded audio doesn't create an awkward space in your design.

2. **Click the Plugin button on the Media tab in the Insert panel or choose Insert⇨Media⇨Plugin.**

   The Select File dialog box appears.

3. **In the File Name field in the Select File dialog box, enter the path to the audio file that you want to embed and click OK.**

   If the file is outside your current root directory, Dreamweaver MX asks whether you want to copy the file to your site root. Click Yes.

4. **Enter a width and height of 2 in the W and H text fields in the Plugin Property inspector.**

5. **Click the Parameters button to open the Parameters dialog box.**

6. **In the Parameters dialog box, click the Add (+) button to add a new parameter.**

7. **Click in the Parameter column and type** hidden.

8. **Type** true **in the Value column.**

   Steps 7 and 8 hide the audio playback controls.

9. **Click OK to complete the process and close the dialog box.**

Linking to an audio or video clip

A simple and relatively trouble-free way to include audio and video clips on a Web page is to link the page to an audio or video file. Users can click the link if they want to hear or watch the clip. This selection opens a player outside the browser where the user can control playback.

You follow the same steps to create a link to an audio or video file as you do to create a link to a Web page (see Book II, Chapter 2); the only difference is that you specify a media file instead of a URL for the link.

Adding Other Media

Dreamweaver MX enables you to easily insert a number of other multimedia formats into your Web pages, including ActiveX, Java Applets, Macromedia Flash MX, and Shockwave. After inserting any of these media formats, you can set the control and playback features of the media in the Parameters dialog box. Additionally, you can fine-tune the media action on your page by using the Behaviors panel to create triggering actions that cause the media to play, stop, and execute other functions.

Follow these directions to insert other media:

1. **In the Document window, click the location in your page where you want to add a multimedia file.**

2. **Select the Media tab in the Insert panel to view all the object types that you can insert, as shown in Figure 7-7.**

   Alternatively, you can choose Insert⇨Media from the main menu and select the media type that you want to use from the drop-down list.

Book II
Chapter 7

Advanced Web
Page Design
Techniques

Figure 7-7:
Your
embedded
media
options.

3. **On the Media tab of the Insert panel, click the icon of the type of media file you want to insert.**

   The Select File dialog box appears.

   For Applet, Macromedia Flash MX Flash, and Shockwave files: In the File Name field in the Select File dialog box, enter the path to the media and click OK. Your file is inserted, and the associated Property inspector appears. You can change the selected file in the Plugin Property inspector by typing a new name in the Src text field or by browsing in the Src folder to select a file. Select the Embed check box if you want Netscape Navigator users to have access to the Applet, Flash movie, or Shockwave object.

   For ActiveX: An ActiveX placeholder is inserted, and the ActiveX Property inspector appears. Enter the name of the ActiveX object you want to play in the Class ID text field. Select the Embed check box if you want Netscape Navigator users to have access to the ActiveX object.

4. **In the Property inspector for your selected media, enter dimensions in the W and H text fields to size the Media placeholder to any dimensions you choose.**

5. **In the Property inspector for your selected media, click the Parameters button to open the Parameters dialog box, where you can add parameters appropriate to the selected media type.**

See your documentation for Macromedia Flash MX and other multimedia programs for details on formatting and playing files that you create with these programs on your Web pages.

Bringing Animation to Your Web Pages

Using Dreamweaver MX, you can play the role of animation director and add eye-catching motion and activity to any page in your site.

Creating animation in Dreamweaver MX hinges on manipulating a *timeline*. You use the timeline to define which objects show up on your page, how they are positioned, and what other media are playing anytime a user is viewing your Web page. The timeline enables you to change all these parameters from one second to the next, creating a motion-rich page — without the drudgery of generating true animation.

Only Web users with Internet Explorer 4.0 (or later) or Netscape Navigator 4.0 (or later) can view timeline animations.

Understanding timeline basics

You can use the Timelines panel to record and play back Dreamweaver MX animation. You can open the Timelines panel, shown in Figure 7-8, by choosing Window⇨Others⇨Timelines from the main menu.

Behavior Channel   Timeline Controls

Figure 7-8:
The
Timelines
panel in
Dreamweaver
MX.

Frame

Animation Channel

Book II
Chapter 7

Advanced Web
Page Design
Techniques

The Timelines panel includes the following features:

✦ **Timeline controls:** This area consists of the Timeline Name drop-down list, the Rewind button, Back button, Current Frame Number text field, Play button, Frame Rate (fps) text field, Autoplay check box, and Loop check box. These controls enable you to select which timeline you want to view and to control the playback of the timeline. (See Table 7-1, later in this chapter, for more information on these controls.)

✦ **Behavior channel:** The Behavior channel, which is the first row of the Frames area of the Timelines panel (marked with a "B" at the left), enables you to attach behaviors to specific frames of animations in the timeline you select. You can use the Behavior channel to make an audio file start to play when the animation reaches a particular frame, for example.

✦ **Frames:** This area of the panel displays the frame numbers for your selected timeline. You can click any frame number to display that frame. The current frame is indicated by the pink playback head. Clicking and dragging the playback head plays the frames as you drag.

✦ **Animation channels:** This area enables you to add layers and animate layers on a channel. You can create multiple channels that run simultaneously or start and stop at frames you choose.

You cannot animate the same layer on different channels simultaneously. For the scoop on layers, check out Book II, Chapter 5.

Utilizing the functions of the timeline

Dreamweaver MX can't render animation like you see in the movies, but it can help you create motion on your Web pages without giving you a headache. Here's what the timeline can accomplish:

✦ **Simple animation:** You should create animations that display in a Web browser at approximately 15 frames per second (fps) to achieve a uniformity of motion on a wide variety of computers. (Animated films run at 24 fps.) Note that the display rate is approximate and is based on the capabilities of the user's system. See the section, "Adding and deleting objects on a timeline," later in this chapter, for details.

✦ **Layer manipulation:** This includes the ability to change a layer's position, size, visibility, and z-index (stacking position).

✦ **Behavior triggering:** This allows you to set up a series of behaviors, such as Show or Hide layer, to execute at various points along the timeline.

We don't have the space to cover layer manipulation or behavior triggering in this chapter, but you can find out about these techniques by reading *Dreamweaver MX For Dummies,* by Janine Warner and Ivonne Berkowitz, published by Wiley Publishing, Inc.

✦ **Image revelation:** You can change the source of an image to show and hide several images over a period of time, effectively creating a Web slide show. (You don't need to use layers to create this type of animated effect — just images.)

Adding, editing, and deleting timelines

Creating a timeline is a snap! To create a new timeline, choose Modify⇨Timeline⇨Add Timeline from the main menu. Deleting them is similarly easy. First, just select the timeline from the drop-down list in the Timelines panel and then choose Modify⇨Timeline⇨Remove Timeline from the main menu.

If you want to rename a timeline, you can do it at any time in Dreamweaver MX. To rename a timeline, follow these steps:

1. **Open the timeline that you want to rename by choosing Window⇨Timelines and selecting the timeline you want to rename from the Timeline Name drop-down list.**

2. **Choose Modify⇨Timeline⇨Rename Timeline.**

   The Rename Timeline dialog box, shown in Figure 7-9, appears.

Figure 7-9:
Renaming
your
timeline.

3. **Enter a new name in the Rename Timeline dialog box and click OK.**

   Alternatively, you can enter a new name directly in the Timeline Name field. The name must be a single word that begins with a letter and consists only of alphanumeric characters.

Book II
Chapter 7

Adding and deleting objects on a timeline

The first step in creating a timeline animation is to add the layer or image that you want to animate to a timeline. Added objects can be deleted at any time.

To add an object to a timeline, follow these steps:

1. **Choose Window⇨Others⇨Timelines to access the Timelines panel.**

2. **In the Timelines panel, select the timeline you want to work on from the Timeline Name drop-down list.**

3. **In the Document window, select the layer or image you want to animate.**

4. **Add your selection to the timeline by using one of the following methods:**

   • Choose Modify⇨Timeline⇨Add Object to Timeline. Doing this adds an animation bar (a representation of the first and last frames of an object's animation, and all the frames in between) to one of the channels (each numbered row in the Timelines panel is called a channel). The animation bar starts at the frame position of the playback head. The first animation bar you create is placed on Animation Channel 1, the second animation bar is placed on Channel 2, and so on. You can have more than one animation bar on a channel, but bars can't overlap on a channel.

- Drag the layer or image to an channel on the timeline. You can drag the layer to any channel and any start frame, as long as there's not already an animation bar there.

Regardless of the method you choose, a 15-frame animation bar is created with keyframes included on the first and last frames, as shown in Figure 7-10. The name of the layer or image labels the newly created animation bar. You use keyframes to establish important parts of your animation like where an object or layer is on the page at a particular time. When you animate a layer moving across the screen, you only have to set up where the layer is when the animation bar starts and where the layer is when the animation bar ends — Dreamweaver MX "tweens" the locations in between.

TIP

Name your layers and images something more descriptive than the default names (Layer 1 or Image 1) so that you can better distinguish animation bars in a timeline.

5. **Repeat Steps 2 through 4 to add other layers and images to the timeline.**

Keyframes

Figure 7-10:
Keyframes
are added to
the Timeline
automatically.

To delete an object from a timeline, simply select its animation bar. Then choose Modify⇨Timeline⇨Remove Object from the main menu. In Windows 2000, you can also just press the Delete key.

Moving images across a page using paths

You can move a layer across your Web page by recording a *path* in Dreamweaver MX. A path defines the starting and ending points for the route that you want an image-containing layer to take. Dreamweaver MX supports two kinds of paths: linear (straight line) paths, and freeform (curvy) paths.

Recording a linear path

Create an animation that moves a layer in a straight line as follows:

1. **Choose Window➪Others➪Timelines from the main menu to access the Timelines panel.**

The Timelines panel appears.

2. **In the Timelines panel, select the timeline you want to work on from the Timeline Name drop-down list.**

3. **In the Document window, select the layer you want to animate.**

The current location of the layer is the starting point for the animation. If you want a different starting point, reposition the layer now.

4. **Drag the layer to the Timelines panel.**

You can drag the layer to any animation channel and any start frame. By default, a 15-frame animation bar is created, with keyframes included on the first and last frames.

5. **Click the ending keyframe in the animation bar and drag it to create the duration of animation you want.**

6. **In the Document window, drag the selected layer to its ending position.**

Dreamweaver MX draws a thin line that displays the animation path. Caffeine junkies will be happy to know that Dreamweaver MX automatically accounts for a shaky hand and makes your line straight.

Dreamweaver MX adds the animation and updates the source code for your page.

Recording a freeform path

To create an animation that moves a layer around a Web page in a freeform path, use the following steps:

1. **Choose Window➪Others➪Timelines from the main menu to access the Timelines panel.**

The Timelines panel appears.

2. **In the Timelines panel, select the timeline you want to work on from the Timeline Name drop-down list.**

**Book II
Chapter 7**

**Advanced Web
Page Design
Techniques**

3. **In the Document window, select the layer you want to animate.**

   The current location of the layer is the starting point for the animation. If you want a different starting point, reposition the layer now. Make sure you select the layer and not an object on the layer.

4. **Choose Modify➪Timeline➪Record Path of Layer.**

   Alternatively, with the layer selected, right-click a frame in a channel and choose Record Path of Layer from the contextual menu.

5. **Click and drag the layer in the Document window, as shown in Figure 7-11, to create any path you want.**

   The path is traced as you drag. The path follows the position of the top-left corner of the layer.

6. **Release the mouse button to stop recording the path.**

   A new animation bar for the recorded path appears in the Timelines panel. The length of the bar corresponds to the time you spent dragging the layer. Intervals where you dragged slowly consist of more keyframes than those intervals where you dragged rapidly.

Figure 7-11:
Recording a
path.

Playing a recorded path

To preview a recorded path in a Web browser, choose File⇨Preview in Browser from the main menu. If you haven't set up a default preview browser, you will be prompted to do so.

A quicker approach, however, is to use the playback controls provided on the Timelines panel. These playback controls enable you to preview your work directly in the Document window. Table 7-1 explains the function of each control.

Table 7-1	Timeline Playback Controls
Timeline Control	*Function*
Rewind button	Moves the playback head backward to the first frame of the selected timeline.
Back button	Backs up the playback head by one frame. Click and hold to play the timeline in reverse.
Frame indicator	Shows the position of the playback head. Enter a frame number to jump to that frame.
Play button	Advances the playback head by one frame. Click and hold to play the timeline start to finish.
fps text field	Sets the frame rate in frames per second (fps) at which the animation plays. To change the default rate of 15 fps, enter a number and press Enter.
Autoplay check box	When selected, causes the selected timeline to begin playing when the page completely downloads in the browser.
Loop check box	When selected, causes the animation to repeat upon reaching the last frame.

Chapter 8: Integrating Dreamweaver MX with Other Macromedia Products

In This Chapter

✔ **Integrating Dreamweaver MX with Fireworks MX**

✔ **Integrating Dreamweaver MX with Macromedia Flash MX**

✔ **Integrating Dreamweaver MX with ColdFusion MX**

✔ **Integrating Dreamweaver MX with FreeHand 10**

✔ **Integrating Dreamweaver MX with Director Shockwave Studio**

With the release of the Macromedia Studio MX suite, Macromedia has brought Fireworks, Flash, Dreamweaver, ColdFusion, and FreeHand closer together than ever before. The applications in the suite have complementary — and in some cases overlapping — capabilities.

In order to take advantage of Dreamweaver MX's integration with Fireworks MX and Macromedia Flash MX, you need to make sure Design Notes are enabled. Design Notes are Macromedia Studio MX's way of tracking changes and establishing links between exported files (such as GIFs or JPEGs) and their source files (Fireworks MX PNG files, for example).

By default, Design Notes are enabled when you establish a new site. If you disable them and then wish to re-enable them, just follow these steps:

1. **In Dreamweaver MX, choose Site⇨Edit Sites.**

   The Edit Sites dialog box appears.

2. **Select the site by clicking it.**

   If you have a site open already, that site is already selected.

3. **Click the Edit button.**

   The Site Definition dialog box opens.

4. **If the Site Definition dialog box opens with the Basic tab selected, click the Advanced tab.**

   The Advanced options appear.

5. Click Design Notes in the Category column.

The Design Notes options appear.

6. Select the Maintain Design Notes check box, as shown in Figure 8-1.

The Maintain Design Notes option is selected by default, but it can be toggled on and off in the Site Definition dialog box.

Figure 8-1: Enabling the Maintain Design Notes option in the Site Definition dialog box.

7. If you are working on the site with others, make sure the Upload Design Notes for Sharing check box is selected.

The Upload Design Notes for Sharing option uploads your Design Notes so that other people working on the site can have access to them. If you're the only person working on a site, you should deselect this option to speed file transfers.

8. Click OK.

Disabling Design Notes is simple: Just deselect the Maintain Design Notes check box.

With Design Notes enabled, you can move seamlessly back and forth between Dreamweaver MX and the other applications in the Macromedia Studio MX suite.

Integrating Dreamweaver MX with Fireworks MX

Fireworks MX is a Web design tool and Dreamweaver MX is an HTML editor, so you may expect that the two applications complement each other well. In fact, the two programs make a dynamite tag team.

The phrase *Roundtrip HTML* refers to the basic interaction between Fireworks MX and Dreamweaver MX. Essentially, if you generate your HTML in Fireworks MX and edit the code in Dreamweaver MX, Fireworks MX recognizes the changes you make in the other application. That goes for links, image maps, behaviors shared by both programs, and edited HTML text in text slices. If you make radical changes to the table structure in Dreamweaver MX, however, Fireworks MX may not be able to reconcile the HTML with the Fireworks PNG source file. In those cases, Fireworks MX will write over your changed code with new code.

In order to take advantage of Roundtrip HMTL, you need to establish a few settings, both in Dreamweaver MX and in Fireworks MX. In Dreamweaver MX, you need to define a local site (see Book II, Chapter 3) and make Fireworks MX your primary image-editing application.

**Book II
Chapter 8**

Integrating Dream-
weaver MX with
Other Macromedia
Products

Making Fireworks MX your primary image editor

If you installed Dreamweaver MX along with the rest of Macromedia Studio MX, Fireworks MX is your primary image-editing application by default. However, if you changed that default setting, here's how to return to the setting of Fireworks MX as your primary image-editing application:

1. **In Dreamweaver MX, choose Edit⇨Preferences or use the keyboard shortcut Ctrl+U.**

The Preferences dialog box appears.

2. **Select File Types / Editors in the Category column.**

The File Types / Editors options appear in the Preferences dialog box, as shown in Figure 8-2.

3. **Select the** `.png` **extension in the Extensions column.**

The extension is highlighted.

4. **Click the plus (+) button over the Editors window.**

If Fireworks MX is already listed in the Editors window, you don't need to click the plus (+) button.

Figure 8-2:
The Dream-
weaver MX
Preferences
dialog box.

5. **If you need to add Fireworks MX to the Editors window, navigate to** `Fireworks.exe` **on your hard drive and double-click it.**

   If Fireworks MX is now the only application listed in the Editors window, it's the primary editor by default ("Primary" is in parentheses next to "Fireworks").

6. **If you have more than one image editor listed in the Editors window, make sure Fireworks MX is highlighted and click the Make Primary button above the Editors window.**

7. **Do the same for the** `.gif`, `.jpg`, `.jpe`, **and** `.jpeg` **extensions.**

8. **Click OK.**

You may need to set a few preferences in Fireworks MX as well. See Book III, Chapter 8 for information on how to set Launch and Edit preferences.

Working with tables

Taking advantage of Roundtrip HTML means more than just setting preferences: You also need to know which application is best to use for particular types of changes. If you wish to make major structural changes to the table that constitutes your HTML page, modify your original Fireworks MX PNG source file and re-export the HTML from there, rather than using Dreamweaver MX to modify the code. Using Fireworks MX to change the table structure ensures that the slices in your Fireworks PNG source file will correspond to the cells in your HTML table.

Here's how to edit a table in Fireworks MX (provided the table was created in Fireworks MX) by launching it from within Dreamweaver MX:

1. **Select the table in Dreamweaver MX.**

   The Property inspector updates to display the parameters of the table.

2. **Click the Fireworks Edit button in the Property inspector.**

   If need be, you can navigate to the source Fireworks PNG file from within the Dreamweaver MX Property inspector. The source file opens in Fireworks MX.

3. **Make edits to the slices or guides as necessary.**

4. **Click the Done button when you're finished editing.**

   The Fireworks MX window closes, and Dreamweaver MX updates the table and images.

Book II
Chapter 8

Integrating Dream-
weaver MX with
Other Macromedia
Products

When you launch and edit a table in Fireworks MX, it may overwrite some changes you may have made to the table structure in your Dreamweaver MX code, if the changes you made in Dreamweaver MX are substantial. A warning notifies you when Fireworks MX will overwrite the existing Dreamweaver MX edits.

When you want to leave the table structure intact but need to rename or reoptimize an image, you can launch Fireworks MX from a selected image rather than a selected table. Editing a .jpeg image from its Fireworks MX PNG source file rather than editing and resaving the already optimized image ensures the highest image quality.

To launch and edit a PNG source file from an optimized image placed in Dreamweaver MX (to change graphic text in a .jpeg image, for example), follow these steps:

1. **Click the optimized image in the Dreamweaver MX Document window.**

   The Property inspector updates to display image parameters.

2. **Click the Fireworks Edit button in the Property inspector, as shown in Figure 8-3, or right-click the optimized image and choose Edit with Fireworks from the contextual menu.**

   If Dreamweaver MX cannot locate the source Fireworks PNG file, you're prompted to navigate to the source file. When you do, the source PNG file opens in Fireworks MX. At the top of the Fireworks MX canvas, the words "Editing from Dreamweaver" show that Roundtrip HTML is in effect.

   Notice at the top left of the Property inspector that the Fireworks MX icon and the designation FW Image identify the selected image as one created in Fireworks MX. Note also the Fireworks MX Src text field at the bottom middle of the Property inspector, which shows the path and name of the source Fireworks MX PNG file.

Figure 8-3:
The Dream-
weaver MX
Property
inspector
for an
image.

3. **Edit the image within the context of your overall page design.**

   The new version of the image will be exported at the specified settings, which you may leave as is or change before clicking Done.

4. **Click the Done button at the top left of the canvas.**

   The Fireworks MX window minimizes. When you look at the Document window in Dreamweaver MX, you see the new image.

You can also launch and edit a GIF or JPEG image directly in Fireworks MX, though it's always best to edit from the source PNG when possible, both to preserve image quality and to keep your source file in sync with your Web page. If you don't have a source PNG (or don't need to keep your source design file up to date) and you just want to tweak an image without changing its width and height, you can do so easily as follows:

1. **Double-click the image's filename or corresponding icon on the Site tab or Assets tab of the Files panel.**

   Fireworks MX launches, and your image appears on the canvas.

2. **Make changes to the image.**

3. **Export the updated GIF or JPEG from Fireworks MX by choosing File⇨Export or using the key command Ctrl+Shift+R.**

   If necessary, navigate to the folder in which you keep the optimized images for your site. A prompt warns you that the file already exists. Click OK to replace the existing file.

4. **Close the file in Fireworks MX.**

   When you close the file in Fireworks MX, an alert asks if you want to save changes to your file. If you want Fireworks MX to save the file as a PNG, click Yes. Otherwise, click No.

You can add a Fireworks MX-generated table to an open Dreamweaver MX document, whether the document is blank or has code already in it:

1. **Click the Fireworks HTML button on the Common tab of the Insert panel.**

   The Insert Fireworks HTML dialog box appears.

2. **Type the pathname or click the Browse button and browse to the Fireworks MX HTML file.**

   If the HTML file you select was not generated by Fireworks MX, an alert informs you, and you won't be able to insert the HTML.

3. **Select the Delete File after Insertion check box if you don't need to save the Fireworks MX-generated HTML.**

   Unless you want a backup copy of the HTML, free from any edits you might make in Dreamweaver MX, you can safely delete it.

4. **Click OK.**

Book II
Chapter 8

Integrating Dream-
weaver MX with
Other Macromedia
Products

If you want to nest tables but still use Roundtrip HTML, one way to do it is to make a large table in Dreamweaver MX and insert Fireworks MX-generated tables in the cells. Then, if you need to change one of the inserted tables, you can select the table and edit it in Fireworks MX.

Integrating Dreamweaver MX with Macromedia Flash MX

You can create Flash buttons and Flash text without actually having Macromedia Flash MX installed on your computer, thanks to Dreamweaver MX's Flash commands. If you've installed Macromedia Studio MX, though, you'll probably prefer to create Flash movies in Macromedia Flash MX and let Dreamweaver MX write the code to embed Flash SWF files in your HTML pages.

Inserting a Flash movie into a Dreamweaver MX document

Inserting a Flash SWF movie into a Dreamweaver MX document is easy, and Dreamweaver MX offers easy access to many parameters of SWF movies directly from the Property inspector, though you can't edit a Flash SWF movie from within Dreamweaver MX.

To insert an SWF file into an existing Dreamweaver MX HTML document, follow these steps:

1. **Click the spot in the page where you want the Flash movie to go.**

2. **Choose Insert⇨Media⇨Flash (or use the keyboard shortcut Ctrl+Alt+F) or click the Flash icon on the Common tab of the Insert panel.**

The Select File dialog box appears.

3. **Navigate to the SWF file and double-click it, or click it once and click OK.**

You can type the name of the file in the File Name text field instead if you prefer. The Select File dialog box closes and your SWF movie is placed where the cursor was last active.

Working with the Property inspector

When an SWF file is selected in the Document window, the Dreamweaver MX Property inspector (shown in Figure 8-4) gives you access to many parameters for the display of the movie, including:

✦ **Width and Height:** Unless specified otherwise here, the SWF will display at the dimensions you set in Macromedia Flash MX's Document Properties dialog box.

✦ **Loop:** You can toggle looping on or off by selecting or deselecting this check box.

✦ **Autoplay:** You can toggle autoplay on or off by selecting or deselecting this check box. When Autoplay is selected, the SWF starts automatically when the HTML page loads in the user's browser window.

✦ **V Space and H Space:** As with GIFs and JPEGs, you can set the vertical and horizontal spacing to provide margins between SWFs and other content that occupies the same table cell.

Figure 8-4:
The Dream-weaver MX Property inspector for SWF movies.

✦ **Quality:** A drop-down list offers four options: High, Auto High, Auto Low, and Low. The Low option sacrifices image quality to increase smoothness in the flow of the animation.

✦ **Scale:** A drop-down list gives you three choices: Show All, No Border, and Exact Fit.

✦ **Align:** A drop-down list offers access to all the options for aligning the SWF within a table cell.

✦ **Background color (Bg):** A background color chosen here overrides the background color as set in Macromedia Flash MX's Document Properties dialog box.

The Property inspector also includes some other handy tools:

✦ **The Flash Edit button:** This button opens the source FLA file in the Macromedia Flash MX application.

✦ **The Reset Size button:** This button restores the SWF to its original dimensions.

✦ **The Play button:** This button allows you to see the SWF file in action without opening the page in a browser window.

✦ **The Parameters button:** This button allows you to customize parameters passed to the SWF.

Book II
Chapter 8

Integrating Dream-
weaver MX with
Other Macromedia
Products

The Flash Edit button in the Property inspector is grayed out if you do not have Macromedia Flash MX installed on your computer. When you want to edit an SWF, you need to go back to the FLA source file to make your changes, then re-export the SWF. This is true except in the case of changing a link in an SWF file, in which case Dreamweaver MX adds a Design Note to pass the new link to the FLA source movie when you next launch and edit the FLA.

Editing a Flash movie in Dreamweaver MX

To edit a Flash movie from within Dreamweaver MX, just follow these steps:

1. **Select the SWF file by clicking it in the Dreamweaver MX Document window.**

   The Property inspector updates to display the Macromedia Flash MX parameters, as shown in Figure 8-4.

2. **Click the Edit button in the Property inspector.**

   If necessary, navigate to the FLA source file in the Locate Macromedia Flash Document File dialog box and double-click the FLA, or click it once and then click the Open button.

   The source file opens in Macromedia Flash MX. The designation "Editing from Dreamweaver" confirms that Macromedia Flash MX was launched from within Dreamweaver MX.

3. **Edit the Flash movie source file.**

4. **Click the Done button at the top left of the Flash stage.**

Macromedia Flash MX exports an updated SWF to the proper directory, saves the FLA file to its current directory, and closes. The new SWF appears in the Dreamweaver MX Document window. If you changed the dimensions of the Flash movie, click the Reset size button to update the Dreamweaver MX code.

Editing a link in an SWF file in Dreamweaver MX

Editing a link in an SWF file is similar to editing a Flash movie, but you need to set up a few things beforehand:

✦ Establish a home page and dependent pages in the Site Map.

✦ Set the Site Map to display dependent files (as in Figure 8-5).

See the Fireworks MX Help files for details on setting up a Site Map.

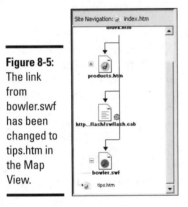

Figure 8-5: The link from bowler.swf has been changed to tips.htm in the Map View.

After you've done that, you can change a link in an SWF by following these steps:

1. **Right-click the link displayed under the SWF in the Site Map and choose Change Link from the contextual menu.**

The Select HTML File dialog box appears.

2. **Navigate to the file to which you want to link and double-click it, or type a URL into the URL text field.**

3. **Click OK.**

 You can also update a link in an SWF while updating the same link in other files by choosing Site⇨Change Link Sitewide from the Site tab of the Files panel. Whether you change the link only in the SWF file or in an SWF file as part of a sitewide update, the FLA source file will not be updated until you launch and edit the SWF from Dreamweaver MX.

Integrating Dreamweaver MX with ColdFusion MX

Dreamweaver MX has fully absorbed ColdFusion MX, in the sense that Dreamweaver MX is now the working environment for ColdFusion MX. In Book VI, we describe how to set up your ColdFusion MX server, as well as concepts in programming; Book II, Chapter 6 offers the information you need to write CFML (ColdFusion Markup Language) using Dreamweaver MX.

Integrating Dreamweaver MX with FreeHand 10

Though you can publish FreeHand 10 documents as HTML (complete with embedded SWF movies, URL links, and Flash actions), FreeHand 10 is not as tightly integrated with Dreamweaver MX as Fireworks MX is.

FreeHand 10 is primarily a print-oriented design application, so it's no surprise that it lacks the kinds of controls Fireworks MX offers for image slicing and optimization.

In other words, if you're designing for the Web, you'll find Fireworks MX a much better tool (not in the least for its solid integration with Dreamweaver MX). Nonetheless, if you ever find yourself with an HTML file published by FreeHand 10, rest assured that you can open and edit that file in Dreamweaver MX, as you can with an HTML file created in any application.

Book II
Chapter 8

Integrating Dream-
weaver MX with
Other Macromedia
Products

Integrating Dreamweaver MX with Director Shockwave Studio

Although Director Shockwave Studio wasn't released with the original Macromedia Studio MX suite, the MX version of Director Shockwave Studio was announced in November of 2002. You can use Dreamweaver MX to place Shockwave movies (SWFs) exported from Director Shockwave Studio in your HTML pages. Though they share the extension .swf, files exported from Director Shockwave Studio and Macromedia Flash MX are not interchangeable, and Dreamweaver MX treats them differently.

To insert an SWF file exported from Director Shockwave Studio into your HTML page, just follow these steps:

1. **Click in the Document window where you want the inserted movie to go.**

2. **Choose Insert⇨Media⇨Shockwave, or use the keyboard shortcut Ctrl+Alt+D, or click the Shockwave icon in the Insert panel's Media tab.**

   The Select File dialog box appears.

3. **Navigate to the SWF file and double-click it, or click once and then click OK.**

   You can type the name of the file in the File Name text field instead if you prefer. The Select File dialog box closes and your SWF movie is placed where the cursor was last active.

At the time of this writing, Dreamweaver MX did not have the capability to launch and edit Director Shockwave Studio movies, though future versions may have such a capability.

Book III

Fireworks MX

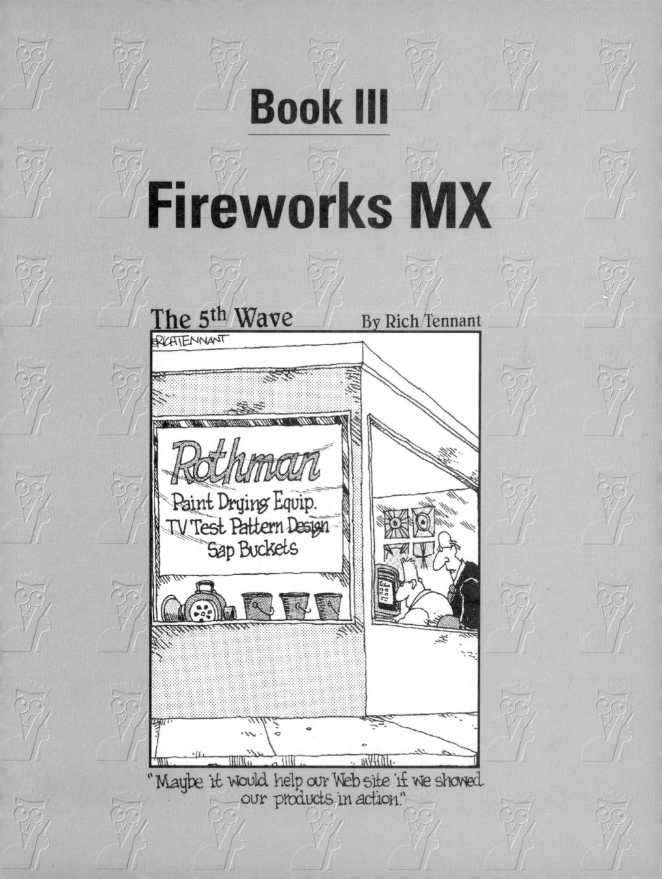

The 5th Wave   By Rich Tennant

ERICATENNANT

Rothman

Paint Drying Equip.
TV Test Pattern Design
Sap Buckets

"Maybe it would help our Web site if we showed
our products in action."

Contents at a Glance

Chapter 1: Introduction to Fireworks MX

In This Chapter

✔ **Understanding Fireworks MX**

✔ **Taking a quick tour of the Fireworks MX interface**

✔ **Customizing your work environment**

✔ **Setting your preferences**

Fireworks MX is the latest version of a graphics creation and editing program designed to streamline the process of making images for the Web. In the days before the original version of Fireworks MX, making graphics for the Web could be a frustrating and time-consuming process of trial and error. Not only that, but the results often looked pretty bad.

With products like Fireworks MX, all that has changed. This chapter gives you a brief introduction and tour of the product and shows you how to set up Fireworks MX to fit your working style.

Understanding the Power of Fireworks MX

The basic process of making graphics for a Web site can be divided into two major parts:

✦ **Creating the images:** This consists of drawing, importing, and manipulating pictures, as well as designing the overall page layout on the Fireworks MX canvas.

✦ **Optimizing the images:** This includes slicing the page layout into pieces, selecting the proper compression format and level for each piece, and exporting the individual pieces.

Fireworks MX has two different tools that make the process of creating graphics for a Web site easier: layers and slices. Layers are a mainstay of graphics development tools, such as Photoshop, and animation programs, such as Macromedia Flash MX, and layers make creating and editing graphics a simpler proposition. Slices, first introduced by Macromedia in the original version of Fireworks MX, offer an efficient way to divide a design into individually optimized Web graphics. Both layers and slices are described in more detail in the following sections.

Making designing easier with layers

We discuss layers in more detail in Book III, Chapter 5, but this section serves as an introduction to the benefits of layers.

Layers act like transparent sheets that can be stacked one on top of the other. You draw a separate element of the image on each transparency. Any area where you haven't put something remains transparent, so layers beneath show through. In a typical file you might have several text layers and many layers of backgrounds, icons, lines, shapes, and so on.

If you ever make mistakes or change your mind about things, layers can save you lots of time as you design your site. Suppose that you're doing calligraphy and illustration on fine paper. If you mess up one part of the image, the whole thing is often ruined because you only have one layer to work with: the paper. Short of cutting a piece out of the paper, you may not be able to delete your mistakes. Layers offer a practical approach to fixing your errors.

Using layers provides many benefits. Some of the most practical advantages include the following:

✦ You can change any element of your design — text, bitmap, or vector shape — without altering or destroying any other element.

✦ You can apply effects to layers that are grouped together, decreasing the amount of time it takes to edit an image. (Of course, you can also apply effects to individual layers.)

✦ You can easily move elements up and down in the stack of layers to change the visual effect on the screen.

✦ You can test new designs and effects in a snap because hiding and showing elements of an image is extremely easy.

Creating slices

We discuss slices in more detail in Book III, Chapter 6, but here's an introduction to the concept of slices. Imagine for a moment that you've created your masterpiece design for a new Web site. Your Fireworks MX file may include lots of different kinds of imagery, including the following:

✦ Logos

✦ Navigation buttons

✦ Header graphics, such as banners

✦ Photos

✦ Drawings

✦ Animations

Before you can create your Web page, you've got to get all of these graphics into a Web-friendly format, which is where slices come in. The idea is simple, yet elegant: include a special layer in the program that can never be removed where you can create guides as to how you want the images to be "sliced" up into separate, individually optimized and hyperlinked images. Figure 1-1 shows that special layer, called the Web Layer, and some slices in action.

Slices provide some key advantages over traditional methods of creating images for the Web:

✦ You can slice a design into more than one image at a time.

✦ You can export multiple files in a single procedure.

✦ You can control exactly where images are sliced, which helps prevent you from making images with overlapping areas.

✦ You have an increased ability to optimize image size (and thereby reduce download time) by selecting the best optimization method for each slice.

Figure 1-1:
The Web
Layer and
Slices.

Slices guarantee that the layout of your Web page appears nearly identical on every user's screen to the design you create in Fireworks MX. (If you have HTML text on your page, the appearance of that text may vary, depending on which browser and platform the user views your page with.)

Taking a Quick Tour of the Fireworks MX Interface

The Fireworks MX interface is set up to make accessing the tools quick and intuitive. When you start Fireworks MX, you'll notice that it doesn't create a new document automatically. To create a new Fireworks MX file (called a PNG file), just follow these steps:

1. **Choose File⇨New.**

   The New Document dialog box appears.

2. **Choose the canvas size for your document.**

   The default width and height are 500 pixels, and the default resolution is 72 pixels per inch. You can enter your own size in the fields provided and change the unit of measurement by selecting one from the drop-down list. You should leave the resolution at 72 pixels per inch unless you're designing for some medium other than the Web, like print.

3. **Select a color for the canvas.**

   The default canvas color is white, but you can choose a custom color by selecting the Custom radio button and then using the eyedropper to choose a color from the color picker. You can also choose to have a transparent background by selecting the Transparent radio button.

4. **Click OK to create your new Fireworks MX document.**

   When you click OK, you see something that looks a lot like Figure 1-2.

The Tools panel: A bird's-eye view

The panel at the top left is the Tools panel, which provides access to all the tools you use to make and modify your graphics. The Tools panel divides tools into groups based on their function, as described in the following list:

✦ **Select:** Contains items used to select an object, as well as items used to crop or otherwise manipulate the canvas.

✦ **Bitmap:** Stores items used to paint, draw, fill, and so on.

✦ **Vector:** Contains items used to create and manipulate vector graphics. (See Book V, Chapter 1 for more on vector graphics.)

✦ **Web:** Holds items like the Slice tool that are designed specifically for getting images ready for the Web.

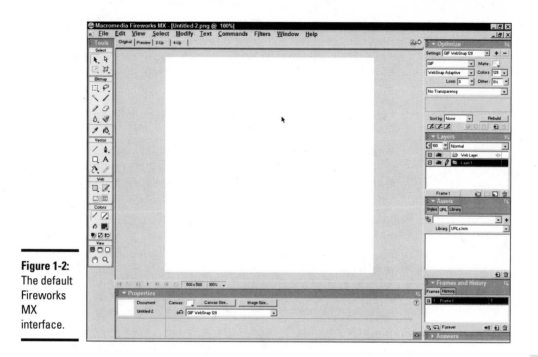

Figure 1-2:
The default
Fireworks
MX
interface.

✦ **Colors:** Stows away basic color management tools.

✦ **View:** Holds tools that you can use to change your view of the canvas or the screen.

An arrow at the lower-right corner of a tool's icon indicates that the tool has one or more specialized variations. You can click on the arrow to activate a pop-up menu that displays icons for the available variations.

The Tools panel: A bug's-eye view

This section gives you the lowdown on the tools you'll likely use the most in the Tools panel. You get to see them in action in subsequent chapters, but for now, here are the highlights for each of the three key categories of tools:

✦ **Select:** The following tools (clockwise from top left) make up the Select section of the Tools panel:

• **Pointer/Select Behind tool:** Use the Pointer tool to select objects on the canvas by clicking on them or clicking and dragging an area that encompasses them. Use the Select Behind tool when you want to click on an object on the canvas that is covered by other objects.

• **Subselection tool:** Use the Subselection tool to select an individual object from a group.

- **Crop/Export Area tool:** Click the Crop tool and select an area on the canvas to crop an image. When you crop an image, you discard everything outside the selected area from your image. After you have selected the area that you want to keep, double-click inside the area to crop. Use the Export Area tool to create a new image from the area you select. After you have selected the area you want to export, double-click inside the area to bring up the Export Preview window.

- **Scale/Skew/Distort tool:** This tool is inactive (as indicated by the dimmed icon) until you have selected an object on the canvas. Click this tool and click and drag the transform handles at the corners of the object to change its size and/or shape.

✦ **Bitmap:** The following tools (clockwise from top left) make up the Bitmap section of the Tools panel:

- **Marquee/Oval Marquee tool:** Click the Marquee tool and click and drag to select a rectangular area on the canvas. If you want to select a circle or oval area, use the Oval Marquee variation. When you select an area, you select all objects that fall completely within the area.

- **Lasso/Polygon Lasso tool:** Click the Lasso tool and click and drag on the canvas to select everything within an irregularly shaped area of the canvas. If the shape you want to select is made up of straight lines, use the Polygon Lasso.

- **Brush tool:** Click this tool to paint on the canvas. See Book III, Chapter 3 for more information about the very versatile Brush tool.

- **Eraser tool:** Click the Eraser tool to erase a swath through any bitmap object on the canvas.

- **Rubber Stamp tool:** Click this tool to copy a selected area of a bitmap to another spot on the canvas. Alt+click on the area that you want to copy, and then click and paint where you want the copy to go.

- **Paint Bucket/Gradient tool:** Click this tool and then click a shape on the canvas to fill the shape with a solid color (Paint Bucket) or gradient. For details about gradients, see Book III, Chapter 4.

- **Eyedropper tool:** Click this handy tool to select a color from the swatches in the color picker or from any object on the canvas by clicking on the desired color.

- **Blur/Sharpen/Dodge/Burn/Smudge tool:** Click this tool and click and drag on the canvas to soften the focus of (Blur) or bring into focus (Sharpen) an area of a bitmap image. Click the Dodge tool and click and drag on the canvas to lighten an area of a bitmap image. Click the Burn tool and click and drag to darken an area of a bitmap image. Click the Smudge tool and click and drag on the canvas to smear a part of an image into another part of the image, as if you were finger painting. You can set the parameters for these tools in the Property inspector.

- **Pencil tool:** Click the Pencil tool and click and drag to draw single-pixel-width lines. If you want control over the thickness and texture of the line you are creating, use the Brush tool.

- **Magic Wand tool:** Click the Magic Wand and click on a bitmap to select areas of solid or similar colors in your image.

✦ **Vector:** The following tools (clockwise from top left) make up the Vector section of the Tools panel:

- **Line tool:** Throw your ruler away! With the Line tool, you can draw a straight line every time. You can adjust the line's thickness, color, and other parameters in the Property inspector.

- **Pen/Vector Path/Redraw Path tool:** Click the Pen tool to create vector graphics by drawing vector paths. You can use the Pen tool to select points and let Fireworks MX connect the dots, or you can draw the shape yourself with the Vector Path tool. You can use the Redraw Path tool to change the shape of a vector graphic by clicking and dragging any of the points that define the shape.

- **Text tool:** Click this tool and click on the canvas to place and edit text on the canvas. See Book III, Chapter 3 for information on how to make the most of the Text tool.

- **Knife tool:** Click this tool and click and drag a line to cut vector paths in two.

- **Freeform/Reshape Area/Path Scrubber (Additive)/Path Scrubber (Subtractive) tool:** Use the Freeform tool to reshape a vector path by pushing or pulling the stroke instead of moving the individual points that define it. Use the Reshape Area tool to pull a vector path as if you had grabbed it with your hand. Use the Path Scrubber tool to change the color, thickness, and various other properties of the vector path. If you have a graphics tablet, you can set the properties to vary based on variations in the pressure or speed you use in drawing.

- **Rectangle/Rounded Rectangle/Ellipse/Polygon tool:** Create vector shapes by clicking these tools and clicking and dragging on the canvas.

Across the aisle: The right-side panels

Five key panels appear on the right-hand side of the screen, opposite the Tools panel. These panels include the following:

Book III
Chapter 1

Introduction to
Fireworks MX

✦ **The Optimize panel:** This panel enables you to set your export options (GIF or JPEG, quality level, and so on). See Book III, Chapter 6 for more information about the Optimize panel.

✦ **The Layers panel:** This panel contains all your layer options and information. The first layer is always the Web layer, which holds information about the coordinates of the slices. (See Book III, Chapter 6 for more about slices.)

✦ **The Assets panel:** This panel provides a way to centralize and organize links from Web objects to Web pages. Fireworks MX can actually generate your entire Web page — images, code, and all.

✦ **The Frames and History panel:** This panel gives you access to the Frames area, where you can navigate easily among the frames in your document. You use frames to make button rollovers and animations. (See Book III, Chapter 5 for more details.) This panel also allows you to view the History area, which is a list of your most recent actions.

✦ **The Answers panel:** This panel provides links to the Macromedia Web site, where you can find tips, tricks, tutorials, and up-to-date information about Fireworks MX.

The Property inspector

The Property inspector is docked to the bottom of the Document window. This panel changes automatically to reflect the settings for the currently selected tool or object.

The Property inspector allows you to see and adjust the parameters of whatever object or tool you select. If you're working on a text layer, for example, the Property inspector gives you immediate access to and complete control over the font, size, color, and other attributes of the text. When you select a shape, on the other hand, the Property inspector offers you easy access to controls over the shape's size, position on the canvas, color, texture, and more.

If you ever want to hide all the panels temporarily, press F4 or the Tab key. To make the panels visible, press F4 or the Tab key again.

Viewing and Previewing Your Work

While you work, you view the canvas with the Original tab selected. The other three tabs at the top of the canvas allow you to preview what your optimized images will look like:

✦ **Original:** This is the default tab and shows you what the file you are working on looks like.

✦ **Preview:** This view shows you what the page will look like when it is optimized for the Web, based on your current image optimization settings.

✦ **2-Up:** This tab offers previews of what optimized images will look like, but with a little something extra: a side-by-side comparison of two optimization settings.

✦ **4-Up:** By selecting the 4-Up tab, you can preview four different optimization settings on the same image at the same time. You can compare how they look and how big the resulting image file would be at each setting, as well as how long the image would take to download at a particular modem speed.

Because every image compresses a little differently, you can never predict exactly what an image might look like after it is optimized. The longer you work with Fireworks MX, the better you get at narrowing the optimization options before you preview; nevertheless, you may find it more efficient to preview before you export. For more information about the purpose and art of image optimization, see Book III, Chapter 6.

At the top right of the canvas is a feature new in Fireworks MX: a Quick Export button. The Quick Export button allows you to export files to, and even launch, other applications, such as Dreamweaver MX, Macromedia Flash MX, and FreeHand 10. Export options for Macromedia Director Shockwave Studio, Adobe Photoshop, and others are also available from the Quick Export button.

Customizing Your Work Environment

During different phases of the design process, you may find that you refer to some panels constantly but other panels not at all. Unless you have a gigantic monitor set to a high resolution, you'll need to collapse some less-frequently used panels to make room for more-frequently used ones.

Collapsing and expanding panels

Every panel's name is displayed at the left on the top dark gray bar in the panel. To the left of the name sits a handy little arrow that points down to indicate the panel is expanded and points to the panel name if the panel is collapsed.

You can expand or collapse a panel in two ways:

✦ Click the name of the panel.

✦ Click the arrow to the left of the panel name.

When the panel expands, it makes room for itself by forcing the panels below it down — unless it's a panel on the bottom, in which case it forces the panels above it up. If there's not enough room on your monitor to show all the panels open at once, Fireworks MX collapses the panel directly beneath or above the one you expanded.

If you have a panel expanded but still can't see quite enough of it, you can drag the panel open wider or longer by clicking on the left or bottom edge of the panel and dragging it.

In addition to collapsing and expanding panels, you can also open and close panels. Check out Table 1-1, which includes the key commands for closing and opening panels.

Table 1-1	Keyboard Shortcuts for Opening and Closing Panels		
Panel	*Keyboard Shortcut*	*Panel*	*Keyboard Shortcut*
Tools	Ctrl+F2	Styles	Shift+F11
Properties	Ctrl+F3	Library	F11
Answers	Alt+F1	URL	Alt+Shift+F10
Optimize	F6	Color Mixer	Shift+F9
Layers	F2	Swatches	Ctrl+F9
Frames	Shift+F2	Info	Alt+Shift+F12
History	Shift+F10	Behaviors	Shift+F3

Moving, docking, and grouping panels

When you open Fireworks MX for the first time, all the panels are docked and grouped in a default configuration. (Refer to Figure 1-2 to see this default configuration.) However, undocking and moving panels and putting them in custom groups is easy.

To move a panel, follow these steps:

1. **Click the gripper at the top left of the panel.**

The gripper is the five dots on the dark gray bar at the top of the panel.

2. **Drag the panel to the spot on the screen where you would like it to go.**

3. **Release the mouse button.**

You now see the panel in the position you selected, in its own window, as shown in Figure 1-3.

Figure 1-3:
An
undocked
panel.

Book III
Chapter 1

Introduction to
Fireworks MX

When you move a panel, you automatically undock it, but you don't auto-matically dock it somewhere else when you release the mouse button. The panel remains floating in the Fireworks MX window until you dock it.

To dock a panel, follow these steps:

1. **Place your cursor over the gripper at the top left of the panel.**

The gripper is the five dots on the dark gray bar at the top of the panel.

2. **Drag the panel to a docking area.**

A docking area is anywhere along the outer edge of the Document window or adjacent to a docked panel. When you have dragged the panel over a docking area, a rectangle appears on the screen to give you a preview of the space the panel would occupy if you docked it there.

3. **Release the mouse button.**

The panel is docked in its expanded state.

Fireworks MX allows you the option to consolidate or group panels, which provides a nice way to put the panels you like using together.

To group a panel with another panel, follow these steps:

1. **Click the Panel options icon (the three white lines and arrow) at the top right of the panel you want to add to a group.**

   The Panel options menu appears.

2. **Select the Group Layers With option.**

   An additional pop-up menu appears.

3. **Choose the panel you want to group the currently selected panel with.**

   The panel you added appears as a tab in the panel to which you added it.

Follow these steps to remove a panel from a group:

1. **Click the tab of the panel you want to separate from the group.**

2. **Click the Panel options icon at the top right of the panel.**

   The Panel options menu appears.

3. **Select the Close Panel Group option.**

   This closes not only the panel you want to close, but also any other panels in that group.

4. **Reopen any panels from the group that you didn't want to close by choosing them from the Window menu.**

If you have moved your panels around and docked them to accommodate a particular project or document, you can save your panel arrangement by choosing Commands⇨Panel Layout Sets⇨Save Panel Layout and giving your settings a name. You can then retrieve that layout set-up from the same location.

Setting Fireworks MX Preferences

Setting preferences allows you to customize the way Fireworks MX handles certain basic functions and displays certain items. To edit Fireworks MX preferences, choose Edit⇨Preferences or use the keyboard shortcut Ctrl+U.

As you can see in Figure 1-4, there are five tabs in the Preferences window:

 ✦ General

 ✦ Editing

 ✦ Launch and Edit

 ✦ Folders

 ✦ Import

Figure 1-4:
The
Preferences
dialog box.

Setting General preferences

You can select the General tab and customize the following settings:

✦ **Undo Steps:** Set the value from 0 to 999. This setting affects Edit⇨Undo/ Redo and also increases the number of possible steps in the History panel. Be aware, however, that the more undo steps you allow, the more memory Fireworks MX requires. You must close and relaunch Fireworks MX to use the new setting.

✦ **Color Defaults:** Set the default colors for Stroke (a line or border), Fill (the inside of a shape), and Highlight (the color that indicates what you currently have selected). To apply the changes to the default Stroke and Fill colors, you must make the changes via the Set Default Stroke/Fill Colors button in the Tools panel.

✦ **Interpolation:** Choose one of the four methods that Fireworks MX can use to render a change to the image size:

• **Bicubic Interpolation,** the default method, generally yields the highest-quality results.

• **Soft Interpolation** blurs the image slightly.

• **Bilinear Interpolation** gives a sharpness level somewhere in between Bicubic and Soft.

• **Nearest Neighbor Interpolation** sharpens edges.

For more details on changing image size, see Book III, Chapter 2.

✦ **Workspace:** Select this check box if you want to see the icons that appeared on tabs in previous versions of Fireworks MX.

Setting Editing preferences

Select the Edit tab to access these editing preferences in Fireworks MX:

**Book III
Chapter 1**

**Introduction to
Fireworks MX**

✦ **Precise Cursors:** Select this check box if you prefer to use crosshairs as a cursor instead of the custom cursors for each tool.

✦ **Delete Objects when Cropping:** Leave this check box selected if you want to delete objects and pixels that fall outside the area to which you crop your image.

✦ **Brush-Size Painting Cursors:** Select this check box if you want the cursor size to represent the size of stroke you are about to make.

✦ **Bitmap Options:** You have two options here:

- Select the Turn off "Hide Edges" check box if you always want to see the path selection feedback of a selected object.

- Select the Display Striped Border check box to display a striped border around the canvas when you are working in bitmap mode.

✦ **Pen Tool Options:** You have two options here:

- Select the Show Pen Preview check box if you want Fireworks MX to show what your path will look like before you actually draw the line based on the position of your cursor.

- Select the Show Solid Points check box if you want selected points to appear hollow and deselected points to appear solid.

✦ **Pointer Tool Options:** You have several options here:

- Select the Mouse Highlight check box if you want an object's selection feedback (the box that indicates that an object has been selected) to activate when you roll the cursor over that object.

- Select the Preview Drag check box if you want to see an object as you drag it.

- Select the Show Fill Handles check box if you want to be able to drag handles to change the position, width, skew, and rotation of a gradient fill.

- Set the value of the Pick Distance option from 1 to 10 to specify how close in pixels your cursor needs to be to an object for you to select it.

- Set the value of the Snap Distance option from 1 to 10 to specify how close to a grid or guide in pixels an object must be before the object snaps to the grid or guide.

Setting Launch and Edit preferences

You set the Launch and Edit preferences to specify how you want Fireworks MX to act when it's launched from within other applications in the Macromedia Studio MX suite.

The options are the same whether you are choosing options under When Editing from External Application or When Optimizing from External Application:

✦ Select the Ask When Launching option if you want Fireworks MX to ask you whether or not to edit the PNG source file when you launch Fireworks MX from within another application.

✦ Select the Always Use Source PNG option if you want Fireworks MX always to find the source PNG for editing an image from within another application.

✦ Select the Never Use Source PNG option when you never want Fireworks MX to locate and make available for editing the source file for an image you are editing from within another application.

In most cases (with Macromedia Flash MX being an exception), if you edit an image by launching Fireworks MX from within another application, Fireworks MX attempts to locate the source PNG file for editing, regardless of the Launch and Edit preferences.

Setting Folders preferences

Fireworks MX comes with its own effects, textures, and patterns, but the application allows you to access additional materials for use in modifying bitmap images. Select the Folders tab to gain access to the following:

✦ **Photoshop Plug-Ins:** If you have Photoshop plug-ins you want to be able to use in Fireworks MX, select the Photoshop Plug-Ins check box. Use the dialog box to browse to the folder that holds those plug-ins.

✦ **Textures:** If you have additional textures you would like to access from within Fireworks MX, select the Textures check box. Use the dialog box to browse to the folder that has the texture files.

✦ **Patterns:** If you have additional patterns you would like to access from within Fireworks MX, select the Patterns check box. Use the dialog box to browse to the folder that has the pattern files.

If you change these preferences, you need to quit and relaunch Fireworks MX for the changes to take effect.

You can access the effects, textures, and patterns from the Property inspector when you select an object.

Setting Import preferences

Set the Import preferences to tell Fireworks MX how you want to convert Photoshop (.psd) files for editing in Fireworks MX:

**Book III
Chapter 1**

Introduction to
Fireworks MX

+ **Layers:** Three options are grouped under this heading:

  • Select the Convert to Fireworks MX Objects check box if you want Fireworks MX to make each Photoshop layer into an object on its own Fireworks MX layer.

  • Select the Share Layer Between Frames check box if you want each layer of the Photoshop file to be shared across all Fireworks MX frames.

  • Select the Convert to Frames check box if you want Fireworks MX to import each Photoshop layer as a Fireworks MX frame. That can save you a few steps if the Photoshop file has layers that correspond to animation frames or button states.

+ **Text:** Two options are grouped under this heading:

  • Select the Editable check box if you want to edit text layers from the Photoshop file using the Fireworks MX Text tool. The text may look slightly different in Fireworks MX, though it will be close.

  • Select the Maintain Appearance check box if you need the text in Fireworks MX to look identical to the text in Photoshop but do not need to edit the text.

Getting Help

Fireworks MX offers several forms of assistance to users. If you can't find the answer to your question in this book, you have several good options available to you:

+ **The Help menu:** This menu offers links to appropriate parts of the Macromedia Web site and an indexed, searchable online manual.

  Press F1 to access the online manual at any time when you're using Fireworks MX. The online manual is always where we go first when we need to figure out how to do something in Fireworks MX.

+ **Fireworks MX tutorials:** Fireworks MX comes with two built-in tutorials, one on Graphic Design Basics and the other on Web Design Basics. To access them, choose Help⇨Using Fireworks MX, click the Contents tab, and click on the tutorial name. The tutorials are quick, easy, and very helpful to the novice.

+ **The Answers panel:** The Answers panel is an updateable (via the Internet) repository of tips, tricks, and links to appropriate areas of the Macromedia Web site.

+ **The installation CD-ROM:** The CD-ROM from which you installed Fireworks MX contains a couple of searchable, printable PDF files:

- The Using Fireworks MX PDF offers the basics.

- The Extending Fireworks MX PDF describes how you can use JavaScript to control every command and setting in Fireworks MX.

You can copy the PDFs into the Fireworks MX folder to your hard drive so you don't have to rummage around for the installation CD when you have a question the Help menu can't answer.

✦ **Tooltips:** Tooltips are built into the Fireworks MX user interface. Hover the cursor over an interface element to see a brief description of the element's function or capabilities.

If none of these resources gives you an answer to your question, Macromedia offers both free Web-based support (including online forums) and fee-based support via e-mail and telephone.

Chapter 2: Fireworks MX Basics

In This Chapter

✔ **Creating a new Fireworks MX document**

✔ **Changing the view of your document**

✔ **Saving documents**

✔ **Modifying document size**

✔ **An introduction to color management**

*I*n this chapter, we introduce some of the basic processes of working with Fireworks MX. If you're a regular PC user, many of these processes will already be second nature to you. We show you how to create and save a Fireworks document, how to change the magnification of your document, and how to change the size of your document. We also offer an introduction to some issues regarding the way colors are displayed on the Web.

Creating a New Fireworks MX Document

Before you can start creating or editing cool images with Fireworks MX, you need to start the program and either create a brand-new blank document or open an existing image that you want to change. You can open Fireworks MX in several ways:

✦ Select Fireworks MX from the Start menu.

✦ Click the Fireworks MX icon in your taskbar or double-click the icon on your desktop, if you have either of those options available.

✦ Double-click the icon of an existing Fireworks MX .png file.

✦ Double-click the icon of any image associated with Fireworks MX. (During installation, you can choose which file types will be associated with Fireworks MX, including GIFs and JPEGs.)

No matter how you open Fireworks MX, you can create a new Fireworks MX document by following these steps:

1. Choose File⇨New or press Ctrl+N.

The New Document dialog box opens, displaying options for the size and background color of your canvas, as well as the resolution of your document, as shown in Figure 2-1. The default for all these settings is determined by the settings of the most recently opened Fireworks MX document. If those settings are what you want, simply click OK. Otherwise, continue with the following steps.

Figure 2-1:
Set the canvas size and canvas color in the New Document dialog box.

2. **Type numbers in the Width and Height text boxes to set the width and height of your canvas; use the drop-down list to select whether you want the width and height of the canvas measured in pixels, inches, or centimeters.**

   If you're designing for the Web, pixels are most appropriate, because pixels are the basic display units on computer monitors. If you're designing for print, inches or centimeters may work better.

   You can use different units of measurement for the width and height, although it would probably be more confusing than helpful.

3. **Set the canvas color.**

   The default canvas color is white. You can also set the canvas to be transparent, which can be useful if you're making a graphic that has a transparent background. If your Web page is going to use a particular color for the background, click the square to use the eyedropper to choose a color from the color picker, as shown in Figure 2-2.

Figure 2-2:
Use the color picker to select a custom background color for your canvas.

4. **Click OK.**

   Your canvas opens to the specified size, with the specified background color.

Changing Views of Your Document

After you start adding stuff to your canvas, you may find that you want to make adjustments too fine to eyeball with the canvas at 100 percent size. Fireworks MX offers several ways for you to increase and decrease the magnification of your canvas. Changing the magnification doesn't affect your document's size, it just changes your view of it, as if you're looking at your document through a magnifying glass.

To increase the magnification of the canvas so you can make fine adjustments, use one of the following methods:

- ✦ **Choose View⇨Zoom In or press Ctrl+=.** Repeat as necessary to achieve the desired view.

- ✦ **Choose View⇨Magnification and then select a magnification percentage greater than 100 percent.** If you use this method, you can select your magnification percentage directly, rather than stepping through each level. Figure 2-3 shows this selection method.

- ✦ **Click the Magnification drop-down list at the bottom of the canvas and select from the list of pre-set magnification levels.**

If your canvas is larger than the window in which you are viewing it, you can decrease the magnification of the canvas so you can see the entire document by using one of the following methods:

- ✦ **Choose View⇨Zoom Out or press Ctrl+-.** Repeat as necessary to achieve the view you want.

- ✦ **Choose View⇨Magnification and then select a magnification percentage less than 100 percent.** If you use this method, you can select your magnification percentage directly, rather than stepping through each level.

- ✦ **Click the Magnification drop-down list at the bottom of the canvas and select from the list of pre-set magnification levels.**

Several of the most common magnification levels can be accessed in one step with the key commands listed in Table 2-1.

Figure 2-3:
Changing
the canvas
magnif-
ication.

Table 2-1	Magnification Shortcuts
Magnification Percentage	*Key Combination*
50%	Ctrl+5
100%	Ctrl+1
200%	Ctrl+2
300%	Ctrl+3
400%	Ctrl+4
800%	Ctrl+8
1600%	Ctrl+6

Saving Documents

You may have read this elsewhere, but it bears repeating: Save early and
save often. We can't think of anything worse than working for hours on an
image, getting it just perfect, and having a power outage or other mishap
wipe out all that work in one cruel second.

Spare yourself the frustration of losing your work and save your documents
often by choosing File➪Save or by pressing Ctrl+S.

You can still use the Undo command after you have saved, so it never really hurts to save your document. However, if you are concerned with preserving intermediate versions of a document, you can save versions, rather than saving over your previous work. If you want to try several different approaches to a design but don't want to clog one file with all of the approaches, use the Save As command and name the file with a slight variation. (For example, if your file is named `homepage.png`, you could name a second version `homepage_v02.png`.)

To save a version of your document, follow these simple steps:

1. **Choose File⇨Save or press Ctrl+S to save the file in its current state, with its current name.**

2. **Choose File⇨Save As or press Ctrl+Shift+S.**

   The Save As dialog box appears, as shown in Figure 2-4.

Figure 2-4: Use the Save As command to save iterations of your work.

Book III Chapter 2

Fireworks MX Basics

3. **Type a new filename.**

   If you have already named the file, the current name is filled in for you, so you need to modify the filename in order to save the current version of the document.

4. **If you are editing a non-PNG file and want to save the file in its original format, use the drop-down list to select the format.**

5. **Click OK.**

   The new version of the file is now open and ready for modification.

Modifying Document Size

You can modify the size of your Fireworks MX document in two fundamentally different ways. With these methods, you're changing the actual dimensions of the document, not just the magnification of the canvas:

✦ **Changing the image size:** When you change the image size, Fireworks MX recreates the entire document, including everything on the canvas, at a different height and/or width.

✦ **Changing the canvas size:** When you change the canvas size, you do not change the size of the objects on the canvas, you only change the size of the space on which you put the material, as if you cut the top, bottom, or sides off a printed picture. You can use the crop tool to change the canvas size or you can use a dialog box.

Changing the image size

When you change the image size of your document, you change the dimensions of the canvas and of everything on the canvas. If you shrink your image, Fireworks MX discards some of the data when it reorders the pixels to make the image smaller.

If you increase the size of your image, Fireworks MX *interpolates* data, which entails performing sophisticated calculations to decide what color of pixels to add and where to add them in order to make a larger version of the image.

You can choose which method Fireworks MX uses to interpolate or resample pixels:

✦ **Bicubic interpolation:** Bicubic interpolation is the default method and generally yields the highest-quality results with the widest variety of images by taking an average of the nearest 16 pixels in the original image size to create a new pixel in the resized image.

✦ **Soft interpolation:** This method blurs the image slightly. Why would you want the resized image to be slightly blurred? Because resizing can result in visual inconsistencies in the image called *artifacts*. Blurring the image takes the edge off the artifacts, rather like a soft-focus lens makes a starlet's skin look smoother.

✦ **Bilinear interpolation:** The bilinear method gives a sharpness level somewhere in between Bicubic and Soft.

✦ **Nearest-neighbor interpolation:** This method sharpens edges, so it works best on images that don't have subtle gradients. If you use this method on a bitmap of a sunset, for example, you'll get "banding," noticeable stripes of color areas that no longer blend into one another.

When you shrink your image, Fireworks MX discards some pixels and adds a few to smooth out the resized image. If you have a 400 x 300 image that you shrink to 240 x 180, and then you enlarge it back to its original size, the image you end up with will not be identical to the original image. However, as long as the size changes aren't extreme, you may not notice much of a difference.

If the Constrain Proportions check box is selected, as it is by default, and you change the width in the Pixel Dimensions part of the window, the height in that part of the window updates automatically, as does the width and height in the Print Size part of the window. If you change the image resolution in the Print Size part of the window, the width and height in both Pixel Dimensions and Print Size updates automatically.

The Pixel Dimensions and Print Size widths and heights are identical, they're just being measured with different units. (You can set Pixel Dimensions and Print Size to use the same units of measurement.)

To change the image size of your document, with the intention of displaying the image online, follow these steps:

1. Choose Modify➪Canvas➪Image Size.

   The Image Size dialog box appears, with the current image size and resolution as the defaults, as shown in Figure 2-5.

Figure 2-5:
Changing the image size.

2. Type new numbers in the Width and Height text boxes in the Pixel Dimensions part of the window to set the new width and height for your image; use the drop-down list to select whether you want to change the width and height of the image based on pixels or percentages.

   If you're designing for the Web, pixels are most appropriate, because pixels are the standard units of computer monitor display. If you're designing for print, inches or centimeters may work better. If you want your new image to have the same *aspect ratio* (the ratio of width to height, for example, 4:3 for an image that is 400 x 300 pixels) as your current image, leave the Constrain Proportions check box selected and skip Step 3. A padlock icon at the right indicates that proportions will be constrained.

   If you want to stretch or squash everything in your image as if it were reflected in a funhouse mirror, deselect the Constrain Proportions check box and proceed to Step 3.

You can use different units of measurement for the width and height, although doing so offers no advantages.

3. Select a method for resampling your image, or leave at the default.

Resampling settings are discussed earlier in this section.

4. Click OK.

The image resizes.

To change the image size of your document for the purpose of printing it, follow these steps:

1. Choose Modify⇨Canvas⇨Image Size.

The Image Size dialog box appears, with the current image size and resolution as the defaults.

2. Set the image resolution for print in the Print Size section of the Image Size dialog box.

Computer screen resolution is standardized at 72 dots per inch. Most printers nowadays print at resolutions of anywhere from 300 dpi to 2400 dpi. If you are designing for the Web and are working with a resolution of 72 dpi, changing the resolution here does not increase the resolution of any of your bitmaps (that's kind of like trying to focus a photograph after you've already taken it), but it ensures that the printout fills the page properly.

3. Type new numbers in the Width and Height text boxes in the Print Size part of the window; use the drop-down list to change the measurement units, if desired.

If the Constrain Proportions check box is selected, as it is by default, and you want the printed image to have the same aspect ratio as the current image, skip to Step 4. You can deselect the Constrain Proportions check box and type new numbers in the Width and Height text boxes if you want to stretch or smash your image.

You can use different units of measurement for the width and height, although doing so offers no advantages.

4. Leave the Resample Image check box selected unless you want to change the image size by changing the image resolution.

If you change the image resolution, you change the number of pixels per inch.

5. Click OK.

The image resizes.

Changing the canvas size

Making the canvas size smaller is akin to removing strips from the outside of a drawing or painting. Whatever is on those strips gets discarded with the strips. In other words, when you reduce the canvas size, you are essentially cropping the image.

Making the canvas size bigger is like sewing extra strips onto the outside edges of a canvas. You add space to the canvas without changing the size of anything already sitting on it.

To reduce the canvas size, follow these steps:

1. **Choose Modify⇨Canvas⇨Canvas Size.**

The Canvas Size dialog box opens, as shown in Figure 2-6. The default width and height when the window opens are the current dimensions of the document.

Figure 2-6:
Use the Canvas Size dialog box to crop your canvas.

2. **Type new numbers for the width and height in the text boxes, and select the measurement units for the width and height.**

Your choice is, as elsewhere, pixels, inches, or centimeters.

3. **Select the anchor area.**

Because you are cutting off part of your canvas, you must set the anchor to tell Fireworks MX which edges of the canvas to discard:

- If you click one of the top three squares, Fireworks MX preserves the top and cuts off any pixels below the height you have set.

- If you click one of the middle three squares, Fireworks MX removes the top and bottom of the existing document.

- If you click one of the bottom squares, Fireworks MX cuts off any pixels above the height you have set.

- If you choose one of the left three squares, Fireworks MX discards any pixels to the right of the width you have set.

- If you choose one of the middle three squares, Fireworks MX chops off the pixels on either side of the width you have set.

- If you choose one of the right three squares, Fireworks MX lops off everything to the left of the width you have set.

4. Click OK.

The canvas resizes.

If you're not sure of the dimensions of the image you want, but you know which area of the current image you want to keep, you can reduce the canvas size by using the Crop tool. See Book III, Chapter 1 for information about how to use the Crop tool.

To increase the canvas size, just follow these steps:

1. Choose Modify⇨Canvas⇨Canvas Size.

A pop-up window opens, showing the current document dimensions.

2. Type the new width and height in the Width and Height text boxes and select the measurement units for the width and height.

You can choose pixels, inches, or centimeters.

3. Select the anchor area.

Because you are appending an area to your canvas, you must set the anchor to tell Fireworks MX where to put the new area:

- If you click one of the top three squares, Fireworks MX adds the space to the bottom of your current canvas.

- If you click one of the middle squares, Fireworks MX adds equal space to the top and bottom of your current canvas.

- If you click one of the bottom squares, Fireworks MX adds space to the top of your current canvas.

- If you click one of the left three squares, Fireworks MX adds space to the right of your current canvas.

- If you click one of the center three squares, Fireworks MX adds space to the left and right of your current canvas.

- If you click one of the right three squares, Fireworks MX adds space to the left of your current canvas.

4. Click OK.

The canvas resizes.

An Introduction to Color Management

The primary colors of light are Red, Green, and Blue (RGB). All the colors you see on a computer monitor are made up of varying amounts of those three colors. When you work in FreeHand 10, you have the option to design using CMYK colors (Cyan, Magenta, Yellow, and Black). CMYK is the process used in offset printing. (See Book IV for more about FreeHand 10.)

Because Fireworks MX is made for Web design, it only uses the RGB color spectrum; all its color options are combinations of red, green, and blue. The following section explains how you use hexadecimal numbers to create different colors using the RGB color spectrum.

Hexadecimal numbers

When you are designing a Web page, you select a background color and HTML text colors. In HTML, colors are specified by using hexadecimal numbers — the # symbol, followed by six digits (from 0 through 9) or letters (A through F). Zero represents the bottom of the scale (zero luminosity) and F represents the top of the scale (full luminosity).

The hexadecimal number's six places operate as three pairs. The first pair represents red, the second pair represents green, and the third pair represents blue. For example, to make the background color for your page white, you would write the following code:

```
<BODY bgcolor="#FFFFFF">
```

In order to make white, you need to set each color to its highest luminosity, which is represented by the pair, "FF." If you wanted to put black text on your page, you could use the following code:

```
<FONT color="#000000">text</FONT>
```

In order to make black, you need to set each color to its lowest luminosity, which is represented by the pair, "00." If you don't understand what the code is all about in those examples above, see Book II on Dreamweaver MX.

The hexadecimal expression of a pure RGB red is #FF0000; a pure green is #00FF00; and a pure blue is #0000FF. The number of possible colors is a bit mind-boggling: It's in the millions. Only a small subset of those possible colors are Web safe, though.

Web safe colors

In the early days of the Web, many computer monitors could display only 256 colors. Because 40 of those colors were reserved for the computer's operating

**Book III
Chapter 2**

**Fireworks MX
Basics**

system or otherwise off-limits, that left 216 colors available for use on Web sites: the *Web safe colors*. When you set your monitor's resolution to the 8-bit display option, your monitor can show only that old set of 256 colors. What happens when you look at an image that has colors that don't fall into that set of 256? Your computer approximates the colors it can't display either by a process called dithering or by changing the colors to ones that it can display.

Dithering is the process of combining two or more colors in order to mimic another color. Offset printing uses an analogous process in order to make many colors out of the four CMYK ink colors. If you look at a color image in a newspaper or magazine through a magnifying glass, you see that it's made up of many little colored dots and hollows. Viewed from a certain distance, those tiny dots blend together to form what appear to be solid colors. For example, you may see orange with your naked eyes, but if you look closely with a magnifying glass, you see alternating yellow and magenta dots on that newspaper or magazine page.

When a computer dithers a color, it patterns two colors to create the illusion of a third color. As with a color photo in a newspaper, this strategy works only to a limited extent. If you look closely, you can see the pattern. If the dithered color is used just for a line or some small page element, the dither may be rather innocuous. If, on the other hand, you select non-Web safe colors for your page background and/or text colors, people who view your site using a monitor set to 8-bit may have a difficult time trying to read the text on your Web site.

If users have their monitors set to 16-bit and they're looking at a 24-bit color, they get a dithered color also, but the higher resolution of 16-bit versus 8-bit means that the computer can choose closer colors, so the dither doesn't look as obvious. Note that the more colors you have in your image, the larger the file size.

So should you use only Web safe colors when you design your Web site? Isn't that terribly limiting? After all, the Web safe colors were not selected by designers, and there are some really ugly ones in the bunch!

Go ahead and use non-Web safe colors, but think about what you're using them for and how likely it may be that the people visiting your site may only be able to see them dithered.

In the early days of the Web, when most Web surfers had 8-bit monitors and used early browsers, designers would predither all their images. That way, images would look essentially the same to all users, whether the users had 8-bit displays or 16-bit displays. Nowadays, browsers have become more sophisticated, and monitors that display at 16-bit and higher are affordable to average computer owners. As a result, designers have decided that in certain cases, it's better to allow inconsistency in the realm of display in order to offer higher image quality to better-equipped users.

Variability and Web design

One of the most frustrating aspects of Web design, especially for people trained in print design, is that many design elements cannot be controlled. Monitor settings (both in terms of number of colors displayed and pixel resolution) vary from user to user, and on Macintosh monitors colors appear lighter than they do on PC monitors. Users can change the size of HTML text in their browsers, and they can drag their browser windows as wide or narrow as they see fit. Not only that, download rates may be anywhere from about 5K with a 56K modem, to twenty times that or more with cable or DSL modems.

As a result, Web design always starts with a consideration of the end user — the average person who's going to visit the site. If your Web site's audience is going to be made up mostly of college students who have high-speed Internet access in their dorms, or people working in large companies who have high-speed Internet access at their desks, you can get away with making image file sizes larger. You also can assume those people have their monitors set to 16-bit (thousands of colors) or 24-bit (millions of colors), because it looks better and all computers sold nowadays come with video cards that can display at least 16-bit color. What you know about your potential end users should affect your choices of colors for page background, HTML text, and GIFs.

If you have a mix of business users and home users, you have to make some compromises in page width, image quality, and other things. If your users are mostly older, you may want to make your default text size a little bigger than average, or you may be satisfied simply to design your page in such a way as to accommodate a larger text size. (See Book II for hints on how to build pages that won't break when users change their settings.) You should always try to choose a text color that contrasts fairly sharply with the background color.

Web designers have a phrase that describes what your design should be able to do so that all users can have a satisfactory experience on your site: Your design should *degrade gracefully*. That is, where you do not want to compromise quality or remove features to bring every user's experience down to the lowest common denominator, make sure that users with the least fancy equipment or with disabilities can still access your important content. For example, blind users will have access to any text on your site via screen reader software (which reads the text on your site aloud) or Braille software and hardware. For more information on accessibility issues and standards, visit the World Wide Web Consortium (W3C) Web site at www.w3.org.

Book III
Chapter 2

Fireworks MX
Basics

In keeping with tradition, though, Fireworks MX still uses the Web safe color palette as its default in the color picker.

In the next chapter, we get into the nitty-gritty of applying all this color stuff to the real-life situations of choosing colors for page backgrounds, HTML text, and the like.

Chapter 3: Working with Text, Shapes, and Images

In This Chapter

✔ Styling text

✔ Creating and editing shapes

✔ Working with images

*I*n this chapter, we explore the power that Fireworks MX gives you to write and edit text, make and manipulate vector shapes, and create and mutate bitmap images. The control that you have with Fireworks MX may sometimes seem overwhelming, but the number of its tools is limited and the concepts behind the tools are simple. And whether you have a clear idea about what you want, or you're interested in experimenting, Fireworks MX suits your needs.

Working with Text

Text is the most common element on most Web pages, much as text is the most common element in magazines and newspapers. Unlike with printed material, though, users can alter the size and appearance of Web text to a certain extent, if you allow them that flexibility. Some of the most important decisions you make in building your Web site involve how you present text on the screen. In general, a finished Web page has two kinds of text:

✦ **HTML text:** The text you see on the Web page that is created with HTML. This type of text is akin to the text in word-processing software such as Microsoft Word.

✦ **Graphic text:** The text that's embedded in an image, such as a JPEG or a GIF file. In other words, it's a *picture* of text.

Which method of presenting text is better for you and people viewing your Web site depends largely on the function of the text.

Some advantages of using HTML text include the following:

✦ HTML text is smaller (in kilobytes) and therefore loads faster in a user's Web browser.

✦ Visitors can vary the size of the text by changing settings in their browsers, although you can use CSS (Cascading Style Sheets) styles to prevent users from varying the text size in most current browsers. You may not want to use this feature because increasing the text size helps people with poor eyesight read your Web pages.

✦ Special software and hardware (in the case of Braille) can make HTML text available to blind users via audio or touch.

Remember, always use an ALT tag for graphic text. The ALT tag should say what the graphic text says, so blind users have access to it.

✦ Visitors to your site can select, copy, and paste HTML text into e-mails or word-processing documents, which can help spread the word you're trying to get out via your Web site.

On the downside, HTML text tends to be limited to very basic fonts — those available on all computers, notably Arial and Times — and can be presented in a limited number of ways.

Graphic text, in contrast, is much more visually dynamic than HTML text, because it's part of an image. That's why graphic text is common for buttons and banners, which need to grab the user's attention. Some of the key advantages to using graphic text include the following:

✦ You can create text using any font that's installed on your computer.

✦ You can apply lots of different effects to text, like glows and drop-shadows.

✦ You have greater control of things like *leading* (the spacing between lines of text) and *kerning* (the spacing between letters).

Of course, using graphic text also has drawbacks. You can't copy and paste text in a graphic, for example. Also, because the graphic text is part of an image, the size (in kilobytes) of the text is larger than that of plain HTML text.

Regardless of the kind of text you're creating, Fireworks MX can be of help. The following sections show how you can use the Fireworks MX text editing tools to create text as part of an image, as well as export text in HTML format.

If you want to include your main HTML text in your Fireworks MX document, or if you want to use placeholder text that will be replaced with final HTML text later in Dreamweaver MX, use the Fireworks MX text default, 12 point Arial or Verdana (with no anti-alias), in your page design. Using one of those settings gives you a good approximation of how the text will look on the HTML page you make from your design.

Creating text with the Text tool

Creating text with Fireworks MX is a snap, which is good because you do a lot of it when you're creating images and page mockups. To create some text, just follow these three easy steps:

1. **Select the Text tool by clicking the capital A in the Vector section of the Tools panel.**

An I-shaped pointer appears, as shown in Figure 3-1.

2. **Move the pointer to the point on the canvas where you want to create the text.**

3. **Click on the canvas and type away.**

You can always move text as well as change its font or color. We cover those details later in this chapter.

If the text you want to add already exists in a word-processing program, open the text document, select the applicable text, and copy it. Then, select the Text tool, click on the canvas in Fireworks MX, and press Ctrl+V to paste the text. Your text appears in the default font.

Book III
Chapter 3

Working with Text, Shapes, and Images

Figure 3-1:
Click the Text tool to reveal an I-beam-shaped pointer.

If you're pasting text into your Fireworks MX document, set the width of the text box before you paste the text in. The default Fireworks MX text box expands outward to the right rather than downward. To set the width of the text box, select the Text tool from the Tools panel, and click and drag diagonally on the canvas to create a text box of the right size. If your text is too long to fit in the box you've created, the box expands downward automatically.

Selecting a font and changing its size

After you create a snippet of text, you can select it for editing in one of three ways:

✦ After selecting the Text tool, select the text you want to edit by clicking and dragging to highlight just the desired text.

✦ Using the Arrow tool, double-click the text you created. Doing so activates the Text tool and makes the text available for editing.

✦ Using the Arrow tool, click once on the text you've created. Doing so selects the entire text box. When you edit the text settings in the Property inspector, Fireworks MX applies the changes to all the text in the box.

After you select text, notice that the Property inspector switches automatically to show the available text properties that you can apply to your selected text, including bold, italic, various text alignments, and effects like drop shadow and glow.

You can change your text to a different font in one of two ways:

✦ Choose a font from the scrolling drop-down list (that's the menu displaying the default font, Arial) in the Text Property inspector. The drop-down list displays all the fonts you have in your machine in alphabetical order. Note that as you scroll through the list, the menu displays the name of the selected font using the font face itself so you can quickly see what each font looks like. Figure 3-2 shows the Text Property inspector.

✦ Choose Text⇨Font and then select from the list of fonts displayed on the screen.

If you have tons of fonts and your favorite is way down the list, you can skip to it by clicking in the scrolling drop-down list in the Text Property inspector and typing the first letter of the font name on your keyboard. This jumps you to the first font available with that letter. You can then press the down-arrow key to find the font you're looking for. Press Enter to apply the font to the selected text.

Figure 3-2:
The Text Property inspector puts all your options within one click.

After you select a font, changing its size doesn't take any time at all. You can change a font size in Fireworks MX in one of two ways:

✦ **Use the Size Box:** The Text Property inspector contains a text box indicating the current size of the font you're working with. To change the text size, simply type the point size you'd like in the text box and press Enter.

✦ **Use the Slider:** Click and hold the arrow at the right of the size box and then slide it up. The text size increases. Similarly, slide it down and the text size decreases, as shown in Figure 3-3.

Figure 3-3:
Use the handy size slider to set your font size.

Adding a little color

By default, all text in Fireworks MX is black. Although black is handy and always in fashion, it's not the right color for every occasion. Changing font color in Fireworks MX is a pretty easy proposition. To change your color the basic way, just follow these steps:

1. Select the Text tool and place the cursor next to the first word that you want to change the color of. Click and drag until you've selected all the text you want to make a different color.

Alternatively, if you're using the Arrow tool, click the text once to select it.

2. Open the palette in the Text Property inspector by clicking the square to the right of the text size slider.

A color palette appears on-screen, showing only Web safe colors by default. Your mouse pointer changes to an eyedropper when you roll over the palette. The System Color Picker, which offers other color options, is discussed later in this section.

3. Using the eyedropper, click a color.

The square is now the color you have selected for your text. More importantly, your selected text is that color as well. If the text appears not to be the same color as the square, that's because the text is high-lighted. Click anywhere on the canvas or click any tool to deselect the text and see the color applied to the text.

If you don't feel like scrolling all the way to the bottom of the screen, you can also change the color of your font by using the Color area of the Tools panel. It works the same way as the pop-up menu in the Text Property inspector, but you save moving that extra inch or so down the screen.

The color picker contains a number of different views. The default view is Web safe color cubes. You can switch views by clicking the right-facing triangle in the top-right corner of the color picker, and then selecting a new view from the list that appears. The other views include the following:

✦ **Swatches panel:** Displays your saved colors. If you have any saved colors, they show up here. If not, the panel displays the Web safe palette.

✦ **Continuous tone:** Shows the colors as they move from lighter to darker left to right across the color picker. These are the same colors as the Web safe color cubes, just arranged differently.

✦ **Windows OS:** Shows the 217 Web safe colors that are also the Windows operating system colors.

✦ **Mac OS:** Shows the system colors for the Mac operating system.

✦ **Grayscale:** Provides a range of grays from light to dark. Be warned though, only six grayscale colors are Web safe!

What if the color you want isn't in the Web safe palette? Well, thankfully, Fireworks MX provides you with a number of different coloring options. On the top of the palette is the System Color Picker (the color wheel near the middle of the top of the window that pops up when you click the color box). You can click the System Color Picker to see your other color options. The color picker offers several other ways for you to choose a color, as shown in Figure 3-4:

✦ **RGB values:** Red, Green, and Blue are the colors that make up all the colors you can see on-screen.

✦ **Hue, Saturation, and Luminosity values:** A different way of telling the computer how to combine red, blue, and green.

✦ **The color matrix:** A visual representation of the Hue (the horizontal axis), Saturation (the vertical axis), and Luminosity (the extra strip on the right) values.

Figure 3-4:
The Fireworks MX color picker.

Using the color matrix gives you the most flexibility in choosing a color in that you can visually pick precisely the color you want. Here's how you use the color matrix:

1. **From the top middle of the color pop-up menu, select the System Color Picker.**

The Color dialog box appears.

2. **Place your cursor over the color you want and click the mouse button.**

You see a cross hair where you clicked. At the center of the cross hair is the color you chose. The higher you go in the matrix, the more saturated the color becomes. If you want to make the color darker or lighter, click on the shade you want in the Luminosity bar next to the matrix, or click and move the slider to the right of the shade. Note that, at this point, you still haven't changed the color of the text on the canvas.

3. **Click OK to apply the color to your text.**

The color is applied to the selected text on the canvas.

If you want to use a color frequently, click the Add to Custom Colors button on the lower right after you select your custom color. That way, whenever you need to use that color, you can click its square in the color picker instead of having to remember its RGB values or trying to find it in the color matrix.

Manipulating text

After you have typed or pasted your text, you can change anything about it, from its color to its position on the page. The process of changing the color is identical to the process of applying color in the first place, and you'll find editing, moving, and deleting text just as easy.

Inserting text

To insert text, just follow these steps:

1. **Choose the Text tool from the Tools panel.**

An I-beam-shaped cursor appears.

2. **Click the place in the text box where you want to add text.**

A blinking vertical line indicates where your new text will be inserted.

3. **Start typing, or use Ctrl+V to paste text that you have copied from elsewhere.**

Deleting text

To delete text, do the following:

1. **Choose the Text tool from the Tools panel.**

2. **Click the place in the text box where you want to delete text.**

3. **Click and drag over the text you want to delete.**

The selected text is highlighted, as shown in Figure 3-5.

4. **Press Delete or cut the text by pressing Ctrl+X.**

The highlighted text disappears.

To delete an entire selection of text, select the Pointer tool, and then click once on the text box that you want to delete. After the text box is selected, press the Delete key to delete the text box and everything in it.

If you realize immediately that you deleted more than you intended, or deleted the wrong chunk of text, use the keyboard shortcut Ctrl+Z to undo the deletion.

Replacing text

To replace text, just follow these steps:

1. **Choose the Text tool from the Tools panel.**

2. **Click the place in the text box where you want to replace text.**

3. **Click and drag over the text you want to delete.**

   The selected text is highlighted, as shown in Figure 3-5.

4. **Start typing, or press Ctrl+V to paste in text you have copied from elsewhere.**

Figure 3-5:
Selecting
text in a text
box.

Take a class from a pro, with this very instructional video featuring Marshall Willenholly, PBA Hall of Famer, Triple Crown winner and 1998 PBA Senior Champion.

Order now and receive five dollars off any additional video.

Moving text

To move text within a text box, do the following:

1. **Choose the Text tool from the Tools panel.**

2. **Click and drag over the text you want to move.**

   The selected text is highlighted, as shown in Figure 3-5.

3. **Choose Edit⇨Cut or press Ctrl+X to cut the text.**

4. **Place the cursor where you want to drop in the text and click.**

   A blinking vertical line indicates where your new text will be inserted.

5. **Choose Edit⇨Paste or press Ctrl+V to paste the text at the insertion point.**

To move a text box, follow these steps:

1. **Choose the Pointer tool.**

2. **Place the cursor anywhere over the text box.**

   An outline appears in red to indicate that your cursor is over the text box.

3. **Click anywhere within the text box and, with the mouse button held down, drag to move the text box.**

   Fireworks MX shows you where the text is moving to.

4. **Release the mouse button when the top left of your text is positioned where you want it.**

   The text is relocated.

Changing text box dimensions

After you have moved your text box, you may find that the text is too wide, too narrow, too long, or too short to fit in its new position in your design. Do you have to change your text? Not necessarily. Fireworks MX allows you to change the length and width of your text box, which may be all you need to do.

To change the width or length of a text box, just follow these steps:

1. **Choose the Pointer tool.**

2. **Place the cursor anywhere over the text box.**

   An outline appears in red to indicate that you have rolled over the text box.

3. **Click anywhere within the text box to select it.**

   The red outline changes to blue to indicate that you have selected the entire text box.

4. **Place the Pointer over one of the resize handles (the squares in the middle of the right-hand or left-hand side or the bottom of the box, depending on whether you want to resize the width or length of the box).**

   The Pointer automatically changes to the Subselection tool.

5. **Click a resize handle and drag the box to the desired width or length.**

6. **Release the mouse button to see the change.**

   If you widen your text box, Fireworks MX automatically shortens it. If you make your text box narrower, on the other hand, Fireworks MX makes the text box longer. If you drag the box longer than it needs to be to hold the text, the bottom of the box snaps to the lowest point your text reaches to at the width you dragged the box to.

Working with Vector Shapes

Fireworks MX gives you two ways to draw on your canvas:

+ **Vector mode:** Uses points, lines, and shapes to define image elements

+ **Bitmap mode:** Uses pixels to define image elements

Each method has advantages and disadvantages, and which mode you use depends on what you are attempting to do.

If you want to make a shape that you can easily tweak, resize, or export to Macromedia Flash MX or FreeHand 10 later, you will want to work in vector mode. When you make a simple vector shape in Fireworks MX, what you are actually creating is a mathematical model of a series of points connected by lines. By adding, subtracting, or moving points, you can change the shape without changing any of its other qualities, such as the line (stroke), width, and texture.

Because a simple vector shape is more a mathematical description of an image than an actual image, its data size is small. Not only that, but a square of a particular color and stroke width and gradient fill is basically the same data size whether it's 10 x 10 pixels or 1000 x 1000 pixels on-screen. That becomes important in Macromedia Flash MX, in which smaller image data sizes mean faster downloads.

Making a good old-fashioned line

The basic building block of a shape is the line. When you first create a line using the Line tool, it is a straight line (though it can be vertical, horizontal, or diagonal). To create a line in Fireworks MX, just follow these steps:

1. **Select the Line tool from the Vector part of the Tools panel.**

2. **Place your cursor over the spot where you would like your line to start.**

When your cursor is over the canvas, it becomes a cross hair. The center of that cross hair is your point of contact with the canvas.

3. **Click where you want your line to start and, holding the mouse button down, move your cursor to where you want your line to end.**

4. **Release the mouse button.**

By default, the stroke of your line is 1 pixel in width. A *stroke* in Fireworks MX is a like a brushstroke in painting. Stroke properties include width, texture, and color. The thicker the brush, the thicker the stroke it makes. Of course, in Fireworks MX, you can make strokes with the Pencil and Pen tools, and with other tools as well.

If you hold down the Shift key while you draw a line, you restrict the angle of the line to 45-degree increments.

Making simple shapes

Fireworks MX has easy-to-use tools for creating rectangles (including squares), ovals (including circles), and polygons. The tools for making all these shapes are grouped with the Rectangle tool in the vector section of the Tools panel. When you click on the Rectangle tool and hold down the mouse button, a pop-up menu displays four tools:

✦ **The Rectangle tool:** Use this tool to create squares and other rectangles.

✦ **The Rounded Rectangle tool:** Use this tool to create rectangles with rounded edges. You may find this tool particularly useful when you're creating buttons for your Web site. You can customize the rectangle roundness in the Property inspector.

✦ **The Ellipse tool:** Use this tool to create round shapes like circles and other ovals.

✦ **The Polygon tool:** Use this tool to create many-sided shapes (up to 360-sided). Use the Property inspector to set the number of sides before you draw on the canvas. The slider includes values from 3 through 25; for values greater than 25, type a number in the field. By default, the Polygon tool creates pentagons. Add three points and you have an octagon, or delete two points to get a triangle.

See the section "Editing, moving, and deleting shapes," later in this chapter, for information on changing shapes.

To make a rectangle, follow these steps:

1. **Select the Rectangle tool from the Vector section of the Tools panel.**

2. **Place your cursor over the point on the canvas where you want the top-left corner of your rectangle.**

   Notice that the cursor has become a cross hair.

3. **Click and drag to the spot where you want the bottom-right corner of the rectangle, as shown in Figure 3-6.**

4. **Release the mouse button.**

   The shape appears on the canvas.

Figure 3-6:
Making a
rectangle
shape.

You can use a variation on these steps to create a square or a rounded rectangle:

+ **Square:** To make a square, follow the preceding directions, but in Step 3, hold down the Shift key while you move the cursor.

+ **Rounded rectangle:** To make a rounded rectangle, follow the preceding steps, but in Step 1, select the Rounded Rectangle tool instead.

To make an oval, follow these steps:

1. **Select the Ellipse tool from the Vector section of the Tools panel by clicking on the Rectangle tool and holding the mouse button down until the pop-up menu with the Ellipse tool displays.**

2. **Place your cursor over the point on the canvas where you want the oval.**

   Your cursor becomes a cross hair.

3. **Click and drag to create the oval.**

An oval doesn't have corners, so you may not be able to get precise placement when you make the shape. That's no big deal, though, because moving the shape is easy, as we describe later in this chapter in the "Editing, moving, and deleting shapes" section.

To make a circle, follow the preceding directions, but hold down the Shift key while you move the cursor.

You can make an equilateral polygon (a shape in which all sides have equal lengths) by following these steps:

1. **Select the Polygon tool from the Vector section of the Tools panel by clicking on the Rectangle tool and holding the mouse button down until the pop-up menu with the Polygon tool displays.**

2. **At the right of the Property inspector, type the number of sides you want the polygon to have, or use the slider next to the Sides text field to set the number of sides.**

   By default, the polygon is five-sided. If you set the number of sides to 3 instead of 5, you draw a triangle. Set the number of sides to 6 and you draw a hexagon. You can make a shape with up to 360 sides — just don't expect us to know what a polygon with 360 sides is called!

3. **Place your cursor over the point on the canvas where you want the shape.**

   Your cursor becomes a cross hair.

4. **Click and drag to create the polygon.**

   The Property inspector changes to give you access to various properties of the polygon, including fill options, stroke options, and effects.

Making complex shapes

Creating squares and circles and polygons may be a snap in Fireworks MX, but what about making shapes too unique to have names, like shapes that have some straight lines and some curved lines — *freeform* shapes? Believe it or not, making odd shapes is just as easy as making regular ones, and it may even be more fun!

The main tool you use to create complex shapes is the Pen tool. Like the Rectangle tool, the Pen tool comes with some variations, which you can access by clicking and holding the mouse button down on the Pen tool. The pop-up menu for the Pen tool in the Vector section of the Tools panel displays the following variations:

✦ **The Pen tool:** Use the Pen tool to place points on the page;
  Fireworks MX connects the dots for you.

✦ **The Vector Path tool:** Use the Vector Path tool to draw as you would
  with a felt-tip marker.

✦ **The Redraw Path tool:** Use the Redraw Path tool to change the length
  or shape of a path you have already created.

To make a freeform shape with straight lines, follow these steps:

1. **Select the Pen tool from the Vector section of the Tools panel.**

2. **Place the cursor over the canvas.**

   Your cursor becomes a fountain pen.

3. **Click to make your starting point.**

4. **Move your cursor and click to create a second point.**

   Fireworks MX connects the dots with a straight line.

5. **Move your cursor and click to create a third point, and, if you like,
   a fourth, fifth, tenth, or one hundred forty-second point.**

6. **If you want a closed shape, click again on your starting point to close
   the shape. Otherwise, double-click the end point to make an open
   shape.**

Making curved lines with the Pen tool can be a little difficult initially. If you
know a few things about the Pen tool, using it to make curved lines will be a
little easier. First of all, you can make two kinds of points with the Pen tool.
Which kind you make determines whether the line connecting the dots is
straight or curved:

✦ **Corner points:** These points anchor straight lines.

✦ **Curve points:** These points anchor curved lines.

If you simply click in various spots to make the shape, you automatically
make corner points. To make a freeform shape with curved lines, as shown
in Figure 3-7, do the following:

1. **Select the Pen tool from the Vector section of the Tools panel.**

2. **Place the cursor over the canvas.**

   Your cursor becomes a fountain pen.

3. **Click to make your starting point.**

4. **Move your cursor and click on a second point. Keeping the mouse button held down, move your cursor.**

   Point handles (solid circles at both ends of a line that has the selected point in the middle) appear, which indicates you have made a curve point. As you move the mouse, Fireworks MX previews the curve between the first and second point.

5. **Release the mouse button to make the curve.**

   Fireworks MX joins your first and second points.

6. **Move your cursor and click and drag to create as many curved lines as you wish.**

7. **If you want a closed shape, click again on your starting point to close the shape. Otherwise, double-click on the end point to make an open shape.**

Figure 3-7: Making a complex shape.

Editing, moving, and deleting shapes

Altering a simple shape is nearly as easy as making a simple shape. If you make a shape using the Rectangle, Rounded Rectangle, Ellipse, or Polygon tool, Fireworks MX thinks of the shape as a group of points. If you want to edit the shape, first you need to ungroup the points so you can move them.

To prepare a straight-sided simple shape (that is, a shape with nothing but corner points, like a rectangle) for editing in order to change the shape, follow these steps:

1. **Select the Subselection tool (the white arrow) from the top of the Tools panel.**

2. **Click anywhere on the line defining the shape.**

   All the points, and a guide line connecting them, highlight. If you try to move any of the points, a pop-up window lets you know that the points are grouped. Click OK to ungroup them or click Cancel and proceed to Step 3. If you don't try to move any of the points, go to Step 3.

3. **Choose Modify⇨Ungroup or use the keyboard shortcut Ctrl+Shift+G to ungroup the points.**

 The shape remains selected.

4. **Click and drag any point in the shape to the new location you want.**

If you want to edit a complex shape (like the one shown in Figure 3-7), you can use the Subselection tool to alter any of the curves:

1. **Select the Subselection tool (the white arrow) from the top of the Tools panel.**

2. **Click anywhere on the line defining the shape.**

 All the points, and the guide lines connecting them, highlight.

3. **If the shape is grouped, choose Modify⇨Ungroup or press Ctrl+Shift+G to ungroup the points.**

4. **Click and drag a curve point to its new location, or click on a curve point to make it active and then click and drag one of the point handles to change the shape of the curve.**

Moving a shape is a piece of cake:

1. **Select the Subselection tool (the white arrow) from the top of the Tools panel.**

2. **Click anywhere on the line defining the shape and, keeping the mouse button held down, drag the shape to your desired location.**

If you click, release the mouse button, and then click and drag a point, you move the point rather than the whole shape. If you change the shape by mistake, press Ctrl+Z to undo the change.

Deleting a shape is a very simple matter indeed. To delete a shape, do the following:

1. **Select the Subselection tool (the white arrow) from the top of the Tools panel.**

2. **Click anywhere on the line defining the shape.**

3. **Press the Delete key or the Backspace key on your keyboard.**

 If you want to cut the shape and paste it somewhere else (in your current document, or in a different document), use the key command Ctrl+X to remove the shape and Ctrl+V to paste it in your desired new location.

Splitting shapes

If you ever have occasion to split one shape into two shapes, you can call upon the services of the Knife tool. The Knife tool is only available when you have an ungrouped shape selected. When you don't have an ungrouped shape selected, the Knife tool is grayed out in the Tools panel.

To split a shape, follow these steps:

1. **Select the Subselection tool (the white arrow) from the top of the Tools panel.**

2. **Click anywhere on the line defining the shape you want to split.**

   All the points, and the guide lines connecting them, highlight. Just as importantly, the Knife tool becomes available. (If the Knife tool remains grayed out in the Tools panel, press Ctrl+Shift+G to ungroup the shape and make the Knife tool available.)

3. **Select the Knife tool from the Vector portion of the Tools panel.**

   When you move your cursor over the canvas, it becomes a blade.

4. **Click and drag the cursor across the points over the guide lines where you want the shape to split, as shown in Figure 3-8.**

   New points show where the cut was made.

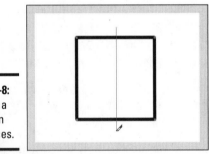

Figure 3-8: Splitting a square in two pieces.

If you hold down the Shift key while dragging, you can constrain the split to 45-degree angles.

Adding a little color to your shapes

You can think of your shapes as having two parts: the stroke (line) that defines the outside, and the inside, which can be empty or filled. The most basic stroke for a shape is a solid color; likewise the most basic inside for a filled shape is a solid color.

You can get pretty fancy with both strokes and fills (adding gradients, textures, and more, which we discuss in Book III, Chapter 4). However, we start with the basics: adding solid colors to strokes and fills.

Adding color to the stroke

The default color of strokes in Fireworks MX is black. So when you add color to the stroke, you're really changing the stroke's color from black to a color of your choosing.

To add or change the color of your stroke, just follow these steps:

1. **Select the Subselection tool from the Tools panel.**

2. **Click anywhere in the stroke.**

   The stroke is highlighted to show that it is selected.

3. **Click on the black square next to the pencil icon in the Stroke part of the Property inspector.**

   The pointer assumes the shape of an eyedropper, and the Fireworks MX color picker appears.

4. **Select a color.**

   The stroke changes color. For a refresher on the color picker, see the "Adding a little color" section, earlier in this chapter.

If your stroke is only 1-pixel wide, the highlight obscures the line and you can't see your change immediately. Don't worry, though. Just click anywhere on the canvas except the shape you just changed to deselect the shape so you can see it. (You can also deselect the shape by clicking Ctrl+D.)

Adding a fill color to the inside of the shape

Fills in Fireworks MX are empty by default. So when we say you add color to the fill, that's exactly what you're doing! Just as with adding color to a stroke, though, after you know how to add a color to the fill, you also know how to change the fill's color.

To add or change a fill color to your shape, just follow these steps:

1. **Select the Subselection tool from the Tools panel.**

2. **Click anywhere in the shape.**

   The stroke highlights to show that the shape is selected.

Book III
Chapter 3

Working with Text, Shapes, and Images

3. **Click on the square with the red line through it (next to the paint bucket icon) in the Fill part of the Property inspector.**

   The pointer assumes the shape of an eyedropper, and the Fireworks MX color picker pops up.

4. **Select a color.**

   For a refresher on the color picker, see the "Adding a little color" section, earlier in this chapter.

To remove an existing fill from your shape, follow the steps above, but at Step 4, click the Transparent button (the square with the red line through it at the top middle of the color picker).

Working with Bitmap Images

Vector images are compact and versatile, but they don't accommodate the complexity of photographic images or illustrations. In a photographic image, each pixel might be a completely different color than any of the pixels around it, so each pixel's color must be defined individually. That makes bitmaps big from a file-size perspective, but for pictures on your Web site (of people, places, or things), bitmaps are the only way to go.

Fireworks MX offers an array of useful tools for making and manipulating bitmap images. You may use the bitmap tools to draw in Fireworks MX, but you're likely to be in bitmap mode mostly when you want to place and tweak imported images like photographs.

Exploring the bitmap drawing tools

The main bitmap drawing tools in Fireworks MX are the Brush and the Pencil. Those tools are somewhat interchangeable and using them is as intuitive as can be. On the other hand, each tool has an amazing amount of flexibility, so although you can start drawing with them quickly, it may take some time for you to become acquainted with their full capabilities.

Most of the flexibility of the tools is centered around the concept of *tips.* In the real world, the sharper a pencil, the thinner a line it draws. The thicker the end of a paint brush is, the thicker the line it makes, and the kind of bristles it has affects the texture of the line it makes. The same is true with the tools in Fireworks MX.

In Fireworks MX, however, each tip is associated with a tool (though all those tools are really just variations of the Pencil and Brush) to form a *stroke category,* as the following list describes:

✦ **Pencil:** 1-Pixel Hard, 1-Pixel Soft, Colored Pencil, Graphite

✦ **Basic:** Hard Line, Hard Rounded, Soft Line, Soft Rounded

✦ **Air Brush:** Basic, Textured

✦ **Calligraphy:** Bamboo, Basic, Quill, Ribbon, Wet

✦ **Charcoal:** Creamy, Pastel, Soft, Textured

✦ **Crayon:** Basic, Rake, Thick

✦ **Felt Tip:** Dark Marker, Highlighter, Light Marker, Thin

✦ **Oil:** Bristle, Broad Splatter, Splatter, Strands, Textured Bristle

✦ **Watercolor:** Heavy, Thick, Thin

✦ **Random:** Confetti, Dots, Fur, Squares, Yarn

✦ **Unnatural:** 3D, 3D Glow, Chameleon, Fluid Splatter, Outline, Paint Splatter, Toothpaste, Toxic Waste, Viscous Alien Paint

The tips run the gamut from basic to out-of-this-world. Figure 3-9 shows strokes made with three of the more complex tips. After you're familiar with the default stroke settings, you may want to customize the tips. The Edit Stroke dialog box offers you an amazing amount of control over stroke parameters like ink amount, flow rate, shape, and sensitivity. See your documentation for details.

If you have a pressure-sensitive graphics tablet, you can set your drawing speed and pressure to modify how the stroke is placed on the canvas. Just enter your desired settings in the Sensitivity tab of the Edit Stroke dialog box.

Figure 3-9:
Lines made with some of the more exotic Brush stroke tips.

Airbrush, Textured

Crayon, Thick

Unnatural, Viscous Alien Paint

To draw a line or shape using the Brush or Pencil tool, follow these steps:

1. **Select the Brush or Pencil tool from the Bitmap area of the Tools panel.**

When you place your pointer over the canvas, the pointer takes the shape of a cross hair. The default tip for the Brush tool is also the default tip for the Pencil tool: 1-Pixel Hard.

2. **Select a color from the color picker in the Property inspector.**

   For a refresher on the color picker, see the "Adding a little color" section, earlier in this chapter.

3. **Select a tip from the Stroke Category pop-up window.**

   Each specialized tip has its own default edge size and texture.

4. **Click and drag on the canvas to make your line or shape.**

   The wider the brush, of course, the more pronounced the effect of a fancy tip. See Book III, Chapter 4 for more information on customizing the Brush edge and texture.

Inserting a bitmap image

Inserting an existing bitmap image into a Fireworks MX document is something you're likely to do often if you're designing a Web page, whether the bitmaps are pictures of your products or pictures of your family.

To insert a bitmap image into your document, you can drag and drop the image onto the canvas from your desktop or a folder, or you can import the image. To import a bitmap image, follow these steps:

1. **Choose File⇨Import or press Ctrl+R.**

   The Import dialog box appears.

2. **Navigate to the folder containing the image you want to insert.**

3. **Double-click the filename, or click the filename and click OK.**

   The Import dialog box closes, revealing the canvas. The cursor changes into the Insertion Pointer — a right angle.

4. **Align the Insertion Pointer with the top left point on your canvas where you want the inserted image to go.**

5. **Click to place the image.**

Selecting areas in a bitmap image

Fireworks MX allows you to select areas within an image in several different ways. The Marquee tool, Lasso tool, and Magic Wand tool will all be familiar to users of Photoshop. If you're new to these tools, read on for a brief rundown.

Using the Marquee tool

The Marquee tool has two guises:

✦ **The Marquee tool:** Use this tool to make rectangular selections.

✦ **The Oval Marquee tool:** Use this tool to make oval-shaped selections.

To select a rectangular or oval part of your bitmap, simply follow these steps:

1. **Select the Marquee tool or the Oval Marquee tool from the Bitmap part of the Tools menu.**

   When you move your pointer over the canvas, it becomes a cross.

2. **Place the center of the pointer over one corner of the area you want to select.**

3. **Click and drag diagonally over the area you want to select.**

   The selected area is delimited by a flashing marquee — the marquee is rectangular if you selected the Marquee tool and oval if you selected the Oval Marquee tool.

Using the Lasso tool

The Lasso tool, like the Marquee tool, has two guises:

✦ **The Lasso tool:** Use this tool to make a freeform selection area.

✦ **The Polygon Lasso tool:** Use this tool to select a polygonal area.

To select an irregular area of your bitmap, follow these steps:

1. **Select the Lasso tool from the Bitmap part of the Tools menu.**

   When you place your pointer over the canvas, it becomes a lasso.

2. **Place the bottom tip of the pointer over the spot on the canvas where you want your selection to start.**

3. **Click and drag to create an outline of the area you want to select, as shown in Figure 3-10.**

   You must close the outline to make the selection. When your pointer is over the spot where you started your selection, a little filled square appears at the bottom right of the pointer. Click to close the selection shape.

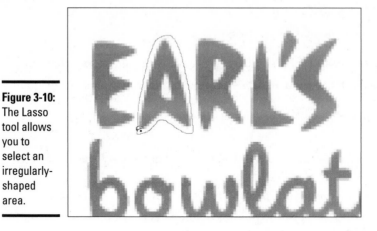

Figure 3-10:
The Lasso
tool allows
you to
select an
irregularly-
shaped
area.

To select a polygonal area of your bitmap, follow these steps:

1. **Select the Lasso tool from the Bitmap part of the Tools menu.**

   When you place your pointer over the canvas, it becomes a lasso.

2. **Place the bottom tip of the pointer over the spot on the canvas where you want your selection to start.**

3. **Click to establish the first point of the area you want to select.**

4. **Move your cursor to the second point of the area you want to select and click.**

   Fireworks MX connects the points with a straight line.

5. **Place your cursor and click on all points making up the polygonal selection.**

   You must close the outline to make the selection. When your pointer is over the spot where you started your selection, a little filled square appears at the bottom right of the pointer. Click to close the selection shape.

Using the Magic Wand

The third bitmap selection tool is known as the Magic Wand tool. The Magic Wand tool selects an area of solid color or of similar colors. (You can set the wand's sensitivity level so it selects areas of more similar or less similar colors.)

To select a contiguous area of similar color in your bitmap, follow these steps:

1. **Select the Magic Wand tool from the Bitmap section of the Tools panel.**

When you place your pointer over the canvas, it takes the form of a magician's wand.

2. **Place the pointer over the part of the canvas you want to select, and click.**

A blinking marquee marks off the selected area. If too much area is selected, you need to make the wand more sensitive. Set the Tolerance level in the Property inspector to a lower number. If not enough area is selected, set the Tolerance level to a higher number (up to 255, at which setting you will probably select your entire bitmap).

Editing bitmaps: The basics

Fireworks MX allows you to manipulate bitmaps in all kinds of crazy and interesting ways, but naturally, it also allows you to do common everyday image-altering as well.

Perhaps the most basic bitmap editing tasks you can do are cropping, resizing, rotating, and distorting an image, which we cover in Book III, Chapter 4, along with basic filtering operations, like Blurring, Sharpening, and making color adjustments.

No introductory chapter on bitmap editing would be complete, though, without a quick look at the Eraser tool. As you may expect, the Eraser tool is the anti-Brush. While the Brush tool adds a line or shape or pattern to a bitmap, the Eraser tool removes a line of pixels from a bitmap.

To erase pixels from your bitmap, follow these steps:

1. **Select the Eraser tool from the Bitmap part of the Tools panel.**

The Eraser tool defaults to a circle, though you can set it to be square-shaped in the Property inspector.

2. **In the Property inspector, type the size, or use the handy slider to set the width of the Eraser.**

The range goes from 1 to 100.

3. **Select the circle shape or square shape by clicking on one or the other.**

4. **Set the Edge by typing a number or using the slider.**

The range goes from 0 to 100. Setting to zero gives a hard edge to your Eraser (a pixel is removed or not), while setting to 100 gives a fuzzy edge to the erased area.

5. **Set the Opacity of the Eraser by typing a number or using the slider.**

   The range goes from 1 to 100 percent. If you set to the Opacity to 100 percent, the Eraser clears all the erased pixels entirely (except at the edges, if you have an edge of greater than 0 set). If you set to an opacity of less than 100 percent, the Eraser creates a translucent effect, allowing whatever is under the bitmap to show through. The lower the opacity percentage, the less the image underneath shows through.

6. **Click and drag on your image with the Eraser tool to rub out those unwanted pixels.**

   The pixels disappear as you drag the cursor over them.

Chapter 4: Transforming Text, Shapes, and Images

In the course of laying out the pages of your Web site, you may want to change the size or color of an image so that it fits more naturally into your design. In this chapter, we show you how to manipulate images, or parts of images, to create effects from subtle to extreme.

Scaling Graphics

When we talk about scaling graphics, we're not talking about changing the size of your overall image (that is, everything on the whole of your canvas). To find out how to change the canvas size, see Book III, Chapter 2. You can change the size of an image element or selected part of an image element in two ways:

♦ **Use the Scale Transformation tool:** Click and drag the image object or selection. Employ this option if you want to figure out the proper size of the image by eyeballing it.

♦ **Change the numbers in the Property inspector:** Type numbers in the width and height boxes. Use this option if you have exact dimensions in mind for your image.

Both methods are fairly simple, and their results are identical (that is, whether you drag an object to a specific width or type that width into the Property inspector, the resized object will look the same).

Using the Scale Transformation tool

You can change the size of an object, either retaining its proportions or distorting it, by using the Scale Transformation tool. To change the size of an object by using the click-and-drag method, follow these instructions:

1. **Click the Selection tool or Subselection tool in the Tools panel and then click the object you want to resize.**

   For more information on selecting image objects or parts of image objects, see Book III, Chapter 3.

2. **Select the Scale tool from the Tools panel or choose Modify⇨ Transform⇨Scale.**

   A box with eight handles and a center point overlays the selected object.

3. **Click and drag one of the handles to scale the object as follows:**

   • **To scale the object while retaining its proportions:** Click one of the corner handles and drag the object to the desired size.

   • **To scale the object and distort its proportions:** Click and drag the middle handle on either the left or right side of the box around the object to change the object's width; or click and drag the center handle on either the top or bottom of the box around the object to change the object's height.

   By default, Fireworks MX continues to display the original box around the object, but it adds a version of the box with a dotted line to show the new dimensions as you drag, as shown in Figure 4-1.

4. **Release the mouse button.**

   Fireworks MX redraws the image to your selected size.

Figure 4-1:
Resizing an image using the click-and-drag method.

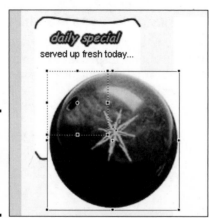

5. **Click and drag to reposition the image, if necessary.**

   The cursor changes into a four-pointed arrow when you place it over the redrawn image, which indicates that you can move the image. (See Figure 4-2.)

Resizing by entering numerical values

Sometimes you have a space with a defined width and height into which you want to place images of that exact width and height. If the images are not already sized to fit that space and you have calculated the exact proportions or you aren't worried about distorting the images, use the following method to resize the images.

To change the width and/or height of an image by typing in a new value for the width and/or the height, just follow these steps:

1. **Using the Selection tool or Subselection tool, click the object you want to resize.**

   See Book III, Chapter 3 for more information on selecting image objects or parts of image objects.

2. **In the Property inspector, double-click or click and drag over the number in the Width field to highlight it, as shown in Figure 4-3, and type in a new number.**

   If you cannot see the Width and Height fields, your Property inspector may be collapsed. To expand the panel, click once on the downward-pointing arrow at the bottom right corner of the panel. If the Property inspector is not visible on-screen, press Ctrl+F3 to open it.

3. **If you are not going to change the height, press Enter to implement the width change.**

   Fireworks MX redraws the selection at the new width.

4. **If you are going to change the height, select the number in the Height field and type a new value.**

5. **Press Enter or click in another value field.**

   Fireworks MX updates the height of the selection.

Figure 4-3:
The highlighted number is about to be replaced.

Distorting and Skewing Images

Changing the width but not the height of an image object, or changing the object's height but not width, distorts the object along one axis. What if you want to stretch one corner of an object but leave the rest of the object more or less intact, or perform some other unusual stretching or shrinking? The Distort and Skew transformation tools are at your disposal.

What's the difference between skewing and distorting? Skewing is actually a particular kind of distortion:

✦ **Distorting:** Stretching or shrinking one or more sides of an image object.

✦ **Skewing:** Distorting an image object by stretching or shrinking three of its four sides at once but not changing the dimensions of the fourth side. Skewing can create the illusion of perspective.

The Distortion tool is far more versatile than the Skew tool:

✦ You can use the Distortion tool to resize along one axis, in which case you are scaling the object.

✦ You can use the Distortion tool to stretch or shrink three sides of an object at once, in which case you are skewing the object.

✦ You can use the Distortion tool to create more complex forms of image manipulation by both scaling and skewing the object, for example.

Distorting an image

To distort an object using the Distortion transformation tool, follow these steps:

1. **Click the Selection tool or Subselection tool in the Tools panel and then click the object you want to distort.**

2. **Select the Distort tool from the Tools panel or choose Modify⇨ Transform⇨Distort.**

    If you are selecting from the Tools panel, click and hold on the Scale tool in the Tools panel and select the Distort tool from the pop-up menu. A box with eight handles and a center point overlays the selected object.

3. **Click and drag any handle.**

    By default, Fireworks MX continues to display the original box around the object, but it adds a version of the box with a dotted line to show the new dimensions as you drag, as shown in Figure 4-4. The cursor becomes a double-sided arrow as you place it over a center or middle handle.

    Note that when you try to drag handles too far (that is, if you try to drag a middle left handle above the top left handle, for example), the dotted line will stretch to wherever you drag the handle, but when you release the mouse button, the image snaps to the farthest allowable point in the direction you dragged. In short, a handle may not cross other handles.

4. **Click and drag any other handles.**

    You can stretch and squash the image by dragging as many handles as many times as you want.

5. **Press Enter or double-click anywhere in the canvas window.**

    Fireworks MX updates the selection.

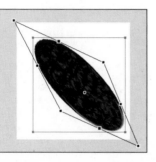

Figure 4-4:
Distorting an image to create a weird effect.

Skewing an image

To skew an image, follow these simple steps:

1. **With the Selection tool or Subselection tool, click the object you want to skew.**

2. **Select the Skew tool from the Tools panel or choose Modify⇨ Transform⇨Skew.**

   If you are selecting from the Tools panel, click and hold on the Scale tool in the Tools panel and select the Skew tool when the pop-up menu displays the Skew and Distort tools. A box with eight handles and a center point overlays the selected object.

3. **Click and drag any handle:**

   • The center handles on the top and bottom can skew a side of the image left or right.

   • The middle handles on the left and right can skew a side of the image up or down.

   • The corner handles behave differently depending on if you drag them along the left-right axis or along the up-down axis, but no matter which axis you drag along, they *spread* the selected side of the image along that axis. For example, if you select the top left corner and drag up, the bottom left corner stretches down proportionally.

   By default, Fireworks MX continues to display the original box around the object, but it adds a version of the box with a dotted line to show the new dimensions as you drag, as shown in Figure 4-4. The cursor becomes a double-sided arrow as you place it over a center or middle handle. The arrow indicates in which directions you can drag the handle.

4. **Press Enter or double-click anywhere in the canvas window.**

   Fireworks MX updates the selection.

Distorting and skewing text

In Fireworks MX, distorting text is as easy as distorting images. To distort a text block, just follow these steps:

1. **Click the Selection tool or Subselection tool in the Tools panel and then click the text block you want to distort.**

   You can also select the text block using the Text tool, but you cannot distort only part of a text block. You can, however, Shift+click two text boxes and distort them together.

2. **Select the Distort tool from the Tools panel or choose Modify⇨ Transform⇨Distort.**

   If you are selecting from the Tools panel, click and hold on the Scale tool in the Tools panel and select the Distort tool from the pop-up menu. A box with eight handles and a center point overlays the selected object.

3. **Click and drag any handle.**

   By default, Fireworks MX continues to display the original box around the object, but it adds a version of the box with a dotted line to show the new dimensions as you drag. The cursor becomes a double-sided arrow as you place it over a center or middle handle.

   Note that when you try to drag handles too far (that is, if you try to drag a middle right handle above the top right handle, for example), the dotted line will stretch to wherever you drag the handle, but when you release the mouse button, the image snaps to the farthest allowable point in the direction you dragged. In short, a handle may not cross other handles.

4. **Click and drag any other handles.**

   You can stretch and squash and drag as many handles as many times as you want.

5. **Press Enter or double-click anywhere in the canvas window.**

   Fireworks MX updates the selection as shown in Figure 4-5.

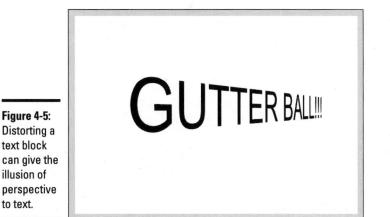

Figure 4-5:
Distorting a
text block
can give the
illusion of
perspective
to text.

To skew a text block, follow these simple steps:

1. **Using the Selection tool or Subselection tool in the Tools panel, click the text block.**

   You can also select the text block using the Text tool, but you cannot distort only a part of a text block.

2. **Select the Skew tool from the Tools panel or choose Modify⇨ Transform⇨Skew.**

   If you are selecting from the Tools panel, click and hold on the Scale tool in the Tools panel and select the Skew tool when the pop-up menu displays the Skew and Distort tools. A box with eight handles and a center point overlays the selected object.

3. **Click and drag any handle.**

   By default, Fireworks MX continues to display the original box around the object, but it adds a version of the box with a dotted line to show the new dimensions as you drag. The cursor becomes a double-sided arrow as you place it over a center or middle handle. The arrow indicates in which directions you can drag the handle.

   The center handles on the top and bottom can skew a side of the image left or right. The middle handles on the left and right can skew a side of the image up or down.

   The corner handles behave differently depending on if you drag them along the left-right axis or along the up-down axis, but no matter which axis you drag along, they *spread* the selected side of the image along that axis. For example, if you select the top left corner and drag up, the bottom left corner will stretch down proportionally.

4. **Press Enter or double-click anywhere in the canvas window.**

   Fireworks MX updates the selection.

Rotating and Flipping Graphics and Text

As is the case with resizing, Fireworks MX allows you to rotate and flip everything on the canvas at once, but it also allows you to select individual graphic elements (image objects) and rotate or flip them independently.

Rotating graphics

You can rotate a graphic in two ways:

✦ **Rotate a preset amount:** Fireworks MX offers a quick way to rotate a graphic either 90 or 180 degrees around its center point.

✦ **Rotate any amount:** You can click and drag to rotate an image around its center point, or even move the point and rotate the image around a point not at the image's center.

To rotate a graphic by 90-degree increments, follow these simple steps:

1. **Select the object by using the Selection tool or Subselection tool.**

   For more information on selecting image objects or parts of image objects, see Book III, Chapter 3.

2. **Choose how you want rotate the object:**

   • **To rotate the object 180 degrees (turning it upside down):** Choose Modify⇨Transform⇨Rotate 180 Degrees.

   • **To rotate a graphic 90 degrees clockwise (to turn it sideways to the right):** Choose Modify⇨Transform⇨Rotate 90 Degrees CW, or use the key command Ctrl+Shift+9.

   • **To rotate a graphic 90 degrees counter-clockwise (to turn it sideways to the left):** Choose Modify⇨Transform⇨Rotate 90 Degrees CCW, or use the key command Ctrl+Shift+7.

Rotating an object freehand requires a couple of extra steps, but it gives you much finer control over the degree of rotation. To rotate an object any amount about its center axis, just follow these steps:

1. **Select the object.**

2. **Choose Modify⇨Transform⇨Free Transform (or Scale, Skew, or Distort).**

   You can also use the keyboard shortcut Ctrl+T to access the Free Transform command.

3. **Place your cursor over the canvas.**

   The cursor changes into a rounded arrow, as shown in Figure 4-6.

4. **Click and drag the cursor in any direction.**

   If you drag down or to the right, the image rotates clockwise; if you drag up or left, the image rotates counter-clockwise.

5. **Press Enter or double-click anywhere in the canvas window.**

   Fireworks MX updates the selection.

If you hold down the Shift key while rotating your graphic, you can restrict the angle of the rotation to 15-degree increments.

**Book III
Chapter 4**

**Transforming Text,
Shapes, and Images**

Figure 4-6:
Rotating a
bowling pin
image so it
appears to
be falling.

Rotating text

In Fireworks MX, rotating text is pretty much like rotating a graphic. To rotate a text block in 90-degree increments, follow these steps:

1. **Click the Selection tool or Subselection tool in the Tools panel and then click the text block.**

You can also select the text block using the Text tool, but you cannot distort only a part of a text block.

2. **Choose how you want to rotate the text as follows:**

- **To rotate the text block by 180 degrees (turning it upside down):** Choose Modify➪Transform➪Rotate 180 Degrees.

- **To rotate a text block 90 degrees clockwise (to turn it sideways to the right):** Choose Modify➪Transform➪Rotate 90 Degrees CW, or use the key command Ctrl+Shift+9.

- **To rotate a text block 90 degrees counter-clockwise (to turn it sideways to the left):** Choose Modify➪Transform➪Rotate 90 Degrees CCW, or use the key command Ctrl+Shift+7.

To rotate text freehand, follow these simple steps:

1. **Use the Selection tool or Subselection tool to select the text block you want to rotate.**

You can only distort the entire text block.

2. **Choose Modify➪Transform➪Free Transform (or Scale, Skew, or Distort).**

You can also use the keyboard shortcut Ctrl+T to access the Free Transform command.

3. **Place your cursor over the canvas.**

   The cursor changes into a rounded arrow.

4. **Click and drag the cursor in any direction.**

   If you drag down or to the right, the text block rotates clockwise; if you drag up or left, the image rotates counter-clockwise.

5. **Press Enter or double-click anywhere in the canvas window.**

   Fireworks MX updates the selection.

Flipping images

Fireworks MX allows you to flip images vertically and horizontally. Both manipulations are a snap.

To flip an image horizontally (making it a mirror image of what it was originally) or vertically (turning it upside down), follow these simple steps:

1. **Select the object you want to flip.**

2. **Choose Modify⇨Transform⇨Flip Horizontal to make a mirror image of the object; choose Modify⇨Transform⇨Flip Vertical to turn the object upside down.**

   Depending on which choice you make, your selection either flips horizontally, as shown in Figure 4-7, or vertically, as shown in Figure 4-8.

**Book III
Chapter 4**

Transforming Text,
Shapes, and Images

Figure 4-7:
The left image of the bowling pin has been duplicated, moved, and flipped horizontally to make the image of the bowling pin on the right.

Figure 4-8:
The left image of the bowling pin has been duplicated, moved, and flipped vertically to make the image of the bowling pin on the right.

Flipping text

Fireworks MX allows you to flip text blocks vertically and horizontally. Both manipulations are a piece of cake.

To flip a text block horizontally (making it a mirror image of what it was originally) or vertically (turning it upside down), follow these simple steps:

1. **Select the text block you want to flip with the Selection tool or Subselection tool.**

    You can also select the text block using the Text tool, but you cannot distort only a part of a text block.

2. **Choose Modify⇨Transform⇨Flip Horizontal to make a mirror image of the text block; choose Modify⇨Transform⇨Flip Vertical to turn the text upside down.**

    Your selection flips horizontally or vertically.

Adding Gradients and Textures to Shape Fills and Bitmap Selections

In Book III, Chapter 3, we show you how to fill a vector shape with a color. In this section, you find out how to treat your shape to a fancier filling: a gradient and/or a texture. Gradients and textures can add the illusion of depth to your images. They also increase the file size of your images because they are difficult to compress, so use them sparingly.

Introducing gradients

A *gradient* is a subtle blend of one color into another. A classic example of a gradient in nature is a sky at sunset (or sunrise, if you ever wake up that early). Near the horizon, the sky is a deep, bright orange; straight up, the sky is a dark blue. In between those two colors is a bunch of transitions: from bright orange to pale orange to pale blue to dark blue. The transitions are so subtle, it's difficult to say where one color leaves off and another begins. That's a gradient.

Fireworks MX ships with a wonderful array of useful gradient patterns, which you can access via a drop-down list in the Property inspector:

✦ Linear	✦ Bars
✦ Radial	✦ Ripples
✦ Ellipse	✦ Waves
✦ Rectangle	✦ Satin
✦ Cone	✦ Folds
✦ Starburst	

While the black-and-white of this printed page may not quite do these gradients justice compared to what they look like in full color, you can still get a pretty good idea of the variety of the gradients, as shown in Figure 4-9.

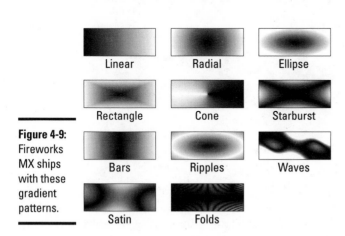

Figure 4-9: Fireworks MX ships with these gradient patterns.

Linear Radial Ellipse

Rectangle Cone Starburst

Bars Ripples Waves

Satin Folds

You can choose any colors to make your gradients, but Fireworks MX also has the following handy preset gradient options:

✦ Black, White   ✦ Red, Blue

✦ Blue, Red, Yellow   ✦ Red, Green, Blue

✦ Blue, Yellow, Blue   ✦ Silver

✦ Cobalt Blue   ✦ Spectrum

✦ Copper   ✦ Violet, Orange

✦ Emerald Green   ✦ White, Black

✦ Pastels

To add a preset gradient fill to a vector shape, follow these steps:

1. **Click the shape to select it.**

2. **Click and hold the Fill Categories box next to the Paint Bucket icon in the Property inspector.**

3. **Select a gradient type from the drop-down list, as shown in Figure 4-10.**

The default colors for gradients are black and white. If those are the colors you want for your gradient, congratulations! You're done! If not, continue with the next step.

Figure 4-10:
Selecting
a gradient
type from
the Fill
Options
drop-down
list.

4. **Click the Fill Color box next to the Paint Bucket icon in the Property inspector.**

A pop-up window, as shown in Figure 4-11, appears:

• At the bottom is a preview pane, which shows what the gradient pattern will look like when applied to the shape. (The selected pattern in Figure 4-11 is Cone.)

• In the middle of the window lies the Preset drop-down list, as described in the previous list.

• At the top of the window is a simpler preview strip that shows color but not pattern information. Above and below that strip are sliders.

The sliders above give you control over the opacity of each color in the gradient; the sliders below give you control over the amount of each color in the gradient.

Figure 4-11: The gradient pop-up window has controls for color and opacity, a list of gradient Presets, and a Preview pane.

5. **Select a Preset.**

   The preview panes and the selected shape update.

   Notice that different presets have different numbers, or instances, of colors. The Cobalt Blue Preset, for example, creates its opalescent glow with two instances each of three colors.

6. **Click anywhere outside the pop-up window to make it disappear.**

To add a user-defined gradient fill to a vector shape requires a number of steps, but it can be as simple or complex a process as you wish. Just follow these steps:

1. **Select the shape.**

2. **Click and hold the Fill Categories box next to the Paint Bucket icon in the Property inspector.**

3. **Select a gradient type from the drop-down list, as shown in Figure 4-10.**

   The default colors for gradients are black and white.

4. **Click the Fill Color box next to the Paint Bucket icon in the Property inspector.**

   A pop-up window appears, as shown in Figure 4-11.

Book III
Chapter 4

Transforming Text, Shapes, and Images

5. Click the left color slider, as shown in Figure 4-12.

When you place the cursor over a slider, it becomes a solid black arrow with no stem. When you click and release the slider, the familiar color picker pops up. If you need a refresher on the color picker, see Book III, Chapter 3.

6. Select a color from the color picker.

Your cursor is an eye-dropper in the color picker window.

Figure 4-12:
At left, picking the first color of the gradient. At right, adding a color to the gradient.

7. If you want more than two colors in your gradient, click anywhere between the two default color sliders. If not, skip to Step 12.

Note that your cursor becomes an arrow with a small plus sign (+) when you move it between the existing color sliders. After you click, a new slider appears, and your cursor becomes a solid black arrow with no stem until you move it off the new slider.

By default, the color of the new slider is the color in the strip directly above where you clicked.

8. If you want to change the color of the new slider, click it and release.

When you click and release, the familiar color picker pops up.

9. Select a color using the eyedropper.

10. If desired, move the new color slider left or right to change where the new color blends with the other colors.

11. If you want more than three colors in your gradient, repeat Steps 7 through 10.

12. Click the right color slider.

13. Select a color using the eyedropper.

14. **If you want to, move any of the sliders horizontally to adjust where their respective colors fall in the gradient.**

15. **If desired, adjust the opacity of the entire gradient or vary the opacity of different parts of the gradient.**

By default, the opacity of both ends is set to 100 percent (no background shows through). You can add and adjust opacity sliders just as you can color sliders, and they work in more or less the same way.

When you click an opacity slider, a pop-up window displays a slider that goes from 0 percent at the left (no gradient shows in front of the background) to 100 percent at the right.

16. **Click anywhere outside the pop-up window to make it disappear.**

After you've added a gradient fill to your shape, you can rotate, skew, move, and change the width of the gradient. See your documentation for details.

To remove a color slider or opacity slider (you must have at least two colors to make a gradient, of course), click and drag it up out of the gradient pop-up window. When you release the mouse button, the slider will be gone, and you'll have a less complex gradient fill.

To add a gradient fill to a bitmap selection, follow these steps:

1. **Select the part of the bitmap image you want to fill.**

In most cases, the Magic Wand tool is the best candidate for this job. For more information on selecting parts of image objects, see Book III, Chapter 3.

2. **Click the Color box next to the Paint Bucket icon in the Colors section of the Tools panel.**

The color picker pops up.

3. **Click the Fill Options button at the bottom of the pop-up window.**

A new pop-up window with a drop-down list appears in place of the color picker.

4. **Select a gradient pattern from the drop-down list.**

5. **Follow Steps 4 thorough 6 in the steps that describe adding a preset gradient fill to a vector shape or Steps 4 through 6 in the steps that describe adding a user-defined gradient fill to a vector shape.**

6. **Click the Paint Bucket tool and then click anywhere in the selected area to apply the gradient fill.**

Adding textures

Adding textures to your fills and bitmap selections is even easier than adding gradients. You can even have fills with both a gradient and a texture, though we find that combining gradients and textures often diminishes the graphic power of both in a given image.

To add a texture to a vector shape, follow these steps:

1. **Click the shape to select it.**

   If the shape is transparent, you'll need to add a color or gradient fill. If the shape has a transparent fill (no fill), the Texture list box will be inactive.

2. **Click and hold the Texture arrow under the Edge list box in the Property inspector.**

   A drop-down list displays the built-in textures. If you have additional textures, select Other from the menu and browse to the texture you want to use.

3. **Select a texture from the drop-down list.**

   When you release the mouse button, the texture is applied to the shape fill with the default opacity of 50%.

4. **Type a value or drag the slider next to the Texture list box to set the opacity of the texture.**

   A setting of 0 does not show any of the texture, and a setting of 100 shows the texture at full (100 percent) opacity.

Adjusting Color Information and More with Filters

Fireworks MX has plenty of useful presets and defaults for the novice user, and enough tweakability to satisfy most any pro. Pros will especially appreciate the amount of control Fireworks MX gives users in the area of color adjustment.

You can accomplish many of the effects described in this section in two basic ways:

✦ **Using Live Effects:** This is a bit like making everything you look at appear yellow by putting on a pair of sunglasses. You're not changing the colors of whatever you're looking at, you're putting something between you and the object to change the appearance of the object. Live effects can be turned off and on without changing the pixels that make up the object to which the effects are applied. If the object in your Web page design is something that may change later or be repurposed elsewhere, perhaps with different effects applied, you can use Live Effects to apply *non-destructive* changes to the object in a particular PNG file. Live Effects can be applied only to whole objects.

✦ **Using Filters:** This method is considered *destructive,* because it alters the pixels in the bitmap. This is like making everything you see yellow by painting everything yellow. Though the process is destructive, it is not permanent — as long as you have the Undo command available.

We show you how to use the Filters method in the following three sections. For more about Live Effects, see Book III, Chapter 7.

Fine-tuning your colors

We touch briefly on the color adjustment tools at the end of Book III, Chapter 3, but here we go into a bit more detail. The color adjustment controls available from the Filters menu are as follows:

✦ **Brightness/Contrast:** Controls the overall luminosity of a selection and the contrast of color shades within a selection.

✦ **Curves:** Offers a way to modify very specific colors without affecting others.

✦ **Hue/Saturation:** Controls the tones and intensities of colors within a selection.

✦ **Invert:** Allows you to reverse the colors in a selection to make something analogous to a photographic negative.

✦ **Levels:** Like curves, levels allows you to modify colors, but it does so by letting you adjust shadows, mid-tones, and highlights of one of the three individual color channels (red, green, or blue) or all channels together.

✦ **Auto Levels:** In theory, an optimal image has an even distribution of dark tones, medium tones, and light tones. Auto Levels sets levels automatically so that shadows, mid-tones, and highlights are evenly distributed in your image.

To change the brightness or contrast of a graphic or selection, just follow these steps:

1. **Select a graphic or part of a graphic.**

For more information on selecting image objects or parts of image objects, see Book III, Chapter 3.

2. **Choose Filters⇨Adjust Color⇨Brightness/Contrast.**

A dialog box with separate sliders for brightness and contrast appears.

3. **If you wish to lighten or darken your selection, click and drag the Brightness slider.**

   The default position is at the center. You can drag left down to –100 units to darken the selection, or you can drag right up to 100 units to lighten the selection. If the Preview check box is selected, as it is by default, you can see the change to your selection when you release the mouse button.

4. **If you want to alter the relationship between the dark and light pixels in your selection, click and drag the Contrast slider.**

   The default position is at the center. You can drag left down to –100 units to reduce the contrast in the selection, or you can drag right up to 100 units to increase the contrast in the selection. If the Preview check box is selected, as it is by default, you can see the change to your selection when you release the mouse button.

5. **Click OK.**

All colors on a computer monitor are formed from the combination of the three color channels, red, green, and blue. You can change the curves for the individual color channels or for the combination of all channels. Curve adjustments can be made for bitmaps only, not shapes. If you want to adjust the curve of a shape, convert it to a bitmap first. To change the curve of the RGB channels, follow these steps:

1. **Select a graphic or part of a graphic.**

   For more information on selecting image objects or parts of image objects, see Book III, Chapter 3.

2. **Choose Filters⇨Adjust Color⇨Curves.**

   A dialog box with a grid appears, as shown in Figure 4-13. The grid's horizontal axis shows the original brightness of the pixels in your selection. The grid's vertical axis shows the new brightness of the pixels.

Figure 4-13:
The default setting in the Curves dialog box is a diagonal line.

3. Choose a channel from the drop-down list.

Your choices are RGB (all channels), Red, Green, or Blue.

4. Click anywhere along the line in the grid and drag to adjust the curve.

When you click on the line, Fireworks MX generates a handle automatically. The end points always remain where they are, but you can add handles anywhere else on the line and drag them to new points. You can delete handles by dragging them up out of the dialog box. You can type a numerical value into the Input and Output text fields instead of dragging the line, if you prefer.

If the Preview check box is selected, as it is by default, you can see the changes when you release the mouse button after dragging a handle.

Clicking the Auto button restores the line to its original setting.

5. Click OK.

To change the hue, saturation, and/or lightness of a graphic or selection, just follow these steps:

1. Select a graphic or part of a graphic.

For more information on selecting image objects or parts of image objects, see Book III, Chapter 3.

2. Choose Filters➪Adjust Color➪Hue/Saturation.

A dialog box with separate sliders for Hue, Saturation, and Lightness pops up.

3. If you want to change the basic color of your selection, click and drag the Hue slider.

The default position is at the center. You can drag left down to –180 degrees or you can drag right up to 180 degrees. (You can think of the slider as a flattened circle, like a map of the Earth is a flattened globe.) If the Preview check box is selected, as it is by default, you can see the change to your selection when you release the mouse button.

4. If you want to alter the intensity of the colors in your selection, click and drag the Saturation slider.

The default position is at the center. You can drag left down to –100 units to reduce the color saturation in the selection, or you can drag right up to 100 units to increase the color saturation in the selection. If the Preview check box is selected, as it is by default, you can see the change to your selection when you release the mouse button.

**Book III
Chapter 4**

Transforming Text, Shapes, and Images

5. **If you want to alter the luminosity of the colors in your selection, click and drag the Lightness slider.**

The default position is at the center. You can drag left down to –100 units to reduce the lightness of the selection, or you can drag right up to 100 units to increase the lightness of the selection. A setting of –100 gives you black, and a setting of 100 gives you white. If the Preview check box is selected, as it is by default, you can see the change to your selection when you release the mouse button.

6. **Click OK.**

If you want to change the hue and/or saturation of black or white pixels, select the Colorize check box and then make your adjustments.

To invert the colors of a graphic or any selection, follow these simple steps:

1. **Select a graphic or part of a graphic.**

2. **Choose Filters➪Adjust Color➪Invert, or use the key command Ctrl+Alt+Shift+I.**

The colors of your selection are inverted, as in a photographic negative.

The Levels command allows you to make color corrections to an image or selection by altering the balance of highlights, mid-tones, and shadows. The graphical representation of the distribution of shades is called a Histogram.

To adjust the Levels of an image or image selection, follow these steps:

1. **Select a graphic or part of a graphic.**

For more information on selecting image objects or parts of image objects, see Book III, Chapter 3.

2. **Choose Filters➪Adjust Color➪Levels.**

The Levels dialog box appears, as shown in Figure 4-14.

Figure 4-14:
The Levels dialog box includes a Histogram.

3. **Choose a channel from the drop-down list.**

Your choices are RGB (all channels), Red, Green, or Blue.

4. **Click and drag the Input shadows slider (the black triangle at the left under the Histogram) as needed.**

Note that the shadows slider cannot be dragged farther right than the mid-tones slider, because shadows must always be darker than mid-tones. The slider scale goes from 0 (no brightness, which is black) to 255 (full brightness, which is white). The mid-tones slider moves automatically when you move the shadows slider.

5. **Click and drag the Input mid-tones slider (the gray triangle in the middle under the Histogram) as needed.**

The mid-tones slider cannot be dragged farther left than the shadows slider nor farther right than the highlights slider. The mid-tones slider's scale goes from 0 to 10.

Dragging the mid-tones slider to the right generally darkens the selection, and dragging it to the far left can create something resembling a posterization effect, in which transitions between colors are abrupt rather than smooth.

6. **Click and drag the Input highlights slider (the white triangle at the right under the Histogram) as needed.**

The highlights slider cannot be dragged farther left than the mid-tone slider, because highlights must be lighter than mid-tones.

7. **Click and drag the Output shadows and highlights sliders as needed.**

These sliders can be moved past each other. Moving the darkness slider all the way to the right and the lightness slider all the way to the left inverts the colors in the selection.

8. **Click OK.**

If you click Cancel, your adjustments will not be implemented. If you click the Auto button, Fireworks MX sets the optimal color balance automatically.

To let Fireworks MX set the optimal levels automatically, you can click the Auto button in the Curves and Levels dialog boxes, or you can select a graphic or part of a graphic and then choose Filters⇨Adjust Color⇨ Auto Levels.

Blurring and sharpening

Blurring a graphic or selection can add a sense of softness to an image; sharpening, on the other hand, can add a sense of solidity or hyper-reality to an image. *Note:* The Sharpen command cannot correct a blatantly out-of-focus photo; nothing can.

To blur an image or part of an image using Fireworks MX presets, simply follow these steps:

1. **Select a graphic or part of a graphic.**

   For more information on selecting image objects or parts of image objects, see Book III, Chapter 3.

2. **Choose Filters⇨Blur⇨Blur.**

   For a more pronounced effect, choose Filters⇨Blur⇨Blur More.

3. **Click OK.**

You can also use the Blur tool from the Tools panel to "paint" a blur across your image. If you want to blur multiple small parts of an image, you may find the Blur tool more effective.

If you want more control over the amount of blur of your image, you can employ the Gaussian Blur filter. Just follow these steps:

1. **Select a graphic or part of a graphic.**

2. **Choose Filters⇨Blur⇨Gaussian Blur.**

   The Gaussian Blur dialog box appears.

3. **Click and drag the slider to set the radius of the blur.**

   The radius can be set from 0.1 (hardly noticeable blur) to 250.0 (near total blur).

4. **Click OK.**

To sharpen an image or selection using Fireworks MX presets, just follow these steps:

1. **Select a graphic or part of a graphic.**

2. **Choose Filters⇨Sharpen⇨Sharpen.**

   For a more pronounced effect, choose Filters⇨Sharpen⇨Sharpen More.

3. **Click OK.**

If you want more control over the amount and manner of the sharpening, you can use the Unsharp Mask filter. This filter works by strengthening the contrast between adjacent pixels, which makes for more sharply defined edges between areas of color. Actually, that's the way all the Sharpen filters work, but with Unsharp Mask, you can create your own settings for three aspects of the sharpening process:

✦ **Sharpen Amount:** This is the amount of contrast introduced between adjacent pixels.

✦ **Pixel Radius:** This is the size of the area around each pixel that gets sharpened.

✦ **Threshold:** This setting determines which pixels get sharpened based on the existing contrast levels in the selection or image.

To sharpen an image or selection using the Unsharp Mask filter, follow these steps:

1. **Select a graphic or part of a graphic.**

For more information on selecting image objects or parts of image objects, see Book III, Chapter 3.

2. **Choose Filters⇨Sharpen⇨Unsharp Mask.**

The Unsharp Mask dialog box pops up.

3. **Click and drag the Sharpen Amount slider.**

The slider goes from 1 percent (not very much) to 500 percent (very strong contrast).

4. **Click and drag the Pixel Radius slider.**

The slider goes from 0.1 (hardly noticeable) to 250.0 (very strong effect).

5. **Click and drag the Threshold slider.**

The slider goes from 0 (change all pixels) to 255 (change no pixels).

6. **Click OK.**

Using the other filters: Convert to Alpha and Find Edges

The Convert to Alpha filter makes your selection transparent. The lighter the pixel, the more transparent it becomes. White pixels, for example, seem to disappear, allowing the background to show through fully. Black pixels, on the other hand, remain black and completely opaque.

To convert a selection to Alpha, follow these simple steps:

1. **Select a graphic or part of a graphic.**

2. **Choose Filters⇨Other⇨Convert to Alpha.**

    The selection is converted.

3. **Click anywhere on the canvas or use the key command Ctrl+D to deselect your selection.**

The Find Edges filter makes a photograph look like a line drawing by greatly simplifying the color information in the image.

To use the Find Edges filter, just follow these steps:

1. **Select a graphic or part of a graphic.**

    For more information on selecting image objects or parts of image objects, see Book III, Chapter 3.

2. **Choose Filters⇨Other⇨Find Edges.**

    The selection takes on the appearance of a line drawing.

3. **Click anywhere on the canvas or use the key command Ctrl+D to deselect your selection.**

Using Extras: Lite Versions Bundled with Fireworks MX

Fireworks MX allows you to use third-party filters as plug-ins, and initial shipments of Fireworks MX included "lite" versions of Eye Candy 4000 (Bevel Boss, Marble, and Motion Trail) and Alien Skin Splat (Edges). These versions of the third-party software are not full-featured (hence the "lite" appellation), though grayed-out menu options give you a sense of what the full-featured version of the software can do.

Because these lite versions are not officially part of Fireworks MX, we do not cover them in this book. You can find information about the fully-functioning versions of these filters at www.alienskin.com.

Chapter 5: The Power of Layers and Frames

In This Chapter

↙ **Introducing layers and frames**

↙ **Managing layers**

↙ **Using layers for masking**

↙ **Using the Web layer**

↙ **Blending**

↙ **Managing frames**

↙ **Using frames to create rollovers and animated GIFs**

*E*verything you put on your canvas in Fireworks MX — everything you draw or type or paste or import — exists in a layer. In turn, every layer exists in a frame. Initially this seems simple enough, but it is more involved than it first appears. Layers can be shared by frames, and a single layer can contain a single object (a bitmap, shape, or text) or multiple objects. Things can actually get pretty complex in a large file, where you can have dozens of bitmaps, shapes, and text blocks.

Layers give you a way to organize your Fireworks PNG image so that you can easily turn groups of objects on or off (that is, make the groups of objects visible or hide them), put objects on top of or beneath other objects, lock groups of objects so they can't be modified, and find things easily.

Frames, on the other hand, offer a way to organize layers so you can export multiple states of buttons (different versions of the button such as those that appear when the button is rolled over or clicked by the user) and animated GIFs quickly and easily.

The *canvas* is at the bottom of the stack of layers. It is not really a layer itself — it can't be expanded or collapsed, made visible or invisible, locked or unlocked, or deleted.

The *Web Layer,* the repository for slices and hotspots, is always the top layer, as you can see in Figure 5-1. You create slices in the Web Layer in order to cut your page design into individual images. After images have been sliced, they can be optimized, exported, and placed in HTML pages, where they may be hyperlinked. You create hotspots in the Web Layer to make images that can be exported for your Web page along with some HTML code that specifies areas in the image that are hyperlinked. The Web Layer can be made visible or invisible, and it can be locked and unlocked, but it cannot be deleted.

Figure 5-1:
The Layers panel displays a stack of layers in their collapsed state.

Managing Layers

Fireworks MX uses the concept of folders to describe how a layer functions. (Notice the folder icon next to the layer name in Figure 5-1.) So you can think of a layer as a receptacle for "files" (image objects and text objects). The individual "files" can be copied or moved to other layers, deleted, named, renamed, and so on.

Take a closer look at the Layers panel. Looking left to right at an unexpanded layer, you can see the following across four columns:

✦ **The Expand/Collapse button:** A plus sign (+) in the box indicates that the layer is collapsed. A minus sign (–) in the box indicates that the layer is expanded. Click the control to toggle between expanded and collapsed views of the layer.

✦ **The Show/Hide layer button:** An eye appears in this column when the layer is visible on the canvas. When the layer is invisible on the canvas, the column is empty. Click in the column to toggle the layer's visibility on the canvas off and on. Note that when you export images from your PNG, only visible objects are exported.

✦ **The Lock/Unlock button:** If you click on this column of a collapsed layer, a lock appears, indicating that none of the objects on that layer can be edited. If you click once on the layer name (in the fourth column) or turn on the Show/Hide layers button (in the second column), a pencil appears in the third column, indicating that the layer is active. If the layer is active, you can edit the objects in the layer. Only one layer can be active at a time.

✦ **The layer name:** By default, Fireworks MX names each layer for the order in which it was created. The first layer is called Layer 1, the second layer is called Layer 2, and so on. (To find out how to give the layer a more meaningful name, check out the "Renaming a layer" section, later in this chapter.) When the layer is active, the layer name is highlighted.

Adding and deleting layers

When you add a new layer to your PNG, the new layer always gets added above the currently selected layer. You can add a layer in two easy ways:

✦ Click the Add/Duplicate Layer button (the folder with the plus sign on it) at the bottom middle of the Layers panel.

✦ Choose New Layer from the Layer Options menu.

In either case, the New Layer dialog box appears, with the layer's default name highlighted. You need to type a new name for the layer and select the Share Across Frames option if you're making a multiple-frame document and you want the objects on the new layer you created to be visible on the other frames of your document. The newly created layer is active until you click another layer.

To delete a layer, click it in the Layers panel and drag it to the Delete button (the garbage can icon) at the bottom right of the Layers panel. You can also click the layer and then click the Delete button in the Layers panel.

Making a layer active

As noted previously, only one layer can be active at a time. However, many objects on a layer can be editable simultaneously, which can come in handy when you want to move several objects the same amount and in the same direction. In order to change any object in a layer, you need to make the layer active:

✦ **Make a layer active:** Click an object on the canvas that's in that layer, or click in the name column of that layer in the Layers panel.

✦ **Make a layer inactive, but not locked:** Click an object on the canvas that's not in that layer, or click the name column of another layer in the Layers panel.

Sometimes when you have an object from one layer selected and you click an object on another layer to make it active, the item you're trying to select won't highlight. Why not? Look closely: You have selected a new layer, just not the one you want. Often you find yourself in this position if you have a very large object on the bottom layer of your file — when you try to click something in front of it, Fireworks MX thinks you're trying to click the large object on the bottom layer and highlights it instead of the smaller object (the one you're trying to select) in front of it. Luckily, you can just click on the object you want to select in the Layers panel to make it active.

Expanding and collapsing layers

Because files can contain many layers, and layers can contain many objects, *and* you have only so much room for the Layers panel, Fireworks MX allows you to expand and collapse a layer as needed:

✦ **Expand a layer:** Click the plus (+) button in the first column of that layer. Each object in that layer appears on its own line below the layer name. Each object has its own Show/Hide button, as well as a thumbnail of the object and a name.

✦ **Collapse a layer:** Click the minus (–) button. If the layer is active, it will remain so until you click another layer or an object on the canvas that resides on another layer.

Figure 5-2 shows the Layers panel with some layers collapsed and one layer expanded to show the objects it contains.

Figure 5-2: Selecting an object on the canvas also selects it in the Layers panel.

Making a layer visible or invisible on the canvas

The more complicated your designs get, the more you'll be *showing* and *hiding* layers, that is, making them visible or invisible. Luckily, showing and hiding layers is simple:

✦ **Make a layer visible (show a layer):** Click in the second column or the name column of the Layers panel.

✦ **Make a layer invisible (hide a layer):** Click the Hide layer button (the eye icon) in the second column.

If you export your design as images (so you can use the images in a Web page), objects on hidden/invisible layers will not be exported. In other words, what you see on the canvas when you export is what you will get in your exported images folder.

Locking and unlocking a layer

Sometimes when you have a lot of overlapping objects, selecting some objects without selecting others can get difficult. One way to prevent objects from being moved or deleted is to lock the layer they're on. You can't lock individual objects, but you can move objects from one layer to another (say, from an unlocked layer to a locked layer).

✦ **Lock a layer:** Click in the third column. If the column is blank when you click in it, the lock appears. If the column has a pencil in it, the pencil changes to a lock, and the pencil appears in an adjacent layer, if there is one.

✦ **Unlock a layer:** Click on the lock in the third column of that layer. Unlocking a layer does not automatically make it active.

Renaming a layer

By default, each layer is named for the order in which it was created. The first layer is called Layer 1, the second is called Layer 2, and so on. If you have only a couple of layers in your document, that naming scheme may be sufficient. If you have dozens of layers, on the other hand, you'll want to place similar objects together on layers and then name the layers so you can tell with a quick glance at the Layers panel where the objects are.

To rename a layer from its default name, just follow these simple steps:

1. **Double-click the layer name.**

   A window with one text field appears, as shown in Figure 5-3. The current name is in the text field, in a highlighted state.

2. **Type a new name.**

   You don't need to click in the text field, because the current layer name is already highlighted. If you want to keep part of the current name, use your mouse to select the part of the name you want to replace or remove and type over or delete it.

3. **If you have multiple frames in your document and you want this layer to be visible in the other frames, select the Share Across Frames check box.**

   Otherwise, move on to Step 4.

4. **Press the Enter key.**

Figure 5-3:
Type a new layer name in the text field.

Moving a layer in front of or behind other layers

As you add layers to your PNG file, they stack up. The higher a layer appears in the Layers panel, the closer the objects in that layer are to the front of the canvas. Likewise, within a layer, the higher an object appears, the closer it is to the front of the canvas.

Figure 5-4 illustrates the relationship between objects, their position on the canvas, and their position in the Layers panel. The before part (on the top) of Figure 5-4 shows the bowling ball in front of both pins, and in the Layers panel, the object named "bowling ball" is above the "pin" objects. The after part (on the bottom) of Figure 5-4 shows the large pin in front of the bowling ball. The ball, in turn, is in front of a smaller bowling pin. In the Layers panel, the ball object is between the pin objects.

You can change the order of a layer or object as follows:

✦ **Move a layer or object in front of another:** Click the name column of the layer or object and drag it up. A black horizontal line appears when you roll over a spot where you can place the layer or object. Release the mouse button to drop the layer or object in its new location.

✦ **Move a layer or object behind another:** Click the name column of the layer or object and drag it down. A black horizontal line appears when you roll over a spot where you can place the layer or object. Release the mouse button to drop the layer or object in its new location.

Figure 5-4:
Moving a
layer in the
Layers
panel,
before (top)
and after
(bottom).

Merging layers

Sometimes in the process of creating a PNG document, you'll find that you need all the objects you've made but you don't need them to be on so many layers. If you want to move one or two objects from one layer to another, you can do so using the method described in the section "Moving a layer in front of or behind other layers." If, on the other hand, you want to move all the objects in one layer to another, and there are quite a few objects in each layer, you're better off merging the layers.

To merge all the objects on one layer into a single bitmap object in the layer immediately underneath, follow these steps:

1. **Click in the name column of the layer in the Layers panel.**

   Make sure all the objects in the layer are highlighted. (If they're not, you may have clicked an object in the layer instead of the layer itself.)

2. **If necessary, drag the layer so it's on top of the layer you want to merge into.**

   You use the Merge Down command later in this process, so you need to make sure the two layers are one on top of the other.

3. **Click the Options menu icon at the top right of the Layers panel.**

   The Layers panel's Options menu pops up.

4. **Select Merge Down from the Options menu.**

   The selected layer merges into the one below it. Note that the objects in the upper layer are combined into a single bitmap object in the new layer. Text in the new object is not editable, and vector shapes in the new object are now bitmaps.

You can also use the key command Ctrl+E to merge a layer into the one below it, or choose Modify➪Merge Down.

To merge all the layers together into one, do the following:

1. **Click in the name column of any layer in the Layers panel.**

2. **Choose Modify➪Flatten Layers.**

   Your document now has a single layer. Each object remains separate from the others.

Using Layers for Masking

A *mask* is a layer that you create specifically to let some areas of an image show while other areas are hidden. Fireworks MX uses two kinds of masks — bitmap masks and vector masks (you can use text as a vector mask). What both kinds of masks have in common is what they do: When you lay a mask over an image, the mask blocks out parts of the image and lets other parts show through. Which parts show through and which are blocked out is determined by the shape of the mask, as Figure 5-5 demonstrates.

Figure 5-5:
This image
was created
by masking
a pile of
bowling
balls with a
bowling pin.

When you use a *bitmap mask,* the grayscale values of the mask determine what, and how much, shows through. The lighter the pixel, the more the object or objects beneath show through. The darker the pixel, the less the stuff underneath shows through.

A *vector mask,* on the other hand, uses the shape outline of the vector object like a cookie cutter. However, Fireworks MX gives you a lot more flexibility than you have with a real cookie cutter! For example, you can *anti-alias* (smooth out jagged edges) and even feather (blur) the edges of your mask, or you can change the size of your mask at any time after you have created it.

Fireworks MX offers many ways to create masks. We cover the basics here, but you can always refer to the Fireworks MX Help files if you're interested in exploring masks more in-depth.

Creating a bitmap mask

To make a bitmap mask using an existing bitmap, follow these steps:

1. **If you want to mask multiple objects, group them by selecting them and using the key command Ctrl+G.**

2. **Select the object you want to use to make the mask.**

   You can select multiple objects to make a mask by Shift+clicking them, but if you do, Fireworks MX automatically makes a vector mask, not a bitmap mask. See the section "Creating a vector mask" if you want to make a vector mask using multiple bitmap objects.

3. **Choose Edit⇨Cut, or use the key command Ctrl+X.**

   Cut? That's right. You paste the shape in a couple of steps.

4. **Select the layer, object, or group you want to be visible through the mask by selecting it in the Layers panel or on the canvas.**

   The layer, object, or group is highlighted.

5. **Choose Edit⇨Paste as Mask.**

   All the parts of the masked image that fall outside the masking object disappear. In the Layers panel, the mask icon shows up in the third column, while a link icon and thumbnail of the mask shape show up next to the thumbnail of the masked image.

6. **If necessary, select Alpha channel in the Property inspector.**

   When the mask is selected in the Layers panel, the Property inspector offers two options for a bitmap mask: Mask to Alpha Channel and Mask to Grayscale (the default), as shown in Figure 5-6. Mask to Alpha Channel uses the transparency of the mask bitmap, and Mask to Grayscale uses the brightness of the pixels in the mask bitmap.

Figure 5-6:
You can change the Mask To setting in the Property inspector.

You can hide a mask temporarily by clicking it in the Layers panel and then choosing Disable Mask from the Layers panel's Options menu. The mask icon disappears from the Show/Hide object column and a red X appears over the mask, indicating the mask is disabled. To re-enable the mask, simply click on it.

To make a bitmap mask by creating an empty mask and modifying it, follow these steps:

1. **Select the object you want to mask by clicking it on the canvas or in the Layers panel.**

2. **Click the Mask button at the bottom of the Layers panel or choose Modify⇨Mask⇨Reveal All.**

   The Mask icon is the rectangle with a dotted circle inside. Reveal All means the mask you have made will be completely transparent until you modify it.

3. **Select a paintbrush or other drawing tool and draw on top of the bitmap.**

   Wherever you draw, the mask blocks the image behind.

What if you want to do the opposite: Reveal what's underneath only where you draw? Easy! Just follow these steps:

1. **Select the object you want to mask by clicking it on the canvas or in the Layers panel.**

2. **Choose Modify⇨Mask⇨Hide All.**

   Hide All means the mask you have made will be completely opaque until you modify it, so when you first apply it, your masked object will seem to have disappeared.

3. **Select any color other than black.**

   Because the opaque areas of the mask are represented as black, the areas that you want to show through must be drawn using any other color.

4. **Select a paintbrush or other drawing tool and draw on top of the bitmap.**

   Wherever you draw, the mask reveals the image behind.

You can delete a mask by clicking it in the Layers panel and then choosing Delete Mask from the Layers panel's Options menu. When you delete a mask, a pop-up window gives you the option to apply the mask before deleting it, which will change the masked image.

Book III
Chapter 5

The Power of Layers and Frames

Creating a vector mask

To make a vector mask, such as the one shown in Figure 5-7, follow these steps:

Figure 5-7:
A vector star-shaped mask with bevels and drop-shadows added to make the image "pop."

1. **Select a text block or vector shape by clicking on the shape on the canvas or in the Layers panel.**

   The object is highlighted on the canvas and in the Layers panel.

2. **Drag the shape or text over the object or objects you want to mask.**

   The layer with the shape doesn't have to be on top of the layers with the objects you want to mask, but it's easier to position the shape if you can see it!

3. **Choose Edit⇨Cut, or use the key command Ctrl+X.**

   You paste the shape in a couple of steps, so you need to cut it here.

4. **Select the layer or object you want to be visible through the mask by clicking it in the Layers panel or on the canvas.**

   The layer or object is highlighted.

5. **Choose Edit⇨Paste as Mask.**

   All the parts of the masked image that fall outside the mask shape or text disappear. In the Layers panel, the mask icon shows up in the third column, and a link icon and thumbnail of the mask shape appear next to the thumbnail of the masked image, as shown in Figure 5-8.

Figure 5-8:
An active mask in the Layers panel.

Using the Web Layer

The Web Layer was the greatest innovation of the original version of Fireworks, and if it no longer seems revolutionary, it's still as handy a feature as you'll come across in making Web pages. The Web Layer allows you to cut your page layout into *slices,* which are pieces of your layout, held in place by HTML, that end up as individual images on your Web page. The Web Layer also allows you to name and optimize each slice individually, which means that you can find the best balance of file size and image quality for each piece of your layout. Just as importantly, because it's a repository for slice information, the Web Layer allows you to save slice coordinates, dimensions, and optimization settings along with everything else in your PNG file.

You never have to leave the Fireworks MX application to ready your images for the Web, and you don't have to write down or remember your image size, placement, and optimization settings if you ever need to remake an image. The Web Layer also allows you to see at a glance where your slices are, which helps you recreate your page design in HTML. For details about slices and image optimization (including when to use GIFs and when to use JPEGs), see Book III, Chapter 6.

Standard HTML pages are built on a grid system of cells organized into rows and columns. The rows and columns make up a *table*. You can have multiple tables on a Web page, and you can even have tables within tables within tables. You can set the height of each row and the width of each column individually, but you can't make a round cell or a triangular table.

If you use Fireworks to make your HTML, each slice you make in your PNG ends up as an image that fills a table cell in your Web page. It is possible to combine multiple images in a single cell, but Fireworks is not made to work that way.

Think of your Web page design as a rectangular sheet cake. The decorations on top of the cake can be all kinds of shapes, but when you cut the cake, you probably make rectangular slices, cutting right through text, slicing a single icing rose into four pieces, and so on. You ignore the design on the surface of the cake because you're more interested in slicing the cake quickly and controlling the size of each piece. You might make a few specially-cut pieces if somebody really wants the blue rose near the top or the exclamation points from the text that says, "Happy Birthday!!!"

When you are cutting up a Web page, you will want certain pieces to remain intact (a corporate logo or a navigation button, for example), but other objects will fit the HTML grid structure better if they are sliced into pieces or included with other objects on a single piece. If you have an object with round edges, you need to slice it into rectangles so it can be reconstructed on a Web page, like the bowling ball shown in Figure 5-9. The bowling ball will be recreated in HTML as three stacked rectangles. The middle slice in Figure 5-9 is selected, so its name and image compression type appear at the top left of the slice.

Figure 5-9:
A bowling ball divided into multiple slices so it can be recon-structed on a Web page.

Using the Slice tool

The Slice tool, which can be found in the Web area of the Tools panel, looks like a utility knife on a green square with red lines on each side. When you employ the Slice tool, the slices you create are added automatically to the Web Layer.

To make a slice in your PNG file, follow these steps:

1. **Select the Slice tool from the Web area of the Tools panel.**

2. **Click and drag diagonally on the canvas to make a rectangle.**

The slice shows up as a green overlay on the canvas.

Using the Polygon Slice tool

You may have noticed that the Slice tool has a partner: the Polygon Slice tool. You can probably guess that the Polygon Slice tool allows you to make non-rectangular slices. But wait! Didn't we say that slices and images must be rectangular? The short answer is that the Polygon Slice tool doesn't create a non-rectangular slice — it creates a rectangular slice with a *polygonal hotspot* (a polygonal area that can be hyperlinked in combination with some HTML code) inside.

So what's the difference between a polygonal hotspot made by the Polygon Slice tool and one made by the Polygon Hotspot tool? The Polygon Hotspot tool doesn't make a slice, it just makes an irregularly-shaped linkable area in a slice. (A slice may contain many hotspots, each linked to a different page.) The Polygon Slice tool, on the other hand, makes both hotspots and slices. If you have a map of the United States, and you want each state to link to its own HTML page, use the Polygon Hotspot tool to make linked areas in the shape of each state. (For more information on the Polygon Hotspot tool, see Book III, Chapter 6.) If you just have a few irregularly shaped buttons, you can use the Polygon Slice tool to make a linkable image.

To make a polygonal slice, follow these steps:

1. **Select the Polygon Slice tool from the Slice tool menu in the Web area of the Tools panel.**

If the regular Slice tool is showing, click and hold the Slice tool button to reveal the pop-up menu so you can select the Polygon Slice tool.

2. **Click on a series of points to make a polygonal shape.**

Fireworks automatically draws straight lines to connect each point to the last. You do not need to click the first spot to close the shape.

Working with Objects

In the world of Fireworks MX, an *object* is any self-contained bitmap, vector shape, or text block that can appear on the canvas. The object may include blank space, and you can make a single object out of many objects (as you do when you merge layers, which we discuss earlier in this chapter). In general, anything in your design that you want to be able to edit individually should be left as a single object.

Renaming an object in the Layers panel

By default, each object is named for its type (path, bitmap, and so on) but can be individually renamed. As with layers, being able to name objects in the Layers panel becomes crucial as you add more elements to your design. The Layers panel does contain thumbnails of each object, but if you have multiple similar objects in several places on the canvas, you may want a way to tell the objects apart in the Layers panel.

To rename an object, double-click the File icon or the current name of the object and type a new name in the pop-up window. Renaming an object makes it active. When the object is active, the line around the icon is highlighted and the column reverses to a black background with white text.

Moving an object between layers

You may want to move an object from the layer it was originally created on to a different layer. For example, you may want an object to be stacked on top of or under other items on the canvas and have other objects in the layer remain exactly where they are. Luckily, moving an object from one layer to another is a snap.

To move an object from one layer to another, click the name column of the object in the Layers panel and drag it to a new location. A black horizontal line appears when you roll over a spot where you can place the object. Release the mouse button to drop the layer or object in its new location.

Setting an object's opacity/transparency

You can set each object's transparency independently by using a slider in the Layers panel. By default, objects are completely opaque, and the opaque object completely blocks out whatever objects are underneath it, as in Figure 5-4. You can make the objects on a layer semi-transparent, which allows the objects underneath to show through by an adjustable amount.

The extreme ends of the Opacity/Transparency slider are 100 percent opaque (which can also be thought of as 0 percent transparent) and 0 percent opaque (100 percent transparent).

To adjust the transparency of a layer, follow these simple steps:

1. **Click the name column of the object you want to adjust, or click the object on the canvas, to select the object.**

   The object is highlighted on both the canvas and in the Layers panel.

2. **Click and drag the Opacity/Transparency slider to adjust how opaque the object will be.**

The Opacity/Transparency slider is located near the top right of the Layers panel. (You can find an identical slider in the Property inspector.)

The available range of opacities goes from 100 percent (completely opaque, nothing shows through) to 0 percent (completely transparent, objects underneath show through completely).

3. **Release the mouse button when you get to the setting you want.**

You can also type a number from 0 to 100 into the text field next to the slider to set the object's transparency. Remember to press the Enter key to apply the new setting.

Fireworks MX can do a few fancier tricks with opacity. For example, you can set an opacity gradient, so some parts of your object are more transparent than others. See the next section on blending for more information on this topic.

Blending

Blending one object with another has to do with varying the transparency of the top object so some of the bottom object shows through. But blending in Fireworks MX involves more than just adjusting opacity. You can use a dozen blending modes in conjunction with the Opacity control and the colors of your objects to produce different blending effects:

+ **Normal:** The default blending mode, normal, actually means there's no blending going on at all.

+ **Multiply:** This mode multiplies the value of each pixel of the top object with each pixel of the objects underneath, which generally results in a darker color.

+ **Screen:** This mode divides the value of each pixel of the bottom object by each pixel of the object on top and produces a lighter color.

+ **Darken:** This mode replaces pixels of the top object that are lighter than the pixels in the object underneath with the darker pixels from below.

+ **Lighten:** This mode replaces pixels of the top object that are darker than the object underneath with the lighter pixels from the object below.

+ **Difference:** This mode subtracts the darker color from the color with more brightness, regardless of which is on top.

+ **Hue:** This mode replaces the luminance and saturation of a pixel on top with those of the pixel underneath.

**Book III
Chapter 5**

The Power of Layers and Frames

✦ **Saturation:** This mode replaces the hue and luminance of a pixel on top with those of the pixel underneath.

✦ **Color:** This mode replaces the luminance of a pixel on top with that of the pixel underneath, but keeps the shading of the top pixel the same.

✦ **Luminosity:** This mode replaces the hue and saturation of the pixel on top with those of the pixel underneath, leaving the luminance of the pixel on top.

✦ **Invert:** This mode changes the colors of the pixels in the object underneath to their opposites, regardless of the colors of the object on top.

✦ **Tint:** This mode adds gray to the areas of overlap.

✦ **Erase:** This mode removes all pixels in the overlapping areas, leaving a hole in the canvas. Any objects underneath the object with a blend mode of erase will be invisible where the objects overlap.

Layers can have blending modes, but the blending mode settings of individual objects on the layer override the settings of the layer they're on. That means different objects on the same layer can have individualized blend settings. The blending mode of a *group* of objects, however, overrides the blending modes of individual objects within the group. Removing the blending mode of the group restores the blending modes of the individual objects.

To blend an existing object with whatever is under it, just follow these steps:

1. **Select the object you want to blend by clicking it on the canvas or in the Layers panel.**

2. **Select a blending mode from the drop-down list in the Layers panel.**

   When you release the mouse button, the blend mode takes effect.

3. **If you want, adjust the transparency of the object by typing a value between 1 and 100 in the text field next to the blending mode menu or by using the Opacity/Transparency slider.**

Any objects that you put under the blended object will be affected by (or will affect) the blended object where both objects overlap.

You can also establish a blend's opacity and mode *before* you create an object by setting the properties of a drawing tool in the Property inspector, as shown in Figure 5-10. (***Note:*** Not all tools permit this.) Your settings will apply every time you use that tool. Remember, individual object blend settings override the blend settings of the layer the objects are on.

Figure 5-10:
You can set a tool's blending mode by using the tool's Property inspector.

To set the blend before you draw, follow these steps:

1. **Use the key command Ctrl+D or choose Edit➪Deselect to make sure you don't have any objects selected.**

If you have an object selected, you might accidentally change its blend mode when you're trying to set one for the object you're about to create.

2. **Select a drawing tool, such as a paintbrush.**

Some tools cannot have their blends changed from the default, Normal.

3. **Select a color for the tool.**

See the section on adding color in Book III, Chapter 2 if you don't know how to select a color for the tool. You can always change the color of the object later, but that can get complicated, especially if you have a special blend mode and opacity set.

4. **Select a blending mode from the drop-down list in the Layers panel or from the identical list in the tool's Property inspector.**

5. **If desired, set an opacity for the tool by dragging the Layers panel's opacity slider or typing a value in the Layers panel's text field.**

Alternatively, you can set the opacity in the tool's Property inspector in the same way.

6. **Use the tool to make your vector shape or bitmap.**

The tool's blend and opacity settings remain in effect until you change them. After you create an object, you can always adjust its blend and opacity settings. You may want to create a new layer (see the section "Adding and deleting layers") before making a new object. If you don't make a new layer, remember that the object's blend settings override the layer's blend settings.

Managing Frames

Given all that you can do with layers, you may be wondering why you would need these things called "frames." *Frames* are essentially sets of layers that enable you to do two things that layers alone can't accomplish:

✦ Export multiple button states (different versions of the button such as those that appear when the button is rolled over or clicked by the user) simultaneously

✦ Create and export animated GIFs (files that contain multiple GIF images displayed in sequence)

You can think of layers as stacked one on top of the other; frames, on the other hand, are better visualized as a series, each following the previous in the same location but at a later time, like a flip book. Each frame is distinct from the others. A given frame may share layers or objects with other frames, but the shared layers or objects are usually different from one frame to the next (the objects are a different color, have a different effect applied to them, or are at different coordinates). These differences make up multiple button states or animated GIFs.

Like layers, frames can be duplicated, added, and deleted. You must have at least two frames in your Fireworks PNG file in order to export buttons with rollover states or animated GIFs.

Adding frames

By default, your Fireworks PNG has a single frame, which contains all the layers in the file. To add a frame to your file, just follow these steps:

1. **Choose Add Frames or Duplicate Frame from the Options menu at the top right of the Frames panel.**

Choose Duplicate Frame if you want the objects in the current frame to be copied to the new frames. Choose Add Frames if you want to add empty frames to your file. Either the Add Frames or Duplicate Frame dialog box (shown in Figure 5-11) appears, both of which have identical parameters.

Duplicate Frame

Number: 1

Insert new frames:
- ◯ At the beginning
- ◯ Before current frame
- ⦿ After current frame
- ◯ At the end

OK   Cancel

2. Enter a number or click the arrow next to the text field to use a slider to set the number of frames you would like to add.

The slider goes from 0 through 10, but you can type in values higher than 10:

- For a simple rollover, you want one additional frame, for a total of two frames in your file.

- If you want your button to have an on state as well as a highlight (rollover) and normal state, you want two additional frames, for a total of three frames.

- If you want a highlight-while-on state, you want three additional frames, for a total of four frames.

If your animated GIF has more than 20 frames, the file size may be prohibitively large. For complicated animations, you're better off using Macromedia Flash MX.

3. Select one of the options for where the new frames should be added in reference to the current one.

You have the following options:

- **At the Beginning:** The first new frame becomes Frame 1 and the remaining frames are numbered sequentially, regardless of how many frames you currently have in your document, and regardless of which frame is currently active.

- **Before Current Frame:** The frames are added before the currently active frame.

- **After Current Frame:** The frames are added after the currently active frame.

- **At the End:** The new frames are the last frames, no matter how many frames you already have or which frame is currently active.

4. Click OK.

Deleting and editing frames

To delete a frame, click the frame in the Frames panel and drag it to the garbage can icon at the bottom right of the Frames panel. To delete multiple frames simultaneously, Shift+click all the frames in the Frames panel that you want to delete and, while the frames are highlighted, click the garbage can icon at the bottom right of the Frames panel.

You can select a frame for editing two ways:

✦ **Click the frame in the Frames panel.**

✦ **Click and hold the frame indicator at the bottom left of the Layers panel.** A drop-down list appears, giving you easy access to all the frames in your document. Simply select the frame you want to edit.

Renaming frames

Renaming frames is a simple matter: Double-click the frame's name in the Frames panel and type the new name in the text field that appears.

Using Frames to Create Rollovers and Animated GIFs

Now that you know how to make and manage frames, you're ready to use them! In this section we cover how to create rollovers and animated GIFs, both of which can add interest to your Web site.

Creating a rollover

Creating a button rollover is really just a matter of making two (or three or even four) versions of a button graphic, each on its own frame. Dreamweaver MX allows you to generate rollover code pretty easily, but you can also have Fireworks MX make the rollover code along with the HTML.

To make a simple button rollover, follow these steps:

1. **Make a button, or set of buttons, using the processes outlined in Book III, Chapters 3 and 4.**

   The button can have text or an icon, it can have a shape or bitmap under the text or icon, and it can be any shape or size you like (but you probably want to keep it on the small side to limit file size and leave room on your page for content). For easy housekeeping, keep all the buttons for which you want to have additional states on the same layer.

2. **Make sure the layer on which you have your buttons is not shared across frames.**

By default, objects on layers are not shared across frames. If a layer is shared across frames, changes to any objects in that layer will be reflected in all frames. If a layer is shared across frames, the Shared icon (which resembles a ladder with arrows on both sides) appears to the right of the layer name.

To disable sharing across frames, double-click the layer and deselect the Share Across Frames check box.

3. **Add one frame after the current frame by clicking the New/Duplicate Frame button in the Frames panel or by choosing Add Frames from the Frames panel's Options menu.**

4. **In Frame 2, edit the objects that make up your button to create a high-lighted rollover state.**

   The highlighted rollover state is the image that will swap in when the user rolls the cursor over the button.

   You can make the text a different color or add a glow to it, or you can make the vector shape or bitmap a different color. There are too many options to mention here, really. Just make sure the difference is notice-able when the user moves a cursor over the button.

5. **Make a slice overlaying the button graphic.**

   See Book III, Chapter 6 for details on making slices.

6. **Click and release the mouse button in the middle of the slice to access the Add Behavior pop-up menu, and choose the Add Simple Rollover behavior.**

   When a slice is active, you can see the Target icon in the middle of the slice. When you place your cursor over the target, it becomes a hand.

If you want to test the rollover, click on the Preview tab at the top of the canvas to make the Preview pane active. Place your cursor over your button in the Preview pane to see the Rollover behavior in action. Next move the cursor off the button to see the button return to its normal state — that behavior is part of a Simple Rollover.

Adding an on state (for when the user is on the Web page the button repre-sents) and a highlight-while-on state (for when the user rolls over the button on the Web page the button represents) are as simple as repeating Steps 3 and 4 above, and adding more behaviors via the Behavior panel. See Book III, Chapter 7 for further details.

Creating an animated GIF

You may find that the easiest way to create an animated GIF is to build one frame, duplicate it, edit that frame, duplicate it, and so on. Fireworks MX has a display mode called onion-skinning, which is especially handy for building animated GIFs. With onion-skinning turned on, illustrated in Figure 5-12, you can see the frame you're working on, plus dimmed versions either of the next frame, the previous and next frames, or all frames. That can be very useful in helping you pace your animation to get the illusion of smooth motion.

Figure 5-12:
You can see the current frame plus other frames with onion-skinning on.

To activate onion-skinning, just follow these steps:

1. **Click the Onion-skinning button at the lower left of the Frames panel.**

The Onion-skinning menu pops up.

2. **Select one of the four options:**

- **Show Next Frame:** Select the Show Next Frame option if you already have your frames set up and want to check frames two at a time.

- **Before and After:** Select the Before and After option if you want to see the previous and next frames as well as the current frame.

- **Show All Frames:** Select the Show All Frames option to see all the frames at once.

- **Custom:** Select the Custom option if you want to set the number of frames visible at once and to customize their transparencies.

3. **Leave the Multi-Frame Editing option selected if you want to be able to edit the objects in the visible but not current frames.**

Use the Select Behind tool to select objects in frames other than the current one.

When you duplicate a frame, you duplicate the objects in it. When you edit an object in a frame, though, you change only that instance of it. In our bowling ball animation, shown in Figure 5-12, we rotated the ball (as well as moved it left) in each frame to give the illusion that the ball is rolling. If we wanted to, we could have the ball be a different color in each frame as well.

Setting the frame rate

The frame rate is the speed at which each frame follows the previous frame. You can set the rate to be the same all the way through the animation, or you can set individually the amount of time each frame stays on-screen.

To set a constant frame rate, follow these steps:

1. **Click the first frame and Shift+click the last frame in the Frames panel to select all the Frames.**

All the frames highlight.

2. **Double-click the frame delay column (the right-hand column) of any frame in the Frames panel.**

The Frame Delay dialog box appears.

3. **Type a number in the Frame Delay text field to set the amount of time in hundredths of a second that each frame will remain on-screen.**

If you want the frames to be on-screen for more than a second, the number you type should be over 100. For example, if you type 350, each frame will be on-screen for 3.5 seconds. You won't get much of an illusion of motion at that frame rate, however! The less time each frame is on-screen, the more frames of your animation will appear each second. The more frames per second, the smoother the animation looks. But the more frames you have in your animation, the bigger the file.

4. **Press Enter.**

To change the amount of time one frame stays on-screen, follow these steps:

1. **Double-click the frame delay column (the right-hand column) of any frame in the Frames panel.**

The Frame Delay dialog box appears.

2. **Type a new number in the Frame Delay text field to set the amount of time in hundredths of a second that the frame will remain on-screen.**

3. **Press Enter.**

To loop or not to loop

Fireworks MX allows you to loop your animation, which causes it to automatically start over at the beginning after playing the last frame. You can have the GIF loop indefinitely, you can set it to play once (stopping at the last frame), or to play a designated number of times and then stop on the last frame.

The default for animated GIFs is to loop endlessly. To make a GIF that stops at the final frame, just follow these steps:

1. **Click the GIF Animation Looping button at the bottom of the Frames panel (just to the right of the Frame Delay icon).**

   The Looping pop-up menu appears.

2. **Select a number of times you want the animation to repeat, or select No Looping if you want it to play only once.**

   Because you're setting the amount of times for it to repeat, if you select 1, that means the animation will play twice through and stop. Note that after you have made your choice, the choice appears next to the Loop button, as shown in Figure 5-13.

The Frames panel, shown in Figure 5-13, shows what mode of onion-skinning is on, if any, and on which frames (first column); it also shows the frame name (second column), frame delay (third column), and looping information (bottom).

Figure 5-13:
The Frames panel shows the frames' settings.

Previewing animated GIFs

You can preview animated GIFs in the Preview pane. The available controls are as follows:

✦ Go to first frame

✦ Play/Stop

✦ Go to last frame

✦ Go back one frame

✦ Go forward one frame

A quick word about animated GIFs versus SWFs

Macromedia Flash Player, the browser plug-in which users must have to view SWF files, has a remarkable penetration rate. As of this writing, nearly 98 percent of Web users have some version of the plug-in. That means if you have an SWF file on your page, chances are very high that any visitors will see it.

Unlike animated GIFs, Flash movies can include synchronized audio and can incorporate dynamic content. SWFs can show fades, dissolves, and motion effects more smoothly (and often more efficiently, in terms of file size) than animated GIFs.

Nevertheless, you may on occasion want to put a simple animation on your page, and creating

it with Macromedia Flash MX would be overkill. The Flash plug-in may have a nearly 98 percent rate of installation, but users don't even need a plug-in to view animated GIFs. In addition, making an animated GIF in Fireworks MX is often easier than making an SWF or an animated GIF using Macromedia Flash MX.

Be aware also that Macromedia Flash MX can import PNG files as well as animated GIFs, so if you plan to edit your animation in Macromedia Flash MX, you don't need to export it from Fireworks MX.

The animation plays at the frame rate you have set for it, and conveniently, you can adjust the frame rate in the Frames panel without leaving the Preview pane. Your animation will loop in the Preview pane, even if it's set not to loop for export. Onion-skinning is not visible in the Preview pane.

Chapter 6: Slicing Up Content for the Web

In This Chapter

✔ Investigating the advantages of using slices

✔ Creating and editing slices

✔ Optimizing your content for the Web

✔ Previewing slices

✔ Exporting images

*A*fter you have designed your page, you need to figure out how to translate your design to the Web. If you're planning to export HTML as well as images from Fireworks MX and plan not to mess with the code afterward, that's okay. When you want to make changes to the page, you can do so in Fireworks MX and then re-export the HTML and images.

Regardless of your skill level or your site maintenance needs, you'll want to slice and optimize your images, and luckily doing so is easy.

Exploring the Advantages of Using Slices

When we introduced the Web Layer in the previous chapter, we offered the analogy that a design for a Web page is like a sheet cake. Of course, when you slice a cake, the point is to eat it. When you slice a page layout, like the one in Figure 6-1, the aim is to optimize (reduce the file size of) your images so you can reconstruct your design with HTML in such a way as to balance image quality with download time.

Slicing your design offers two advantages:

✦ **Individually optimized images:** Each sliced image can be compressed by a different amount using the most appropriate method, giving you maximum control over the balance between image quality and download time.

✦ **Gradual download:** The browser displays each sliced image as it is downloaded to the user's computer, so the page appears to build gradually. Users are much more engaged by watching this process than by staring at a blank screen waiting for a complete page to load all at once!

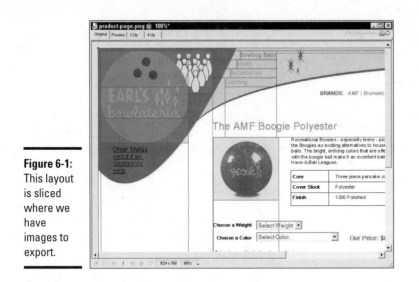

Figure 6-1:
This layout is sliced where we have images to export.

When you use slices in combination with frames, you gain other advantages. The main advantage is that you can export multiple images simultaneously from a single slice, which is the easiest way to make buttons that change based on user actions. (See the "Exporting Images" section, later in this chapter, for the details.)

A Web page made up of a single image may be simple to make but may take too long to download on a modem because the image file is so large. That's where slices come in. Although there's no minimum or maximum number of slices that you can make on a page, you don't want to make too many slices. Having lots of teeny-weeny images can result in a page that loads *too* gradually. It's a question of balance.

Every image tag in a Web page's HTML code results in a call to the Web site's host server. The more images you have on your page, the more requests for images the browser has to make, and the more images the server has to send. That can feel like having a waiter bring you a salad one piece of lettuce at a time — with you having to request each piece!

Creating and Editing Slices

In Book III, Chapter 5, we cover the basics of how to make a slice, but here we give you some more details. So you don't have to flip back to the previous chapter, here's a reminder on how to make a slice in your Fireworks PNG file:

1. **Select the Slice tool from the Web area of the Tools panel.**

2. **Click and drag diagonally on the canvas to make a rectangle.**

   The slice shows up as a green overlay on the canvas.

The default appearance of the slice is as a bright green semi-transparent overlay. You can change the default color of slices in the Preferences settings. You can also change the color of an individual slice in the Property inspector when you have the slice selected. Changing a slice color does not affect the underlying image in any way.

One handy feature of the Slice tool is its snap feature. If you have navigation buttons on the left side of your page, you may want the buttons all to be the same width to simplify your HTML. When you have a single slice made for your first button and you click and drag to make the slice for the second button, Fireworks MX will snap to the identical width when your cursor is within a few pixels of it. Of course, you can also make sure they're the same width by typing a value into the width text field, or by copying and pasting the slice.

Naming a slice

When you name a slice, you're doing more than making it easy to identify in the Layers panel — you're also naming the image for export. For that reason, when you name a slice, you want to avoid using spaces or any special characters that are illegal in filenames. You should also limit any name to no more than 27 characters (otherwise, Macintosh users will not get to see the image).

To name or rename a slice, just follow these steps:

1. **Double-click the current name of the slice in the Layers panel.**

   A text field pops up, as shown in Figure 6-2. By default, slices are named "Slice."

Figure 6-2:
Naming a
slice that
contains a
top
navigation
button.

2. **Type a new name for the slice.**

3. **Press Enter.**

You may notice that when a slice is selected, the Property inspector gives you access to the slice's name, dimensions, position on the page, and more. You can also change the name of the slice in the Property inspector rather than in the Layers panel.

Moving a slice

After you have created a slice, you may find yourself needing to move it, for example, if you move some elements in your design a few pixels one way or the other, and the underlying image you're trying to slice has shifted. You can choose between three basic ways of moving a slice:

✦ Move a slice by clicking and dragging the slice. (In most cases, you'll probably want to use this method.)

✦ Use the arrow keys to move a slice.

✦ Change the X and Y coordinates of the slice in the Property inspector.

To move a slice using the click-and-drag method, just follow these steps:

1. **Click the slice on the canvas.**

   You can click anywhere on the slice except the corners and the center. Clicking a corner or the center of a slice gives you special options.

2. **Hold down the mouse button and drag the slice to its new location.**

You can also use the arrow keys to move a slice:

1. **Select the slice by clicking it on the canvas or in the Layers panel.**

2. **Press the appropriate arrow key.**

   Each time you press an arrow key, the slice moves by one pixel. If you hold down the Shift key and then press an arrow key, the slice moves by ten pixels.

Sometimes when you want to line something up along one axis, the easiest way to do that is to select slices and type the new X or Y coordinate for each slice. The top left corner of the canvas always has the coordinates (0, 0), and coordinates are expressed in the form (X, Y). If your design is 800 pixels wide and 600 pixels high, the bottom right corner has the coordinates (800, 600).

To move a slice when you know the exact pixel coordinates to which you want to move it, follow these steps:

1. **Select the slice by clicking it on the canvas or in the Layers panel.**

   The Property inspector changes to give you access to slice parameters.

2. **If you want to change the slice's horizontal position, type a numerical value in the Property inspector text field labeled X: and press Enter.**

   Your slice shifts left if you type in a lower number or right if you type in a higher number.

3. **If you want to change the slice's vertical position, type a numerical value in the Property inspector text field labeled Y: and press Enter.**

   Your slice shifts up if you type in a lower number or down if you type in a higher number.

Resizing a slice

Sometimes after you make a slice, you decide you need to resize the underlying image. After you resize the image, you want to resize the slice. You may also need to resize a slice if you draw the slice quickly and don't make it big enough. As with moving a slice, resizing a slice can be done by clicking and dragging or by typing new values.

To resize two dimensions of a slice at once using the click-and-drag method, follow these steps:

1. **Click a corner of the slice.**

   You must click a handle at one of the corners in order to resize the slice. If you click anywhere inside the slice (except the exact center) and drag, you move the slice instead of resizing it.

2. **Drag the handle on the corner of the slice to the desired new location.**

If you only want to change the height, click and drag the top or bottom border of the slice. If you only want to change the width, click and drag the left or right border of the slice. Note that when your cursor is over the border, it changes into the Resize cursor, two parallel lines with an arrow pointing outward from each line, as shown in Figure 6-3.

When you're creating slices, their edges snap to edges of already created slices, so you may find it difficult to get the edge of a slice where you want it. You can zoom in until you reach a magnification at which you can resize the slice so it doesn't snap to the edge of the other slice, or you can use the text fields in the Property inspector to change the selected slice's dimensions.

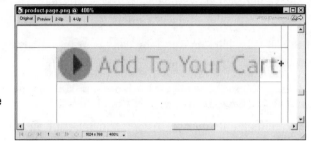

To resize a slice by typing new values, follow these steps:

1. **Select the slice by clicking it on the canvas or in the Layers panel.**

    The Property inspector changes to give you access to the slice's parameters.

2. **If you want to change the slice's width, type a new numerical value in the text field labeled W: and press Enter.**

    If you increase the width, you add pixels to the right side of the slice. If you decrease the width, you take pixels away from the right side of the slice.

3. **If you want to change the slice's height, type a new numerical value in the text field labeled H: and press Enter.**

    If you increase the height, you add pixels to the bottom of the slice. If you decrease the height, you take pixels away from the bottom of the slice.

Duplicating a slice

If you have a series of buttons, each of which is to be the same width and height, you can make one slice and then duplicate it as many times as you need. Of course, you also need to move each duplicated slice to overlay a different button and name each slice according to the button it overlays. To duplicate a slice, just follow these steps:

1. **Select the slice by clicking it on the canvas or in the Layers panel.**

2. **Choose Edit⇨Duplicate or use the key command Ctrl+Alt+D.**

    A duplicate slice appears on top of, but slightly offset from, the slice you duplicated.

    If you Clone the slice instead of duplicating it (Edit⇨Clone or Ctrl+Shift+D), the new slice appears directly on top of the old one.

You can also copy and paste a slice, though that's essentially the same as cloning, except that it takes an extra step!

3. **Move the slice to its proper location.**

   See the "Moving a slice" section, earlier in this chapter, for instructions.

Optimizing Your Images for the Web

In order to understand the process of optimization, you need to know about image compression. When you compress an image, you reduce its file size by reducing the amount of data in the file. The two main types of image compression are

 ✦ **Lossy:** Some data is discarded from the image to make the file smaller.

 ✦ **Lossless:** The data in the image is described in a more efficient way, which makes the file smaller.

The two main compression methods used to format images for the Web are

 ✦ **JPEG:** A lossy method, best used for photographs, gradients, and other complex, variegated images.

 ✦ **GIF:** A generally lossless method, best used for images with large areas of flat color, like company logos. It also allows for images with transparent backgrounds.

Not sure which compression method to use for a particular slice? That's where the Preview panes come in. You can use a Preview pane any time you have slices. They show you what the image will look like at your chosen compression setting (or settings). See the section, "Previewing Slices," later in this chapter, for the details.

One way to deal with compression is to make a setting when you first make the slice and then make the fine adjustments later. It doesn't really matter, though. You can just leave each slice at the default setting until you're ready to export.

Working with the options in the Optimize panel

Take a look at the Optimize panel, shown in Figure 6-4, as it appears when it is expanded and a slice is selected. You click the Options button (the icon with the three lines and the arrow) at the top right of the Optimize panel to access the Options menu. The items in the Options menu vary depending on the file type you have selected in the Export file format drop-down list.

Figure 6-4:
The
Optimize
panel with
a default
JPEG
setting
selected.

When you have JPEG selected, the Options menu offers the following:

✦ **Save Settings:** This option allows you to preserve your current compression setting as a preset, which you can then select from the Settings menu in the Optimize panel. Presets (custom or not) can be useful for *batch processing* images (automating the export of multiple images that use the same settings).

✦ **Delete Settings:** This option does what you would expect — it deletes your custom compression settings.

This option deletes *all* the settings. To remove an individual setting, select it from the Settings drop-down list and click the button with the minus sign (–) just below the Options menu in the Optimize panel.

✦ **Optimize to Size:** This handy option allows you to set a target file size for your slice. Fireworks MX then makes the appropriate compression settings to produce a file of your specified size.

✦ **Export Wizard:** The Export Wizard walks you through the steps of exporting an image with a series of dialog boxes.

✦ **Progressive JPEG:** If you have this option selected when you export a slice, your JPEG will contain two versions of your image. The first is a low-resolution version of the image that loads relatively quickly to a browser. The second, which fills in over the first, is a higher-resolution version. Although the time it takes for this type of image to become visible is shorter, the overall download time is longer.

If your JPEG needs to be large (in terms of width and height) *and* high-quality, you should consider exporting it as a progressive JPEG.

Flash MX cannot dynamically import progressive JPEGs.

✦ **Sharpen JPEG Edges:** Select this option if image clarity is a priority (if, for example, you have small text in the image). Note that clarity makes for larger file sizes.

✦ **Show Swatch Feedback, Load Palette, Save Palette:** These options apply to 8-bit graphics (including GIFs; JPEGs are a 24-bit format). Custom palettes are sets of colors to which you can limit images. See your documentation for further details.

✦ **Help, Group Optimize With, Close Panel Group:** These options don't relate to JPEGs per se. See Book III, Chapter 1 for more information about general panel options.

When you have GIF selected from the Export File Format menu, the Options menu makes some JPEG-specific options unavailable but offers the following GIF-specific (8-bit graphic specific) options:

✦ **Interlaced:** An interlaced GIF is similar to a Progressive JPEG. A low-resolution version of the graphic loads first (and fast), and the image slowly transitions until it is at its maximum resolution. As with Progressive JPEGs, the image loads faster initially, but the final version of the image doesn't load as quickly as it would if it weren't interlaced. (You can also export an interlaced PNG.)

✦ **Remove Unused Colors:** When this option is selected, as it is by default, Fireworks MX removes any color from the image's palette that isn't used by the image. Smaller palettes mean smaller file sizes.

Under the Optimize panel name is the Settings drop-down list, which offers seven default settings (two for JPEGs and five for GIFs). You can choose between two default settings for JPEGs:

✦ **JPEG — Better Quality:** Makes a high-quality image, which results in a bigger file size and a longer download time.

✦ **JPEG — Smaller File:** Makes a small file, with a corresponding loss in image quality.

For information about the default GIF settings, see the section, "Making a GIF," later in this chapter.

Under the Settings drop-down list is another drop-down list, the Export File Format list. If you use a default setting from the Settings list above, Fireworks MX automatically shows the file format in the lower menu. Otherwise, you select the export file format. We only look at JPEGs and GIFs, because they are by far the most common Web formats, but the full list of file formats that Fireworks MX can export is noted in the sidebar, "Other export file types."

The rest of the parameters in the Optimize panel vary based on what export file format you choose, so we discuss them in the following sections in the context of how to export JPEGs and GIFs.

**Book III
Chapter 6**

**Slicing Up Content
for the Web**

Other export file types

Fireworks MX can export these other image types in addition to JPEGs and GIFs:

✓ **PNG:** The native file format for Fireworks MX is PNG. You should be aware that Fireworks MX stores extra information in PNGs that is not available to other applications opening the same file. PNGs can have transparent backgrounds and can be viewed in some browsers. PNG is a Flash MX-friendly format.

✓ **WBMP:** A 2-bit format (black and white only) created especially for wireless devices like PDAs and cell phones.

✓ **TIFF:** This format is often used for print materials.

✓ **BMP:** Bitmap is the native image format for PCs.

Making a JPEG

Because JPEG is a lossy compression method, you will want a fair amount of control over just how much data gets discarded from your image. The higher the amount of compression, the lower the image quality — but also the smaller the file size and consequently the faster the download time. Fireworks MX gives you a few options so you can maximize image quality while minimizing file size.

Using the default JPEG settings

To use a default setting is easy. Just follow these steps:

1. **Select the slice by clicking it on the canvas or in the Layers panel.**

2. **Select either JPEG — Better Quality or JPEG — Smaller File from the Settings drop-down list in the Optimize panel.**

   The Image Type, Quality, and Smoothing drop-down lists update according to your chosen setting. You can further refine these settings if you like, as outlined in the following section.

Using custom JPEG settings

To make or edit a custom JPEG setting, follow these steps:

1. **Select the slice by clicking it on the canvas or in the Layers panel.**

2. **Select JPEG from the Export file format drop-down list in the Optimize panel.**

3. **Type or use the Quality slider to set the image quality.**

   You can enter any whole number from 0 to 100, with 0 representing the lowest quality and 100 the highest.

   If part of your image needs to be a higher quality than the rest, follow the next set of instructions, which describe using the Selective Quality option.

4. **Set the smoothing, if necessary.**

   Smoothing blurs the image a little, reducing its quality but also reducing its file size. You can type or select any whole number from 1 through 8, with 1 representing the least blurring and 8 representing the most blurring.

The Selective Quality option in the Optimize panel allows you to compress different parts of your image by different amounts. In some cases, using Selective Quality can be a great alternative to cutting a photograph into different slices set at different compression levels.

Here's how to use the Selective Quality option:

1. **Click Original above the canvas if you are not already viewing the Original pane.**

2. **Use a Selection tool to select the area of the image that you want to compress differently than the rest of the image.**

   Make sure you're in the Original view, not in a Preview pane.

3. **Choose Modify⇨Selective JPEG⇨Save Selection as JPEG Mask.**

   Your JPEG mask shows up as a pink overlay.

4. **Select JPEG from the drop-down list in the Optimize panel, if it's not already selected.**

5. **Click the Selective Quality button (the pencil and paper) in the Optimize panel.**

   The Selective JPEG Settings dialog box, shown in Figure 6-5, appears.

6. **Make sure the Enable Selective Quality check box is selected in the Selective JPEG Settings dialog box (it is checked by default).**

7. **Type a number from 0 to 100 in the text field.**

   Zero represents the lowest quality; 100 represents the highest quality. This number should, of course, be different from the number in the Quality field discussed previously.

8. **Change the overlay color if you don't like the default overlay color.**

The overlay color does not affect the exported image.

9. **Select the Preserve Text Quality check box if you want to preserve the quality of any text within your selection, regardless of the overall compression settings.**

   This is a handy shortcut that you can use with or without a JPEG mask.

10. **Select the Preserve Button Quality check box if you want to preserve the quality of any buttons within your selection, regardless of the overall compression settings.**

11. **Click OK or press Enter.**

Figure 6-5:
The Selective JPEG Settings dialog box offers a few simple options.

Making a GIF

Okay, when we said the GIF compression method is generally lossless, we meant this: You can make lossless GIFs, but you can also make lossy GIFs if you need to. GIFs compress image data in a couple of ways:

✦ **By keeping track of the data more efficiently:** GIFs group adjacent pixels of the same color in each row of the image so the pixels can be described as a group instead of as individual pixels. The fewer colors you have in each row, and the more pixels of the same color are together in a line, the better GIF compression works.

✦ **By limiting the number of colors in an image:** You can create custom palettes (sets of colors) or use the specialized built-in palettes that Fireworks MX offers. If you compress your image with a palette that doesn't contain all the colors in the image, Fireworks MX substitutes colors from the palette, effectively reducing the number of colors in the GIF as compared to the source image.

Sometimes you can simulate the appearance of the lost color by dithering two colors from the palette. The section on Web safe colors in Book III, Chapter 2 has more about dithering.

Using the default GIF settings

Fireworks MX offers several default settings for GIFs:

✦ **GIF Web 216:** This setting limits the colors in your GIF to the basic Web safe palette.

✦ **GIF Web Snap 256:** This setting limits the number of colors in your GIF to 256, while snapping any colors close in appearance to Web safe colors to the Web safe palette.

✦ **GIF Web Snap 128:** This setting limits the colors in your GIF to 128, while snapping any colors close in appearance to Web safe colors to the Web safe palette.

✦ **GIF Adaptive 256:** This setting limits the colors in your GIF to the 256 most common in the GIF. Other colors are changed to the closest color in the palette. This setting will give you the highest fidelity GIF version of your image.

✦ **Animated GIF Web Snap 128:** This setting is the same as GIF Web Snap 128, but for animated GIFs.

Using custom GIF settings

To make a basic GIF that doesn't use a Fireworks MX default setting, just follow these steps:

1. **Select a slice by clicking it on the canvas or in the Layers panel.**

2. **Select GIF from the Export file format drop-down list in the Optimize panel, which is shown in Figure 6-6.**

The Optimize panel shown in Figure 6-6 displays the setting for a top navigation button. Note that transparency appears as a checkerboard pattern in the palette.

3. **Set the compression mode by selecting one from the Indexed palette drop-down list.**

For Web images, choose from the top four:

- Adaptive
- WebSnap Adaptive
- Web 216
- Exact

4. **Type a number in the Colors: text field or use the slider to set the number of colors in your palette, if you're not compressing using the Web 216 or Exact settings.**

Figure 6-6:
A button's settings in the Optimize panel.

The fewer colors you have in your palette, the smaller the file size of your image. If you have fewer colors in the palette than in your image, however, Fireworks MX must substitute colors, deteriorating image quality. If your image has more than 256 colors, you may get better results using a JPEG setting.

5. **If there are more colors in your image than in your palette, and if you prefer dithering to straight one-for-one color substitutions, type a percent in the Dither: text field or use the slider to set a percentage from 1 to 96.**

   The more you dither, the fewer colors you need in your palette. Unfortunately, dithering can look bad up close and increases the file size.

Making a transparent GIF

To make a GIF with transparent areas, which allows the HTML page background color or background image to show through, follow these steps:

1. **Select a slice by clicking it on the canvas or in the Layers panel.**

2. **Select GIF from the Image Type drop-down list in the Optimize panel, if GIF is not already selected.**

3. **Select Index Transparency from the Transparency drop-down list.**

   The default is No Transparency. Even when you don't have a background in your PNG file, you still need to select Index Transparency to make a GIF with transparent pixels.

4. **Select the eyedropper button with the equal sign (=) to select a color in the palette or on the canvas that you want to make transparent.**

   The three transparency eyedropper buttons are at the bottom left of the Optimize panel. The selected color becomes transparent in the palette in the Optimize panel. If you're viewing a preview pane, the transparency will appear (or disappear, as it were) on the canvas.

5. **Use the eyedropper with the plus sign (+) to select additional colors to make transparent, if desired.**

You can use the eyedropper with the minus sign (–) to restore opacity to a color that has been made transparent, if necessary.

Previewing Slices

You can optimize your slices as you make them, or you can make all your slices first and then optimize them all at once. Either way, if you're having trouble deciding on the best method or amount of compression to use on a slice, you can use one of the three Preview panels to help you make an informed decision:

✦ **Preview:** This view shows a single version of your canvas, where you can see what your slices will look like and how big their files sizes will be at your current compression settings. Click on a slice to preview it.

✦ **2-Up:** This panel puts two versions of your canvas side-by-side, so you can compare the original image with a compressed version of the image, or you can compare two compressed versions to each other. Click on a slice on either side to preview it on both sides.

✦ **4-Up:** This divides the work area into quadrants, so you can compare three compression settings at once to the original image, or you can compare four different compression settings to each other at once. Click a slice in any quadrant to preview the settings in all quadrants.

In the Preview panes, slices that are not currently selected look slightly pale, as if viewed through a fogged-up window. Selected slices look as they will when exported, given their current settings (including transparencies, which appear as checkerboards, as shown in Figure 6-7).

The Preview pane

You can select the Preview pane by clicking the Preview tab at the top left of the image's window, right above the canvas.

The Preview pane previews more than just the appearance of your image; it also shows you the image's projected file size *and* the amount of time it would take for a file that size to download at a particular download speed. (The default is 56 Kbps, or the approximate speed of a 56 Kbps modem.)

In Figure 6-7, you can see the file size and download time stats at the top right above the canvas. Because a 56 Kbps modem can download at a rate of 5K per second, and this image is a little over 0.5K, the download time shows as 0 sec (less than 1 second).

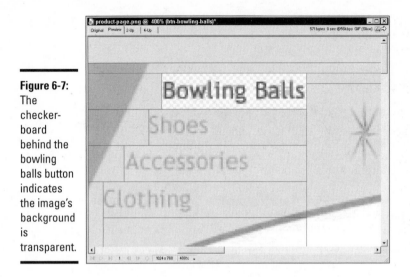

Figure 6-7:
The
checker-
board
behind the
bowling
balls button
indicates
the image's
background
is
transparent.

When you change the settings in the Optimize panel, the size and download time information at the top of the Preview pane update automatically. The Optimize panel works the same way, whether you're looking at a Preview pane or the default Original pane.

The 2-Up view

You can select the 2-Up view simply by clicking the 2-Up tab at the top left of the image's window, above the canvas.

The 2-Up view sets two versions of the canvas side by side. At the bottom of each pane is an indicator of which view is in the pane and some of its vital statistics. In Figure 6-8, the pane on the left shows what the image would look like as a JPEG with the settings as shown at the bottom of the pane, and the pane on the right shows what the image would look like if exported as a GIF with the settings as shown at the bottom of the pane.

You can click in either pane to select the slice, and then adjust its settings in the Optimize panel. You can set the magnification of both panes several ways:

✦ You can use the Magnifying tool in the View section of the Tools panel.

✦ You can choose Zoom In, Zoom Out, or a preset Magnification setting from the View menu.

✦ You can select a zoom setting from the drop-down list at the bottom of the panes.

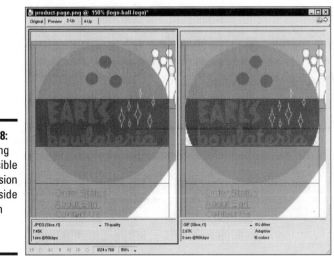

Figure 6-8:
Comparing
two possible
compression
settings side
by side in
the 2-Up
view.

You can use the Hand tool from the View section of the Tools panel to move the canvas. When you move the canvas in one pane, the canvas also moves in the other pane.

To select a different slice than the one currently selected, click the Selection tool and then click a slice in either pane or in the Layers panel. The slice becomes active in both panes simultaneously.

The 4-Up view

You can select the 4-Up view by clicking the 4-Up tab at the top left above the canvas. When you first open the 4-Up view, the top left quadrant displays the Original view, and the other three panes have identical compression settings. To change the settings in one pane, click in the pane to select it, and then change its settings in the Optimize panel. In fact, the concept, properties, and processes of using the 4-Up view are identical to those of the 2-Up view; you just get an extra two panes.

Figure 6-9 shows the 4-Up view. Comparing the three compression settings, it seems the one that best balances visual quality with file size is the GIF pane at the bottom right.

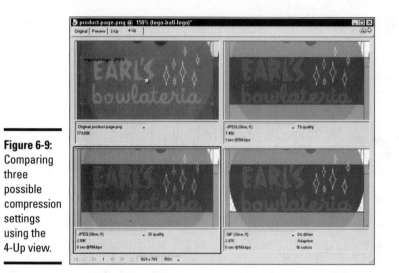

Figure 6-9:
Comparing three possible compression settings using the 4-Up view.

Relating Hotspots and Slices

Slices can only be rectangular, which is fine if your buttons are rectangular. But what if you want to create non-rectangular HTML links to other Web pages? You have two choices:

✦ **Use the Polygon Slice tool to make a polygonal slice.** This works best if the area that you want to use as a hyperlink is fairly isolated from other slices. See Book III, Chapter 5 for details.

✦ **Use a Hotspot tool to draw hotspots on an image.** Fireworks will create the underlying image plus what is known as an *image map*. An image map is some HTML code representing coordinates for hyperlinked polygonal hotspots. *Hotspots* are areas on an image that have been coded to respond to user actions.

Typically, the hotspots are hyperlinked to Web pages. In Figure 6-10, the bowling ball could be linked to a page about bowling balls, while the pin could be linked to a page with a list of bowling alleys. Hotspots are great, but use them sparingly so you don't add too much code to your HTML or tax the user's processor with too many instructions.

If that all sounds too technical, don't worry. You don't need to know all the ins and outs of HTML to make an image map — Fireworks MX takes care of that for you. All you have to do is create hotspots in the shapes you want, and export HTML with your images. See Book III, Chapter 7 for details.

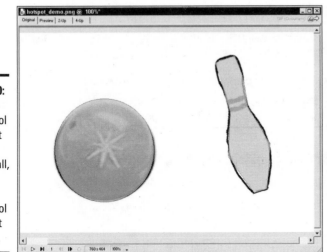

Figure 6-10:
The Circle Hotspot tool works best for a bowling ball, and the Polygon Hotspot tool works best for the pin.

Exporting Images

You can export images in two ways: one by one or all at once. You can have Fireworks MX generate HTML at the same time as you export your images, or you can export the images only and write the code yourself in Dreamweaver MX. (The code Fireworks MX generates is less efficient and more difficult to edit than code you would write.)

Exporting a single image

To export a single image, follow these steps:

1. **Right-click a slice to activate a shortcut menu.**

2. **Select Export Selected Slice.**

An Export dialog box appears, with default values set for exporting a single image.

3. **Navigate to the folder into which you want to put your image.**

4. **Leave the Save as Type setting at the default, Images Only.**

5. **If necessary, rename the image.**

6. **Leave the Slices setting at the default, Export Slices.**

7. **Leave the Selected Slices Only and Current Frame Only check boxes selected.**

8. **Click the Save button on the right.**

Exporting multiple image slices

To export all the image slices in a PNG file at once, if you plan to write the HTML yourself, follow these steps:

1. **Choose File⇨Export or use the key command Ctrl+Shift+R.**

The Export dialog box appears, with default values set for exporting multiple images and HTML, as shown in Figure 6-11.

Figure 6-11:
The Export dialog box set to export HTML and images.

2. **Select Images Only from the Save as Type drop-down list.**

The options below the Save as Type drop-down list update to reflect your selection.

3. **Leave the Slices setting at the default, Export Slices.**

4. **Select the Selected Slices Only check box and deselect the Include Areas without Slices check box if you need only the sliced images to build your HMTL page.**

5. **If you have rollover images that you want to export, make sure that the Current Frame Only check box is deselected.**

6. **Click the Save button.**

Exporting an animated GIF

When you export an animated GIF, you'll notice that beyond the default Images Only option in the Save as Type drop-down list, there's also a Macromedia Flash MX SWF option. Although that option does allow you to make some additional settings, chances are that if the ultimate format of the animation is to be an SWF file, you would be better off opening the PNG file in Macromedia Flash MX and exporting from there. Why? Because Macromedia Flash MX offers more powerful authoring and editing tools, many more export parameters than Fireworks MX, and ActionScript for adding complex interactivity to your animation.

To export an animated GIF, follow these simple steps:

1. **Make sure you have selected Animated GIF in the Optimize panel's Image Type drop-down list.**

2. **Choose File⇨Export or use the key command Ctrl+Shift+R.**

The Export dialog box appears, with default values set for exporting animated GIFs.

3. **Navigate to the folder into which you would like the GIF to go.**

4. **Leave the default Images Only setting in the Save as Type drop-down list.**

5. **Click Save.**

There's lots more to the Export function than we've outlined in this section. For information on exporting HTML and other export options, see the section about advanced export functions in Book III, Chapter 7.

**Book III
Chapter 6**

**Slicing Up Content
for the Web**

Chapter 7: Advanced Fireworks MX Tools

In This Chapter

✔ **Using advanced export options**

✔ **Using hotspots to create image maps**

✔ **Making three- and four-state button rollovers**

✔ **Bringing interactivity to your pages with behaviors**

F ireworks MX, like all the applications in the Macromedia Studio MX suite, is deep and rich. In this chapter, we introduce some of the application's more advanced capabilities, such as the following:

✦ Exporting HTML code with JavaScript. (*JavaScript* is a coding language that you can use to make elements of your Web page change based on user feedback, among other things.) If you have added behaviors to your Fireworks MX PNG, you've added JavaScript to the HTML that Fireworks MX will generate.

✦ Creating image maps with hotspots.

✦ Setting up button behaviors that go beyond simple rollovers. (See Book III, Chapter 5 for instructions on how to create simple button rollovers.)

✦ Using the Image Swap behavior to make an image on your Web page change when the user rolls over a separate image.

Using Advanced Export Options

In Book III, Chapter 6, we describe how to export images, but not how to export HTML or other types of files. If you're designing a Web page and you have behaviors or hotspots in your Fireworks PNG file, you will want to export HTML along with your images, because the HTML and JavaScript code make hotspots and behaviors work in Web pages.

The first step in exporting any type of file from Fireworks MX is to choose File➪Export or press Ctrl+Shift+R to bring up the Export dialog box. The Save as Type drop-down list in the Export dialog box, shown in Figure 7-1, offers access to an array of extra options:

Figure 7-1:
The Export dialog box offers different options, depending on which Save as Type option you choose.

+ **HTML and Images:** Exports HTML code as well as images.

+ **Images Only:** Exports images at your chosen optimization settings.

+ **Dreamweaver Library (.lbi):** Exports library items as well as images. (Library items are snippets of HTML code you can use in Dreamweaver MX to make site maintenance easier.)

+ **CSS Layers (.htm):** Allows you to export layers, frames, or slices as Cascading Style Sheet layers, so Fireworks MX generates both images and CSS-based HTML code. You can make pop-up menus on your pages using CSS Layers, which you can't do with HTML alone. Fireworks MX has tools that you can use to make complex pop-up menus. See your documentation for details.

+ **Director (.htm):** Exports either layers or frames as images that can be imported into Macromedia Director Shockwave Studio for use in Shockwave movies. (Director Shockwave Studio is not part of the Macromedia Studio MX suite.)

+ **Layers to Files:** Exports each layer in the current frame as a separate image file, which can be useful if you're planning to use the layers to build an animation in another application.

+ **Frames to Files:** Exports each frame as a separate image file, which can be useful if you're planning to use the frames to build an animation in another application.

+ **Lotus Domino Designer:** Exports either the top four layers, the top four frames, or the first four frames of each slice as separate files. Domino is an IBM Web application server/collaboration tool.

+ **Macromedia Flash SWF:** Exports an SWF file, which can be viewed via the Flash browser plug-in and imported into Flash MX. Macromedia Flash MX is a much more flexible authoring tool for SWFs.

✦ **Illustrator 7:** Exports either the current frame, leaving layers intact, or exports a document in which frames have been converted to layers.

✦ **Photoshop PSD:** Exports the PNG as a layered Photoshop document (PSD). You can choose to maintain editability of text layers and effects, which may result in variations in appearance between the two files, or to maintain the appearance by giving up editability of text and effects. Remember, your PNG's Web layer won't be exported.

Although you may want to export any of these types of files, in this section we focus on the HTML and Images option, which is the one that you're likely to use most often.

Readying your PNG for HTML export

If you're using Fireworks MX to generate your HTML code, chances are you have buttons in your design that you want linked to other pages on your site. Or perhaps you have one or more hotspots in your PNG, and you want those hotspots to link to other pages on your Web site. Naturally, Fireworks MX makes it easy for you to add URLs to create the hyperlinks for buttons and hotspots. All you need to do is plan ahead: You should have HTML document names for all the pages to which you want to link from your current page.

To add a URL to an existing slice in the document's Web layer (see Book III, Chapter 6 for information on creating slices), just follow these steps:

1. **Select the slice by clicking it on the canvas or in the Layers panel.**

The Property inspector is updated to show information about the selected slice.

2. **Click in the Link text field in the Property inspector.**

If you have added links to other slices, those links appear as drop-down list choices in the Link text field.

3. **Type a URL.**

If you are linking to a page on your own site and all your HTML pages are in the same folder, simply type the name of the HTML document (for example, `index.htm` or `help.htm`). You must type the name of the document exactly as it appears. (If you type `index.htm` but your home page is actually `index.html`, the link will not work.)

If you are linking to a page not on your site, include the complete URL (such as `http://catalog.dummies.com/booksanddownloads.asp`).

4. **Press Enter or click anywhere on the canvas.**

Book III
Chapter 7

Advanced
Fireworks MX Tools

To add a URL to an existing hotspot, just follow these steps:

1. **Click the hotspot on the canvas or in the Layers panel to make it active.**

   The hotspot is highlighted on the canvas and in the Layers panel.

2. **Click in the Link text field in the Property inspector.**

   If you have added links to other slices, those links will appear as drop-down list choices in the Link text field.

3. **Type a URL.**

   If you are linking to a page on your own site and all your HTML pages are in the same folder, simply type the name of the HTML document (for example, `index.htm` or `help.htm`). You must type the name of the document exactly as it appears. (If you type `index.htm` but your home page is actually `index.html`, the link will not work.)

   If you are linking to a page not on your site, include the complete URL (such as `http://catalog.dummies.com/booksanddownloads.asp`).

4. **Press Enter or click anywhere on the canvas.**

Exporting HTML with your images

If you want, you can tell Fireworks MX to generate the HTML along with the optimized images for your Web page and let that be the end of it. If you plan to make any changes to the HTML in Dreamweaver MX or another HTML editor, however, you can set some options to control the way Fireworks MX sets up tables in the HTML it generates, which can make your Web page maintenance a little easier down the line.

To export HTML and images that you plan not to update, or that you plan to update in Fireworks MX rather than Dreamweaver MX, follow these steps:

1. **Set up a folder structure for your Web site on your hard drive.**

   You should have a master folder that holds every file for your site. Inside the master folder, you may wish to put an `images` folder, which can hold all your images, keeping them separate from the HTML documents. You can have your HTML documents and image files all mixed together in the master folder, but if you have lots of images, you'll find the image files easier to locate and work with if you create a separate folder for them.

2. **Check to make sure all the right layers are visible (or not visible) in your PNG file.**

   Remember, only visible layers and objects are included in the exported image files.

3. In Fireworks MX, choose File⇨Export or press Ctrl+Shift+R.

The Export dialog box appears.

4. Navigate to the Web site's master folder.

If you haven't created a master folder for your Web site, you can create a folder by clicking the standard Windows Create New Folder icon to the right of the Save In drop-down list.

5. Type a name for your page in the File Name text field if the default is not what you want your HTML page to be named.

The default HTML file extension in the Macromedia Studio MX suite is .htm, but .html is also acceptable.

6. Select HTML and Images from the Save as Type drop-down list.

The options below this drop-down list update to reflect your choice.

7. Select Export HTML File from the HTML drop-down list.

If you select Copy to Clipboard instead of making an HTML page, Fireworks MX exports the code to a temporary location (your PC's Clipboard), from which the code can be pasted into an existing document. If you select Copy to Clipboard, you can simply open any type of text document and press Ctrl+V to paste the HTML into the file.

Export HTML File has myriad options available. See the upcoming section, "Setting the Export HTML File options," for information.

8. Select Export Slices from the Slices drop-down list.

If you haven't made slices in your PNG file but you have placed guides in the file, you can select the Slice Along Guides option, and Fireworks MX cuts up your design based on the guides.

9. Leave the Current Frame Only check box deselected unless you have multiple frames in your document, at least one of which you do not want to export.

10. Leave the Include Areas without Slices option selected unless you have a plan to deal with areas you didn't slice.

If you're using a background image, for example, or you want to use transparent spacer GIFs, you may not need images from the nonsliced areas — if there are any.

11. Select the Put Images in Subfolder check box if you want your images to be exported to a folder inside your site's master folder.

It's important to decide when you export where your images are going to live, because your HTML document will include links to the images. The links will be expressed as pathnames to the images relative to the location of the HTML document.

12. **Click the Save button.**

Setting the Export HTML File options

When you click the Options button in the Export dialog box, the HTML Setup dialog box opens, as shown in Figure 7-2. In the HTML Setup dialog box, you can view and modify the default settings that determine the structure of the exported HTML document.

Figure 7-2:
The HTML Setup dialog box opens when you click Options in the Export dialog box.

You can access settings on the three tabs in the HTML Setup dialog box:

✦ **General:** Allows you to change the default HTML style — different HTML editors have different styles of writing and displaying the code — and file extension, as well as to choose whether or not Fireworks MX should put comments in the HTML document. (*Comments* are notes in the HTML source code that typically contain information about the structure of the code, like "Left navigation starts here." Comments are not displayed by the browser.) Select the Lowercase File Name check box if you want to make the names of the HTML file and all exported images all lowercase, even if you might have named images with uppercase and lowercase letters in your PNG.

✦ **Table:** Allows you to customize the way Fireworks MX sets up tables. The default is that Fireworks MX puts a one-pixel high spacer row at the top and a one-pixel wide spacer column on the right to hold the design in place. You can choose to have Fireworks MX nest tables (put one table inside another) instead. You can also tell Fireworks MX to recreate parts of your design that lack objects as cells with background-transparent spacer GIFs in the HTML, to leave the cell empty, or put in a non-breaking space. A spacer GIF is a one-pixel by one-pixel transparent image that you can set to any height and width in your HTML to hold open an otherwise empty table cell.

✦ **Document Specific:** Allows you to customize image naming based on table structure and/or image function. For example, for slices with multiple frames, Fireworks MX appends _f2, _f3, and so on, to the file-name. If the images from Frame 2 of your PNG are buttons in their rollover state, you may prefer to have Fireworks append -o or -over to the filename.

The Set Defaults button on the Document Specific tab allows you to save any new settings you make, which is particularly useful if you like to use a specific naming convention for button rollovers and on states. When you adjust the Document Specific settings to your liking and click Set Defaults, your adjusted settings become the new default Document Specific settings.

Setting Up Image Maps and Button Rollovers

Fireworks MX writes image maps and JavaScript into the HTML code you export, provided you have hotspots (which Fireworks MX uses to make image maps) or behaviors (which Fireworks MX uses to make JavaScript) in your PNG. The following two sections outline how to set up image maps (which allow you to make several distinct hyperlinks from a single image) and complex button behaviors (which make the button image change based on a user action like rolling the mouse over the image or clicking on the image).

Fireworks MX can show slices and hotspots overlapping, but you should be careful not to overlap either. Fireworks MX will not export any part of a slice that's under another slice. (The slice on top includes the overlapped area; the slice underneath is cut off.) Likewise, whichever hotspot is on top in the Layers panel overrides the hotspot underneath.

Creating image maps with hotspots

The three hotspot tools allow you to create hotspots shaped like rectangles, circles, or polygons. You can also use the Polygon Slice tool to create a hotspot, though as a rule you should use the hotspot tools unless you are making a single, isolated hotspot. (For more information on the Polygon Slice tool, see Book III, Chapter 6.)

To create a circular or rectangular hotspot using a hotspot tool, just follow these steps:

1. **Select a hotspot tool from the Web section of the Tools panel.**

Click and hold on the Rectangle Hotspot tool for the pop-up menu containing the Circle Hotspot tool, if necessary.

2. **Click and drag the area you want to be a hotspot.**

3. **Type a URL in the Link text field in the Property inspector and press Enter.**

   You can add URLs as you make the hotspots, or you can create all of your hotspots and then select each one and add a URL in the Property inspector.

4. **Make more hotspots as needed.**

When you create hotspots using the Polygon Slice tool, you're actually making rectangular images with linked areas inside. As a result, Fireworks MX makes a separate image map for each slice. That's fine if you're only making one polygonal slice, but if you're making several adjacent hotspots, you're better off using the Polygon Hotspot tool or making your image map in Dreamweaver MX. (See Book III, Chapter 6 for information about how to use the Polygon Slice tool.)

Making a polygonal hotspot is only a little bit more involved than making a rectangular or circular hotspot. To make a polygonal hotspot, just follow these steps:

1. **Select the Polygon Hotspot tool from the Web section of the Tools panel.**

   Click and hold on the Rectangle Hotspot tool for the pop-up menu containing the Polygon Hotspot tool.

2. **Click on the canvas to establish the first point of your polygon.**

3. **Click on a second point.**

   Fireworks MX draws a line connecting the points.

4. **Continue to click until you have drawn the shape you want.**

   You don't need to click again on the first point to close the shape. Be aware that the more points you make, the more code is required to reproduce your hotspot as an image map, so you may want to avoid making hotspots that have more than six or seven points. Note how the polygonal hotspot for the bowling pin in Figure 7-3 sacrifices perfect coverage of the pin to make a simpler shape, which means less code.

5. **Type a URL in the Link text field in the Property inspector and press Enter.**

   You can add URLs as you make the hotspots, or you can create all of your hotspots and then select each one and add a URL in the Property inspector.

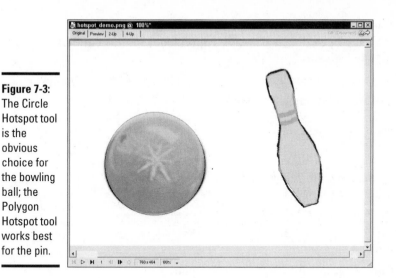

Figure 7-3:
The Circle Hotspot tool is the obvious choice for the bowling ball; the Polygon Hotspot tool works best for the pin.

6. **Click the Polygon hotspot tool and then deselect the last hotspot you made by using the key command Ctrl+D or choosing Select⇔Deselect.**

Deselecting ensures that you won't inadvertently add an extra point to your Polygon hotspot.

When it comes time to export your images, you need to export HTML as well as images in order to get the image map that Fireworks MX makes from your hotspots. See "Exporting HTML with your images," earlier in this chapter, for more details.

Dreamweaver MX has its own tool for creating hotspots and image maps. You can also use that tool to edit hotspots and image maps generated by Fireworks MX. See Book II, Chapter 7 for more details.

Creating advanced button rollovers

In Book III, Chapter 5, we discuss how to use frames in conjunction with text and drawing tools to make the images for a simple button rollover, which provides all the information you need if you plan to use Dreamweaver MX to generate the rollover code.

If you want to export the rollover code for a two-state button (normal and rollover/highlight) from Fireworks MX, you need to add a behavior to the slice by taking these steps:

1. **Right-click the slice for which you want to create rollover code, or click the behavior handle (the round icon) in the center of the selected slice.**

A contextual menu appears.

2. **Choose Add Simple Rollover.**

A second way to add rollover behavior to a button is to use the Behavior panel:

1. **If the Behavior panel is not currently open, choose Window⊅Behaviors or use the keyboard shortcut Shift+F3.**

2. **Click the Add Behavior (+) button at the top left of the Behaviors panel.**

A menu appears.

3. **Choose Simple Rollover from the menu.**

You have set up a behavior that swaps the image in Frame 1 with the image in Frame 2 when a user rolls a cursor over the button on your Web page. The behavior also swaps the image back when the user moves the cursor off the button.

If you want to check out your rollover in action without building your Web page, click the Preview tab at the top of the canvas and move your cursor over the slice.

If you want to include a down state for your button, and you have a third frame in your PNG with the image for an additional button state, follow the preceding steps to add a rollover state and then do the following:

1. **Click the Add Behavior button at the top left of the Behaviors panel.**

A menu appears.

2. **Choose Set Nav Bar Image from the menu.**

The Set Nav Bar Image window appears.

3. **Click OK.**

Now, when a user clicks the mouse on the button in your exported HMTL, the button will change from the rollover state to the down state.

Figure 7-4 shows what the Behaviors panel looks like after you add the Simple Rollover and Set Nav Bar Image behaviors.

Figure 7-4:
Use the Add
Behavior
button to
add a
behavior
and use the
minus
button to
remove a
behavior
from a slice.

If the three-state button is linking to another page, adding a down state doesn't give you much bang for your buck because the linked page may appear in the browser window before the user even has a chance to notice that the button changed.

You may want to include an over-while-down state for your button (sort of an extra rollover) if you are using the down state of the button to indicate the current page. If so, make sure you have a fourth frame with the image for an extra button state, add the Rollover and Set Nav Bar Image behaviors as discussed previously, and then do the following:

1. **Double-click the Set Nav Bar Image line in the Behaviors panel.**

   The Set Nav Bar Image dialog box appears.

2. **Select the Include Over While Down State (Frame 4) check box.**

   If the button is for the current page, select the Show Down Image Upon Load check box as well.

3. **Click OK.**

Bringing Interactivity to Your Pages with Behaviors

Fireworks MX can generate JavaScript that does more than merely change the state of a button. For instance, you can set a behavior that swaps one image for another image elsewhere on the page when you roll over a button or hotspot. You can also use Fireworks MX to generate pop-up menus.

The Swap Images behavior

A button rollover is an image swap — you swap the image for one button state with the image for another state. But you can roll over a button and have an image other than the button image swap. If you want the image swap and page download to be pretty quick, you should limit the number of images to be swapped and limit the file size of each swapped image.

To add the Swap Image behavior to a trigger slice and target slice, create the frames, images, and slices, and then follow these steps:

1. **Click the slice that you want to use to trigger the image swap.**

You can click the slice either on the canvas or in the Layers panel.

2. **Click the Add Behavior (+) button at the top left of the Behaviors panel.**

A menu appears.

3. **Choose Swap Image.**

The Swap Image dialog box, shown in Figure 7-5, appears.

Figure 7-5:
The Swap Image dialog box allows you to choose the swapped image by name or position on the page.

4. **Select the targeted slice by clicking its name (in the box on the left) or by clicking its representation (in the box on the right).**

When you click in either box, both boxes update to show your selection.

5. **Using the Frame No. drop-down list, select the frame number the rollover should trigger.**

The drop-down list shows all the frames in your PNG file.

You can also select the Image File radio button and navigate to an existing image file outside your PNG to swap in. Be aware, though, that for the rollover to work correctly in all browsers, the default target image and swapped target image must be the same height and width.

6. **Leave the Preload Images and Restore Image onMouseOut check boxes selected.**

Preloading the swapped image ensures there won't be a delay the first time the user rolls over the button that triggers the swap. The trade-off is that the Web page takes longer to load initially.

Restoring the image to default prevents the swapped image from "sticking." If you want the swapped image to remain in place until the user rolls over another button, deselect the Restore Image onMouseOut check box.

7. **Click OK.**

A line on the canvas from the center of the trigger slice to the target slice shows that one slice triggers a behavior in the other, as shown in Figure 7-6.

Figure 7-6:
A line from the behavior handle of the trigger slice connects to the target slice.

You can have multiple buttons trigger a rollover in the same slice, and you can have a single button trigger rollovers in multiple slices. Of course, the more big rollovers you have on the page, the longer the page takes to load. On the other hand, rollovers provide useful feedback (and instant gratification) to the user, and Fireworks MX makes producing them a snap.

Generating pop-up menus

Pop-up menus are a great way to cram a lot of navigation into a small space because they only appear when a user rolls over a button or hotspot.

Fireworks MX allows you to specify many of the parameters of the menus' appearance. To start with, you can choose whether the links in your pop-up menus are made of text or images. In a nutshell, that choice boils down to this:

✦ **Linked text:** This option ensures faster download but less control over the appearance of the text, because the text is HMTL.

✦ **Linked images:** This option makes for a slower download but gives you more control over the appearance of the text, because the text is graphic.

You can also customize the position of the menu relative to the slice that triggers it, the color of the text and cell background for both normal and rollover states, and more. In fact, there are so many options, we can't cover them all here! After you've got the basics, though, you'll be poised to explore all the options, if you so desire.

To make a basic one-level pop-up menu with linked text, follow these steps:

1. **Select a slice by clicking it on the canvas or in the Layers panel.**

2. **Click the Add Behavior (+) button at the top left of the Behaviors panel.**

A pop-up menu appears.

3. **Choose Set Pop-up Menu from the Add Behaviors pop-up menu.**

The Pop-up Menu Editor, shown in Figure 7-7, appears, with the Content tab active by default.

4. **Click under the Text column of the Pop-up Menu Editor and type the text as you would like it to appear in your menu.**

Figure 7-7:
The Content tab of the Pop-up Menu Editor, with a few items added.

5. **Press Tab or click under the Link column of the Pop-up Menu Editor, and type or select the URL or filename for the page you want your text to link to.**

   If you have any existing links already on your page, they appear in a drop-down list in the Link column.

6. **If you want the link to open in a new window or different frameset, tab over to or click in the Target column to set the target for the link.**

   If you simply want the linked page to open in the user's current browser window, leave this column blank, as shown in Figure 7-7. For information on other Target options, see the discussion of links in Book II, Chapter 2, or the discussion of framesets in Book II, Chapter 6.

7. **Repeat Steps 4 through 6 for each item in your menu.**

   You can add rows to the list of menu items by clicking the Add Menu button.

8. **Click the Next button at the bottom of the Pop-up Menu Editor.**

   The Appearance tab becomes active.

9. **Leave the Cells: selection at the default of HTML.**

   If you want to use images instead of HTML text, you need to click the Image button. Each navigation item is in its own table cell.

10. **Select Vertical Menu or Horizontal Menu from the drop-down list.**

11. **Select the Font face, size, style, and alignment.**

    Of course, this isn't necessary if you're using graphics rather than HTML text.

12. **Select the Text color and Cell background color for the Up (normal) state.**

    If you don't want to use the defaults, click on the color boxes to view the color palette. At the bottom of the dialog box, you can see a preview of your menu, as shown in Figure 7-8.

13. **Select the Text color and Cell background color for the Over (rollover) state.**

    If you don't want to use the defaults, click on the color boxes to view the color palette. At the bottom of the dialog box, you can see a preview of your menu.

14. **Click the Next button at the bottom of the Pop-up Menu Editor.**

    The Advanced tab becomes active.

15. **Adjust any of the parameters in the Advanced tab as needed.**

Figure 7-8:
The preview shows what the menu will look like after you change each parameter.

All these settings can be previewed at the bottom of the dialog box, except Menu Delay:

- **Cell Width and Cell Height:** By default, Fireworks MX sets the Cell Width and Cell Height automatically, based on the content, but you can select Pixels from the drop-down list and type in a custom width and/or height.

- **Cell Padding and Cell Spacing:** Cell Padding is the space between the edges of the cells and the text within the cells. The default Cell Padding setting is 3. Cell Spacing is the space between the edge of one cell and the edge of an adjacent cell. The default Cell Spacing setting is 0.

- **Text Indent:** Text Indent is the number of pixels from the left (in a vertical menu) or from the top (in a horizontal menu) to the text, not including the gaps introduced by cell padding and cell spacing. The default Text Indent setting is 0.

- **Menu Delay:** Menu Delay is the amount of time your menu stays on-screen after the user's mouse rolls off the menu. It is adjusted in milliseconds (ms), or thousandths of a second. The default, 1000 ms, is one second.

- **Border:** The border of your pop-up menu can be turned on or off, and the colors that make up the border are customizable.

16. **Click the Next button at the bottom of the Pop-up Menu Editor.**

The Position tab becomes active.

17. **Click a Menu Position icon.**

The X and Y coordinates, which represent the top left corner of the menu relative to the slice, update. You can type your own values for the X and Y coordinates if you want to customize them.

18. **Click Done.**

The Preview pane that you access at the top of your canvas does not allow you to see the pop-up menu in action. In order to preview your pop-up menu in action, you must choose File⇨Preview in Browser or use the key command F12. Any Web browser installed on your computer can be used to preview your menu, as long as you have JavaScript enabled on that browser.

Pop-up menus are a tricky business, and their appearance can vary in different browsers. Be sure to test all your target browsers to make sure they display the menus acceptably.

When you make a slice active that has a pop-up menu behavior attached, an outline shows on the canvas in Fireworks MX where the pop-up menu will appear when the user rolls over the slice.

To edit the pop-up menu, click the behavior handle (the round icon in the middle of the slice) and choose Edit Pop-up Menu, or double-click the Behavior in the Behaviors panel.

Chapter 8: Integrating Fireworks MX with Other Macromedia Products

In This Chapter

✔ **Integrating Fireworks MX with Macromedia Flash MX**

✔ **Integrating Fireworks MX with Dreamweaver MX**

✔ **Integrating Fireworks MX with FreeHand 10**

✔ **Integrating Fireworks MX with Director Shockwave Studio**

*W*ith the release of the Macromedia Studio MX suite, Macromedia has brought Fireworks MX, Macromedia Flash MX, Dreamweaver MX, ColdFusion MX, and FreeHand 10 closer together than ever before. Fireworks MX and ColdFusion MX don't really work together, but the rest of the applications in the suite have complementary, and in some cases, even overlapping capabilities.

We explore some of those capabilities in the next few pages but start by pointing out one of the new features you'll find in Fireworks MX: the Quick Export button, shown at the upper-right corner of the canvas in Figure 8-1.

Figure 8-1: In Fireworks MX, the Quick Export button is a small Fireworks MX icon with an arrow at the right.

— Quick Export button

When you click the Quick Export button, a contextual menu appears (see Figure 8-2) that offers one-click access to the following:

+ **Dreamweaver MX:** Export HTML, Update HTML, Copy HTML to Clipboard, and Launch Dreamweaver

+ **Macromedia Flash MX:** Export SWF, Copy, and Launch Flash

+ **FreeHand 10:** Export to FreeHand, Copy Path Outlines, and Launch FreeHand

+ **Director:** Source as Layers, Source as Slices, and Launch Director

+ **Preview in Browser:** View in Primary Browser, View in Secondary Browser, and Set Primary and Secondary Browser

+ **Export to:** Photoshop, GoLive, FrontPage, and Illustrator

The Quick Export button may include additional options, depending on what exports you may have done previously from your Fireworks PNG file.

Figure 8-2:
The Quick Export button gives you one-click access to several options.

When you export using the Quick Export button, you may use defaults, but you also have access to all the regular options available from the Export dialog box. See Book III, Chapter 7 for information on advanced export options.

Integrating Fireworks MX with Macromedia Flash MX

You can open, edit, and export animated GIFs in both Macromedia Flash MX and Fireworks MX. If you're creating an animated GIF only as an alternative to an SWF (for users who come to your Web page who don't have the Flash plug-in), you'll want to use Macromedia Flash MX to generate the GIF and SWF (Shockwave Flash) animations. Macromedia Flash MX was built as a powerful animation program, which means that it offers more flexibility, more sophisticated animation tools, and more advanced export options for animations than Fireworks MX.

Exporting files from Fireworks MX to Macromedia Flash MX

Sometimes all the sophistication and flexibility that Macromedia Flash MX provides is more than you want or need. You may find Fireworks MX a more congenial environment for creating or editing simple, silent, non-interactive animations for the Web, whether as animated GIFs or SWFs.

Fireworks MX can export SWFs, but behaviors won't be exported from Fireworks MX with the SWF. Nor will masks, live effects, some text formatting, and numerous other features of your PNG. If you want to work with elements of your PNG in Macromedia Flash MX, you don't need to export it — you can simply import it into Macromedia Flash MX. (See Book V, Chapter 10 for details on the advantages of and restrictions on importing Fireworks MX PNGs.)

Nevertheless, if you want to export a simple SWF animation from Fireworks MX, it's a snap. Just follow these steps:

1. **Choose File⇨Export, or use the key command Ctrl+Shift+R.**

The Export dialog box appears.

2. **Change the filename from the default, if necessary.**

3. **Select Macromedia Flash SWF from the drop-down list.**

4. **Click the Options button if you plan to import the file into Macromedia Flash MX for editing; otherwise, click OK.**

The Options button gives you control over objects, text, JPEG quality, frame rate, and which frames to export:

- **Objects:** Choose Maintain Paths if you want vector shapes to be editable, but you don't mind if their appearance shifts a little. Choose Maintain Appearance if you want the shapes to look identical, but you don't need to edit them within Macromedia Flash MX.

- **Text:** Choose Maintain Editability if you want to be able to change the text after the SWF has been imported into Macromedia Flash MX. Choose Convert to Paths if you want the text to appear the same in Macromedia Flash MX and don't plan to edit it.

**Book III
Chapter 8**

**Integrating
Fireworks MX with
Other Macromedia
Products**

- **JPEG Quality:** Type a number between 1 and 100 or use the slider to select a number to set the optimization for JPEGs. For more information on setting JPEG Quality, see Book III, Chapter 6.

- **Frames:** Choose All if you want all the frames in your PNG to be in the exported SWF. If you want only a select series of frames to be exported, choose From, and in the text fields, type the number of the first and last frame in the PNG that you want in the SWF.

- **Frame Rate:** Type the number of frames per second at which you want your exported SWF to run.

Of course, you can also click the Quick Export button and choose Macromedia Flash⇨Export SWF, as shown in Figure 8-3.

Figure 8-3:
Taking the Quick Export shortcut to export a multiple-frame PNG as an SWF is easy.

You can't import or open SWFs in Fireworks MX, but what you *can* do with SWFs (in Macromedia Flash MX) is a little mind-boggling: You can create panels and commands for Fireworks MX. In fact, the Align panel is an SWF and the Document Driven Graphics Wizard is also an SWF created in Macromedia Flash MX. For more information on commands, check out the "Extending Fireworks MX" PDF on the Macromedia Studio MX installation CD or browse to www.macromedia.com/support/fireworks.

Importing files into Macromedia Flash MX from Fireworks MX

If you want to design a Macromedia Flash MX-based Web page, you can do so in Fireworks MX, but you'll need to import the PNG into Macromedia Flash MX and create the interactivity in Macromedia Flash MX.

Macromedia Flash MX can import PNG files, either as flattened files (with or without *alpha transparencies,* which are transparent or semi-transparent areas) or as sets of editable Library items. Macromedia Flash MX can't import slice information, Live Effects, or JavaScript behaviors, but it can preserve different button states on their respective separate frames. For more information on what Macromedia Flash MX can and cannot import in a PNG, see Book V, Chapter 10.

And of course, Macromedia Flash MX can import JPEGs and regular GIFs, so you can export those formats from Fireworks MX for easy import into Macromedia Flash MX.

Macromedia Flash MX cannot dynamically load progressive JPEGs. See Book III, Chapter 6 for information on progressive JPEGs.

Macromedia Flash MX can import SWFs that were created in and exported from Fireworks MX, but keep in mind that many benefits of SWFs are not available in SWFs exported from Fireworks MX. (See the section "Exporting files from Fireworks MX to Macromedia Flash MX.") If you want interactivity in your SWF, you're better off designing objects in Fireworks MX (or FreeHand 10) and then importing the Fireworks MX PNG (or FH10 file) into Macromedia Flash MX. Of course, you also have the option to author the movie using only Macromedia Flash MX.

Integrating Fireworks MX with Dreamweaver MX

**Book III
Chapter 8**

**Integrating
Fireworks MX with
Other Macromedia
Products**

Fireworks MX is a Web design tool and Dreamweaver MX is an HTML editor (XML editor, ColdFusion editor, and so on). The two programs have overlapping capabilities, and they have complementary capabilities. Not only that, but they're designed to work together to make Web page creation and modification a breeze.

Basically, if you generate your HTML in Fireworks MX and edit the code in Dreamweaver MX, Fireworks MX recognizes the changes you make in the other application. That goes for links, image maps, behaviors shared by both programs, and HTML text. Macromedia coined the term *Roundtrip HTML* to describe the way the two programs work together.

Setting preferences

You need to establish a few settings, both in Dreamweaver MX and in Fireworks MX, to work with Roundtrip HTML. In Dreamweaver MX, you need to define a local site (see Book II, Chapter 3) and make Fireworks MX your primary image-editing application (see Book II, Chapter 7).

In Fireworks MX, you should set a few preferences. Just follow these steps:

1. **Choose Edit⇨Preferences or use the key command Ctrl+U.**

The Preferences dialog box appears.

2. **Click the Launch and Edit tab to make it active.**

   You use the two drop-down lists for specifying the treatment of Fireworks MX source files: When Editing from External Application and When Optimizing from External Application.

3. **Select one of the three options from the When Editing from External Application drop-down list.**

   - **Always Use Source PNG:** This option means that when you launch Fireworks MX from within another application, the original PNG source file for the Web page or table will open in Fireworks MX.

   - **Never Use Source PNG:** If you select this option, when you launch Fireworks MX from within another application, the exported GIF or JPEG you select will open in Fireworks MX.

     JPEG is a lossy format, so if possible, you'll want to edit the image from the original source file. For more information about lossy compression, see Book III, Chapter 6.

   - **Ask When Launching:** Choosing this option means that every time you launch Fireworks MX from within another application, you will be prompted to specify whether you want to edit the PNG source file or the exported optimized image.

4. **Select one of the three options from the When Optimizing from External Application drop-down list.**

   The options are identical to those in the When Editing from External Application drop-down list.

5. **Click OK.**

Editing PNGs

When you're editing your HTML in Dreamweaver MX, you may find that it's not working quite the way you wanted it to. You may add text to one cell and find that it creates a misalignment of an image in the adjacent cell in the table that makes up your page. Perhaps you need to slice an image differently. In cases like these, you'll want to edit your PNG source file, instead of making massive changes in Dreamweaver MX that can make your PNG source file out of sync with the HTML page it represents. Luckily, you can launch and edit your Fireworks MX PNG source file from within Dreamweaver MX by following these steps:

1. **Click the optimized image in the Dreamweaver MX document window.**

   The Property inspector updates to display image parameters.

2. **Click the Fireworks Edit button in the Property inspector, as shown in Figure 8-4, or right-click the optimized image and choose Edit with Fireworks from the contextual menu that appears.**

   If Dreamweaver MX cannot locate the PNG automatically, the Find Source dialog box appears. Click Yes, because you want to locate the PNG source file for the image you selected for editing. Navigate to the source file in the Open dialog box and either double-click the PNG file's icon or click the file's icon and click Open. The source PNG file opens in Fireworks MX. At the top of the canvas, the words "Editing from Dreamweaver" show that Roundtrip HTML is in effect.

3. **Edit the image and/or slice as needed.**

4. **Adjust any Optimization settings if necessary.**

   See Book III, Chapter 6 for information about optimizing images.

   The new version of the image will be exported at the new settings you specify or at the previous settings if you opt not to change them.

5. **Click the Done button at the top left of the canvas.**

   The Fireworks MX window closes, and the new image is visible in the Document window in Dreamweaver MX.

Figure 8-4:
The Dream-
weaver MX
Property
inspector
for an image
includes an
Edit with
Fireworks
button.

Book III
Chapter 8

Integrating
Fireworks MX with
Other Macromedia
Products

Working with tables

When you export HTML from Fireworks MX, you export code that tells a browser where each slice goes by establishing a table with cells arranged in rows and columns to correspond with your slices. If you want to take advantage of Roundtrip HTML, make sure your Export settings include Dreamweaver HTML as the HTML Style (see Book III, Chapter 7 for details). If you want to make major changes to the table structure after you start editing the HTML in Dreamweaver MX, whether or not that requires reslicing images, you should launch from Dreamweaver MX and edit the table in your Fireworks MX PNG source file:

1. **Select the table in Dreamweaver MX.**

   The Property inspector updates to display the parameters of the table.

2. **Click the Fireworks Edit button in the Property inspector.**

   If need be, you can navigate to the source PNG file from within the Dreamweaver MX Property inspector by clicking the File icon next to the Edit button. The source file opens in Fireworks MX.

3. **Make edits to the slices, guides, and images as necessary.**

   You can even edit the HTML in text slices if you wish.

4. **Click the Done button (to the left of the Editing from Dreamweaver icon at the top of the canvas) when you are finished editing.**

   The Fireworks MX window closes, and Dreamweaver MX updates the table and images.

If you have made substantial changes to table structures in Dreamweaver MX, though, Fireworks MX may not recognize the code. In that case, when you launch and edit the table in Fireworks MX, Fireworks MX will overwrite the changes you made in Dreamweaver MX. A prompt notifies you when Fireworks MX will overwrite the existing Dreamweaver MX edits.

What if you accidentally delete the PNG source file, or you don't have a copy of it in the first place? A feature new to Fireworks MX called Reconstitute Table can save the day. Fireworks MX can make an existing HTML table with image slices into an editable PNG — as long as no tables are nested in the table you want to reconstitute — and can even import behaviors and pop-up menus created in Fireworks MX or Dreamweaver MX. If you have multiple, non-nested tables on the page (tables stacked one on top of the other, for example), Fireworks MX opens a PNG for each table.

To create new PNGs from an HTML file with multiple, non-nested tables, follow these steps:

1. **Choose File⇨Reconstitute Table.**

   The Open dialog box appears.

2. **Navigate to the HTML file and double-click to open it or select the file and then click Open.**

   Each non-nested table in the HTML opens in its own window, with slices named and in place, and rollover behaviors attached.

To create a new PNG from the first table in an HTML file that has multiple tables, follow these steps:

1. **Choose File⇨Open.**

The Open dialog box appears.

2. **Navigate to the HTML file and double-click to open it or select the file and then click Open.**

   The first table in the file opens in Fireworks MX, with slices named and in place, and rollover behaviors attached.

To add the first table in an HTML file with multiple tables to an existing PNG, follow these steps:

1. **Choose File⇨Import.**

   The Open dialog box appears.

2. **Navigate to the HTML file and double-click it or select the file and click Open.**

   The insert pointer appears when you place the cursor over the canvas.

3. **Place the pointer at the top left corner of where you want the imported table to go and click.**

   The table — slices, images, JavaScript, and all — appears. Objects are spread in layers based on table structure.

You can also import XHTML and UTF-8 encoded files. (See the Using Fireworks MX PDF on your Macromedia Studio MX installation disk for details.) After you export the reconstituted table from Fireworks MX, you can take advantage of Roundtrip HTML from that point on.

**Book III
Chapter 8**

**Integrating
Fireworks MX with
Other Macromedia
Products**

Integrating Fireworks MX with FreeHand 10

FreeHand 10 is a vector graphics application, so it shares many capabilities with Fireworks MX. The main difference between the programs is that FreeHand 10 is made to be used primarily for print design (and as such has more extensive drawing capabilities) and Fireworks MX is made to be used primarily for Web page design.

Print and Web design jobs use different color modes:

✦ **CMYK:** Offset printing, the four-color process used to create most mass-produced printed materials, utilizes the color mode CMYK (*C*yan, *M*agenta, *Y*ellow, and blac*K*).

✦ **RGB:** Though some Web graphics may be made using the Grayscale or other modes, by and large graphic production for the Web uses the RGB (*R*ed, *G*reen, *B*lue) mode, because RGB is the mode used for computer monitors.

Changing an image from one mode to another requires a *conversion* process. If you have designed a page in Fireworks MX but want to repurpose the design for a print piece, you should import it into FreeHand 10 to perform the conversion from RGB to CMYK. Some colors may shift slightly, because the two modes do not share all colors. For more information, see Book IV, Chapter 6.

Despite the differences in color mode for print and Web design jobs, document portability between FreeHand 10 and Fireworks MX is pretty seamless. You can open FreeHand 10 files (.fh10) in Fireworks MX and Fireworks MX PNGs in FreeHand 10. Some features of Fireworks MX PNGs may not be available or translate to FreeHand 10, and some FreeHand 10 options and settings may not be available when you open an FH10 document in Fireworks MX, including Live Effects and slices. (See the Fireworks MX Help files for a complete list.)

Importing FreeHand 10 files into Fireworks MX

To import a FreeHand 10 file (or any FreeHand file from version 7 or later) into Fireworks MX, follow these steps:

1. **Choose File⇨Import or use the key command Ctrl+R.**

   The Import dialog box appears.

2. **Navigate to the FreeHand 10 file and double-click it or select it and then click the Import button.**

   The Vector File Options dialog box, shown in Figure 8-5, appears.

Figure 8-5:
The Vector File Options dialog box allows you to set various options when you import a FreeHand file into Fireworks MX.

3. **Adjust any settings that you wish to change from the file-specific defaults:**

- **Scale:** Scale sets the scale of the imported file using a percentage. If you change the scale, the width and height change automatically to reflect the scaling percentage. Bitmap objects are not affected by this setting.

- **Width and Height:** You can set the width and height of the imported file by typing numbers in the text fields and selecting pixels, inches, or centimeters from the drop-down lists.

- **Resolution:** Standard screen resolution is 72 dpi (pixels/inch). If the file you're importing is at another resolution, you may want to import it at the standard screen resolution, because files at print resolution tend to be bigger and slower, and the final resolution of your Web images will be 72 dpi.

- **Paths and Text:** Select the check boxes for paths and text if you want them to be anti-aliased (for smoothed edges) on import, and select Crisp, Strong, or Smooth from the drop-down list to control the anti-aliasing. You can change these settings later from the Property inspector.

  You can use the File Conversion settings to control how Fireworks MX imports multi-page documents.

- **Include Invisible Layers:** By default, layers that are turned off in FreeHand 10 do not get imported. Select the Include Invisible Layers check box if you want to import objects on layers that are turned off.

- **Include Background Layers:** Select the Include Background Layers check box if you want the objects on the background layer of the FreeHand 10 file to be imported into Fireworks MX.

  The Render as Images settings allow you to convert complicated shapes and fills to bitmaps.

4. **Click OK.**

The Vector File Options dialog box closes and the pointer changes to the right-angled Insert cursor when you place it over the canvas.

5. **Put the cursor where you want the top-left corner of the imported file to go and click.**

The imported files objects are placed in the current frame of the Fireworks MX document.

Book III
Chapter 8

**Integrating
Fireworks MX with
Other Macromedia
Products**

If you don't want to import the whole FreeHand 10 file, you have a couple options. If you have enough room on your monitor to have Fireworks MX and FreeHand 10 open side-by-side, you can drag and drop shapes and bitmaps from one application to the other.

Alternatively, you can copy and paste vectors and bitmaps from one application to the other. To copy and paste a vector object from Fireworks MX to FreeHand, just follow these steps:

1. **Select a vector shape in Fireworks MX by clicking it on the canvas or in the Layers panel.**

2. **Choose Edit⇨Copy or use the keyboard shortcut Ctrl+C.**

   If you want to copy only the outline of the shape, you can use the Fireworks MX command Copy Path Outlines from the Edit menu or from the Quick Export button.

3. **Paste the shape into an open FreeHand 10 document by choosing Edit⇨Paste from the FreeHand 10 menu or using the key command Ctrl+V.**

   Your vector shape, including outline and fill information, appears in the FreeHand document.

When you copy and paste or drag a vector shape with a FreeHand 10 pattern fill into Fireworks MX, where the pattern fill is not available, the fill will be lost.

Exporting Fireworks MX files into FreeHand 10

To export a Fireworks MX vector graphic file for use in FreeHand 10, follow these steps:

1. **Choose File⇨Export, use the key command Ctrl+Shift+R, or click the Quick Export button and choose FreeHand⇨Export to FreeHand.**

   The Export dialog box appears.

2. **Navigate to the folder where you'd like the exported file to go.**

3. **Name the file, if necessary.**

   You don't need to include an extension in the name; Fireworks MX will add the extension automatically, based on the type of file you choose to export.

4. **Select Illustrator 7 from the Save as Type drop-down list.**

   Illustrator 7 is a vector-based page layout application much like FreeHand 10. The Illustrator 7 format can be read by many vector-based design programs, including FreeHand 10.

5. **Click Options to change any Illustrator 7 export parameters from their defaults as necessary:**

    - Choose either Export Current Frame Only (if you want to export only one frame from your PNG and preserve the layer names in FreeHand) or Convert Frames to Layers (if you want all the frames of the PNG to appear as layers in your FreeHand file).

    - You want to leave the FreeHand Compatible check box selected, of course.

6. **Click OK.**

    The Illustrator Export Options dialog box closes.

7. **Click the Save button in the Export dialog box.**

Integrating Fireworks MX with Director Shockwave Studio

The MX version of Director Shockwave Studio (Macromedia's flagship multimedia authoring application) wasn't released with the original Macromedia Studio MX suite, but Fireworks MX and Director Shockwave Studio 8 can work together nicely if, for example, you want to edit a Director Shockwave Studio bitmap cast member using the capabilities of Fireworks MX. (In Director Shockwave Studio, objects such as bitmaps, shapes, and text are referred to as cast members.) Macromedia's Web site gives you access to a Fireworks Import Xtra, which you need to download and install if you are working with Director Shockwave Studio version 8 or earlier.

You can use Fireworks MX to create GIFs, JPEGs, 32-bit PNGs (with or without transparencies), and HTML (with interactive and/or animated content), all of which can be imported into Director Shockwave Studio.

The Quick Export button allow you easy access to two export modes in Director Shockwave Studio:

- ✔ **Source as Layers:** This mode exports each layer. You should use this mode for layered PNG files or animations.

- ✔ **Source as Slices:** This mode exports slices and behaviors in the form of optimized images and HTML with JavaScript. You should use this mode for rollover buttons or other interactive content.

The Trim Images selected box is selected by default when you export to Director Shockwave Studio. The Trim Images option is available in the Export window for both modes and crops each layer or frame to remove space outside the objects in each layer or frame. In other words, if your canvas is 800 x 600 pixels, and you have an animation that uses only 25 percent of the canvas, Trim Images will crop the extra 75 percent out of each layer it exports.

You can also launch Fireworks MX from within Director Shockwave Studio to edit and optimize cast members. To do so, you want first to set Fireworks MX as your external image-editor by choosing File⇨Preferences⇨Editors from within Director Shockwave Studio and selecting Fireworks MX for bitmap graphics.

Book III
Chapter 8

Integrating
Fireworks MX with
Other Macromedia
Products

Book IV

FreeHand 10

The 5th Wave   By Rich Tennant

Contents at a Glance

Chapter 1: Introduction to FreeHand 10

In This Chapter

✔ **Introducing FreeHand 10**

✔ **Appreciating vector graphics**

✔ **Navigating the interface**

✔ **Introducing the drawing tools**

*W*hen you installed Macromedia Studio MX on your computer and saw the FreeHand 10 icon on your Start menu, you may have been less than impressed. After all, everything else is an MX version, which sounds like some hot turbocharged Italian sports car, and this puppy's only version 10. If that's an issue with you, fear not intrepid graphic illustrator, because FreeHand 10 is packed full of features that you can use to create graphics for print and for the Web. You use FreeHand 10 to create vector-based illustrations. And if you're in the mood, or your client — you know, those people who pay the bills — requests it, you can include bitmap images in your document. With FreeHand 10, you can create your own vector images, add text to the file, and then save the document for future editing in one of the native FreeHand 10 formats, or export the document for use in another program.

In this chapter, you get to know FreeHand 10 up close and personal. We show you what you can do with FreeHand 10 and give you a tour of the interface. In reading this chapter, you gain an appreciation for the drawing tools that you use to create vector objects. We also show you how to come to grips with those pesky inspectors and panels that are lurking about the interface just waiting for you to try your hand at FreeHand 10.

Introducing FreeHand 10

First and foremost, FreeHand 10 is an illustration program. You use FreeHand 10 to create illustrations for use in a variety of applications. FreeHand 10 has sophisticated drawing tools that you use to create shapes for your illustration. The shapes range from ho-hum circles and rectangles to sophisticated shapes that you create with the Pencil tool. You can specify the color of the shape (known as a *fill*) and whether the shape has an outline (known in FreeHand-speak as a *stroke*).

The shapes you create with the drawing tools are vector-based. What? You say you don't know what a vector is, Victor? Well, if you have to know right now, you can fast-forward to the section, "Understanding the Role of Vector Graphics."

You combine the shapes you create with text objects, and if your design requires, you can add a photograph to the illustration. Photo-realistic images are also known as bitmaps, which you should not confuse with the Windows-only BMP image format, which also goes by the name of bitmap.

When you have many objects in a document, it can be hard to select individual shapes. And sometimes you've got so many objects, it's hard to see the vectors for the bitmaps or text objects. The designers of FreeHand 10 give you an easy way to segregate a busy document: layers. When you select a layer, you can add objects to the layer and then arrange them just the way you want. When you've got it just right, you can lock the layer and begin working on another layer. No matter what you do on the new layer, you can't inadvertently mess up your locked layer — until you unlock it, that is.

Prior versions of FreeHand allowed you to create documents with vector objects and bitmaps for print. With FreeHand 10, you have increased support for creating objects for the Web. You can export your document, or just selected objects from your document, in a wide variety of formats. And if it has been a long day and you've had all the FreeHand 10 you can handle, you can save the document in FreeHand 10's native FH10 format for another day's work. When you save a document in FreeHand 10's native format, you can edit all objects in the document and, if needed, add more or delete existing objects.

Using Illustration Tools for the Web

When you have a program with as much power as FreeHand 10, you can create documents for Web pages. The sophisticated drawing tools in FreeHand 10 make it possible for you to create the basis for Web page buttons that you can add to a document you're creating in Dreamweaver MX, or for that matter, buttons for a Flash movie. You can assign links to the buttons. When you're finished with the document, you can export selected objects, or an entire document, in Web-friendly image formats.

The illustration tools in FreeHand 10 also make it possible for you to create artsy-fartsy interfaces for your Flash movies and banners for your Web pages. If you create FreeHand documents with multiple pages, you can also export the whole thing as a Macromedia Flash SWF movie.

Understanding the Role of Vector Graphics

Vector objects are comprised of lines and curves that are redrawn mathematically, which results in a small file size. Vector-based graphics are resolution-independent, which means you can increase their size without losing image fidelity. By contrast, bitmaps cannot be enlarged without losing fidelity. Figure 1-1 shows an enlarged vector object alongside an enlarged bitmap.

Vector object   Bitmap

Figure 1-1: Bitmaps become grainy when enlarged (right), but vector objects remain razor sharp when enlarged (left).

When you create a vector object, you have point-by-point control over the shape of the object. Vector objects have straight points and curve points. You can specify which type of point is created when you create free-form shapes with the Pencil tool. When you use the shape tools, the point type is predetermined, but you can change them in a heartbeat. A curve point has handles that you can click and drag to modify the shape. Figure 1-2 shows a vector object with straight and curve points.

Book IV
Chapter 1

Introduction to
FreeHand 10

Curve points

Straight point

Figure 1-2:
You define
the shape of
a vector
object by
modifying
the points.

Investigating the FreeHand 10 Interface

The FreeHand 10 interface has many components. When you launch
FreeHand 10 and create a new document, you get an interface with a document window, a toolbar docked on the side of the interface, a status bar
(Windows only) at the bottom of the interface, and some panels and inspectors tastefully arranged about the workspace. The FreeHand 10 workspace
is shown in Figure 1-3.

When you launch the Windows version of FreeHand 10, a wizard appears,
prompting you to select a task. If you don't like wizards and prefer using
menu commands to create new documents, open existing files, and so on,
the next time you launch FreeHand 10, deselect the Show This Screen When
Starting FreeHand option, and the wizard will never bother you again, unless
you uninstall and then reinstall FreeHand 10.

Exploring the document window

In the center of the interface, you find what looks like a blank piece of paper
that the Macromedia designers have put a border and a drop shadow
around so you can find it. This is the document you are creating, and unless
you're creating illustrations of polar bears in a blizzard, the document won't
stay white and blank for long.

The area outside of the document is known as the *pasteboard*. No, you can't
paste sticky notes on it to remind yourself to pick up milk on your way
home, but you can use it as a staging area for items you intend to use in the
document, but don't quite know where yet. Objects outside of the document
area will not be printed or exported, but they are saved with the FreeHand
10 document.

Tools   Blank document   Collapsed panel groups

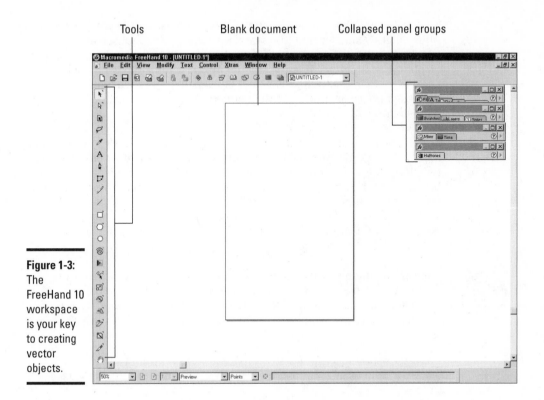

Figure 1-3:
The
FreeHand 10
workspace
is your key
to creating
vector
objects.

Around the border of the document, you find a vertical and horizontal scroll-bar that you use to pan to different parts of the document. Scrollbars come in handy when you magnify the document. When you create a document with multiple pages, you use the horizontal scrollbar to pan to a different page.

FreeHand 10 has lots of contextual menus. Contextual menus contain commands and options relevant to a selected item or workspace. You access the commands in a contextual menu by right-clicking.

Using the drawing tools

On the left side of the interface, you find the toolbar, which shows various tools neatly stacked in a single column. On the toolbar, you find your drawing tools and other tools that you use to modify vector objects, move them, reshape them, and more. We know you're probably chomping at the bit to find out what these tools do. Don't worry. We show you how to use most of the drawing tools in Book IV, Chapter 2. The other tools are discussed in detail throughout Book IV as they pertain to different tasks you perform with FreeHand 10.

**Book IV
Chapter 1**

**Introduction to
FreeHand 10**

The problem with the single vertical column is that unless your desktop size is just slightly smaller than the state of Texas, you cannot see all your tools, which of course makes the hidden tools very hard to use. We suggest you display your tools as a floating toolbar. When you display your tools as a floating toolbar, the toolbar is neatly labeled *Tools* — a feat which earned the designers an award for truth in advertising — and your tools are divided into two columns.

To arrange your tools as a floating toolbar, click the border to the left of any tool, drag the tools into the workspace, and drop them at a convenient location. If you don't like the spot you've dropped the tools, you can click the title bar and then drag and drop to reposition the toolbar. Figure 1-4 shows how the tools look as a floating toolbar.

To select a tool, click its icon. If you're not sure what a particular tool does, hold your cursor over the tool until a Tooltip appears.

Tooltips are enabled by default. If you prefer to work without Tooltips, you can turn them off by choosing Edit⇨Preferences. In the Preferences dialog box, click the Panels tab and then deselect the Show ToolTips option.

Tools

Figure 1-4:
You have access to all tools when you display your tools as a floating toolbar.

Many of the tools have keyboard shortcuts, which is a convenient way to quickly change from one tool to another. Some of the tools have two keyboard shortcuts, a letter and a number. Table 1-1 shows the keyboard shortcuts for frequently used tools listed in the order in which they appear on the toolbar.

Table 1-1		Keyboard Shortcuts for Tools	
Tool	*Shortcut*	*Tool*	*Shortcut*
Pointer	V or 0 (zero)	Subselect	A or 1
Page	D	Lasso	L
Text	T	Pen	P or 6
Bezigon	B or 8	Pencil	Y or 5
Line	N or 4	Rectangle	R
Polygon	G or 2	Ellipse	O or 3
Freeform	F or 9	Knife	K or 7
Hand	H	Zoom	Z

Working with toolbars

In addition to the drawing tools, you have other tools to simplify your life as a FreeHand 10 illustrator. They're tucked away as menu commands, but you can get them anytime you need them by choosing Window⇨Toolbars and then selecting one of the following:

+ **Menu:** This toolbar is open by default and duplicates many menu commands. On this toolbar, you find icons to open a document, save a document, print a document, import graphics, open frequently used panels, and more.

+ **Text:** You use this toolbar to format text objects in your documents. You choose font style, font size, font color, and specify paragraph alignment, along with other options that are discussed in Book IV, Chapter 3.

+ **Controller:** You use the Controller toolbar to test a document you plan to export as a Flash movie. You use the VCR-like controls to play the movie and use the other icons to export the movie.

+ **Status:** This toolbar is only available in Windows and is used to change the magnification of the document, navigate to another page in a multi-page document, and change document preview mode. This toolbar also has a window that displays information about selected objects.

+ **Info:** When you choose this toolbar, you see information about objects you select. The toolbar displays the type of object selected, the current position of the cursor, as well as the object's coordinates when you drag it to a different position in the document.

✦ **Xtra Operations:** You use this toolbar to transform and distort the path of one or more selected objects in your document. We show you how to use the available options from this toolbar in Book IV, Chapter 5.

✦ **Xtras:** You use this toolbar to access FreeHand 10 plug-in tools, such as the Arc tool and Fisheye Lens tool. We show you how to use these tools in Book IV, Chapter 5.

✦ **Envelope:** You use this toolbar to transform shapes or object groups by applying an envelope to them.

When you choose one of these toolbars, it appears as part of the main toolbar at the top of the interface. However, you can drag the toolbar into the workspace if this suits your working preference. If you exit FreeHand 10 and leave several toolbars in the workspace, FreeHand 10 doesn't clean up after you; the software assumes you're perfectly capable of keeping your workspace tidy and assumes you want the toolbars in these positions. Every time you launch FreeHand 10, the workspace is laid out as you last left it.

Perusing the panels

When you launch FreeHand 10, you find several panel groups hanging around the workspace. Panel groups are combinations of panels that you use to create or modify items for your FreeHand document. For example, the Color Mixer panel gives you all the tools you need to mix up a sky-blue-pink, or any other color your artistic muse or client requires.

Panel groups are free-floating in the workspace. Each panel within a group has its own tab. If you don't like a panel group's position, you can grab it by the scruff of its neck (that would be the title bar) and drag it to a different location. You can collapse panel groups when you are finished with them, or close them entirely to clear the workspace. You can also create custom panel groups to suit your working preferences. You have the following panels at your beck and call:

✦ **Layers:** You use the Layers panel to add layers to a document and manage layers within a document. We show you how to work with layers in Book IV, Chapter 2.

✦ **Styles:** You use the Styles panel to duplicate, edit, or delete styles being used in your document. The Styles panel displays default text and object styles, which you can modify to suit your document.

✦ **Swatches:** You use the Swatches panel to create a color palette for objects in your document. We show you how to use the Swatches panel in Book IV, Chapter 6.

✦ **Navigation:** You use the Navigation panel to assign URL links to objects and text in your FreeHand documents.

✦ **Color Mixer:** You use the Color Mixer to mix a color. You can mix the color using the CMYK (Cyan, Magenta, Yellow, Black) color model, RGB (Red, Green, Blue) color model, HLS (Hue, Lightness, Saturation) color model, or the system color picker. After you mix a color, you can add it to the Swatches panel, a task we show you how to perform in Book IV, Chapter 6.

✦ **Tints:** You use the Tints panel to specify the percentage or hue of the original color. We show you how to tint reds, greens, blues, and other popular rainbow colors in Book IV, Chapter 6.

✦ **Halftones:** Halftones are used when you add screened objects to a document. You use Halftones when you are preparing a document for a postscript-printing device at a service center. Halftones are beyond the scope of this book.

✦ **Align:** You use the Align panel to align objects in your document. We show you how to get your objects in alignment (without using a chiropractor) in Book IV, Chapter 4.

✦ **Transform:** You use the Transform panel to move, rotate, scale, skew, or reflect a selected object. We show you how to fold, spindle, and otherwise mutilate objects with the Transform panel in Book IV, Chapter 4.

When you launch FreeHand 10, the panel groups are all lined up on the right side of the workspace. You can bring the panels to life using any of the following methods:

✦ Choose Window⇨Panels and then choose the name of the panel you want to open.

✦ Click a panel tab.

You can move a panel group to any desired position in the workspace by clicking the panel title bar and then dragging and dropping it to the desired position. Figure 1-5 shows two panels side by side. The panel on the left is the shy reclusive type as it is currently collapsed, while the panel on the right is strutting its stuff in the expanded position.

Book IV Chapter 1

Introduction to FreeHand 10

Figure 1-5:
A tale of two panel groups.

You can change a panel group's status by doing any of the following:

+ Double-click a collapsed panel's title bar to expand the panel.

+ Click the Maximize button to expand a collapsed panel.

+ Click the Minimize button to collapse an expanded panel.

+ Double-click an expanded panel's title bar to collapse the panel.

+ Close a panel by clicking the Close button. When you do this, the panel disappears from the face of the document window; the only way you can reopen the panel is by choosing Window➪Panels and then choosing the panel you want to open.

Here are a few final tips on how to navigate and manage panels:

+ If you use a panel group frequently, collapse the panel group and move it to a convenient position in the workspace.

+ When you have a panel group open with the Windows version of FreeHand 10, you can switch between panels by pressing Ctrl+Tab.

+ To clear the workspace of all panel groups, choose View➪Panels.

+ To display hidden panels, choose View➪Panels.

Inspecting the inspectors

Inspectors look like panels. In fact, they reside within their own panel group. Inspectors give you information about an object. For example, the Object inspector gives you the current coordinates of an object and its dimensions. But inspectors do much more than inspect the object. If you're not satisfied with any of the parameters an inspector displays, you can change the parameters, which will change the object in one fell sweep. For example, if you want to change an object's dimensions, open the Object inspector and enter new values. In other Macromedia Studio MX programs, the tasks performed by individual FreeHand 10 inspectors are handled en masse by the Property inspector. You can call on the following inspectors as needed:

+ **Object:** You use this inspector to display the object's width, height, and position within the document. You can change any of these parameters by entering new values; a task we show you in Book IV, Chapter 4.

+ **Stroke:** You use this inspector to display information about an object's stroke (outline). If you don't like what you see, you can change the stroke by choosing different options. We show you how to modify strokes in Book IV, Chapter 6.

✦ **Fill:** You use this inspector to show the current fill (color) of an object. You can use the inspector to modify the object's fill as well. We show you how to define an object's fill in Book IV, Chapter 2.

✦ **Text:** The text inspector tells you everything you need to know about a selected block of text, except if you spelled it right. You also use this inspector to modify the way text looks, a feat of prestidigitation we show you in Book IV, Chapter 3.

✦ **Document:** This inspector gives you information about the document such as its orientation, size, and so on. We document the Document inspector in Book IV, Chapter 2.

You open inspectors in the same manner as you open panels, as described in the previous section, "Perusing the panels."

Modifying groups

Macromedia's FreeHand 10 design team worked long and hard to come up with an optimum layout for panels and inspectors. They grouped panels and inspectors in a logical manner. However, like everything else, the way panels are grouped is not cast in stone, and if you're one of those folks who like different strokes, you can change the way panels and inspectors are grouped:

1. **Choose Window⇨Panels or Window⇨Inspectors.**

2. **Select the name of the panel or inspector you want to group differently.**

The panel or inspector appears. Alternatively, you can click the panel's or inspector's tab to select it.

3. **Click the arrow near the upper-right corner of the panel or inspector.**

4. **Choose Group** *name* **with, where** *name* **is the name of the panel or inspector.**

5. **Choose the name of the panel group you want to group the panel or inspector with, as shown in Figure 1-6.**

The panel or inspector is added to the group you specified and banished from its former home.

You can create a new panel group by selecting a panel, clicking the arrow in the panel's upper-right corner, and then choosing New Panel Group from the menu.

Figure 1-6:
You can
group a
panel or
inspector in
a different
group.

 FreeHand 10 has contextual menus, lots of them. Contextual menus contain commands and options relevant to a selected item, or workspace. You access the commands in a contextual menu by right-clicking.

Chapter 2: Understanding FreeHand 10 Basics

In This Chapter

✔ **Creating a new document**

✔ **Working with text**

✔ **Adding shapes to the document**

✔ **Using the Pen tool**

✔ **Adding color to a shape**

✔ **Introducing layers**

✔ **Saving documents**

*W*hen you need to create an illustration with FreeHand 10, you start by launching the program and creating a new document. After that, you can begin creating your masterpiece. This process can involve getting the word out by adding text, creating artwork by making standard shapes with the shape tools or freeform shapes with the Pen tool, and setting a dividing line between elements in your illustration with the Line tool. When you create objects for your illustrations, you can outline the object by defining a stroke and add color to the object by defining the object's fill. After you've created the document, you can save it for future editing and refinement. When your document is complete, you export the document to its intended destination.

In this chapter, you get an overview of typical FreeHand 10 workflow. We also show you which tools you can use to create objects for your illustrations and point you in the right direction for additional information and tips.

Creating FreeHand 10 Documents

The default size for a FreeHand 10 document is 612 x 792 points (8½ x 11 inches), which is letter size. You can modify the document size and add pages to the document by using the Document inspector. You also use the Document inspector to set the bleed value and final output resolution of the document. You can also modify parameters, such as the page orientation, and the way thumbnails are displayed in the Document inspector. If you want, you can also create a Master Page to maintain the continuity of all pages in the document. A Master Page has elements that will be used on every page of the document, such as a text header with the client's logo. We show you how to create Master Pages in the "Creating a Master Page" section, later in this chapter.

Creating a new document

You begin a FreeHand 10 project by creating a new document. Creating a new document gives you a blank page that you use to assemble the artwork for your illustration. You can create a new document one of two ways:

✦ Choose File⇨New Document.

✦ Click the New Document icon that looks like a blank letter.

After you create a new document, it appears in the center of the Document window, as shown in Figure 2-1.

Modifying documents with the Document inspector

You use the Document inspector to change the orientation of the document, change the size of the document, and so on. To open the Document inspector, shown in Figure 2-2, choose Window⇨Inspectors⇨Document.

Figure 2-1:
Every
FreeHand 10
project
starts with
a blank
document.
It's a
FreeHand
law.

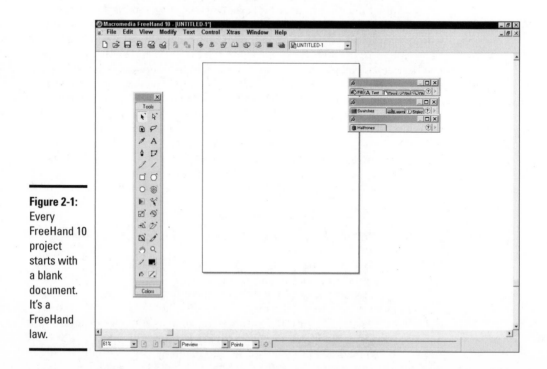

Figure 2-2:
Use the
Document
inspector to
change the
size of the
document.

Changing the document size and orientation

If you need to change the size of a document, you use the Document inspector. You can choose from a standard document size, or create a custom size. You also use the inspector to change the document orientation from portrait (vertical) to landscape (horizontal). To modify the document size and orientation, follow these steps:

1. **Choose Window⇨Inspectors⇨Document.**

The Document inspector opens (refer to Figure 2-2).

2. **Click the triangle to the right of the Page Size field.**

The Page Size drop-down list appears.

3. **Choose one of the preset options.**

The first five presets are European sizes. The available presets are as follows:

- **A3:** Creates a document sized 841.89 x 1190.55 points.

- **A4:** Creates a document sized 595.27 x 841.29 points.

- **A5:** Creates a document sized 419.52 x 595.27 points.

- **B4:** Creates a document sized 708.66 x 1000.60 points.

- **B5:** Creates a document sized 498.89 x 708.66 points.

- **Legal:** Creates a document sized 612 x 1008 points.

- **Letter:** Creates a document sized 612 x 792 points.

- **Tabloid:** Creates a document sized 792 x 1224 points.

- **Web:** Creates a document sized 550 x 400 points, which incidentally is the default size for a Flash movie. The default orientation for this preset is Landscape.

- **Custom:** Choose this preset, and the x and y fields become available. You can then enter values in these fields to create a document of the desired size.

The measurements in the preceding list are shown in points, the default FreeHand 10 unit of measurement. You will see different values if you change to a different unit of measurement. For example, if you change the unit of measurement to inches, Letter size is 8.5 x 11 inches.

4. Click the desired orientation button.

You can choose from Portrait to create a document that is taller than it is wide, or Landscape to create a document that is wider than it is tall.

5. Click the Close button to apply your changes.

The document is reconfigured to the size and orientation you specified.

Creating a Master Page

If you need to create a multipage document that you want to use as a Flash movie or as a storyboard, you can use the Document inspector to create a Master Page that you can apply to any or all pages in the document. A *Master Page* is like a template; it has common items and attributes that are applied to all children of the Master Page. To create a master document, follow these steps:

1. Choose Window⇨Inspectors⇨Document.

The Document inspector opens.

2. Click the arrow near the upper-right corner of the inspector.

The menu shown in Figure 2-3 appears.

Figure 2-3:
You create Master Pages and add pages using this menu.

3. Choose New Master Page from the menu.

FreeHand 10 creates a blank page entitled New Master Page-01. If you don't like the name, there's not much you can do about it; the designers of FreeHand 10 make sure the name is cast in stone.

4. Create the elements that you want to appear on all pages that use this Master Page.

For example, you can create a text header with your client's logo.

5. **To finish the page, click the triangle to the right of the Page Title window at the top of the Document window and choose the default document page.**

   Unless you are editing a previously saved document, the default page is named `Untitled`. The document pages inherit the filename of the FreeHand 10 document when you save the document.

You can create as many Master Pages as needed for a document by follow-ing the preceding steps. New Master Pages will be appended by the next available Master Page number.

To format an existing page using a Master Page, follow these steps:

1. **Choose Window⇨Inspectors⇨Document.**

   The Document inspector opens.

2. **Navigate to the page you want to format using a Master Page.**

   You navigate to the page by clicking its thumbnail in the Document inspector, or by using the Hand tool to scroll from one page to another in the Document window.

3. **Click the triangle to the right of the Master Page field and select the desired Master Page from the drop-down list.**

   The page inherits the characteristics of the selected Master Page.

Adding pages to a document

If you use FreeHand 10 to create storyboards or Flash movies, you can add as many pages as you need to get the job done. When you add pages, you can format them using a previously created Master Page. To add one or more pages to your document, follow these steps:

1. **Choose Window⇨Inspectors⇨Document.**

   The Document inspector opens.

2. **Click the arrow near the upper-right corner of the inspector.**

   The pop-up menu appears.

3. **Choose Add Pages.**

   The Add Pages dialog box, shown in Figure 2-4, appears.

Figure 2-4:
Adding
pages to
your
document.

Add Pages

Number of new pages: 1

Page size:

Letter

x 612   y 792

Bleed size: 0

Make child of Master Page:

Master Page-01

OK   Cancel

4. **Enter a value for the number of pages you want to add.**

5. **Accept the default document page size, or select the Page Size radio button and select a different page size from the drop-down list.**

6. **Click the triangle to the right of the Make Child of Master Page field, and then select a Master Page from the drop-down list.**

When you choose this option, the new page inherits the characteristics of the Master Page used to create the page the new document is being created from. This option is unavailable if you've changed the page size. If you don't want to use a Master Page to format the document, select the Page Size radio button and you can then choose one of the preset document sizes, or choose Custom to enter your own values for document size.

7. **Click OK.**

FreeHand 10 adds the pages to your document. Alternatively, you can click Cancel to void the operation.

You can also duplicate a page, remove a page, or convert the current page to a Master Page by choosing Window➪Inspectors➪Document, clicking the arrow near the upper-right corner of the inspector, and then choosing the appropriate command from the pop-up menu.

Editing a Master Page

You're on the home stretch of a project when all of a sudden your boss or client rears his or her head and wants you to change the document. You mumble some choice words under your breath and then remember you've formatted most of the pages in the document using a Master Page. When you edit a Master Page, all instances of pages to which the master is applied are updated as well. To edit a Master Page, follow these steps:

1. **Select a page that you formatted using a Master Page.**

2. **Choose Window⇨Inspectors⇨Document.**

   The Document inspector opens.

3. **Click the Edit button.**

   FreeHand 10 refreshes the Document window to display the Master Page.

4. **Edit the Master Page as needed.**

5. **To apply your changes, click the triangle to the right of the document title window and select another document.**

   All pages formatted with the Master Page are updated to reflect your edits.

Changing the Document inspector thumbnail display

When you create a document with multiple pages, you can display thumbnails of the pages in the Document inspector. When you view pages in this manner, you can use the Page tool (a mahvelous device we show you how to use in the next section, "Using the Page Tool") to rearrange the order of the pages. Follow these steps to modify the way thumbnails are displayed in the Document inspector:

1. **Choose Window⇨Inspectors⇨Document.**

   The Document inspector opens.

2. **Click one of the buttons at the lower-left corner of the inspector:**

   - The first button displays each page as tiny thumbnails.
   - The second button displays each page as medium-size thumbnails.
   - The third button displays a thumbnail of the selected page only.

3. **Click the Close button to apply your changes.**

   The next time you open the Document inspector, the page thumbnails are displayed according to the button you selected.

You can also use the Document inspector to set Bleed and Resolution. When you print a document, FreeHand 10 places registration marks (printable area) and trim marks according to the document size you specify. When you enter a bleed value, the registration marks are moved in from the edge of the page without changing the document size. If you add a bleed value to the document, remember to increase the page size by that amount in your printer's setup dialog box, otherwise you'll get this error message: "This document will not fit in the selected page size." Refer to your printer manual to determine the maximum resolution it is capable of producing as well as how to modify the page size.

Using the Page Tool

When you create a multipage document, you use the Page tool to rearrange the order of pages and select pages. You find the Page tool that looks like a document with an arrow in it with the FreeHand 10 tools, as you can see in Figure 2-5. To use the Page tool on a multipage document, do the following:

1. **Deselect all objects, place your cursor inside the Document window, and then right-click.**

   The contextual menu appears.

2. **Choose View⇨Fit All.**

   FreeHand 10 refreshes the Document window to display all pages in the document.

3. **Select the Page tool.**

4. **Click a page to select it.**

   After selecting a page, you can move it to a different position. This is like rearranging the papers on your desk, but you can't get messy and overlap document pages. You must create a space for a page. Figure 2-5 shows a multipage document being rearranged with the Page tool.

You can also use the Document inspector to rearrange pages. Open the Document inspector and then switch to a view that shows thumbnails of all the pages in your document. Click a page thumbnail to select it and drag it to a new location.

Page tool   Bounding box of page being moved

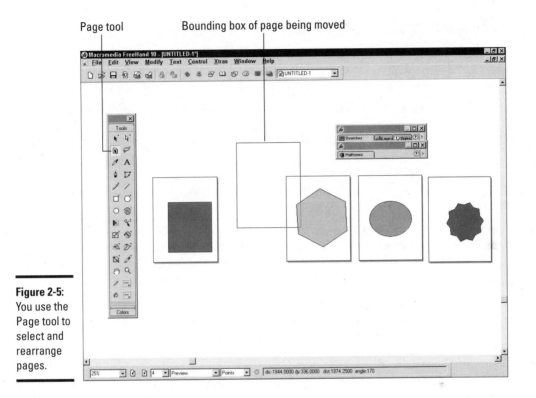

Figure 2-5:
You use the
Page tool to
select and
rearrange
pages.

Opening Existing Documents

We know. We haven't shown you how to save a document yet, and here's a
section about opening them. Well, when you first begin working with
FreeHand 10, you may need to open existing FreeHand 10 documents created by someone else, and you usually open existing documents before you
can edit and save them, so here goes. To open an existing document, follow
these steps:

1. **Choose File⇨Open.**

   The Open dialog box appears.

2. **Navigate to the folder where the file is located.**

3. **Select the file and then click Open.**

   FreeHand 10 displays the document and associated pages in the
   Document window. You can now edit the document.

Using the Document Grid

When you create documents, you may need to enlist FreeHand 10 visual aids to help you place objects with precision. Visual aids are a definite benefit if you're dealing with a small monitor, or if you're working with a large monitor, but you have managed to work your way into wearing trifocal glasses.

Your first line of optic defense is the document grid, which is a series of equally spaced vertical and horizontal dotted lines. To view the document grid, choose View⇨Grid⇨Show. You can use the grid intersections as anchor points for items you add to a document. You can toggle the grid on and off at will, as well as modify other grid parameters.

After you enable the grid, you can give it a magnetic personality by choosing View⇨Grid⇨Snap to Grid, which causes objects you create to snap to grid intersections. If you're creating an illustration for duck hunters, enabling the Snap to Grid feature is another way to get your ducks in a row.

After you display the grid, you can modify the grid spacing to suit the document you are creating:

1. **Choose View⇨Grid⇨Edit.**

   The Edit Grid dialog box appears.

2. **Enter a value in the Grid Size field.**

   This is the new grid spacing using the default document unit of measure.

3. **Select the Relative grid check box.**

   This option is disabled by default. Choosing this option causes objects when moved to snap to the same relative position within different grid spaces. Do not select this option if you want objects to snap to grid intersections.

4. **Click OK to apply the changes.**

   FreeHand 10 resizes the grid to the value you specified.

Using Rulers

FreeHand 10 has yet another visual aid you can use: rulers. To view rulers, choose View⇨Page Rulers⇨Show.

You can modify the rulers' unit of measure by choosing View⇨Page Rulers⇨Edit.

Creating guides

After you display rulers, you can create guides to further aid in aligning objects in your document. You can create as many vertical and horizontal guides as you need. You do not need to delete guides when you print the documents, because guides are unprintable. You can create guidelines by dragging them from the rulers, and if needed, position them precisely using menu commands.

To create a guide, follow these steps:

1. **Click one of the rulers and drag into the Document window.**

Click the horizontal ruler to create a horizontal guide; click the vertical ruler to create a vertical guide. As you drag, a blue line designates the guide's current position. You can use the opposite ruler to view the current location of the guide.

2. **Release the mouse button when the guide is in the desired position.**

A FreeHand 10 guide is added to your document. If the guide isn't positioned perfectly, you can click it and drag it to a new position. If you need to precisely position a guide, please refer to the next section, "Editing guides."

If you have both the grid and guides showing, the workspace can become a bit cluttered. We recommend that you use one or the other.

You can customize the way that guides behave as follows:

✦ **Snap to guides:** Objects snap to guides by default. To disable snapping to guides, choose View➪Guides➪Snap to Guides. To enable snapping, choose the command again.

✦ **Hide and show guides:** When you add guides to a document, they are visible by default. You can hide guides by choosing View➪Guides➪Show. To view hidden guides, choose the command again.

✦ **Lock and unlock guides:** When the guides are positioned the way you want them, you can lock them by choosing View➪Guides➪Lock. To unlock all guides, choose the command again.

Editing guides

If in spite of your best efforts, a guide is in the wrong place, you can precisely position it where you want. To reposition an improperly placed guide, follow these steps:

1. **Choose View➪Guides➪Edit or double-click the guide that you want to edit.**

The Guides dialog box, shown in Figure 2-6, opens. If you have multiple guides in your document, they are listed by type and position.

Page buttons

Figure 2-6:
You can
move a
guide
precisely
using the
Guides
dialog box.

Guides

Page: 1

Type	Location	
Vertical	484	Release
Vertical	230.833	
Horizontal	353.417	Remove
Horizontal	558.583	
Vertical	85.4166	Add...
		Edit...
		OK
		Cancel

2. **Select the guide you want to edit.**

The guide is highlighted. If you double-clicked a guide to open the dialog box, the guide is already selected. If you have a multipage document, you also need to enter the number of the page whose guides you want to edit or use the buttons at the top of the dialog box to navigate from one page to another.

3. **Click the Edit button.**

The Guide Position dialog box opens, showing the coordinate of each guide.

4. **In the Location field, enter the position (coordinate) where you want the guide to appear, and then click OK.**

The Guide Position dialog box closes and the new location is recorded in the Guides dialog box.

5. **Click OK to reposition the guide.**

The Guides dialog box closes and the guides get a move on.

When you choose View➪Guides➪Edit Guides, you can use the Guides dialog box to add a guide, remove a guide, or release a guide.

Adding Text to Your Illustration

When you use FreeHand 10 to create an illustration, you can use the Text tool to add text to vector and bitmap objects. You can do so much with text in FreeHand 10 that it truly boggles the mind. This section gets you up and running with the Text tool, but we show you the whole enchilada on text in Book IV, Chapter 3. To add text to your document, follow these steps:

1. **Select the Text tool, which looks like a capital letter A.**

2. **Click the location where you want the text to appear in your document.**

3. **Type.**

   It's really that simple.

4. **When you're finished typing, click anywhere outside of the text block.**

   The Text tool reverts to the Pointer tool, which you can now use to move the text block to another location.

After you create text, you can change text characteristics to create wonderfully artistic text for your illustration. We show you how to do everything with text — short of writing the next Great American Novel — in Book IV, Chapter 3.

Creating Predefined Shapes

The easiest way to add vector shapes to your illustrations is by using the shape tools. In this section, we show you the tools you can use to add shapes to your illustrations, as well as how to add the shape to a document. Some of the tools have parameters that you can define, such as the number of sides in a polygon. We show you how to set these parameters and more in Book IV, Chapter 4.

You can use the following tools to add shapes to your illustrations:

✦ **Rectangle tool:** You use this tool to add rectangles (and squares) to your illustrations. The rectangles can have rounded corners or not.

✦ **Polygon tool:** You use this tool to add star-like shapes to your illustrations. In fact, you can specify whether you use the tool to draw a polygon or a star. You can also specify the number of sides for the polygon.

✦ **Ellipse tool:** You use this tool to draw ovals (or circles), or as high-brow designers refer to them, ellipses.

✦ **Spiral tool:** You use this tool to add spirals to your documents. Spirals look like springs. You can specify the direction the spiral rotates, the number of rotations, and where the spiral emanates from.

To add a shape to your document, follow these steps:

1. **Select a drawing tool.**

If you click the tool once, you draw a shape using the last settings specified for the tool. If the tool has definable parameters, you can choose new parameters by double-clicking the tool. Tools that have modifiable parameters have an inverted L to the upper right of their icons. The drawing tools are shown in Figure 2-7, along with the boxes you use to color shapes and outlines.

Figure 2-7: You use these tools to add shapes to your illustrations and color them.

2. **Click the place inside the document where you want the shape to appear and then drag diagonally to create the shape.**

   As you drag, FreeHand 10 creates a preview of the shape. If you hold down the Shift key while creating a shape, the shape width and height remain equal. In other words, if you hold down the Shift key while using the Rectangle tool, you create a square; hold down the Shift key while using the Ellipse tool, and you create a circle.

3. **Release the mouse button when the shape is the desired size.**

   FreeHand 10 adds the shape to your document. After creating a shape, you can move it to a different location with the Pointer tool, or you can modify the shape by selecting it and then opening the Object inspector. We show you how to modify a shape using the Object inspector in Book IV, Chapter 4.

Creating Custom Shapes with the Pen Tool

You use the Pen tool to create freeform vector objects. The Pen tool gives you point-to-point control over the shape you create. You can use the Pen tool to create an open path or a closed path (the beginning and ending points meet to create an outline). You can even use the Pen tool to trace an image on another layer. (We show you how to add layers to a document in the upcoming section, "Working with Layers.")

To create a shape with the Pen tool, follow these steps:

1. **Select the Pen tool.**

2. **Click the place in the document where you want to add the first point.**

   When you click, you create a straight point; if you click and drag, you create a curve point. You create a straight point when you want to create a straight line segment, a curve point when you want a curved line segment.

3. **Click the spot where you want the second point to appear.**

   Remember to click and drag if you want a curve point. A curve point has handles that you use to modify a curved line segment. You modify handles with the Subselection tool. The Subselection tool is covered in detail in Book IV, Chapter 4.

4. **Continue adding points to define your shape.**

5. **To complete an open path, double-click to define the last point; to complete a closed path, click the first point.**

   Your shape is finished. Now you can use the Pen tool to create another shape or to modify the shape that you just created.

Using the Line Tool

You use the Line tool to create straight lines. You can modify the line style and width using the Stroke inspector, a task we describe in the upcoming section, "Creating Outlines."

To use the Line tool, follow these steps:

1. **Select the Line tool.**

2. **Click the point where you want the line to begin and then drag to create the line.**

   As you drag the tool across the document, FreeHand 10 creates a preview of the line. If you hold down the Shift key while using the tool, you constrain the line to horizontal if you're dragging from left to right, vertical if you're dragging from top to bottom, or to 45 degrees from the horizontal axis if you're dragging diagonally across the document.

3. **Release the mouse button when the line is the desired length.**

   FreeHand 10 creates a straight line using the old tried and true method of following the shortest distance between the beginning and ending points.

Coloring Shapes

If you use a shape tool that creates a closed path, or use the Pen tool to create a closed path, you can add color to the shape by defining a fill. To add color to a shape, you use the Fill color box.

Using the Fill color box

The Fill color box is near the bottom of the Tools toolbar, yet it's one of the most important tools in the whole lot. After all, a shape without color is kind of drab. Of course, you can opt for the minimalist look and create a shape with no fill and a stroke, in which case, you get an outline.

To define a fill for an object, follow these steps:

1. **Click the Fill color box.**

   The pop-up color palette appears.

2. **Move your cursor over the palette.**

   Your cursor becomes an eyedropper. As you move your cursor over the color swatches, the window in the upper-left corner of the palette refreshes and displays the color your cursor is currently over. A ToolTip displays the color's hexadecimal value and RGB value, as shown in Figure 2-8.

3. **Click a color to select it or click the No Color button if you want a shape with just an outline (stroke).**

   The swatch in the Fill color box refreshes to show the color you selected. This color is used to fill any new shapes you create until you select a different fill color. If you select no color, a diagonal red slash (/) appears in the Fill color box.

Figure 2-8:
You can add color to an object by defining a fill.

Changing a shape's fill color

If a shape's fill color doesn't suit your (or you client's) fancy, you can easily change it. You can also create a custom fill using the Fill inspector, a colorful operation we show you how to do in Book IV, Chapter 4.

Follow these steps to change a shape's fill color:

1. **Select the shape.**

2. **Click the Fill color box, as shown in Figure 2-8.**

   The pop-up color palette appears and your cursor becomes an eyedropper as you move it over the palette.

3. **Click a color to select it.**

   The swatch in the Fill color box changes to the color you selected, as does the color of the shape you selected. *Remember:* You can revert from a filled shape to an unfilled shape by clicking the No Color button. If you select No Color, the diagonal red slash appears in the Fill color box.

Creating Outlines

You can create an object with no fill, select a stroke color, and you've got an outline. If you create an object with no fill and no stroke, well . . . you've got nothing. But seriously, you use the Stroke color box to select an outline color for an object. If you need to change the stroke width, or style, you use the Stroke inspector, which is covered in detail in Book IV, Chapter 4.

Using the Stroke color box

You use the Stroke color box to choose a color for the outlines of the shapes you add to your illustration. You can select any color from the pop-up color palette or the System Color Picker (covered in Book IV, Chapter 6), or you can choose to go sans stroke.

Follow these steps to select a stroke color:

1. **Click the Stroke color box that has an icon that looks like a pencil.**

   The pop-up color palette appears.

2. **Move your cursor over the palette.**

   Your cursor becomes an eyedropper. As you move your cursor over the color swatches, a ToolTip displays the color's hexadecimal and RGB values. The window in the upper-left corner of the color palette refreshes to show the color your cursor is currently over.

3. Click a color to select it.

If the shape you are creating won't have a stroke, click the No Color button. After you select a color, the palette closes, and the selected color is displayed in the Stroke color box. If you click the No Color button, a diagonal red slash appears in the Stroke color box. The color you choose is applied to all shapes you create until you follow the preceding steps to select another stroke color.

Changing an object's stroke color

If you create an object and the object's outline (stroke) is not to your liking, you can change it at any time. You can also add a stroke to a shape that doesn't have one.

To change the stroke color of an object:

1. Select the object.

2. Click the Stroke color box.

The pop-up color palette appears.

3. Click a color to select it.

To remove a stroke from an object, click the No Color button. You can also choose a color from the System Color Picker by clicking the System Color Picker button to the right of the No Color button. After you select a color, the pop-up color palette closes and the color is applied to the object's outline.

Working with Layers

Layers are like thin sheets of clear plastic on top of your illustration. You can see what's underneath the plastic. In FreeHand 10, you use layers to segregate your objects. You can also use layers to trace an object on a lower layer, such as a complex bitmap image. Layers simplify your life as a FreeHand 10 illustrator, especially when you create a document with a lot of stuff.

When you create a new document, FreeHand 10 gives you three layers to work with: Foreground, Background, and Guides. Only objects on the Foreground layer, or layers above the separation line, are printable. The separation line is a horizontal black line in the Layers panel.

You use the Layers panel to create and otherwise manage layers. To open the Layers panel, choose Window⇨Panels⇨Layers. The Layers panel is shown in Figure 2-9.

**Book IV
Chapter 2**

**Understanding
FreeHand 10 Basics**

Hide/unhide layers

Display as outlines

Lock/unlock layers

Figure 2-9:
Use the
Layers
panel to
manage the
layers in
your
document.

Printable layers

Nonprintable layers

Creating layers

You can create a new layer whenever you need it. When you create a new layer, it becomes the drawing layer until you select another layer to work with. You create a new layer by following these steps:

1. **Choose Windows⇨Panels⇨Layers.**

The Layers panel opens.

2. **Click the arrow in the upper-right corner of the panel.**

The Layers panel menu appears.

3. **Choose New.**

FreeHand 10 creates a new layer with the default name of Layer followed by the next available layer number, such as Layer-1.

4. **Enter a new name for the layer and then press Enter.**

This step is optional. You can rename the layer at any time. We strongly advise you to get in the habit of naming layers, especially if you're creating documents with multiple layers.

You can duplicate the currently selected layer and all objects on it by opening the Layers panel, clicking the arrow in the upper-right corner of the panel, and then choosing Duplicate from the menu.

If you don't like the default layer name, you can rename the layer by following these steps:

1. **Choose Window⇨Panels⇨Layers.**

The Layers panel opens.

2. **Double-click the layer you want to rename.**

The layer name is highlighted.

3. **Enter a new name for the layer and then press Enter.**

The layer is renamed and enters a witness protection program.

After you select a layer, it becomes the active layer. You can use the Layers panel, which is shown in Figure 2-9, to perform any of the following tasks:

✦ **Hide and unhide objects:** Click the check mark in the left column to hide all objects on the selected layer. Click the column again to unhide the layer.

✦ **Display objects as outlines:** To display objects on a selected layer as outlines, click the filled dot center column of the Layers panel. The filled dot becomes hollow and the outline of each shape is displayed.

✦ **Lock and unlock layers:** Click the open padlock icon in the third column to lock the layer. After you lock a layer, the icon changes to a closed padlock and you cannot edit or select objects on the layer. Click the padlock again to unlock the layer.

✦ **Hide and display layers:** Click the arrow near the upper-right corner of the Layers panel and choose All Off from the Layers panel menu to hide all layers or choose All On to display all hidden layers.

Editing layers

When you use layers to organize a complex illustration, objects on top layers eclipse underlying objects on lower layers. You use the Layers panel to rearrange the order of layers and to perform other tasks, such as merging layers. You can also merge objects into a single layer when you've got everything just the way you want it.

To edit layers, choose Window⇨Panels⇨Layers and perform any of the following tasks:

✦ **Move layers:** Select a layer and drag it to a different position to change the way objects are displayed.

✦ **Make layers non-printable:** Select a layer and drag it below the separation line to make the layer non-printable.

✦ **Move objects between layers:** You can move an object to a different layer by selecting it in the Document window, and then in the Layers panel, click the name of the layer to which you want to move the object.

✦ **Merge layers:** To merge several layers into a single layer, select the layers, click the arrow in the upper-right corner of the Layers panel, and choose Merge Selected Layers from the Layers panel menu.

✦ **Merge foreground layers:** To merge all foreground layers into a single layer, click the arrow in the upper-right corner of the Layers panel, and then choose Merge Foreground Layers.

✦ **Remove layers:** You can remove a selected layer by clicking the arrow in the upper-right corner of the Layers panel and then choosing Remove from the Layers panel menu. If the layer you are removing contains objects, FreeHand 10 displays a warning dialog box to that effect. Click Yes to delete the layer.

Saving Documents in FreeHand 10

When you finish creating a document, or you've had all the fun with FreeHand 10 that you can handle for the day, save your document. You can save the document as a FreeHand 10 file, a FreeHand 10 template, or an Editable EPS file. Save the document as a FreeHand 10 file and you can edit the elements in the document when you reopen it. When you open a document saved as a template, you can use the elements in it as the basis for a new document. Saving a document as a template is useful if you do repetitive work for a client that uses the same elements in all the documents, such as the client's logo and address. You add additional elements to the template as needed and use the Save As command to save the revised template as a document. When you save the file as an Editable EPS file, you can work with the file in another illustration program that supports the EPS format, such as CorelDraw. When you save a document in any of these formats, you can later reopen and edit the document. *Note:* You are limited to saving a single page document when you choose the Editable EPS format.

Saving FreeHand 10 files

You can save a FreeHand document whenever you need to. When you save a document that has been edited since it was last saved, an asterisk (*) appears after the document's name in the document title bar. To save a document, follow these steps:

1. **Choose File⇨Save.**

The Save Document dialog box opens.

2. **Enter a name for the document and navigate to the folder where you want to save the file.**

3. **Choose the file format you want the document saved as.**

   You can choose from the following: FreeHand 10 Document (.fh10), FreeHand 10 Template (.ft10), or Editable EPS (.eps).

4. **Click the Save button.**

   FreeHand 10 saves the document to the specified folder.

When you save a previously saved file, the Save Document dialog box does not appear, and the file is saved using the same filename in the same location as the previous iteration of the file.

You can save your work using a different filename. This option is handy when you're making lots of edits and saving a file frequently. You can save a master version of the file, and then save a working version of the file using a different filename. If you run into a computer glitch and the working version of the file becomes corrupt, you can always revert to the master copy of the file. You also use the Save As command to save a FreeHand template that you have added elements to in order to create a new document. To save a file using a different filename:

1. **Choose File⇨Save As.**

   The Save Document dialog box opens.

2. **Enter a name for the document and navigate to the folder where you want to save the file.**

3. **Choose the file format you want the document saved as.**

   You can choose to save the document in one of the following formats: FreeHand 10 Document (.fh10), FreeHand 10 Template (.ft10), or Editable EPS (.eps).

4. **Click the Save button.**

   FreeHand 10 saves the renamed document to the specified folder.

Computers can be cranky creatures and are subject to system overloads, which may cause your machine to crash when you least expect it. In order to avoid losing hours of work, we advise you to save your work early and save your work often.

Exporting files in other formats

You can create FreeHand 10 illustrations for a wide variety of uses. You can create images for the Web, illustrations for print, and Flash movies, to name a few. When you need to use the finished illustration for a specific application, you export the file in the necessary format. You also save the original as a FreeHand 10 document. To export a file, follow these steps:

1. **Choose File⇨Export.**

    The Export dialog box appears.

2. **Enter a name for the file and specify the folder to which you want the file saved.**

3. **Choose the export file format. You can choose to export the file as one of the following:**

    - A bitmap file using the BMP, GIF, JPEG, PNG, or TIFF file formats.

    - A vector file using the EPS or EMF file format.

    - A Flash movie using the SWF format. You can import the end result into Macromedia Flash MX, or embed the movie in an HTML document for viewing on the Internet.

    - A FreeHand 5, 7, 8, or 9 file. If you export a file with PNG images, they will not display if you choose version 7 or earlier.

    - An Adobe Illustrator file, versions 1.1, 3.0/4.0, 5, or 8.8.

    - A PICT file (Macintosh only).

    - A DXF file for use in 3D applications.

    - A PDF file for viewing with the Adobe Acrobat Reader. The file may also be printed from the Acrobat Reader.

    - An RTF file for use in a word processing application.

4. **Click the Save button.**

    FreeHand 10 exports the file in the format you specify.

Chapter 3: Using the FreeHand 10 Text Tools

In This Chapter

✔ **Creating text**

✔ **Editing text**

✔ **Creating text styles**

✔ **Creating text columns**

✔ **Converting text to paths**

✔ **Aligning text to a path**

*I*f you need to add text to an illustration, you use the Text tool. If you want the text to jump up and get someone's attention, FreeHand 10 gives you the tools to create really cool looking text. You can convert text to vector objects, align text to paths, and much more. In fact, you can do so many cool things with text in FreeHand 10, it would take forty or fifty pages to show you all of them. Unfortunately, we don't have that much space, but this chapter shows you the important features of working with text in FreeHand 10, so you'll have plenty to work with.

In this chapter, we show you how to stylize your text by modifying fonts, point size, and more. We explain how to use the Text inspector to modify your text, as well as how to format your text. And if you want to make your text jump through hoops, we show you how to do that by aligning text to a path.

Creating Text Using the Text Tool

When you need to add text to an illustration, the first step is to call on the Text tool. After you select the Text tool, you can create an auto-expanding text block that grows wider as you enter more text, or you can create a text block that is sized to fit a specific area of the illustration, in which case FreeHand 10 automatically wraps text to a new line as needed. You can specify the font size, color, and other text attributes before or after you enter text.

Creating auto-expanding text blocks

When you select the Text tool and create text in the document, the default text block (box) is auto-expanding, which means the block gets wider as you enter more text. To create an auto-expanding block of text, follow these steps:

1. **Select the Text tool.**

   The Text tool is the handsome-looking tool that's identified by a capital A. As you move the tool into the Document window, your cursor becomes an I-beam.

2. **Click the spot in your illustration where you want the text block to begin.**

   A flashing vertical line signifies that FreeHand 10 is ready for you to enter text.

3. **Begin typing.**

   Your words of wisdom appear in the document.

4. **Press Enter to create a new line.**

   Any text you type now appears on a new line. If you want a text block that wraps text from line to line, you need to create a fixed-size text block, which we show you how to create in the next section.

5. **Click anywhere outside of the text box when you are finished entering text.**

   The Pointer tool is selected.

Creating fixed-size text blocks

When you create a fixed-size text block, you constrain the text to the size of the block. When text reaches the side of the box, FreeHand 10 automatically wraps new text to the next line. To create a fixed-size text block, follow these steps:

1. **Select the Text tool.**

2. **Click the point in the illustration where you want the text to appear and then drag diagonally to define the size of the text box.**

   As you drag, FreeHand 10 displays a dashed rectangle that gives you a preview of the box's current size.

3. **Release the mouse button when the text box is the desired size.**

   FreeHand 10 creates a rectangular bounding box.

4. **Begin typing.**

   When you enter enough text to reach the side of the text box, Freehand 10 wraps the text to the next line.

5. **Click anywhere outside of the text box when you finish entering text.**

   FreeHand 10 reverts to the Pointer tool that you can now use to resize or move the text box. Figure 3-1 shows an auto-expanding text box and a fixed-size text box.

You can add additional text to a text block by selecting the Text or Pointer and then double-clicking the text block at the point where you want to add text. If you double-click a text block with the Pointer tool, it reverts to the Text tool.

Figure 3-1:
A tale of two text blocks.

> Auto-expanding text block
>
> Fixed-size text block

You can remove any empty text blocks from your document by choosing Xtras⇨Delete⇨Empty Text Blocks.

Using Text Rulers

When you create text, FreeHand 10 displays a text ruler above the text. The text ruler is similar to the ruler you find at the top of the workspace of popular word processing programs. You use the text ruler in a similar manner. You can change the indent of paragraph text and change the position of tabs by dragging the icons at the top of the text ruler. After you finish entering text and select another tool, the text ruler is no longer visible. To view the text ruler, double-click the text block with the Pointer tool. Figure 3-2 shows a block of text with its attached text ruler.

First line indent marker

Tab markers

Left indent marker

Figure 3-2:
Use the text ruler to change the indent of paragraph text and the position of tabs.

Right indent marker

Fixed-size text block

TIP

Text rulers are enabled by default. Choose View⇨Text Rulers to hide text rulers from view. Choose the command again the unhide text rulers.

Checking the Spelling of a Text Selection

If you're like many designers, when you enter text, your fingers are flying across the keyboard, especially when you have copious amounts of text to stuff into a document. Sometimes your fingers are moving so fast that you transpose letters and end up with some spelling errors. To safeguard against exporting a document with spelling errors, you can spell check your text selections:

1. **Choose Text⇨Spelling.**

   The Spelling dialog box appears.

2. **Click the Start button.**

   FreeHand 10 begins checking your document for spelling errors. If it finds a spelling error, the suspect word is highlighted in the field at the top of the dialog box. Possible substitutes are listed in a field underneath the suspect word, as shown in Figure 3-3.

Figure 3-3:
Checking for misspelled words.

3. **If the spell checker finds a word not listed in its dictionary, you can choose one of the following options:**

   - **Ignore:** If you choose this option, the spell checker ignores the word and checks the rest of the document for errors.

   - **Change:** Choose this option when you select a word from the suggestions list so that the spell checker can replace the suspect word with the one you select.

   - **Ignore All:** If you choose this option, the spell checker ignores this and all future instances of the suspect word. This option is handy when your document has several instances of a person's name or something else that would not be found in the dictionary but is spelled correctly.

- **Change All:** Choose this option when you select a word from the suggestions list so that the spell checker can replace this and all future occurrences of the suspect word.

- **Add:** If you choose this option, the spell checker adds the suspect word to its dictionary.

After you choose an option, the spell checker continues searching the rest of the document for misspelled words.

You can find and replace text and other objects in your FreeHand 10 documents by choosing Edit⇨Find and Replace⇨Text. Follow the prompts in the dialog box to quickly locate text in your document.

Editing Blocks of Text

After you create a block of text, you can move it with the Pointer tool or resize a fixed-size text block. You can also convert an auto-expanding text block to a fixed-size block and vice-versa.

Moving and deleting text

After you create a block of text, you can move or delete it as needed by following these steps:

1. **Select the block of text with the Pointer tool.**

A bounding box appears around the perimeter of the text box.

2. **To move the selected text box, click it and drag it to a new location.**

The text box is moved.

3. **To delete the text box, press the Delete or Backspace key.**

The text box is gone. Alternatively, you can delete a selected text box by choosing Edit⇨Clear.

Resizing text boxes

If you create fixed-size text boxes, you can modify the width and height as needed. To resize a fixed-size text box, select the text box with the Pointer tool and do one of the following:

✦ **Resize a text box:** To resize the text box, click and drag the corner handle: The text reflows to the new dimensions of the text box.

✦ **Proportionately resize a text box:** To proportionately resize the text box, click the handle on any corner, and then while holding down the Shift key, drag away from the center of the text box to make it larger, or towards the center to make it smaller. Text inside the box reflows to the new dimensions.

When you resize a text box using one of these methods, the text size remains unchanged. You can resize the text as you resize the text box by doing the following:

1. **Select the text box with the Pointer tool.**

   FreeHand 10 draws a bounding box around the text box.

2. **Click the handle at any corner of the text box, and while holding down the Shift and Alt keys, drag the handle until the text box is the desired size.**

   The text box is proportionately resized and the text is resized as well.

If you drag the middle handle on either side, or the center top or bottom handle, you don't resize the text, you change the text spacing. If you move either of these handles towards the center of the text box, individual characters overlap, leaving you with a jumbled, illegible mess.

Changing text box characteristics

You can change the characteristics of a text box at any time. For example, if you have a fixed-size text box, you can convert it to an auto-expanding text box and vice-versa.

To convert an auto-expanding text box to a fixed-size text box, follow these steps:

1. **Select the text box with the Pointer tool.**

2. **Double-click one of the middle handles on the sides of the text box and one of the middle handles on the top or bottom of the text box.**

   You can now resize the text box by clicking any corner handle and dragging. *Remember:* You can proportionately resize the text box by holding down the Shift key while dragging.

To convert a fixed-size text box to an auto-expanding text box, follow these steps:

1. **Select the text box with the Pointer tool.**

2. **Double-click one of the middle handles on the sides of the text box and one of the middle handles on the top or bottom of the text box.**

FreeHand 10 shrink-wraps the box around the text inside. When you add additional text to the box, it will expand to accommodate the additional text. *Remember:* You can create a new line by pressing Enter.

Formatting Text

When you create text for a FreeHand 10 document, you can format the text before you create it or select all the text in the text box after the fact and do your formatting then. You can specify the font style, font size, font color, paragraph alignment, and much more.

You have three tools at your disposal for choosing text attributes: menu commands, the Text inspector, and the Text toolbar. We give you a brief overview of the menu commands and the Text toolbar, but we focus on the Text inspector, FreeHand 10's formatting powerhouse:

✦ **Menu commands:** You can use the menu to specify font type, font size, style, paragraph alignment, leading, baseline shift, and case (capitalization). To format selected text using a menu command, choose Text, choose a category from the menu, and then choose the desired command from the submenu.

✦ **The Text toolbar:** You use the Text toolbar to select a font, specify the font size and paragraph alignment, and so on. You can even use the Text toolbar to attach text to a path, as described in the upcoming section, "Working with Text and Paths." The Text toolbar is shown in Figure 3-4, and like other FreeHand 10 toolbars, you can leave it floating in the workspace or dock it below the menu bar.

Figure 3-4:
The Text toolbar, a typist's best friend.

Font size   Bold   Flow inside path
Font style   Leading   Italic   Attach to path
Detach from path
Convert to paths
Text alignment

✦ **The Text inspector:** You can choose your font type, style, size, and alignment using the Text inspector. You can choose these parameters before or after creating a text box. To open the Text inspector, choose Window➪Inspectors➪Text. After you open the inspector, which is shown in Figure 3-5, choose from one of the five buttons to specify parameters when working with text:

   • **Character:** You use this section of the Text inspector to choose a font type, font size, style, paragraph alignment, leading, kerning, and baseline shift. You can also apply effects to text in this section, as well as choose a text style.

   • **Paragraph:** You use this section of the Text inspector to specify paragraph spacing and indentation, and answer the age-old question: "To hyphenate or not to hyphenate?"

   • **Spacing:** You use this section of the Text inspector to scale characters and specify spacing between letters and words.

   • **Columns and Rows:** You use this section of the Text inspector to display a block of text as columns and rows.

   • **Adjust Columns:** You use this section of the Text inspector to specify how text flows between columns and rows.

Paragraph

Character

Figure 3-5:
You use
the Text
inspector to
format text
and much
more.

Columns and rows

Adjust columns

Spacing

Choosing a font type, size, and style

You can choose a font style and size before you begin typing or after you create a block of text. If you choose the font style after creating your text, you have the added benefit of seeing a preview of the font, as it will be applied to your text. To choose a font style, follow these steps:

1. **Create a block of text.**

   You know the drill. Select the Text tool, click inside the document, and type.

2. **Click anywhere outside of the text box to deselect the Text tool.**

   The block of text is still selected, and the Pointer tool is now the active tool.

3. **Choose Window⇨Inspectors⇨Text.**

   The Text inspector appears in the Document window.

4. **Click the Character button.**

   The character section of the Text inspector is displayed.

5. **Click the triangle to the right of the Font Name field and scroll through the drop-down list.**

   The fonts you have installed on your system show up in the Font Name drop-down list. As you scroll through the list, the first few words of the selected text are displayed with the font style applied, as shown in Figure 3-6.

Font type

Font style

Font size

Figure 3-6: Choosing a font type in the Text inspector.

Leading
Kerning
Baseline shift
Styles menu
Text effects

Paragraph alignment

6. **Click a font name to select it.**

7. **Select a size from the Text Size drop-down list.**

   You can also enter your own value in this field if you want the text to be sized differently than the preset values. If you type a value into this field, you must press Enter to apply the size.

8. **Select one of the following options from the Style drop-down list:**

   • **Plain:** Choose this default style if you like plain — yawn — ho-hum text.

   • **Bold:** Choose this style to boldface the text.

   • **Italic:** Choose this style to italicize the text.

   • **BoldItalic:** Choose this style to boldface and italicize the text.

9. **Close the panel to apply the characteristics to the text.**

   If needed, you can also use this section of the Text inspector to apply effects to text, apply a style to the text, and more.

 If you like to mix and match font types, styles, and so on, within a block of text, double-click the text to activate the Text tool and then select the letters or words in the block of text that you want to style differently. After selecting the letters or words, open the Text inspector to set the parameters for the text selection.

Creating text styles

When you add text to a document, FreeHand 10 uses the default Normal Text style to format the text. You can modify the text using menu commands or the Text inspector, however, the changes only apply to the block of text you are creating. If you're creating a document with lots of text that spans different pages, formatting each new block of text can become a nuisance, especially when they're all the same. After you decide on text formatting options for a document, you can save the formatting as a style, which you can then apply to any block of text with a click of the mouse. To create a text style, follow these steps:

1. **Select the Text tool and create a block of text.**

2. **Format the text using the font style, size, and other attributes that will remain constant throughout the document.**

3. **Choose Window⇨Panels⇨Styles.**

   The Styles panel, shown in Figure 3-7, opens.

Figure 3-7:
You can create a custom text style using the Styles panel.

4. **Click the arrow in the upper-right corner of the panel and choose New from the Styles panel menu.**

   A new entry appears in the Styles panel with the default name of Styles, appended by the next available style number (Style-1, for example). If you're creating more than one style for the document, you can rename the style to better reflect what the style applies to.

5. **To rename the style, double-click its name, type a new name, and then press Enter.**

   The style is renamed.

After you create a text style, you can apply the style to any text block on any page in your document. To apply a text style, follow these steps:

1. **Select the block of text to which you want to apply a style.**

2. **Choose Window➪Panels➪Styles.**

   The Styles panel opens and all styles currently in use for the document are displayed.

3. **Click the name of the style you want applied to the text.**

   The text is formatted to the style's parameters.

Choosing a text color

If language can be colorful, so should text. When you add color to text, you accentuate the text and make it stand apart from other elements in an illustration. You can apply the same color to an entire block of text, or select individual letters from a block of text and choose a different color. To specify the color for a block of text, follow these steps:

1. **Select the block of text with the Pointer tool.**

   If you only want to apply a color to an individual letter or word in a text block, double-click the text block to activate the Text tool and then select the letter or word you want to select a color for.

**Book IV
Chapter 3**

**Using the FreeHand
10 Text Tools**

2. **Click the Fill color box.**

   The pop-up palette appears.

3. **Click a color to select it.**

   You've got colorful text!

Some illustrators like to choose a different color for the first letter in a paragraph to draw the viewer's eye to the paragraph. You can also draw attention to the first letter in a paragraph by specifying a larger font size.

Aligning your text

When you create a block of text, the default alignment is to align the text to the left side of the text block. You can modify the text alignment to suit the illustration that you are creating. You can change the text alignment at any time:

1. **Using the Pointer tool, select the block of text whose alignment you want to modify.**

2. **Choose Window⇨Inspectors⇨Text.**

   The Text inspector opens.

3. **Click the Character button.**

4. **Click the appropriate button to apply one of the following alignments to the selected text:**

   - **Left:** Aligns the text to the left side of the text box; this is the default alignment. The right side of the text will be ragged.

   - **Center:** Aligns each line of text to the center of the text box.

   - **Right:** Aligns text to the right side of the text box. The left side of the text will be ragged.

   - **Justify:** Spaces the text so that it flows to fill the text box, leaving no ragged edges.

5. **Close the Text inspector or choose another parameter to modify.**

   Your text is aligned.

Changing paragraph settings

When you create several paragraphs of text in a block, you can change the formatting of the paragraphs to suit your illustration. You can modify the paragraph indentation and how the tabs are spaced using the Text inspector:

1. **Select the block of text whose paragraph settings you want to modify.**

2. **Choose Window⇨Inspectors⇨Text.**

   The Text inspector opens.

3. **Click the Paragraph button.**

   The Paragraph section of the Text inspector opens, as shown in Figure 3-8.

Above

Below

Figure 3-8:
Use the
Paragraph
section to
set
paragraph
indents and
more.

Left indent
Right indent
First line indent

4. **Enter a value in the Left and Right Indent fields.**

   These values determine how far a paragraph indents from the left and right borders of the text box. A positive value indents the text inside the text box, and a negative value places the text outside the text box or column.

5. **Enter a value in the First Line Indent field.**

   This value determines how far the first line of a paragraph indents from the left indent of the paragraph.

6. **Enter a value in the Above field or in the Below field, or both.**

   The values you enter in these fields determine how much space appears above or below the paragraph. If you enter values in both fields, FreeHand 10 creates a space above and below each paragraph in the text box.

7. **Select the Hang Punctuation check box to place punctuation, such as quotation marks, outside of paragraph margins.**

8. **Select the Hyphenate check box to enable automatic hyphenation for the block of text.**

9. **Close the Text inspector to apply the changes or choose another text parameter to modify.**

   Your changes are applied to the selected block of text.

You can display a line between each paragraph by choosing an option from the Rules section of the Text inspector when specifying paragraph options. If you choose to display rules, make sure the Show Borders option in the Object inspector is enabled. You'll also need to open the Stroke inspector to choose a stroke style for the rules.

Formatting text in columns and rows

If you like your text neatly arranged, you can do that in FreeHand 10. You can format a block of text to be displayed in rows and columns, which is the equivalent of creating a table. After you format text into columns and rows, you can control how the text flows between columns and rows. Follow these steps to format a block of text into columns and rows:

1. **Select the block of text you want to format into columns and rows.**

2. **Choose Window⇨Inspectors⇨Text.**

The Text inspector opens.

3. **Click the Columns button.**

The Columns section of the Text inspector opens, as shown in Figure 3-9.

Figure 3-9: You can format a text block into rows and columns.

4. **Enter a value in the Columns field.**

This determines the number of columns in the text box.

5. **Enter a value in the Column Spacing field.**

This value determines the distance between columns.

6. **Enter a value in the h field.**

   This value determines the height of each table cell.

7. **Enter a value in the Rows field.**

   This value determines the number of rows in the text box.

8. **Enter a value in the Row Spacing field.**

   This value determines the amount of space between the rows in the text box.

9. **Enter a value in the w field.**

   This value determines the width of each cell.

10. **Click the desired Flow button.**

    The option you choose determines how the text flows within the table. The left button flows text down all rows in a column and then into the next column. The right button flows text across all rows and then down to the next column.

If the text isn't flowing between rows and columns to your liking, you can modify text flow by opening the Text inspector and then clicking the Balance Columns button. Select the Balance Columns check box to balance the flow between columns.

To display a border around rows and columns, choose one of the Rules options for each row and column. If you choose to display rules, make sure the Show Border option is enabled in the Object inspector. You also have to select a stroke style from the Stroke inspector.

Scaling text horizontally

You can adjust the width of characters in a text block to suit your design. You can make characters wider or narrower. This option gives you a bit of artistic latitude when a font is almost, but not quite, perfect for your needs. To scale text horizontally, follow these steps:

1. **Using the Pointer tool, select the block of text you want to scale.**

   If you select a block of text with the Pointer tool, the changes will be applied to all text and subsequent text you enter in the text block. To scale individual words in a text block, double-click the text block with the Pointer tool and then select the word(s) or character(s) you want to scale.

2. **Choose Window⇨Inspectors⇨Text.**

The Text inspector appears.

3. **Click the Text Spacing button.**

The Text spacing section of the Text inspector opens.

4. **In the % field, enter the value by which you want the text scaled.**

This value is a percentage of the text's original size. Enter a value larger than 100 to increase the text width, or lower than 100 to shrink the text.

5. **In the Spacing % fields, enter values in the Min, Opt, and Max fields for Words and Letters:**

- **Word:** The values you enter for Word affect the space between words in a selected block of text. A value of 100 is the standard spacing for words. Values less than 100 move words closer together, and values higher than 100 move words apart.

- **Letter:** The values you enter for Letter affect the spacing between letters. The standard letter spacing is 0. Enter a higher value for more space between letters and a lower value to move letters closer together.

To precisely space letters and words, enter the same value for Min, Opt, and Max.

6. **In the Keep Together field, enter a value for the number of lines to be kept together when scaling text columns.**

Enter a value of 2 to prevent the first or last line of a paragraph being isolated at the top or bottom of a column.

7. **Select the Selected Words check box to prevent a line break when scaling selected text.**

8. **Close the Text inspector or select another text option to modify.**

The selected text is scaled by the value specified.

Copying attributes between text blocks

If you're like many illustrators, you'll be working on a document, get a blinding flash of insight, and come up with a better design for something. If this happens when you're creating a new block of text, you can quickly copy the attributes from the new block of text to other text blocks in your document. You can copy settings from the Text Character, Spacing, and Paragraph sections of the Text inspector. To copy attributes from one text block to another, follow these steps:

1. **Select the text block whose attributes you want to copy.**

2. **Choose Edit⇨Copy Attributes.**

The attributes are copied to the Clipboard.

3. **Select the text block to which you want to paste the attributes.**

4. **Choose Edit⇨Paste Attributes.**

FreeHand 10 pastes the copied attributes to the selected block of text.

Adding visual effects to text

You can create some pretty snazzy text using FreeHand 10 by selecting an exciting font and then modifying it with the Text inspector. If you need more pizzazz than that, you can apply visual effects to text. You can choose from effects like the ever-present drop shadow, or other unique effects, such as highlighting text. However, you can only apply one effect to each block of text. Figure 3-10 shows the effects that you can choose from.

Figure 3-10: You can achieve interesting results by applying an effect to text.

Highlight
Inline
Shadow
Strikethrough
Underline
Zoom

Follow these steps to add a visual effect to text in a document:

1. **Double-click a block of text with the Pointer tool.**

The text is selected and the Text tool is active.

2. **Select the text to which you want to apply a visual effect.**

You can select an individual letter, a word, or the entire text block.

3. **Choose Window➪Inspectors➪Text.**

   The Text inspector makes an appearance.

4. **Click the Effects button and choose one of the following:**

   - No Effect
   - Highlight
   - Inline
   - Shadow
   - Strikethrough
   - Underline
   - Zoom

5. **Close the Text inspector or choose another text parameter to modify.**

   FreeHand 10 applies the effect to the selected text.

Adjusting the Spacing and Position of Characters and Lines

When you create paragraph text, you have more options than just font type, size, and alignment. You can also specify the space between paragraph lines, which is known as *leading*. Another parameter you can modify is *kerning*, which is the space between two characters. You can also modify the *baseline shift* of a word or letter in a block of text, which causes the selected word or letter to be raised above or below the baseline of the other characters in the text block.

Adjusting leading

To adjust leading for a block of text, follow these steps:

1. **Select a block of text with the Pointer tool.**

2. **Choose Window➪Inspectors➪Text.**

   The Text inspector opens.

3. **Click the Character button.**

4. **Enter a value in the Leading field.**

   Enter a number to specify the leading value. The value is applied according to the option you select in Step 5.

5. **Choose one of the following options from the Leading Type drop-down list:**

   - **Plus (+):** Specifies a point value to be added to the current font size.

   - **Equal (=):** Specifies leading equal to a value.

   - **Percent (%):** Specifies leading as a percentage of the current font size.

6. **Close the inspector to apply your changes, or select another text parameter to modify.**

   The change is applied to the selected text box.

Adjusting kerning

To adjust kerning for a block of text, follow these steps:

1. **Select a block of text with the Pointer tool.**

   This determines the kerning for the entire block of text, also known as *range kerning*. To modify kerning between individual words or characters, double-click the block of text and place your cursor between the characters or words for which you want to modify kerning.

2. **Click the Character button.**

3. **Enter a value in the Kerning field and then press Enter.**

   The value you enter is a percentage of the space of the letter M for the text font. To decrease the kerning between words or characters, enter a negative value, such as –10, which will decrease the kerning by 10 percent.

4. **Close the Text inspector, or choose another text parameter to modify.**

   Your specified kerning is applied to the text.

Adjusting baseline shift

You can modify baseline shift by following these steps:

1. **Select the Pointer tool and double-click the text block that contains the word or character whose baseline shift you want to modify.**

   Your cursor becomes an I-beam.

2. **Select the word or character whose baseline shift you want to modify.**

   The word or character is highlighted.

**Book IV
Chapter 3**

**Using the FreeHand
10 Text Tools**

3. **Choose Window⇨Inspectors⇨Text.**

   The Text inspector appears.

4. **Click the Character button.**

5. **In the Baseline Shift field, enter the value by which you want the baseline shifted.**

   By default, this value is in points. (If you've changed to a different unit of measurement, for example, pixels, the value will be in pixels.) To shift the selected text above the baseline, enter a positive value. To shift the selected text below the baseline, enter a negative value. For example, entering a value of –15 shifts the selected text 15 points below the baseline.

6. **Close the Text inspector, or choose another text parameter to modify.**

   The text is shifted by the amount specified.

Working with Text and Paths

When you create a line of text, it flows in a line from point A to point B. This is the time-honored standard for creating text. But wait, you're an illustrator, and FreeHand 10 is an illustration program. You say you want text that swoops and swirls like a roller coaster? Or perhaps you want your text characters to look a little different. If that's your artistic vision, we show you how to achieve it in the upcoming sections.

Converting text to a path

You can convert a block of text, or a single letter, into a path. When you do this, the letter or text block is no longer editable as text, but you can have a field day distorting the text by manipulating points with the Subselection tool or by using the Freeform tool. (We show you how to use the Subselection tool in Book IV, Chapter 4.)

Here's how you convert text to a path:

1. **Select the block of text that you want to convert to a path.**

   This technique works best with single letters or initials, for example, the letters used to make a client's logo. This technique also works best if the text is large.

2. **Choose Text⇨Convert to Paths.**

   FreeHand 10 converts the text to a vector object. Figure 3-11 shows a letter after being converted to paths. The converted letter has been further modified with the Freeform tool.

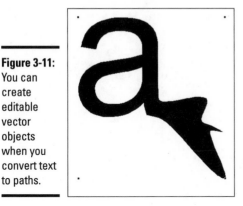

Figure 3-11:
You can
create
editable
vector
objects
when you
convert text
to paths.

Aligning text to a path

If you or your client have the hankering for an illustration with unique text, you can easily achieve this goal by attaching text to a path. You create text that swoops and swirls by attaching text to an open path, or you can create stylized text by attaching it to a closed path, such as an ellipse. To align text to a path:

1. **Select the text and the path.**

You can select both objects by dragging the Pointer tool around the text and the path, or by selecting either the text or the path, and then selecting the other while holding down the Shift key.

2. **Choose Text⇨Attach to Path.**

The text develops a magnetic attraction for the path.

Aligning text to both sides of an oval

Another effect that you can achieve with FreeHand 10 is attaching text to the top and bottom of an oval — okay, an ellipse for you sticklers. If you have a client that wants you to display text above and below a logo, this is the path — pun intended — to take. To attach text to the top and bottom of an oval, follow these steps:

1. **Create an oval.**

For more information on creating ovals, see Book IV, Chapter 4.

2. **Use the Text tool to create a block of text.**

Create the text that appears above and below the ellipse in the same text block. Press Enter after you create the text that appears above the ellipse, and then type the second line of text.

**Book IV
Chapter 3**

**Using the FreeHand
10 Text Tools**

3. **Select the oval, and then while pressing the Shift key, select the text.**

4. **Choose Text⇨Attach to Path.**

   The text on the first line attaches to the top of the oval, and the text on the second line attaches to the bottom of the oval, as shown in Figure 3-12.

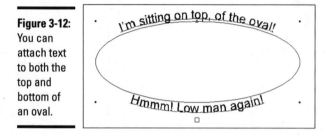

Figure 3-12: You can attach text to both the top and bottom of an oval.

If you have an object in your illustration and you want a block of text to flow around it, select the text and the object and then choose Text⇨Run Around Selection. When the Run Around Selection dialog box opens, click the second button, and then enter the distance you want the text to appear from the object in the text fields.

If you attach text to both sides of an oval and it doesn't align as desired, you may have to do one of the following:

✦ If the text disappears, choose Window⇨Inspectors⇨Object. After the Object inspector opens, choose None from the Top and Bottom text alignment menus.

✦ If the text flows in the wrong direction, Alt+click the path to select it and then choose Modify⇨Alter Path⇨Reverse Direction.

You can flow text inside an object. Create an object, such as an ellipse or polygon, and then create a block of text. Select the text and object, and then choose Text⇨Flow inside Path. Whoosh! The text appears inside the shape.

Modifying the alignment of text along a path

After you attach text to a path, you can modify where the text aligns to the path. You can modify which side of the path text appears on, as well as move the text to a different point along the path. To modify the alignment of text along a path, follow these steps:

1. **Using the Pointer tool, select the text whose alignment along a path you need to change.**

2. **Choose Window⇨Inspectors⇨Object.**

   The Object inspector opens.

3. **Select the Show Path check box if you want the path displayed as well as the text.**

4. **From the Top and Bottom Alignment drop-down list, select one of the following:**

   - **None:** Select this option if text you attach to a path is not visible.

   - **Baseline:** Aligns the baseline of the text to the path.

   - **Ascent:** Aligns the text to the bottom of the path.

   - **Descent:** Aligns the text to the top of the path.

5. **From the Orientation drop-down list, select one of the following options:**

   - **Rotate around path:** Orients the text with the rotation of the path.

   - **Vertical:** Orients the text vertically to the path.

   - **Skew Horizontal:** Skews the text horizontally along the path.

   - **Skew Vertical:** Skews the text vertically along the path.

6. **In the Inset section, enter a value in the Left field, and then press Enter to move the text to a different position along the path.**

   This is the distance you want the text offset to the right along the path. If the text is attached to an oval, enter a negative value to move the text to the left.

   When you enter a value in the Left field, the value in the Right field is automatically updated. For example, if you enter a value of 10 in the Left field, this value is added to the Right field. The value in the Right field is where the text ends. If you're a math whiz, you can enter a value in the Right field, however, it's easier to enter a value in the Left field.

If you prefer, you can change the text alignment along a path by manually moving it. To manually align text along a path, follow these steps:

1. **Use the Pointer tool to select the block of text whose alignment to a path you want to modify.**

   The text is selected and a small triangle appears to the left of the text, as shown in Figure 3-13.

2. **Click the triangle and drag the text to a new location along the path.**

   As you drag the triangle, FreeHand 10 creates a gray shape the size of the text that gives you a preview of the current location of the text along the path.

3. **Release the mouse button when the text is in the desired location.**

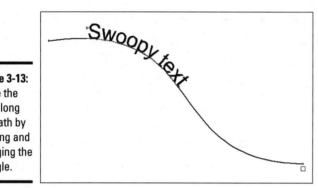

Figure 3-13:
Move the text along the path by clicking and dragging the triangle.

Chapter 4: Creating Illustrations with FreeHand 10

In This Chapter

✔ **Creating shapes**

✔ **Selecting objects**

✔ **Modifying shapes**

✔ **Creating groups**

✔ **Arranging and aligning objects**

✔ **Slicing objects**

When you create a FreeHand 10 illustration, you have a multitude of options to work with. However, with a bit of practice, you can create some interesting shapes for your illustrations and then modify them to suit your artistic muse or your client's vision. The results you can achieve are only limited by your imagination and sense of experimentation. The FreeHand 10 tools, although many, are relatively simple to use, which gives you the freedom to concentrate on your creation without having to worry about an overly complicated tool.

In this chapter, we show you how to create a FreeHand 10 illustration using the marvelous array of tools. We explain how to use the available tools to create shapes and then use panels or tools to modify those shapes. In Book IV, Chapter 5, we show you how to transform the shapes you create to put your own unique touch on an illustration.

Using Predefined Shapes

In Book IV, Chapter 2, we introduce the shape tools. The shape tools look kind of ho-hum when you see them on the toolbar; but when you click one of them and use it to add a shape to your illustration, things start looking up. And if you double-click an innocuous little tool button, you may get a menu with tool options that allows you to modify the base shape into something truly cool. In this section, we show you how to use the shape tools to create shapely shapes. We also point out which tools have additional options. Figure 4-1 shows the shape tools and the shapes you can create with them.

Drawn with Rectangle tool

Drawn with Polygon tool in Star mode

Rectangle tool

Polygon tool
Spiral tool

Figure 4-1:
Cool shapes
are just a
click and
drag away
with these
tools.

Ellipse tool

Drawn with Spiral tool

Drawn with Ellipse tool

Drawn with Polygon tool
in Polygon mode

Creating rectangles and squares

If you need a rectangle in your illustration, or its equally dimensioned cousin, the square, you use the Rectangle tool. Rectangles make wonderful borders for Web site headers or frames for text. If your illustration calls for rectangles with rounded corners, the Rectangle tool can give you this as well. To add a rectangle to your illustration, follow these steps:

1. **Select the Rectangle tool (refer to Figure 4-1).**

If you're creating a garden-variety rectangle, you can just click and drag inside the document. If you want a rectangle with pizzazz, read on.

2. Double-click the Rectangle tool.

The Rectangle Tool dialog box appears.

3. Enter a value for the corner radius.

Enter a low value for gently rounded corners, or a high value for corners with curves that rival those of an Italian sports car.

4. Click OK.

The dialog box goes on hiatus until you double-click the tool again.

5. Click and drag inside the document to draw the rectangle.

As you drag, FreeHand 10 draws a bounding box to give you a preview of the shape's current size. If you hold down the Shift key while dragging, you constrain the shape to a square. If you hold down the Alt key, the shape is created from the center outward.

6. Release the mouse button when the shape is the desired size.

FreeHand 10 creates the rectangle.

Creating polygons

If you like many-sided shapes, the Polygon tool's got your name written all over it. Actually, it has a polygonal shape emblazoned on it, but you can satisfy your need for many-sided shapes with this tool. You can create polygons and star-shaped objects with the Polygon tool. You'll also be happy to know that you can specify how many sides the shape has. To create a polygon, follow these steps:

1. Select the Polygon tool (refer to Figure 4-1).

You can create a polygon using the tool's current settings by clicking and dragging inside the document. For other options, you need to open the Polygon Tool dialog box.

2. Double-click the Polygon tool.

The Polygon Tool dialog box opens, as shown in Figure 4-2.

**Book IV
Chapter 4**

Creating Illustrations with FreeHand 10

Figure 4-2: You can create a polygon or star with the Polygon tool.

3. **Drag the slider to specify the number of sides.**

Alternatively, you can enter a value higher than 3 in the field. The slider stops at 20, but you can manually enter any number in the field. (If you create a polygon with lots of sides, it ends up looking like a circle.)

4. **Select the Polygon or Star radio button.**

This determines whether you draw a polygon or a star. If you select Star, you can specify the angle of the sides by following the next step. If you select Polygon, you're done; go to Step 7.

5. **In the Star Points section, select Automatic or Manual.**

If you select Automatic, FreeHand 10 determines the angle based on the number of sides you specify.

6. **If you specify Manual, drag the slider to specify the angle of the star sides.**

As you drag the slider, the preview window refreshes to show you the star's shape with the current settings.

7. **Click OK.**

The dialog box closes.

8. **Click and drag inside the document to create the shape.**

As you drag, FreeHand 10 creates a preview that shows the current size of the shape. Hold down the Shift key while dragging to create a shape that is as wide as it is tall. Hold down the Alt key to draw the shape from the center out.

9. **Release the mouse button when the shape is the desired size.**

A star is born. That is, unless you choose the Polygon option.

Creating ellipses

The ellipse is a wonderful shape, a curved wonder that makes ends meet. If your illustration calls for a circular shape, the Ellipse tool is right up your alley. And if you're creating an illustration of a bowling alley, you use the Ellipse tool to create a bowling ball and then use the Rectangle tool to create an alley. To create a shape with the Ellipse tool:

1. **Select the Ellipse tool.**

It's the tool with a circle for an icon. (Refer to Figure 4-1.) The Ellipse tool has no parameters to modify.

2. **Click the spot in the document where you want to create an ellipse and then drag diagonally.**

As you drag the tool, FreeHand 10 creates a preview of the shape's size. If you hold down the Shift key while dragging, you constrain the shape to a circle. If you hold down the Alt key, you create the shape from the center out.

3. **Release the mouse button when the ellipse is the desired size.**

FreeHand 10 creates the ellipse.

Creating spirals

Spirals are fun shapes that you can use to good effect when creating whimsical illustrations. You can use a spiral to create a reasonable facsimile of a corkscrew, just the thing if your client sells fine — or not so fine — wines. To add a spiral to an illustration, follow these steps:

1. **Select the Spiral tool. (It looks like a wound-too-tight spring.)**

You can create a spiral using the tool's current settings by dragging in the document. If you want a custom spiral, take the following steps.

2. **Double-click the tool.**

The Spiral dialog box opens, as shown in Figure 4-3.

Figure 4-3:
You use this dialog box to specify how your soaring spiral swirls.

3. **In the Spiral Type section, select one of the following options:**

- Click the left button to create a spiral with an evenly spaced, concentric radius.

- Click the right button to create a spiral with an expanding radius that becomes wider with each spiral. If you choose this option, drag the slider to set the expansion rate. Alternatively, you can enter a value in the text field.

4. **Choose one of the following options to specify the manner in which FreeHand 10 draws the spiral:**

   - **Rotations:** Choose this option to specify the number of rotations the spiral has, regardless of its size. When you choose this option, set the number of rotations by dragging the slider. Alternatively, you can enter a value in the text field.

   - **Increments:** Choose this option to create more rotations as the spiral grows larger. When you choose this option, specify the spacing between each interval by dragging the slider or by entering a value in the Increment Width text field. To create a shape with expanding spirals, enter a value in the Start Radius text field.

5. **Choose one of the Draw From options:**

   - **Center:** Choose this option, and you draw the spiral by clicking the center point and then dragging to place the spiral's ending point.

   - **Corner:** Choose this option, and you draw the spiral by clicking to place one ending point of the spiral and then dragging to set the other.

   - **Edge:** Choose this option, and you draw the spiral by clicking to create the end point and then clicking to set to center point.

6. **Click a Direction button to determine which way your spiral swirls.**

   Click the left button for a counterclockwise spiral, the right button for a clockwise spiral.

7. **Click OK.**

   The Spiral dialog box closes.

8. **Click anywhere in the document and then drag to define the size of the spiral.**

   As you drag, FreeHand 10 creates a preview of the spiral's current size. Hold down the Alt key to draw the spiral from the center, regardless of the option you choose in the Spiral dialog box.

9. **Release the mouse button when the spiral is the desired size.**

   FreeHand 10 draws the spiral.

Creating Freeform Shapes with the Pencil Tool

If you're a designer who likes diversity, FreeHand 10 gives it to you in spades. In addition to the shape tools and the Pen tool (discussed in Book IV, Chapter 2), you can also add freeform shapes to FreeHand 10 illustrations using the Pencil tool. You can use this tool to create anything from a simple squiggly line to an expressive calligraphic stroke. To use the Pencil tool, follow these steps:

1. **Select the Pencil tool.**

To create a line using the tool's current settings, click inside the document and drag to create the shape.

2. **Double-click the Pencil tool.**

The Pencil Tool dialog box, shown in Figure 4-4, opens.

Figure 4-4:
You can choose the width of your pencil stroke and more by varying these settings.

3. **Select one of the following Tool Operation options:**

- **Freehand:** Select this option to draw a simple line the width of the currently selected stroke.

- **Variable Stroke:** Select this option to create an artistic brush-like stroke with the tool.

- **Calligraphic Pen:** Select this option to create a stroke that looks like it was created with a calligrapher's pen.

4. **Drag the slider next to the Precision field.**

This setting determines how much FreeHand 10 smoothes the line as you draw. Choose a low value to smooth minor variations as you draw, or choose a high value to follow minor variations as you draw. Alternatively, you can enter a value in the text field.

5. **Select the Draw Dotted Line check box.**

This setting is optional. If you select it, FreeHand 10 creates a dotted line preview as you draw. This option speeds redraw and is recommended if you use FreeHand 10 on a computer with a slower processor.

6. **Select the Auto Remove Overlap check box.**

This is another optional setting. Choose it, and FreeHand 10 removes unnecessary overlapping lines to create a composite path.

Book IV
Chapter 4

Creating
Illustrations with
FreeHand 10

7. **If you choose any option other than Freehand, the Width field is available.**

   If you are creating a line with the Variable Stroke option, drag the Min and Max sliders. This determines the minimum and maximum width of the stroke; in other words, the amount of variation in the stroke's width. Alternatively, you can enter a value in each field. If you choose the Calligraphic Pen option, go to Step 8.

8. **If you choose the Calligraphic Pen option, select the Fixed or Variable radio button.**

   This option determines if your stroke is fixed width or variable. If you choose Fixed, drag the slider to determine the width of the stroke. If you choose Variable, the Min and Max sliders become available. Drag each slider to determine the minimum and maximum width of the stroke. Alternatively, you can enter values in these fields.

9. **If you chose the Calligraphic Pen option, click and drag the Angle slider to choose a setting.**

   This setting is measured in degrees and determines the pencil's angle of attack. Alternatively, you can enter a value between 0 and 360 in the text field.

10. **Click OK.**

    The Pencil Tool dialog box closes.

11. **Click and drag inside the document to create a line.**

    If you hold down the Alt key while drawing, the tool is constrained to a straight line. If you hold down the Alt and Shift keys, you create a straight line that is constrained to 45 degree increments.

12. **If you choose the Variable Stroke or Calligraphic Pen option, you can vary the stroke by ⅛ of the tool's Width setting by doing one of the following as you draw:**

    - To decrease the stroke width, press the left-arrow key.

    - To increase the stroke width, press the right-arrow key.

    - If you draw with a pressure-sensitive tablet, vary the pressure you apply to the tablet to vary the stroke width.

13. **Release the mouse button when the line is the desired length.**

    FreeHand 10 freehands the line. At this point, you can add to the line by placing the tool over the last or first point. Your cursor becomes a plus sign (+), indicating that the path can be extended.

Selecting Objects

When you create a document and add stuff (a technical term for objects) to the illustration, you place the stuff where you think it belongs. Thankfully, your initial placement isn't cast in stone. If you need to move, or otherwise modify, an object, you have to select it. If the object you're modifying is a path, you can select individual points along the path. In the upcoming sections, we show you how to use the selection tools to select stuff.

Using the Pointer tool

You use the Pointer tool to select an object or several objects in your document. To use the Pointer tool, select it (it's the handsome looking tool with the solid left-pointing arrow for an icon) and do one of the following:

✦ Click an object to select it. If the object has no fill, click the object's stroke.

✦ Click and drag a marquee around several objects to select them.

✦ Click an object, and then while holding down the Shift key, click other objects to add them to the selection.

After selecting an object or group of objects, dots appear to signify the border of each object or group. You can now drag the objects to a different location or use one of the inspectors to change the parameters of the object(s). If you select a path, the dots that comprise the path appear.

If you are using a tool other than the Pointer tool, you can momentarily select the Pointer tool by pressing and holding the Ctrl key. Use the tool to select objects; release the Ctrl key to revert to the previous tool.

The Pointer, Subselection, and Lasso tools share common settings. By default, objects or points must be completely encompassed by a marquee in order to be selected. You can vary the sensitivity of these tools by doing the following:

1. **Double-click the Pointer tool, Subselection tool, or Lasso tool.**

The tool's dialog box appears.

2. **Select the Contact Sensitivity option.**

Select this option if you want the ability to select objects that are only partially encompassed by a marquee. This option is deselected by default.

3. **Click OK.**

   The new settings are applied to the three selection tools and remain in effect until you open the dialog box and choose a different option.

Using the Subselection tool

You use the Subselection tool to select individual objects, select individual points along a path, or select an object that is nestled within a group. To make a selection with the Subselection tool, follow these steps:

1. **Select the Subselection tool.**

   It's the tool with the icon that looks like a hollow arrow pointing left. You find it right next to the Pointer tool at the top of the toolbox.

   To momentarily select the Subselection tool while using the Pointer tool, hold down the Alt key. After using the Subselection tool, release the Alt key to revert to the Pointer tool.

2. **To make a selection, do one of the following:**

   • Click an object. This selects an object, even when it's in a group.

   • Click a path to select it.

   • Click an individual point along a path. Note that you must first select the path, and then select the point.

   • Select a group of points by dragging a marquee around them.

3. **After creating a selection, you can move it with the Pointer tool.**

To momentarily select the Subselection tool while using a tool other than the Pointer tool, hold down the Ctrl+Alt keys. Release the keys to return to the previously used tool.

To modify a path between two points, select the path with the Subselection tool and then click and drag anywhere between two points. As you drag, FreeHand 10 modifies the path between the two points.

Using the Lasso tool

You use the Lasso tool to select objects. This tool works differently than the other selection tools. To make a selection with the Lasso tool (the tool that looks like a cowboy's lariat), follow these steps:

1. **Select the Lasso tool.**

2. **Click and drag to define a marquee around the objects you want to select.**

FreeHand 10 creates a dashed bounding box, giving you a preview of the selection area.

3. **Release the mouse button when the bounding box surrounds the objects you want to select.**

   The objects are selected. You can now move the objects with the Pointer tool or modify them with one of the inspectors.

Editing Objects with the Object Inspector

The FreeHand 10 Object inspector is a multifaceted workhorse you use to change a variety of parameters, depending on the object you select. If you select a point, the Object inspector displays the type of point selected (curve or straight) and the position of the point. If you select an object, the Object inspector displays the object's x- and y-coordinates in the document, as well as the object's dimensions. To change an object's position and size, follow these steps:

1. **With the Pointer tool, select the object whose characteristics you want to modify.**

2. **Choose Window⇨Inspectors⇨Object.**

   The Object inspector opens and displays the selected object's dimensions and location.

3. **To change the position of the object, enter new values in the x and/or y fields.**

4. **To change the object's dimensions, enter new values in the Width and/or Height fields.**

   Note that this does not resize the object proportionately.

5. **Press Enter to apply the changes.**

   The object is resized and/or repositioned. You can close the inspector, or leave it floating in the workspace.

Grouping and Ungrouping Objects

At times, it's advantageous to create a group of objects. When you select several objects and create a group, the group behaves as a single object. You can move the group with the Pointer tool, resize the group with the Object inspector, and modify the stroke and fill of every object in the group with the Fill and Stroke inspector. If you need to edit an individual object in a group, you select it with the Subselection tool and then perform the needed task.

**Book IV
Chapter 4**

**Creating
Illustrations with
FreeHand 10**

You can create a group at any time, for example, when you've arranged several elements to create an illustration of a face. You can create a group by selecting objects from different layers. When you do this, the objects are moved to the current drawing layer, yet they retain their stacking order. To create a group, follow these steps:

1. **Select the objects you want to group.**

   You can select objects with the Pointer tool, Subselection tool, or Lasso tool.

2. **Choose Modify⇨Group.**

   Four dots appear to signify the border of the group.

After you have created a group, you can select an individual object in the group by doing one of the following:

✦ Select the Subselection tool and click the object you want to select.

✦ Select the Pointer tool, hold down the Alt key, and click the object you want to select.

If you have objects underneath other objects in a group, you can select them by holding down the Ctrl and Alt keys while right-clicking to cycle through the objects in the group.

To ungroup objects, follow these steps:

1. **Select the object group with the Pointer tool.**

2. **Choose Modify⇨Ungroup.**

   The group is disbanded, and you can now edit each object individually. Yoko goes into hiding.

After you create a group, you can nest another object or group by selecting the object or group, selecting the object or group you want to nest the item in, and then choosing Modify⇨Group.

Arranging Objects

When you add objects to an illustration, they are stacked on top of each other, and the object on top of the stack eclipses objects below it. You can change the stacking order of objects at any time by following these steps:

1. **Select the object whose order in the stack you want to rearrange.**

2. **Choose Modify⇨Arrange and then choose one of the following commands from the submenu:**

- **Bring to Front:** Moves the object to the front of the stack.
- **Move Forward:** Moves the object ahead of the next object in the stack.
- **Move Backward:** Moves the object behind the next lower object in the stack.
- **Send to Back:** Moves the object to the back of the stack.

After applying one of the Arrange commands, the object's order in the stacking layer is changed.

When you use the Arrange command, you modify the stacking order on the drawing layer. If there are layers above or below the drawing layer (the currently selected layer), objects on those layers will affect the overall appearance of your illustration. In order to achieve the desired result, you may have to move the object to another layer. For more information on layers, see Book IV, Chapter 2.

TIP

You can also modify the stacking order by cutting or copying an object, selecting an object in the document, and then choosing Edit⇨Paste in Front or Edit⇨Paste Behind.

Aligning Objects with the Align Panel

When you have several objects in a document, you may need to align them. This is a fairly easy process using FreeHand 10's object chiropractor: the Align panel. You use the Align panel to align objects to each other or to the document. You can also use the Align panel to distribute objects relative to the other objects in the selection or relative to the document. When you choose one of the distribution options, the objects are spaced equally. You can also use the panel to align points along a path.

To align objects, follow these steps:

1. **Select the objects or points you want to align.**

2. **Choose Window⇨Panels⇨Align.**

The Align panel, shown in Figure 4-5, appears. The panel consists of three rectangles in the left window that give you a visual representation of the currently selected options. The left window has nine squares in the center and four mitered edges. You can align the objects by double-clicking one of these squares or mitered edges. For example, if you double-click the mitered edge at the top of the window, objects are aligned to the top; double-click the mitered edge on the left side and objects are aligned to the left. If you double-click the square in the top right corner, objects are aligned to the top and right; double-click the square in the center and objects are aligned to the center. If you click a square or edge, the rectangles are aligned in the Align panel that gives you a preview of what the final alignment will look like in the Document window when you double-click the desired square or edge.

Horizontal alignment menu

Figure 4-5:
You use this panel to bring your objects into alignment.

Vertical alignment menu

3. **Select the Align to Page check box to align or distribute objects relative to the page.**

   This aligns selected objects relative to the page. For example, objects can be aligned to the top and right corner of the page. If this option is not selected, objects are aligned or distributed relative to their current positions in the document. For example, if you have selected several objects in the document, and you double-click the left edge with the Align to Page option selected, the objects are aligned to the left border of the document. Without this option, the objects are aligned to the leftmost object in the selection.

4. **To align the selected objects, do one of the following:**

   • Click one of the squares or edges in the alignment window.

   • Select one of the following options from the Horizontal drop-down list: No Change, Align Top, Align Center, or Align Bottom.

   • Select one of the following options from the Vertical drop-down list: No Change, Align Left, Align Center, or Align Right.

5. **To distribute the selected objects, do the following:**

   • Select one of the following options from the Horizontal drop-down list: No Change, Distribute Tops, Distribute Centers, Distribute Bottoms, or Distribute Heights. For example, if you select the Distribute Tops option, the objects are equally spaced according to the top of each object.

- Select one of the following options from the Vertical drop-down list: No Change, Distribute Lefts, Distribute Centers, Distribute Rights, or Distributes Widths. For example, if you select the Distribute Lefts option, selected objects are distributed (spaced) according to the left side of each object.

6. **Click the Apply button.**

   The objects are aligned or distributed according to the options you select. If the alignment or distribution isn't as you'd expect — this may happen the first few times you use the tool — choose Edit➪Undo, and then perform the alignment or distribution again.

Slicing Objects with the Knife Tool

You can use the Knife tool to create two paths from a closed path, such as a circle or rectangle, or you can use the tool to slice an open path in two. For example, you can use the Knife tool on a circle or oval to create a curved path that otherwise would be difficult to create.

After you slice an object or path one time, you are left with two editable paths. If you use the Knife tool to take several swipes at the shape, you're left with a lot of editable paths. You can vary the Knife tool settings to vary the width of the slice, and whether the tool makes a straight slice or free-hand slice.

To use the Knife tool, follow these steps:

1. **Select the object or path you want to slice.**

2. **Select the Knife tool.**

   You can use the tool using the previous settings or change the settings.

3. **Double-click the tool to change the settings.**

   The Knife Tool dialog box, shown in Figure 4-6, appears.

Figure 4-6:
You can specify slice and dice settings for the Knife tool.

4. **Select one of the following Tool Operation options:**

   - **Freehand:** Select this default option to make a freehand cut. You can switch to a straight cut by holding down the Alt key, or constrain the tool to 45 degree increments by holding down the Alt and Shift keys.

   - **Straight:** Select this option to make a straight cut. Hold down the Shift key to constrain the tool to horizontal when dragging left to right, vertical when dragging up or down, or 45 degrees from the horizontal when dragging diagonally.

5. **Drag the Width slider to determine the tool's effective cutting area.**

   A value of 0 creates a thin cut, while higher values create two cuts separated by the width you choose. Alternatively, you can enter a value in the Width text field.

6. **Select one of the following check boxes:**

   - **Close Cut Paths:** Select this check box, and FreeHand 10 closes the paths you create with the tool and displays the stroke and fill of the original path.

   - **Tight Fit:** Select this check box, and the tool closely follows the path you draw with your mouse or tablet.

7. **Click OK.**

   The Knife Tool dialog box closes.

8. **Click and drag across the object.**

   As you drag, FreeHand 10 displays the tool's path.

9. **Release the mouse button to complete the operation.**

   FreeHand 10 slices and dices the shape into paths.

After you use the Knife tool, you have two (or more) paths. To select an individual path, select the Pointer tool and then click anywhere outside of the document to deselect any selected paths. You can then click a path to select it, and then move it to a different location or modify it with one of the inspectors.

Chapter 5: Transforming Text, Shapes, and Images

In This Chapter

✓ Importing bitmaps

✓ Scaling objects

✓ Modifying an object's shape and position

✓ Tracing images

✓ Combining shapes

✓ Using Xtras tools

Thanks to the diversity of the software toolset and menu commands, FreeHand 10 allows you to put your own stamp of creativity on your designs by using preset shapes and then modifying the shapes to suit your creative muse (and your client). In addition to modifying shapes, you can combine two or more shapes to create something truly unique.

In this chapter, we show you how to modify shapes with tools and menu commands. We also show you how to create new shapes by blending one shape into another, by using the Combine menu commands to connect shapes, by cutting one shape from another, and more.

Working with Bitmap Images

Vector objects are FreeHand 10's claim to fame; however, sometimes you have to add a photo-realistic bitmap image to an illustration. No matter how good a graphic artist you are, you'll find it hard to create a realistic image of a supermodel using strokes and fills. So if you use FreeHand 10 to create illustrations for clients like talent agencies or clothing manufacturers, you'll need to incorporate bitmaps into your work.

You can import images that have been saved in the following formats: TIFF, GIF, JPEG, PICT, PNG, Targa, and BMP. After you have a bitmap image in an illustration, you can modify the bitmap using certain menu commands and Xtras tools. For example, you can scale, skew, flip, or rotate the bitmap. You can also use the drawing tools to augment a bitmap image. For example, you can use the Rectangle tool to create a snazzy border for a bitmap. You can also use the Text tool to plop some text on top of the bitmap. To import a bitmap, follow these steps:

1. **Choose File⇨Import.**

   The Import Document dialog box appears.

2. **Navigate to the folder that contains the bitmap you want to import.**

3. **Select the bitmap file and then click the Open button.**

   Your cursor becomes a right angle. This signifies the upper-left corner of the bitmap image you are importing.

4. **Click the spot in the document where you want the bitmap to appear.**

   The bitmap is placed in the document and the Pointer tool becomes active. You can now move, scale, skew, flip, or rotate the bitmap.

 To create a snazzy border for the bitmap, use the Rectangle tool to create a rectangle slightly bigger than the bitmap. Choose Modify⇨Arrange⇨Send Backward to move the rectangle behind the bitmap. You can then use one of the Xtras tools or operations to modify the rectangle (Emboss works well) and then group the bitmap and rectangle. We show you how to use the Xtras tools in the upcoming section, "Using the Xtras Tools to Change a Shape."

Modifying Objects

A bitmap of a supermodel is joy forever, but so are vector objects, especially when you modify them to perfection. You have a great deal of latitude in how you can modify an object after you create it. You can scale, skew, flip, or rotate an object using menu commands or tools. In the upcoming sections, we show you how to accomplish these object makeovers without breaking a sweat. The tools you can use to modify objects are part of the FreeHand 10 tool set. Figure 5-1 shows the tools you commonly use to modify objects.

If you're a perfectionist, you probably prefer to move and resize objects with mathematical precision. Don't be alarmed. There are others like you in the world. In fact, many of them are graphic designers, which is why Macromedia created menu commands to scale, resize, and move objects. The cool thing about these commands is that when you invoke one, the others all pop up in the Transform panel. Talk about convenience. In the upcoming sections, we show you how to use each command.

Pointer tool

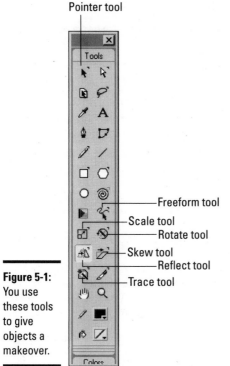

Freeform tool
Scale tool
Rotate tool
Skew tool
Reflect tool
Trace tool

Figure 5-1:
You use
these tools
to give
objects a
makeover.

Scaling graphics

Sometimes you make things just a bit too large and you've got to cut
them down to size, or vice-versa. For an object in your illustration, you cut it
down to size (or make it bigger) by scaling it. You can scale an object manually, or use a menu command.

Scaling graphics manually

You can scale an object manually as follows:

1. **Select the object whose size you want to change.**

2. **Select the Scale tool.**

Your cursor becomes a cross hair with a circle in the middle. When you
use the Scale tool, you can resize the object from a corner, or from the
center out.

3. **To resize the object, do one of the following:**

   - **To resize the object from a corner:** Click any corner and drag left, right, up, or down.

   - **To resize the object from the center:** Click the center of the object and drag left, right, up, or down.

   - **To resize the object proportionately:** Click either the corner or center of the object, and then while holding down the Shift key, drag toward the object to shrink it, away from the object to increase its size.

   As you drag the tool, FreeHand 10 displays the outline of the shape's current size.

4. **Release the mouse button when the shape is the desired size.**

   FreeHand 10 resizes the object.

Using the Scale command

To resize an object with mathematical precision, you can use the Scale command. To resize an object using this command, follow these steps:

1. **Select the object you want to scale.**

2. **Choose Modify⇨Transform⇨Scale or double-click the Scale tool in the Tools panel.**

   The Transform panel opens to the Scale section, as shown in Figure 5-2.

Figure 5-2:
You can use the Transform panel to scale and make copies in one fell swoop.

3. **Enter a value in the Scale field.**

   This value is the percentage of the object's original size. Enter a value larger than 100 to increase the object's size; enter a value lower than 100 to decrease the size.

4. **Select one or more of the following check boxes:**

   - **Contents:** Scales the contents of a clipping path with the rest of the path.
   - **Fills:** Scales the object fill as you scale the object.
   - **Strokes:** Scales the object's stroke as you scale the object.

5. **Select the Uniform check box to scale the object proportionately.**

   This is the default scaling option. If you deselect this check box, the h and v fields appear. To scale the object vertically, enter a value in the v field; to scale the object horizontally, enter a value in the h field, or enter the desired values in both fields to scale both dimensions.

6. **In the Center section, enter values in the x and/or y fields.**

   Changing the value in either field moves the object's center of rotation.

7. **Enter a value in the Copies field to create copies of the object as you scale it.**

   When you enter a value in this field, FreeHand 10 leaves the original object unaltered and creates the number of copies you specify. Each copy will be incrementally larger or smaller, creating copies that are sized incrementally along a path between the original object and the last copy.

8. **Click the Scale button.**

   FreeHand 10 scales the object, and if you enter a value in the Copies field, it blends the copies with the original.

If you like really radical transformations, select an object, then select the Freeform tool. Move your cursor toward the object, and then click and drag to modify the shape. FreeHand 10 morphs the shape like it was made of virtual Silly Putty.

Skewing and distorting objects

In this section, we show you how to skew. Skewing is great fun. And if you skew up, you can undo the change. If you wanted to make an image of a car look like it was accelerating or rapidly coming to a halt, you could skew the image to the left or right.

Skewing an object manually

To skew an object manually, follow these steps:

1. **Select the object you want to skew.**

2. **Select the Skew tool (refer to Figure 5-1).**

You can skew an object vertically or horizontally, relative to a side of the object, or relative to the center of the object.

3. **To skew the object, do one of the following:**

    *   Click above or below the object and drag left or right to skew the object horizontally, or drag left or right and up or down to skew the object vertically and horizontally relative to the side from which you are skewing.

    *   Click to the right or left of the object and drag up or down to skew the object vertically, or drag up or down and left or right to skew the object vertically and horizontally relative to the side from which you are skewing.

    *   Click inside the object and drag left or right to skew horizontally, or drag up or down to skew vertically, or drag up or down and drag left or right to skew horizontally and vertically relative to the center of the object.

    As you skew the object, FreeHand 10 creates an outline of the shape's current configuration.

4. **Release the mouse button when the shape has been skewed to perfection.**

    FreeHand 10 skews the shape.

Using the Skew command

If you or your client has a skewed outlook on an illustration, you can easily get this point across to your viewing audience by skewing one or more objects with the Skew command. You use the command to precisely skew — as opposed to skewer, something the Knife tool is good at — an object horizontally or vertically. To use the Skew command, follow these steps:

1. **Select the object you want to skew.**

2. **Choose Modify⇨Transform⇨Skew or double-click the Skew tool.**

    The Transform panel opens, conveniently bookmarked at the Skew section, as shown in Figure 5-3.

Figure 5-3:
You can really skew up when you use this command.

3. **Enter a value in the h and/or v fields.**

   These values are in degrees. Enter a positive value in the h field to skew the object to the right; enter a negative value to skew the object to the left. Enter a positive value in the v field to skew the object up; enter a negative value to skew the object down.

4. **Select one or both of the following check boxes:**

   • **Contents:** Select this check box to skew the contents of a clipping path along with the rest of the path.

   • **Fills:** Select this check box to skew a Tiled fill along with the rest of the object.

5. **In the Center section, enter values in the x and/or y fields.**

   If you enter a different value in either of these fields, the object's center of rotation changes. FreeHand 10 uses this center when skewing the object.

6. **Enter a value in the Copies field.**

   If you enter a value, FreeHand 10 does not skew the original object and creates the number of copies specified. The original object is unchanged and each copy is skewed by the specified amount; the last copy is skewed to a value that is the product of the number of copies and the skew value you specify.

7. **Click the Skew button.**

   The object gets skewed.

Rotating objects

No self-respecting graphics program would leave a graphic designer without a means of rotating an object. FreeHand 10 doesn't surprise you here. You can rotate an object or group with the Rotate tool. And if you like to rotate your objects with a degree of precision (pun intended, a circle after all is 360 degrees), you can use a menu command to do that.

Rotating objects manually

If you prefer menu commands, fast-forward to the "Using the Rotate command" section. If you prefer freeform rotation, follow these steps:

1. **Select the object you want to rotate.**

2. **Select the Rotation tool (refer to Figure 5-1).**

   You can use the tool to rotate an object using a corner or the center as the point of reference.

3. **To rotate the object, do one of the following:**

   - Click any corner and drag to rotate the object relative to the corner point clicked. If you click beyond the corner boundary of the object, FreeHand 10 uses the spot you click as the center of rotation.

   - Click the center of the object and drag to rotate the object relative to its center.

   As you drag the tool, FreeHand 10 creates an outline of the object's current position and a diagonal line to show you the angle of rotation.

4. **Release the mouse button when you have rotated the object to the desired position.**

   FreeHand 10 redraws the object in its new position.

Using the Rotate command

When you need to put a different spin on an object, you can use the Rotate command. You specify the number of degrees the object rotates, and you can even spin some copies of the original object. Follow these steps to use the Rotate command:

1. **Select the object you want to rotate.**

2. **Choose Modify⇨Transform⇨Rotate or double-click the Rotate tool.**

   The Transform panel appears with the Rotate section selected, as shown in Figure 5-4.

Figure 5-4:
It spins! It copies! It's the Rotate command.

3. **Enter a value in the Rotation Angle field.**

   This is the number of degrees you want the object to rotate. Enter a negative value to rotate the object in a clockwise direction.

4. **Select one of the following check boxes:**

   - **Contents:** Select this check box to rotate the contents of a clipping path with the rest of the path.

   - **Fills:** Select this check box to rotate a Tiled fill with the rest of the object.

5. **In the Center section, enter values in the x and/or y fields.**

   If you enter a different value in either of these fields, the object's center of rotation changes. FreeHand 10 spins an object around the center of rotation.

6. **Enter a value in the Copies field.**

   If you enter a value, the original object is not rotated and FreeHand 10 creates the number of copies you specify, rotating each copy by the amount specified. The last copy is rotated to an angle that is determined by the number of copies and the degree of rotation. For example, if you create three copies with a rotation of 15 degrees, the last object is rotated 45 degrees.

7. **Click the Rotate button.**

   FreeHand 10 spins the object.

Flipping objects

We're sure you've seen those cute pictures of identical twins standing next to each other. They look like bookends. If you want the bookend effect in a FreeHand 10 illustration, you can flip a copy of an object. Or you can flip an object to point it in the opposite direction. In this section we give you instructions to flip for.

Reflecting objects manually

You can flip an object with the Reflect tool. When you flip an object, you create a mirror reflection of the object. Hmmm . . . guess that's why they call it the Reflect tool. In any event, if you need to flip an object to keep your illustration from being a flop, follow these steps:

1. **Select the object you want to flip.**

2. **Select the Reflect tool (refer to Figure 5-1).**

   You specify the centerline for flipping the object by clicking a spot in the document.

3. **Click to the left or right of the object to specify the centerline FreeHand 10 uses to flip the object.**

   If you hold the mouse button, FreeHand 10 creates a vertical line to show you the centerline and an outline of the shape's position.

4. **Drag up or down to rotate the reflected object from the centerline.**

   As you drag, FreeHand 10 moves the outline to give you a preview of the reflected object's current position.

5. **Release the mouse button.**

FreeHand 10 flips the object and places it on the other side of the spot you clicked, at a distance equal to the object's former position from the centerline.

Using the Reflect command

You can flip an object vertically or horizontally with the Reflect command. And if your design calls for it, you can use the command to create a mirror image alongside of or below the original. To use the Reflect command, do the following:

1. **Select the object you want to reflect.**

2. **Choose Modify⇨Transform⇨Reflect or double-click the Reflect tool.**

The Transform panel appears, and it's in a reflective state of mind, as shown in Figure 5-5.

Figure 5-5:
Objects will flip over the Reflect command.

3. **Enter a value between 0 and 90 to reflect the object horizontally; enter a value between 90 and 180 to reflect the object vertically.**

4. **Select one or both of the following check boxes:**

   - **Contents:** Select this check box to reflect the contents of a clipping path along with the path.

   - **Fills:** Select this check box to reflect a Tiled fill with the rest of the object.

5. **Enter a value of 1 in the Copies field.**

By default, this field has a value of 0. Entering a value of 1 will create a mirror image of the original along with the original for a bookend effect.

6. **Enter values in the x and y fields to determine the center axis along which the object is reflected.**

Unless you're a math whiz, it's easier to double-click the object and then drag the center handle (it looks like a gear) to the desired position.

7. **Click the Reflect button.**

The Transform panel says, "Om," and the object is reflected.

If you like transforming objects with menu commands, you can save your-self some time by keeping the Transform panel in your workspace. To open the Transform panel, choose Windows⇨Panels⇨Transform. After the panel is open, click the appropriate button to move, rotate, scale, skew, or reflect a selected object. After you complete the transformation, double-click the panel's title bar to collapse it and then drag it to a convenient out-of-the-way spot in the workspace.

You can also open the Transform panel by double-clicking the appropriate tool.

Using the Move command

You can move objects anywhere in your document with the Pointer tool. However, when precision is needed, only a good menu command will do; in this case the Move command. If you need any object in your document to get a move on with precision, follow these steps:

1. **Select the object you want to move.**

2. **Choose Modify⇨Transform⇨Move.**

The Transform panel appears with the Move section selected, as shown in Figure 5-6.

Figure 5-6:
When you click the Move button, the object's gonna move.

3. **Enter a value in the x field and/or y field.**

This is the distance in pixels (or the unit of measure you specify for the document) you want the object to move along each axis.

4. **Select one or both of the following check boxes:**

- **Contents:** Select this check box to move the contents of a clipping path with the rest of the path.

- **Fills:** Select this check box to move a Tiled fill with the rest of the object.

5. Enter a value in the Copies field.

If you enter a value in this field, FreeHand 10 does not move the original object and creates copies equally spaced along a path between the original object's position and the position that results by applying the values entered in each field.

6. Click the Move button.

FreeHand 10 moves the object and makes the number of copies you specify.

You can also nudge a selected object by pressing one of the arrow keys on your keyboard. Hold down the Shift key while moving the object to increase the nudge distance by a factor of ten.

Scaling, Skewing, and Rotating with the Pointer Tool

When you first glance at the Pointer tool, you wouldn't think it's a tool of steel. But like mild-mannered Clark Kent from the Daily Planet, this tool has the strength of three tools: the Rotate tool, the Scale tool, and the Skew tool. And just like Clark Kent after he jumps into a phone booth and becomes the Man of Steel, the Pointer tool doesn't perform its other duties in a rigid manner. In fact, you can use the tool to scale, skew, and rotate in a freeform manner. To transform an object with the Pointer tool, follow these steps:

1. Select the Pointer tool.

2. Double-click the object you want to transform.

When you double-click the object, a bounding box with eight handles at the perimeter appears. A circular handle in the center that looks like a gear also appears, as shown in Figure 5-7.

Transformation handles

Figure 5-7:
Freeform an object with the Pointer tool.

Center of rotation handle

3. **After double-clicking the object, you can do any of the following to transform the object's shape:**

- **To change the object's height:** Move your cursor toward the handle on the center top or bottom of the object. When your cursor becomes a two-headed vertical arrow, click and then drag up or down.

- **To change the object's width:** Move your cursor toward the handle on the middle right or left of the object. When your cursor becomes a two-headed horizontal arrow, click and then drag right or left.

- **To scale the object:** Move your cursor toward any corner point. When your cursor becomes a dual-headed diagonal arrow, click and then drag toward the object or away from it. Hold down the Shift key while dragging to scale the object proportionately.

  When scaling an object proportionately with the Pointer tool, be sure to release the mouse button before releasing the Shift key; otherwise the object may not scale proportionately.

- **To move the object's center of rotation:** Click the handle that looks like a gear and drag it to a different location. You can drag the handle anywhere in the document.

- **To rotate an object:** Move your cursor beyond the object's bounding box. When your cursor becomes a curved two-headed arrow, click and drag to rotate the object. FreeHand 10 rotates the object relative to its center of rotation, the little gear-like handle that you can move anywhere to change the center of rotation.

- **To skew the object horizontally:** Move your cursor between the center and one of the corner points on the object's top or bottom. When your cursor becomes two horizontal lines with arrows going in opposite directions, click and drag left or right. If you also move your cursor up or down, the object will rotate and skew at the same time.

- **To skew the object vertically:** Move your cursor between the center and one of the corner points on the left or right side of the object. When your cursor becomes two vertical lines with arrows going in opposite directions, move your cursor up or down. If you move your cursor left and right at the same time, the object rotates around its center point and skews at the same time.

4. **Release the mouse button when the object is transformed to the desired shape.**

   Faster than a speeding bullet, the Pointer tool transforms the object.

Book IV
Chapter 5

Transforming Text, Shapes, and Images

5. You can now drag other handles to further change the object, or double-click anywhere beyond the object's bounding box.

If you double-click beyond the bounding box, the super Pointer tool swoops into a phone booth and resumes its former guise as the mild-mannered Pointer tool. The object is still selected.

You can also display handles to manipulate an object by selecting the object and then choosing Modify➪Transform➪Activate Handles. But double-clicking the object is faster.

Using the Trace Tool

You use the Trace tool to trace all or part of a bitmap image. When you use the Trace tool, you transform the pixels in the bitmap into vector paths and shapes. The default settings for the Trace tool are optimized to produce good results without taxing your system. However, you can modify the settings if you have a powerful processor and lots of memory. Follow these steps to use the Trace tool:

1. Double-click the Trace tool (refer to Figure 5-1).

The Trace Tool dialog box opens, as shown in Figure 5-8.

Figure 5-8:
You can
specify the
degree of
accuracy
with which
the Trace
tool traces.

2. From the first Color Mode drop-down list, select an option.

You can use as few as 2 colors to trace a bitmap, or as many as 256. Choosing a higher value creates more vector objects, and your computer takes longer to perform the operation.

3. **Select Colors or Grays from the next Color Mode drop-down list.**

   If you select Grays, a color image is converted to grayscale.

4. **If you're tracing a color image, select the RGB color model or CMYK color model from the third Color Mode drop-down list.**

   Select the RGB color model if your illustration will be displayed on a monitor; select CMYK if your illustration will be printed.

5. **From the Resolution drop-down list, select Low, Medium, or High.**

   Selecting Medium or High results in a more faithful rendition of the original bitmap, however, this produces more vector objects and takes longer for your computer and printer to process.

6. **From the Path Conversion drop-down list, select one of the following options:**

   - **Outline:** Select this option, and FreeHand 10 traces the outline of objects in the bitmap. If you select this option, the Path Overlap field opens. Select None for tracing text objects and line art, select the Loose option to trace contiguous areas of color, or select the Tight option for best results when tracing images like JPEGs with millions of colors.

   - **Centerline:** Select this option, and FreeHand 10 traces the center of strokes. Use this option when you are tracing a vector illustration with lots of line work and few fills. If you select this option, the Uniform Lines option is selected by default. Deselect the Uniform Lines option to create paths with varying stroke widths.

   - **Centerline/Outline:** Select this option to trace an object with the end result being vector objects with both strokes and fills. Contiguous areas of color will be outlined with a stroke. If you select this option, enter an Open Path Below value between 2 and 10 pixels. When tracing, FreeHand 10 leaves any paths below this value open.

   - **Outline:** Select this option to trace an outline of the bitmap.

7. **Drag the slider to specify a value for Trace Conformity.**

   You can specify a value between 0 and 10. Select a low value for a loose rendering of the original bitmap; a higher value for a more precise rendering of the image with more points.

8. **Drag the slider to specify a value for Noise Tolerance.**

   This setting determines how FreeHand 10 deals with muddy areas of color, scan lines, or other noise in a low-quality image. You can specify a value between 0 and 10. Choose a higher value to remove more noise from the original.

9. Drag the slider to set a value for Wand Color Tolerance.

This value determines how FreeHand 10 treats neighboring areas of color. If you choose a low value, FreeHand 10 blends colors of similar hues; if you choose a high value, FreeHand 10 creates more colors when tracing.

10. Click OK.

The Trace Tool dialog box closes.

11. Click one corner of the area you want to trace and then drag the tool to define the area you want traced.

As you drag the tool, FreeHand 10 creates a dotted marquee showing you the current selection area. Hold down the Shift key to constrain the selection to a square area.

12. Release the mouse button when you have selected the desired area.

FreeHand 10 traces the object.

Creating New Shapes by Combining Shapes

Did you ever wish you could combine a rectangle with a triangle and an oval to create a freeform sculpture? With FreeHand 10, you can combine shapes and then create something new by choosing a menu command. To combine two or more shapes into a new shape, follow these steps:

1. Select the shapes you want to combine.

You can select as many shapes as you need. The shapes must overlap, unless you're using the Blend command.

2. Choose Modify⇨Combine and then choose one of the following commands from the submenu:

- **Blend:** Creates a blend between the selected shapes. When you choose this command, FreeHand 10 creates new shapes between the original shapes.

- **Union:** Joins the selected objects into a single path. If you choose this command with filled objects, the new object inherits the fill of the object that was highest in the stack.

- **Divide:** Creates new shapes where the shapes intersect.

- **Intersect:** Creates a new shape that encompasses the area where the original shapes overlap.

- **Punch:** Cuts the object highest in the stack out of the objects underneath.

- **Crop:** Creates new paths by cropping to the area where the paths overlap.

- **Transparency:** Creates new shapes where the shapes intersect. The new shapes have a degree of transparency that allows the color of the underlying object to show through. When you choose this command, a dialog box appears that allows you to specify the degree of transparency.

After you choose one of the Combine commands, FreeHand 10 creates new shapes. Figure 5-9 shows the different shapes you can create with the commands.

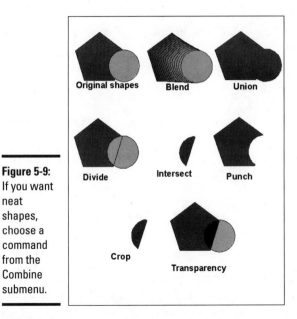

Figure 5-9: If you want neat shapes, choose a command from the Combine submenu.

Using the Xtras Tools to Change a Shape

You use the Xtras tools to create interesting shapes and modify existing ones. Instead of using a whole lot of pages to write about each tool, in the next sections, we show you how to use some of the more popular Xtras tools. We leave it to you to explore the others at your own leisure. To use an Xtras tool, choose Windows⇨Toolbars⇨Xtras Tools, and the toolbar shown in Figure 5-10 appears.

Arc   Smudge   Mirror
        3D
        Rotation | Shadow | Chart

Figure 5-10:
Xtras, come
and get your
Xtras tools.

        Spiral |Roughen| Bend

Fisheye   Eye-   Graphic
lens   dropper   hose

Using the Arc tool

You use the Arc Xtras tool to create . . . you guessed it: Arcs. To use the Arc tool, follow these steps:

1. **Double-click the Arc tool.**

   The Arc Tool dialog box opens.

2. **Select one of the following options: Create Open Arc, Create Flipped Arc, or Create Concave Arc.**

   When you select an option, a window in the dialog box gives you a preview of the arc the option creates.

3. **Click and drag.**

   As you drag the tool, a preview of the shape is created.

4. **When the arc is the desired shape, release the mouse button.**

Using the 3D Rotation tool

You use the 3D Rotation tool to give a garden-variety shape, such as a rectangle, perspective. The tool is interactive; you click and drag until you get the result you want. Follow these steps to use the 3D Rotation tool:

1. **Select the shape to which you want to give perspective.**

2. **Select the 3D Rotation tool from the Xtras toolbar.**

3. **Click and drag.**

   As you drag, FreeHand 10 draws a preview of the shape.

4. **Release the mouse button when the shape is as desired.**

   FreeHand 10 completes the 3D rotation.

You can modify the settings for the 3D Rotation tool by double-clicking it and modifying the settings in the 3D Rotation dialog box.

Using the Smudge tool

You use the Smudge tool to create ghost images of an object. It almost looks like someone repeatedly mashed a rubber stamp while moving along a straight line; each image is more faded than the last until the effect fades away. To use the Smudge tool, follow these steps:

1. **Select the object you want to smudge.**

2. **Select the Smudge tool from the Xtras toolbar.**

   Your cursor becomes a pointing finger.

   Double-click the Smudge tool to open the Smudge Tool dialog box. Within this dialog box, you can specify the final stroke and fill colors by dragging a color swatch from the Swatches, Tint, or Color Mixer panels into the appropriate field in the Smudge Tool dialog box.

3. **Click and drag in the direction you want the smudges to appear.**

   As you drag, an outline of the shape signifies the current position of your cursor and a straight line is drawn from the object's original position to the current position of the cursor. The straight line indicates the path of the smudges.

4. **Release the mouse button when the smudge path is acceptable.**

   FreeHand 10 creates some smudges.

Using the Shadow tool

You use the Shadow tool to create a drop shadow for a vector object in your document. You use the tool interactively by simply clicking where you want the shadow to appear. To create a shadow, follow these steps:

1. **Select the object you want to create a shadow for.**

2. **Select the Shadow tool from the Xtras toolbar.**

3. **Click and drag.**

   As you drag, FreeHand 10 creates an outline of the shadow's current position and a straight line from the corner of the original object to the shadow.

4. **Release the mouse button when the shadow is in the desired position.**

   FreeHand 10 creates a shadow using a tint of the original fill.

**Book IV
Chapter 5**

**Transforming Text,
Shapes, and Images**

You can vary the opacity of the shadow and change several other parameters by double-clicking the Shadow tool and then specifying different parameters in the Shadow dialog box.

Two other useful tools are on the Xtra Tools toolbar: the Bend tool and the Graphics Hose tool. The Bend tool bends vector objects. If you need to add many identical graphic elements, such as flowers or leaves, to an illustration, the Graphics Hose tool is the tool you need. Double-click the Graphics Hose tool to fill the graphic hose with preset objects from the Contents list, set your parameters, and then click away.

Using Xtras Operations to Modify Shapes

You use the Xtras Operations toolbar to modify shapes and more without a lot of extra work. Many of the tools on this toolbar are duplicated as menu commands. To open the Xtras Operations toolbar, shown in Figure 5-11, choose Window⇨Toolbars⇨Xtras Operations.

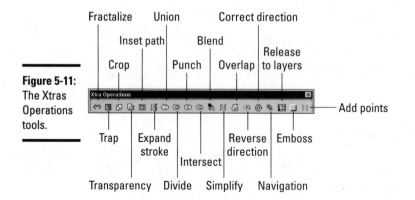

Figure 5-11: The Xtras Operations tools.

Most of the tools shown in Figure 5-11 have been covered previously. We urge you to experiment with the others, but unfortunately, we have no more space left to cover them. We're going to squeeze in an introduction to one more tool though: the Emboss tool.

The Emboss Xtras Operations tool is cool for things like buttons and just plain old fancy objects. The Emboss tool has so many options, it would take a half-hour long infomercial — The Amazing Emboss-a-matic — to explain them all. We give you the condensed version of how to use the Emboss tool:

1. **Select the object you want to emboss.**

2. **Double-click the Emboss tool from the Xtras Operations toolbar.**

The Emboss dialog box opens, as shown in Figure 5-12.

Figure 5-12:
You can
choose
settings for
the Emboss
tool.

3. **Click a button to select an emboss style. The available styles are: Emboss, Deboss, Chisel, Ridge, or Quilt.**

The buttons look just like the effect you get when you apply the effect to an object.

4. **From the Vary drop-down list, select Color or Contrast.**

If you select the Color option, the Highlight and Shadow fields become available. Click each color swatch to choose a color from the pop-up palette.

5. **Drag the slider to choose a Depth setting.**

6. **Enter a value in the Angle field.**

This determines the angle from which the light source comes. Alternatively, you can click and drag the dial slider.

7. **Click the Apply button to preview the object with the current settings.**

If the object is embossed to your liking, proceed to Step 8; otherwise, choose different settings and click the Apply button to preview the object with the new settings.

8. **Click OK.**

The object gets embossed.

Chapter 6: Exploring the Color Management Tools

In This Chapter

✔ **Working with color**

✔ **Creating a color palette**

✔ **Mixing a color**

✔ **Using the Eyedropper tool**

✔ **Modifying strokes and fills**

When you create a FreeHand 10 illustration, you can work with as much or as little color as you want. Right up front, you are advised to shy away from a monochrome palette, unless you're creating an illustration of a polar bear in a snowstorm or a piece of coal in an unlit room with no windows at midnight. But seriously, you can use color sparingly if you're creating an illustration for the Web, or you can use lots of color if you're creating illustrations for print. FreeHand 10 gives you a wide variety of color tools to work with. You can mix colors, create color palettes, load color palettes, and more. If you like bright, vibrant objects that look three dimensional in your illustrations, you can use the Fill inspector to create a gradient fill (a blend of two or more colors).

In this chapter, we show you how to use the FreeHand 10 color tools to add vibrancy to every illustration you create. We explain how to work with the different color models to mix up colors, as well as how to use the Swatches panel to create a color palette for your document. If you prefer to stick with a given color, but want lighter variations of it, we detail how to do this with the Tints panel.

Before you begin creating an illustration, consider its final destination. Are you creating an illustration for print or for the Web? If you're creating an illustration for print, choose colors from the CMYK palette. If you are having a service center print the illustration, find out what system they use for color matching and choose all your colors from that color system. We show you how to choose from a color system in the section, "Using the Swatches Panel."

If you're creating an illustration for monitor viewing, use colors from the RGB color model. If you're creating a document for Web viewing, remember the old Zen maxim: Less is more. If your viewing audience accesses the Internet using dial-up modems, the fewer colors you use, the smaller the file size, and thus the quicker the download time.

Using the Color Mixer

You use the Color Mixer to mix up any color of the rainbow for your objects. Hey, talk about truth in advertising. You can mix a color using one of three color models, or you can use the System Color Picker to add a splash of color to your illustration. The neat thing about the Color Mixer is that you're dealing with values. If you have a set of values for a color (say for example that lovely chartreuse your client uses for a logo), you can match that color exactly by entering the values in the appropriate section of the Color Mixer. In the next few sections, we explain how to use each color model to mix up a shade of chartreuse, or whatever other color you fancy for your illustration. To open the Color Mixer, shown in Figure 6-1, choose Window⇨Panels⇨Color Mixer.

After mixing a color, you can apply it to an object or add it to the Swatches panel. We cover these colorful tasks in the upcoming section, "Working with the Color Mixer."

Figure 6-1:
You can mix a color using one of three color models.

Add to Swatches panel

Mixing a CMYK color

When you mix a color using the CMYK color model, you mix percentages of Cyan, Magenta, Yellow, and blacK. If your document is destined for print, this is the color model you should choose. Follow these steps to mix a color using the CMYK color model:

1. **Choose Window⇨Panels⇨Color Mixer.**

The Color Mixer previously shown in Figure 6-1 opens.

2. **Click the CMYK button.**

The Color Mixer is reconfigured to mix a color in CMYK mode, as shown in Figure 6-2.

Color component values

Figure 6-2:
CMYK color:
A little dab'll
do ya.

Color value sliders

Original color   Mixed color

Add to
Swatches panel

3. **Drag the sliders to mix the color.**

As you drag the sliders, the color swatch on the right side at the bottom of the panel changes to reflect the current values. The values in each field update as well. Alternatively, you can enter known values in each field to match a known color.

Mixing an RGB color

When you create illustrations that will be displayed on a Web site or as part of a CD-ROM presentation, you use the RGB (*R*ed, *G*reen, *B*lue) color model. You have 256 values (values from 0 to 255) of each color to work with. For example, if you create an RGB color with the following values (R=255, G=0, B=0), you get bright red; the following values yield bright blue (R=0, G=0, B=255), the values for white are (R=0, G=0, B=0), and so on. When you combine the possible permutations, you end up with millions of colors. To mix an RGB color, follow these steps:

1. **Choose Window➪Panels➪Color Mixers.**

The Color Mixer opens (refer to Figure 6-1).

2. **Click the RGB button.**

The Color Mixer is reconfigured, as shown in Figure 6-3.

3. **Drag the sliders to mix the color.**

As you drag the sliders, the color swatch on the right side at the bottom of the panel changes to reflect the current values. The values in each field also update. Alternatively, you can enter values in the text fields, which by the by, is the proper way to match a known color value.

Color component values

Figure 6-3:
A dash of
red, green,
and blue.

Color value sliders

Original   Mixed
color   color

Add to
Swatches panel

Mixing an HLS color

FreeHand 10 uses HLS (*H*ue, *L*ightness, *S*aturation) color; you may see this
color model referred to as HSB (*H*ue, *S*aturation, *B*rightness) in other programs. When you mix a color using the HLS color model, you choose a Hue,
specify how Light the color is, and how Saturated the color is. The HLS
model is actually a color wheel. The hue is a value between 0 and 360
degrees. Values for Light and Saturation vary between 0 and 100. To mix an
HLS color, follow these steps:

1. **Choose Window⇨Panels⇨Color Mixer.**

   The Color Mixer opens (refer to Figure 6-1).

2. **Click the HLS button.**

   The Color Mixer is reconfigured, as shown in Figure 6-4.

HLS color wheel

Figure 6-4:
You can mix
a color from
the HLS
color wheel.

Color component values

Original   Mixed
color   color

Add to
Swatches panel

3. **Click inside the color wheel and drag to select a hue.**

As you drag, the color swatch at the bottom of the panel changes to reflect the color your cursor is currently over. The values in the Hue and Saturation fields update as well.

4. **Drag the slider to select a value for lightness.**

The values vary from 0 (black) to 100 (white). Alternatively, you can enter a value in the Lightness field.

5. **To specify saturation, enter a value in the Saturation field.**

You can enter a value between 0 and 100. Low values create a grayer variation of the color; higher values increase saturation, creating a more vibrant color. Alternatively, you can drag the point in the color wheel, towards the center to decrease saturation, or away from the center to increase saturation.

After you mix up a color, click the button for another color mode to see the component values for the new color in that color mode.

Mixing a color from the System Color Picker

Your operating system uses specific colors to display the icons, buttons, and text of the software you use. (If you use FreeHand 10 on a Macintosh machine, you choose a color from the Apple Color Picker, which oddly enough contains more colors than Candy Apple Red or Granny Smith Green.) You can use a color from the System Color Picker in your FreeHand 10 illustrations. To mix a color from the System Color Picker, follow these steps:

1. **Choose Window⇨Panels⇨Color Mixer.**

The Color Mixer opens (refer to Figure 6-1).

2. **Click the RGB or CMYK button.**

Choose the color mode you're using for the document. After you select a color from the System Color Picker, it is converted to the color model you choose.

3. **Click the System button.**

The Color dialog box opens, as shown in Figure 6-5.

4. **Click a color to select it.**

The swatch on the right corner at the bottom of the panel refreshes to show the color you select. The component values for the color are displayed in the text fields for the color mode you choose.

Figure 6-5:
You can
choose a
color from
the System
Color
Picker.

Working with the Color Mixer

After you use the Color Mixer to mix the perfect hue, you can apply it directly to an object, use it for the current fill color, or add it to the Swatches panel. We show you how to use the Swatches panel to create a color palette in the upcoming section, "Using the Swatches Panel."

Using the Color Mixer to apply color to an object

When you mix a color with the Color Mixer, you can apply it directly to an object in your document. To apply a color from the Color Mixer to an object, follow these steps:

1. **Click the swatch on the right side at the bottom of the Color Mixer.**

A square appears at the end of your cursor.

2. **While holding down the mouse button, drag toward the object you want to apply the color to.**

3. **Release the mouse button when your cursor is over the object.**

The color is applied to object.

Using the Color Mixer to change the current fill or stroke color

If you're getting ready to create several objects and you want to use the same stroke or fill color on these objects, you can replace the current stroke or fill color with one you mix in the Color Mixer. To use a color mixed in the Color Mixer as the current fill or stroke color, follow these steps:

1. **Select a non-drawing tool (the Pointer tool is a good choice) before mixing your color.**

If you select a drawing tool and then mix a color, all selected objects change to that color. When you draw a new object, the fill stroke colors revert to the previous colors.

2. **Click the swatch on the right side at the bottom of the Color Mixer.**

   A square appears at the end of your cursor.

3. **While holding down the mouse button, drag towards the Fill or Stroke color box.**

4. **Release the mouse button when your cursor is over the Fill or Stroke color box.**

   The swatch in the Fill color box or Stroke color box changes to the color you mixed in the Color Mixer. If you have an object in the document selected, its fill or stroke color changes as well.

Adding a color to the Swatches panel

If you mix a color you're going to use repeatedly in the document, you can add it to the Swatches panel. To add a color from the Color Mixer to the Swatches panel, follow these steps:

1. **Choose Window➪Panels➪Color Mixer.**

   The Color Mixer opens.

2. **Mix a color.**

   If you don't know how to mix a color, you didn't read the preceding section, "Using the Color Mixer." Caught ya. After you stop blushing, please read the "Using the Color Mixer" section.

3. **Click the Add to Swatches button at the lower-left corner of the Color Mixer panel.**

   The Add to Swatches dialog box opens.

4. **Accept the default name for the color or enter one of your own.**

   FreeHand 10 uses the component values to name the color. When the color is added to the Swatches panel, a small rectangular swatch of the new color is added as well. If you give the color a unique name, it will be easier to find if you're creating an illustration with lots of colors. To give the color a unique name, type the color and then press Enter.

5. **Choose Process or Spot.**

   This option refers to how the color is separated for the output device. Process colors are printed on four separate pages using the four process (CMYK) inks. Spot colors are not separated and are printed on a separate plate.

6. **Click Add.**

   The color is added to the Swatches panel.

Creating Color Tints

When you create a color tint, you create a lighter variation of the original color. You create a color tint by varying the percentage of the original color with the Tints panel. After you create a color tint, you can apply it directly to an object, add the tint to the Swatches panel, or use it as the current fill or stroke color. To create a color tint, follow these steps:

1. **Create a color using the Color Mixer panel.**

2. **Click the Tints tab.**

The Tints panel opens, as shown in Figure 6-6.

Figure 6-6:
To tint or not
to tint, that
is the
question.

Tint value windows

Original   Tinted
color   color

Add to
Swatches panel

3. **Drag the slider to specify the percentage of the original color that will be used to create the tint.**

As you drag the slider, the swatch at the bottom right of the panel updates to display the new tint. Compare this to the swatch on the bottom left of the panel, which is the original color. Alternatively, you can tint the color by clicking one of the squares (tints of the original color in 10 percent increments) or by entering a value in the field.

4. **After creating the tint, do one of the following:**

- Click the color swatch in the lower-right corner of the panel, and then drag and drop the color on an object in the document.

- Click the color swatch in the lower-right corner of the panel, and then drag and drop the color on the Fill color box to replace the current fill color with the tint, or drag and drop the color on the Stroke color box to replace the current stroke color with the tint. If you have an object selected while doing this, the object's stroke or fill color is changed as well.

- Click the Add to Swatches button to add the tint to the Swatches panel. After you click the button, the Add to Swatches dialog box appears. For more information on adding a color to the Swatches panel, read the "Adding a color to the Swatches panel" section, earlier in this chapter.

If the Color Mixer and Swatches panels are open at the same time, you can click the color swatch at the bottom of the Color Mixer panel, and drag and drop it into the Swatches panel, and the color is added to the palette. You can drag and drop a color from the Tints panel as well.

Using the Swatches Panel

When you create an illustration that uses the same colors on each page or for several objects, mixing the color each time you need it is time-consuming and counterproductive. You can save a considerable amount of time if you add the colors you use frequently to the Swatches panel. You also use the Swatches panel to use colors from preset color systems. This option is handy if you're creating a document that will be printed by a service center that uses a known color system to match colors. If you're creating a document for a Web page, you can also choose a color from the Web safe color library. Another option you have with the Swatches panel is saving the current color palette for future use. To open the Swatches panel, shown in Figure 6-7, choose Window⇨Panels⇨Swatches.

Figure 6-7:
You use the
Swatches
panel to
create a
color palette
and more.

Book IV
Chapter 6

Exploring the Color
Management Tools

The Swatches panel that is shown in Figure 6-7 already has colors added to it. The default colors when you create a new document are None, Black, White, and Registration. You cannot rename or delete these colors. Black is a spot color that is used for the black separation plate when printing a process color. The registration color is used for crop or trim marks and prints solid on separations.

You can differentiate color types in the Swatches panel as follows:

✦ **Process colors:** The names of process colors are italicized.

✦ **Spot colors:** The names of spot colors are displayed with plain type.

✦ **RGB colors:** RGB colors display a triangular icon with red, green, and blue spheres after the color's name. Colors derived from the HLS color wheel or the System Color Picker are displayed as RGB colors as well.

✦ **CMYK colors:** CMYK colors are displayed with no icon.

After you open the Swatches panel, you can do any of the following:

✦ **Apply a color to an object:** You can apply a color to an object by selecting it and then dragging and dropping it on an object. Alternatively, you can apply a color by selecting an object, and then clicking the desired color's name in the Swatches panel.

✦ **Modify a color:** You can modify a color in one of two ways:

• **Color Mixer panel:** You can modify a color by opening the Color Mixer panel and then dragging and dropping a color from the Swatches panel to the left side of the color swatch at the bottom of the Color Mixer panel.

• **Tints panel:** You can modify a color by opening the Tints panel and then dragging and dropping a color from the Swatches panel to the left side of the color swatch at the bottom of the Tints panel.

✦ **Change the stroke color:** You can change the current stroke color by selecting a color from the Swatches panel and then dragging and dropping it on the Stroke color box.

✦ **Change the fill color:** You can change the current fill color by selecting a color from the Swatches panel and then dragging and dropping it on the Fill color box.

Adding preset colors to the Swatches panel

You can add a color to the Swatches panel from the Color Mixer or Tints panel as outlined earlier in the chapter. If you fast-forwarded to this section and need to know how to add a color to the Swatches panel from the Color Mixer, read the section, "Adding a color to the Swatches panel"; to add a tint to the Swatches panel, read the section, "Creating Color Tints." In this section, we show you how to add colors to the Swatches panel from preset color matching systems. To add a color from a preset color matching system to the Swatches panel, follow these steps:

1. **Choose Window➪Panels➪Swatches.**

The Swatches panel opens.

2. **Click the triangle at the upper-right corner of the panel and choose one of the preset color matching sets.**

   If the document you're creating will be printed by a service center, find out the system they use for color matching. For example, they may use one of the Pantone or Munsell matching systems. If the document you're creating will be displayed on a Web page, choose Web Safe Color Library. After you choose a color matching system, the available colors appear in the Library window.

3. **Click a color to select it.**

   You can add additional colors to the selection by clicking them while holding down the Ctrl key.

4. **Click OK.**

   FreeHand 10 adds the selected color(s) to the Swatches panel using the color's default library name.

Renaming a color

You can rename any color in the Swatches panel, except the default colors: None, Black, White, and Registration. If you give a color a unique name, you'll have an easier time selecting it from the Swatches panel. To rename a color, follow these steps:

1. **Choose Window➪Panels➪Swatches.**

   The Swatches panel opens.

2. **Double-click the color you want to rename.**

   The color's name is highlighted.

3. **Type a new name for the color and then press Enter.**

   The color is renamed.

Exporting a color palette

When you create an ideal color palette, you can export the palette for future use. This option is handy if you do work for a client that uses specific color combinations for their text and logo. You create the palette by adding colors to the Swatches panel as outlined previously in this chapter in the "Adding a color to the Swatches panel," "Creating Color Tints," and "Adding preset colors to the Swatches panel" sections. After you create the palette, you can export it by following these steps:

1. **Choose Window➪Panels➪Swatches.**

   The Swatches panel opens.

2. **Click the triangle near the upper-right corner of the panel.**

   The Swatches panel menu opens.

3. **Choose Export.**

   The Export Colors dialog box, shown in Figure 6-8, opens.

Figure 6-8:
You can
create a
custom
color library
from the
Swatches
panel.

4. **Select the colors you want to export.**

   To select a color, click it. Hold down the Shift key to add contiguous colors to the selection, or hold down the Ctrl key to add noncontiguous colors to the selection.

5. **Click OK.**

   The Create Color Library dialog box appears.

6. **Enter a name in the Library Name field.**

   This is the name that will appear on the Swatches menu. Choose a meaningful name that describes the type of colors in the library, or enter the name of the client you use the colors for.

7. **In the Filename field, accept the default name of CUSTOM, or enter another name for the library.**

   If you intend to store more than one library, change the name to one that reflects the contents of the library.

8. **Click Save.**

   FreeHand 10 saves the library and it appears on the Swatches menu.

Adding custom colors to the Swatches panel

After you save a color palette as a library, you can use any or all colors from the palette in new illustrations by adding them to the Swatches panel. To add colors from a custom library to the current Swatches palette, follow these steps:

1. **Choose Windows⇨Panels⇨Swatches.**

   The Swatches panel opens.

2. **Click the triangle near the upper-right corner of the panel.**

   The Swatches menu opens.

3. **Select the custom color library by clicking its name.**

   The Library dialog box opens.

4. **Select the colors you want to add to the Swatches panel.**

   Select an individual color by clicking its swatch. To add contiguous colors to the selection, hold down the Shift key and click the colors you want to add. To add noncontiguous colors to the selection, hold down the Ctrl key and then click the colors you want to add.

5. **Click OK.**

   The colors are added to the Swatches panel.

Using the Eyedropper Tool

You use the Eyedropper tool to sample a color. You can sample the color from an object in your document, the Stroke color box, the Fill color box, or from the following panels: Color Mixer, Tints, and Swatches. To sample a color with the Eyedropper tool, follow these steps:

1. **Select the Eyedropper tool.**

   It's the tool with an eyedropper for an icon.

2. **Sample a color by doing one of the following:**

   - Click an object in the document window.
   - Click a color swatch in any of the following panels: Color Mixer, Swatches, or Tints.

   After you sample a color, hold down the mouse button and drag and drop the color to any of the following:

   - **A different object in the document:** Do this when you sample a color from one object that you want to apply to another.

- **An object in the document:** Do this when you want to sample a color from a panel.

- **The color swatch in the Color Mixer panel:** Do this when you want to modify a color using the Color Mixer.

- **The color swatch in the Tints panel:** Do this when you want to tint an existing color.

- **The Swatches panel:** Do this when you want to add a sampled color to the Swatches panel.

3. **Release the mouse button.**

   The sampled color is applied to the object or added to the panel you dropped it on.

Modifying Strokes with the Stroke Inspector

You use the Stroke inspector to change the color of a stroke, its width, and other parameters. If the stroke is a single line, you can add arrowheads to the head and/or tail of the stroke. The Stroke inspector has enough options to fill up a whole lot of pages. You'll never use many of the options, so we spare you a lot of excess verbiage and save ourselves from an early onset of carpal tunnel syndrome by showing you how to modify a basic stroke in this section. To modify a stroke with the Stroke inspector, follow these steps:

1. **Select the stroke you want to modify.**

   You select a single line, or modify an object's stroke (outline) by selecting the object.

2. **Choose Windows⇨Inspectors⇨Stroke.**

   The Stroke inspector, shown in Figure 6-9, opens.

3. **Click the triangle to the right of the stroke color name and select a color from the drop-down list.**

   The colors in this list are the colors you have stored in the Swatches panel. Alternatively, if you have the Tints or Color Mixer panel open, you can click the swatch from the panel and then drag and drop it on the current stroke color swatch in the Stroke inspector.

4. **Select an option from the Width drop-down list.**

   Alternatively, you can enter the desired value in the Width field.

5. **Click a button in the Cap section to determine the path end.**

   The available options are: Butt, Round, or Square.

6. **Click a button in the Join section to determine how path ends join.**

   The available options are: Mitered, Round, and Bevel.

Figure 6-9:
You can modify a stroke's appearance with the Stroke inspector.

Stroke color   Stroke type

Width

Bevel

Butt | Square | Round

Round   Mitered

7. Enter a value in the Miter Limit field.

This value is applicable if you choose a Miter join. Enter a value between 1 and 57. If the line length exceeds this value, it will be squared off instead of mitered.

8. To have a dashed stroke, select an option from the Dashed drop-down list.

9. To apply an arrowhead to an open path, select an option from the Arrowheads drop-down lists.

Use the left Arrowheads drop-down list to select an arrowhead for the start of the path; use the right Arrowheads drop-down list to select an arrowhead for the end of the path. You can select different arrowheads for each end of the path. You can also have an arrowhead at one end of the path and no arrowhead at the other.

The settings you specify are applied to the selected stroke. When you create a new stroke, the stroke is created using the previous settings.

You can use the Stroke inspector to set stroke settings for all future strokes you create. Deselect all objects in the document, select a non-drawing tool, such as the Pointer tool, and then set stroke characteristics as outlined in the previous steps. The characteristics will be applied to all future strokes until you modify the settings in the Stroke inspector.

If you like artistic brush strokes, select a path, open the Stroke inspector and then select Brush from the Stroke Type drop-down list. You can make the stroke look like it was painted with an artist's brush or an airbrush.

**Book IV
Chapter 6**

**Exploring the Color
Management Tools**

Modifying Fills with the Fill Inspector

When you add color to a shape, you give it a fill. You can modify the fill at any time using the Fill inspector. The Fill inspector is filled with all manner of different fill options. In fact, it has so many options; it would fill a chapter of its own. In the upcoming sections, we show you the most commonly used fill options.

Creating a Basic fill

You can create or modify a Basic fill with the Fill inspector. A Basic fill is pretty simple; it only has one color. When your design calls for a Basic fill, here's how you create one with the Fill inspector:

1. **Select the object whose fill you want to modify.**

   Alternatively, deselect all objects in the document, select a non-drawing tool, and the fill you create is applied to all future shapes you create.

2. **Choose Window⇨Inspectors⇨Fill.**

   The Fill inspector opens.

3. **From the Fill Type drop-down list, select Basic.**

   The Fill inspector is reconfigured, as shown in Figure 6-10. The default fill color of black is selected.

Figure 6-10:
Basic fills
are . . .
basic.

4. **Choose a color from the Fill drop-down list.**

   These are the colors currently in the Swatches panel. Alternatively, you can select a color by clicking the swatch in the Color Mixer or Tints panel and then dragging and dropping it on the current color swatch in the Fill inspector.

   After you select a color, it is applied to the selected object, or if you have no objects selected, the fill will be applied to all closed paths you create until you modify the fill.

Creating a Gradient fill

When you create a gradient fill, you blend two or more colors; you can create a graduated gradient fill, a radial gradient fill, or a contoured gradient fill. Figure 6-11 shows a comparison of the three types.

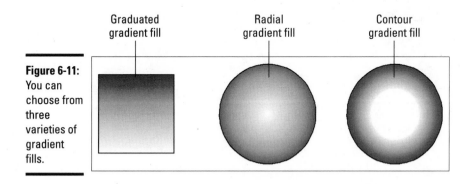

Graduated gradient fill   Radial gradient fill   Contour gradient fill

Figure 6-11: You can choose from three varieties of gradient fills.

When you create a gradient fill, you specify each color in the fill and where the color is blended. To create a gradient fill, follow these steps:

1. **Select the object to which you want to apply the gradient fill. The object must have a closed path.**

   Alternatively, you can deselect all objects in the document, and the fill you create will be applied to closed paths you create from this point forward.

2. **Choose Window⇨Inspectors⇨Fills.**

3. **From the Fill Type drop-down list, select Gradient.**

   The Fill inspector is reconfigured, as shown in Figure 6-12.

4. **Click the appropriate button to determine the fill type.**

   You can choose Graduated, Radial, or Contour. The default gradient fill blends black and white, but you can choose any color.

5. **Click the color swatch at either end of the color ramp and choose a color from the pop-up palette.**

   The color swatch refreshes to show the color you selected. Alternatively, you can click the color swatch in the Color Mixer or Tints panel and then drag and drop the color onto the color swatch on the color ramp.

Book IV Chapter 6

Exploring the Color Management Tools

Graduated

Radial

Contour

Figure 6-12:
You can
create a
colorful fill
by choosing
the gradient
option.

Color ramp

Color points

6. **To add additional color points to the gradient, click the color swatch at the right side of the color ramp and then drag and drop it to the desired position on the color ramp.**

   You can add as many points as needed to define your fill. After adding another color point, you can select a different color by using any of the methods outlined in Step 5. If you need to move a color pointer, click the color pointer and drag it to a different position on the color ramp. To remove a color point, click it and drag it off the color ramp.

   You can also drag a color from the Swatches panel and drop it in the desired position on the color ramp. You can use the Eyedropper tool to sample a color and then drop it on the color ramp as well.

7. **If you choose a Graduated fill, set the following options:**

   • **Linear or Logarithmic:** Select Linear or Logarithmic from the Taper drop-down list. Linear gradients blend the colors in equal increments. Logarithmic gradients blend the colors in ever-widening bands.

   • **Taper angle:** Drag the circular dial to specify the gradient taper angle. Hold down the Shift key while dragging to constrain the changes to 45-degree increments. Alternatively, you can enter a value in the text field.

8. **If you choose a Radial fill, drag the square in the middle of the right-hand window to set the center point of the fill, as shown in Figure 6-13.**

   This is the fill's center; the colors radiate from this point. To reset the fill center point, click inside the right window while holding down the Shift key.

Figure 6-13:
You set the
center point
of the fill by
dragging the
square.

Drag to set
fill center point

9. **If you choose a Contour fill, set the following options:**

   • Click the square in the center of the right-hand window to determine the center point of the fill.

   • Drag the taper slider to determine the area of the center color. Choose a low value for a wide area of center color; a high value to create a small area of center color. Alternatively, you can enter a value in the taper text field.

Creating a Tiled fill

When you create a tiled fill, you copy a shape from within the document and use it to create a fill that displays the copied object tiled within another object. You can specify how large the tiled object is and change the fill's position within the object. To create a tiled fill, follow these steps:

1. **Select the object that you want as the basis for your tiled fill.**

2. **Choose Edit⇨Copy.**

   The object is copied to the Clipboard.

3. **Select the object you want to fill.**

4. **Choose Window⇨Inspectors⇨Fill.**

   The Fill inspector opens.

5. **From the Fill Type drop-down list, select Tiled.**

   The Fill inspector is reconfigured to create tiled fills.

6. **Click the Paste In button.**

   The copied shape is pasted into the window and is tiled within the object you are filling.

7. **To resize the object, enter values in the x and y fields.**

   Enter values lower than 100 to make the object smaller and values larger than 100 to increase the size of the tiled object. As you enter values, the object's fill changes to reflect the new parameters. Enter the same value in each field to resize the object proportionately.

8. **Enter values in the x and y Offset fields.**

   The values you enter move the fill within the object to which it is applied. Enter positive x values to move the tiled fill to the right, and negative x values to move the tiled fill to the left. Enter positive y values to move the fill up, and negative y values to move the fill down.

9. **Drag the circular dial to set the fill's angle.**

   Hold down the Shift key to constrain the changes to 45-degree increments. Alternatively, you can enter a value in the Angle field. Figure 6-14 shows the Fill inspector being used to create a tiled fill and the object the tiled fill is being applied to.

Filled object   Fill scale

Figure 6-14:
It's not
ceramic,
but it is tile.

Fill angle

Fill offset

You can also modify colors in your documents by choosing Xtras⇨Colors and then choosing a command from the submenu. You can use these commands to lighten, darken, or desaturate process colors, as well as randomize colors, sort named colors, and more. We urge you to experiment with these powerful commands to further your use of color in FreeHand 10.

Chapter 7: Integrating FreeHand 10 with Other Macromedia Products

In This Chapter

✔ Integrating FreeHand 10 with Fireworks MX

✔ Integrating FreeHand 10 with Macromedia Flash MX

✔ Integrating FreeHand 10 with Dreamweaver MX

Macromedia Studio MX is a complete package that offers graphic designers and Web designers a wonderful set of tools to work with. The applications share some common components, and the interfaces are similar, which means you don't have to reinvent the wheel when you decide to branch out from one Macromedia Studio MX application to another. In addition to sharing common interface elements, Macromedia applications can use items created in another Macromedia application. For example, you can create a multipage FreeHand 10 document and export it as a Flash movie. You can also take advantage of FreeHand 10's superior illustration tools to create objects that would be difficult or impossible to create with other Macromedia applications. You can then export the objects for use in a Fireworks MX document that will be used in a Dreamweaver MX Web design, or incorporate the objects in a Flash movie or application. You can also publish a FreeHand 10 document as HTML that you can modify in Dreamweaver MX.

In this chapter, we show you some of the ways FreeHand 10 integrates with other Macromedia applications. We explain how to export illustrations as images for the Web and how to export a multipage document for use as a Flash movie.

Integrating FreeHand 10 with Fireworks MX

When you create artwork in FreeHand 10, you can export it for use in a Fireworks MX document. You can do this if you prefer the drawing toolset in FreeHand 10, but you also need to use the enhanced Web graphics features in Fireworks MX to create documents for Web pages. Fireworks MX also features enhanced optimization tools that enable you to optimize an image for an intended destination, producing a document with the smallest possible file size with acceptable image quality. You can export documents as image files, or as AI or EPS files, that can be opened in Fireworks MX. For information on file types you can open in Fireworks MX, refer to Book III, Chapter 8.

Even though you can export a FreeHand 10 document as a PNG file, when you open the file in Fireworks MX, all objects and layers are flattened and cannot be edited.

You can also get FreeHand 10 objects into Fireworks MX by dragging and dropping. To do this, create your artwork in FreeHand 10 and then launch Fireworks MX. You then need to size both application windows so that they are tiled side by side. At this point, you can drag an object from a FreeHand 10 document into a Fireworks MX document.

Integrating FreeHand 10 with Macromedia Flash MX

If you've used Macromedia Flash MX, you know the software has a wonderful toolset for creating animations; however, traditional graphic illustrators may find the drawing tools somewhat quirky. Even though Macromedia Flash MX has a powerful Pen tool that enables you to create open and closed paths, if your background is in graphic illustration, you'll find that the FreeHand 10 toolset is more powerful. In this regard, you can create a multipage document using the FreeHand 10 drawing tools to create characters that change from page to page. In the upcoming sections, we show you how to animate the artwork you create in FreeHand 10 and export the document as a Flash SWF movie file.

Creating animations

When you want to animate objects that you intend to use in Flash movies, you place the objects on separate layers. You can animate objects, groups, or blends. If you want to animate a single object and make it appear to move from one point of the page to another, follow these steps:

1. **Select the object you want to animate, press the Alt key, and drag to duplicate the object.**

   As you drag, FreeHand 10 creates a preview of the duplicate's current position.

2. **Release the mouse button when the duplicate object is in the desired position.**

   After you create the duplicate, you can use any tool to modify the shape. Do this when you want the shape to morph during the animation. For that matter, you can create a different object instead of creating a duplicate, and then follow the remaining steps to morph from one shape to another.

3. **Select the original and the duplicate objects.**

4. **Choose Xtras⇨Create⇨Blend.**

   FreeHand 10 creates a blend between the original and the duplicate objects.

5. **Select the blend.**

6. **Choose Xtras⇨Animate⇨Release to Layers.**

   The Release to Layers dialog box appears.

7. **Accept the default Sequence option and click OK.**

   FreeHand 10 releases the objects to layers.

After you release the blend to layers, you can preview the animation as it will appear in the Macromedia Flash Player. *Note:* The animation sequence is determined by the stacking of layers, and goes from the bottom layer up. Objects on the Background layer are shown on all frames of the animation.

To preview the animation as a Flash movie, follow these steps:

1. **Choose Control⇨Test Movie.**

   FreeHand 10 creates an SWF file and opens the movie in another window. When the window opens, the animation begins to play.

2. **After the movie begins, you can control the movie by choosing Control and then choosing one of these commands:**

   - **Play:** Restarts the movie after you stop it.
   - **Stop:** Stops the movie.
   - **Rewind:** Rewinds the movie to the first frame.
   - **Step Forward:** Advances the movie to the next frame.
   - **Step Backward:** Rewinds the movie to the previous frame.
   - **Export:** Opens the Export Movie dialog box.
   - **Movie Settings:** Opens the Movie Settings dialog box.

   After you preview the movie, you can fine-tune the document by selecting the FreeHand 10 document from the Document Title drop-down list.

Using ActionScript

When you create a document in FreeHand 10 with the intention of exporting it as a Flash movie, you can integrate ActionScript in the Flash movie. ActionScript adds a degree of interaction to a Flash movie. You can assign ActionScript to objects in your FreeHand 10 movie that cause the movie to

Book IV
Chapter 7

**Integrating
FreeHand 10 with
Other Macromedia
Products**

advance to another frame, stop, enable users to drag an object from one place to another, and so on. You choose which event causes the ActionScript to execute; for example, the downstroke or upstroke of a mouse click. The ActionScript is embedded in the Flash movie you export. You can assign one of the following actions to an object in a FreeHand 10 document:

✦ **Go To:** Advances the movie to another frame or scene.

✦ **Play:** Plays the movie frame by frame.

✦ **Stop:** Stops the movie.

✦ **Print:** Prints the frame.

✦ **Full Screen:** Displays the movie in Full Screen mode, regardless of the document size.

✦ **Start/Stop Drag:** Causes the object to be draggable, based on the event you choose; for example, when a user presses the mouse button.

You can assign ActionScript to a bitmap image or object in your FreeHand 10 document by following these steps:

1. **Select the object to which you want to assign ActionScript.**

2. **Choose Window⇨Toolbars⇨Xtras Operations.**

Alternatively, you can also choose Window⇨Panels⇨Navigation. Either way, the Xtras Operations toolbar appears in the workspace.

3. **Click the Navigation button that looks like a link.**

The Navigation dialog box appears, as shown in Figure 7-1.

Figure 7-1:
You can add ActionScript to objects in a FreeHand 10 document.

4. **Select an action from the Action drop-down list.**

You can select any of the actions listed in the previous bullet list.

5. **Select the event that triggers the action from the Event drop-down list.**

For more information on ActionScript events, refer to Book V, Chapter 8.

6. **If the action you select requires parameters, the Parameter drop-down list becomes active. Select the parameter that suits the way you want the action to execute.**

   For more information on ActionScript parameters, refer to Book V, Chapter 8.

7. **Close the Navigation dialog box.**

   The action is added to the object. Test the movie to make sure the action executes properly.

Exporting Flash movies

After you create an animation and add ActionScript to objects in the document, you can export the document as a Flash movie. You can export the movie for the Flash 4 or Flash 5 Player. To export your document as a Flash movie, follow these steps:

1. **Choose File⇨Export.**

   The Export Document dialog box appears.

2. **From the Save as Type drop-down list, select Macromedia Flash SWF.**

3. **Click the Setup button.**

   The Movie Settings dialog box, shown in Figure 7-2, appears.

4. **In the Objects section, select compression options from the Path Compression and the Image Compression drop-down lists.**

   The default compression setting is Medium. Select a higher setting to create a smaller file size with lower image quality. Select a lower setting for higher image quality at the expense of a larger file size.

Figure 7-2:
You can specify settings for your Flash movie.

**Book IV
Chapter 7**

**Integrating
FreeHand 10 with
Other Macromedia
Products**

5. If your document has dashed lines, you can convert them to individual objects by selecting the Trace Dashed Strokes option.

If you select this option, FreeHand 10 creates an individual object for each dash. This results in a larger file size, but you can edit each dash as an object if you import the movie into Macromedia Flash MX.

6. Select one of the following options from the Text drop-down list:

- **Maintain Blocks:** Select this option if you want to be able to edit the text when you import the file into Macromedia Flash MX.

- **Convert to Paths:** Select this option, and FreeHand 10 converts text objects to paths that cannot be edited as text in Macromedia Flash MX. This results in a smaller file size.

- **None:** Select this option, and FreeHand 10 does not export text objects with the Flash movie.

7. In the Frames section, select a Page option.

This determines how many pages of the document are exported as frames. Select the All option to export all pages, or enter specific page numbers in the From and To fields.

8. Select one of the following options from the Animation drop-down list:

- **Layers and Pages:** Select this option to export all layers and the pages you specify as frames. This option results in a single SWF file. Each exported page can be used as a scene in Macromedia Flash MX.

- **Layers:** Select this option to export each page as a separate SWF file. Layers on each page are converted to frames.

- **Pages:** Select this option to export each page of the document in a single SWF file. Layers on each page are flattened to a single image.

- **None:** Select this option to export each page of the FreeHand 10 document as a single SWF file. Layers on each page are flattened to a single image in the Flash movie.

9. Accept the default frame rate of 12 fps (frames per second) or enter a different value.

This value is the number of frames that result in one second of playback in the Flash movie. Enter a lower value for a smaller file size that may cause jerky motion when the movie is played; enter a higher value for smoother motion at the expense of a larger file.

10. Select the Autoplay option (enabled by default), and the movie begins playing as soon as it loads into the Macromedia Flash Player.

Deselect this option if you have added ActionScript that causes the movie to begin playing when a user clicks an object in the Flash movie.

11. **Select the Full Screen Playback option, and the exported Flash movie expands to fill the user's screen.**

The user can exit full-screen mode by pressing the Esc key.

12. **Select an option from the Compatibility drop-down list.**

The default Flash 5 option enables the movie to be viewed successfully in the Macromedia Flash 5 Player or greater. Select the Flash 4 option if you think your audience may be using older versions of the Macromedia Flash Player.

13. **Select the Protect from Import option, and the movie cannot be imported into Macromedia Flash MX, or any previous version of Flash.**

This option prevents other animators from dissecting your handiwork in Macromedia Flash MX, or previous versions of the software. Do not select this option if you intend to use the exported Flash movie as part of another production you are editing in Macromedia Flash MX.

14. **Select the High Quality Printing option (the default option) to allow users to print frames from the Flash movie at high resolution (Flash 4 Player or newer).**

If you deselect this option, the resolution for printing defaults to screen resolution (72 dpi).

15. **Click OK.**

The Movie Settings dialog box closes.

16. **Enter a name for the file and specify the folder to which you want the file saved.**

17. **Click the Save button.**

FreeHand 10 exports the file as an SWF movie.

Integrating FreeHand 10 with Dreamweaver MX

The artwork that you create in FreeHand 10 can be exported in formats you can use in a Dreamweaver MX HTML document. You can export documents as JPEG or GIF files. You can also export documents as SWF files that you can then embed in Web pages you create within Dreamweaver MX.

In addition, you can add navigation links to objects in your FreeHand 10 documents and then publish the document as an HTML file. If this piques your curiosity, please read the following sections.

Adding navigation links

You can add a navigation link to any object in a FreeHand 10 document. This option is handy when you intend to publish the document as an HMTL file.

Book IV
Chapter 7

Integrating
FreeHand 10 with
Other Macromedia
Products

To add a navigation link to an object in a FreeHand 10 document, follow these steps:

1. **Select the object to which you want to add the link.**

You can add a link to a text object, a path, or a bitmap image. However, if you assign a link to an open path, you don't give the user much of a target area to click.

2. **Choose Window⇨Xtras Operations.**

The Xtras Operations toolbar appears in the workspace.

3. **Click the Navigation button (it looks like a link from a chain).**

The Navigation dialog box opens, as shown in Figure 7-3.

Figure 7-3:
You use the Navigation dialog box to create a hyperlink.

4. **In the Link field, enter the URL you want linked to the object.**

This is the Web page that appears in the user's browser when the link is clicked. If the Web page is at the same Web site, you only need to enter the filename of the page you want opened when the link is clicked; for example: `myPage.htm`. If the file is in a different directory, you need to enter the relative path to the file; for example, `htmldocs/myHtmldoc.htm`. If the Web page resides at another Web site, you need to enter the absolute path to the Web page, such as `http://www.dasdesigns.net/about.htm`.

5. **Close the Navigation dialog box.**

The link is assigned to the object and will be written as HTML code when the document is published as an HTML file.

Publishing a document as HTML

When you create a FreeHand 10 document that you intend to use as a Web page, you can publish the document as an HTML file that you can edit in Dreamweaver MX. When you publish a FreeHand 10 document as an HTML file, FreeHand 10 writes the HTML code needed to display the objects and bitmaps in the document in a Web browser, as well as to create any links you assigned to objects in the document. To export a FreeHand 10 document as an HTML file, follow these steps:

1. **Choose File➪Publish as HTML.**

The HTML Output dialog box opens.

2. **Click the Setup button.**

The HTML Setup dialog box appears, as shown in Figure 7-4.

3. **In the Document Root field, enter the folder where the files for your Web site are stored.**

If you're using the file in a Web site you've already created in Dreamweaver MX, store the file in the same directory as your Dreamweaver MX HTML documents.

4. **Select one of the following options from the Layout drop-down list:**

- **Positioning with Layers:** Select this option, and FreeHand 10 creates HTML code that positions the objects using HTML layers. This option precisely places each object in the document. Browsers capable of decoding HTML 3.0 or greater support layers.

- **Positioning with Tables:** Select this option, and FreeHand 10 creates an HTML document with a table. Each object in the document is placed in a table cell. Overlapping objects are sliced or combined to fit table cells. Most popular Web browsers support tables.

5. **Select the option applicable to the language in your document from the Encoding drop-down list.**

The default, Western (Latin 1), is the proper encoding format for the English language.

6. **Select one of the following options from the Vector Art drop-down list: GIF, JPEG, PNG, or SWF.**

This option determines which format FreeHand 10 uses when converting paths in your document to images that will be displayed in a Web browser.

Book IV
Chapter 7

Integrating
FreeHand 10 with
Other Macromedia
Products

7. **Select one of the following options from the Images drop-down list: GIF, JPEG, PNG, or SWF.**

   The option determines the file format FreeHand 10 uses to convert bitmap images in your document into images that are displayed when the HTML document is loaded into a Web browser. If the image has millions of colors, choose JPEG. If the image has large areas of solid color, choose GIF.

8. **Click OK.**

   The HTML Setup dialog box closes.

9. **Select an option for Pages.**

   You can publish all pages as HTML documents, or specify a range of pages to publish.

10. **Select the Show Output Warnings option (selected by default), and FreeHand 10 displays the HTML Output Warnings dialog box when converting the document to HTML.**

    The HTML Output Warnings dialog box warns you of any potential anomalies that would prevent the page from displaying properly in a Web browser.

11. **Select the View in Browser or HTML Editor option.**

    This option is selected by default. When the document is converted, FreeHand 10 displays the document in your default Web browser. You can specify another Web browser or HTML editor by clicking the Browse button and then using the Open dialog box to navigate to the folder where the EXE file for the browser or HTML editor is located.

12. **Select the Save as HTML option.**

    FreeHand 10 converts the file to HTML format. The file is displayed in your default browser if you choose this option. If the file is displayed in a browser, you can check to make sure the links are working properly. When the file is saved, FreeHand 10 creates a folder named FreeHand 10 HTML Output that is stored in the folder you specified in the HTML Setup dialog box in Step 3. Within the FreeHand 10 HTML Output folder is a subfolder named Images that stores the vector and bitmaps artwork from the document.

After you publish a document as HTML, you can edit the file by opening it in Dreamweaver MX, modifying the document to suit the Web site it will be displayed at, and then uploading the file to a Web site. When you upload the HTML file, you will have to upload any associated images from the Images folder as well.

Book V

Macromedia Flash MX

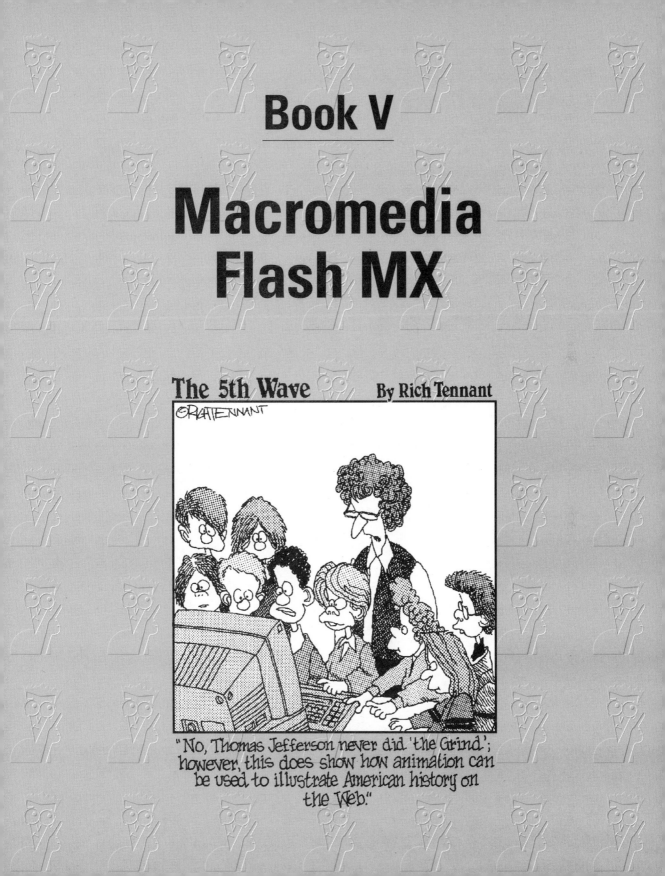

The 5th Wave   By Rich Tennant

"No, Thomas Jefferson never did 'the Grind'; however, this does show how animation can be used to illustrate American history on the Web."

Contents at a Glance

Chapter 1: Introduction to Macromedia Flash MX

In This Chapter

✔ Familiarizing yourself with Macromedia Flash MX

✔ Introducing vector graphics

✔ Investigating basic movie making principles

✔ Creating a Flash document file

✔ Exploring the Macromedia Flash MX interface

✔ Viewing movies

✔ Setting preferences in Macromedia Flash MX

✔ Getting help

*I*f you are creating a Web site, Macromedia Flash MX isn't a necessity. If this is the case, the question becomes: When and why do you use Macromedia Flash MX? The answer is simple: You use Macromedia Flash MX when you want your Web site to make greater use of animation, sound, and interactive graphics. This chapter provides an introduction to Macromedia Flash MX and its capabilities.

Understanding What Macromedia Flash MX Is and How It Works

If someone asks you what Macromedia Flash MX is, you can quickly say, "It's a Web animation program." However, that statement, while true, doesn't do justice to Macromedia Flash MX's wide-ranging capabilities.

Recognizing what Macromedia Flash MX can do

Macromedia Flash MX is a rich program. It is fully programmable and uses its own language, called ActionScript. Only your creativity limits what you can do with Macromedia Flash MX. The following list points out Macromedia Flash MX's major features and may help you decide if you want to use Macromedia Flash MX on your Web site:

✦ Animate text and graphics, including changing their color and visibility.

✦ Create your own graphics or import graphics from another program, such as Macromedia FreeHand 10 or Fireworks MX.

✦ Design Web buttons, still or animated, that link users to other pages or sites or perform other programmed actions.

✦ Add sound and video to your Web site.

✦ Add interactivity to your site by enabling viewers to choose where they go and what they see or hear. You can also create forms for viewers to fill out, poll their interests, and customize a site for each viewer.

✦ Create a user interface, including scrollbars, check boxes, list boxes, forms, and more.

If you wish, you can design an entire Web site using Macromedia Flash MX. For example, you can use Flash buttons to create your menu and place the content of your Web site on the Timeline. Macromedia Flash MX gives you complete artistic freedom when designing your site, while designing in HTML can be limiting. For example, HTML significantly limits your placement of objects. On the other hand, when using Macromedia Flash MX, you need to be careful that the site displays quickly and is easy to navigate. Also, updates and server-side connectivity may be more complex and time-consuming with Macromedia Flash MX.

Creating content for a Web site in Macromedia Flash MX

Using Macromedia Flash MX has two components. First you create the Flash document and publish it to a format that a browser can read. Then you (or others) view the Flash content in a browser. To create Flash content, you follow these basic steps:

1. **Create your Flash animation in Macromedia Flash MX and save it as a Flash document.**

   This document has an .fla extension and is often called an FLA file. (Chapters 2 through 6 and Chapters 8 and 9 in Book V explain the features Macromedia Flash MX offers for creating Flash documents.)

2. **Use the Publish command in Macromedia Flash MX to save your FLA file as a Flash movie.**

   The Flash movie has an .swf extension and is often called an SWF file. When you publish the movie, Macromedia Flash MX also generates the HTML code that you need to insert the SWF file into your Web page. See Book V, Chapter 7 for detailed instructions.

You sometimes see an FLA file referred to as a movie file. However, current Macromedia usage is to call the SWF file a movie. You sometimes see the SWF file called a Shockwave file, which explains the letters SWF. However, Macromedia no longer uses this terminology for the SWF file.

3. **Insert the HTML code into your Web page (or create a new Web page and add the HTML code).**

   The HTML code refers to the SWF file.

After these three steps, you follow the procedures you use for any Web site — uploading the HTML and SWF files.

Using Macromedia Flash MX on a Web site

In order to view a Flash movie, you need the Macromedia Flash Player. Macromedia Flash Player 6 is the latest player as of this writing. After you have the Macromedia Flash MX player installed, your browser automatically uses the player to display the Flash animation. The Macromedia Flash Player is a free download from the following Web site:

```
www.macromedia.com/shockwave/download/index.cgi?P1_Prod_Version=ShockwaveFlash
```

Although the vast majority of people who access your Web site will have the Macromedia Flash Player on their computers already, it is a good idea to include a button or link on your Web site that connects to this URL so that people can easily find and download the player if they need it.

Appreciating the Unique Nature of Vector Graphics

Most graphics that you see on a Web site are bitmap files. A *bitmap* is a graphic image that's made up of many tiny dots (bits), which are very close together. The various colored dots create the pattern that your eyes see as a picture. When the dots are displayed on a computer screen, they're called pixels. To get a bitmap graphic into Macromedia Flash MX, you import it. See Book V, Chapter 3 for more about importing graphics.

Bitmap graphics can create very large file sizes (although compression can make the files smaller). Large file sizes mean that your Web page takes longer to display in a Web browser. Also, bitmaps don't scale very well. If you need to enlarge a bitmap, you start to see the individual dots, which results in a grainy graphic image.

Macromedia Flash MX creates vector graphics. Unlike bitmaps, *vector graphics* are defined by equations that specify location, direction, and color. White space is not recorded. The equations result in small file sizes, and that means quick display on your Web site. Moreover, vector graphics are easily scalable. No matter how large or small you make your graphic, it always looks clear.

Not all graphics can be created using vectors. Photographs and other complex designs usually need bitmaps to be displayed in all their glory. Often you will use a combination of bitmap and vector graphics.

Exploring Basic Movie Making Principles

Macromedia Flash MX uses a classic movie making structure:

+ **The Stage:** The Stage contains all your content, which includes graphics and text.
+ **Frames:** A frame represents a small unit of time, such as $\frac{1}{12}$ of a second. Each frame contains a tiny section of the animation.
+ **The Timeline:** The Timeline contains all the frames. You use the timeline to manipulate your content over time, and thus create the animation.

The Stage

The Stage, shown in Figure 1-1, is a simple rectangle on which you place all your content. You change the content on the Stage from frame to frame to create animation. You generally use the drawing and editing tools in the Toolbox to draw and edit the content on the Stage. In this respect, Macromedia Flash MX is a graphic program like many others. You can create text, circles, lines, and so on, and you can specify the color of the objects that you create. You can save the graphics in standard Web site bitmap formats — JPEG, GIF, and PNG.

In the section, "Setting document properties," later in this chapter, we explain how to specify the size and color of the Stage.

The Timeline

You can think of the Timeline (see Figure 1-1) as the frames in a film reel. The difference is that Macromedia Flash MX's Timeline is electronic, rather than on film. Each frame covers a specific period of time. The default frame rate is 12 frames per second (fps), which means that each frame covers $\frac{1}{12}$ of a second. You use the frames in the Timeline to control the flow of the animation. You click a frame to make it current. By specifying which frames contain animation, you determine when animation starts and stops. Book V, Chapter 5 explains more about working with the frames in the Timeline.

The Toolbox

Layer list

Current scene   Timeline   Menus   Stage   Zoom control box

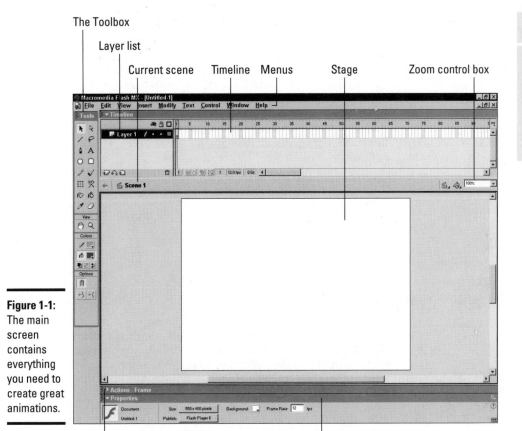

Figure 1-1:
The main
screen
contains
everything
you need to
create great
animations.

Actions panel (collapsed)   Properties panel (partially expanded)

Layers

In Figure 1-1, you can see the layer list, which includes the default Layer 1,
to the left of the Timeline. Layers are covered in Book V, Chapter 4, but for
now you should understand that you can separate the content on the Stage
into layers. Layers help organize your content so that your graphics and
animations don't "bump" into each other. You should also use separate
layers for ActionScript and sounds.

Scenes

A scene is simply a way to organize the Timeline. You can use the default
Scene 1 (see Figure 1-1) and ignore scenes altogether. However, when your
animations become more complex, scenes help you keep track of your
movie structure. Scenes are further discussed in Book V, Chapter 5.

Creating a Flash Document File

The first step to creating a Flash document is to start Macromedia Flash MX. In most cases, you have a shortcut on your desktop. Double-click it to start Macromedia Flash MX. If you don't have a shortcut, choose Start⇨Programs⇨ Macromedia⇨Macromedia Flash MX.

When you start Macromedia Flash MX, you're immediately in a new movie. To open an existing movie, choose File⇨Open, locate the FLA file, and double-click it. You often start by creating or importing graphics.

To save a Flash document as an FLA file for the first time, choose File⇨Save. Choose a location on your hard drive or network, type a name, and click the Save button. After the first save, just choose File⇨Save to save your latest changes.

Taking a Quick Tour of the Macromedia Flash MX Interface

The Macromedia Flash MX interface exists to help you create animation. While the interface has several components and is very customizable, you will soon find it easy to use. Refer to Figure 1-1 to see one way of viewing the interface.

Menus

Most of the commands that you use in Macromedia Flash MX are on the menus. Macromedia Flash MX doesn't make extensive use of the toolbars that are so familiar from other programs. Here is a summary of the menu items and their main features:

✦ **File:** Open, close, and save files; import and export files; print a Flash document; publish documents (to create SWF movie files); close Macromedia Flash MX.

✦ **Edit:** Undo and redo commands; cut, copy, and paste; delete, duplicate, and select objects on the Stage; copy and paste frames from the Timelines; edit symbols, which is covered in Book V, Chapter 3; set preferences; create keyboard shortcuts.

✦ **View:** Zoom in and out, change how Macromedia Flash MX displays objects and text, choose which parts of the screen you want to display, snap objects to pixels on the Stage or other objects.

✦ **Insert:** Insert symbols, insert and delete frames on the Timeline, insert layers, create animation (see Book V, Chapter 5).

✦ **Modify:** Edit layers, scenes, the Stage, symbols, frames, and graphic objects on the Stage.

✦ **Text:** Format text.

✦ **Control:** Play and rewind animation, test movies and scenes, activate some interactive features, mute sounds.

✦ **Window:** Display panels and toolbars.

✦ **Help:** Get help on Macromedia Flash MX and ActionScript.

Most of the menu commands are discussed in detail in the rest of this book.

Table 1-1 lists some of the commonly used keyboard shortcuts for the menu commands. After you get used to them, you'll find that they're faster than using the menu. Later in this chapter, we explain how you can create your own keyboard shortcuts.

It may be helpful to photocopy this table and post it up near where you work.

Table 1-1	Handy Keyboard Shortcuts
Menu Command	*Keyboard Shortcut*
File⇨New	Ctrl+N
File⇨Open	Ctrl+O
File⇨Save	Ctrl+S
File⇨Import	Ctrl+R
Edit⇨Undo	Ctrl+Z
Edit⇨Redo	Ctrl+Y
Edit⇨Cut	Ctrl+X
Edit⇨Copy	Ctrl+C
Edit⇨Paste	Ctrl+V
Edit⇨Paste in Place	Ctrl+Shift+V
Edit⇨Copy Frames	Ctrl+Alt+C
Edit⇨Paste Frames	Ctrl+Alt+V
View⇨Hide Panels	F4
Insert⇨Convert to Symbol	F8
Insert⇨New Symbol	Ctrl+F8
Insert⇨Frame	F5
Insert⇨Keyframe	F6
Modify⇨Group	Ctrl+G

(continued)

Table 1-1 *(continued)*

Menu Command	Keyboard Shortcut
Modify⇨Break Apart	Ctrl+B
Control⇨Play	Enter
Control⇨Rewind	Ctrl+Alt+R
Control⇨Test Movie	Ctrl+Enter
Window⇨Align	Ctrl+K
Window⇨Color Swatches	Ctrl+F9
Window⇨Actions	F9
Window⇨Library	Ctrl+L or F11

Timeline

The Timeline doesn't tell you *what* is happening; it tells you *when* something is happening. However, the Timeline does give you clues about the content of your animation. Figure 1-2 shows a Timeline with plenty of action. (Book V, Chapter 5 is all about using the Timeline to create animation.)

Figure 1-2: A busy Timeline.

If the Timeline isn't displayed, choose View⇨Timeline. Note that each layer has its own Timeline, so that you can see the sequence of events separately for each layer. (See Book V, Chapter 4 for more information about the Timeline, layers, and the layer list.) The Timeline has the following features (see Figure 1-2):

✦ **Layer list:** The layer list helps you organize your content. For example, Figure 1-2 shows separate layers for different objects, sounds, and actions (ActionScript programming).

✦ **Insert a layer:** Use the New Layer button to add a new layer.

✦ **Delete a layer:** Use the Delete Layer button to delete a layer.

✦ **Playhead:** The playhead indicates the current frame.

✦ **Current frame:** The Current frame box also displays the current frame.

✦ **Frame rate:** The Frame rate box displays the current frame rate, which is the number of frames that play per second in an animation.

✦ **Elapsed seconds:** The Elapsed seconds box displays the number of seconds that have passed from the beginning of the movie to the current frame, at the current frame rate.

✦ **Action:** A small *a* in a frame indicates that the frame contains ActionScript to control the animation.

✦ **Keyframe with no content:** A *keyframe* is a frame that contains a change in the animation. If you insert a keyframe but don't put anything in that keyframe, the Timeline displays an unfilled circle.

✦ **Keyframe with content:** When a keyframe contains any object, the Timeline displays a filled circle.

✦ **Sound:** When you insert sound into an animation, its wave appears on the Timeline.

✦ **Motion tween:** A motion tween is motion animation that Macromedia Flash MX calculates automatically from the first and last keyframes. The Timeline shows motion tweens in light blue.

✦ **Shape tween:** A shape tween is shape (morphing) animation that Macromedia Flash MX calculates automatically. The Timeline shows shape tweens in light green.

Toolbox

The Toolbox includes all the tools you need in order to create and edit graphics. The Toolbox contains four sections:

✦ **Tools:** Select, draw, and edit graphic objects and text

✦ **View:** Pan and zoom

✦ **Colors:** Specify the color of lines and fills

✦ **Options:** Specify options for the buttons in the Tools section

Figure 1-3 shows the Toolbox in detail, and you can also see the options for the Brush tool. See Book V, Chapter 2 for further explanation about the Toolbox.

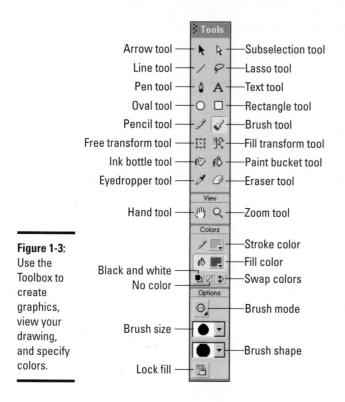

Figure 1-3:
Use the
Toolbox to
create
graphics,
view your
drawing,
and specify
colors.

All the tools in the Toolbox have keyboard shortcuts. It's very convenient to pick a tool using your left hand on the keyboard while your right hand is on the mouse (or perhaps vice versa if you're left-handed). Table 1-2 lists keyboard shortcuts for many of the tools in the Toolbox.

Table 1-2	Keyboard Shortcuts for Toolbox Tools		
Tool	*Shortcut*	*Tool*	*Shortcut*
Arrow	V	Brush	B
Subselection	A	Free Transform	Q
Line	N	Fill Transform	F
Lasso	L	Ink Bottle	S
Pen	P	Paint Bucket	K
Text	T	Eyedropper	I

Tool	Shortcut	Tool	Shortcut
Oval	O	Eraser	E
Rectangle	R	Hand (Pan)	H
Pencil	Y	Zoom	M, Z

Panels

You use panels to specify settings (such as colors) or to view information about objects. You can access the panels from the Window menu, and panels also have their own Options menus. Click the Menu icon on a panel to display the menu.

You can organize the Macromedia Flash MX screen for your convenience. For certain tasks, you may want one group of panels open, for other tasks, you may want a different group available, or none at all. Here are some guidelines for working with panels:

✦ **Save panel layouts:** If you like to work with certain panels open most of the time, you can save panel configurations. Just display the panels you want and choose Window⇨Save Panel Layout. Type a name for the layout and click OK. The next time you want to see that layout, choose Window⇨Panel Sets. You'll see your layout listed on the submenu. Choose it to restore your panel layout.

✦ **Dock:** The panels can be docked at the edge of the screen so that they don't cover up the Stage. To dock a panel, drag it by its *grabber* (the five dots next to the name of the panel) to the right or bottom of the screen until it displays a rectangular border. (See Figure 1-4.) To undock a panel, drag the grabber away from the edge of the screen.

✦ **Hide/Display panels:** Press F4 or the Tab key to hide all the panels and then get them back again.

✦ **Stack:** You can stack panels one on top of the other to save space. Drag the panel by its grabber beneath another panel. (See Figure 1-4.)

✦ **Collapse and expand:** You can collapse a panel to just a title bar when you need more space on your screen — this option makes it easy to reopen the panel when you need it again. You can either click the panel's title bar or click the collapse/expand arrow at the left side of the title bar. (See Figure 1-4.)

Specific panels are covered throughout the book as appropriate. For example, Chapter 2 includes a discussion of colors as well as the panels that you need to use to create and work with colors.

Collapse/Expand arrow

Grabber   Title bar

Docked, expanded panel

Docked, collapsed panel
Menu icon

Figure 1-4:
Panels are
somewhat
like dialog
boxes. Use
them to
specify
settings and
display
information
about
objects.

Undocked panel

The Property inspector

The Property inspector is a special panel that you use almost all the time.
The Property inspector is context-sensitive, which means that it changes
depending on what you are doing. For example, if you are working with text,
you see all the possible text properties, as shown in Figure 1-5. If you select
a rectangle, you see the properties of that shape. Usually, you keep the
Property inspector open at the bottom of the screen, either expanded or
collapsed. The Property inspector has its own special expand/collapse
arrow at its lower-right corner that you use to display additional properties.

Figure 1-5:
The
Property
inspector
lets you
inspect and
change the
properties
of your
objects.

Expand/Collapse arrow

To set the properties of an object, select it and enter the properties in
the appropriate boxes of the Property inspector. Specific details about the
Property inspector are explained throughout the rest of the book in the
context of the topics of each chapter.

Library

Every Flash document file has its own Library. Whenever you import a
graphic, video, or sound, Macromedia Flash MX saves it in the Library. If you
save a graphic object as a symbol (see Book V, Chapter 3 for details), it goes
in the Library as well. The Library stores every object that you might use
again. These objects all have names so that you can easily find them.

To use any object from the Library, click the keyframe on the Timeline
where you want it to appear and drag the object from the Library onto the
Stage. (Keyframes are explained in Book V, Chapter 5.) You can drag an
object from the preview window or from the item's listing. Figure 1-6
shows a Library with several types of objects.

To keep your Library from becoming overwhelming, use the Library tools:

✦ **Use folders:** Organize your Library items into folders. To create a new
folder, click the New Folder icon. Then drag items onto the folder's
name. Double-click a folder to expand or collapse it.

✦ **Sort:** You can alphabetize Library items by any column. Click the heading of the column. To reverse the sort order, click the Sort Order icon.

✦ **Rename:** Double-click any item and type a new name.

✦ **Delete:** Select an item and click the Delete (Trashcan) icon. Macromedia
Flash MX warns you that this action cannot be undone.

✦ **Update:** If a sound, video, or bitmap file that you have imported has
changed, you can update the Library to use the latest version of that
file. Click the Menu icon and choose Update.

Button symbol   Menu

Figure 1-6:
The Library
contains
named
objects that
are saved
with a Flash
document
file.

Preview box

Sort order
(ascending
or descending)

Graphic symbol

Movie clip symbol

Sound

Expanded folder

Delete (trashcan)

View item properties

New folder

New symbol

You are not limited to using items in your current document's Library. You
can open a Library from any Flash document and drag any of its items into
your movie. Choose File⇨Open as Library and choose the file. The new
Library opens as a stacked panel on your current Library panel.

If you want some sample Library items to look at, choose
Window⇨Common Libraries. You find a good assortment of sounds and
symbols that come with Macromedia Flash MX.

Viewing the Stage

As you work, you often need to zoom in to see part of the Stage more closely
or zoom out to see the entire Stage. You may also want to *pan* — to move
the display in any direction.

Below the right side of the Timeline you can find the Zoom drop-down list,
as shown in Figure 1-7. Click the arrow to set the zoom percentage.

Figure 1-7:
Use the
Zoom drop-
down list to
see objects
on the Stage
more clearly.

Another way to zoom in and out is to use the Zoom tool in the View section of the Toolbox, which is shown in Figure 1-8:

1. **Choose the Zoom tool.**

The Options section displays the plus and minus icons.

Figure 1-8:
The View
section of
the Toolbox.

2. **Choose the plus icon to zoom in or the minus icon to zoom out.**

3. **Click anywhere on the Stage to zoom in or out.**

To pan, choose the Pan tool, in the View section of the Toolbox, and drag on the Stage in any direction. You can also use the scrollbars to pan.

Setting Movie and Macromedia Flash MX Preferences

Macromedia Flash MX offers lots of opportunities to customize the way it looks and functions. It's worthwhile to take a look at these features to make your work flow as smoothly as possible.

Setting document properties

One of the first things you do when you start a movie is set the size and color of the Stage, along with other properties that apply to the entire Macromedia Flash MX document. You can adjust these settings using the Property inspector or the Document Properties dialog box. To use the Property inspector, follow these steps:

1. **Choose Window⇨Properties to display the Property inspector if it isn't already open.**

If the Property inspector isn't expanded, click its title bar.

2. **Click the Stage to make sure no other object is selected.**

The Property inspector looks like the one shown in Figure 1-9.

Figure 1-9:
The Property inspector when no objects are selected.

3. **To change the Stage size, click the Size button.**

The Document Properties dialog box, shown in Figure 1-10, opens.

Figure 1-10:
The Document Properties dialog box.

4. **Type the new width and height of the Stage in the Dimensions text fields and click OK.**

5. **To change the frame rate (the speed at which Macromedia Flash MX plays the frames), type a new number in the Frame Rate text field.**

The default is 12 frames per second (fps).

6. **To change the Stage color, click the Background box. Choose a new color from the Color palette.**

   For more about colors, see Book V, Chapter 2.

If you use the Document Properties dialog box, you have more options. Follow these steps:

1. **Choose Modify⇨Document.**

   The Document Properties dialog box, shown in Figure 1-10, appears.

2. **To change the Stage size, type the new width and height of the Stage in the Dimensions text fields.**

   As a shortcut, click the Match Printer button to set the Stage size to match the current paper size, or click the Match Contents button to set the Stage size to the minimum size needed to encompass all the objects.

   To get the smallest possible Stage size, put all your objects at the upper-left corner of the Stage.

3. **To change the units used on the ruler, use the Ruler Units drop-down list and select an option.**

   You can choose from pixels (the default), inches, centimeters, millimeters, and points.

Setting preferences

You can customize a number of settings to suit your personal needs. The main switchboard is the Preferences dialog box, shown in Figure 1-11 with the General tab selected.

Figure 1-11:
The
Preferences
dialog box.

Preferences

| General | Editing | Clipboard | Warnings | ActionScript Editor |

General

Undo Levels: `100`

Printing Options: ☐ Disable PostScript

Selection Options: ☑ Shift Select
☑ Show Tooltips

Panel Options: ☐ Disable Panel Docking

Timeline Options: ☐ Disable Timeline Docking
☐ Span Based Selection
☐ Named Anchor on Scene

Highlight Color: ◉ Use this color
◯ Use layer color

Font Mapping Default: `_sans`

[OK] [Cancel] [Help]

The General tab has a variety of miscellaneous options:

✦ **Undo Levels:** This is the number of commands that Macromedia Flash MX remembers so you can undo them. You can enter any value from 0 to 300. The default is 100.

✦ **Printing Options — Disable PostScript:** This option disables PostScript output when you print to a PostScript printer in Windows. Check this box only if you have trouble printing to a PostScript printer.

✦ **Selection Options — Shift Select:** By default you have to press Shift to select more than one object. If you don't press Shift, the first object is deselected. Uncheck this item to enable you to select additional objects without pressing Shift.

✦ **Selection Options — Show ToolTips:** This option shows ToolTips over toolbars and buttons when you pass your cursor over them. Uncheck this check box to make the ToolTips disappear.

✦ **Panel Options — Disable Panel Docking:** This option prevents panels from docking. Docked panels lock to the side of the Macromedia Flash MX window without covering up the Stage where you work.

✦ **Timeline Options — Disable Timeline Docking:** This option prevents the Timeline from docking.

✦ **Timeline Options — Span Based Selection:** This option allows you to click between two keyframes to select the entire section between them, as in Flash 5.

✦ **Timeline Options — Named Anchor on Scene:** Selecting this option automatically creates a named anchor at the beginning of each scene. A named anchor enables Web site users to use their browser's Back and Forward buttons to navigate within a Flash movie, from anchor to anchor.

✦ **Highlight Color:** This option sets the color of the box around selected symbols and groups. Select the Use This Color option to specify another color, or select the Use Layer Color option to use the layer's outline color.

✦ **Font Mapping Default:** This option specifies which font to use when you open a Flash document that contains a font you don't have installed.

The Editing tab contains options related to the Pen tool and text, as follows:

✦ **Pen tool — Show Pen Preview:** When this option is checked, Macromedia Flash MX displays a preview of the line or curve segment before you click the next point. This is a helpful option for visualizing the final result of the graphic.

✦ **Pen tool — Show Solid Points:** Uncheck this option to show unfilled points at vertices.

✦ **Pen tool — Show Precise Cursors:** This option means that you will see a small cross hair rather than the default pen-shaped cursor, which can be handy for more precise placement of points.

✦ **Vertical text — Default Text Orientation:** This option sets vertical text as the default, and is useful for some Asian fonts.

✦ **Right to Left Text Flow:** This option sets the default for vertical text so that vertical lines flow from right to left. (Used for some Asian fonts.)

✦ **No Kerning:** This option removes kerning from vertical text.

The Pen tool and text are covered in Book V, Chapter 2.

The Clipboard tab enables you to set preferences for bitmaps, gradients, and text pasted in from FreeHand 10, which is the subject of Book IV:

✦ **Bitmaps — Color Depth:** This option sets the color depth for bitmaps copied to the Clipboard — for Windows only.

✦ **Bitmaps — Resolution:** This option sets the resolution of bitmaps copied to the Clipboard — for Windows only.

✦ **Bitmaps — Size Limit:** This option specifies a size limit in kilobytes for RAM (memory) used for a bitmap on the Windows Clipboard. If you have large images, you can increase this number. The default is 250K.

✦ **Bitmaps — Smooth:** This option applies anti-aliasing to bitmaps in Windows to smooth their edges.

✦ **Gradients:** This option specifies the quality of gradients that you copy to the Windows Clipboard for use in other applications.

✦ **FreeHand Text:** This option enables text pasted from FreeHand 10 to be edited in Macromedia Flash MX.

The Warnings tab lists situations in which Macromedia Flash MX displays a warning message. The checkboxes are all checked by default. If you find a warning unnecessary, uncheck the appropriate check box.

The ActionScript Editor tab customizes how ActionScript looks and functions in the Action panel:

✦ **Automatic Indentation and Tab Size:** By default, ActionScript you type in Expert mode is indented. The default tab size (indentation) is four spaces. You can remove or change the tab size.

✦ **Code Hints and Delay:** Code hints provide a pop-up menu to help you complete your code based on what you're typing. You can remove code hints or delay their display.

✦ **Text:** This option specifies text font and size in the ActionScript editor.

✦ **Syntax Coloring:** This option sets the colors for each syntax type of code.

When you finish specifying preferences, click OK.

Creating your own keyboard shortcuts

You can change any shortcut and create your own. To create shortcuts, choose Edit⇨Keyboard Shortcuts to open the Keyboard Shortcuts dialog box, as shown in Figure 1-12.

Figure 1-12:
Use the
Keyboard
Shortcuts
dialog box
to customize
shortcuts.

You can't change the set of shortcuts that come with Macromedia Flash MX. However, you can create a duplicate set of shortcuts and modify the duplicate. Give the duplicate a new name, such as MyShortcuts.

The buttons at the top of the Keyboard Shortcuts dialog box help you manage your shortcuts:

✦ **Duplicate Set:** Duplicates a shortcut set

✦ **Rename Set:** Renames a set of shortcuts

✦ **Delete Set:** Deletes a set of shortcuts

After you have a new set of shortcuts, choose from the Commands drop-down list the types of commands you want to change. You can change any of the four types of commands:

+ **Drawing Menu Commands:** Commands from the menu

+ **Drawing Tools:** Tools in the Drawing toolbox

+ **Test Movie Menu Commands:** The menu that appears when you choose Control⇨Test Movie

+ **Actions Panel Commands:** Commands that control the look and functioning of the Actions panel

Click the plus sign (+) on the list to display all the commands and their current shortcuts. To create a new shortcut, follow these steps:

1. **Choose the command you want.**

2. **Click the Add Shortcut button.**

   Macromedia Flash MX adds a new shortcut.

3. **On your keyboard, press the keys for the shortcut you want to use.**

   You must include Ctrl. If that shortcut is already assigned, the command is displayed. You can decide to override the shortcut or choose another one.

   • If you want to use that shortcut, click Change.

   • If you don't want to use that shortcut, with the empty shortcut selected on the Shortcuts list, click Remove Shortcut.

4. **To change another shortcut, repeat Steps 1 through 3.**

5. **Click OK.**

Getting Help

If you need more help than you can find in this book, use Macromedia Flash MX's Help system and tutorials.

For more information on Macromedia Flash MX, see *Macromedia Flash MX For Dummies,* by Gurdy Leete and Ellen Finkelstein. For some great Macromedia Flash MX techniques, see *50 Fast Macromedia Flash MX Techniques* by the same authors (both books published by Wiley Publishing, Inc.).

To open Help, choose Help⇨Using Flash. The opening screen looks like Figure 1-13.

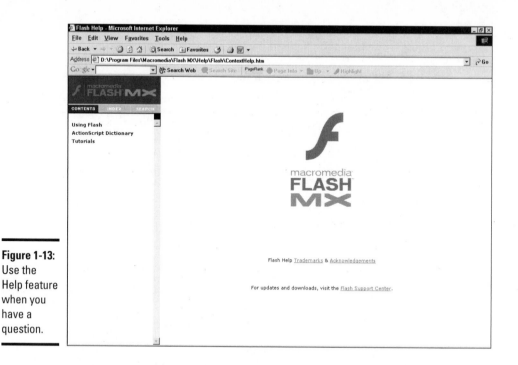

Figure 1-13:
Use the
Help feature
when you
have a
question.

Using Flash

The Using Flash section of Help is the main manual. You can access it in three ways by clicking the three tabs at the top:

✦ **Contents:** This tab displays a list of topics. Choose the one you want, then choose a subtopic.

✦ **Index:** This tab displays an alphabetical list. Click a letter of the alphabet and then choose a topic.

✦ **Search:** Enter a search word or phrase. Put a plus sign (+) between words. Click List Topics and double-click the topic you want.

Tutorial

Macromedia Flash MX includes both a set of lessons and a tutorial. Choose Help➪Lessons➪Introduction to start with the lessons, which are more basic than the tutorial.

To try the tutorial, choose Tutorials from the main Help screen. (See Figure 1-13.) If you have the printed manual, find the tutorial in Chapter 1. (The printed tutorial is easier to use than the electronic version.)

Chapter 2: Using the Graphics Tools

This chapter shows you how to use the drawing and editing tools in Macromedia Flash MX to create graphics and text. In order to produce great animation, you need great graphics, so read on.

Choosing When To Use Flash Tools

Book V, Chapter 1 explains the difference between vector and bitmap graphics. You should use the Macromedia Flash MX drawing tools when you want to create vector graphics for fast download times.

To create more detailed graphics, you may want to use Fireworks MX or FreeHand 10 because they have more advanced creation and editing tools. You may also want to use these programs to edit existing bitmaps. On the other hand, you may have bitmaps, such as a photograph or complex logo, that's only available as a bitmap. To use any bitmap, import it. (See Book V, Chapter 3 for the scoop on importing graphics.)

Creating Shapes and Text

You use the Toolbox to create shapes and text in Macromedia Flash MX. See Figure 2-1 for the details of the Toolbox. The Tools section of the Toolbox offers many tools for creating and editing images. Most tools have options that specify how the tool works.

When creating shapes in Macromedia Flash MX, you need to keep in mind what happens when two or more shapes touch:

✦ If the shapes are the same color, they combine. You can use this technique to create complex shapes.

✦ If the shapes are different colors, the top shape replaces and cuts out the bottom shape.

✦ If you use the Pencil or Line tool to intersect any other shape, the line and other shape are cut at their intersection.

If you don't see the Toolbox, choose Window⇨Tools.

Figure 2-1: The Toolbox contains graphic creation and editing tools.

Line tool

The Line tool draws straight lines. You can continue to draw connected lines to create any shape you want.

To draw a line, follow these steps:

1. **Choose the Line tool from the Toolbox.**

2. **From the Property inspector, choose a color by clicking the Stroke Color box.**

    If the Property inspector is not visible, choose Window➪Properties.

    You can also find the Stroke Color box in the Colors section of the Toolbox. A *stroke* is another word for a line or the outline of any shape in Macromedia Flash MX.

3. **Type a stroke weight (width) in the Stroke Height box of the Property inspector or click its arrow and use the slider to choose a stroke weight.**

4. **Choose a stroke style from the Stroke Style box of the Property inspector.**

    If you want to create a custom stroke style, click the Custom button in the Property inspector.

5. **Click the Stage where you want to start the line and drag (with the mouse button down) to the ending point.**

6. **Release the mouse button.**

To constrain the line to multiples of 45 degrees, press Shift while dragging.

Oval tool

An oval has both a stroke (outline) and a fill color. Use the Oval tool to draw ovals and circles:

1. **Choose the Oval tool from the Toolbox.**

2. **From the Property inspector, choose a stroke color by clicking the Stroke Color box and choosing a color.**

    If the Property inspector is not visible, choose Window➪Properties.

    You can also find the Stroke Color box in the Colors section of the Toolbox. As with the Line tool, you can also set a stroke weight and style.

3. **From the Property inspector, choose a fill color by clicking the Fill Color box.**

4. **Click the Stage where you want the upper-left of the oval to be and drag (with the mouse button down) diagonally to the lower-right.**

5. **Release the mouse button.**

To create a perfect circle, press Shift as you drag the mouse.

Rectangle tool

Like an oval, a rectangle has both a stroke and a fill. You can draw rectangles and squares with the Rectangle tool as follows:

1. **Choose the Rectangle tool from the Toolbox.**

2. **From the Property inspector, choose a stroke color by clicking the Stroke Color box and choosing a color.**

   If the Property inspector is not visible, choose Window⇨Properties.

   You can also find the Stroke Color box in the Colors section of the Toolbox. As with the Line tool, you can also set a stroke weight and style.

3. **From the Property inspector, choose a fill color by clicking the Fill Color box.**

4. **If you want to draw a rectangle with rounded corners, click the Rounded Rectangle Radius button in the Options section of the Toolbox, type a radius, and press Enter.**

5. **Click the Stage where you want the upper-left of the rectangle to be and drag (with the mouse button down) diagonally to the lower-right.**

6. **Release the mouse button.**

To create a square, press Shift as you drag the mouse.

Pencil tool

The Pencil tool is somewhat like a real pencil. You can draw artistic shapes with it. To draw with the Pencil tool, follow these steps:

1. **Choose the Pencil tool from the Toolbox.**

2. **From the Property inspector, choose a stroke color by clicking the Stroke Color box and choosing a color.**

   If the Property inspector is not visible, choose Window⇨Properties.

   You can also find the Stroke Color box in the Colors section of the Toolbox. As with the Line tool, you can also set a stroke weight and style.

3. **Click the Pencil Mode button in the Options section of the Toolbox. Choose one of the following:**

    -   **Straighten:** Straightens wiggly lines and changes sloppy rectangles, ovals, and triangles to perfect ones.

    -   **Smooth:** Smoothes out curved lines.

    -   **Ink:** Slightly smoothes and straightens, but mostly leaves your drawings the same.

4. **Click the Stage where you want the drawing to start and drag on the Stage.**

    You can draw angles and curves.

5. **Release the mouse button.**

To constrain each line segment to 90-degree angles, press Shift as you drag the mouse. To refine how the options work, choose Edit⇨Preferences and click the Editing tab. Use the Smooth Curves and Recognize Shapes drop-down lists. When you're done, click OK.

Pen tool

You can use the Pen tool to draw straight lines and curves. The Pen tool offers the greatest editing control and the most control over curves. Using the Pen tool takes some practice, but soon you'll find it to be very flexible.

To better see how a Pen tool drawing will look, choose Edit⇨Preferences and click the Editing tab. Select the Show Pen Preview check box. Click OK.

Follow these steps to work with the Pen tool:

1. **Choose the Pen tool from the Toolbox.**

2. **From the Property inspector, choose a stroke color by clicking the Stroke Color box and choosing a color.**

    If the Property inspector is not visible, choose Window⇨Properties.

    You can also find the Stroke Color box in the Colors section of the Toolbox. As with the Line tool, you can also set a stroke weight and style.

3. **You can draw either straight segments or curves:**

    -   **To draw a straight segment:** Click the start point and click the end point. Do not drag. Click additional points to add segments. Double-click to finish.

    -   **To draw a curve:** Click the start point and move the mouse in the desired direction, then click and drag in the direction of the curve. Continue clicking and dragging to create additional curves. Double-click to finish.

To close a figure, place the cursor near the start point until you see a small circle, and then click. Press Shift as you draw to constrain the lines or curves to 45-degree angles.

Brush tool

The Brush tool fills areas with a brush-like effect. You can vary the shape and width of the stroke. The Brush tool creates fills, so you use the Fill Color button to set the color. To draw with the Brush tool, follow these steps:

1. **Choose the Brush tool from the Toolbox.**

2. **From the Property inspector, choose a fill color by clicking the Fill Color box and choosing a color.**

If the Property inspector is not visible, choose Window⇨Properties.

You can also find the Fill Color box in the Colors section of the Toolbox.

3. **Choose a Brush mode by clicking the Brush Mode button in the Options section of the Toolbox and choosing one of the following options:**

- **Paint Normal:** Paints wherever you brush, including over other objects on the same layer. (See Book V, Chapter 4 for more on layers.)

- **Paint Fills:** Fills enclosed and blank areas, but doesn't cover strokes.

- **Paint Behind:** Paints blank areas of the Stage, but doesn't cover fills or strokes.

- **Paint Selection:** Fills in a selected area. (Later in this chapter, we explain how to select objects.)

- **Paint Inside:** Paints inside any enclosed area where you start your brush or on the Stage if you don't start in an enclosed area. Doesn't cover strokes.

4. **Choose a brush size by clicking the Brush Size drop-down list in the Options section of the Toolbox.**

5. **Choose a brush shape by clicking the Brush Shape drop-down list.**

If you have a pressure-sensitive pen and tablet, you see a pressure button in the Options section. You can then dynamically vary the width of the brush according to how much pressure you put on the pen as you draw.

6. **Click the start point, then drag to draw with the brush.**

Press Shift as you draw to constrain your shapes to 90-degree angles.

Paint Bucket tool

The Paint Bucket tool fills enclosed shapes. You can create the enclosed shape with many of the other Toolbox tools. You can also use the Paint

Bucket tool to change the color of existing fills. To fill an enclosed area, follow these steps:

1. **Choose the Paint Bucket tool from the Toolbox.**

2. **From the Property inspector, choose a fill color by clicking the Fill Color box and choosing a color.**

If the Property inspector is not visible, choose Window⇨Properties.

You can also find the Fill Color box in the Colors section of the Toolbox.

3. **From the Gap Size button in the Options section of the Toolbox, select an option if you need to fill in a shape that is not completely enclosed.**

You can choose from Don't Close Gaps to Close Large Gaps.

4. **Click inside the enclosed area to fill the shape.**

Ink Bottle tool

The Ink Bottle tool outlines an existing shape or changes the color of an existing stroke (outline):

1. **Choose the Ink Bottle tool from the Toolbox.**

2. **From the Property inspector, choose a stroke color by clicking the Stroke Color box and choosing a color.**

If the Property inspector is not visible, choose Window⇨Properties.

You can also find the Stroke Color box in the Colors section of the Toolbox. You can also set a stroke weight and style.

3. **Click anywhere on the shape.**

If the shape has no stroke outline, Macromedia Flash MX adds a stroke. Otherwise, Macromedia Flash MX changes its color, width, and style to the settings you choose.

Text tool

Sooner or later, you may need to explain what all those animations you have created mean, so you'll probably need some text. Macromedia Flash MX offers many text options, both simple and advanced. To create text, follow these steps:

1. **Choose the Text tool from the Toolbox.**

2. **In the Property inspector, shown in Figure 2-2, specify the font, size, color, and other properties.**

If the Property inspector is not visible, choose Window⇨Properties.

3. **Click on the Stage as described next and start typing.**

   - To specify the width of the text (when creating a paragraph), click at the upper-left corner where you want the text to start and drag to the right margin.

   - To create text that expands as you type (for a single line of text), just click.

Figure 2-2: Use the Property inspector to set the properties of your text.

You can specify the following text properties in the Property inspector:

✦ **Text type:** Use the Text Type drop-down list to specify one of three types of text:

   - **Static:** Regular text.

   - **Input:** Text that users type in their browser. Input text is one way of making your Web site interactive. Use input text for forms or to enable users to set values that affect the animation.

   - **Dynamic:** Text that is displayed from another source, such as another Web site, another movie (SWF) file, or an external file. Great for weather, sports scores, and so on.

✦ **Font:** The font or typeface. Select from the drop-down list.

✦ **Font size:** Type a number or use the slider to choose a size.

✦ **Color:** Click the Text (fill) Color box to choose a color.

✦ **Bold/Italic:** Click the Bold button or the Italic button to make the text bold or italic.

✦ **Justify:** Click one of the Justify buttons to make the text justified on the left, center, right, or full (justified on left and right).

✦ **Character spacing:** Adjust the *tracking,* which is the spacing between letters.

✦ **Character position:** Select Superscript to create text above the normal position or Subscript to create text that is below the normal position.

✦ **Auto Kern:** *Kerning* is the spacing between certain letters such as A and V that may appear too far apart. Select the Auto Kern check box to turn kerning on; deselect it to turn kerning off.

✦ **Format:** Click the Format button to open the Format Options dialog box, where you can set paragraph formatting:

  • **Indent:** The indentation of the first line of a paragraph.

  • **Line Spacing:** The spacing between lines, measured in points. If your text is 18 points, set a line spacing of 18 points to double-space the text.

 Click the Expand/Collapse arrow at the lower-right corner of the Property inspector for more advanced text options.

Modifying Shapes and Text

If you create something on a computer, you'll inevitably have to change it. Sometimes you change your mind, and other times you just need to make adjustments to get the effect you want.

Arrow tool

The first step in changing an object is to select it. To select an object or group of objects, choose the Arrow tool and use one of these techniques:

✦ To select one object, click the object.

✦ To select several graphic objects that touch each other, double-click one of the objects. (This doesn't work with symbol instances. See Book V, Chapter 3 for more information.) To select a rectangle's stroke and fill, double-click the fill.

✦ To select several objects that do not touch, click off the objects and drag diagonally to create a bounding box around the objects you want to select. Macromedia Flash MX selects all objects that are completely inside the box.

See the section, "Reshaping with the Arrow tool," later in this chapter, for information on reshaping objects using the Arrow tool.

The Arrow tool has a Snap button in the Options section of the Tools toolbox. When you click it, objects that you move snap to other objects so that you can attach two objects precisely. The Snap option also snaps new objects that you create to existing objects.

Lasso tool

Another way to select your objects is to lasso 'em. Use the Lasso tool when you want to select a number of objects but can't get them in a rectangular bounding box. You can drag the mouse and create a free-form shape or use straight-line segments:

1. **Choose the Lasso tool from the Toolbox.**

2. **Choose the type of lassoing you want:**

- **To lasso free-form:** Click anywhere on the Stage and drag around the objects you want to select, and then release the mouse button.

- **To lasso with straight-line segments:** Choose the Polygon button from the Options section of the Toolbox. Click anywhere on the Stage and continue to click at each segment's end point. Double-click to finish.

Moving and copying objects

You can move and copy objects on the Stage in many ways. The best method varies with the circumstances and your personal preferences.

✦ **Select and drag:** Use the Arrow tool to select an object. Then move the cursor over the object until you see the four-arrow cursor. Click and drag to move the object. Hold the Ctrl key while you drag to copy the object.

✦ **Arrow keys:** Select an object and use the arrow keys to move the object one pixel at a time in the direction of the arrow.

✦ **Property inspector:** Select an object and open the Property inspector. Click the Expand/Collapse arrow at the lower-right corner to display the expanded panel. Use the X and Y text fields to set a new location for the object.

✦ **Cut, copy, and paste:** Select an object and press Ctrl+X to move (cut) it or Ctrl+C to copy it. If you want, click another layer or frame. Then press Ctrl+V to paste the object.

Eraser tool

To delete any object, select it and press Delete on the keyboard. However, to erase part of any object, use the Eraser tool:

1. **Choose the Eraser tool from the Toolbox.**

2. **Select the eraser size and shape from the Eraser Shape drop-down list in the Options section of the Toolbox.**

3. **To specify how the Eraser tool works, choose an option from the Eraser mode button:**

   • **Erase Normal:** Erases anything you drag across.

   • **Erase Fills:** Erases only fills.

   • **Erase Lines:** Erases only strokes.

   • **Erase Selected Fills:** Erases only selected fills.

   • **Erase Inside:** Erases only fills where you first click. Use this option to erase only fills inside an enclosed area, but leave other fills alone.

4. **With the Faucet option (in the Options section of the Toolbox) *not* selected, click and drag to erase.**

TIP

To erase an entire fill, select the Faucet option (in the Options section of the Toolbox) and click the fill. This method is equivalent to selecting a fill and pressing Delete.

Reshaping with the Arrow tool

You can reshape and modify objects using the Arrow tool when the objects are not selected. You can reshape both end points (including corners) and middles (whether straight or curved), as shown in Figure 2-3:

✦ **End points:** Place the cursor over the end point of a line or curve segment. You see a small corner shape near the cursor. Click and drag to change the location of the end point.

✦ **Middles:** Place the cursor over the middle of any line or curve segment. You see a small curved shape near the cursor. Click and drag to reshape the segment.

Figure 2-3:
You can reshape end points and middles of fills and lines with the Arrow tool.

Subselect tool

The Subselect tool looks like the Arrow tool, but the Subselect tool is a white (instead of black) arrow. Both the Arrow tool and the Subselect tool reshape objects, but the Subselect tool uses a more sophisticated technique. When you are using the Subselect tool, the shape displays anchor points that you can move or delete. When you click an anchor point, *tangent lines* — lines that are parallel to the curve at the anchor point — appear and enable you to change the direction of the curve. You can reshape strokes or fills created with the following tools:

+ Pen

+ Pencil

+ Line

+ Oval

+ Rectangle

+ Brush

To reshape objects with the Subselect tool, follow these steps:

1. **Choose the Subselect tool from the Toolbox.**

2. **Click a stroke or the edge of a fill to display the anchor points.**

3. **Drag any anchor point to modify the shape.**

4. **To change the direction of a curve, select its anchor curve and then drag the tangent line's handles (the dots at either end of the tangent line).**

To delete an anchor, select it and press Delete.

Free Transform tool

The Free Transform tool is the heavyweight of editing tools — it can do almost anything. To use this tool, choose the Free Transform tool from the Toolbox and select an object. The object displays a special bounding box that includes handles and a central *transformation point,* as shown in Figure 2-4.

Figure 2-4:
When you use the Free Transform tool on an object, the object displays a bounding box with handles and a central transformation point.

You can use the Free Transform tool in the following ways:

✦ **Move:** Place the cursor over the object. When you see the four-arrow cursor, click and drag.

✦ **Rotate:** Place the cursor just outside (but not on) any corner handle. When you see a circular arrow cursor, click and drag.

✦ **Scale while maintaining proportion:** Place the cursor on any corner handle. When you see a broken two-arrow cursor, click and drag inward or outward.

✦ **Scale either the height or width:** Place the cursor on any side handle. When you see a two-arrow cursor, click and drag inward or outward.

✦ **Skew (slant either horizontally or vertically):** Place the cursor anywhere on the bounding box, but not on a handle. When you see the parallel line cursor, click and drag in any direction.

✦ **Move the transformation point:** Place the cursor on the transformation point at the center of the bounding box. When you see a small circle cursor, click and drag in any direction. The transformation point is used as a base for rotation and scaling.

✦ **Taper:** Choose the Distort option of the Free Transform tool from the Options section of the Toolbox. Place the cursor on any corner handle and press Shift as you click and drag inward or outward. (See Figure 2-5 for an example of tapering.)

Figure 2-5:
Tapering the
fish makes
its back end
wider.

Figure 2-5:
Tapering the
fish makes
its back end
wider.

✦ **Distort:** Choose the Distort option of the Free Transform tool from the Options section of the Toolbox. Click and drag any handle to distort the bounding box. (See Figure 2-6 for an example of distortion.) *Note:* The Distort option works on shapes, but not on symbols (see Book V, Chapter 3 for more on symbols), text, or groups. (Groups are explained later in this chapter.)

✦ **Warp:** Choose the Envelope option of the Free Transform tool from the Options section of the Toolbox. Drag any anchor point or tangent line handle to warp the bounding box.

The Envelope option, shown in Figure 2-7, works on shapes, but not on symbols (see Book V, Chapter 3 for more on symbols), text, or groups. (Groups are explained later in this chapter.)

Figure 2-6:
Distort the
upper-right
corner of
the goldfish
and it looks
more like a
shark!

Figure 2-7:
You can fine-
tune shapes
with the
Envelope
option of the
Free
Transform
tool.

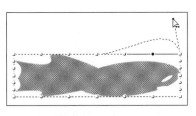

Straightening and smoothing with the Arrow tool

You can straighten lines and smooth curves with the Arrow tool. Both processes reduce the number of changes in direction. You can repeat the process until Macromedia Flash MX can't straighten or smooth any more. Follow these steps:

1. **Choose the Arrow tool from the Toolbox.**

2. **Select the shape you want to modify.**

3. **To straighten, click the Straighten button from the Options section of the Toolbox. To smooth, click the Smooth button.**

4. **Continue to click the option button until you like the result.**

Optimizing curves

A process called *optimizing curves* is similar to smoothing curves. Optimizing a curve reduces the number of individual elements the curve contains and can help reduce the size of your Flash document file. Follow these steps to optimize curves:

1. **Select the object that you want to optimize.**

2. **From the main menu, choose Modify⇨Optimize.**

The Optimize Curves dialog box, shown in Figure 2-8, appears. You can select Use Multiple Passes for a slower, more thorough approach. If you select the Show Totals Message check box, the amount of optimization displays after you close the dialog box.

Figure 2-8:
The
Optimize
Curves
dialog box.

3. **Choose the amount of smoothing by using the slider in the dialog box.**

4. **Click OK.**

Carefully check the results after optimizing. Sometimes small objects disappear! If you don't like the results, choose Edit⇨Undo and try again with a different Smoothing setting.

Softening edges

To create a soft look around the edges of a shape, follow these steps:

1. **Select a shape.**

2. **From the main menu, choose Modify⇨Shape⇨Soften Fill Edges.**

   The Soften Fill Edges dialog box opens, as shown in Figure 2-9.

Figure 2-9:
The Soften
Fill Edges
dialog box.

3. **In the Soften Fill Edges dialog box, set the distance.**

   The distance is the width of the softened part of the edge, in pixels (by default).

   Macromedia Flash MX uses the units that you set in the Document Properties dialog box to measure the distance. Choose Modify⇨ Document to change the measurement units.

4. **Enter the number of steps, that is, the number of concentric rows in the softened edge.**

5. **Select Expand or Inset.**

   The Expand option creates the softened edges outside the shape.
   The Inset option creates the softened edges within the shape.

6. **Click OK.**

Flipping

A great way to make symmetric shapes is to draw half the shape, copy it,
and flip the copy either vertically or horizontally. You can then move the
two shapes together, as shown in Figure 2-10. To flip an object, follow
these steps:

1. **Select the object.**

2. **From the main menu, choose Modify⇨Transform⇨Flip Vertical or Flip Horizontal.**

Figure 2-10:
This shape
was created
by copying
the crescent
moon,
flipping it
horizontally,
and then
moving the
two shapes
together.

Transferring properties with the Eyedropper

The Eyedropper tool transfers stroke and fill properties from one object to
another. To transfer properties, follow these steps:

1. **Choose the Eyedropper tool from the Toolbox.**

2. **Select a stroke or fill.**

   If you select a stroke, the Ink Bottle tool is activated. If you select a fill,
   the Paint Bucket tool is activated.

3. **Click another stroke or fill.**

Macromedia Flash MX transfers the properties of the stroke or fill to the second object.

Grouping

Often, you want to work with several objects at one time. Instead of having to select them all each time you want to move or copy them, you can group them and work with them as one object. To group objects, select them and choose Modify⇨Group.

You can edit one element of the group by following these steps:

1. **Choose the Arrow tool from the Toolbox.**

2. **Double-click the group.**

Macromedia Flash MX dims other objects on the Stage.

3. **Edit any element of the group.**

4. **To return to regular editing, double-click any blank area on the Stage with the Arrow tool.**

Alternatively, you can choose Edit⇨Edit All.

To ungroup objects, select the group and choose Modify⇨Ungroup.

Breaking apart objects

You can break apart text into letters, and then break apart the letters into shapes. After letters are broken apart into shapes, you can edit them like any other shape. You can also break apart symbols (see Book V, Chapter 3), groups, and bitmaps. (See the "Working with bitmap fills" section, later in this chapter, for more information.)

Aligning objects

To get a professional look, you may want to make sure that objects are properly aligned and equally distributed. To align and distribute objects, follow these steps:

1. **Select the objects.**

2. **Choose Window⇨Align.**

The Align panel, shown in Figure 2-11, appears.

Figure 2-11:
Use the
Align panel
to align and
equally
space
objects,
such as
buttons for
your Web
site.

3. **Choose the options you want in the Align panel:**

   • Use the top row to align the selected objects horizontally or vertically.

   • Use the middle row to evenly distribute objects horizontally or vertically by their edges.

   • Use the Match Size buttons to match the size of selected objects by width, height, or both.

   • Use the Space buttons to distribute objects by the spaces between them.

   • Use the To Stage button to align or distribute objects relative to the Stage.

To center an object on the Stage, click the To Stage button on the Align panel. Then click the middle Align Vertical and Align Horizontal buttons. However, if you haven't panned or scrolled your display, you can use a quicker method — cut and paste the object. Macromedia Flash MX pastes the object at the center of the display.

Working with Colors

By default, Macromedia Flash MX works with a Web safe palette of 216 colors. These colors are likely to appear the same in all browsers. However, you can create your own colors. You can also design gradients that vary from one color to another. Another technique is to fill objects with bitmap images, explained at the end of this chapter in the "Working with bitmap fills" section.

Creating solid colors

You can create a solid color when you need to take more artistic license than the standard Web safe palette allows:

1. **Choose Window⇨Color Mixer.**

   The Color Mixer panel, shown in Figure 2-12 with the Solid option active, opens.

Figure 2-12:
The Color Mixer panel is the place to create new colors.

You can specify colors using the RGB (Red, Green, Blue) or HSB (Hue, Saturation, Brightness) systems. You can see the current system by the letters next to the text fields in the panel. In Figure 2-12, you can tell that the RGB system is active, because the text fields are labeled R, G, and B. To choose a different system, click the menu icon in the upper-right corner of the panel to open the panel's menu and choose the color system you want. You can also use the color space in the panel to specify a color.

2. **Select Solid from the Fill Style drop-down list.**

3. **Click the Stroke Color or Fill Color icon (to the left of the Stroke or Fill box), depending on whether you want to change a stroke or a fill.**

   You can use this color later for either a stroke or a fill if you save it as a swatch, as outlined in Step 6.

4. **Type the color specifications in the text fields or click a color in the color space and use the slider to make the color lighter or darker.**

5. **Use the Alpha slider or text field to set the transparency of the color.**

   A higher alpha percent is more opaque.

6. **To save the color, create a color swatch by clicking the menu icon in the upper-right corner of the panel and choosing Add Swatch.**

Your new color is now displayed in the Stroke Color or Fill Color box in the Property inspector and in the Colors section of the Toolbox. You can use any of the tools to work with that color. If you add a color swatch, you can continue to use that color later by choosing it from the color palette that opens when you click the Stroke Color or Fill Color box.

Creating gradients

Gradients blend one color (lighter with darker) or many colors in either a linear or radial (circular) pattern. Gradients give the appearance of shading and three dimensions. To create a gradient, follow these steps:

1. Choose Window⇨Color Mixer.

The Color Mixer panel, shown in Figure 2-13 with the Linear gradient option active, opens.

Figure 2-13:
Use the
Color Mixer
panel to
create
gradients.

2. From the Fill Style drop-down list, select Linear or Radial to specify the type of gradient you want to create.

3. Choose a pointer underneath the horizontal gradient bar.

The pointer becomes black when you select it so that you know it is active.

4. Use one of these methods to select a color for that pointer:

• Click the Fill Color box and choose a color.

• Specify a color using one of the methods of creating a new color specified previously.

• Use the color space to specify a color.

5. Repeat Steps 3 and 4 for all the pointers.

You add a pointer when you want to add a new color to the gradient. Three pointers results in a three-color gradient. To add a pointer, click just beneath the gradient bar where you want the pointer to appear. To delete a pointer, drag it off the gradient bar.

6. To save the gradient, click the Options menu icon in the upper-right corner of the Color Mixer panel and choose Add Swatch.

Editing fills

After you create your gradient or bitmap fills, you may decide you want to change them. (Bitmap fills are explained in the next section.) To edit a fill, follow these steps:

1. **Choose the Fill Transform tool from the Toolbox.**

2. **Click a gradient or bitmap fill.**

Macromedia Flash MX places a boundary and editing handles around the fill, which varies with the type of fill, as shown in Figure 2-14.

Figure 2-14:
When you transform a fill, you see an editing boundary around the fill.

3. **Make one or more of the following changes:**

- **Move the fill's center:** Drag the small circle at the center of the fill.

- **Change the fill's width or height:** Drag the square handle inward or outward.

- **Rotate a fill:** Drag the circle on the editing boundary (the endmost circle for a radial gradient).

- **Scale a bitmap fill:** Drag the corner square boundary inward or outward.

- **Scale a radial gradient:** Drag the middle circular handle on the editing boundary inward or outward.

- **Skew a bitmap fill:** Drag a circular handle on the top or side.

Working with bitmap fills

You can create a fill with a bitmap that you have imported. (See Book V, Chapter 3 for more on importing bitmaps.) To create a fill with a bitmap image, follow these steps:

1. **From the main menu, choose File⇨Import.**

The Import dialog box appears.

2. **Choose the bitmap file you want and click Open.**

The bitmap appears on the Stage.

3. **From the main menu, choose Modify⇨Break Apart.**

4. **Choose the Eyedropper tool from the Toolbox.**

5. **Click the bitmap image.**

The Paint Bucket tool is activated and the Fill Color button (in the Colors section of the Toolbox and in the Property inspector) displays the bitmap image.

6. **Click the object you want to fill.**

You may have to move the bitmap image you imported if it covered your object. Notice that the bitmap is tiled — repeated throughout the filled area.

Chapter 3: Working with Symbols

A *symbol* is any object or group of objects, an animation, or a Web button. You give the symbol a name and save it in the Library. (See Book V, Chapter 1 for a discussion of the Library.) In this chapter, you find out about symbols and how to use them.

Appreciating the Importance of Symbols

You need to know about symbols if you want to work in Macromedia Flash MX. The following are the three types of symbols:

✦ **Graphic:** The simplest type of symbol, and a useful way to save groups of objects that you want to reuse. You can also animate graphic symbols.

✦ **Movie clip:** A little movie that you put inside your big movie. You can apply ActionScript, Macromedia Flash MX's programming language, to a movie clip or within a movie clip to specify how it functions. The movie clip has its own Timeline, and you generally insert it on the main Timeline to let it play. Movie clips can be placed inside each other, or *nested.* Movie clips are useful for building complex animation and an interactive Web site.

✦ **Button:** You use buttons when you want your site viewers to click to go to another page or create some other effect. You use ActionScript to specify what happens when a viewer clicks a button.

The rest of this chapter explains now to create and work with graphic, movie clip, and button symbols.

Symbols are the building blocks of complex graphics and animation in your Flash documents. Symbols have the following qualities:

✦ You can easily use symbols again and again by dragging them from the Library onto the Stage.

✦ They reduce your file size (for faster browser display) because Macromedia Flash MX only stores the symbol definition once and remembers one object instead of many.

✦ Symbols (or text or grouped objects) are required for most animation.

✦ Symbols keep their integrity, so you can put other objects in front of them or behind them without the objects being joined or cut out.

Working with Graphic Symbols

You usually create a graphic symbol from objects you have already created. For example, you may have a background consisting of a sky, grass, flowers, and the sun. Saving them as a symbol reduces file size and ensures that if you copy or move the background, all its components come along for the ride.

Working with instances of symbols

When you drag a symbol from the Library, the copy on the Stage is called an *instance*. You can have many instances of one symbol in a Flash document. You can change an instance so that it differs from its original symbol. To change an instance, follow these steps:

1. **Select the instance by clicking it on the Stage.**

2. **Use the Property inspector to do one or more of the following:**

   • Change the brightness, color, or transparency by selecting an option from the Color drop-down list. Select Advanced from the Color drop-down list to change both color and alpha (transparency) at the same time.

   • Change an instance's type (graphic, movie clip, or button) by selecting an option from the Symbol Behavior drop-down list.

   You can also change the properties of an instance using ActionScript. For more information on ActionScript, see Book V, Chapter 8. If you need to refer to a symbol instance in your ActionScript, you can give it a name, so that each instance of a symbol has a unique name. Select the instance and enter the name in the Instance Name text field of the Property inspector.

3. **Use the Free Transform tool (or other editing tools) in the Toolbox to rotate, scale, or skew the instance.**

Creating graphic symbols

To create a graphic symbol from existing objects, follow these steps:

1. **Select the objects you want to convert to a symbol.**

2. From the main menu, choose Insert⇨Convert to Symbol or press F8.

The Convert to Symbol dialog box, shown in Figure 3-1, appears.

Figure 3-1:
Convert an
object into a
symbol.

Convert to Symbol
Name: gr_jagged   OK
Behavior: ○ Movie Clip   Registration: Cancel
          ○ Button
          ⦿ Graphic   Advanced   Help

3. In the Name text field, enter a name for the symbol.

Some people start the names of their symbols with a code indicating the type of symbol. For example, you could start your graphic symbols with `gr_` and then add the name of the symbol. This type of nomenclature automatically alphabetizes your symbols by their type and helps to make clear which type of symbol you are using.

4. Select Graphic from the Behavior list of symbol types.

5. Click OK.

The objects you selected are now one object, surrounded by a selection border. The symbol has also been stored, automatically, in the Library.

You can also achieve the same result by creating an empty symbol and then adding your objects:

1. From the main menu, choose Insert⇨New Symbol to open the Create New Symbol dialog box.

Make sure no objects are selected when you do this step. The Create New Symbol dialog box is the same as the Convert to Symbol dialog box (refer to Figure 3-1).

2. In the Name text field, enter a name for the symbol.

3. Select Graphic from the Behavior list of symbol types.

4. Click OK.

You now find yourself in symbol-editing mode and are no longer on the main Timeline.

5. Draw the objects for your graphic symbol.

All these objects become part of your symbol.

6. Choose Edit⇨Edit Document to exit symbol-editing mode and return to the main Timeline.

The symbol is now in the Library and disappears from the screen.

Using graphic symbols

To insert an instance of a symbol, drag it from the Library onto the Stage. You can drag from the symbol's icon in the Library list or from its preview at the top of the Library window.

You can also use a graphic symbol (and any other type of symbol) from another Flash document file:

1. **Choose File⇨Open as Library.**

2. **Choose the file that contains the symbol you want.**

3. **Click the Open button.**

   Macromedia Flash MX opens another Library window.

4. **Drag symbols from the new Library window onto the Stage.**

Editing graphic symbols

If you change the original symbol, every instance of the symbol that you have inserted is also changed. This feature can save you lots of time if you need to change the shape of all your buttons, for example. To edit a symbol, follow these steps:

1. **Select any instance of the symbol on the Stage.**

   Although you start by selecting an instance of the symbol, when you edit it as described in Step 2, you are editing the symbol, not the instance.

2. **Right-click the symbol instance and choose one of the following:**

   - **Edit in place:** This option allows you to edit a symbol while still viewing other objects on the Stage. The other objects are dimmed so you can distinguish them from the symbol.

   - **Edit:** If you select this option, you perform your edits in symbol-editing mode, which allows you to edit a symbol separately from the main Stage and Timeline. You see only the symbol.

   - **Edit in New Window:** Opens a new window where you edit the symbol. You see only the symbol.

3. **Edit the symbol by changing its color, shape, or effects.**

4. **Choose Edit⇨Edit Document to return to the main Timeline, or if you chose Edit in a New Window, click the window's Close button.**

   You see all the instances of the symbol change to reflect the edits.

To get back to individual objects, you can break apart any instance of a symbol. Select the instance and choose Modify➪Break Apart.

Creating and Working with Movie Clip Symbols

Movie clips can be used for a number of reasons and in a number of different ways:

✦ Use a movie clip to create animation that you want to insert or load onto the main Timeline.

✦ Use a movie clip whenever you need to control its functioning with ActionScript. (For more information on ActionScript, see Book V, Chapter 8.) For example, you can use ActionScript to control the size or color of a movie clip. You can also put ActionScript inside a movie clip to tell it to stop at a certain frame. You cannot control a graphic symbol with ActionScript.

✦ You can use movie clips to create interface elements, such as check boxes, radio buttons, and scroll bars. This type of movie clip is called a *component* and is covered in Book V, Chapter 8.

✦ You can also use movie clip symbols whenever you want to insert animation into the main Timeline but keep a copy in the Library for reuse. Figure 3-2 shows a movie clip in symbol-editing mode that will be an animation of a bouncing ball. If you want several bouncing balls on your Web site, you can drag the movie clip onto the Stage as many times as you want.

You can create a movie clip symbol from scratch or convert animation that you have created on the main Timeline to a movie clip. To create a movie clip symbol from scratch, follow these steps:

1. **From the main menu, choose Insert➪New Symbol to open the Create New Symbol dialog box.**

Make sure no objects are selected when you do this step.

2. **In the Name text field, enter a name for the symbol.**

3. **Select Movie Clip from the Behavior list of symbol types.**

4. **Click OK.**

You now find yourself in symbol-editing mode and are no longer on the main Timeline, as shown in Figure 3-2. In Figure 3-2, you can see the movie clip icon and the name of the movie clip, bouncing ball, just below the layer list.

5. **Create the objects or animation for your movie clip symbol.**

6. **Choose Edit⇨Edit Document to exit symbol-editing mode and return to the main Timeline.**

   The symbol is now in the Library and disappears from the screen.

Sometimes you create some animation on the main Timeline and later realize you need to turn it into a movie clip:

1. **On the layer listing, click the first layer on the list, press Shift, and then click the last layer.**

   All the layers are now selected. See Book V, Chapter 4 for coverage of layers.

2. **Choose Edit⇨Copy Frames.**

3. **Make sure no objects are selected and choose Insert⇨New Symbol.**

   The New Symbol dialog box appears.

Figure 3-2:
Creating a
symbol in
symbol-
editing
mode.

4. **In the Name text field, enter a name for the symbol.**

5. **Select Movie Clip from the Behavior list of symbol types.**

6. **Click OK to close the dialog box and enter symbol-editing mode.**

7. **Click the first frame of the Timeline.**

    This is the Timeline for the movie clip, not the whole movie.

8. **Choose Edit⇨Paste Frames.**

9. **Choose Edit⇨Edit Document to return to the main Timeline of the movie and exit symbol-editing mode.**

    The movie clip symbol is now saved in the Library.

10. **Delete the original animation by selecting all the layers (as you did in Step 1) and choosing Insert⇨Remove Frames.**

You drag a movie clip onto the Stage just like a graphic symbol. Editing a movie clip is also the same as for graphic symbols. See the previous section, "Working with Graphic Symbols," for detailed steps.

Working with Button Symbols

Buttons are a major component of Web sites. You can use buttons as links to move to other pages and sites, and some buttons trigger more complex actions, such as stopping music or starting an animation.

A button has four *states* that you define when you create the button:

+ **Up:** The appearance of the button when the mouse cursor is not over the button.

+ **Over:** The appearance of the button when the mouse cursor is over the button, but not clicking it.

+ **Down:** The appearance of the button when the button is being clicked.

+ **Hit:** The area of the button that responds to the mouse. This area is invisible. The hit state is often the same as the down state, because it just defines the active area of the button.

A common technique is to design a button that changes color or size when the cursor passes over the button and then changes again when clicked. This technique provides feedback that the button has responded to the user. Figure 3-3 shows a button's four states.

Figure 3-3:
Four states
of a button:
up, over,
down, and
hit. Notice
how the up,
over, and
down states
have slightly
different fills.

Creating simple button symbols

Creating a button involves designing the look of the button for the first three
states and the size of the button for the Hit state. Often, you add text to the
graphic so that people know what the button is for. Follow these steps to
create a button:

1. **Choose Insert⇨New Symbol.**

The Create New Symbol dialog box appears.

2. **In the Name text field, type a name for the button.**

3. **From the list of behaviors, select Button and click OK.**

You now see the button timeline. The dot in the Up frame indicates that
the frame is a keyframe. (See Book V, Chapter 5 for more information on
keyframes.) The Up frame is active.

4. **Draw the button for the Up state.**

You can create the graphic with Macromedia Flash MX's drawing tools,
an imported graphic, or an instance of a symbol.

Place the graphic for all the button states at the center of the display.
(Book V, Chapter 2 explains how to center objects.) If the button images
aren't all in the same place, the button shifts when the viewer passes
the cursor over or clicks the button.

5. **Click the Over frame and choose Insert⇨Keyframe.**

The graphic you created for the Up state is still on the Stage.

6. **Draw the button for the Over state.**

Use the graphic for the Up state and change it (or leave it the same if
you want) or delete the graphic and draw a new one in its place.

7. **Click the Down frame and choose Insert⇨Keyframe.**

8. **Create the graphic for the Down frame (as in Step 6).**

9. **Click the Hit frame and choose Insert⇨Keyframe.**

10. **Create the shape that defines the active area of the button.**

This shape should completely cover all the graphics of the other states. Usually a rectangle or circle is enough. If you ignore the Hit frame, Macromedia Flash MX uses the boundary of the objects in the Up frame.

If you use text for the button, viewers have to hit the letters precisely unless you create a hit area around the text.

11. **Choose Edit⇨Edit Document to return to the regular Timeline.**

To place a button on the Stage, drag it from the Library to create an instance of the symbol. To edit a button, see the instructions for editing graphic symbols.

Adding pizzazz to buttons

Buttons don't have to be simple. You can make your buttons more interesting in the following ways:

✦ **Add a sound:** You add a sound to a button's Timeline in symbol-editing mode in the same way you add a sound to a frame on the main Timeline. See Book V, Chapter 6 for information on adding sounds.

✦ **Add animation:** Create a movie clip symbol as described in the section "Creating and Working with Movie Clip Symbols," earlier in this chapter. Click the keyframe of the button's Timeline that you want to contain the movie clip; for example, click the Over keyframe. Delete any existing graphic and drag a movie clip symbol containing animation from the Library onto the screen.

✦ **Add interactivity:** In order for the button to do something, it needs some ActionScript. Drag an instance of the button onto the Stage and select it. Then use the Actions panel to add ActionScript to the button. See Book V, Chapter 9 for specific information about using ActionScript.

Testing buttons

After you have created a button, you should drag an instance of it onto the Stage and test it. To test simple buttons, follow these steps:

1. **Choose Control⇨Enable Simple Buttons.**

2. **Pass the cursor over the button and click it to see if the effects work.**

3. **In order to select the button by clicking it, choose Control⇨Enable Simple Buttons again to disable the button.**

If your button contains movie clips, you need to test the entire movie to test the button. Choose Control⇨Test Movie and test the button. To close the movie window, click its Close button.

Chapter 4: Making Your Life Easier with Layers

In This Chapter

✔ Getting familiar with layers

✔ Working with layers

✔ Changing layer options

✔ Using folders to manage layers

*L*ayers are a way to organize your Flash document. Layers are an important part of creating a movie for the following reasons:

✦ **Layers keep objects from bumping into each other.** If you draw two circles and overlap them, they either merge, or one creates a cut out of the other. However, if you put them on two separate layers, they each remain whole.

✦ **Each animated object must be on its own layer.** So if you want more than one object on the Stage at one time, you need to create a new layer.

✦ **ActionScript and sounds should have their own layer.** This allows you to easily find and troubleshoot any problems as well as avoid potential conflicts.

✦ **Special types of layers let you create special effects:**

 • **Mask layers:** Mask layers create a "keyhole" through which you can see layers beneath it.

 • **Guide layers:** Guide layers direct animation along a path.

In addition, you can use layers for your own organizational purposes. For example, you can put text on a separate layer. Then, if you want to focus on just the text, you can hide all the other layers. In this chapter, we explain how to create and manage layers.

Layers add a third dimension to the organization of your Flash document. The Stage lays out your graphics in the horizontal (X axis) and vertical (Y axis) dimensions. Using layers is like adding a Z axis, enabling you to put graphics on top of each other as if on successive transparent sheets.

The Timeline, of course, adds the fourth dimension, time. Layers are intimately connected to the Timeline. For each layer, Macromedia Flash MX adds a row of frames in the Timeline.

Working with the Layer List

You work with layers on the layer list, which is to the left of the Timeline, as shown in Figure 4-1. The layer list contains the following features:

✦ **Default layer:** You start a new movie with the default layer, Layer 1.

✦ **Active layer:** The active layer is highlighted. When you create objects, they go on the active layer.

✦ **Show/Hide Layers:** You can show or hide objects on any layer by clicking the Show/Hide icon for that layer.

✦ **Lock/Unlock Layers:** You can lock any layer so that objects cannot be selected or edited. Click the Lock icon for that layer. To unlock a layer, click the Lock icon again.

✦ **Display Outlines:** You can display objects on a layer as outlines. Each layer uses a different outline color. Outlines may help you see objects on all layers more clearly. Click the Outlines icon for any layer.

✦ **Insert Layer:** To insert a layer, click the Insert Layer button below the layer list.

✦ **Insert Motion Guide:** To add a motion guide layer, click the Insert Motion Guide button below the layer list. See the "Using guide layers" section, later in this chapter, for more information on guide layers.

✦ **Insert Layer Folder:** You can organize layers into folders. Click the Insert Layer Folder button below the layer list.

✦ **Delete Layer:** To delete a layer, select it and click the Delete Layer button or drag the layer to the Delete Layer button.

Default, active layer

Show/Hide layers

Lock/Unlock layers

Display outlines

Figure 4-1:
Use the
layer list to
manage
your layers.

Delete layer

Insert layer folder

Add motion guide

Insert layer

Working with Layers

When you open a new movie, it has one layer, called Layer 1. As you
work, you create, delete, move, and copy layers. You also name your layers.
Choose a naming system that makes sense to you. *Note:* If the names are too
long, you won't be able to see the whole name in the layers list, so don't get
too extravagant. You can drag the right border of the layer listing to the
right to see more of the layer names.

Creating layers

When you need to create a new layer, click the Insert Layer button at the
bottom of the layer list (refer to Figure 4-1) or choose Insert⇨Layer. The
new layer appears above the active layer and becomes the active layer.

Right after you create a new layer is a good time to rename the new layer as
something meaningful. Double-click the layer name, type a new name, and
then press Enter.

Using layers

When you draw an object, it appears on the active layer, which is the layer that is highlighted and has a pencil icon next to its name in the layer list. To draw on a different layer, click the name of the layer you want to use. When you click a new layer, Macromedia Flash MX selects all the objects on that layer. To deselect them, click any empty area (on the Stage or in the gray space around the Stage).

Editing layers

You often need to make changes to layers or move objects from one layer to another. Keeping your layers organized is an important part of keeping your entire movie under control.

Selecting layers

When editing layers, you may want to select more than one layer at a time, such as when you need to move more than one layer at a time. To select a group of layers that are all together, click the first layer name on the layer list, press Shift, and click the last layer of the group. To select layers that are not together, click the first layer, press Ctrl, and click any additional layers that you want to select.

Moving objects from one layer to another

Often you draw objects before realizing they need to be on a separate or different layer. For example, you can only have one object on a layer that you are animating. If you draw additional objects on that layer, you should move them to another layer. First create a new layer, if necessary. To move objects from one layer to another, follow these steps:

1. **Select the objects that you want to move.**

   The layer containing the objects is also made current.

2. **Choose Edit⇨Cut.**

3. **Click the layer to which you want to move the objects.**

4. **Choose Edit⇨Paste in Place.**

   The objects appear in the same location as before, but they are now on the new layer.

Distributing to layers

A great feature is the ability to distribute all objects on a layer to separate layers. For example, if you want to animate each letter of a word, you should put each letter on a separate layer. Say you want to animate the letters of the word *now* so that each letter flies onto the Stage separately:

1. **Select the text or objects.**

   In this example, select the word *now*.

2. **If you are working with text, choose Modify⇨Break Apart.**

   You see a separate box around each letter. Each letter is now a separate object.

3. **Choose Modify⇨Distribute to Layers.**

   Each object or letter is now on a separate layer. Macromedia Flash MX automatically creates the layers for you. In the "now" example, Macromedia Flash MX creates three layers, named n, o, and w for each of the three letters.

   The objects also remain on their original layer. You can delete that layer if you wish and keep only their copies on the individual layers.

Renaming layers

If the content of a layer changes, you should rename the layer to something appropriate to its content. To rename a layer, double-click the layer name, type the new name, and press Enter.

Deleting layers

To delete a layer, select the layer and click the Trashcan button at the bottom of the layer list. (Refer to Figure 4-1.)

Deleting a layer deletes *everything* on that layer. Be aware that you may not be able to see everything on the layer, because you see only what is on the Stage in the current frame. To see what is on a layer throughout the Timeline, follow these steps:

1. **Right-click the layer name and choose Hide Others.**

2. **Click the first frame on the Timeline.**

3. **Press Enter to run the animation.**

Copying layers

You can copy an entire layer, and if you do, all the objects on that layer are copied as well:

1. **Select the layer.**

   Selecting the layer selects all the objects on the layer.

2. **Choose Edit⇨Copy Frames.**

3. **Choose Insert⇨Layer to create a new layer.**

4. **Choose Edit⇨Paste Frames.**

Reordering layers

Macromedia Flash MX displays objects in the order of their layers, from the top down. In other words, objects on the top layer appear in front of objects on the next layer on the list. You can reorder the layer list to change which objects appear in front on the Stage. See Figure 4-2 for an example.

Figure 4-2: By changing the layer order, you change which objects appear in front on the Stage.

To move a layer to a different spot in the layer list, drag its name to the desired location.

Using guide layers

A *guide layer* is a special type of layer that is invisible when your Flash document is published and played as a movie. Guide layers have two main purposes:

✦ **Drawing guide:** You can place gridlines on the Stage to help you lay out the objects on the Stage or import a bitmap and use it as a guide to help you draw using the graphics tools. The content on the guide layer will be invisible when the movie is published, but it helps you draw on a visible layer.

✦ **Motion guide:** You can place a path on a guide layer that controls the animation of an object, as shown in Figure 4-3.

Figure 4-3:
The path on the guide layer determines the path of the ball.

To create a guide layer, follow these steps:

1. **Click the Insert Layer button on the layer list.**

2. **Right-click the layer and choose Guide from the contextual menu.**

   The layer icon changes to the guide icon that looks like a dotted arc and a circle.

3. **To link a guide layer to an existing layer, drag its name onto the bottom edge of the existing layer.**

   When you use a guide layer as a motion guide, you need to link the guide layer to the layer containing the objects you want to guide (called the guided layer). The guided layer's icon is highlighted and Macromedia Flash MX indents the guided layer underneath the guide layer, as you see in Figure 4-3. (You may need to try this a couple of times before it works.)

Using mask layers

A *mask layer* hides everything on its connected masked layers, except inside a filled shape or text object. Masks are often used to create a spotlight effect, where you see only what is in the spotlight and everything else is hidden. You can see this effect in Figure 4-4, where the circular mask hides everything outside of the circle. The circle is on a mask layer, and what you see inside the circle is on two masked layers.

To create a mask layer, follow these steps:

1. **On the top layer of the layer list, create the objects you want to be visible through the mask.**

2. **With the top layer selected, click the Add Layer button at the bottom of the layer list.**

3. **Draw a shape, such as a circle, on this new layer.**

4. **Right-click the new layer and choose Mask from the menu.**

   The masked layer is locked and indented. The mask layer is also locked, as shown in Figure 4-4.

Figure 4-4:
The circular mask hides everything except what is inside the circle.

To edit a mask or masked layer, click the lock next to the layer name. Unlocking these layers removes the mask effect. After you have finished editing, click the lock column next to the layers' names again to redisplay the mask effect.

To link a layer to a mask layer, drag the layer directly underneath a mask layer. The layer is indented. To display the mask effect, make sure it is locked by clicking it under the Lock column of the layer list.

Changing Layer Options

You can control the visibility, editability, and display of objects on layers. These tools are very helpful when you are trying to isolate certain objects for editing or animation.

Altering the visibility of objects

You can hide all the objects on a layer. If you have a lot of objects on the Stage and want to edit objects on one layer, you can hide other layers that you don't need to see at the moment.

Don't forget about objects on hidden layers. They still show up in your published movie.

To hide a layer, click beneath the eye icon on the layer's row. An X appears in the eye column to show you that the layer is hidden. Click the X to unhide the layer.

To hide all layers except one, right-click the layer you want to see and choose Hide Others from the contextual menu that appears.

Locking and unlocking layers

You can lock the objects on a layer so that you cannot edit them. You may find yourself inadvertently selecting objects that you want to leave alone. This can get very annoying, but you can easily avoid the situation by locking that layer.

To lock a layer, click beneath the lock icon on the layer's row. A lock appears in the lock column. Click the lock to unlock the layer.

To lock all layers except one, right-click the layer and choose Lock Others from the contextual menu that appears.

Displaying objects as outlines

If you get confused about which objects are on which layers, you may want to briefly display objects as outlines. Objects on each layer can be displayed as outlines of a different color, so that you can tell which layer an object is on. However, text never appears as outlines but displays in the outline color.

To display objects as outlines, click beneath the outline icon on the layer's row. A colored box appears in the outline column. Click the box to fully redisplay the layer.

Setting layer properties

Many of the layer controls discussed in this chapter are combined in the Layer Properties dialog box, as shown in Figure 4-5. Most of the time you just use the controls on the layer list or the contextual menu that you see when you right-click a layer. However, the Layer Properties dialog box does have some unique features.

Figure 4-5:
The Layer
Properties
dialog box.

To open the Layer Properties dialog box, select the layer you want to modify and choose Modify⇨Layer. You can use this dialog box to do the following:

✦ **Rename the layer:** Type a new name in the Name text field.

✦ **Show/Hide the layer:** Select or deselect the Show check box.

✦ **Lock/Unlock the layer:** Select or deselect the Lock check box.

✦ **Change the type of layer:** You can turn a layer into a guide, guided, mask, masked, or normal layer.

♦ **Change the outline color:** Click the Outline Color swatch and choose a new color.

♦ **Turn outlines on/off:** Select or deselect the View Layer as Outlines check box.

♦ **Change layer height:** Select a percentage from the Layer Height drop-down list.

When you finish making changes, click OK to close the Layer Properties dialog box.

Using Folders to Manage Layers

If you have many layers, you can organize them into folders. For example, you may want to put all your layers containing text in one folder.

To create a folder, click the Insert Layer Folder icon at the bottom of the layer list. A new folder appears above the current layer. Double-click the folder name and enter a name that describes its contents.

Here's how to manage folders:

♦ **Put layers in a folder:** Drag layers onto the folder's row.

♦ **Remove a layer from a folder:** Drag the layer above the folder name or to another location where it doesn't darken a folder.

♦ **Collapse and expand individual folders:** Click the arrow at the left of the folder's icon.

♦ **Expand and collapse all folders:** Right-click the layer list and choose Expand All Folders or Collapse All Folders from the menu.

♦ **Hide or lock an entire folder and its layers:** Click beneath the eye or lock icon on the folder's row.

♦ **Reorder folders:** You can change the order of folders, which also changes the order of its layers. Just drag any folder up or down.

♦ **Delete folders:** Select the folder and click the Trashcan icon.

Deleting a folder deletes all the layers in the folder and everything on those layers. Macromedia Flash MX warns you of this if you try to delete a folder.

Chapter 5: Creating Animation

In This Chapter

✔ Touring the Timeline

✔ Understanding frames and keyframes

✔ Creating animation frame-by-frame

✔ Creating tweened animation

✔ Creating interactive animation

✔ Working with scenes

M acromedia Flash MX is basically an animation program, so this chapter on animation is central to the whole purpose of Macromedia Flash MX. In this chapter, we provide the information you need to create motion and shape animation.

Getting Familiar with the Timeline

The Timeline lays out your animation in time. In order to animate, you need to be thoroughly familiar with the Timeline and its special coding, as shown in Figure 5-1.

Figure 5-1:
The Timeline provides a great deal of information about your animation.

As you can see in Figure 5-1, every fifth frame on the Timeline is numbered. Each layer has its own row in the Timeline. (For more information on layers, see Book V, Chapter 4.)

If the Timeline isn't visible, choose View➪Timeline. You can collapse the Timeline by clicking its Collapse/Expand arrow at the left side of its title bar.

Understanding the frame rate

The frame rate is the speed at which Macromedia Flash MX plays the animation. The default frame rate is 12 frames per second (fps). You can have only one frame rate per document. To change the frame rate, follow these steps:

1. **Double-click the Frame Rate box at the bottom of the Timeline.**

   The Document Properties dialog box appears.

2. **In the Frame Rate text field, enter a new number in frames per second.**

3. **Click OK.**

When you use a frame rate that is too slow, the animation appears jerky. Increasing the frame rate may make animation appear smoother, but a frame rate that is too fast can appear blurred. The default frame rate of 12 fps is a good place to start.

The Internet connection rate and the size of the file also affect the rate of animation. A large file (often due to large graphics or sounds) and a slow Internet connection can make the animation stutter. Your viewers will get the best results if you reduce the size of the file as much as possible. In Book V, Chapter 7, we explain how to optimize files for the Web.

Working with the Timeline

You can work with the Timeline in the following ways:

✦ **Go to a frame:** Click the frame on the Timeline to go to a particular frame. If you want to work on a specific layer, click the frame in that layer's row.

✦ **Change size and appearance of the frames:** To modify the frames, click the Frame View button in the upper-right corner of the Timeline and choose one of the options from the menu. You can change the width and height of the frames, turn coloring of frames on and off, and choose to display a small thumbnail of the frame's content in each frame.

✦ **Add a label or comment to a frame:** To add a label or comment, select a frame and type a label name in the Frame Label text field of the Property inspector.

✦ **Select frames:** Click a frame and drag across the frames you want to select. (You can also click the first frame, press Shift, and click the last frame you want to select to select all the frames in between.)

✦ **Copy and paste frames:** Select the frames you want to copy, choose Edit⇨Copy Frames from the menu, click where you want the frames to go, and choose Edit⇨Paste Frames.

✦ **Move frames:** Select the frames you want to move and drag them to the desired location.

✦ **Add a frame:** To add a frame, right-click on the desired frame and choose Insert Frame from the menu.

✦ **Delete frames:** Select the frames you want to delete. Right-click and choose Remove Frames.

✦ **Add a keyframe:** Right-click on the desired frame and choose Insert Keyframe from the menu.

✦ **Change the length of an animation:** Press Ctrl and click and drag the first or last keyframe of the animation to the right or left.

✦ **Scroll along the Timeline:** Use the horizontal scroll bar to scroll along the Timeline. Use the Vertical scroll bar (which appears when you have too many layers to display) to scroll through the layers.

Onion skinning

When you animate an object, you can display some or all of the animated frames at once, using an effect known as *onion skinning*. Onion skinning produces overlapping translucent images like the translucent layers of an onion. See Figure 5-2 for an example of onion skinning.

To work with onion skinning, use the buttons under the Timeline:

✦ **Onion skin:** Turns on onion skinning and adjusts the Onion markers to customize the number of frames that display the effect.

✦ **Onion skin outlines:** Displays single-color outlines of your animation.

✦ **Edit multiple frames:** Enables you to edit any of the frames on the Timeline, regardless of the current frame.

✦ **Modify onion markers:** Displays a menu so you can always show the markers (even when onion skinning is off), anchor the markers so they don't follow the playhead (current frame marker), and set the number of frames that the markers cover.

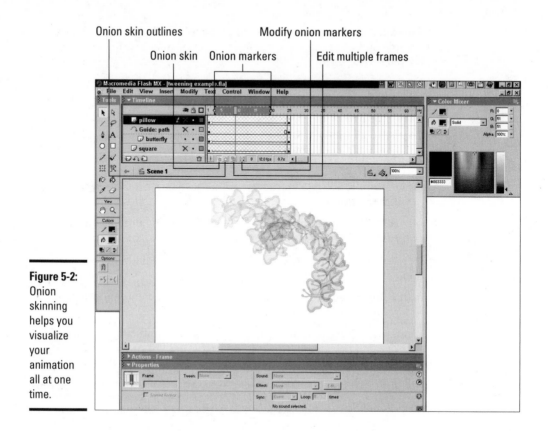

Onion skin outlines

Modify onion markers

Onion skin   Onion markers

Edit multiple frames

Figure 5-2:
Onion
skinning
helps you
visualize
your
animation
all at one
time.

Using Frames and Keyframes

A frame is actually a unit of time, based on your frame rate. You can place content on any frame, but you can only change content on a keyframe. Use a keyframe whenever you want to start or stop an animation or make any object appear or disappear.

To introduce any new object onto the Stage, you must have a keyframe. Insert a keyframe and click the keyframe on the layer where you want the object to appear. Then do one of the following:

✦ Draw something by using the Macromedia Flash MX drawing tools. (See Book V, Chapter 2.)

✦ Import a bitmap. (See Book V, Chapter 3.)

✦ Drag an object onto the Stage from the Library. (See Book V, Chapter 1.)

You can create two types of animation in Macromedia Flash MX:

✦ **Frame-by-frame:** In frame-by-frame animation, each frame is a keyframe and contains a slight change in your objects so that when you play the Flash document, you see a smooth animation. This type of animation is time-consuming and creates bigger files, but it may be necessary to create complex effects. Cartooning is mostly done using frame-by-frame animation.

✦ **Tweening:** In tweening, the first and last frames of the animation are keyframes, and Macromedia Flash MX calculates everything in between. You can tween motion and shapes *(morphing)*. Tweening is faster to create than frame-by-frame animation and creates small file sizes.

Creating Animation Frame-By-Frame

When your animation does not have a simple pattern, such as movement of one object in a direction or the change of one shape to another shape, you need to use frame-by-frame animation. A common example of frame-by-frame animation is cartooning where a figure needs to move in complex ways or a mouth moves in synchrony with speech.

To create frame-by-frame animation, follow these steps:

1. **Right-click a frame in the current layer where you want the animation to start and choose Insert Keyframe from the menu that appears.**

2. **Draw or import your image.**

Book V, Chapter 2 is all about creating graphics. To import an image, choose File➪Import.

3. **Right-click the next frame and choose Insert Keyframe again.**

4. **Change the graphic slightly to create the second frame of the animation.**

5. **Repeat Steps 3 and 4 as necessary until you have completed your animation.**

See Figure 5-3 for an example of frame-by-frame animation.

During the process, press Enter to play back your animation and check your work.

Figure 5-3:
This frame-
by-frame
animation of
the legs
moving is
shown
using onion
skinning.

Creating Tweened Motion Animation

Motion tweening moves a single symbol instance, text object, or grouped set of objects either in a straight line or along a path that you draw (often with the Pencil tool).

Although you can motion tween only one object at a time on any layer, you can tween other objects on other layers to create the overall look of many objects being animated.

You can also change the size, rotation, skew (slant), color, and transparency of symbol instances as you motion tween them. To make these changes to text or groups, convert them to symbols. See Book V, Chapter 3 for a discussion of symbols.

Preparing to tween

You can only put one object — symbol instance, text, or group — on the layer where you are animating. The first step is to create the object you want to animate and make sure that nothing else is on that layer. Often, you create a new layer just for your animation.

Decide how you want your object to move. Do you want its color, size, or rotation to change? After you have decided, you are ready to tween.

The Macromedia Flash MX Controller is like a control panel for a tape or video player. The Controller is helpful when you animate because it offers controls for rewinding and playing your animation. To open the Controller, choose Window⇨Toolbars⇨Controller.

Creating a simple tween

Before you tween, open the Property inspector by choosing Window⇨ Properties. To create a simple motion tween that moves the object along a straight line, follow these steps:

1. On your animation layer, insert a keyframe where you want the animation to start.

2. Click the keyframe and create the object or objects you want to animate.

You cannot tween plain graphics. If necessary, turn your object or objects into a symbol (see Book V, Chapter 3) or a group (see Book V, Chapter 2). Text is fine as it is. You can also import a graphic or drag an instance of a symbol from the Library onto the Stage.

3. Insert a keyframe where you want the animation to end.

The longer the span of frames is, the slower the animation. You can always adjust the length of a tween later, as explained in the "Working with the Timeline" section, earlier in this chapter.

4. Click the last keyframe and move the object to its new location.

At this point, you can also change the object's color and transparency by using the Color drop-down list of the Property inspector. In addition, you can use the Free Transform tool or other Macromedia Flash MX commands to change the object's size, rotation, and skew, as shown in Figure 5-4.

5. Select the range from keyframe to keyframe by clicking the first keyframe and dragging to the last keyframe.

If the span of frames is too long to show, click the first keyframe, scroll to the last keyframe, press Shift, and click the last keyframe.

You can click anywhere between the keyframes and get almost the exact same result as the technique in Step 5. The last keyframe isn't tweened, but the result looks the same when you play the animation.

6. From the Tween drop-down list of the Property inspector, select Motion.

If you changed the object's size, select the Scale check box in the Property inspector to tween the size.

Figure 5-4:
A simple motion tween including scaling. Onion skinning shows all the frames outlined.

7. **If you want to rotate the object during the tween (in addition to any rotation you created in Step 4), select CW (clockwise) or CCW (counterclockwise) from the Rotate drop-down list in the Property inspector, and then enter the number of rotations in the Rotation Count text field.**

   To test your animation, click the first keyframe and press Enter or use the Controller to rewind and play your animation.

You can accelerate or decelerate the speed of the tween. To accelerate from beginning to end, enter a value between –1 and –100 in the Ease text field of the Property inspector. To decelerate, use a value between 1 and 100.

See Figure 5-4 for an example of a ball that moves along a diagonal line. The ball also becomes smaller, so that it appears to recede in the distance as it moves.

Motion tweening along a path

To tween along a path that is not a straight line, you need to draw the path on a guide layer. (See Book V, Chapter 4 for the steps to create a guide layer.) Your animation is on the guided layer that is associated with the guide layer. Figure 5-5 shows an example of a motion tween along a path.

Figure 5-5:
The butterfly
moves
along its
path. Here
you see the
effect
shown with
onion
skinning on.

To create an animation that moves along a path, follow these steps (which
start just like the steps for simple motion tweening):

1. **On your animation layer, insert a keyframe where you want the
   animation to start.**

2. **Click the keyframe and create or import the object or objects (symbol
   instance, group, or text) you want to animate.**

3. **Insert a keyframe where you want the animation to end.**

4. **Select the range from keyframe to keyframe by clicking the first
   keyframe and dragging to the last keyframe, or click anywhere
   between the two keyframes.**

5. **From the Tween drop-down list of the Property inspector, select
   Motion.**

6. **In the Property inspector, select the Snap check box to snap the
   object to the path.**

7. **If you want the object to rotate in the direction and angle of the
   path, select the Orient to Path check box.**

8. **Right-click the object's layer and select Add Motion Guide.**

   The new layer is added. The layer is labeled Guide, and the object's layer is indented beneath it.

9. **On the guide layer, draw your path.**

10. **Click the first keyframe of the object's layer and drag the object by its registration point (a small plus or circle) to the beginning of the path until the registration point snaps to the path.**

11. **Click the last keyframe of the object's layer and drag the object by its registration point to the end of the path until the registration point snaps to the path.**

12. **Press Enter to play the animation.**

If you need to change your path, use the Macromedia Flash MX editing tools to edit the path you created. You can use the Arrow or Subselection tools to edit the path. (See Book V, Chapter 2 for details.)

Objects on a guide path are not visible in the published movie. However, you often don't want to see the path even in your document, so you can more easily visualize the animation. Just click the eye column of the guide layer to hide it.

Creating Tweened Shape Animation

If you want your objects to change shape, you need shape tweening, often called *morphing*. Unlike motion tweening, shape tweening works only with plain vector objects, usually ones that you create with the Macromedia Flash MX drawing tools. You cannot shape tween a symbol instance, text, or a group, unless you break them apart by choosing Modify⇨Break Apart.

To turn text into shapes, choose Modify⇨Break Apart twice. The first time only breaks apart the text into individual letters. The second time you choose Modify⇨Break Apart, you create shapes from the individual letters. However, remember that you can have only one animated object on a layer. You can break apart text once, and then choose Modify⇨Distribute to Layers to put each letter on a separate layer. If you want to shape tween the letters, break apart each letter a second time.

Creating a simple shape tween

To shape tween a shape, follow these steps:

1. **On a new layer, right-click the frame where you want the animation to start and select Insert Keyframe.**

2. **Create the beginning shape.**

3. **Insert a keyframe where you want to end the animation.**

4. **With the second keyframe selected, create the ending shape.**

You can create the end shape by erasing the first shape and drawing a new one or by modifying the first shape.

5. **If you want to change color, you can simply choose another color for the ending shape from the Color palette in the Property inspector.**

6. **If you want to change transparency, open the Color Mixer panel (Window⇨Color Mixer) and change the Alpha percentage in the Alpha text field.**

You can also change the color in the Color Mixer.

7. **Click between the keyframes or select the entire span of the tween.**

8. **Select Shape from the Tween drop-down list of the Property inspector.**

9. **From the lower section of the Property inspector, select Angular from the Blend drop-down list if your tween shape has straight lines and sharp corners. Select Distributive for more curvy shapes.**

You may need to click the Collapse/Expand arrow at the lower-right corner of the Property inspector to display the lower section of the Property inspector.

10. **To play the animation, click the first keyframe and press Enter.**

Using shape hints for more control

When you create your first shape tween, you may find that Macromedia Flash MX calculated the transformation differently than you imagined it. You can give Macromedia Flash MX cues, called *shape hints,* that tell it which part of the original shape moves where, as shown in Figure 5-6.

Figure 5-6:
Shape
hints tell
Macromedia
Flash MX
where
points on
your
beginning
shape will
end up.

To use shape hints, follow these steps:

1. **Create a shape animation as described in the section, "Creating a simple tween."**

2. **Click the first keyframe of the animation.**

3. **Choose Modify➪Shape➪Add Shape Hint or press Ctrl+Shift+H.**

   A small red circle with the letter "a" inside it appears on the Stage.

4. **Drag the shape hint to the desired area in your shape.**

5. **Click the ending keyframe of the animation.**

   You again see a small circle with the letter "a" inside it on the Stage.

6. **Drag the shape hint to the area in your shape where you want the beginning hint to move.**

7. **Repeat Steps 3 through 6 to place additional shape hints.**

8. **Press Enter to play the animation and check the results.**

If you want, you can remove or hide existing shape hints:

✦ To remove a shape hint, drag it off the Stage.

✦ To display and hide shape hints, select the layer and keyframe with the shape hints and choose View➪Show Shape Hints.

You may get better results if you place the hints counterclockwise, starting from the upper-left corner of your shape.

Adding Basic Interactivity to Animation

You often need to control how your animation works. For example, you may want some animation to loop or to stop at a certain point. You may also want to enable viewers to control the animation. Buttons commonly allow users to stop the animation (perhaps some introductory animation for your Web site) or turn off the sound. You introduce interactivity and control by using ActionScript, the Macromedia Flash MX programming language.

The following sections offer a few ideas for using ActionScript in animation. We cover interactivity in detail in Book V, Chapter 9.

Go To

You don't need to play your animation from beginning to end. You can add ActionScript (often simply called *actions*) to control the playing of the frames. The goto action tells the movie to go to a different frame. At that point, you can tell the animation to stop or to play.

Say that you want your animation to play from Frames 1–24, but then you want the last half to loop over and over again. On Frame 24, you can add a goto action and tell Macromedia Flash MX to go to Frame 12 and play. The animation goes to Frame 24, and then loops back to Frame 12 again. In this situation, the first 11 frames play only once, but Frames 12 through 24 play over and over in a loop.

In another situation, you may want animation to play from Frames 1–24 and then go to Frame 50 and stop. You may be using Frame 50 to display a menu. In this case, you use the goto and stop actions.

Stop

Sometimes, you just want to stop the animation. For example, movie clips automatically loop. If you want them to play just once and then stop, you add a stop action in the last frame. For any animation, you can add a stop action at the end to make sure that everything stops at the same time.

Play

After you stop an animation, you may want to play it again. You can use the play action to play a movie when certain conditions are met. If the conditions are not met, the movie does not play (due to a stop action).

On (mouse event)

The on action is used for buttons, which are explained in Book V, Chapter 3. To add interactivity, you specify what happens when the button is clicked or released, when a mouse cursor passes over or off the button, or when a mouse cursor is dragged over or off the button. For example, a common use of the on action would be to specify that when the button is clicked, you go to a different frame or URL, such as another page on the Web site.

Working with Scenes

A *scene* is a section of an animation. You can divide up your animation into scenes, each with its own Timeline. The scenes play back in the order you set. The purpose of creating a scene is to help you organize your animation. By default, you work in Scene 1. The current scene name is displayed beneath the layer list. To create a new scene, choose Insert⇨Scene.

To manage your scenes, choose Window⇨Scene. The Scene panel opens, as shown in Figure 5-7.

Figure 5-7:
The Scene panel helps you manage scenes.

You can use the Scene panel to work with scenes in the following ways:

✦ **Change scene order:** Drag a scene's name in the Scene panel to a new location to change the order of the scenes.

✦ **Rename a scene:** Double-click a scene's name, type a new name, and press Enter to rename a scene.

✦ **Add a scene:** Click the Add Scene button at the bottom of the Scene panel to add a scene.

✦ **Delete a scene:** Select a scene and click the Delete Scene button at the bottom of the Scene panel to delete a scene.

✦ **Duplicate a scene:** Select a scene and click the Duplicate Scene button at the bottom of the Scene panel to create a copy of a scene.

✦ **View a scene:** Select the scene in the Scene panel to view the scene.

Chapter 6: Adding Sound and Video

In This Chapter

✔ Introducing sound and video formats

✔ Working with sounds

✔ Working with video clips

*Y*ou can make the Web experience richer by adding sound and video to your Web pages. Sounds can range from a simple clicking noise when a user clicks a button to music and narration. You can also include video in your Web site.

Exploring Sound and Video Formats

Both sound and video files come in many formats. Before you can use sound or video, you need a file that Macromedia Flash MX can import.

Sound file formats

You can use the following sound file formats in Macromedia Flash MX:

✦ **AIFF:** This is the standard sound format for Macintosh computers. These files usually have filenames with the `.aif` or `.ief` extensions.

✦ **WAV:** This is the standard format for Windows machines. These files usually have filenames with a `.wav` extension.

✦ **MP3:** This is a highly-compressed format that maintains high quality sound.

Certain MP3s use a kind of compression that Macromedia Flash MX cannot import. Also, if the MP3 is over 160 Kbps, you need to install QuickTime before you can import the file.

A sound file has several properties that affect its quality and size. You can often adjust these properties to reduce file size without noticeably affecting quality. For sophisticated adjustments, you probably need a sound-editing program. Here are the basic properties of a sound file:

✦ **Sample rate:** The *sample rate* is the number of times in kilohertz (kHz) that an audio signal is sampled when it's recorded digitally. A higher sample rate results in higher quality sound but also yields a larger file size.

✦ **Bit rate:** The *bit rate* is the number of bits (pieces of data) used for each audio sample. Sixteen-bit sounds are clearer, but 8-bit sounds are smaller and may be good enough for simple sounds, such as a button click.

✦ **Channels:** *Channels* are the number of streams of sound in a file and are either mono or stereo. Mono may be just fine and uses half the amount of data as stereo.

You can find a sound's properties when you import the sound into Macromedia Flash MX, as explained in the upcoming section, "Importing sounds."

Video file formats

The type of video formats you can use depends on some other software that supports their playback:

✦ **If you have QuickTime 4 or later installed:** You can import AVI, MPEG (MPG), MOV, and DV formats.

✦ **If you have DirectX 7 or later installed:** You can import AVI, MPEG (MPG), and WMV/ASF (Windows Media File) formats.

Because video files are usually very large, they are always compressed by using a *codec*. The word *codec* stands for compression/decompression. The same codec decompresses the video file when it is used. You need to have the codec that was used for the video file on your computer in order to import the video file. The same applies to the audio track in a video file.

Working with Sounds

Working with sounds in Macromedia Flash MX involves at least two steps — importing the sound and placing it in a movie. You can also edit sounds in Macromedia Flash MX.

Importing sounds

To import a sound, follow these steps:

1. **Choose File⇨Import.**

The Import dialog box appears.

2. **Select the sound file you want to import and click Open.**

   The sound goes into the Library.

To see a sound's properties, open the Library and right-click the sound. Choose Properties from the menu that appears.

Placing a sound in a movie

After a sound is in the Library, you can place it in your movie. You need to decide when it starts, when it ends, or whether you want to loop the sound.

To place a sound, follow these steps:

1. **Create a new layer for the sound by choosing Insert⇨Layer.**

2. **Right-click the frame and choose Insert Keyframe.**

   This inserts a keyframe on the sound's layer where you want the sound to start.

3. **Press Ctrl+L to open the Library.**

4. **Drag the sound to the Stage.**

   The sound extends to the next keyframe, if one exists.

5. **To specify settings for the sound, open the Property inspector by choosing Window⇨Properties.**

6. **Expand the Property inspector, as shown in Figure 6-1, using the Expand/Collapse arrow in the lower-right corner.**

Figure 6-1:
Specifying
sound
settings.

Properties				
Frame	Tween: None	Sound: meditate.mp3		
<Frame Label>		Effect: Custom	Edit...	
Named Anchor		Sync: Event Loop: 0 times		
		44 kHz Stereo 16 Bit 41.7 s 667.5 kB		

7. **From the Sound drop-down list, choose the sound for which you want to specify settings.**

   All the sounds you have imported are listed.

8. **To create a special effect, select an effect from the Effect drop-down list:**

   • **None:** No special effect (the default).

   • **Left channel:** Plays the sound from the left speaker.

- **Right channel:** Plays the sound from the right speaker.

- **Fade left to right:** Starts playing from the left speaker and moves to the right speaker.

- **Fade right to left:** Starts playing from the right speaker and moves to the left speaker.

- **Fade in:** Starts playing softly and increases the volume.

- **Fade out:** Starts playing loudly and decreases the volume.

- **Custom:** If you edit the sound, as explained in the next section, your sound has a custom effect.

9. **Select a synchronization type from the Sync drop-down list:**

- **Event:** Plays the sound from its first keyframe until it ends, even if the movie stops. Replays the sound whenever that keyframe plays. The entire sound downloads before it plays. This choice is ideal for button sounds that you want to play whenever the button is clicked. Event is the default synchronization type.

- **Start:** Plays the sound like the Event option, but if the keyframe is replayed before the sound is finished, the Start option doesn't replay the sound.

- **Stop:** Stops playing the sound.

- **Stream:** Synchronizes the sound with the animation, shortening or lengthening the animation to match the length of the sound. Macromedia Flash MX may skip frames if necessary. The sound stops when Macromedia Flash MX plays the last frame containing the sound. Also, the sound stops when the movie stops, and it doesn't continue playing after the frame or frames it occupies. The bandwidth for streamed sound is shared with other streamed data, so that the quality may be lower than for event sounds. Also, sound samples may be dropped to allow for synchronization with the frames.

10. **If you want to loop (repeat) the sound, enter the number of loops in the Loop text field.**

11. **Press Enter to play the animation and hear the sound.**

   Press Ctrl+Enter to test the movie if you have more-complex animation.

Editing sounds

Macromedia Flash MX contains its own simple sound-editing tool. For example, you can delete some of the beginning or end of the sound if you don't need it. You can also change the volume. To edit a sound, follow these steps:

1. **Click a frame that contains a sound.**

2. **Open the Property inspector by choosing Window↷Properties.**

If necessary, click the Collapse/Expand arrow at the lower-right corner to expand the Property inspector fully.

3. **Click the Edit button.**

The Edit Envelope dialog box, as shown in Figure 6-2, appears.

You can edit the sound as follows:

- **Change the volume:** Drag an envelope handle (see Figure 6-2) up to increase volume or down to decrease volume. Click an envelope line to add a handle so that you can change the volume at that location.

- **Delete the beginning of the sound:** Drag the Time In control to the right.

- **Delete the end of the sound:** Scroll to the end of the sound and drag the Time Out control (the ending control) to the left.

You can use the Zoom In and Zoom Out buttons (see Figure 6-2) to change the magnification in the Edit Envelope dialog box. You can also use the Frames and Seconds buttons to change the display between frames and seconds.

Envelope handle   Left channel/speaker

   Effect drop-down list   Left volume envelope

Figure 6-2:
You can edit
sounds in
the Edit
Envelope
dialog box.

Play   Zoom in   Frames

Stop   Zoom out ⌐ ⌐Seconds

Right channel/speaker

Time In control

Setting sound properties

You can control the properties of a sound to further compress it. If you need to specify different properties for different sounds, set the properties when you place the sound in your movie:

1. **Open the Library by choosing Window⇨Library.**

2. **Double-click the sound.**

   The Sound Properties dialog box, as shown in Figure 6-3, appears.

   The top part of the dialog box lists the sound's name, original location, and statistics. At the bottom of the dialog box, use the Compression drop-down list to select the file format you want:

   • **Default:** Leaves the sound unchanged.

   • **ADPCM:** Enables you to convert stereo to mono and to choose a sampling rate and bit rate. Used for short sounds.

   • **MP3:** Enables you to convert stereo to mono and to choose a bit rate and quality. MP3 is an efficient compression method and is used for longer, more-complex sounds, especially music.

   • **Raw:** Enables you to convert stereo to mono and to choose the sampling rate. Raw uses no compression.

   • **Speech:** Enables you to choose a sampling rate. This option uses compression specially designed for speech.

   As you choose an option, you see the resulting statistics at the bottom of the dialog box.

3. **Click the Test button to hear the result of your choice.**

Figure 6-3:
You can set properties of individual sounds in the Sound Properties dialog box.

You can also set sound properties for all sounds at once when you publish your movie. (See Book V, Chapter 7.)

Working with Video Clips

A new feature of Macromedia Flash MX is the ability to embed video clips in your Flash movie. A video clip can be live action or animation created with an animation program that outputs a video file format. *Note:* Macromedia Flash MX may not be able to handle very long video files. You also have no direct control over the video frames.

To use a video, follow these steps:

1. **Right-click a frame and choose Insert Keyframe or select a keyframe.**

2. **Choose File➪Import.**

The Import dialog box appears.

3. **Choose the video file you want and click the Open button.**

The Import Video Settings dialog box, as shown in Figure 6-4, appears.

Figure 6-4:
Adjust the quality and scaling of a video file in the Import Video Settings dialog box.

4. **To compress the video, drag the Quality slider to the left.**

Macromedia Flash MX automatically compresses video files, but using the Quality slider compresses the file further.

5. **To choose the frequency of keyframes in the video clip, drag the Keyframe Interval slider.**

A video keyframe is separate from a Timeline keyframe. A *video keyframe* stores the entire image data as compared to the changes from the previous frame that are stored in regular frames. A greater frequency of video keyframes ensures greater accuracy but enlarges the size of the file. You can choose a value from 0 to 48. A keyframe interval of 1 inserts a video keyframe in every frame — so use an interval of 1 only for very small video files.

A keyframe interval of 0 adds a single keyframe at the beginning of the video stream and no other keyframes. A value of 0 inserts no keyframes.

6. **To scale the movie, drag the Scale slider.**

   Use the Scale slider to reduce the scale of the movie. Full-frame video files may be 640 x 480 and will function more smoothly on the Web at a smaller size.

7. **Select the Synchronize Video to Macromedia Flash Document Frame Rate option to match the video frame rate to the Flash movie frame rate.**

   If your video seems to display poorly, try deselecting this option.

8. **From the Number of Video Frames to Encode Per Number of Flash Frames drop-down list, select a ratio.**

   The default is 1:1, which plays one video frame for each Flash frame. A ratio of 1:2 would play one video frame for every two Flash frames. A 1:2 or higher ratio reduces file size, but reduces smoothness of playback as well.

9. **If the Import Audio check box is available, select it to include the audio.**

   If the video file has an audio track that uses a codec not available on your computer, you see a warning that you cannot import the audio.

10. **Click OK.**

    If the video clip is longer than the span of keyframes into which you are placing the video, a message displays, asking if you want to add enough frames necessary to play the entire clip.

11. **Click Yes to add the frames.**

You can also import a video file directly into the Library by choosing File⇨Import to Library. One reason to do this is to insert the video into a movie clip symbol (see Book V, Chapter 3 for a discussion of movie clip symbols). You can then control the video by adding ActionScript to the movie clip.

The Import Video Settings dialog box, as shown earlier in Figure 6-4, shows a logo for Sorenson Spark. Sorenson Spark is a video codec built into Macromedia Flash MX. A Pro Edition with expanded capabilities is available at www.sorenson.com/sparkpro.html.

Chapter 7: Publishing Movies

After you finish creating your Flash document, you need to publish it in SWF movie format. You then use HTML code to insert the SWF movie on a Web page so that browsers can display the animation. In this chapter, we explain how to get your animation onto your Web site.

Publishing Movies the Simple Way

If you don't need to change any settings, you can immediately publish your file by choosing File➪Publish. For more control, choose File➪Publish Settings to open the Publish Settings dialog box, as shown in Figure 7-1.

Figure 7-1: Use the Publish Settings dialog box to publish your movies.

By default, Macromedia Flash MX creates two files: The SWF file and an HTML file that contains the HTML code needed for your Web page. You can also export your document to other formats by selecting the format you want on the Formats tab. We discuss the HTML code and other export formats in "Generating HTML and Graphics," later in this chapter.

Macromedia Flash MX creates all these files by using the name of your Flash document and tacking on various filename extensions. If you want to specify the filenames, deselect the Use Default Names check box and enter your own names in the text fields.

To post your movie on your Web site, you use the HTML code either by itself or within another Web page. Then you upload both the Web page and the SWF file as you would any other Web page and image.

Macromedia Flash MX has a lot more options for you to tweak. To set these options, click the other tabs of the Publish Settings dialog box and select the options you want before clicking the Publish button.

Click the Flash tab, as shown in Figure 7-2, to see the options for creating the SWF file. You can set the following options:

✦ **Version:** Saves in previous version formats for backward compatibility.

✦ **Load Order:** Controls the loading order of layers in your document for the first frame (which usually takes the longest to display).

Changing the load order can affect how your ActionScript code functions.

Figure 7-2:
Use the Flash tab of the Publish Settings dialog box to set options for the SWF movie file.

✦ **Generate Size Report:** Creates a text file that details the size of the frames of your movie, so that you can make adjustments if a movie is loading slowly.

✦ **Protect from Import:** Helps prevent the SWF file from being imported into an FLA file that others could then modify.

Never trust that your SWF is completely safe. Tools to undo this option are available on the Web.

✦ **Omit Trace Actions:** Reduces file size by deleting trace actions if you used them in your ActionScript to help you debug your code.

✦ **Debugging Permitted:** Enables you to use the Macromedia Flash MX Debugger feature to debug errors in ActionScript.

The debugger allows you to troubleshoot ActionScript problems from within your browser. You can protect this feature with a password.

✦ **Compress Movie:** Compresses your Flash document, especially text and ActionScript. *Note:* This feature is only compatible with the Flash Player 6.

✦ **Password:** Enables you to set a password for debugging so that those without the password cannot debug your movie.

✦ **JPEG Quality:** Sets the quality of bitmaps. Higher quality looks better, but means a larger file size.

✦ **Audio Stream:** Sets the audio compression for all stream sounds in the movie, if you haven't set individual settings in the Sound Properties dialog box. Click the Set button to set the compression. See Book V, Chapter 6 for more information on stream sounds.

✦ **Audio Event:** Sets audio compression for all event sounds in the movie.

✦ **Override Sound Settings:** Overrides settings in the Sound Properties dialog box and applies settings here to all sounds in your movie.

Optimizing Movies for Speed

As you work, you should always design for fast display on a Web site. You can't control the speed of your viewers Internet connections or how fast their computers' processors are, but you can definitely control the size of your movie file. Before you publish your document, you may want to look it over from within Macromedia Flash MX and see how you can make it more efficient. After you publish and test the movie on a Web page, you may find that you need to make some adjustments for faster download. The following four sections offer some tips for optimizing your movies for speedy display.

Simplifying graphics

You can simplify the graphics in your movie and greatly increase its speed. Here are some pointers:

✦ **Use tweened animation:** Tweened animation is faster than frame-by-frame animation. (See Book V, Chapter 5.)

✦ **Don't animate bitmaps:** Macromedia Flash MX needs to store the location of each pixel in a bitmap, and that greatly increases file size. In fact, avoid bitmaps altogether as much as possible.

✦ **Turn everything into symbols:** Even backgrounds should be symbols. You can also put symbols inside of symbols. (See Book V, Chapter 3.)

✦ **Group objects:** Groups also reduce file size. (See Book V, Chapter 2.)

✦ **Optimize curves:** Optimizing curves reduces the number of lines in your graphics. (See Book V, Chapter 2.)

✦ **Use solid lines:** Avoid dashed and dotted lines. Especially avoid custom lines. (See Book V, Chapter 2.)

✦ **Use the Pencil tool rather than the Brush tool:** The Brush tool requires your document to store more information. (See Book V, Chapter 2.)

✦ **Use the Web-safe color palette:** Avoid custom colors. (See Book V, Chapter 2.)

✦ **Use solid fills rather than gradients as much as possible:** Gradients are more complex to calculate.

✦ **Avoid transparency:** As much as possible, avoid using alpha values of less than 100 percent.

Optimizing text

Text takes up more bytes in your file than vector graphics. Here are some options for reducing the load:

✦ **Reduce the number of fonts:** Use simpler fonts, fewer font styles (bold, italic), and fewer fonts overall. Use device fonts (sans, serif, and typewriter) if possible.

The three device fonts display correctly in any browser and on any computer.

✦ **Put text into your HTML document:** Not all text needs to be in your Flash document. If you can put some of your text in HTML format, you'll get faster download times.

Minimizing the size of sound files

Sound and music can really hog up the download stream. (See Book V, Chapter 6 for details about working with sounds.) You can use the following techniques to minimize the size of sounds:

✦ **Compress sounds:** Use the Sound Properties dialog box (right-click the sound in the Library and choose Properties) to fine-tune settings for individual sounds or use the sound settings on the Flash tab of the Publish Settings dialog box, described earlier in this chapter. Use the MP3 format whenever possible.

✦ **Remove silent areas:** Edit sounds to remove unnecessary beginnings and endings by adjusting the Time In and Time Out controls.

✦ **Reuse sounds:** You can reuse a sound with different in and out points or loop different parts of the same sound.

✦ **Don't loop streaming sound:** It's not necessary, and the browser continually downloads it.

Testing download time

Macromedia Flash MX can simulate various Internet connection speeds and give you feedback on which frames may cause a delay in download time. Don't miss out on this excellent tool. If the results indicate delays, go back and adjust your movie until everything displays quickly. You don't want to lose your Web site visitors because they get impatient while waiting for your Flash movie to download! Follow these steps to test your movie's download time:

1. **Choose Control⇨Test Movie.**

2. **From the menu bar of the new window, choose Debug and choose a download speed.**

3. **From the menu bar of the new window, choose View⇨Bandwidth Profiler.**

The Bandwidth Profiler is shown in Figure 7-3.

Figure 7-3:
The Bandwidth Profiler shows you which frames will display slowly on a Web site.

4. Choose View⇨Show Streaming to simulate playing the animation over an Internet connection.

Watch for any jerkiness and listen for any breaks in the sound.

5. Choose View⇨Streaming Graph to see all the frames that may cause delays or View⇨Frame by Frame Graph to see the size of each frame.

These are just two ways of viewing the information. You can use either view. Click on any bar (which represents a frame) to see the information for that frame. Frames that extend above the red horizontal line may cause a delay in the display of the movie.

6. Click the Close button of the SWF window when you are finished.

A short delay in the first frame is often acceptable as Macromedia Flash MX downloads all the information. After the first frame, you should try to avoid any delays because they result in pauses or uneven animation.

Although the best solution is to minimize delays, another possible choice is a preloader, a short animation that plays over and over while the main animation is loading. If you want your viewers to get to your movie quickly, work to reduce file size rather than using a preloader. If the artistry and special effects are primary, then use a preloader.

Generating HTML and Graphics

When you publish your Flash document, you also generate the HTML code that you need to create a Web page that plays your animation. You can also export your movie in several other graphic and animation formats.

Creating HTML code

You can use the HTML code that Macromedia Flash MX generates to create a new Web page that contains nothing else, or you can insert the HTML code into an existing Web page that may contain many other components. On the HTML tab of the Publish Settings dialog box, you can specify the following settings:

✦ **Template:** Specifies the content of the HTML file. The Flash Only (the default) option includes only `<OBJECT>` and `<EMBED>` tags. Other templates add code to detect earlier Flash Players or offer other features. To see what each template does and which formats you need to choose, select the template and click the Info button.

✦ **Dimensions:** Controls the size of the movie in the browser. The default option, Match Movie, matches the width and height of your Stage. You can also specify the size in pixels or by percent.

✦ **Playback: Paused at Start:** Pauses the movie until your viewer clicks a button (that you have coded to start the movie) or right-clicks and chooses Play. By default, this option is off, so that the movie plays automatically.

✦ **Playback: Loop:** Repeats the movie over and over. By default, this option is on.

✦ **Playback: Display Menu:** On by default, this option displays a shortcut menu if viewers right-click. The menu allows viewers to play, loop, and print the movie. However, not all viewers know that this shortcut menu exists.

✦ **Playback: Device Font:** Substitutes anti-aliased fonts (that look smoother) for fonts not available on the user's computer. Not checked by default.

✦ **Quality:** Sets the quality of playback. Choose one of the following:

   • **Low:** Uses no anti-aliasing (smoothing).

   • **Auto low:** Starts at low quality and switches to the highest quality that the user's computer (detected by the Macromedia Flash Player) can handle.

   • **Auto high:** Starts at high quality and switches to a lower quality if the user's computer (detected by the Macromedia Flash Player) cannot handle high quality.

   • **Medium:** Uses some anti-aliasing, but doesn't smooth bitmaps.

   • **High:** Uses anti-aliasing for everything except tweened bitmaps (the default).

   • **Best:** Uses anti-aliasing for text, unanimated bitmaps, and tweened bitmaps.

✦ **Window Mode:** Specifies how the movie's window relates to the rest of the page in Internet Explorer 4.0 and higher on the PC. Choose Window (a separate window), Opaque (an opaque background), and Transparent (a transparent background).

✦ **HTML Alignment:** Aligns the movie in the browser window. You can choose Default (centered), Left, Right, Top, or Bottom.

✦ **Scale:** Specifies how the movie is placed in its boundaries when you use the Pixels or Percent option of the Dimensions setting and the width and height are therefore different from the movie's original size. The choices are Default (Show All), No Border, Exact Fit, and No Scale.

✦ **Flash Alignment:** Specifies how the movie fits in the movie window (not the browser window). The Horizontal setting can be Left, Center, or Right. The Vertical setting can be Top, Center, or Bottom.

✦ **Show Warning Message:** Displays warning messages if there are problems during publishing.

Creating graphic files

You can create GIF, JPEG, and PNG graphic files from a frame of your Flash movie. Each type of graphics file has its own options. Macromedia Flash MX creates the image from your first frame unless you give another frame the #Static label.

To add a label to a frame, click the frame and open the Property inspector (Window⇨Properties). Expand the Property inspector by using the Collapse/Expand arrow at the bottom-right corner. Type the label name in the Frame text field. You can name a frame anything you want. Certain names, such as the #Static label, have specific meanings for how Macromedia Flash MX functions, as just described.

GIF files

GIF files have limited colors but allow transparency. Choose GIF on the Formats tab of the Publish Settings dialog box. Then click the GIF tab where you have the following settings:

✦ **Dimensions:** Select the Match Movie option to match the size of the Stage. Deselect and type the new dimensions to use a different size.

✦ **Playback:** Select either the Static (a single image) or Animated (an animated GIF of the entire movie) option. If you select Animated, you can choose to loop continuously or repeat a specified number of times.

✦ **Options:** You have several options to choose from:

• **Optimize Colors:** Select the Optimize Colors option to remove unused colors.

• **Interlace:** Select the Interlace option to load in increments of greater resolution (starting from fuzzy).

• **Smooth:** Select the Smooth option to anti-alias the artwork.

• **Dither Solids:** Select the Dither Solids option to approximate colors not available on the GIF color palette.

✦ **Transparent:** Allows you to set transparency (alpha) of the background.

✦ **Dither:** Defines the type of dithering. You can choose Ordered dithering, which provides good-quality dithering without much increase in file size, or you can choose Diffusion dithering, which provides top-quality dithering for the 216 Web colors but makes for a larger file size.

✦ **Palette Type:** Defines the GIF color palette. If you choose an adaptive palette, a unique color palette is created for the GIF. You can then choose the maximum number of colors. If you choose a custom palette, click the ellipsis button and choose a palette file. To save a palette of colors that you use in Macromedia Flash MX, choose Window⇨Color Swatches, click the Options Menu button, and choose Save Colors.

JPEG files

JPEG files allow for many colors but do not allow transparency. They decompress when downloaded, taking up more memory. Choose JPEG on the Formats tab of the Publish Settings dialog box. Then click the JPEG tab, where you have the following settings:

✦ **Dimensions:** You can match the size of the Stage or specify another size.

✦ **Quality:** Choose the quality. Higher quality means a better picture but a larger file size.

✦ **Progressive:** Displays the JPEG file in increments of greater resolution (starting from fuzzy) as it downloads in a browser.

PNG files

PNG files offer many colors and transparency, too. Choose PNG on the Formats tab of the Publish Settings dialog box. Then click the PNG tab, where you have the following settings:

✦ **Dimensions:** You can match the size of the Stage or specify another size.

✦ **Bit Depth:** Controls the number of colors the image can contain and the availability of transparency (alpha). More colors — and adding transparency — increase the file size.

✦ **Options:** You have several options to choose from:

  • **Optimize Colors:** Select the Optimize Colors option to remove unused colors.

  • **Interlace:** Select the Interlace option to load the PNG file in increments of greater resolution (starting from fuzzy).

  • **Smooth:** Select the Smooth option to anti-alias the artwork.

  • **Dither Solids:** Select the Dither Solids option to approximate colors not available on the GIF color palette. Same as for GIF images (explained previously).

✦ **Dither:** If you choose an 8-bit depth, use the same Dither settings as for GIF images. This option is not available for other bit depths.

✦ **Palette Type:** If you choose an 8-bit depth, use the same Dither settings as for GIF images.

✦ **Max Colors:** Same as for GIF images.

✦ **Palette:** Same as for GIF images.

✦ **Filter Options:** Determines the method of compression, the method of combining pixels in the image. Choose from the following options:

  • **None:** No compression.

  • **Sub:** Filters adjoining pixel bytes, going horizontally.

  • **Up:** Filters vertically.

  • **Average:** Uses both horizontal and vertical.

  • **Path:** Creates an algorithm using the three nearest pixels to predict the next pixel.

  • **Adaptive:** Provides the most accurate colors.

Creating QuickTime movies

QuickTime is a video format that plays on the QuickTime player. To use QuickTime movies, you need to have QuickTime 4, 5, or 6 installed.

The Macromedia Flash Player doesn't always keep up with QuickTime versions. A movie that you create in Macromedia Flash MX may not work with the latest version of QuickTime.

Choose QuickTime on the Formats tab of the Publish Settings dialog box. Click the QuickTime tab, where you have the following settings:

✦ **Dimensions:** You can match the size of the Stage or specify another size.

✦ **Alpha:** If you have combined a QuickTime movie with a Flash movie, this option sets the transparency of the Flash track within the QuickTime movie. A QuickTime movie can contain a separate layer with the Flash movie. The Auto option makes the Flash track transparent only if it is on top of other tracks. The Alpha-transparent option always makes the Flash track transparent. The Copy option makes the Flash track opaque, hiding all content behind it.

✦ **Layer:** Specifies how the Flash track is layered with the QuickTime content. Choose from Auto (Flash track on top if Flash content appears in front, otherwise on the bottom), Top (Flash track on top), and Bottom (Flash track at the bottom).

✦ **Streaming Sound:** Select the Use QuickTime Compression check box to export sound to a QuickTime soundtrack. Click Setting to specify how the sound is compressed.

✦ **Controller:** Creates a control panel to play the movie. Choose None if you have created your own controller or don't want viewers to have any control. The Standard option displays the QuickTime controller. The QuickTime VR option offers special panoramic and 3-D viewing features.

✦ **Playback:** Select the Loop check box to repeat the movie, the Paused At Start check box to let viewers use the Controller to start the movie, or the Play Every Frame check box to disable skipping frames and sound to maintain timing.

✦ **File:** The Flatten (Make Self-Contained) option combines the Flash movie with imported content into a QuickTime movie. If you don't select the Flatten check box, the QuickTime movie references the Macromedia Flash MX SWF file.

Creating self-playing movies

Self-playing movies are called *projectors*. A projector doesn't require a separate Macromedia Flash Player and is ideal when you are putting a Flash movie on a CD-ROM. To create a projector, choose Windows Projector or Macintosh Projector on the Formats tab of the Publish Settings dialog box. Then click the Publish button. The result is a file with an .exe extension (for PCs) or an .hqx extension (for Macs). The projector file is larger than an SWF file.

Exporting movies and images

Export a movie or image, instead of publishing it, when you need to use it in another application. For example, you can export a frame as a GIF file and insert it into a PowerPoint presentation. If you already have the HTML code and just want to update an SWF file, you can export instead of publish:

1. **Select the frame you want to export, if you are exporting an image.**

2. **Choose File➪Export Image or File➪Export Movie.**

3. **Type a name for the image or movie.**

4. **From the Save as Type drop-down list, select a file type.**

5. **Click Save.**

A dialog box may appear if the format you choose has settings that you can specify. These settings are the same as you have when you publish a file and are explained in the section, "Generating HTML and Graphics," earlier in this chapter. You can export the following file types:

+ Adobe Illustrator (`.ai`)
+ Encapsulated PostScript (`.eps`)
+ Drawing Exchange Format (`.dxf`)
+ Windows Bitmap (`.bmp`)
+ Metafile (`.emf`/`.wmf`)
+ FutureSplash Player (`.spl`)
+ Graphics Interchange File (`.gif`)
+ Joint Photographic Experts Group (`.jpeg`/`.jpg`)
+ QuickTime (`.mov`)
+ PICT Sequence (`.pct`)
+ Portable Network Graphic (`.png`)
+ Video for Windows (`.avi`)
+ Windows Audio (only) (`.wav`)

Chapter 8: Getting Interactive with ActionScript

*F*lash documents are fully programmable using the built-in language, ActionScript. Before we go any further, let's be clear: You don't need to be a programmer to use ActionScript. Nonprogrammers can do a lot with ActionScript. However, if you are a programmer, you certainly have an advantage. In this chapter, we explain how a nonprogrammer uses ActionScript.

Exploring the Role of ActionScript

ActionScript gives you the ability to control your movies. Here are some things you can do with ActionScript:

✦ Create a button to take your viewers to another Web page.

✦ Loop a movie clip through a small range of frames.

✦ Let your viewers drag objects on your Web site to new locations. (An example would be a site where viewers drag images of furniture onto a floor plan to see if it fits.)

✦ Create a preloader, a short animation that plays while a longer movie loads.

✦ Set the properties, such as location and size, of movie clip instances. (See Book V, Chapter 3 for an explanation of movie clips and instances.)

✦ Create an animated *mask* (a shape that hides everything on the Stage except what is just behind the shape).

✦ Play or stop animation.

In certain cases, you need to use ActionScript. For example, a button is useless without some ActionScript. You can create wonderful animation with no ActionScript at all, but adding ActionScript opens many possibilities for your Web site, and it's easy to use after you get some practice.

Because ActionScript tells your movie what action to take, the code is often called *actions.* Adding ActionScript is the same as adding actions.

ActionScript is very similar to JavaScript, a programming language used on Web pages.

Using Actions in Your Movies

Macromedia Flash MX offers a wide variety of actions that you can use, the basics of which we cover here. You can get more information several ways:

✦ Choose Help⇨ActionScript Dictionary.

✦ Take a tutorial by choosing Help⇨Using Flash⇨Tutorials⇨Introduction to ActionScript Tutorial.

✦ Pick up a copy of *Macromedia Flash MX ActionScript For Dummies* by Doug Sahlin, published by Wiley Publishing, Inc.

To add actions, you use the Actions panel (Window⇨Actions), which is shown in Figure 8-1 as it appears when you select a frame.

Figure 8-1: Using the Actions panel.

The Actions panel has the following features:

✦ **Title bar Expand/Collapse arrow:** Use this arrow to expand the Actions panel, as shown in Figure 8-1, and to collapse the Actions panel so that you see only the title bar.

✦ **Actions list:** Choose actions and other ActionScript components from this list.

✦ **Script pane:** Displays ActionScript.

✦ **Code box Expand/Collapse arrow:** Click this arrow to expand and collapse the ActionScript text field.

✦ **Parameters:** Choose the parameters from this section. Many actions require parameters.

✦ **Insert a target path:** Click this button to open a dialog box where you can choose from named instances in the drawing if you need to refer to another object.

✦ **View options menu:** Switch between Normal mode, in which you choose actions from the Actions list adding parameters from the Parameters section, and Expert mode, where you type your ActionScript from scratch.

Movie Control actions

The first grouping of actions in the Actions panel, which you can open by choosing Window➪Actions, contains the movie control actions. These actions control the Timeline of a movie, and you can choose from the following actions:

✦ goto: This action tells your movie to go to a different frame. You can specify the frame by number, label, with an expression that calculates the frame number, or by using the Next Frame or Previous Frame parameters. You can choose the Go To and Play option (the default), which continues to play at the new frame, or you can choose Go To and Stop option, which stops at the new frame.

✦ on: This action defines the mouse event that triggers the action. It is used for buttons and automatically added when you are adding ActionScript to a button.

✦ play: This action tells a movie to start playing.

✦ stop: This action stops a movie from playing.

✦ stopAllSounds: This action stops any sounds from playing.

Browser/Network actions

The Browser/Network category contains actions that connect your movie to the world outside it. You have the following choices:

✦ `fscommand`: This action is an advanced command that enables you to control other applications. You can use this command to execute JavaScript on the Web page.

✦ `getURL`: This action creates a hyperlink to another Web page or Web site.

✦ `loadMovie`: This action loads an SWF file or JPEG image.

✦ `unloadMovie`: This action unloads a loaded movie.

Movie Clip Control actions

Movie clip control actions control movie clips, of course. Here are the movie clip control actions:

✦ `duplicateMovieClip`: This action makes a copy of a movie clip.

✦ `onClipEvent`: This action specifies the event that triggers a movie clip action. It is inserted automatically when you add an action to a movie clip.

✦ `removeMovieClip`: This action deletes a movie clip, usually one created with the `duplicateMovieClip` action.

✦ `setProperty`: This action sets various size, visibility, and position properties of a movie clip.

✦ `startDrag`: This action makes a movie clip draggable on the browser screen. You can add this action to a button inside a movie clip, so that the movie clip responds to the mouse.

✦ `stopDrag`: This action stops a drag that was started with `startDrag`.

✦ `updateAfterEvent`: This action updates the display of a movie clip after a specified event, such as dragging.

Advanced actions

If you're ready to do a little programming, you can use many more options. For example, ActionScript contains a large number of built-in *methods*, which modify symbol instances. ActionScript programmers create *variables* that store values and use them later on in the script. You can create code that executes only if and when certain conditions exist. For more information, see Macromedia Flash MX's ActionScript dictionary, which you can access by choosing Help⇨ActionScript Dictionary.

To help you understand what you've written, you can (and should) add comments that explain what is going on. *Comments* are lines within the ActionScript code that are ignored when the code is processed. To add a comment, place two forward slashes (//) before the comment text.

When you're ready to write your own ActionScript code, click the View Mode button in the Actions panel and choose Expert Mode. In Expert Mode, you type your ActionScript from scratch in a larger text field.

✦ You can use operators such as + and *or* to calculate values

✦ You can use built-in functions to obtain information about objects before you change them.

✦ You can change certain properties of objects with setProperty, such as:

- Alpha (transparency)
- Height
- Rotation
- Visibility (yes or no)
- Height and width
- X and Y location
- X and Y scale

See "Creating Movie Clip Actions," later in this chapter, for an example of using the setProperty action. After you become familiar with ActionScript, all sorts of possibilities will come to your mind. The sky's the limit!

Creating Frame Actions

You can add actions to three places: frames, buttons, and movie clips. When you add actions to movie clips, you add it to the instance (copy) of the movie clip symbol that you insert on the Stage. You can also insert actions on the Timeline of movie clips.

Movie clips have their own Timeline and therefore their own set of frames.

If you add an action to a frame, the action is executed when the animation reaches that frame. For example, if Frame 20 has an action to go to Frame 1, when Frame 20 is loaded, the movie jumps to Frame 1. You can use frame actions to load a movie clip at a certain frame, stop a movie from running, or to automatically send the user to another URL or another frame.

To add an action to a frame, follow these steps:

1. **Create a new layer.**

   A common name for this new layer would be Actions. (You can put actions on existing layers, but we recommend a special layer for actions so that you can easily find them.)

2. **Click a keyframe on the new layer.**

   Because the action means a change occurs in that frame, you need a keyframe. If necessary, insert a keyframe by right-clicking and choosing Insert Keyframe from the menu that appears.

3. **If it is not open already, open the Actions panel by choosing Window⇨Actions.**

   (Refer to Figure 8-1.) If the panel is open but collapsed, click the Expand/Collapse arrow on the Actions panel's title bar. (Notice that the title bar of the Actions panel says Actions - Frame because you have clicked a keyframe.)

   See Book V, Chapter 1 for more on managing panels.

4. **To choose an action, from the left pane of the Actions panel click a category (such as Actions) and a subcategory (such as Movie Control), and then double-click the action you want (or drag it to the Script pane).**

   If the action needs parameters to specify how it works, text fields appear at the right side of the Actions panel.

5. **Type the required parameters in the parameter text fields or choose them from the drop-down lists.**

   Each action will require different parameters. The appropriate parameters for an action appear when the ActionScript is inserted and when you highlight a line of ActionScript containing that action. For information about the parameters required for any action, choose Help⇨ ActionScript Dictionary and locate the action from the alphabetical list.

Some parameters display an Expression check box at the right. Select the check box if you want the parameter to be considered as an expression, which means that the ActionScript can calculate its value. Macromedia Flash MX defines an *expression* as any combination of ActionScript symbols that represent a value. Deselect the check box if you want the parameter to be considered literally. (For example, the word "Hello" should be considered literally as a string of text.) Also, in many cases, you need to refer to another object, such as a movie clip. Click the Insert a Target Path button to get a list of appropriate objects.

To get the Actions panel out of the way, click the Collapse/Expand arrow on its title bar. Press Ctrl+Enter to test your movie and see the result of your ActionScript.

For a more detailed list of actions, see the section earlier in this chapter, "Using Actions in Your Movies."

For example, to add a `goto` action that sends the movie from the last keyframe to Frame 20 and plays from there, follow these steps:

1. **If Frame 20 is not a keyframe, right-click Frame 20 and choose Insert Keyframe.**

2. **Click the last keyframe.**

3. **Open the Actions panel (choose Window⇨Actions or click the Actions panel's open arrow).**

4. **On the left pane of the Actions panel, click Actions, and then click Movie Control.**

5. **Double-click goto.**

6. **On the right pane of the Actions panel, make sure that the Go To and Play option is chosen. (It's the default.)**

7. **Use the Scene drop-down list if you want to go to another scene.**

8. **Select from the Type drop-down list if you want to specify the frame other than by number.**

    For example, you can specify a frame by label.

9. **In the Frame text field, enter 20.**

10. **Test the movie (Ctrl+Enter) to check that it goes from the last keyframe to Frame 20.**

Creating Button Actions

Buttons are your key to interactivity on your Web site. Buttons are especially attuned to the actions of the mouse. You can add ActionScript to a button that executes an action when the user passes the mouse pointer over the button or clicks it. For information on creating buttons, see Book V, Chapter 3.

To add an action to a button, follow these steps:

1. **Create the button, or if you created the button earlier, drag an instance from the Library onto the Stage.**

2. **Select the button and open the Actions panel, if it is not already open, by choosing Window⇨Actions.**

If the panel is open but collapsed, click the Expand/Collapse arrow on the Actions panel's title bar. (Notice that the title bar of the Actions panel says Actions - Button because you have selected a button.)

3. **From the left pane of the Actions panel, choose a category (such as Actions) and subcategory (such as Browser/Network) in the left pane, and then double-click an action (such as** getURL**).**

The getURL action sends the user to the URL that you specify.

4. **To change the options that relate to the mouse, click the default** on (release) **statement in the Script pane, as shown in Figure 8-2. Select the check boxes that you want to use to execute the action.**

When you add an action to a button, the code automatically includes an option that determines what type of mouse action activates the ActionScript. Because the mouse option determines when the action takes place (such as when the mouse button is released), it is called an *event.* The available events are listed immediately after these steps.

Figure 8-2:
Adding an
action to a
button.

5. **If the action requires parameters, click the line of code that contains the action itself and enter the necessary information in the parameter text fields.**

For more information about the parameters required by each action, consult the ActionScript dictionary. Choose Help⇨ActionScript Dictionary.

You can choose from the following button events:

+ **Press:** The action is executed when the viewer clicks the mouse button.

+ **Release:** The action is executed when the viewer releases the mouse button. This is the most commonly used button event, because the release of the mouse button means that the viewer has completed the click.

+ **Release Outside:** The action is executed when the viewer releases the mouse button outside the hit area.

+ **Key Press:** The action is executed when the viewer presses the specified key. Use this in addition to a mouse event to enable viewers to use the keyboard instead of the mouse. A commonly used key is the Enter key.

+ **Roll Over:** The action is executed when the viewer passes the mouse cursor over the button's hit area, but doesn't click.

+ **Roll Out:** The action is executed when the viewer leaves the hit area.

+ **Drag Over:** The viewer passes the mouse cursor over the button's hit area while holding down the mouse button.

+ **Drag Out:** The viewer leaves the hit area while holding down the mouse button.

As an example, to add a `getURL` action to a button that functions when the button is clicked, follow these steps:

1. **Create the button.**

   For instructions, see Book V, Chapter 3.

2. **From the Library (Window⇨Library), drag an instance of the button onto the Stage.**

   The button should have a border around it, indicating that it is selected.

3. **Open the Actions panel (choose Window⇨Actions or click the Actions panel's open arrow).**

   The Actions panel should say Button on its title bar. If it doesn't, click the button again.

4. **From the left pane of the Actions panel, click Actions and then click Browser/Network. Double-click `getURL`.**

   Your code should look like this:

```
on (release) {
    getURL("");
}
```

5. **With the second line of code highlighted, enter the URL in the URL Parameter text field.**

   If the URL is within a Web site, it can be local, meaning that you don't need `http://`. If you want the button to send viewers to another site, you need the full URL, including the `http://`.

6. **From the Window drop-down list in the Parameters section, select an option.**

   These are the same options used with the `<A>` tag in HTML:

   - `_self`: Opens the URL in the same window.
   - `_blank`: Opens the URL in a new window.
   - `_parent`: When frames are used and one file is nested inside another, opens the URL where the inner file was.
   - `_top`: When frames are used, loads the URL in the topmost frame, and the new page fills the entire window.

7. **From the Variables drop-down list, select an option that specifies what Flash does with any variables that you have created using ActionScript.**

   These options allow you to send data to a CGI script, for example, and are equivalent to the Method option of the Form tag in HTML. Choose one of the following options:

   - **Don't send:** This option doesn't send any data.
   - **Send using Get:** This option sends data using the `get` method, which is used for small amounts of data.
   - **Send using Post:** This option sends data using the `post` method, which is used for larger amounts of data.

8. **Choose Control⇨Test Movie and click the button to check if the `getURL` action works.**

   If you used a local URL, the button won't work unless the movie is published and uploaded to the domain for that URL.

Creating Movie Clip Actions

You add an action to a movie clip as an object on the Stage, in the same way you add an action to a button. Actions in movie clips work on the movie clip's Timeline, not on the main movie's Timeline. To add actions to a movie clip, follow these steps:

1. **Create the movie clip, or if you created the movie clip earlier, drag an instance of the clip from the Library onto the Stage.**

See Figure 8-3 for an example of a movie clip action. In this case, whenever the viewer moves the mouse (the clip event), the height of the ball automatically changes to 450 pixels.

2. **Select the movie clip and open the Actions panel, if it is not already open, by choosing Window⇨Actions.**

If the panel is open but collapsed, click the Expand/Collapse arrow on the Actions panel's title bar. (Notice that the title bar of the Actions panel says Actions - Movie Clip because you have selected a movie clip.)

3. **Click a category (such as Actions) and subcategory (such as Movie Clip Control) in the left pane, and then double-click an action (such as** setProperty**).**

The setProperty action sets properties such as size, visibility, and location. See the "Advanced actions" section, earlier in this chapter.

4. **To change the options that relate to the mouse, click the default** OnClipEvent **(Load) statement in the Script pane.**

Figure 8-3:
The ball is a movie clip with an action.

5. **Check the event that you want to use to trigger the action.**

The events are listed after these steps.

6. **If the action requires parameters, click the line of code that contains the action itself and enter the necessary information in the parameter text fields.**

To find out about the parameters for each action, choose Help➪ ActionScript Dictionary and choose the action from the alphabetical list.

You can choose from the following movie clip events:

✦ **Load:** The action is executed when the movie clip loads into memory.

✦ **EnterFrame:** The action is executed when the movie clip enters a frame.

✦ **Unload:** The action is executed in the first frame after the movie clip is removed from the Timeline (which usually happens as a result of some ActionScript code).

✦ **Mouse down:** The action is executed when the viewer clicks the mouse button.

✦ **Mouse up:** The action is executed when the viewer releases the mouse button.

✦ **Key down:** The action is executed when any key is pressed.

✦ **Key up:** The action is executed when any key is released.

✦ **Data:** The action is executed when data is received from a `loadVars` or `loadMovie` action.

As an example, to add an action to a movie clip that suddenly increases its size (to humorous effect) when the user moves the mouse, follow these steps:

1. **Create the movie clip.**

For instructions, see Book V, Chapter 3.

2. **From the Library (Window➪Library), drag an instance of the movie clip onto the Stage.**

The movie clip should have a border around it, indicating that it is selected.

3. **Open the Actions panel (choose Window➪Actions or click the Actions panel's open arrow).**

The Actions panel should say Movie Clip on its title bar. If it doesn't, click the movie clip again.

4. From the left pane of the Actions panel, click Actions and then click Movie Clip Control. Double-click `setProperty`.

Your code should look like this:

```
onClipEvent (load) {
    setProperty("", <not set yet>, "");
}
```

5. Select the first line of code in the Script pane and choose `mouseMove` from the list of events.

The ActionScript will be executed when the user moves the mouse.

6. Select the second line of code in the Script pane.

7. From the Property drop-down list in the Parameters area of the Actions panel, select `_height (Height)`.

The ActionScript will change the height (vertical distance) of the movie clip.

8. Click in the Target text field in the Parameters area, then click the Insert a Target Path button.

The Insert Target Path dialog box opens.

9. Select the movie clip from the list that appears.

You may see only "This," which means the selected movie clip. You can also give the movie clip an instance name by selecting it and entering a name in the Instance Name text field of the Property inspector. Then you can type the movie clip's instance name in the Target text field of the Actions panel, instead of using the Insert Target Path dialog box.

10. Select the Expression check box next to the Target text field.

You want the name of the movie clip to represent the actual movie clip. The ActionScript won't work unless the Expression check box is selected.

11. In the Value text field in the Parameter area of the Actions panel, type a value for the height of the movie clip in pixels (by default) or the current unit of measurement.

You can change the unit of measurement by choosing Modify⇨Document.

12. Choose Control⇨Test Movie and move the mouse to check if the `setProperty` action works.

Chapter 9: Creating Interfaces with Components and Forms

In This Chapter

✔ **Adding components**

✔ **Creating forms with Macromedia Flash MX**

Macromedia Flash MX is not limited to creating animation. You can use Macromedia Flash MX to develop an entire interface, including buttons, menus, forms, scrollbars, and more. Macromedia Flash MX includes a set of interface elements called components that you can use to efficiently add interfaces and interactivity to your Web site. In this chapter, we investigate how you can use components and create forms with Macromedia Flash MX.

Macromedia Flash MX can create very innovative interfaces. As long as you keep your Macromedia Flash MX interfaces user-friendly and easy to understand, your viewers will appreciate the new look and feel. Scrollbars created with Macromedia Flash MX are a lot cooler than the ones created in most professional programs because you can customize how they look and function. Creating scrollbars and other interface elements for your Web page with Macromedia Flash MX may actually be easier than with other, more complex programming environments, although some of these techniques require a bit of ActionScript programming to make them fully functional.

Components are actually movie clip symbols that contain a set of defined parameters and properties. (For an explanation of movie clip symbols, see Book V, Chapter 3.) You can specify the values of these parameters and properties when you create your Flash document. Using these components ensures that your interface items work together and in a similar manner. Because of the programming that has been done in advance to create the parameters and properties, you need to do less programming for each Flash document you create.

You can customize the appearance of components to match the rest of your Web site's style. If you know some ActionScript, you can even create your own components, and you can find components that Flash developers have created on Flash resource Web sites.

Adding Components

Components can be as simple as a check box or as complex as an entire graphical user interface. Macromedia Flash MX comes with the following components:

✦ **Radio buttons:** Radio buttons are small round buttons. Users can select one choice from several options.

✦ **Check boxes:** Users can select or deselect each check box.

✦ **Push buttons:** Clicking a button makes something happen, like a button symbol in Macromedia Flash MX. (See Book V, Chapter 3 for more information on working with buttons.)

✦ **Combo boxes:** Combo boxes provide drop-down menu lists.

✦ **List boxes:** List boxes enable you to offer users a scrolling list of choices.

✦ **Scroll panes:** Scroll panes enable you to create scrollable windows for movie clips.

✦ **Text scrollbars:** These are scrollbars that you can add to a text field, letting the user scroll through the text.

The procedure for working with a component is similar for all the components. However, individual items vary. The general procedure is as follows:

1. **Open the Components panel by choosing Window⇨Components.**

The Components panel is shown in Figure 9-1.

Figure 9-1:
The
Components
panel
contains
interactive
components.

2. **Drag one of the components onto the Stage.**

3. **With the component still selected, open the Property inspector, if it isn't open already, by choosing Window⇨Properties.**

If the Property inspector is open but collapsed, click the Expand/Collapse arrow on its title bar.

4. **Click the Parameters tab.**

The Property inspector with the Parameters tab displayed is shown in Figure 9-2.

Figure 9-2:
After you place a component on the Stage, you set its parameters in the Property inspector. Here you see the Property inspector when a check box is selected.

5. **In the Instance Name text field of the Property inspector, type an instance name.**

By naming each instance of the component, you can refer to it in your ActionScript.

6. **Set the parameters for the component in the Property inspector by clicking each parameter and entering the value to its right.**

Repeat this procedure with all the components. The individual requirements of the components are listed in the next several sections.

Use the Align panel, which is accessed by choosing Window➪Align, to line up and evenly distribute a series of components, such as radio buttons or check boxes.

You can resize components using the Free Transform tool, but they are not all infinitely flexible. For example, you can change the width of a check box, but not its height.

Check boxes

The CheckBox component allows users to select one or more choices from a list. Each item on the list has a small box next to it that has a check inside when the user clicks on box. The CheckBox component has the following parameters:

✦ **Label:** The Label parameter determines the text that is attached to the component.

✦ **Initial Value:** The Initial Value parameter determines if a specific component is initially selected. For example, if you set the initial value of a check box to `true`, the viewer first sees the check box with a check inside it.

✦ **Label Placement:** The Label Placement parameter places the text relative to the rest of the component. You can choose Left or Right.

✦ **Change Handler:** The Change Handler parameter enables you to specify the name of a function (written in ActionScript) that is executed when the check box is selected or deselected.

Radio buttons

Radio buttons are like check boxes, except that users can only select one at a time in any group of radio buttons. When a radio button is selected, it has a dot inside its circle. The RadioButton component has the following parameters:

✦ **Label:** The Label parameter determines the text that is attached to the component.

✦ **Initial State:** The Initial State parameter determines if a radio button is initially selected.

✦ **Group Name:** Say that you want to poll your users to see if they like to swim and if they like to run. You want a Yes or a No for each. To create such independent groups of radio buttons, enter a Group Name parameter. Users can select one radio button in each group. For example, if you have four radio buttons, you can put two into a group named Swim and two into a group named Run. You can then label buttons Yes and No in each group and ask users "Do you like to swim?" for the buttons in the Swim group and "Do you like to run?" for the buttons in the Run group. Users can then answer Yes or No to each question.

✦ **Data:** Use the Data parameter to store data related to that button. For example, if you want to know if a user selected the radio button named Yes, you can put Yes in the Data field and use ActionScript to execute an action (perhaps go to a specific Web page) if a user selected the Yes radio button.

✦ **Label Placement:** The Label Placement parameter places the text relative to the rest of the component.

✦ **Change Handler:** The Change Handler parameter enables you to specify the name of a function (written in ActionScript) that is executed when the radio button is selected or deselected.

Push buttons

Push buttons are very similar to the buttons you create in Macromedia Flash MX. The main reason to use a push button component would be to create a consistent look with other components. However, the included parameters may make them quicker to use and require less code. They have a Label parameter that places text on the button and a click handler that uses a function you write to specify what happens when a user clicks the button.

Combo boxes

A combo box is a menu list of items with a scroll bar to its right. Users can scroll through the list of items and choose one, as shown in Figure 9-3.

Figure 9-3:
A combo
box is a
scrollable
menu.

Where do you live?

North America
South America
Europe
Africa
Asia
Australia

Like radio buttons, combo boxes have Change Handler and Data parameters. You add the labels for the menu items in the Values dialog box as follows:

1. **With the combo box selected, open the Property inspector, if it isn't open already, by choosing Window⊅Properties or click the Expand/Collapse arrow on the Property inspector's title bar.**

2. **Click the Labels row in the Parameter list, and then click the right side of the row to open the Labels dialog box.**

   The Values dialog box is shown in Figure 9-4.

3. **To add a new menu item, click the plus (+) sign and type the label.**

   You can click any label to edit it.

4. **When you're done, click OK.**

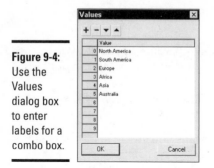

Figure 9-4:
Use the
Values
dialog box
to enter
labels for a
combo box.

The Editable parameter in the Parameter list specifies if the combo box is editable. If this parameter is set to `true`, users can enter text to search for a matching item. If it is set to `false`, users can only select an item.

The Row Count parameter in the Parameter list determines how many items must be in the combo box before the scroll bar is displayed. The default is eight items.

List boxes

A list box is like a combo box, except that (unlike a combo box) it can't be edited by the user, and you can allow users to select multiple items. To allow this, set the Select Multiple parameter to `true`. You add the labels as described in the section, "Combo boxes."

Scroll panes

Scroll panes are rather unusual. They allow you to put movie clips (and only movie clips) inside a scrollable pane. The advantage is to display large movies or images without taking up a lot of space, as shown in Figure 9-5. No programming is necessary. The movie clip must be in the Library, but it doesn't need to be on the Stage.

Figure 9-5:
A scroll
pane allows
you to
display a
movie clip
in a very
small space.

You can load JPG images into a scroll pane using ActionScript.

You also need to give the movie clip the Export for ActionScript option in the Linkage Properties dialog box:

1. **Open the Library by choosing Window⇨Library and then right-click the movie clip.**

2. **Choose Linkage.**

   The Linkage Properties dialog box opens.

3. **In the Identifier text field, enter a linkage name for the movie clip.**

   Usually, the linkage name is the name of the movie clip.

4. **Click the Export for ActionScript option. The Export in First Frame option should also be selected.**

5. **Click OK.**

Select the scroll pane and display the Property inspector. The ScrollPane component has the following parameters:

✦ **Scroll Content:** Enter the linkage name of the movie clip.

✦ **Horizontal Scroll:** You can set the horizontal scroll bar to `auto` (the default — a scroll bar displays only if necessary), `true` (always), or `false` (no scroll bars).

✦ **Vertical Scroll:** You can set the vertical scroll bar to `auto` (the default — a scroll bar displays only if necessary), `true` (always), or `false` (no scroll bars).

✦ **Drag Content:** Set this parameter to `true` to allow users to drag the movie clip (pan it) to see the hidden portion without using the scroll bars. (The default is `false`.)

Text scroll bars

The ScrollBar component lets you place text inside a scrolled area. If the text is too long, users can scroll to see the rest of the text. Text scroll bars are somewhat complex to use because you need to use input or dynamic text.

Input text is text that users type in. *Dynamic text* is text that you supply or that is streamed from the Web into your movie, and the text is dynamically displayed in your movie.

To create a text field with a scroll bar, follow these steps:

1. **With the Text tool, draw a text field on the Stage.**
2. **Display the Property inspector, if it isn't open already, by choosing Window⇨Properties.**
3. **Select Dynamic Text or Input Text from the Text Type drop-down list.**
4. **Enter an instance name in the Instance Name text field.**
5. **With Snap to Objects enabled (choose View⇨Snap to Objects), drag the scroll bar component from the Components panel or the Library close to the side of the text field.**

   The scroll bar should automatically snap to the text field and resize itself.

The scroll bar has two parameters:

✦ **Horizontal:** If this parameter is set to `true`, the scroll bar is horizontal. If it's set to `false`, the scroll bar is vertical.

✦ **Target Text Field:** This should be the same as the instance name of the text field, so that the scroll bar knows to which text field it belongs.

Setting component properties

You can set the color and text properties of a component using ActionScript. You can also globally set properties of all the components in your movie. Finally, you can create *skins,* graphic elements that affect how components look. These methods are beyond the scope of this book. For more information, see Flash Help.

Creating Forms with Macromedia Flash MX

You can create forms that users can complete online. You can capture the information that users input into the forms and either use it elsewhere on your site or send it to a server and place it in a database. Forms are a great way to collect data about your users.

Collecting data within a Flash movie

You can collect data within a Flash movie to personalize the site. For example, if a user enters a name (Joe) and favorite book genre (science fiction), you can send the user to a page (or Flash frame) that incorporates the user's input, such as a page with the message shown in Figure 9-6.

Figure 9-6:
This Flash
form stores
the user's
name and
interest and
responds
based on
the results.

Creating this type of form requires some ActionScript. In general, advanced ActionScript is not covered in this book, but here we give you the ActionScript needed to accomplish this form.

To create this form, start a new movie and follow these steps:

1. **Use the Text tool to create the labels (such as First Name and Favorite Book Genre) on a separate layer, using the default static text.**

   You set the type of text in the Text Type drop-down list of the Property inspector.

2. **Next to each text field you just created, create a new text field.**

3. **Select Input Text from the Text Type drop-down list in the Property inspector.**

4. **Click the Show Border Around Text button in the Property inspector.**

   You want a border so that users know where to enter their text.

5. **For each text field, choose an instance name and enter it in the Instance Name text field of the Property inspector.**

   We use the instance names `firstname` and `favorite`; these names are used later in the ActionScript.

6. **Use the Components panel to drag a push button onto the Stage.**

7. **In the Property inspector, type a label for the button, such as** Done, **and change the Click Handler to Done.**

The Click Handler, Done, is used in the ActionScript as a function to tell Macromedia Flash MX what to do when the button is clicked. Your screen should be similar to the top image in Figure 9-6.

8. **Insert a new keyframe in Frame 2 of all the layers.**

9. **On the text layer of Frame 2, rearrange the text fields, as in the bottom image of Figure 9-6.**

These text fields should have the same instance names as they did in Frame 1.

10. **Select each of the text fields with instance names and change their text type to Dynamic from the Text Type drop-down list of the Property inspector.**

Dynamic text comes from another location and is dynamically placed into the SWF file when viewed. In this case, viewers input text in Frame 1 and the text they input is inserted into the dynamic text fields in Frame 2.

11. **Open the Actions panel.**

12. **Click the View Mode button and choose Expert mode.**

13. **Add a new layer and name it Actions.**

14. **Click Frame 1 of the Actions layer and type the following in the ActionScript Script pane:**

```
stop();
this.firstname.text = "";
this.favorite.text = "";
function done() {
    _global.myName = this.firstname.text;
    _global.myFave = this.favorite.text;
    gotoAndStop(2);

};
```

This ActionScript stops the animation on Frame 1 so that nothing happens until the viewer clicks Done. The next two lines reference the text fields on the current Timeline (using "this") to empty the two text fields in case they already contain text. The function, Done, creates two variables, myName and myFave and sets them equal to the text in the firstname and favorite input text fields. These variables are global so you can use them again in Frame 2. Finally, the ActionScript moves the playhead to Frame 2 and stops there.

15. **Click Frame 2 of the Actions layer and type the following in the ActionScript Script pane:**

```
stop();
this.firstname.text = myName;
this.favorite.text = myFave;
```

This code stops the animation and sets the two dynamic text fields in Frame 2 to the global variables you created in Frame 1. As a result, the text that viewers input in Frame 1 appears here in Frame 2.

16. **Choose Control⇨Test Movie to see how the form works.**

17. **Fill in the form and click the Done button.**

As you can see, although this form requires some ActionScript, it doesn't require very much. You can modify this ActionScript for your own needs.

The form created in this example is very simple. You can add many other features, such as a Thank You page and form validation.

Posting form data

In the example in Figure 9-6, you may have wondered how you would know to send the user the list of books. In order to accomplish this task, you need to post the data from the form to a Web server. You also post data when you want to collect visitors' names, e-mail addresses, and so on, in order to create a database of visitors.

Posting form data is complex because you need a script (often a CGI script, but there are several kinds) on the server to manage the data. The script sets the requirement for the format of the data you send.

As with HTML forms, you specify a method of sending the information (get or post are the only two options) and a URL. You can use the loadVariables function to load variables to a CGI script. Here is an example:

```
loadVariables("http://www.website.com/cgi-bin/scriptname.cgi", "", "POST")
```

For more information, choose Help⇨ActionScript Dictionary and look up the loadVariables or loadVars functions.

Chapter 10: Integrating Macromedia Flash MX with Other Macromedia Products

In This Chapter

✔ Integrating Macromedia Flash MX with Fireworks MX

✔ Integrating Macromedia Flash MX with Dreamweaver MX

✔ Integrating Macromedia Flash MX with FreeHand 10

✔ Integrating Macromedia Flash MX with ColdFusion MX

All the Macromedia Studio MX products covered in this book are extremely useful for creating Web sites. If you are responsible for an entire site — content, art, interface, and server-side programming — you can bring the capabilities of the entire Macromedia Studio MX suite to bear on your site.

The integrated interface means that the programs look and work similarly. For example, the Property inspector basically serves the same purpose in Fireworks MX, Dreamweaver MX, and Macromedia Flash MX. FreeHand 10 also has similar features, but breaks the Property inspector into several inspectors. Menus and panels have a similar look and feel so you can easily find the command you're looking for.

In addition to similar interfaces, the programs also share common tool icons. When you look for the Pen tool in Macromedia Flash MX, it looks the same as the Pen tool in FreeHand 10 and Fireworks MX. Nope, sorry, you won't find a Pen tool in Dreamweaver MX, it's only got WYSIWYG (What You See Is What You Get) tools for inserting graphic objects.

Integrating Macromedia Flash MX with Fireworks MX

Macromedia Fireworks MX is a full-featured Web graphics program. Its native format is PNG, which is a bitmap file format. Fireworks MX can also work with vector images. You can export Fireworks MX vector and bitmap images to Macromedia Flash MX's SWF movie format and then import them into Macromedia Flash MX.

You can also use the quick export feature to copy an object from Fireworks MX to the system Clipboard, and then paste it into Macromedia Flash MX, or you can export selected objects as SWF files. (SWF is an acronym for Small Web File.) SWF files are generically referred to as Flash movies. You activate the Quick Export feature by clicking the icon in the upper-right corner of the Fireworks MX Document window.

Importing a Fireworks MX PNG into Macromedia Flash MX

You can import into Macromedia Flash MX both PNG files and the SWF files created in Fireworks MX by choosing File⇨Import. When you import a Fireworks MX PNG file into a Flash document, you have a tremendous amount of latitude. You can choose to import the file as a movie clip and retain layers, maintain paths as editable objects, and maintain text as editable. Additionally, you can decide to flatten the PNG file into a single bitmap.

If you import a graphic from Fireworks MX, you can start the editing process from within Macromedia Flash MX. Select the graphic and click Edit in the Property inspector (Window⇨Properties). Macromedia Flash MX opens Fireworks MX, where you can edit the image. In fact, there's even this spiffy Editing from Flash icon, in case you go on an extended break and when you return, you forget what you were doing.

If you import the PNG file into Macromedia Flash MX and flatten it to a single bitmap, when you edit the file from within Macromedia Flash MX, Fireworks MX opens the original PNG file, and you can then edit every object to your heart's content. When you're done editing, click the Done button and Fireworks MX updates the image in Macromedia Flash MX. It's known as *roundtrip editing*. Now is that cool or what? Figure 10-1 shows a PNG file being edited in Fireworks MX.

Some software is horribly invasive. If you've installed other software after you installed the Macromedia Studio MX suite, this software may declare itself as the default editor for PNG files. If this happens, you may have to use your operating system to change the associated program for PNG files to Fireworks MX, or reinstall the Macromedia Studio MX suite. If this is not feasible, you'll have to choose the Edit With option in Macromedia Flash MX and navigate to the `Fireworks.exe` file.

Figure 10-1:
Roundtrip
editing:
From
Macromedia
Flash MX to
Fireworks
MX and
back to
Macromedia
Flash MX.

As with other Macromedia products, the interface for Fireworks MX is very similar to the one you know in Macromedia Flash MX. So when you are roundtrip editing, it's not like you have to learn a new toolset or anything. You have a similar toolbox, similar panels, and the familiar Property inspector, for example. The similar interface makes it easy to switch between programs without getting confused.

Cutting and pasting between Macromedia Flash MX and Fireworks MX

Another option is to cut and paste between Macromedia Flash MX and Fireworks MX. If you're creating a graphic symbol in Macromedia Flash MX and it's just not working out, you can use the graphic tools in Fireworks MX to smooth out the lumps in your graphic by following these steps:

1. **Choose Edit⇨Cut.**

   Macromedia Flash MX cuts the object to your system Clipboard.

2. **Launch Fireworks MX.**

3. Choose File➪New.

Fireworks MX is so smart, it knows how big the object you cut from Macromedia Flash MX is, and the document is just the right size.

4. Choose Edit➪Paste.

Fireworks MX pastes the object into the new document.

5. Edit the object in Fireworks MX.

You can use the Fireworks MX editing tools to modify the object you cut from Macromedia Flash MX, add objects, and even add layers. However, make sure you've got everything where you want it, because when you select everything in Fireworks MX and then cut it and paste it back into Macromedia Flash MX, the objects you added are flattened and cannot be edited. The better solution is to follow Step 6 onward.

6. After you've finished editing in Fireworks MX, choose File➪Save.

The Save dialog box opens.

7. Enter a name for the file and navigate to the folder where you want to save the file.

Fireworks MX saves the file in its native PNG format.

8. Exit Fireworks MX.

9. In Macromedia Flash MX, choose File➪Import.

The Import dialog box appears.

10. Select the file you just saved in Fireworks MX and click the Open button.

The Fireworks PNG Import Settings dialog box opens.

11. Choose the settings that best suit the Flash document you're working on.

If you want the ability to edit individual objects from the Fireworks MX file in Macromedia Flash MX, make sure you don't flatten the image. Import the file as a movie clip and retain layers. If you were editing a symbol when you cut the object from Macromedia Flash MX, select the Import into New Layer in Current Scene option, and Macromedia Flash MX imports the PNG file into the symbol you're editing and retains each object from the Fireworks MX PNG file as individual objects. You can now move individual objects as needed, or create additional layers for the objects.

Integrating Macromedia Flash MX with Dreamweaver MX

The Dreamweaver MX interface is also similar to the Macromedia Flash MX interface, with panels and a Property inspector. You can use Dreamweaver MX to create HTML code that holds your SWF files. It's easy to insert SWF files into Dreamweaver MX Web pages — just click the Flash icon from the toolbar in the Common or Media tab. You can also use Dreamweaver MX to generate Flash buttons for use in HTML and CFML pages.

You can open, create, edit, and optimize Macromedia Flash MX files directly from Dreamweaver MX. Finally, Dreamweaver MX now supports ActionScript editing. You can create server-side ActionScript in Dreamweaver MX and save a document as a Macromedia Flash MX AS (ActionScript), ASR (ActionScript Remote), or ASC (ActionScript Communication) file.

When you have a Macromedia Flash MX file in a Dreamweaver MX document and it's not up to snuff, you don't have to exit Dreamweaver MX and reopen the original FLA file, edit it, and then publish the file again. That would be way too much work. In fact, we're exhausted from just typing the last few sentences. Fortunately, there's a much simpler way. When you're working on a Dreamweaver MX HTML file that has an SWF movie embedded within it, you can edit the Macromedia Flash MX file by following these steps:

1. **Select the Macromedia Flash MX file in the Dreamweaver MX HTML document.**

It's the gray rectangle with an F emblazed on it. Note that you must be working in Design or Code and Design view to do this.

2. **Open the Property inspector.**

For more information on the Dreamweaver MX Property inspector, see Book II, Chapter 1.

3. **Click the Edit button.**

Dreamweaver MX launches Macromedia Flash MX, and the Locate Macromedia Flash Document File dialog box appears.

4. **Navigate to the folder where the native FLA file that you published the SWF movie from is stored.**

5. **Select the appropriate file and then click the Open button.**

   The native FLA file that you published the Flash movie as is opens in Macromedia Flash MX, and lo and behold, an icon that says Editing from Dreamweaver appears.

6. **Edit the file in Macromedia Flash MX as needed.**

7. **After editing the file, click the Done button.**

   This publishes the movie again and updates the file in Dreamweaver MX. Before exiting, you may want to choose Control⇨Test Movie to make sure all is in order.

That's roundtrip editing from Dreamweaver MX to Macromedia Flash MX. Too cool.

Integrating Macromedia Flash MX with FreeHand 10

Although at one time FreeHand 10 was used mostly to create graphics for printed media, such as magazines, it now has many features that are very valuable to Web site use. FreeHand 10 can create complex vector graphics beyond anything you can create with Macromedia Flash MX. You can easily import FreeHand 10 graphics into Macromedia Flash MX by choosing File⇨ Import.

When you import FreeHand 10 graphics, you have a great deal of control over the how the graphics appear in Macromedia Flash MX. You can do the following:

✦ Assign pages of FreeHand 10 documents to Macromedia Flash MX scenes or keyframes.

✦ Assign FreeHand 10 layers to Macromedia Flash MX layers or keyframes, or choose to import the entire FreeHand 10 graphic as one layer (flattened).

✦ Convert lens fills (for example, Magnify and Transparency) to Macromedia Flash MX equivalents.

✦ Import symbols from the FreeHand 10 Library directly into your Macromedia Flash MX Library.

You can use the Flash Navigation panel in FreeHand 10 to test SWF files before you export them to Macromedia Flash MX. FreeHand 10 has an anti-alias display mode that uses Macromedia Flash MX's anti-alias feature to show you how your FreeHand 10 artwork will look in Macromedia Flash MX.

You can apply hyperlinks and Flash actions to graphics and text from within FreeHand 10.

FreeHand 10's animation feature means that you can create animations in FreeHand 10 and use them in Macromedia Flash MX. This enables you to use the FreeHand 10 vector drawing tools to create a character, and bring it to life in FreeHand 10, and then export it as a Flash 4 or Flash 5 SWF file. After all, vector illustrations are FreeHand's claim to fame.

You can export FreeHand 10 documents as SWF files. Furthermore, you can view FreeHand 10 documents as temporary SWF files, a process similar to choosing Control⇨Test Movie in Macromedia Flash MX. FreeHand 10 opens a Macromedia Flash Player window, and you can see how your FreeHand 10 document will look as an SWF file.

When you create files in FreeHand 10 with the intention of using them in Flash documents, make sure you use the RGB color model. (See Book IV, Chapter 6 for more about color management in FreeHand 10.) FreeHand 10 files created with the CMYK color model are converted to RGB when you import them into Macromedia Flash MX. Macromedia Flash MX generally does a pretty good job of making the transformation, but if you're a stickler for detail and you want what you see in FreeHand 10 to be what you get in Macromedia Flash MX, stick with the RGB color model when choosing colors for fills and strokes.

In spite of the fact that FreeHand 10 and Macromedia Flash MX are distant cousins, if you try to copy an object from Macromedia Flash MX with the hope of pasting it into FreeHand 10 for some hands-on editing, you can paste the file just fine, but all you can edit is the stroke of the object you created in Macromedia Flash MX. The fill acts just like a bitmap and refuses to yield to the FreeHand 10 editing tools.

Integrating Macromedia Flash MX with ColdFusion MX

When you need to coordinate Flash applications with server-side ActionScript code, you use ColdFusion MX. ColdFusion MX supports server-side ActionScript that you can use to create your Macromedia Flash Remoting MX applications, making it easier to program both sides of the equation (server-side and client-side) in one programming language. *Server-side ActionScript* is a document stored in a directory at the Web server as opposed to ActionScript in the Flash movie.

Another plus when you use the Macromedia Studio MX suite is the fact that you can use ColdFusion MX as a testing server. When you start creating server-side ActionScript in Dreamweaver MX that dovetails with an application you're creating in Macromedia Flash MX, you don't have to upload everything to the Web server to test your application. You can use ColdFusion MX as a local server and test the Flash application (which, as you may remember, is embedded in an HTML file, the pearl in Dreamweaver MX's oyster), by testing the HTML document in Dreamweaver MX to make sure all is well.

You can also connect databases with Flash movies to provide personalized or continually updated information to viewers and add special features, such as text search and dynamic charting, to Flash movies.

Integrating Macromedia Flash MX with other Macromedia products

Macromedia also has two other Flash-related products that you should know about — Macromedia Flash Communication Server MX and Macromedia Flash Remoting MX. These products are for advanced users who want to build communications applications in Macromedia Flash MX and integrate Macromedia Flash MX with applications built in ColdFusion MX or other server-side systems.

Macromedia Flash Communication Server MX

Macromedia Flash Communication Server MX is a new Macromedia program that enables programmers to develop communications applications for Web sites. Some of the possibilities include the following:

- Video teleconferencing
- Video broadcasting for presentations
- Audio messaging
- Text messaging
- Live chat rooms
- Polling
- White boards
- Message boards (discussion groups)

To write the programming code, you can use Dreamweaver MX to create server-side ActionScript. A number of prebuilt components are available as downloads from Macromedia's Web site to make it easy to create communications application. For further information, go to:

```
www.macromedia.com/software/
    flashcom
```

If the previous paragraphs have piqued your interest, you may want to consider downloading the trial version of Macromedia Flash Communication Server MX. After you download the trial version and install it, you can peruse sample applications that Macromedia has already created for you. If you have a Web cam hooked up to your computer, you can test the video capabilities of Macromedia Flash Communication Server MX. The Macromedia

Flash Player acts as the conduit between your Web camera and the Macromedia Flash Communication Server MX. You can download the trial version of Macromedia Flash Communication Server MX at:

```
www.macromedia.com/software/
    flashcom/download/
    components/license.html
```

Macromedia has created some ready-built Macromedia Flash Communication Server MX components. The ActionScript in these babies is longer than most short stories, but don't fret, you don't have to write it; Macromedia Flash geeks have already done that for you. After you download the Macromedia Flash Communication Server MX components and install them, you have a new sub-group in the Components panel called Communications Components, as shown in the following figure. Instead of creating the graphics and ActionScript (which is very complicated), you can just drag one of these components from the Components panel into your Flash application, and you're good to go. You can download the Macromedia Flash Communication Server MX components at:

```
www.macromedia.com/software/
    flashcom/download/
    components/index.html
```

Macromedia Flash Remoting MX

Macromedia Flash Remoting MX offers tools for programmers to connect Macromedia Flash MX with a Web server application built with ColdFusion MX, .NET, or Java. You can integrate Macromedia Flash MX with databases and Web services by using special ActionScript commands. You can use your elegant Macromedia Flash MX artwork as the interface to display data from databases. For more information, go to:

```
www.macromedia.com/software/
    flashremoting
```

Macromedia Flash Remoting MX is an excellent tool you can use to create dynamic Flash applications. For example, if you want to create a Flash application that displays a slide show, you can use the Flash UI ListBox or ComboBox component and create a function to populate the ListBox or ComboBox with the titles and file names of the images you want to load. The down side is that if you need to change the images, you have to edit the Flash movie and enter new values in the ListBox or ComboBox. However, if you use Macromedia Flash Remoting MX, you can access a database that stores the titles and filenames of the images and loads them into the Flash application through a ColdFusion MX component you created in Dreamweaver MX. The ColdFusion MX Component (or CFC as the ColdFusion geeks refer to them) is the conduit between your Flash application and the database. If you've dabbled in ColdFusion MX and feel comfortable with ActionScript, this is your ticket to creating dynamic Flash applications. A cool Flash interface with Macromedia Flash Remoting MX and the odd ColdFusion MX Component or four adds up to something very special.

Macromedia Flash Remoting MX can be accomplished with any server that has ColdFusion MX installed. If you're creating Macromedia Flash Remoting MX applications for a client that has a ColdFusion MX server, you can test the application on your local machine

(continued)

(continued)

using the version of ColdFusion that ships with the Macromedia Studio MX application. But the first step is to download the Macromedia Flash Remoting MX Components you find at:

```
www.macromedia.com/software/
  flashremoting/downloads/
  components
```

After you download and install the components, you may be a bit disappointed, because there's no new components installed in Macromedia Flash MX. That's true, but a whole lot of actions are added to the Actions panel that you find in the Remoting book, as shown in the following figure.

Book VI

ColdFusion MX

The 5th Wave   By Rich Tennant

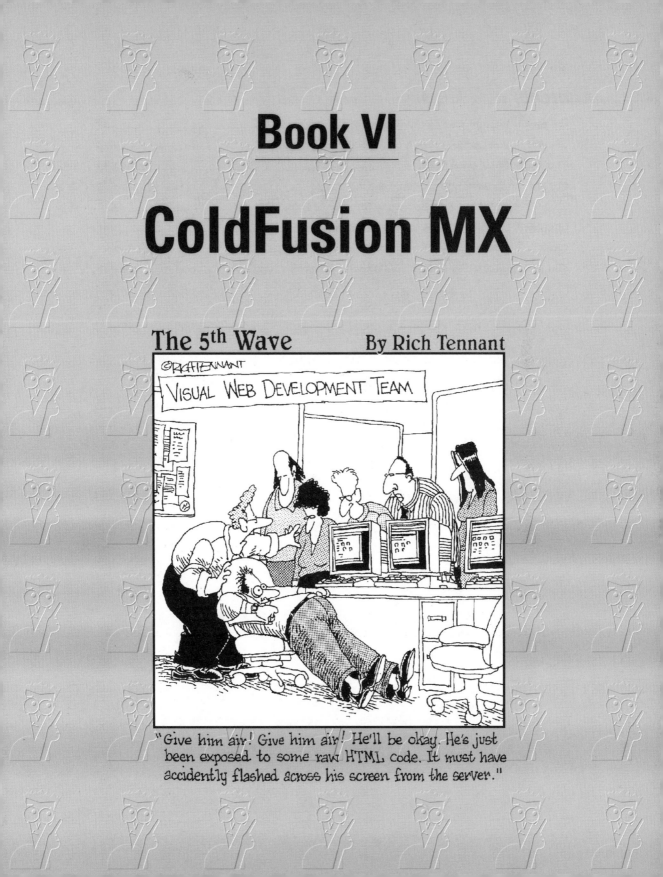

"Give him air! Give him air! He'll be okay. He's just
been exposed to some raw HTML code. It must have
accidently flashed across his screen from the server."

Contents at a Glance

Chapter 1: Introduction to ColdFusion MX

In This Chapter

✔ **Defining dynamic Web sites**

✔ **Understanding the components of ColdFusion MX**

✔ **Beginning to work with the ColdFusion MX application server**

✔ **Working with databases**

✔ **Integrating ColdFusion MX with the rest of Macromedia Studio MX**

ColdFusion MX is a rapid development environment for creating dynamic — not to mention compelling — Internet applications. Three main components make up ColdFusion MX:

✦ An application server

✦ An administrative tool

✦ A custom scripting language

Together, these three components give you a diverse set of tools that make ColdFusion MX the quickest and easiest way to bring dynamic, interactive, database-driven content to your Web site. (A *database* is a program, such as Microsoft Access, that is used to collect information in tabular format, meaning rows and columns.) In this chapter, we give you a basic introduction to each of the three components, as well as an overview of what makes a Web site dynamic.

Creating Dynamic Web Sites

Web pages are wonderful. You can create a page using HyperText Markup Language (HTML), upload it to a *Web server* (a program such as Microsoft IIS or Apache that enables people to view your Web site), and it is ready to be viewed by the world. If you know HTML, this approach is simple, but it can create problems as your Web site expands in size and complexity. As your Web site grows, you may find yourself wanting to do one or more of the following:

✦ Display Web pages for a variety of different products or services using the same look and feel (each page having the same banner, company logo, background image, and so on).

✦ Sort and display the same content in different ways. For example, you may want to highlight sports articles over news articles on a page if a user is more interested in sports than news.

✦ Customize content based on actions a user takes on a site.

✦ Personalize content based on preferences a user sets when visiting your site.

✦ Allow users to perform complex searches of documents and databases.

✦ Create shopping carts and user accounts that keep track of purchases and other shipping information.

If you've ever wanted to do any of these things, then you're longing to create a *dynamic* Web site. Dynamic Web sites use a *Web application server,* such as ColdFusion MX, to extend the capabilities of a standard Web server by creating custom content for each browser request. A Web application server can also connect to a database to retrieve information used to build pages, or it can save information submitted by the user.

To demonstrate what we're talking about, check out the Web site for Earl's Bowlateria, which is shown in Figure 1-1. Earl has an online store that contains hundreds of products. Earl's a busy guy, so he doesn't want to create a static page for every product in his large inventory. That would mean that whenever he put bowling balls on sale, Earl would have to go through all his pages and change every single price listed for bowling balls! How tedious and time-consuming.

However, Earl can instead use the ColdFusion MX application server and a database to drive his Web site, which allows him to use a single ColdFusion MX page to do the following:

✦ Look up the price and product information about any of his products.

✦ Insert the data from the database into a product template. A *template* is a bit of HTML and CFML code that gets combined with data from a database to help construct a Web page. Several templates may make up one individual page.

✦ Display the product page for an item that the user requests via a Web browser.

The idea behind creating a dynamic Web site is that you try to create the least number of templates to represent the largest number of pages on the site. That way, when you change something on the site, you don't have to make the change yourself on every single page.

Figure 1-2 shows a different product from Earl's Bowlateria. If you compare Figure 1-2 to Figure 1-1, you can see that the products are different, but the *architecture* (design) of the two pages is identical.

Figure 1-1:
Earl's
Bowlateria.

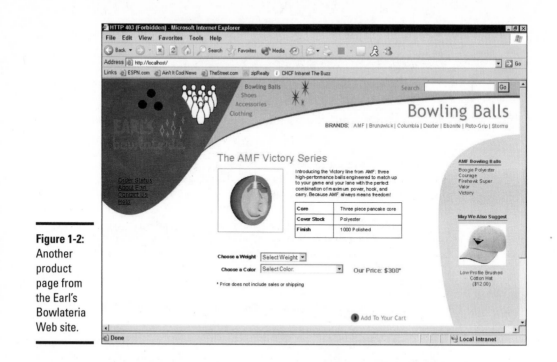

Figure 1-2:
Another
product
page from
the Earl's
Bowlateria
Web site.

Exploring the Components of ColdFusion MX

The workhorse of ColdFusion MX is the application server, which provides a fast, reliable platform for your Web applications. In order to make the most of this powerful application server, you need to be able to configure and control it, which you do by using the following:

✦ **ColdFusion Administrator:** The ColdFusion Administrator allows you to configure the server to meet your specific needs.

✦ **ColdFusion Markup Language (CFML):** ColdFusion Markup Language (CFML) can be used to communicate instructions to the application server.

The ColdFusion MX Application Server is built on top of the Java 2 Platform, Enterprise Edition (J2EE). For more information on J2EE, where it came from, and who supports it, check out the Sun Web site at `java.sun.com`.

Understanding the role of the Web application server

An application server executes the business logic of your Web application. By *business logic,* we mean the way in which you want something to run for your business — in this case, how you want your Web site to display content. Your business logic may be as simple as verifying (ensuring that users have entered all the required information) the data that the user enters in a form on your Web page and inserting it into a database. No matter what sort of task you need to accomplish, if it requires any sort of logical processing (conversion of CFML code to HTML), the application server is the component of ColdFusion MX that does the work.

The infrastructure of most Web applications can be divided into three parts, which are commonly referred to as a 3-tier architecture:

✦ **Display Tier:** A Web browser

✦ **Application Tier:** ColdFusion MX

✦ **Database Tier:** Any compatible database

The application server is responsible for managing the interactions between all three of these tiers. It accepts inputs from the Display Tier, interprets the CFML in the Application Tier, and brokers requests to databases at the Database Tier.

Investigating CFML

In a 3-tier application, the application server executes all the business logic, as we discuss in the previous section. In ColdFusion MX, you use the ColdFusion Markup Language (CFML) to build that business logic.

CFML provides the instructions for each page as it is processed by the application server. Like HTML, CFML uses *tags,* which instruct the application server as to what kind of functions to perform. Built-in tags can handle many common tasks required by Web applications, including the following:

✦ Page formatting

✦ Form validation

✦ Database access

✦ Generating and sending e-mail

✦ User security

✦ Generating charts and graphs

In addition to tags, CFML also includes hundreds of built-in functions (best to think of them as tools built into ColdFusion MX) that you can use to test and manipulate your data. By adding CFML tags and functions to your pages, you build the instructions for the application server. We cover CFML in more detail in Book VI, Chapter 4.

The ColdFusion Administrator

ColdFusion Markup Language provides the application server with instructions for each page, but some information, such as a database connectivity, is only configured once for the entire server. The ColdFusion Administrator is used to control server-wide settings, such as the following:

✦ Database connections

✦ Variable scopes (check out Book VI, Chapter 3 for more information on what variable scoping means in the context of ColdFusion MX)

✦ Debugging options

✦ Security settings

✦ Application logging

The ColdFusion Administrator not only is used to set up your server, but also is an invaluable maintenance tool for reporting on things going on in your Web site. We cover the administrative tool, including how to use it to optimize the speed of your Web site, in more detail in Book VI, Chapter 2.

Setting Up the ColdFusion MX Environment

To begin working with ColdFusion MX, you need access to a working server. You may want to find an Internet service provider (ISP) that already runs ColdFusion MX, or you can install your own server right on your desktop PC. Be aware that ColdFusion has traditionally been available for both the Unix and Windows environments, but Macromedia Studio MX is a Windows- and Macintosh-only product.

Finding an ISP

If you need to get a site up and running as soon as possible, hosting your Web application at an ISP saves you the trouble of installing and configuring your own server. You generally have limited control over the server configuration at an ISP, but that drawback is usually outweighed by the other benefits of using an existing server.

A large number of ISPs have offered ColdFusion hosting for years, and many of these providers are upgrading to ColdFusion MX. You need to check the version of ColdFusion the ISP supports before you sign up. Here are some of the more well-known ColdFusion ISPs:

✦ **CrystalTech:** www.crystaltech.com

✦ **CFDynamics:** www.cfdynamics.com

✦ **Definitive Web Solutions:** www.dwsgroup.com

✦ **Edge Web Hosting:** www.edgeWebhosting.net

Installing the application server

Installing your own application server on your personal computer is a great way to learn about ColdFusion MX. The Developer Edition is designed for a single user machine for personal development. You would want to install ColdFusion MX Professional on a Web server that is going to be put into production. (For more information on ColdFusion MX Professional, check out Macromedia's ColdFusion MX site at www.macromedia.com/software/coldfusion.)

The setup wizard on the Macromedia Studio MX CD walks you through the installation process. To set up ColdFusion MX, just follow these steps:

1. **Insert the Macromedia Studio MX CD into your CD-ROM drive.**

The auto-run utility brings up an interactive menu from which you can install all the Macromedia Studio MX programs.

2. **Click Install ColdFusion MX Developer Edition.**

The Welcome screen appears.

3. **Click Next at the initial installation screen.**

4. **Select the I Accept the Terms in the License Agreement radio button on the Licensing Agreement screen, and then click Next.**

5. **Fill out the form on the Customer Information screen, and then click Next.**

ColdFusion MX requires that you input your name, organization, a valid serial number, and a previous serial number if you're upgrading from a previous version at this screen. It also requires you to choose whether or not you want the product to be available to all users on your computer or just for your user account. We suggest making it available for all users, as this means you won't have to reinstall the program if another user logs onto your desktop PC.

6. **Select a Web server from the Web server drop-down list, and then click Next.**

At this screen, ColdFusion MX scans your system to see if you have any Web servers installed and displays them, as shown in Figure 1-3. For personal development on a single machine, we recommend selecting the Standalone option (as you may or may not have another Web server installed on your machine), though certainly it will work with Microsoft's Internet Information Server (IIS) and others.

Figure 1-3:
Selecting a
Web server.

7. **Choose a directory where you want to install the product.**

By default, ColdFusion MX installs the product in `C:\CFusionMX`, and the Web files in `C:\CFusionMX\wwwroot`. You can change this by clicking the Change button. Otherwise, you can just click the Next button to install into the default directories.

As a general rule, if you've got a partitioned drive (meaning a `C:` drive and a `D:` drive that are both hard drives), then it's a good idea to install your Web files on the `D:` drive. This makes it harder for potential hackers to find any other information on your computer, should you be attacked.

8. **Click Next in the Custom Setup window.**

At the Custom Setup screen, if you want install only select components, you can click on the hard drive icon with the arrow pointing down to remove components from the install.

9. **Enter your passwords, and then click Next.**

As shown in Figure 1-4, ColdFusion MX requires a password for both the ColdFusion Administrator and the ColdFusion MX Remote Development

Services (RDS), which is used for debugging and remote database connections, as well as editing files remotely. The easiest method is to choose a password for the administrator account and then select the Use the Same Password as Above check box.

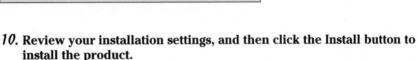

**Book VI
Chapter 1**

**Introduction to
ColdFusion MX**

Figure 1-4:
Entering
passwords.

10. **Review your installation settings, and then click the Install button to install the product.**

Installation will take a few minutes, and the progress will be shown as the installation is occurring.

11. **After the installation is complete, click the Finish button to complete your installation.**

Configuring the application server

After the installation is complete, you can test and configure your application server by loading the ColdFusion Administrator:

1. **Load the ColdFusion Administrator.**

Do this using the shortcut in the Start menu or navigating directly to `localhost:8500/CFIDE/administrator/index.cfm` by typing this URL into your Web browser (the administrator is a Web-based application).

2. **Enter your password.**

Use the username and password for the administrator (as opposed to RDS) that you created during the installation process to log on to the administrator, as shown in Figure 1-5.

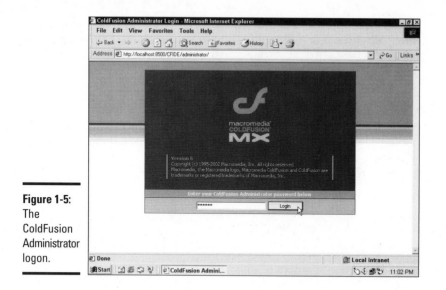

Figure 1-5:
The
ColdFusion
Administrator
logon.

You may want to take care of some administrative tasks, such as the following, right away:

✦ Set up database connections.

✦ Configure e-mail.

✦ Set debugging options.

These tasks and others related to setting up your site are covered in more detail in Book VI, Chapter 2.

If you're using another Web server, such as IIS or Apache, you also need to make sure that that application server is running properly as well, and that it has as its default directory the same location where you installed ColdFusion MX.

Introducing Databases

Databases are often an integral part of any dynamic site, and ColdFusion MX is no exception. A *database,* in very general terms, is simply a structured set of data. The power of a database is in the ability to organize data for easy retrieval when requested. If you've ever used a spreadsheet program, such as Microsoft Excel, then you've probably created a structured collection of data that could, in fact, be a database.

Databases are generally made up of the following elements:

✦ **Tables:** The containers for similar sets of data, made up of columns, rows, and cells. For example, a table might contain records (a collection of rows in a table) of all your products.

✦ **Cells:** The individual blocks that make up the table. Cells contain only a single piece of data and are grouped by columns and rows.

✦ **Columns:** The vertical block of cells that groups the data in the table into categories. Using our previous example of the product table, the data entered into columns in that table might include things like Name, Price, and Description.

✦ **Rows:** The horizontal block of cells in a table that contains the information for each individual record, spanning all the columns. Using the example of the product table, a row contains all the information about a single product, such as `Silver Streak Bowling Ball`, `$200`, and `The finest pure silver bowling ball money can buy`.

Databases come in all shapes and sizes, from the simple to the complex. Following are the most common database types:

✦ **Flat file:** A text file that contains a single set of columns and rows, with the data usually being separated by commas or tabs. A CSV (Comma Separated Values) is an example of a flat file.

✦ **Relational:** A collection of tables with common data elements (values in like-named columns) between them, providing expanded collection and reporting capabilities. Usually requires a query language to retrieve information from the database.

As you become more comfortable with ColdFusion MX, you begin to see (and of course, we show you!) just where databases can be extremely useful. For now, you can whet your appetite by checking out Figure 1-6, which shows an example of a database table in Microsoft Access. Relational database design, which is central to harnessing the power of ColdFusion MX, is covered in more detail in Book VI, Chapter 6.

Figure 1-6:
A typical
Microsoft
Access
table.

Taking a Quick Tour of ColdFusion MX in Dreamweaver MX

Dreamweaver MX has been specially designed to make writing ColdFusion MX pages easier. The great thing about Dreamweaver MX is its ability to flip back and forth between Code view and Design view:

+ **Design view:** Enables you to see a visual representation of your page, just as it would appear in a Web browser.

+ **Code view:** Gives you direct control over the code. If you've used previous versions of ColdFusion or HomeSite (the HTML editor that is part of previous versions of ColdFusion), you may notice that the Code view in Dreamweaver MX looks similar to those products.

+ **Split screen mode:** Displays both the code and the graphical representation on your screen, as shown in Figure 1-7.

Figure 1-7:
Dreamweaver MX in split screen mode.

When you're using Code view, many features are available to you that are made specifically for ColdFusion MX development:

✦ CFML toolbars

✦ CFML function auto-complete

✦ CFML validation

✦ Code view that works similarly to previous versions of Homesite and ColdFusion Studio

✦ Debugging commands

✦ ColdFusion MX server connection

✦ Drag and drop components

✦ Database access

These features are covered in more detail in Book II, Chapter 6.

Chapter 2: Working with the ColdFusion Administrator

In This Chapter

✔ **Understanding the ColdFusion Administrator**

✔ **Creating data sources**

✔ **Configuring an e-mail server**

✔ **Logging events on the Application Server**

✔ **Using debugging options**

*B*efore you begin writing code for your Web application, it's a good idea to familiarize yourself with the ColdFusion MX server. If you are running your own server, you have the ability to set things up just the way you want. Even if you're using a preconfigured server at your Internet service provider, you will want to know how the server is configured to aid in your development process.

This chapter walks you through a few important tasks that are accomplished in the ColdFusion Administrator.

Exploring the Functionality of the ColdFusion Administrator

The ColdFusion Administrator is a Web application that helps the human administrator to manage the server by controlling a wide array of server settings. Although several of the server settings are aimed at giving the developer important information to assist in the writing of CFML (ColdFusion Markup Language) pages, the ColdFusion Administrator *does not create* CFML pages.

Many of the tasks in the ColdFusion Administrator are directly related to tasks that a ColdFusion MX developer carries out. For example, a developer cannot create a form that sends e-mail if the server is not configured to send e-mail. After a server is configured properly with the ColdFusion Administrator, the CFML developer can create a Web application that utilizes the many features of the application server.

Table 2-1 shows how the server settings correspond to actual CFML pages.

Table 2-1	How the ColdFusion Administrator Helps the Developer
ColdFusion Administrator's Function	*What the Developer Does with That Function*
Configures the e-mail server	Creates Web pages to send e-mail.
Sets up data sources (connections to databases)	Adds, edits, and deletes information in databases.
Sets up search collections	Uses CFML to perform searches on documents and databases.
Sets ups debugging options	Outputs all the queries, variables, and processes at the bottom of the rendered ColdFusion MX page so that developers can monitor and fix their code.
Defines Web services	Creates Web services. A Web service is a bridge from your application server to another server with an application that you want to be able to access from within your application. This is a new feature to ColdFusion MX.

Logging On to the ColdFusion Administrator

Before you can work with any of the administrative tools in ColdFusion Administrator, you must first log on, which is a two step process:

1. **Launch the ColdFusion Administrator.**

Because the administrator is a Web application, you access it with your browser. The default URL of the logon page is `http://servername/cfide/Administrator/index.cfm`, where `servername` is the IP number or fully qualified domain name of your server. If you are using the ColdFusion MX Web server, it uses port 8500, so the URL becomes `http://localhost:8500/cfide/Administrator/index.cfm`.

When you enter this URL, the logon screen appears, as shown in Figure 2-1.

2. **Enter your password.**

When you installed ColdFusion MX, you were asked to provide a password for the administrator. Similarly, if you're using ColdFusion Administrator at your ISP, your ISP should have provided you with a password to log on to the ColdFusion Administrator. No username is required, and all administrative users use the same password.

Figure 2-1:
The
ColdFusion
Adminis-
trator Logon
screen.

If you're working in a secure development environment (or in RDS), you can turn off the password protection by clicking the CF Admin Password hyperlink under the Security section in the left navigation frame of the ColdFusion Administrator. This just means that you'll have one less password to have to worry about!

Working with the ColdFusion Administrator

The ColdFusion Administrator tasks are divided into five sections. Each of these sections, and its associated tasks, is listed as a series of text links on the left-hand side of all Administrator pages. The sections, shown in Figure 2-2, are as follows:

✦ **Server Settings:** The tasks in this section control how the ColdFusion MX server behaves. The settings here affect overall server performance.

✦ **Data & Services:** These tasks control how the ColdFusion MX server connects to and exposes databases, Verity search indexes (collections of data used to power ColdFusion MX's built-in search engine), and Web services.

✦ **Debugging & Logging:** This section has tasks used to set debugging and logging options, as well as tools to analyze your system and schedule tasks.

✦ **Extensions:** Tasks here allow you to install and remove components that extend the ColdFusion MX server's capabilities.

✦ **Security:** The security tasks include setting passwords and controlling access to resources.

Section Name

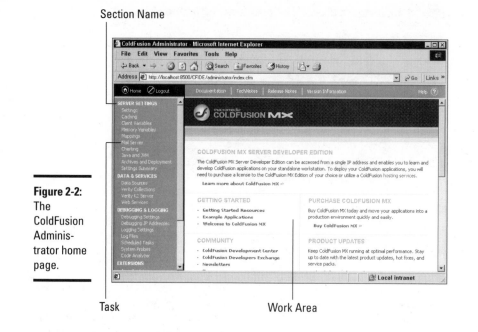

Figure 2-2:
The
ColdFusion
Adminis-
trator home
page.

Task

Work Area

Creating Data Sources

When you want to use information from a database in your Web application, you need to register the database with the ColdFusion MX server. This registration process creates a data source. Each data source has a unique name that you use in your CFML to connect to the underlying database.

Many popular databases, such as Microsoft Access, Microsoft SQL, and MySQL, can be registered as data sources. After your data source has been set up, you can use the <CFQUERY> tag to access the data. We show you how to do this in more detail in Book VI, Chapter 4.

Setting up a data source

The exact procedure for setting up a data source varies, depending on the type of database you're registering. We outline the process below for creating a connection between the ColdFusion MX server and Microsoft Access. Access is the most common database that is used with ColdFusion MX. If you are registering a different type of database, the process will be different after Step 4. Here's how you do it:

1. **Under the Data & Services section in the left navigation frame of the ColdFusion Administrator home page, click the <u>Data Sources</u> link.**

This brings up the Data Sources main page, as shown in Figure 2-3.

Figure 2-3:
The Data
Sources
main page.

2. **In the table titled Add New Data Source, enter a name for your data source in the Data Source Name text field.**

   As a general rule, this name should not include any spaces.

3. **From the Driver drop-down list, select the database driver that matches your database.**

   We use Microsoft Access for this example.

4. **Click the Add button.**

   The Data Source Driver Information page, shown in Figure 2-4, appears. On this page, you enter specific information about your database.

5. **Click the Browse Server button to find the database file that you want to register.**

   In this case, the file is a Microsoft Access database, which has the file-name extension .mdb.

6. **Leave the System Database File field blank.**

   From this field, you can choose to use Windows NT security by selecting a system database (you click the Browser Server button to select a system database). In reality though, very few people use this feature, due in large part to concerns about possible holes in Windows NT security. If you do want to use it, though, the default location for this file is C:\winnt\system32\system.mdw.

7. **Select the Use Default Username check box to use the ODBC default if you do not want to pass a username and password from your <CFQUERY> tag.**

Figure 2-4:
The Data
Source
Driver
Information
page.

8. **(Optional) Enter a descriptive note in the Description text field.**

9. **Click the Submit button.**

   Your new data source is verified automatically. Look for a confirmation message that says OK just below the data sources title in the main working area.

Your new data source will appear in the Connected Data Sources table at the bottom of the page. If the data source was created successfully, the data source name should be highlighted in green, and the status will be OK. If this is not the case, check the top of the page for an error message describing what went wrong.

To use a Microsoft Access database on Windows 98 or Windows Me, you must set up an ODBC (Open Database Connectivity) connection with Windows, an then use the JDBC-ODBC (Java Database Connectivity-Open Database Connectivity) driver from within ColdFusion MX. The Microsoft Access driver and the ODBC driver that come with ColdFusion MX will not work on Windows 98/Me because these drivers require services that are not available under Windows 98/Me.

Other data source tasks

In addition to creating data sources, the Administrator is also used to edit, verify, and delete existing data sources. Each of these operations is represented by an icon in the Connected Data Sources table, which is shown in Figure 2-5.

Edit

Figure 2-5:
The
Connected
Data
Sources
table.

Verify Delete

The following list highlights what each of the data source operations does:

✦ **Edit:** Brings you to the data source settings page.

✦ **Verify:** Verifies that the data source is operational and updates the Status column.

✦ **Delete:** Begins the process of removing the data source.

Connecting to a Mail Server

Although ColdFusion MX is not a mail server, it can connect to an existing mail server to provide e-mail services to your Web application. This can be exceptionally useful if, for example, you want to send a confirmation e-mail to a customer when they purchase a product or sign up for a newsletter. ColdFusion MX supports both sending and retrieving e-mail using the SMTP (Simple Mail Transport Protocol) and POP3 protocols, respectively.

ColdFusion MX uses a spooled architecture to handle sending e-mails. You may be familiar with spooling, because it is commonly used for network printers. E-mail spooling uses the same concept to manage the sending of e-mail in a timely manner. When ColdFusion MX encounters an e-mail request while building a Web page, it sends the request to the spool as it is received. As soon as the e-mail is successfully placed on the spool, ColdFusion MX continues to create the output page. The spool sends e-mail messages in the order they were received, without holding up the processing of your CFML. Using the spool allows ColdFusion MX to build pages quickly, regardless of the speed of the e-mail server being used.

Use the following steps to set up a connection to an e-mail server:

1. **From the left navigation frame, click the** <u>**Mail Server**</u> **link under the Server Settings section.**

The Mail Server Settings page, shown in Figure 2-6, appears.

Figure 2-6:
The Mail
Server
connection
settings
page.

2. **In the Mail Server text field, enter the IP address or the fully quali-fied domain name (**`yourdomain.com`**, for example) of your mail server.**

3. **Enter the port that the mail server uses in the Server Port text field.**

   Normally, mail servers use port 25, which is the default value.

4. **(Optional) Enter a new time in the Connection Timeout text field.**

   Connection timeout specifies the number of seconds the ColdFusion MX server should wait for a response from the mail server before logging an error. The default value is 60 seconds. Leave this alone, unless you know that you will be connecting to a slow mail server.

5. **In the Spool Interval text field, enter a length of time in seconds.**

   The *spool interval* determines how often the messages on the spool will be sent to the mail server. The default value of 15 seconds will attempt to empty the spool four times a minute and can be left as is.

6. **Enable the Verify Mail Server Connection option by selecting the check box.**

   When this option is enabled, the Administrator attempts to connect to the mail server when you click the Submit Changes button. If a connec-tion cannot be established, you will receive an error at the top of the page. You'll also get a message if the verification succeeded.

7. **Click the Submit Changes button to set up your e-mail server.**

   Be sure that the gray bars enclosing the button turn green, signifying success. If they turn red, look for an error message at the top of the page.

Even if you validate your mail server, it is a good idea to send a test message from your Web application. A valid connection to the mail server does not guarantee that the Web application will send e-mail properly. If you try sending mail to yourself and it's not successful, you'll know because you never got the message.

Controlling Logging on Your Site

Basic logging is set up automatically when you install ColdFusion MX. The logs created by the ColdFusion MX server give the administrator information about how well the server is handling its many tasks. Log entries are grouped together by type into separate log files, as shown in Figure 2-7.

Two tasks are related to log files: Logging Settings and Log Files. You see these two task items in the list along the left-hand side of the Administrator page. The Logging Settings task allows you to customize the following:

- ✦ Control where logs are stored

- ✦ Specify how big a log can get before it is archived

- ✦ Control how many archives should be kept

- ✦ Specify what sort of information is logged

To view the actual log entries, click the <u>Log Files</u> hyperlink in the left navigation frame. This will present a list of all of the logs on the server. Table 2-2 describes the most common log files.

Figure 2-7:
The logging page in ColdFusion Administrator.

Table 2-2	Common Log Files and Their Contents
Filename	*Description of Contents*
`application.log`	All errors that are reported to the end user
`mail.log`	Errors generated by the SMTP mail server
`server.log`	Internal server errors generated by ColdFusion MX

You can view any log by clicking the Action button with the magnifying glass, or just by clicking on its name. These buttons are in the Actions area of the Log Files page. The following four actions are available:

✦ **View:** Displays the contents of the log in the browser.

✦ **Download:** Downloads the raw log file.

✦ **Archive:** Creates a numbered copy of the log and clears the current log.

✦ **Delete:** Removes the log. A new one may be created by the server as needed.

When you create an archive with the archive button, the log file is renamed. The new name is just the old name with a digit at the end (1 if it is the first archive, 2 if it is the second, and so on). The important thing to note is that archive files do not show up in the Log File page.

Debugging Options for Building Your Site

During the development of your Web application, you will most likely encounter errors. Some errors are quickly fixed, while others require checking your CFML line by line to find the source. This process of hunting down and fixing errors is called *debugging*.

ColdFusion MX can help you with the debugging process by including debugging data at the bottom of each page it generates. The debugging data includes information about the following:

✦ **Exceptions (Server Errors):** Errors that occurred when your ColdFusion MX page made a request to the server.

✦ **Execution times for each page template:** How long it takes all the code on a page to be read and then processed.

✦ **SQL Queries and Stored Procedures:** The actual queries that are made to the server. This shows you how many queries were made, and what the specific queries were.

✦ **Page Variables:** Shows all the page variables that are active for a given page. You can select from the nine different variable types (cookies, application, and so on).

To enable debugging, simply select the Enable Debugging check box on the Debugging Settings page. The Debugging IP Address page allows you to select which desktop PCs, by IP number, are sent the debugging info. If you leave it blank, the information is sent to all PCs that view the pages.

If you are using Internet Explorer 4 (or above) or Netscape Navigator 6 (or above), check out the dockable debugging window. Just select `dockable.cfm` from the Select Debugging Output Format drop-down list on the Debugging Settings page. This option puts all of the debugging info into a Dynamic HTML collapsible tree (much like the Windows Explorer), which can be displayed in a pop-up window or in a frame right along side your CFML pages.

Chapter 3: ColdFusion MX Basics

In This Chapter

✔ **Exploring ColdFusion MX architecture**

✔ **Working with the application server**

✔ **Understanding the power of CFML tags**

✔ **Calling functions**

✔ **Using variables**

✔ **Building expressions**

ColdFusion MX is an application development suite that helps you create Web applications quickly and easily. When you use ColdFusion MX, you are actually using several tools in concert:

+ **An application server:** This software processes requests from a ColdFusion MX file and returns HTML to the end-user's browser.

+ **An editing tool:** This tool allows you to create and edit your own sites using the ColdFusion tag and scripting language. The script editor is described in more detail in Book VI, Chapter 4.

+ **An administration tool:** This tool can be used to manage various elements of your application, including data sources, mail servers, and logs. You can read more about the ColdFusion Administrator in Book VI, Chapter 2.

Together, these three items provide developers with a power suite of tools to create custom HTML for every site visitor, based on user input and other data.

On its own, a Web server can only read files and deliver them to the browser. In order to rapidly build a robust Web application, the ColdFusion MX Application Server makes use of the ColdFusion Markup Language (CFML). CFML uses tags, which are very similar in structure to HTML tags (such as `<HTML>`, `<BODY>`, and `<TABLE>`), and functions to provide simple, yet powerful, tools to instruct the ColdFusion MX Application Server. The combination of CFML and the application server give you, the ColdFusion MX developer, the ability to provide the end user with a wide array of features:

✦ Database driven pages

✦ E-commerce

✦ Advanced security

✦ Search engines on your site

This chapter focuses on the real magic behind ColdFusion MX — the ColdFusion MX Application Server and the scripting language used to drive it. Get comfy in that computer chair, grab a cup of coffee, and prepare to make your sites come alive!

Understanding the ColdFusion MX Application Server Model

The World Wide Web is built on a client-server architecture. Both client (browser) and server perform specialized tasks, and together they create what is known as the Web. The browser's job is to interface with the user and make requests of the server. The server needs to be able to handle the user's request, and possibly thousands of other simultaneous user requests, and return the proper response. The Web server may only need to read an HTML file to create the response, or it may pass the request on to the ColdFusion MX Application Server for advanced processing.

The ColdFusion MX Application Server works in conjunction with a standard Web server and can be installed alongside most of today's popular Web servers, including the following:

✦ Microsoft IIS

✦ Netscape Enterprise Server

✦ iPlanet Enterprise Server

✦ Apache Web Server

✦ ColdFusion Internal Web Server

When the Web server receives a request for a ColdFusion page, identified by its `.cfm` or `.cfml` extension, the request is passed on to the ColdFusion MX Application Server. The application server interprets the CFML embedded in the page, processes the instructions, and returns the result to the Web server, which sends the final response to the end-user's Web browser. Figure 3-1 shows how these transactions take place.

Figure 3-1:
The
ColdFusion
MX
Application
Server
model.

The ColdFusion Markup Language (CFML) is the language that allows ColdFusion MX to create dynamic Web sites. Most ColdFusion pages will contain a mix of CFML and HTML. Each language has its own uses within the ColdFusion page. HTML is commonly used for the following tasks:

✦ Controlling overall page layout

✦ Building tables

✦ Displaying forms

✦ Setting colors and styles

✦ Implementing menus, rollovers, and other advanced browser features

You can use CFML to make a portion of your page customizable, based on user input, in the following ways:

✦ Retrieve and display data from a database

✦ Create dynamic forms

✦ Build complex navigation

✦ Control user sessions (a user's time visiting the site) and security

Getting Acquainted with CFML

ColdFusion Markup Language (CFML) is a tag-based language that incorporates many of the features found in traditional programming languages, including the following:

✦ **Functions:** Tools in the language that perform specific operations

✦ **Variables:** Values that are used in areas of your site that can change, depending on condition

✦ **Expressions:** Collections of variables, functions, and operators (such as + and &) that are used to generate some specific desired action

In the following sections, you find a more detailed introduction to each of these concepts, plus some practical examples that you can use to dive right into using CFML.

Introducing CFML tags

CFML tags are very similar to HTML tags, only more powerful. CFML instructs the ColdFusion MX server in how to handle the ColdFusion page, just as HTML tags instruct the browser in how to display a Web page. In the end, though, the CFML will be converted into HTML and will not be there when the page is displayed in a browser.

The format of CFML tags follows a few simple rules:

✦ CFML tags are enclosed in angle brackets (< and >).

✦ CFML tags begin with the letters `cf`.

✦ CFML tags can come in pairs, meaning they have a closing tag that starts with a slash (/) in addition to their starting tag.

✦ CFML tags may contain additional modifiers within the tag that allow you to specify more information about what the tag should do.

✦ CFML tags are case insensitive, so `<cfoutput>` is the same as `<CFOUTPUT>`.

ColdFusion MX contains over 100 tags, which enable you to do everything from querying a database to making a form. We include the ten most common CFML tags in Table 3-1, with their respective functions.

Table 3-1	Common CFML Tags
CFML Tag	*Function*
`<CFINCLUDE>`	Grabs another file to be included in your page.
`<CFOUTPUT>`	Outputs content to the screen (both HTML and variables).
`<CFQUERY>`	Sets up and sends a query to a database.
`<CFLOOP>`	Loops through a dataset (generally, these are generated from a `<CFQUERY>`).
`<CFSET>`	Allows you to create a variable and its value.
`<CFIF>`, `<CFELSE>`, `<CFELSEIF>`	The three tags in combination enable you to create conditional operations. (For example, if this, then do that, if not, then do this other thing.)
`<CFFORM>`	Creates a more feature-rich HTML `<FORM>`.
`<CFINSERT>`	Specifies the database, database table, and content to insert.
`<CFCASE>`, `<CFSWITCH>`	Evaluates an expression, and then allows you to choose different responses based on the value of the expression.
`<CFPARAM>`	Allows you to test for a given parameter, and if it does not exist, assign a default value and data type for it.

When the ColdFusion MX Application Server processes the page, all the CFML tags are replaced with the results of the operation. The resulting HTML page should never contain any of your CFML tags. Figure 3-2 shows how this operation occurs.

Identifying the role of the pound sign (#)

The `CFOUTPUT` tag makes special use of the pound sign (#). When a text expression is included between two pound signs, it lets the ColdFusion MX Application Server know to look for a value that corresponds to the name of the variable within the pound signs. (See Book VI, Chapter 5 for more on variables.) For example, if you have a variable named `myname` and you want it to be output to the screen, you could use the following bit of CFML code:

```
<CFOUTPUT> Hello, my name is #myname#. </CFOUTPUT>
```

The text enclosed by the `<CFOUTPUT>` tags is unchanged by the server, unless pound signs surround it.

In addition to simply looking for variables, ColdFusion MX can evaluate expressions within the pound signs, as the example in the next section shows.

Figure 3-2:
CFML gets
parsed at
the server
and
rendered
as HTML.

```
                         <tr>
                                <td colspan="2" valign="top">
                                        <a href="/press/view.cfm?itemid=20137"><img src="/images/main_arrow.gif"
width="11" height="13" alt="" border="0" vspace="0" hspace="0" align="absmiddle"></a>
                                        <a href="/press/view.cfm?itemid=20137" class="mainsecondary" >Higher
Copayments for Prescriptions Drive Patients to Use Less</a>
                                </td>
                        </tr>
                        <tr>
                                <td colspan="2">
                                        <table cellpadding="5" cellspacing="0"  border="0">
                                                <tr>
                                                        <td valign="top" width="100" align="center">
                                                                <a href="/press/view.cfm?itemid=20137"><img
src="/images/archive/bullseyepills.gif" alt="" border="0" hspace="2" vspace="2"></a>
                                                        </td>
                                                        <td>Increasing copayments for prescription drugs causes patients to
reduce their use of medication and switch to lower-cost drugs, according to a study in the October 9 edition of <i>JAMA</i>
that was conducted by RAND and commissioned by CHCF. The higher copayments drive up the proportion of prescription drug
costs that patients pay, while offering a one-time chance to cut insurance plan expenses significantly, according to the
study. The measures that have been put in place by health plans do have the effect of lowering drug expenditures. But just
about all of the cost savings accrue to the health plan and not to the patient.<br>
                                                                <a href="/press/view.cfm?itemid=20137"><img
src="/images/press_release.gif" alt="" border="0" hspace="2" align="absmiddle"><br><br></td>
                                                </tr>
                                        </table>
                                </td>
                        </tr>

                        <tr>
                                <td colspan="2" valign="top">
```

If you want to display a pound sign within a `<CFOUTPUT>` tag, just put two pound signs together, and they will be displayed as one. For example, the following expression prints `Dial #0 for an Operator`:

```
<CFOUTPUT> Dial ##0 for an Operator</CFOUTPUT>
```

Putting a tag to work

Creating a ColdFusion page can be as simple as writing a few lines of code that answer the age old question, "What is two plus two?" We created a brief example that demonstrates how to answer the question as a ColdFusion page. Here's the code:

```
<HTML>
<HEAD>
    <TITLE>CFML Tags</TITLE>
</HEAD>
<BODY>
    <CFOUTPUT>two plus two equals #2+2#</CFOUTPUT>
</BODY>
</HTML>
```

The preceding sample looks a lot like HTML because most of it is HTML. The addition of the CFML tag, `<CFOUTPUT>`, and a `.cfm` extension to the filename of the page turns a simple HTML page into a ColdFusion page. Here are the steps to create your own `.cfm` page:

1. Open your favorite HTML text editor.

Dreamweaver MX in Code view works well.

2. Enter the text of the sample CFML page (from the preceding example).

3. Save your work as `four.cfm` in a directory running the ColdFusion MX Application Server.

On IIS in Windows, this is generally `C:/inetpub/wwwroot`. Check out Book VI, Chapter 2 for more information on setting up your ColdFusion MX Application Server.

4. Load the page in your browser.

If you saved the page in the default location (like wwwroot), the URL should be `http://localhost/four.cfm`, as shown in Figure 3-3.

Figure 3-3:
Two plus two equals four!

Of course, the HTML that is sent to the browser is what's really important. If you view the source of your page as it is displayed in the browser, you see that the `<CFOUTPUT>` tags have been removed, and that the simple addition (2+2) between the pound signs has been replaced by the sum. The HTML should look like this:

```
<HTML>
<HEAD>
    <TITLE>CFML Tags</TITLE>
</HEAD>
<BODY>
two plus two equals 4
</BODY>
</HTML>
```

Working with variables

When you are writing CFML, you may want to store information in memory for later use, which is exactly what a variable does. A *variable* is a named container used to temporarily store information.

Sometimes, the value of a variable comes from an external source, such as a Web form, and other times you create the variables yourself. In ColdFusion MX, you can use the <CFSET> tag to create a variable. A <CFSET> tag looks like this:

```
<CFSET team_name="Pin Pals">
```

This tag sets the value of a variable called team_name to the text string "Pin Pals".

Naming variables

You can name your variables just about anything you want, but you should always follow a few rules:

+ Variables must consist of letters, numbers, and underscores only.

+ Variables should not start with a number.

+ Variables should not contain spaces.

+ Variables are case insensitive. (LAST_NAME is the same as last_name.)

Usually, you want to choose a name that is clear and concise. The name should be long enough to fully describe the contents of the variable, but not so long that it takes too long to type. Table 3-2 summarizes some good and bad choices for variable names.

Table 3-2	Variable Names	
Bad Name	*Good Name*	*Reason*
add	address	The name add is too short and could be confusing.
CustomerBilling AddressLine1	billAddress1	Long names are hard to type.
x	age	The name x does not describe the value.
First Name	FirstName or First_Name	Variables cannot have spaces in their names.

Understanding variable scope

Each variable used in your ColdFusion pages belongs to a particular *scope* (in what area the variable exists), as summarized in Table 3-3. The scope determines the following:

✦ How the variable was created.

✦ How long the variable is available.

✦ Where the variable can be used.

Table 3-3	Common Scope Types
Scope	*Description*
Variables	The default scope holds user-defined variables that are available only on the page where they are created.
Request	The Request scope holds variables that are available to any page used during a single HTTP request.
Form	Variables created in an HTML form are placed in the Form scope.
Cookie	End-user browser cookies are made available to ColdFusion MX in the Cookie scope.
Session	The Session scope holds variables that are available to each user during a single browser session.
Application	Variables in the Application scope are available to all users of the Web application.

All variables belong to one scope or another. If you do not explicitly declare the scope (you do this by adding the scope as a precursor to the variable name, so a form variable would look like this: FORM.myvariable), the default scope, Variables, is used. Two different scopes can contain variables of the same name without a problem. Each variable in a scope is held in a separate area of the computer's memory from variables in other scopes. A variable named Form.username, created by an HTML form, would not conflict with Cookie.username, a variable linked to the browser cookie.

Exploring data types

Variables can hold a variety of types of information. The type of information stored in a variable, which is called its *data type,* determines how ColdFusion MX evaluates the variable. A number of variable types are available in ColdFusion MX, and variables can be generated and represented in a variety of ways. All variable types will fall into one of the following four categories (these categories are explained further in Book VI, Chapter 4):

✦ **Simple:** Simple variables hold a single value. You can read and write a value directly from a simple variable. Numbers, text strings, dates, and Boolean (true/false) values are stored in simple variables.

✦ **Complex:** Complex variables can hold more than one value. ColdFusion arrays and queries are complex variables. Complex variables often hold multiple simple variables. A database query, for example, might hold a list of names and numbers, each of which is a simple value by itself, but when they are combined into a single query, become a complex variable.

✦ **Binary:** The binary data type is used to hold information that is used directly by the computer, such as image files. Binary data is usually unreadable by humans and requires computer processing to become useful.

✦ **Objects:** Objects are variables that contain data, as well as methods to manipulate that data, all wrapped up into a single variable. ColdFusion MX supports several different types of objects, including COM objects, ColdFusion components, JavaBeans, and Web Services.

You don't need to declare a data type for a variable, but as a practice, it's a good idea to do so for more complex variables.

Utilizing expressions

An *expression* is a grouping of variables, constants, operators, and/or function calls that can be evaluated by the ColdFusion MX Application Server to give a single value. Simple expressions can be created with a single variable, but others may involve several function calls. The result of an expression can be assigned to a variable or used to determine what action a CFML page must take.

The following <CFSET> tag assigns the result of the expression score+10 to the variable final_score.

```
<CFSET final_score=score+10>
```

The preceding expression consists of a variable (score) a constant (10) and the addition operator (+). Other expressions might make use of function calls. For example, the following expression between the # signs is used by the <CFOUTPUT> tag to display the formatted date. It consists of two function calls, Now() and DateFormat(), called in succession.

```
<CFOUTPUT>Today is #DateFormat( Now(), "d/m/yy" )#</CFOUTPUT>
```

Chapter 4: Understanding CFML Basics

In This Chapter

✔ **Building a site architecture**

✔ **Utilizing page templates**

✔ **Controlling the display**

✔ **Using databases to generate pages**

✔ **Outputting data**

Y ou may be surprised by the types of complex Web applications that can be built by using basic ColdFusion MX concepts. You can use templates to break each page into smaller segments, which not only helps keep your code manageable, but also allows you to make quick updates to your site. The benefits of your templates can be maximized by storing content in a database. The combination of templates and a database can help you build large, content-rich sites with just a few ColdFusion MX pages.

Setting Up Your Page Architecture

Just as an architect creates blueprints of a building before it is constructed, a ColdFusion MX page can, and should, be planned out before it is built. To a Web designer, *page architecture* deals with how the elements of the page lay out graphically. As the Web developer, you need to consider how the CFML builds the page as well as the aesthetics of the final output.

Understanding template basics

The best way to think of a *template* is as a snippet of code that gets used over and over again for a specific purpose. For example, say a site has several hundred products for sale. The product pages all generally look the same. Only the product content changes. Rather than make several hundred pages, all of which would look the same and contain 99 percent of the same content, you could more easily use one page over and over again to create each product page when that specific product is displayed. When you break up your site into templates, you do the following:

✦ Reduce the overall number of pages you have to manage.

✦ Reduce your maintenance burden because you can make a change to one template and have it affect a large number of viewable pages on the site.

Today, most high-traffic sites, such as www.cnn.com or www.yahoo.com, that have tens of thousands of Web pages are driven by a surprisingly low number of templates.

Determining just how to break a single CFML (ColdFusion Markup Language) page into a series of templates can be more of an art than a science. One of the most common ways to break up a page is shown in Figure 4-1.

The page is broken into four sections, all of which will be different templates:

✦ **Header:** The area that appears at the very top of the page.

✦ **Navigation:** The area that includes links to the other pages in the site, usually found on the left-hand side of the page.

✦ **Content:** The area that includes most of the site content, generally appearing to the right of the navigation area.

✦ **Footer:** The area that appears at the bottom of the page and usually includes links, privacy information, and copyright information.

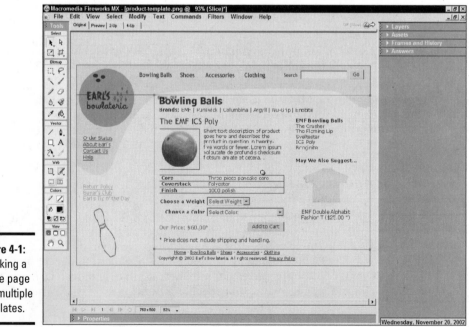

Figure 4-1:
Breaking a single page into multiple templates.

Each section becomes an individual ColdFusion MX file and contains a mix of HTML and CFML. The most important thing to remember is that after the page templates are all put together, they need to equal a properly formatted HTML page, with the correct number of `<HEAD>`, `<BODY>`, `<TABLE>`, `<TR>`, and `<TD>` tags.

It may not seem all that helpful to break one page into four smaller template pages, but the ability to reuse a piece of a page as a template gives you a lot of options. For example, the footer is usually the same on every page of a Web site. This makes it a great candidate to be extracted to a separate template file. After you have isolated the footer text in its own template file, you can include it in as many pages as you'd like. Then, if you ever need to make a change to the footer, you only need to change the footer template file, and the footer will be automatically updated on all the pages that utilize the footer template.

Using <CFINCLUDE>

The easiest way to build a single HTML page from several templates is with the `<CFINCLUDE>` tag. You can use this tag in any ColdFusion MX page. Take a quick look back at Figure 4-1. To create this page, we might have a page called `index.cfm`, and within it, we'd use four `<CFINCLUDE>` tags to compose the page. The tag takes the following form:

```
<CFINCLUDE TEMPLATE="footer.cfm">
```

The `TEMPLATE` attribute specifies the name and location of the footer file on the ColdFusion MX server. The footer file, `footer.cfm` in this example, is also a ColdFusion MX page, and can use all of the ColdFusion MX tags, functions, and variables that are available in the main page (the page with the `<CFINCLUDE>` tag).

The contents of the file `footer.cfm` could look something like this (a standard copyright with a link to a copyright page):

```
<I>Copyright 2003, Earl's Bowlateria.</I>
    <A href="copy_info.cfm">All rights reserved</A>
```

The text of `footer.cfm` is actually quite simple, because it is used to print only a single line on each page. Because this file will be included as part of the larger page, it does not need to be a complete HTML page, so you don't need to include `<HTML>` or `<BODY>` tags, because those are included in the file that originated the request for the template, which is as follows:

```
<HTML>
<BODY>
    <!--- body of HTML page here --->

<CFINCLUDE TEMPLATE="footer.cfm">
</BODY>
</HTML>
```

Building static `include` files can save you time when it comes to building and maintaining a site, but you can do a whole lot more with them! Each template that is included in the main page has access to all the variables, functions, and queries of the main page. This allows you to create a footer that uses CFML to generate dynamic output. For more information on how to use variables and functions, check out Book VI, Chapter 5.

Another common way to use the `<CFINCLUDE>` tag is to isolate database queries, user-defined functions, and other CFML. When a site is controlled by a database, it is very common to have each page use a query (a request to a data source) to retrieve necessary information from the database. (Queries are described in more detail later in this chapter.) Placing queries in included templates has several distinct advantages:

✦ **They're easier to work with during development:** If your queries are all in a common location and have descriptive terms in the filename (`qry_getproducts.cfm` for example), finding the right query to build a page or edit becomes easier.

✦ **They're easier to find for maintenance:** A common development practice is to put your queries in a single location. This makes finding the right query to work on substantially easier.

✦ **They're easier to protect for security:** Again, putting them in a single location, external to your main ColdFusion pages, makes them harder to find for anyone who may try to get access to your databases by stealing your queries.

Using Conditional Processing

Each ColdFusion MX Web application can receive information from a variety of sources:

✦ **User action:** A user clicks somewhere on a site.

✦ **User submitted forms:** A user submits a form from the site.

✦ **Database queries:** Data is retrieved from a database.

✦ **The Web application server:** ColdFusion MX keeps information resident in the server at all times and makes that information available to CFML.

+ **E-mail servers:** Yes, ColdFusion MX can interact with an e-mail server!

+ **COM objects, Java Beans, and Web services:** These advanced services can all pass information to CFML. For more information on these advanced concepts, check out *ColdFusion MX For Dummies*, by John Paul Ashenfelter and Jon Kocen (published by Wiley Publishing, Inc.).

The information received from these sources can be of varying degrees of importance, and sometimes the information is not in a format that the end user can understand. CFML gives you several ways to control the flow of your page, based on the current set of information. Three of the most useful flow control tags are <CFIF>, <CFELSE>, and <CFSWITCH>.

Using <CFIF> and <CFELSE>

The <CFIF> tag is the most common way to control the flow of a page in CFML. The <CFIF> tag is used in CFML in a way that is very similar to how the word "if" is used in English.

The <CFIF> tag is designed to test whether some condition is true or false. This is called a test expression. Any HTML or CFML between the <CFIF> tag and the closing </CFIF> tag is to be evaluated if the test expression is TRUE. Often two values in the test expression are compared to each other, as you can see in the examples later in this section. Other times, the test expression is like those in Table 4-1, which shows some test expressions and their meanings.

Table 4-1	Test Expressions
Expression	*Meaning*
Variables.first_name IS "Earl"	The variable first_name has a value of "Earl".
Form.quantity GT 10	The quantity field of the Web form is greater than 10.
Day(Now()) is 1	The current day of the month is 1.

Book VI, Chapter 5 provides more details on how functions and variables — like those in Table 4-1 — work together.

If the expression is true, the code between the <CFIF> tags is processed, if it is false, the code is skipped. In the following example, if the quantity in the form element is greater than (GT) 10, the line "You qualify for the bulk discount" is displayed on the page:

```
<CFIF Form.quantity GT 10>
You qualify for the bulk discount.
</CFIF>
```

So, what happens if the user inputs a quantity that isn't greater than 10? In this case, nothing will be displayed. Suppose, however, that you want to send a different message if someone chooses fewer than 10 items. In that case, you can use the ⟨CFELSE⟩ tag, which allows you to set the alternative condition to display if the ⟨CFIF⟩ condition isn't true.

Take a look at the following code snippet, which shows how you can construct a ⟨CFELSE⟩ element within your ⟨CFIF⟩ tag (the stuff in between the ⟨!--- and the ---⟩ are code comments to help you understand the flow of the code):

```
<CFIF Form.quantity GT 10>
    <!--- first option --->
    You qualify for the bulk discount.
<CFELSE>
    <!--- second option --->
    If you buy 10 items, you will qualify for the bulk
    discount.
</CFIF>
```

You might think of the ⟨CFIF⟩-⟨CFELSE⟩-⟨/CFIF⟩ combination as, "*If* the test expression is true, do the first option, *else* do the second option." Only one option can happen, the first *or* the second, never both.

Using ⟨CFELSEIF⟩

If you need to test more than one condition, you can use ⟨CFELSE⟩ or ⟨CFELSEIF⟩ to extend the basic ⟨CFIF⟩ tag. Suppose that you have a Web form that asks for the user's age. The form passes the age information to the ColdFusion MX server processing in a variable, which can be tested before printing the proper response. The ⟨CFELSEIF⟩ tag allows you to insert more test expressions into the logic structure:

```
<CFIF Form.age LT 13>
    <!--- first option --->
    You are too young to place an order.
<CFELSEIF Form.age LT 18>
    <!--- second  option --->
    You must have parental permission before ordering.
<CFELSEIF Form.age GT 59>
    <!--- third option --->
    You qualify for the Senior Discount.
<CFELSE>
    <!--- last option --->
    Thank you for your order.
</CFIF>
```

Again, only a single option will be executed. If the user is under 13, the first option will be printed and all of the other tags will be skipped. If the user is not under 13, the next expression is checked. Each expression is checked, in order, until one evaluates to true. Only if none of the expressions are true will the <CFELSE> option be run. It is important to know that when one test is met, the following conditions are not even checked. There is no need.

You don't need to have a <CFELSE> tag, but it is a good idea to include one every time you use a <CFELSEIF> tag. Even if you don't think the <CFELSE> tag will ever be executed, it can be a useful error tracking tool.

<CFSWITCH>

Sometimes you need to be able to handle a lot of different situations in a single page. The <CFSWITCH> tag compares a single test expression to a series of cases that are indicated by <CFCASE> tags and then executes the one that returns TRUE. Suppose that you need to apply special shipping and/or tax rates depending on the state from which an order originates. This is a good candidate for the <CFSWITCH> tag because one variable, #Form.State#, needs to be compared to a bunch of different state abbreviations.

Book VI
Chapter 4

Understanding
CFML Basics

Here's how the code could be represented for a selection of states:

```
<CFSWITCH EXPRESSION="#Form.State#">
    <CFCASE value="CA">
        8% tax for orders within California.
    </CFCASE>

    <CFCASE value="NY">
        6% tax for orders shipped to New York.
    </CFCASE>

    <CFCASE value="AK,HI">
        $10 additional shipping for orders shipped to Alaska
and Hawaii.
    </CFCASE>

    <CFDEFAULTCASE>
        Standard shipping rules apply.
    </CFDEFAULTCASE>
</CFSWITCH>
```

Adding additional cases to the switch tag is as easy, and you can have as many as you want. The <CFDEFAULTCASE> is usually put at the end, and it occurs when none of the other cases are met.

Using SQL Queries

Databases can be a powerful addition to your Web development toolbox. Whether you are storing customer information, Web site content, or document *metadata* (a description of some kind of data), a database gives you a way to store, retrieve, and modify your data. For more information on using databases with ColdFusion MX, check out Book VI, Chapter 6.

Many people are familiar with database concepts, even if they do not know it. The table structure of a spreadsheet is a lot like a table in a database. Each table in a database is given a unique name, and it has columns and rows that hold data. All the columns have the same type of information, and each row holds a set of information about a particular entity. Table 4-2 below shows a sample customer database table. Each row corresponds to a different customer, and each column holds a single kind of data.

Table 4-2	A Simple Customer Database Table		
CustomerID	*Name*	*Address*	*PostalCode*
1	Earl	1 Main St.	94110
2	Andrew	14 Evergreen Terrace	06810
3	Maggie	97 Rosemont Ave.	94110

The CustomerID column is an example of a *unique key*. Each time a record is added to the database, the database automatically assigns a CustomerID to the new record. The new CustomerID will not be the same as any other CustomerID in the database. Having a unique identifier not only keeps your database running at optimal speed, it also helps you manage the data. (If you do not know how to set up a unique key in your database, check with a database administrator, or check your database documentation.)

Exploring SQL concepts

When you ask a database to give you information, it is called a *query*. Database queries use a Structured Query Language (SQL). Through queries, you can read, write, and modify data in your database. Consider the following SQL query:

```
SELECT firstname, lastname FROM Employees
WHERE lastname='Smith'
```

This query has several elements:

* **SQL elements:** These items describe actions, conditions, restrictions, and locations. They include the SELECT, FROM, and WHERE clauses.

* **Columns:** In this case, firstname and lastname are columns within a table. This is the data you're interested in retrieving.

* **Tables:** Here, Employees is a table that includes the columns firstname and lastname.

So, in sum, the query effectively states, "Select the `firstname` and `lastname` from the `Employees` table in the database, where the `lastname` is equal to `Smith`."

Table 4-3 shows some other basic SQL queries and what they do.

Table 4-3	Examples of SQL Statements
Statement	*Description*
`SELECT Name, Address FROM Customers`	Gets the name and address for all customers
`SELECT * FROM Customers WHERE PostalCode = 94110`	Gets all data for customers in the 94110 zip code
`DELETE FROM Customer WHERE CustomerID = 3`	Deletes the customer with a CustomerID equal to 3

**Book VI
Chapter 4**

**Understanding
CFML Basics**

Entire books are dedicated to SQL, and we can only begin to scratch the surface here. Macromedia has put a lot of effort into making SQL easy by adding query editors to Dreamweaver MX, so you can get the most out of your database without getting bogged down in SQL syntax. For the database tools of Dreamweaver MX to function properly, you need to be sure your database is set up properly in the ColdFusion Administrator. (See Book VI, Chapter 2 for more information on the ColdFusion Administrator. In addition, check out Book VI, Chapter 6 for more about using SQL.)

Wondering what that asterisk (*) is in that second SQL statement in Table 4-3? The asterisk (*) is a wildcard in SQL terminology. If you use a * following a `SELECT` statement, it will retrieve data from all the columns in the table you specify in the `FROM` clause.

Pick up a copy of *SQL For Dummies,* 4th Edition, by Allen G. Taylor (published by Wiley Publishing, Inc.) for an easy-to-understand, comprehensive guide to the SQL language.

Using <CFQUERY>

ColdFusion MX has a special tag for running SQL queries, `<CFQUERY>`. The attributes you specify in the `<CFQUERY>` tag tell ColdFusion MX what database to connect to and how to connect to it. The body of the `<CFQUERY>` tag contains the SQL that you want to run. Some of the important attributes of the `<CFQUERY>` tag are listed in Table 4-4. The basic format for CFQUERY is listed here:

```
<CFQUERY name="MyQuery" datasource="SomeDatasource">
INSERT YOUR SQL HERE
</CFQUERY>
```

Table 4-4	Common Attributes of the <CFQUERY> Tag
Attribute	*Description*
name	Required: The name you use to refer to this query in CFML.
datasource	Required: The name used to register the database in the ColdFusion Administrator.
username	Optional: Specifies the username used to log on to the data source.
password	Optional: Specifies the password used to log on to the data source.
maxRows	Optional: Limits the number of rows returned by the query.
timeout	Optional: Gives the time, in seconds, that the ColdFusion MX server should wait for a response from the data source before generating an error.

If all the attributes are set up correctly, and the ColdFusion MX server can connect and communicate with the data source, the <CFQUERY> tag will provide you with a set of data from the data source. All of this data will be available to you to use in your pages in the form of variables. Check out Book VI, Chapter 5 for more information on using variables from queries.

Using SQL commands

SQL provides you with a powerful way to get information out of a database. SQL is the predominant language for Web development, and while a complete primer on it is beyond the scope of this book, we want to give you an introduction to some of the critical SQL statements that will enable you to get data from a database.

Creating queries with SELECT

The SELECT keyword is used to retrieve rows of data from a database, and it is always the first word in a SELECT statement. Following the SELECT keyword is the list of columns you want to retrieve data from. If you want data from all of the columns in a table, use an asterisk (*) instead of specific column names. The last required element of a SELECT statement is the name of the table FROM which the data is being retrieved.

Each of the following examples selects a different set of columns from each row of the Customers table:

✦ SELECT Name FROM Customers

✦ SELECT CustomerID, Name FROM Customers

✦ SELECT * FROM Customers

What if you don't want data from every row? The `WHERE` clause is used to filter rows from a query. The following examples use the `WHERE` clause to restrict the rows being returned:

✦ `SELECT Name FROM Customers WHERE CustomerID = 2`

✦ `SELECT CustomerID, Name FROM Customers WHERE PostalCode > 94000`

With the aid of the `WHERE` clause, you can build queries that retrieve only the information you need to build your page. While looping through the query or outputting directly to the screen, each column can be accessed as a variable using pound signs, such as `#name#` or `#CustomerID#`. The use of pound signs to output a variable is described in more detail in Book VI, Chapter 5.

If you find that you are using `<CFIF>` to filter the data generated by `<CFQUERY>`, consider modifying the SQL to do the filtering for you. The database will probably be able to process the filter faster, plus you won't need to transfer useless information between servers.

Creating queries with DELETE

The `DELETE` keyword is extremely powerful, as it can remove all the data from a table in one fell swoop. To delete all the rows from a table, simply issue the following query, where *tablename* is the name of the table:

`DELETE tablename`

While the above statement will work in Microsoft SQL Server 2000 and MySQL, it won't work in Microsoft Access. This is because Access doesn't support all SQL syntax. It uses a limited version of SQL called Jet SQL. For information on which SQL keywords are supported, check out the Microsoft Access Help files.

More commonly, you'll only want to delete a limited number of rows, or maybe only one row. You can filter the `DELETE` command by using the `WHERE` clause, as described in the previous section, "Creating queries with SELECT." The following examples use this technique:

✦ `DELETE Customers WHERE CustomerID = 2`

✦ `DELETE Customers WHERE PostalCode = 94110`

Your `DELETE` commands should always have a `WHERE` clause — this will keep you from accidentally deleting important data. Because it is so easy to delete data by mistake, some developers recommend never deleting data at all. By adding a status column, you can mark each record as "active" or "inactive," and then do periodic maintenance to remove inactive records by hand.

Creating queries with INSERT

Inserting data into a table is probably the toughest of the basic database operations. The elements of the command are similar to the SELECT statement. After the INSERT keyword, you give the table name followed by a list of columns in parentheses. However, unlike a SELECT command, where the database sends you data, now you need to send the data to the database. The information for the new row is placed at the end of the insert statement with the VALUES keyword, as in the following example:

```
INSERT INTO Customers( Name, Address, PostalCode ) VALUES
    ("Chris", "44 South St.", 06810 )
```

The order of the data after the VALUE keyword must match the order of the columns listed before the VALUE keyword.

If you have a column that is automatically generated, such as an ID column, you do not need to specify a value for that column.

Creating queries with UPDATE

Another powerful action is UPDATE. Without a WHERE clause, the UPDATE command updates every row in the data table, which is not usually what you want. The syntax of the UPDATE command starts off with the UPDATE keyword and the name of the data table, just like the INSERT command. However, rather than listing the columns and values separately, the value of each column is SET individually, as in the following example:

```
UPDATE Customers SET name='Margaret' WHERE CustomerID = 3
```

When the UPDATE command is running, the filter is applied first, and then the rows are modified. This means that you can modify a column that was used in the WHERE clause without affecting the results. The following SQL works just fine, and changes the customers name from "Maggie" to "Margaret."

```
UPDATE Customers SET Name='Margaret' WHERE Name = 'Maggie'
```

Outputting Content to the Screen

As you build a page in ColdFusion MX, you have data from Web forms, database queries, and other sources stored in variables. Some of these variables may hold data that you want to display to your users. The <CFOUTPUT> tag gives you the ability to put data from variables into HTML. The <CFOUTPUT> tag can print a single value, or it can be used to loop through the data in a query, displaying multiple rows of data with just one tag.

Using <CFOUTPUT>

Each <CFOUTPUT> tag must have a closing </CFOUTPUT> tag. Between the tags, you can place HTML or CFML. When you place a variable name in between pound signs (#), <CFOUTPUT> displays the value of the variable, not the variable name.

```
<CFSET animal="badger">
<CFOUTPUT>
My <I>favorite</I> animal is the <B>#animal#.</B>
</CFOUTPUT>
```

This CFML snippet would print the text: "My *favorite* animal is the **badger.**"

Exactly how you set up the tag is a matter of style. The following example prints the exact same text, but most developers find the nested tags to be less clear:

```
<CFSET animal="badger">
My <I>favorite</I> animal is the
    <B><CFOUTPUT>#animal#.</CFOUTPUT></B>
```

Looping

The <CFOUTPUT> tag can do a lot more than just print a single variable. When you specify a query in <CFOUTPUT>, the text between the opening and closing tags is repeated for each row of the query, as in the following example:

```
<CFQUERY name="CustomerData" datasource="CustomerDB">
SELECT * FROM Customers
<CFQUERY>
<CFOUTPUT query="CustomerData">
Customer #CustomerID# is named #name#.<BR>
</CFOUTPUT>
```

The columns from the query are available inside the <CFOUTPUT>, just like ordinary variables. However, every time the <CFOUTPUT> tag loops, a new row of data is used, so the values of each column change. If the query returned three rows of data, the <CFOUTPUT> tag would loop three times and print three lines of text.

Chapter 5: Variables, Functions, and Structured Data

In This Chapter

✔ **Working with variables and parameters**

✔ **Using CFML functions**

✔ **Casting data into arrays, lists, and structures**

After you've gotten your feet wet with the basics of ColdFusion MX, it won't be long before you're itching to add even more functionality to your site. This chapter is designed to give you an introduction to some of the more advanced concepts in ColdFusion MX. In reality, working with variables, parameters, and data structures (collections of data in various forms) are concepts that are common to any technology platform. This just happens to be Macromedia's implementation, and as you'll soon find out, the folks at Macromedia tried to make it as easy as possible to pick up.

Working with Variables and Parameters

If you've ever logged on to a Web site by entering a username and password, then you've probably seen a URL that looked something like this:

```
http://www.somesite.com/index.cfm?userID=123456
```

In that URL string, the `userID` is called the variable and `123456` is the value for that variable. Put simply, a *variable* is a value that can change, depending upon differing conditions within your site. In ColdFusion MX, a *parameter* can represent one of many different data types that are supported in the product, such as variables, queries, arrays, and even dates.

More often than not, variables are used by developers to change the way a Web page looks or responds to a user's input. In ColdFusion MX, variables can come from a variety of sources and appear in a variety of different formats. Variables can be created in ColdFusion MX in four different ways:

✦ By using `<CFSET>` or `<CFPARAM>` tags

✦ As a result of a database query using a `<CFQUERY>` tag

✦ Automatically by ColdFusion MX

✦ From within a `<CFSCRIPT>` tag

CFScript is scripting language that is similar to JavaScript and is available to developers from within CFML. Getting into detail about CFScript is beyond the scope of this book, but to learn more about it, check out *ColdFusion MX For Dummies,* by John Paul Ashenfelter and Jon Kocen (published by Wiley Publishing, Inc.).

The best reason to use variables in your site is that they expand your ability to deliver the right content for the right situation dynamically. In this section, we show you how you can begin to use variables to enhance the user experience on your site. For a review of variable type and scope, refer to Book VI, Chapter 3.

In addition to this tutorial and reference, you can also refer to the Using ColdFusion MX Help files, accessible from within Dreamweaver MX by pressing Ctrl+F1. The Help files are an exceptionally good reference tool to understanding both the type and scope of variables.

Creating variables with <CFSET>

The most common way to create a variable in ColdFusion MX is by using a `<CFSET>` tag. With `<CFSET>`, you create the name of the variable, as well as the value (called an expression). The syntax for the `<CFSET>` tag is as follows:

```
<CFSET VariableName = "expression">
```

The following example shows you how you can use `<CFSET>` with the sample ColdFusion MX databases that come with Macromedia Studio MX to retrieve some information about an employee:

1. **In Dreamweaver MX, verify that you have a connection to the CompanyInfo database by opening the Application panel and selecting the Databases tab.**

   You should see the three default databases, as shown in Figure 5-1. If you can't see them, then you need to configure your database connections. For instructions on how to do this, check out Book VI, Chapter 2.

2. **Create a new ColdFusion MX file by choosing File⇨New and selecting Dynamic Page and ColdFusion from the Category and Dynamic Page columns, respectively.**

3. **Create a variable called EmployeeNumber and give it a value of 1.**

Figure 5-1:
You should
see three
active
databases.

Constants are the simplest form of variables because there's no real
varying in them. In the Code view, your code should look as follows:

```
<CFSET EmployeeNumber = "1">
```

There are a number of rules for the naming of variables. The two most
important rules are that variables must start with a letter, and that they
cannot contain spaces. For a complete set of variable naming rules, check
out Using ColdFusion in Dreamweaver MX by choosing Help⇨Using
ColdFusion, and then choosing Developing ColdFusion Applications⇨
Using ColdFusion Variables⇨Creating Variables⇨Variable Naming Rules.

4. **Expand the CompanyInfo database until you see the Employee table.**

You can expand the database to the table level by clicking the plus box
(+) next to the database and then the tables.

If you want to see the data in the Employee table, right-click the table
name and choose View Data from the contextual menu.

5. **Create a query in the Code view to the CompanyInfo database to get
all information from the Employee table where EmployeeNumber =
emp_ID.**

Your query should look like this:

```
<CFQUERY datasource="CompanyInfo" name="GetEmployees">
SELECT * FROM employee
WHERE emp_ID=#EmployeeNumber#
</CFQUERY>
```

You'll notice something interesting is happening here. Within the query, we've included the `EmployeeNumber` variable. Because ColdFusion MX reads code from the top of the page to the bottom, the server first reads that there's a variable called `EmployeeName` and it has a value of 1. Then, when it reads this query, it swaps out `#EmployeeNumber#` with the value (1) that was previously set for the variable.

6. **Output the data to the screen using a `<CFOUTPUT>` tag.**

   If you want to see what the query returns, you need to include a `<CFOUTPUT>` tag, as follows:

```
<CFOUTPUT query="GetEmployees">#firstname#
        #lastname#<BR>#startdate#<BR>#salary#</CFOUTPUT>
```

7. **Press F12 to preview the page.**

   You should get a look at the personnel information of one Ben Frueh, as shown in Figure 5-2.

Figure 5-2:
Ben Frueh,
Employee
Number = 1.

Testing the existence of variables with <CFPARAM>

The `<CFPARAM>` tag is an interesting ColdFusion MX tag because it checks for the existence and type of a local variable on a page. Depending upon whether that variable exists and what type of variable it is, ColdFusion MX either creates a new variable, gives it a default value, or generates an error. The `<CFPARAM>` tag has three elements:

✦ `name`: The name of the variable

✦ `type`: The data type of the variable, such as a number, string, array, query, and so on

✦ `default`: The default value for a variable

The structure for the tag is as follows:

```
<CFPARAM name="SomeName" type="DataType" default="Value">
```

The only value that's required for the `<CFPARAM>` tag is `name`. If you use only the name, the tag tests for the existence of a variable with that name. If it does not exist, ColdFusion MX returns an error message, as shown in Figure 5-3, and stops processing. If you include `type` with the name in the tag, then ColdFusion MX requires both the name and the corresponding data type for the variable to exist, or it generates an error. Finally, you can choose to include just the `name` and the `default` values. In this case, if no variable exists when the page is processed, ColdFusion MX creates the variable with the default value.

Figure 5-3:
This
variable
does not
exist.

Suppose that you've got a product page on your corporate site. On this product page, you want to be able to show products specific to your various target audiences: consumers, educators, and the government. To accomplish this, you include a form on the product page that asks users to select whether they want to view education or government products.

Because a user won't be choosing a product type until they reach the product page, you can use `<CFPARAM>` to evaluate whether or not a variable exists to show specific product information based on a form input. Here's a simple way to do it:

1. **In Dreamweaver MX, create a new page called** `param.cfm` **and save it locally or on a remote testing server (wherever you have the ColdFusion MX server running).**

2. **Create a** `<CFPARAM>` **called** `type` **and give it an empty default value, as follows:**

```
<CFPARAM name="type" default="">
```

While it's not required, it's always a good idea to scope your variables. That way, you're less likely to run into any errors as ColdFusion MX looks for the right scope for the variable you're testing. Scoping is also covered in more detail in Book VI, Chapter 3. So in the previous example, if you scoped the variable, it would look as follows:

```
<CFPARAM name="FORM.type" default="">
```

Adding this tag first is critical, because farther down the page, you need to look for the variable `type`. This tag ensures that the variable exists, whether or not someone has selected a product type from the drop-down list.

When this exercise is complete, try removing this line to see what happens when the variable isn't defined. ColdFusion MX will generate an error and tell you that the variable isn't defined when you first load the page.

3. **Create a drop-down list that allows a user to select a product type.**

Here's a simple version of what that form element looks like:

```
<FORM action="param.cfm" method="post">
<SELECT name="type">
  <OPTION value="">Select One</OPTION>
  <OPTION value="consumer">Consumer</OPTION>
  <OPTION value="education">Education</OPTION>
  <OPTION value="government">Government</OPTION>
</SELECT>
<INPUT type="submit" value="Go">
</FORM>
```

4. **Evaluate whether the variable type exists and show the product information based on the variable value.**

The most straightforward way to do this is to use `<CFIF>` and `<CFELSEIF>`, as shown here:

```
<CFIF type is "consumer">
<UL>
<LI>Consumer Product One</LI>
<LI>Consumer Product Two</LI>
</UL>
<CFELSEIF type is "education">
<UL>
<LI>Education Product One</LI>
```

```
<LI>Education Product Two</LI>
</UL>
<CFELSEIF type is "government">
<UL>
<LI>Government Product One</LI>
<LI>Government Product Two</LI>
</UL>
</CFIF>
```

Refer to Book VI, Chapter 4 on the variety of ways you can use `<CFIF>` and `<CFELSEIF>` to evaluate conditional statements.

You can also use `<CFSWITCH>` and `<CFCASE>` for this very same example. Indeed, as your applications become more complex, you'll want to use `<CFSWITCH>` and `<CFCASE>`, because they process faster, even if `<CFIF>` and `<CFELSE>` are easier concepts to understand. `<CFSWITCH>` is covered in Book VI, Chapter 4.

Book VI
Chapter 5

Variables,
Functions, and
Structured Data

Getting access to variables through `<CFQUERY>`

Consider the query that we used in the variable example in the section, "Creating variables with <CFSET>":

```
<CFQUERY datasource="CompanyInfo" name="GetEmployees">
SELECT * FROM employee
WHERE emp_ID=#EmployeeNumber#
</CFQUERY>
```

This query returns information from all the columns in the employee table, namely:

- ✦ FirstName
- ✦ LastName
- ✦ Dept_ID
- ✦ StartDate
- ✦ Salary
- ✦ Contract
- ✦ emp_ID

Each of these columns becomes a variable that can be output to the screen using a `<CFOUTPUT>` tag. To use them, surround the column name with pound signs (#). So, for example, to output FirstName, you would use #FirstName#.

Using variables generated by ColdFusion MX

ColdFusion MX generates a variety of variables that you can use in your applications. These variables work just like variables that you create, and they're called in a similar fashion. For example, if you want to show the operating system of the server that ColdFusion MX is running on, you can use the following resident variable:

```
<CFOUTPUT>#Server.OS.Name#</CFOUTPUT>
```

For a complete listing of these resident variables that ColdFusion MX generates, check out the CFML reference guide in Using ColdFusion, accessible by pressing Ctrl+F1 within Dreamweaver MX.

Using CFML Functions

Hundreds of different functions are available to ColdFusion MX developers, and they do everything from creating a date to generating random numbers. Although there are numerous ColdFusion MX functions, they nearly all do one of the following four things:

✦ Create new data and data structures

✦ Evaluate some type of data to determine its existence or format

✦ Evaluate some type of data to produce some new type of data

✦ Change the composition of some type of data

To give you some idea of the breadth of functions that are available, Macromedia puts them into 17 different categories, with many functions being represented in more than one category. We list all these categories in Table 5-1, as well as provide a brief description of the kinds of functions found in each group.

Table 5-1	Categories of Functions in ColdFusion MX
Function Category	*What They're For*
Array functions	Creating, evaluating, and manipulating arrays.
Authentication functions	Authenticating a user. This feature is new to MX.
Conversion functions	Converting array, list, XML, and URL information into other formats.
Date and time functions	Creating and formatting dates and times.
Decision functions	Checking whether various objects are defined or meet various criteria.

Function Category	What They're For
Display and formatting functions	Allowing you to style different kinds of data, such as currency, decimal formats, and number formats.
Dynamic evaluation functions	Evaluating different kinds of dynamic data, such as Boolean searches or string expressions.
Extensibility functions	Extending the functionality of ColdFusion MX to other data types, such as a XML.
Full-text search functions	Functions that are used in conjunction with ColdFusion MX's built-in searching tools.
International functions	Setting, converting, and evaluating currency, time, and location for other countries.
List functions	Testing length, sorting, converting to arrays, and appending lists.
Mathematical functions	Performing advanced calculations on data.
Query functions	Manipulating and evaluating ColdFusion MX queries.
String functions	A host of functions that either contain or somehow manipulate string data.
Structure functions	Creating, manipulating, and evaluating ColdFusion MX structures.
System functions	Interacting with or getting information from the server.
XML functions	Reading and transformation of XML documents.

Functions can be called in a few different ways:

✦ **As part of a CFML tag:** An example of this kind of function is `IsDefined`, which checks to see if a variable is defined. The `IsDefined` function looks like this:

```
<CFIF IsDefined("SomeVariable")>
```

✦ **As part of defining a variable:** An example of this kind of function is `arrayNew(n)`, which creates an *array* (a collection of data) in *n* dimensions. The `arrayNew` function is called from within a `<CFSET>` tag, as follows:

```
<CFSET MyArray = arrayNew(1)>
```

✦ **When outputting a variable:** An example of this kind of function is `DateFormat`, which enables you to change the way the date looks. `DateFormat` can be called as follows, where date is a variable that represents a date:

```
#DateFormat(date, "mm-dd-yyyy")#
```

✦ **From within another function:** It's not uncommon that functions support calling other functions to provide some value. Take the following example:

```
<CFSET discountprice = DollarFormat(Evaluate(price -
     (price * discount))) >
```

In this case, we are setting a variable discountprice, using the DollarFormat function and within that function, using the Evaluate function to perform some basic arithmetic functions.

Going through each of the ColdFusion MX functions is beyond the scope of this book, but the following sections show you how to get started with the five most useful ColdFusion MX functions for beginners.

Using the arrayNew function

The arrayNew function, as you might expect from the name, creates a new array. Arrays, which are collections of data, are a great way to capture information and then redisplay it or manipulate it before committing it to a database.

The syntax for arrayNew is as follows:

```
<CFSET AnArray = arrayNew(n)>
```

Using <CFSET> is the most common way to create an array. AnArray is the variable that represents the elements of the array. arrayNew creates the array and (n) represents the number of dimensions (*dimensions* specify the structure of the data) of the array. ColdFusion MX supports up to three dimensional arrays. Figure 5-4 shows a graphical representation of an array in ColdFusion MX.

Figure 5-4: The arrayNew function creates an array for you.

Building arrays is covered in more detail in the section, "Casting Data into Arrays, Lists, and Structures," later in this chapter.

Using the isDefined function

The isDefined function is one of the most popular ColdFusion MX functions because it works so nicely in conditional statements, especially the <CFIF> tag. The syntax for the function looks like this:

```
<CFIF isDefined("someVariable")>
```

This function returns a value of TRUE and FALSE, depending upon whether the variable is defined when the page is being processed. In the example code above, if the value returned is TRUE, then whatever immediately follows that <CFIF> will be executed. If it returns a FALSE value, then the code immediately following the <CFIF> will be not be executed.

TIP

It's quite common to use this function for validating and processing forms. After the user submits the form, you can use isDefined to ensure that all required fields have been filled out. Alternatively, isDefined can be used to instigate some action — updating a database, for example — if a value exists for the form field submitted.

Using the len function

Developers love to use the len (length) function. len is an incredibly simple function, in that all it does is return the length of a string. Much like isDefined, this function becomes exceptionally valuable when doing error handling and processing because if you're looking for a variable that should be of at least some length and len returns a value of zero, you immediately know that the user hasn't filled in the field or made a selection from a menu. Used as part of a <CFIF> statement, the syntax for len is as follows:

```
<CFIF len(string) is not 0>
```

Using the DateFormat function

Everybody likes to use dates in their Web sites, and you can format a date a number of different ways. The DateFormat function in ColdFusion MX allows you to take a date and format it in a variety of ways. To output today's date in mm-dd-yyyy format, you'd use the following:

```
<CFOUTPUT>#dateformat(Now(), "mm-dd-yyyy")#</CFOUTPUT>
```

Incidentally, Now() is a related function that provides you with the server's current date and time. You can format the date in a number of different ways using month, date, and year. Here are the basics:

✦ d: Day of the month, but single digit days aren't preceded by a zero (1, 2, and 13, for example).

✦ dd: Day of the month, and single digit days are preceded by a zero (01, 06, and 23, for example).

✦ ddd: A three-letter abbreviation for day of the week (such as Mon, Tue, and Wed).

✦ dddd: The full name of the day of the week.

✦ m: Month as a single digit, but single digit months aren't preceded by a zero (such as 1, 6, and 11).

✦ mm: Month as two digits, and single digit months are preceded by a zero (01, 04, and 10, for example).

✦ mmm: The month as a three-letter abbreviation (such as Jan, Mar, and Oct).

✦ mmmm: The full name of the month.

✦ y: The year as last two digits, but only one digit for years ending lower than 10 (1, 5, and 23, for example).

✦ yy: The year as last two digits (such as 01, 08, and 98).

✦ yyyy: The year represented by four digits (1998, 2002, and 2014, for example).

Some similar functions to DateFormat are worth checking out in the CFML Reference, which you can get to by pressing Ctrl+F1. They include TimeFormat, CreateDate, Now, and NumberFormat.

Using the Trim function

Trim is another exceptionally simple, but often used and valuable function. Trim removes any leading spaces from either side of data in a string. This is most useful, for example, when processing searches from text form fields, because you can strip out the spaces in a text field entry like "new homes" to create a search string that could look like "newhomes." Here's how the function looks when used to set a variable that comes from a form:

```
<CFSET HomeSearch = trim(form.HomeType)>
```

In the preceding example, the HomeType form input will have any leading or trailing spaces removed, and the resulting input will be assigned to the variable HomeSearch.

Casting Data into Arrays, Lists, and Structures

In the course of building a dynamic Web site, you will often times find yourself looking for different ways to use *structured datasets* — collections of data that fit a predefined structure. These datasets can be used for a variety of activities, such as populating form elements, creating name/value pairs for things like link-text navigation, or even creating altogether new data structures. To help facilitate the use of structured datasets, ColdFusion MX has three different kinds of tools available to developers:

✦ **Lists:** Lists are simple collections of a number of items.

✦ **Arrays:** Arrays are sets of structured data that can be like a structured list, like a spreadsheet (with rows and columns), or an even more complex configuration.

✦ **Structures:** Structures are collections of related data that are put together in a virtual container of sorts to make them easier to use.

This section covers when and how you can add each of these different elements to your dynamic Web site.

All these data structures support the use of queries to populate them. For more information on how to query a database, check out Book VI, Chapter 3.

Creating lists

Lists allow you to take single sets of structured data and output them to a Web page. You can create a list in ColdFusion MX in two ways:

✦ Using a `<CFLOOP>` tag

✦ Using the `ListAppend` function

Creating a list with `<CFLOOP>` is the more common method, but we cover both techniques.

Using <CFLOOP> to create a list

To create a simple list using `<CFLOOP>`, just follow these steps:

1. **Create a `<CFLOOP>` tag in Code view of your ColdFusion MX document.**

The tag should look like this: `<CFLOOP></CFLOOP>`.

2. **Within the `<CFLOOP>` tag, create a variable using the index parameter.**

Call this variable `MyList`, which would make the open tag look like `<CFLOOP index="MyList">`.

3. Create your list.

The list has to be a separated group of values. You use the list parameter to specify the list. The default item delimiter is a comma. Creating a list of some of the authors of this book would look like this:

```
<CFLOOP index="ListElement" list="Damon Dean,Andy
    Cowitt,Scott Zucca">
```

The default delimiter is a comma, but you can use the delimiters parameter to specify different delimiters, such as the colon. To create the same list as in Step 3 with a colon (:) as a delimiter, just use this code:

```
<CFLOOP index="ListElement" delimiters=":" list="Damon
    Dean:Andy Cowitt:Scott Zucca">
```

4. To view the list, add a `<CFOUTPUT>` **tag within the** `<CFLOOP>` **tags and call the variable.**

Figure 5-5 shows the resulting output, and here's the code:

```
<CFLOOP index="MyList" list="Damon Dean, Andy Cowitt,
    Scott Zucca">
<CFOUTPUT>#MyList#<BR></CFOUTPUT></CFLOOP>
```

Figure 5-5:
Three of the
authors of
this book!

Damon Dean
Andy Cowitt
Scott Zucca

You can also use the results of a query to populate a list using `<CFLOOP>`. Consider the following query of the sample CompanyInfo database:

```
<CFQUERY datasource="CompanyInfo" name="GetEmployees">
SELECT firstname FROM employee</CFQUERY>
```

Now, if your `<CFLOOP>` tag looks as follows, you can generate a list of the first names of all the company's employees as a loop:

```
<CFLOOP query="GetEmployees">
<CFOUTPUT>#firstname#<BR></CFOUTPUT>
</CFLOOP>
```

Using ListAppend to create a list

Creating a list with the `ListAppend` function is a more advanced and dynamic way of creating a list. This quick example shows you how to do it:

1. **Create a variable using `<CFSET>` and give it the first value of your list.**

You can use the same variables and lists from the previous example:

```
<CFSET MyList = "Damon Dean">
```

2. **Append the list by using `ListAppend` and `<CFSET>`.**

`ListAppend` asks you to specify the list, and then add the new value. So the code would look as follows:

```
<CFSET MyList = ListAppend(Mylist, "Andy Cowitt")
```

3. **To output the new list, create an output tag and call the new `MyList` variable.**

Your code should look similar to this:

```
<CFOUTPUT>#Mylist#</CFOUPUT>
```

4. **Press F12 in Dreamweaver MX to preview your work.**

Creating arrays

Arrays are, very simply, structured datasets. These datasets can exist in *n* number of dimensions. A one dimensional array looks surprisingly similar to a list. A two dimensional array is akin to a spreadsheet. A three dimensional array is, well, complicated, but if you can imagine data with height, width and depth, then you'd pretty much have the concept. While they're possible, don't even ask about four dimensional arrays, in part because they're really tough to conceptualize, and because ColdFusion MX only supports up to three dimensional arrays.

Creating an array

Creating basic arrays is a fairly straightforward proposition. If you want to create an array with some of the jobs related to the creation of this book, here's how you could do it:

1. **Use the `ArrayNew` function to create an array and give it a dimension.**

To keep things simple, use a one dimensional array, so the code looks like this.

```
<CFSET BookJobs= ArrayNew(1)>
```

2. **Add items to the array using** <CFSET>.

   When adding items to the new array, you use <CFSET> to first specify the array and then integers enclosed in brackets to specify to which element in the array you're going to be assigning a value.

   If the value is a string, you also need to make sure that the array value is enclosed in quotes. If it's another variable, the quotes aren't needed. For this example, you are using strings, so the code looks like this:

   ```
   <CFSET BookJobs[1] = "Writer">
   ```

3. **Fill out the remaining items in your array.**

   Add a few more jobs to complete the array. Here's the remainder of the list:

   ```
   <CFSET BookJobs[2] = "Editor">
   <CFSET BookJobs[3] = "Production Manager">
   <CFSET BookJobs[4] = "Copywriter">
   <CFSET BookJobs[5] = "Illustrator">
   ```

4. **Add a** <CFDUMP> **tag to the bottom of the array and output the array to the screen by pressing F12.**

   The <CFDUMP> tag outputs variables to the screen. It's exceptionally handy for debugging your code. When you add the <CFDUMP> tag, you need to specify the variable you want to dump. So in this case, the code would look as follows:

   ```
   <CFDUMP var="#BookJobs#">
   ```

5. **Press F12, and you should get a screen that looks a lot like Figure 5-6.**

Figure 5-6:
Hooray for
your first
array!

array	
1	Writer
2	Editor
3	Production Manager
4	Copywriter
5	Illustrator

If you want to see an individual item in an array, such as the Copywriter position, you would use the following syntax:

```
<CFOUTPUT>I was the #BookJobs[4]# for Macromedia Studio MX
    All-in-One Desk Reference For Dummies</CFOUTPUT>
```

Using an array

Now that you've created an array, you can do something more with it than just dump it to the screen. A common use for one dimensional arrays is to populate lists in form elements. In the following example, you create a drop-down list using the elements from an array:

1. **Create a new file entitled** `inc_array.cfm` **and include the array information from the previous example in it.**

   Figure 5-7 shows what the code and filename should look like on your screen in Dreamweaver MX. We put this in a separate file so that it can be made available to other forms on the site that might need the same list, and so that, if we ever need to update that array, we would only need to do it in one location.

2. **In a new document, create an include tag to include the array.**

   A CFML tag for this very purpose is called `<CFINCLUDE>`. With the `<CFINCLUDE>` tag, you specify a file that will have its contents swapped in for the tag when the page is processed by the ColdFusion MX server. Here's what it looks like:

   ```
   <CFINCLUDE template="inc_array.cfm">
   ```

Figure 5-7:
Your
inc_array
file.

3. **Convert the array to a list.**

   At present, the array is still just a single comma-separated collection of information. Before it can be output to the screen, it needs to be broken down into its individual elements. To do this, use a function called `ArraytoList`. With `ArraytoList`, you can specify an array and a delimiter (optional), and the function creates a new variable as a list. Here's the code:

   ```
   <CFSET JobsList = ArraytoList (BookJobs, ",")>
   ```

4. **Create a form element.**

   Now that you've got the list settled, you can go about creating the form. Here's some basic code that creates a form element. For the time being, leave all the `<OPTION>` tags out:

   ```
   <FORM action="param.cfm" method="post">
   <SELECT name="job">
   </SELECT>
   <INPUT type="submit" value="Go">
   </FORM>
   ```

5. **Within the `<SELECT>` tags, create a `<CFLOOP>` that takes the list and uses the values in option tags for the drop-down list.**

   Here is the resulting code first, followed by an explanation:

   ```
   <CFLOOP index="FormOptions" list="#JobsList#">
       <OPTION value="#FormOptions#" >#FormOptions#
       </OPTION></CFLOOP>
   ```

   To make this work is a tad bit tricky. First you need to create a `<CFLOOP>` and give the `index` a name. In this case, call it `FormOptions`. Then, you call the new `#JobsList#` variable using a `<CFOUTPUT>` tag to get the list elements. Finally, you create a single option tag and use the `#FormOptions#` index value to output the values and names for each drop-down list.

6. **To preview your page, press F12.**

   Figure 5-8 shows the resulting output.

Figure 5-8: Congratulations, you've used your first array!

Working with a two dimensional array

Two dimensional arrays give you even more options for adding complex datasets to your site without necessarily using a database. To show you what we mean, we walk you through how to create a dynamically generated text navigation by using a two dimensional array.

First, take a look at this array:

```
<CFSET MyTwoDArray = ArrayNew(2)>
<CFSET MyTwoDArray[1][1] = "Home">
<CFSET MyTwoDArray[1][2] = "index.cfm">
<CFSET MyTwoDArray[2][1] = "Products">
<CFSET MyTwoDArray[2][2] = "products.cfm">
<CFSET MyTwoDArray[3][1] = "About Us">
<CFSET MyTwoDArray[3][2] = "about.cfm">
```

A couple of things jump out immediately as being different from the previous arrays in this chapter:

✦ We designated this array as a two dimensional array by adding a 2 in the parentheses following the `ArrayNew` function.

✦ Two sets of numbers are in brackets next to the variable when you're setting the values. Because this is a two dimensional array, two number pairs specify which row things are in (the first number), and which column they're in (the second number). In this case, we've made all the row to column combinations equal, but they don't need to be that way.

After you have created this two dimensional array, you can turn it into a navigation bar. And here's some good news. It's actually easy to do! Just follow these steps:

1. **Make sure that you've included the previous array in your document.**

2. **Create a `<CFLOOP>` tag with an `index` of `count` that starts at one and goes to three, and be sure that the `<CFLOOP>` is enclosed within a `<CFOUTPUT>` tag.**

   The code would look like this:

   ```
   <CFOUTPUT>
   <CFLOOP index="count" from="1" to="3"></CFLOOP>
   </CFOUTPUT>
   ```

3. **Within the `<CFLOOP>` tags, create a link that references the array files within the `href` and the array names within the link.**

In this step, you're adding the code that will output both the name of the link and the corresponding linked file as the loop is being processed. To accomplish this, use the `index="count"` to pull the appropriate name or page by checking the stage of the loop. Note that all the names are in the 1 column and all the files are in the 2 column. Here's the code you would need to do it:

```
<A href="#MyTwoDArray[count][2]#">#MyTwoDArray[count][1]#</A><BR>
```

4. **Press the F12 key to preview your new page.**

   And voilà! You should have three links, as shown in Figure 5-9.

Using structures

Structures are an interesting alternative to arrays because they can contain any number of different kinds of data. Structures contain discreet elements, but they are accessed through names given to the structure. Structures are both powerful containers for data and easier to think about than arrays. Here's a simple example that shows how you can create a structure for employee information:

1. **Create the structure with a `<CFSET>` tag.**

   Like an array, there's a ColdFusion MX function, called `structnew`, that you use to cast a variable as a structure. The following code creates a new structure for employees:

   ```
   <CFSET employee= structnew()>
   ```

2. **Add some data to the structure.**

   For this employee structure, add first name, last name, e-mail address, department, and salary, which requires the following code:

   ```
   <CFSET employee.firstname = "Bob">
   <CFSET employee.lastname = "Smith">
   <CFSET employee.email = "bobsmith@somecompany.com">
   <CFSET employee.department = "IT">
   <CFSET employee.salary= "100000">
   ```

   In a structure, the word to the right of the dot (`firstname` in `employee.firstname`, for example) is called a *key,* and the combination of this key and it's corresponding value is called a key/value pair. New structure items are added to the employee variable, separated by a dot (the same basic syntax that you'd see with form variables, such as `#FORM.first-name#`).

3. **To call the values in a structure, use a `<CFOUTPUT>` tag and specify the value using its key.**

   To output this information to the screen, you can use the following code:

   ```
   <CFOUTPUT>
   Name: #employee.firstname# #employee.lastname# <BR>
   Email: #employee.email# <BR>
   Department: #employee.department# <BR>
   Salary: #employee.salary# <BR>
   </CFOUTPUT>
   ```

4. **Press F12 to preview the page.**

   As shown in Figure 5-10, you should see the information about an employee, Mr. Bob Smith.

Figure 5-10: All about Mr. Smith.

```
Name: Bob Smith
Email: bobsmith@somecompany.com
Department: IT
Salary: 100000
```

You can also cast data from a query into a structure. Imagine that a user logged on to your corporate intranet. After the user was authenticated, the intranet might make a query like the one we used earlier in this chapter:

```
<CFQUERY datasource="CompanyInfo" name="GetEmployeeInfo">
SELECT * FROM employee
WHERE emp_ID=#EmployeeNumber#
</CFQUERY>
```

This would make all the data from the query available as variables that can be copied into a structure.

So, as you can see, structures offer a tremendous amount of flexibility to the developer. There are also a number of functions that can allow you to manipulate the data in a structure. Table 5-2 includes some of these other structure-related functions and what they do.

Table 5-2	Common Structure Functions
Function	*What It Does*
StructNew	Creates a new structure
IsStruct	Tests to make sure a variable is in fact a structure
StructAppend	Appends one structure to another
StructDelete	Removes an item from a structure
StructCount	Counts the number of items in a structure
StructFind	Enables you to find values in a structure
StructKeyList	Provides a list of all the keys in a structure
StructSort	Sorts elements within a structure

Chapter 6: Using Databases with ColdFusion MX

In This Chapter

✔ Investigating relational databases

✔ Understanding Open Database Connectivity

✔ Understanding Object Linking and Embedding

✔ Creating queries in ColdFusion MX

*B*ook VI, Chapter 4 gives you a brief introduction to the some of the basic database concepts in ColdFusion MX. This chapter gives a more in-depth look at what it means to build a database-driven Web site, both conceptually and practically. This chapter also gives you a more detailed description of how you can build a database and add, update, and delete data from that database.

ColdFusion MX comes with some sample databases, but it doesn't include any database products, such as Microsoft Access, Microsoft SQL Server, MySQL, or Oracle.

A number of other interesting tips and tricks are covered in Book VI, Chapter 4, such as how to use the WHERE clauses to filter data. Similarly, we also show you how to use the SQL functions of INSERT, UPDATE, and DELETE in Book VI, Chapter 4.

Understanding Relational Databases

A traditional database is similar to a spreadsheet, where a collection of worksheets make up the entire spreadsheet, usually called a *workbook*. These worksheets, however, don't have any real connection to one another, except for the fact that they're all part of the same workbook. A traditional database is made up of rows and columns, as shown in Table 6-1, and functions in much the same fashion as these spreadsheets. Traditional databases all have a one-to-one relationship between the table and its data, which means that each table has its own set of data, and that data in one table is not connected to the data in any other table.

Table 6-1	A Traditional Database Table	
FirstName	*LastName*	*EmailAddress*
Bob	Smith	bsmith@somecompany.com
Robert	Williams	rwilliams@somecompany.com
Sarah	Kahn	skahn@somecompany.com
Jane	Gasteyer	jgasteyer@somecompany.com

Relational databases have been around since 1970, when E. F. Codd invented them at IBM. In a *relational database,* multiple tables are linked together through the use of data that exists in more than one table (this is usually referred to as cross-referencing).

In contrast to a traditional database, a relational database makes a direct connection between items in one table and items in another table through the use of unique identifiers, or *keys*. This simple concept opens up a wide array of possibilities in database design.

Here's a simple example. Table 6-1 shows four people that all work at the same company, Some Company. Say that the data sits in the Contacts table. You might have another table specifically for addresses of all the companies you do business with, called Companies. These two tables, in the relational style, are shown in Tables 6-2 and 6-3, respectively.

Table 6-2	The Contacts Table		
ContactID	*FirstName*	*LastName*	*EmailAddress*
1	Bob	Smith	bsmith@somecompany.com
2	Robert	Williams	rwilliams@somecompany.com
3	Sarah	Kahn	skahn@somecompany.com
4	Jane	Gasteyer	jgasteyer@somecompany.com

Table 6-3	The Companies Table				
CompanyID	*Organization*	*Address*	*City*	*State*	*Zip*
10	Some Company	1234 Main Street	Some City	CA	94101
11	Another Company	22 Minor Way	Another City	NE	10110

To connect the Contacts table to the Companies table, you need to cross-reference them somehow. To do this, you can use another table. We call that table ContactToCompany, and it includes the data shown in Table 6-4.

Table 6-4	The ContactToCompany Table
ContactID	*CompanyID*
1	10
2	10
3	10
4	10

If you look closely at Tables 6-2 and 6-3, you see that Table 6-4 shows that all the employees in the Contacts table are now being associated with the same address for Some Company through this intermediary table.

Designing your database using cross-reference tables provides many advantages, including the following:

✦ You can represent complex, many-to-many relationships, rather than simple one-to-one relationships.

✦ Updating an individual data element can impact a large number of related records, as in the case of the address. Updating the address automatically updates four other records in the database.

✦ Your databases are more scalable. Relational databases are capable of handling data that is more complex, and therefore can be used for a greater variety of applications.

The net result of using relational databases is that Web developers have been able to build increasingly complex applications based on more advanced database designs. But the great part about relational databases is that they're just as applicable to smaller dynamic sites as well. It's more about the way you think about representing data in a database, rather then the content itself. So as you begin to think of your first dynamic Web site, challenge yourself to start thinking about how you want to collect data about your products, and see if the relational database model makes sense for you.

It wouldn't make sense to walk you through the process of building a relational database because ColdFusion MX is designed to use relational databases, not to build them. However, ColdFusion MX supports the following products that you can use to generate your databases:

✦ Microsoft Access (Windows)

✦ Microsoft SQL Server (Windows)

✦ MySQL (Windows, Mac, Linux, Unix), an OpenSource database server

✦ Oracle (Unix, Windows)

At last check, `www.dummies.com` has more than 50 books related to database development. If you plan to use databases heavily for your Web site, you should point your browser to `www.dummies.com` and check some of them out! Our favorite is *Microsoft SQL Server 2000 For Dummies*, by Anthony T. Mann (published by Wiley Publishing, Inc.).

Understanding ODBC and OLE

Truthfully, you don't really need to know much about Open Database Connectivity (ODBC) or Object Linking and Embedding (OLE) to begin using ColdFusion MX. However, in the interest of clarity, we want you to know what they are. Simply put, ODBC and OLE are different protocols that enable the Web server to communicate with a database. Specifically, here's what they mean:

✦ **ODBC (Open Database Connectivity):** ODBC is the workhorse application programming interface (the method for interfacing between your application and a data source) for accessing a database. We call it workhorse because over the past decade, this has become the method of choice for interacting with Structured Query Language (SQL) databases.

✦ **OLE (Object Linking and Embedding):** OLE is the future of desktop communication. OLE can talk to a database, much like ODBC, but OLE is designed to provide greater integration between your desktop and a host of interactive applications that utilize technologies like Microsoft's ActiveX.

In practical terms, it doesn't make a whole lot of difference which method you use to connect to a database. That being said, most people will agree that OLE does provide a faster connection. However, despite the big push by Microsoft, most people are still using ODBC as their connection method of choice within ColdFusion MX, simply because of its stability and market acceptance. Figure 6-1 shows the ColdFusion Administrator, where you can choose your method of database connection.

Figure 6-1:
Choose to
use OLE or
ODBC to
connect to
your
database.

Creating Queries in ColdFusion MX

Querying a database in ColdFusion MX is done through different CFML tags, depending upon the situation. You use three basic tags to perform database operations (there are others, too, but they're more specialized):

✦ `<CFQUERY>`: This is the most common query tag, and the one with which you will no doubt become exceptionally familiar. `<CFQUERY>` supports the use of SQL (Structured Query Language), and allows you to perform a host of SQL database operations, including `SELECT`, `INSERT`, `UPDATE`, and `DELETE`.

✦ `<CFINSERT>`: CFML includes its only `INSERT` function through the `<CFINSERT>` tag. You can use either `<CFQUERY>` or `<CFINSERT>` to insert data into a database.

✦ `<CFUPDATE>`: Similar to `<CFINSERT>`, this tag allows you to update records in a database.

The details about using each of these tags are covered in the following sections.

Using <CFQUERY>

`<CFQUERY>` is the workhorse tag in ColdFusion MX. You use it when you want to perform any kind of database operation. The structure of `<CFQUERY>` is as follows:

```
<CFQUERY name="somename" datasource="somedatabase"> Insert
    your SQL statement here</CFQUERY>
```

Within this code, `name` is the name you assign to the query, and `datasource` is a mapped database in ColdFusion MX and SQL. The SQL within the tags is passed directly to the database for execution; the resulting dataset is resident in memory while the page is active, and then is made available as a series of variables that correspond to the columns requested from the database.

Book VI, Chapter 4 covers `<CFQUERY>` in more detail, including examples on usage and how to output data from queries to the screen. Also check out Book VI, Chapter 5 for more information on how to use the variables generated from a `<CFQUERY>`.

Using <CFINSERT>

`<CFINSERT>`, to some degree, takes the place of the `INSERT` SQL function. In fact, when you use this tag, all ColdFusion MX is doing is taking the parameters you specify in the tag and turning it into SQL to be executed at the database. The basic structure of the `<CFINSERT>` tag is as follows:

```
<CFINSERT datasource="SomeDatabase " tablename="SomeTable"
    formfields="FormVariable1, FormVariable2, etc ">
```

`<CFINSERT>` is only valuable when you're doing simple inserts to a database. If the queries are more complex and require inputting into more than one table, for example, you'll have to use `<CFQUERY>` and include your SQL there.

Here's an example that you can try with the databases that come with ColdFusion MX to show how `<CFINSERT>` works:

1. **Create a ColdFusion MX page by selecting Ctrl+N in Dreamweaver MX and then save the page to your local testing area on your hard drive.**

2. **Create two form variables using** `<CFSET>`.

   Usually, these variables would be passed from a form to the page, but for this demo, we're just going to create them here in the page. Here's what the code for these two variables looks like:

```
<CFSET form.dept_name = "Web Development">
<CFSET form.location = "San Francisco">
```

3. **Create a** `<CFINSERT>` **tag to put this data into the Departmt table in the CompanyInfo database as follows:**

```
<CFINSERT datasource="CompanyInfo" tablename="Departmt"
    formfields="dept_name, location">
```

The CompanyInfo database comes with ColdFusion MX and is already mapped as a datasource (as shown in Figure 6-2), so you don't have to worry about that step. This database also doesn't need a password, so you won't need to include that parameter in your `<CFINSERT>` tag.

Now, we're sure a couple things immediately popped into your head when you saw this code snippet. One is that the variables are the same name as the columns in the database. To use this tag, you need to map the variable name to the table column. For example, if in your form, you were capturing department as simply `dept`, then you could use a `<CFSET>` tag to convert `dept#` to `dept_name` as follows:

```
<CFSET dept_name = form.dept>
```

Book VI
Chapter 6

Using Databases
with ColdFusion MX

Figure 6-2:
Company-
Info comes
with
ColdFusion
MX.

4. Create an output to see if your update worked.

You want to check to make sure your update worked, so you should create a `<CFQUERY>` that checks the database to see if the record is there. Then, of course, you need to output it to the screen with a `<CFOUTPUT>` tag. Here's the resulting code:

```
<CFQUERY datasource="CompanyInfo" name="CheckUpdate">
SELECT Dept_ID, Dept_Name, location FROM Departmt WHERE
    dept_name ='#dept_name#'
</CFQUERY>

<CFOUTPUT query="CheckUpdate">#Dept_ID#, #dept_name#,
    #location#</CFOUTPUT>
```

5. Press F12 to preview your work.

Using `<CFUPDATE>`

`<CFUPDATE>` is similar in design to the `<CFINSERT>` tag. The difference is that `<CFUPDATE>` is used to update information in an existing row, rather than create a new row in a table. It also shares a similar structure, as follows:

```
<CFUPDATE datasource="SomeDatabase"
    tablename="SomeTable"
    formfields="UniqueID, UpdateVariable, UpdateVariable">
```

The slight difference here is that you need to select the record that you want to update. Take the case of the change we just made to the CompanyInfo table. The output query returned a value of 7 as the Dept_ID. So if we wanted to update that record to reflect that Los Angeles was now where the Web Development department was located, we'd have to do the following:

1. Set location **equal to Los Angeles and** Dept_ID **equal to 7.**

You'll find it best if you do this in a new ColdFusion MX page. Here's what the code would look like:

```
<CFSET form.Dept_ID = 7>
<CFSET form.location = "Los Angeles">
```

2. Create the `<CFUPDATE>` **tag.**

In this case, we specified Dept_ID so that ColdFusion MX knows which record it's looking for. We also need to specify the other field to update, as well as the database and appropriate table. Here's the code to update the two columns:

```
<CFUPDATE datasource="CompanyInfo"
    tablename="Departmt"
    formfields="Dept_ID,location">
```

3. **Press F12 to update the database.**

After you've done this, you can also then run the output query from the previous example to see the change.

<CFUPDATE> is really only good for the most basic of updates to a database. If you need to update more than one record at a time, you're bettter off using <CFQUERY>.

Chapter 7: Advanced ColdFusion MX Features

In This Chapter

✔ Using `<CFFORM>`

✔ Working with sessions and cookies

✔ Sending mail

✔ Creating graphs

✔ Building custom tags

*W*hen you've got the basics of your site running smoothly, you can start taking a closer look at some of the more advanced features in ColdFusion MX. In this chapter, we show you how you can extend the functionality of forms on your site, as well as how to keep information available throughout the duration of a user's visit. We also walk you through how to send mail and make charts, and finally, provide you with all the information you need to create your own CFML tags.

Using `<CFFORM>`

You may be familiar with HTML forms from Dreamweaver MX. But did you know that you can use ColdFusion MX to check form fields for values? You can do precisely that using `<CFFORM>` and `<CFINPUT>` tags. Although `<CFFORM>` and `<CFINPUT>` initially look similar to plain old HTML forms, you can set a number of different parameters with ColdFusion MX forms. These parameters, when read by a ColdFusion MX server, are converted to JavaScript to provide the desired functionality.

Take a look at this brief code snippet:

```
<CFFORM action="form.cfm" method="post" name="MyForm">
<CFINPUT type="text" name="FirstName" required="yes"
   message="This is a required field">
<INPUT type="submit" value="Go">
</CFFORM>
```

This is a simple form that looks almost like any other form you'd see in an HTML page, except for the addition of required ="yes" and message="This is a required field". If you saved this code in a page entitled form.cfm, loaded the page on a ColdFusion MX-enabled server, and clicked the Go button without including a value for the field, you'd get an error message, just like the one you see in Figure 7-1.

Figure 7-1:
An error
message.

If you think the dialog box in Figure 7-1 looks a lot like something you'd see coming from JavaScript, well, you're correct: It is JavaScript! If you view the source of the resulting page, you can see what happened. First, the following code was added to the head of the document:

```
<SCRIPT LANGUAGE="JavaScript" TYPE="text/javascript">
<!--

function _CF_checkMyForm(_CF_this)
{
         if (!_CF_hasValue(_CF_this.FirstName, "TEXT" ))
         {
                  if (!_CF_onError(_CF_this,
   _CF_this.FirstName, _CF_this.FirstName.value, "This is a
   required field"))
                  {
                           return false;
                  }
         }

         return true;
}

//-->
</SCRIPT>
```

All this JavaScript does is check to see if the text field has a value in it. If it does, great, nothing happens. If it doesn't, then the JavaScript code creates a pop-up warning saying, "This is a required field."

The form itself was also changed, as follows:

```
<FORM NAME="MyForm" ACTION="form.cfm" METHOD="POST"
    onSubmit="return _CF_checkMyForm(this)">
<INPUT TYPE="text" NAME="FirstName">
<INPUT type="submit" value="Go">
</FORM>
```

When <CFFORM> was read by the ColdFusion MX server, it collected all the requirements of all the <CFINPUT> tags and then generated all the JavaScript needed for the form validation. Then, it converted the <CFFORM> and <CFINPUT> tags to regular HTML form elements. Finally, it added onSubmit="return _CF_checkMyForm(this)", which calls the JavaScript that is doing the validation.

This feature provides you with an easy and fast way to validate your forms on the browser, before any data is ever submitted, and there are several parameters that you can set. All of these parameters are set in the <CFINPUT> tag, and the most common ones for <CFFORM>, <CFINPUT>, and <CFSELECT> are listed in Table 7-1.

Book VI
Chapter 7

**Advanced
ColdFusion MX
Features**

Because this type of form validation uses JavaScript that is read by a user's browser, if a user chooses to turn off JavaScript in his or her browser, this type of validation won't work.

Form validation done in the manner discussed here is called *client-side validation.* You can also validate forms after the data has been sent to the server, called *server-side validation.* To learn more about server-side validation, check out *ColdFusion MX For Dummies,* by John Paul Ashenfelter and Jon Kocen (published by Wiley Publishing, Inc.).

In addition to <CFINPUT>, <CFSELECT> can also be used to create drop-down lists. Check out <CFSELECT> in the CFML Reference in the ColdFusion MX documentation for a good example of how to use <CFSELECT> with a database query to populate a drop-down list.

Table 7-1   Common Parameters for <CFFORM>, <CFINPUT>, and <CFSELECT>

Tag	Parameter	Description
<CFFORM>, <CFINPUT>, <CFSELECT>	Name	Describes the name of the element.
<CFFORM>	Action	Gives the page to execute when the form is submitted.
<CFFORM>, <CFSELECT>, <CFINPUT>	passThrough	Allows you to pass HTML code that isn't supported by <CFFORM> through to the resulting HTML form.

(continued)

Table 7-1 *(continued)*

Tag	Parameter	Description
`<CFINPUT>`, `<CFSELECT>`	`Required`	Determines whether a value for the field is required or not.
`<CFINPUT>`	`Validate`	Verifies the format of a given value. There are several formats to choose from, including `date`, `eurodate`, `time`, `float`, `integer`, `telephone`, `zipcode`, `creditcard`, and `social_security_number`.
`<CFINPUT>`, `<CFSELECT>`	`Message`	Gives a message to display if validation is unsuccessful.
`<CFSELECT>`	`Query`	Specifies a query to be used to populate the list.

Working with Sessions and Cookies

Before getting into the "how" of sessions and cookies, it would be good to review what both sessions and cookies are and why they can be exceptionally useful in Web development. ColdFusion MX uses two different types of variables:

✦ **Persistent:** Session variables and cookies are examples of persistent variables. These variables are present throughout the user's time on the site and perhaps longer. Session variables are kept in memory, and cookies are kept in a text file on the user's computer.

✦ **Non-persistent:** These variables are present only in a single ColdFusion MX page. By default, all variables are non-persistent variables. Unless they are actively passed from page to page — through a URL string like `page.cfm?itemID=10000`, for example — these variables will be resident only for that single page.

Persistent variables are great because after they've been set, they're always available, and you don't have to worry about passing them from page to page. For things like user IDs, user preferences, contact information, e-mail addresses, and other custom information about a user, persistent variables are a perfect way to store that information. The following sections walk you through how to generate cookies and use session variables, and point out the advantages to each method.

Using session variables

Session variables, variables which are resident throughout a users time on a site, are best used when you have information that you only want to keep available while the user's browser is open and while the user is on your site. For example, you may want to use a session variable for things like a user ID or user preferences. These are global items, in the sense that they're needed throughout the user's time on the site, as opposed to just one section or function of the site.

Follow these steps to create a session variable:

1. **In the ColdFusion Administrator, make sure that session variables are enabled.**

By default, they should be enabled, but it's always a good idea to check. In the ColdFusion Administrator, which is shown in Figure 7-2, you can find session variables by selecting Memory Variables from the left navigation bar under Server Settings.

2. **In your** `Application.cfm` **file, turn on session management.**

You turn on session management by adding a `<CFAPPLICATION>` tag to your `application.cfm` file. You enable it by setting `sessionmanagement="yes"`. You can also specify the timeout here by using the `sessiontimeout` parameter. The code is as follows:

```
<CFAPPLICATION NAME="Name of Application"
    SESSIONMANAGEMENT="Yes"
   SESSIONTIMEOUT="#CreateTimeSpan(days, hours, minutes,
    seconds)#">
```

Book VI
Chapter 7

Advanced
ColdFusion MX
Features

Figure 7-2:
Enabling session variables in the ColdFusion Administrator.

The values that you choose for *days*, *hours*, *minutes*, and *seconds* are all integers.

3. **Create your session variable.**

   Creating a session variable has two components:

   - **Set the variable:** Setting the variable looks like setting any other type of variable, except that the variable name must be preceded by the session scope (this is the same scope that we discuss in Book VI, Chapter 3) followed by a period, as follows:

     ```
     <CFSET session.MySessionVariable = SomeValue>
     ```

   - **Lock the code:** In addition to setting the variable, you also need to lock the code. Locking the code simply means that you're going to make sure that the server keeps your request separate from any others that may be occurring at the same time. To do this, you use a `<CFLOCK>` tag that encompasses the `<CFSET>` tag, as follows:

     ```
     <CFLOCK scope="SESSION" timeout="20" type="EXCLUSIVE">
     <CFSET session.MySessionVariable = SomeValue>
     </CFLOCK>
     ```

     In this code, `scope` is where you want the lock to occur, `timeout` is how long you want the session to remain locked, and `type` is the kind of lock you want to perform. Exclusive locks allow one server request at a time to read or write shared data, where as read-only locks allow more than one request to read shared data. For more information on where you should use exclusive or read-only locks, check out the ColdFusion documentation by pressing Ctrl+F1 in Dreamweaver MX.

ColdFusion MX server is a multi-threading server, which means it can handle more than one request to the server at a time. While that makes the server more powerful, it also can be dangerous when it comes to the transmission and writing of data into memory. To avoid any crossing over of data during simultaneous requests, you use `<CFLOCK>` to make sure that if two requests come in at the same time, they're performed in sequence, rather than simultaneously.

4. **Include the session scope so that you can call the variable in your code when it's set.**

   All session variables need to include the "session." precursor when calling the variable in a `<CFOUTPUT>` tag, as follows:

   ```
   <CFOUTPUT>#session.MySessionVariable#</CFOUTPUT>
   ```

Setting and retrieving cookies

Cookies are a great way to keep information about a user around for an extended period of time so that you can use it when they visit your site a multitude of times. Unlike a session, which expires after a given period of time, a cookie actually is a text file that resides on a user's computer. This text file usually contains some kind of persistent information about the user, such as an e-mail address, site preferences, or perhaps a log of when he or she last was on the site. As a developer, the value in being able to retrieve this information is to deliver a more targeted, user-friendly application.

Not everyone likes cookies. Some people view them as intrusive or even dangerous because they're allowing an outside site the ability to write a file to their computer. Some people even block cookies. Good net etiquette requires that you must always be judicious when using cookies, and be sure to explicitly state in your site's privacy policy just what you're using those cookies to accomplish.

Here's how you can use ColdFusion MX to add a cookie:

1. **Enable cookies in your application.**

Much like sessions, before you can create a cookie, you first have to set up your application to support cookies. This can be done in the `application.cfm` file, using the same `<CFAPPLICATION>` tag that you would use to set up sessions. You need the following three tag values to be set:

- `CLIENTMANAGEMENT="Yes"`
- `CLIENTSTORAGE="Cookie"`
- `SETCLIENTCOOKIES="Yes"`

After these are set, you can get about the business of generating cookies.

2. **On the page you want to set a cookie, create a `<CFCOOKIE>` tag and give it a name.**

ColdFusion MX includes a tag specifically for the writing of cookies. While you can use dots (.) in cookie names, be sure to avoid spaces and vague names. Here's an example of a well-named and well-formed cookie:

```
<CFCOOKIE name="EmailAddress">
```

3. **Assign the cookie a value.**

A cookie value can be just about any kind of string, constant, or variable. It cannot, however, include complex values like arrays or structures. For example, if your site has a newsletter that requires a user's e-mail address, you could include a check box at sign-up that says

"Remember my e-mail address." If you set the cookie value to #email#, then you could retrieve that value when the user returns to the site. The syntax for setting this value would be as follows:

```
<CFCOOKIE name="EmailAddress" value="#email#">
```

4. **Set an expiration date for the cookie.**

Setting the expiration date lets the computer know when to remove the cookie from the user's machine. You can give the expires parameter several possible types of values:

- A specific date (in mm/dd/yy format)

- A specific number of days into the future (1, 2, 30, and so on)

- now, which deletes the cookie

- never, which writes the cookie and never removes it

If you don't want this cookie to expire, the syntax for the cookie would now look as follows:

```
<CFCOOKIE name="EmailAddress" value="#email#"
    expires="never">
```

5. **Add additional parameters to the cookie tag.**

You can choose to specify three other pieces of information through this tag (check out the CFML reference in Dreamweaver MX for more detailed information on these parameters):

- **Domain:** This parameter sets the range for which the cookie's content is valid. The domain name must start with a period (.), and is a required tag if you use the path parameter. The syntax is as follows: domain =".loungeboy.com"

- **Path:** This parameter limits the validity of a cookie to a specific path within a domain. If you use this parameter, then the domain parameter is also required. The syntax is as follows: path="/newsletters"

- **Secure:** This is a simple yes or no flag for the parameter. If yes is selected, then the cookie will only be set if the site is using Secure Socket Layers (SSL). The syntax is as follows: secure="no"

When the page is processed, the cookie will be set. To check to see if your cookie worked locally while you're testing, check out the local cookies directory on your computer, as shown in Figure 7-3.

Book VI
Chapter 7

Advanced
ColdFusion MX
Features

Figure 7-3:
The local
cookies
directory.

Sending Mail

If you want to have users sign up for something on your site — a mailing list
for example — then you're probably going to want to take advantage of
ColdFusion MX's mail tools. Before we describe how to do it, though, be
warned. You're going to need to have access to an e-mail server (SMTP) to
take advantage of this tag, so be sure to check with your Internet service
provider and make sure that you have this kind of service.

After you've got that squared away, sending mail is a breeze. Check out the
code snippet in the following example. In it, we create a very simple little
form that includes first name, last name, and e-mail address, and then with
the step list, we walk you through sending an e-mail. All of this code goes in
the same file, called `mail.cfm`.

Here's the initial `FORM` code:

```
<FORM method="post" action="mail.cfm">
First Name:  <INPUT name="first" type="text"
    maxlength="60"><BR>
Last Name:  <INPUT name="last" type="text"
    maxlength="60"><BR>
Email:  <INPUT name="email" type="text"
    maxlength="60"><BR>
```

```
<INPUT type="submit" value="Send Mail">
</FORM>
```

To make things simple, we post the request to the same page as the form, as indicated by the method="post" and action="mail.cfm" parameters. Certainly you could have your send-mail page separate. To create the mail, follow these steps:

1. Use <CFPARAM> to check for the existence of the three variables in the form and give them default values.

Because the form and the logic required to send the mail are on the same ColdFusion MX page, you first need to make sure that the variables exist. If they don't, ColdFusion MX will return an error for the code in the next step. This code, placed above the <FORM> tag, will check for the existence of the three variables in the form, and if they don't exist, will create them and give them an empty value. Here's the code:

```
<CFPARAM name="email" default="">
<CFPARAM name="first" default="">
<CFPARAM name="last" default="">
```

2. Create a conditional statement that checks for the existence of the variable email.

You really only need the e-mail address to make this work, so we want to make sure that it has a value associated with it. To do this, you can use a simple <CFIF> tag to test for the length of the variable email, as shown here:

```
<CFIF len(first) is NOT 0>
```

Place this <CFIF> after the FORM element in your page. If the length of the variable email is not 0, then you know it must have a value and then you can send a message.

Even though you've tested for the existence of the variable, you haven't tested to see whether or not that e-mail address is "well-formed," meaning it has an at symbol (@) and a dot (.). As it's currently structured, if we put the word "boo" in the e-mail field, it would try to send mail to "boo," which, of course, is not a valid e-mail address.

3. Create a <CFMAIL> tag within the M <CFIF> tag.

With <CFMAIL>, you can specify a number of options. (You can press Ctrl+F1 to access the Macromedia ColdFusion MX reference within Dreamweaver MX to find out more about all the options.) For this message, you only need to be concerned about the following set of parameters:

- **to:** The address the message is being sent to

- **from:** The address you want the message to be shown as coming from

- **subject:** The subject of the message

- **server:** The mail server that's going to send the message

For the `<CFMAIL>` parameters, you can use static values, as well as variables, and the body of the message in between the opening and closing tags.

For an example message, we use `#email#` to specify the destination address and then use `#first#` and `#last#` to personalize the message by addressing it to the recipient. Finally, we include a small note to let the user know the message was sent. Again, this will be part of the `<CFIF>` tag, following the `FORM` element. The resulting code looks like this:

```
<CFMAIL to="#email#" from="damon@loungeboy.com"
    subject="Here's Your Message, #first#"
    server="mail.loungeboy.com">Dear #first# #last#,
Isn't this mailer the coolest thing!
</CFMAIL>
<P style="color: green">Thank you. Your message has
    been sent to <CFOUTPUT>#email#</CFOUTPUT></P>
```

Book VI
Chapter 7

Advanced
ColdFusion MX
Features

4. **Move the message to your testing server and try it out by sending yourself an e-mail.**

   Figure 7-4 shows the e-mail you get in your Inbox.

Figure 7-4:
You've got
mail!

Creating Graphs

Imagine for a moment that you're a world-renowned scientist who's been tracking doggie treat consumption for the year 2002. Table 7-2 below includes some very important information that any dog would be interested in knowing.

Table 7-2	Average Doggie Treat Allocation by Month for 2002		
Month	*Treats*	*Month*	*Treats*
January	54	July	68
February	74	August	68
March	30	September	40
April	25	October	22
May	20	November	28
June	69	December	38

This data is collected from hundreds of different interviews with dog owners and has been saved as a table called Summary in a Microsoft Access database. Now, you want to make this information available on the Internet as part of your ongoing search for funding sources. With ColdFusion MX, you can easily generate charts of this information dynamically:

1. **Create a new page to display the charts and save it to the local machine where your testing server is located.**

2. **Create a query to get the data you want to display graphically.**

   The following query can be used to the get the doggie treat data:

   ```
   <CFQUERY name="TreatSummary" datasource="DoggieTreats">
   SELECT Month, Treats, SummaryID FROM Summary
   ORDER BY SummaryID
   </CFQUERY>
   ```

   Before you can make this query, you need to have a data source set up in ColdFusion Administrator. For details on how to do this, refer to Book VI, Chapter 2.

3. **Set up the parameters of the chart using** `<CFCHART>`.

   Much like `<CFMAIL>`, you can set a number of different options to customize the labels, size, color, and overall appearance of your graphs. The following code snippet only uses a handful of them. Refer to the CFML Reference Guide (Ctrl+F1) for a complete listing of the parameters you can set. Here's one way to configure your chart:

```
<CFCHART chartheight="500" chartwidth="500"
    format="jpg" font="Arial" fontsize="10"
    labelformat="number" show3d="yes">
```

In this snippet, we set the chart to be 500 pixels wide by 500 pixels high, set the graph file format to be a JPEG, set the font to Arial, and set the font size to 10 pixels. Lastly, we set the label format to a number, and we make the graph 3D.

4. **Specify the type of chart you want using** `<CFCHARTSERIES>`.

The `<CFCHARTSERIES>` tag allows you to define the kind of chart you want to display. Again, you can specify a number of different parameters. If you're only interested in making this a simple bar chart, your code would look as follows:

```
<CFCHARTSERIES type="bar">
```

5. **Create a** `<CFLOOP>` **to create all the** `<CFCHARTDATA>` **entries that represent the data for the graph.**

The `<CFCHARTDATA>` tag is used to specify the item/value pairs for the data in the graph. (In this example, January is an item and 54 is a value.) To create these tags, use a `<CFLOOP>` to get all the month and treat pairs into individual `<CFCHARTDATA>` tags. Here's how it looks:

```
<CFLOOP query="TreatSummary" startrow="1" endrow="12">
<CFCHARTDATA item="#Month#" value="#Treats#"></CFLOOP>
```

6. **Make sure that all your code is closed out by including close tags for all the chart functions.**

The `<CFCHART>`, `<CFCHARTSERIES>`, and `<CFCHARTDATA>` tags require closing tags. So all the chart code together should look as follows:

```
<CFCHART chartheight="500" chartwidth="500"
    format="jpg" font="Arial" fontsize="10"
    labelformat="number" show3d="yes">
<CFCHARTSERIES type="bar">
<CFLOOP query="TreatSummary" startrow="1" endrow="12">
<CFCHARTDATA item="#Month#" value="#Treats#"></CFLOOP>
</CFCHARTSERIES>
</CFCHART>
```

7. **Press F12 to see the new graph.**

Figure 7-5 shows the rather unglamorous but nonetheless effective graph that is generated.

Although these specific charting tags are a great new feature for ColdFusion MX, creating dynamic graphs is definitely slow and a processor hog. You should consider carefully whether or not you can live with slow-loading pages to have dynamic graphs.

Figure 7-5:
It's not
glamorous,
but it works.

Building Custom Tags

As diverse as ColdFusion MX is, you may find at times that it can't do exactly what you'd like it to do. In those instances, you might consider taking advantage of ColdFusion MX's custom tags. In ColdFusion MX, you can create your own CFML tags that are read by the server just like any other ColdFusion MX tag. ColdFusion MX custom tags can be made up of CFML code or a scripting language, such as JavaScript or ColdFusion Script.

Here's a good example of a handy custom tag to have around your online store that also shows how custom tags work. This tag, called `<CF_makediscount>`, takes a price and a discount and returns to the page the discounted price.

Here's how you would create the tag if you were doing it from scratch:

1. **Create a structure for the custom tag.**

Before you begin anything, you have to decide how you want the information to be passed to the custom tag. Your tag should follow the following conventions:

- The tag is enclosed by brackets ($<$ and $>$).

- The tag begins with a `CF_` so that ColdFusion recognizes it as a custom tag and looks for it in the custom tag directory (usually `C:\cfusionMX\customtags` on the server).

- The rest of the name of the tag corresponds to the filename that includes the code for the custom tag. So if your tag is `<CF_somename>`, then there should be a file called `somename.cfm` in the ColdFusion MX custom tag directory.

- Any parameters within the tag are passed as variables to the file that contains the tag's code. Accordingly, `<CF_somename name="foo">` will pass the value `foo` to the file `somename.cfm`.

In the `<CF_makediscount>` example, the tag follows this structure:

```
<CF_makediscount price='someprice'
    discount='somediscount'>
```

`somediscount`, by the way, is a decimal value, not a dollar amount.

2. **Create a new ColdFusion MX file called** `makediscount.cfm`.

This file contains the code that evaluates the price and the discount and then returns the resulting discounted price back to the page that's asking for it.

3. **Within the** `makediscount.cfm` **file, create the code needed to return the discounted price.**

Here's the code required to perform the entire operation:

```
<CFIF len(attributes.price) gt 1>
    <CFSET caller.newprice = DollarFormat
    (Evaluate(price - (price * discount))) >
<CFELSE>
    <CFSET caller.newprice = ''>
</CFIF>
```

Here's what's going on this code:

- First, it checks to make sure that, in fact, the tag has passed a value by saying that if the length of the variable is greater than 1, in which case something must be there, then the code assumes it's a valid value. If no value exists, then the code sets the variable `caller.newprice` equal to a null value (a *null value* is an empty value) and passes that empty value back to the page that made the request to the tag.

**Book VI
Chapter 7**

**Advanced
ColdFusion MX
Features**

- When these variables have been passed to the page, the simple equation of `discount price = price - (price * discount)` is performed.

- Performing this equation is also part of setting a new variable, `caller.newprice`, which is sent back to the page that made the call to the custom tag originally.

You may not be familiar with two scopes in the preceding code. The *attribute scope* is used in custom tags to denote the value being passed to the custom tag by the calling page. The *caller scope* sends the value from the custom tag back to the original calling page.

4. **Test the tag by giving it values and outputting the return value to the screen using** `<CFOUTPUT>`.

   Figure 7-6 shows how this tag works on a Web page. In the page, you see places for price, discount, and the resulting discounted price.

After you've tried this and it's successful, you've built your very first custom tag, and you're well on your way to building new tags for all those complex functions on your site!

Figure 7-6:
Discount
pricing!

Chapter 8: Integrating ColdFusion MX with Other Macromedia Products

In This Chapter

✓ Integrating ColdFusion MX with Dreamweaver MX

✓ Integrating ColdFusion MX with Fireworks MX

✓ Integrating ColdFusion MX with Macromedia Flash MX

ColdFusion MX can add a tremendous amount of dynamic power to your Web applications. As a member of Macromedia Studio MX, ColdFusion MX has also become more integrated with other Macromedia products. In this chapter, we provide a brief overview of how Macromedia has chosen to integrate ColdFusion MX with Dreamweaver MX, Fireworks MX, and Macromedia Flash MX. The current versions of ColdFusion MX and FreeHand 10 don't overlap or integrate, feature-wise.

Integrating ColdFusion MX with Dreamweaver MX

Nowhere is the integration effort more apparent than within Dreamweaver MX. ColdFusion Studio, previously its own stand-alone application, has been fully integrated into Dreamweaver MX. This melding of the products provides developers with the best of both worlds: The easy to use, graphical orientation of Dreamweaver has been combined with the dynamic development platform of ColdFusion. You can now find ColdFusion MX tools throughout Dreamweaver MX:

✦ **The Insert panel:** The Insert panel has five tabs that include a wide array of ColdFusion MX tags, functions, and wizard-like tools. These tools are covered in more detail in Book II, Chapter 6.

✦ **The Application panel:** The Application panel allows you to view data in databases, generate queries, and even build ColdFusion components (bits of code that are encapsulated and made available to all the parts of your application). The Applications panel is discussed in depth in Book II, Chapter 6.

✦ **The Code view:** The Code view, which is shown in Figure 8-1, is the development interface that users had grown accustomed to using in previous versions of HomeSite and ColdFusion Studio. Now, this same interface is available directly in Dreamweaver MX.

✦ **The Code panel:** The Code panel includes documentation and tools that were previously available in ColdFusion Studio and have simply been ported to this new interface.

With all these areas of Dreamweaver MX that include ColdFusion MX components, you also have access to many ColdFusion MX features. The following ColdFusion MX features are now fully integrated into Dreamweaver MX:

✦ **Insert variables, functions, and queries:** You can insert variables, functions, and queries through wizards and dialog boxes. You can find the tools to insert these objects on the Insert panel. For example, if you select the CFML Basic tab and click the database icon, you can fill in the blanks and create a `<CFQUERY>` tag to retrieve content from a database.

✦ **Work with databases:** You can select databases and collect record sets from them. To do this, select the Databases tab in the Application panel. If you don't have a site set up, you'll need to configure your Data Sources. Don't worry, Dreamweaver MX provides a checklist for you to follow to do this! You also find more information on how to retrieve data from a database in Book II, Chapter 6.

Figure 8-1:
The Code view in Dreamweaver MX.

✦ **Generate dynamic content:** You can generate dynamic content by accessing different sources through the Bindings tab on the Application panel. You can also set up variables, give them names, and then just drag them right onto your workspace. For more information on how to use variables in ColdFusion MX, check out Book VI, Chapter 5.

✦ **Specify server-side actions:** You can specify a variety of server-side actions through the Server Behavior tab in the Application panel.

✦ **Set connections to remote servers:** You can set connections to remote servers using ColdFusion MX's RDS (Remote Development Services). To use this feature, create a site and specify the RDS connection in the Remote Info category of the Site Definition dialog box, as shown in Figure 8-2. To bring up the Site Definition dialog box, choose Site⇨Edit Sites, and then from the Edit Sites dialog box, select your Web site's name and click the Edit button.

Figure 8-2:
You can specify to use ColdFusion MX's RDS service in the Site Definition dialog box.

✦ **Create and add ColdFusion MX components to your application:** Using components is beyond the scope of this book. However, *ColdFusion MX For Dummies,* by John Paul Ashenfelter and Jon Kocen (published by Wiley Publishing, Inc.), includes hands-on tutorials of how to use components in ColdFusion MX.

✦ **Link directly to the ColdFusion Administrator:** You can link directly from Dreamweaver MX to the ColdFusion Administrator by selecting Modify Data Sources in the Database tab of the Application panel.

✦ **Change the Dreamweaver MX interface:** You can change the product interface to look just like ColdFusion Studio or HomeSite. This procedure is covered in detail in Book II, Chapter 1.

For a more detailed analysis of Macromedia's integration of Dreamweaver MX and ColdFusion MX, check out Book II, Chapter 6.

Integrating ColdFusion MX with Fireworks MX

The integration between Fireworks MX and Dreamweaver MX is both extensive and well-thought-out. ColdFusion MX, however, doesn't play much of a role at all in that integration. In fact, the only place in Fireworks MX where ColdFusion MX is mentioned at all is in the Export feature. In Fireworks MX, if you choose File⇨Export⇨Options, you can set the export extension to a .cfm file for ColdFusion MX.

Be sure to check out the Macromedia Exchange at www.macromedia.com/exchange. Macromedia is always adding new extensions for products, and it's here that you are likely to find any Fireworks MX to ColdFusion MX tools.

Integrating ColdFusion MX with Macromedia Flash MX

One of the best new pieces of product integration in Macromedia Studio MX is between ColdFusion MX and Macromedia Flash MX. In the recent versions of Macromedia Flash and ColdFusion, Macromedia provided developers with a new way to get dynamic data from ColdFusion into the Macromedia Flash interface. This method, which involved creating XML in ColdFusion with the dynamic data and then calling the file through ActionScript, was a good first step, but it was a convoluted way to query a database, and it slowed down your Flash movies.

With the introduction of ColdFusion MX, Macromedia has significantly expanded its integration efforts in an effort to define Macromedia Flash MX as an interactive, Web-compatible display layer that can easily and efficiently communicate with the business logic through ColdFusion MX. In other words, Macromedia is betting the proverbial farm that developers really want to create dynamic sites using Macromedia Flash MX for the display side and ColdFusion MX for the database side.

The result of all this development work can be boiled down to two new features:

✦ **The Macromedia Flash Remoting MX service:** This service allows you to connect directly to an application server, such as ColdFusion MX, and execute server-side ActionScript.

✦ **New query support for ActionScript:** Now, with server-side ActionScript, you can access data directly using two new functions, called `CF.query` and `CF.http`, that are functionally akin to the `<CFQUERY>` and `<CFHTTP>` CFML tags.

In addition to the Flash remoting service, Macromedia also provides another communication server product, the Macromedia Flash Communication Server MX. With this product, Macromedia Flash MX talks to a communication server using ActionScript, and the server in turn communicates with the ColdFusion MX server. For more information on these tools, check out the *Macromedia Flash MX ActionScript Bible,* by Robert Reinhardt and Joey Lott (published by Wiley Publishing, Inc.).

Advanced Macromedia Flash MX and ColdFusion MX integration just isn't easy, and it really goes beyond the scope of this book. If you're looking for a good hands-on guide to these new features, check out *ColdFusion MX For Dummies,* by John Paul Ashenfelter and Jon Kocen.

Macromedia provides developers with the Designer & Developer Center, a fine resource for learning more about Macromedia products and how to use them. You can find the Designer & Developer Center at `www.macromedia.com/desdev`.

Using the Macromedia Flash Remoting MX service

The Macromedia Flash Remoting MX service enables you to use Macromedia Flash MX to connect directly to an application server, such as ColdFusion MX, and it also offers developers greater access to dynamic content and more advanced scripting tools. The basic way in which this interaction takes place between the Flash client and the server is shown in Figure 8-3.

Figure 8-3: The basic concept behind the Macromedia Flash Remoting MX service.

The following steps outline the process of making the connection to the Macromedia Flash Remoting MX service, both on the ColdFusion MX and on the Macromedia Flash MX sides:

1. **Make sure that the remoting service is installed.**

   You can find the installer for the remoting service in the folder
   `D:\Flash MX\Extending Flash MX`, assuming that `D:\` is your
   CD-ROM drive with the Macromedia Studio MX installation disc in it.

2. **To be able to use the service, you need to include the files
   `NetSevices.as` and `NetDebug.as` in your Macromedia Flash
   ActionScript.**

   These two files tell Macromedia Flash MX how to manage the remote
   connection after it's been made and to provide the debugging output
   for the service. `NetBebug` is optional, and really should only be used
   when you're testing your application. Your ActionScript should look as
   follows:

   ```
   #include "NetServices.as"
   #include "NetDebug.as"
   ```

3. **Specify the location for the remote service.**

   Basically, this just means that you need to tell Macromedia Flash MX
   where to look to find the ColdFusion MX application server on the
   machine where your server-side ActionScript resides. Usually, your
   ColdFusion server (and therefore, the Remoting Gateway) is located at
   `http://localhost`, or `http://localhost:8500`. The code in your
   Macromedia Flash MX ActionScript should look like the following:

   ```
   NetServices.setDefaultGatewayURL("http://localhost/
       flashservices/gateway ")
   ```

   The `/flashservices/gateway` part is a built-in virtual directory that
   tells ActionScript to activate the remoting service.

4. **Set the connection.**

   When you're ready, in your ActionScript you need to say "Open,
   gateway," which can be done with the following ActionScript:

   ```
   gatewayConnection =
       NetServices.createGatewayConnection()
   ```

5. **Go get your content!**

   This is where the approaches to getting content diverge. At this point,
   you can choose to either call a ColdFusion MX component or a server-
   side ActionScript file. For every service you call, though, you need the
   following bit of ActionScript:

   ```
   Service = gatewayConnnection.getService("Filename",
       this);
   ```

   Where `service` is the name of the instance you are invoking,
   `gatewayConnection.getService` is the function that gets the

server-side ActionScript file, `filename` is the name of the ActionScript file without the extension, and `this` represents the current instance of the service.

The Macromedia Web site has a great paper written by Stephen Gilson that walks you through a lot of this in more detail. The paper is entitled "Using Macromedia Flash Remoting MX with Macromedia ColdFusion MX," and you can find it by going to the Designer & Developer Center and selecting Flash Remoting MX from the Development Centers drop-down list. You can also find this paper in the ColdFusion MX support documentation area of the Macromedia Web site.

Working with CF.query and CF.http

As part of the new Server-side ActionScript element of the Macromedia Flash Remoting MX service, Macromedia has developed two new functions that you can use to interact with the ColdFusion MX server without having to learn CFML:

◆ `CF.query`: `CF.query` is a server-side ActionScript function that allows you to execute ColdFusion MX queries from within a Flash movie. This functionality allows developers to execute database-driven applications directly from Macromedia Flash MX through server-side ActionScripts. The following syntax shows the arguments that `CF.query` supports in this version:

```
CF.query
   ({
        datasource:"data source name",
        sql:"SQL stmts",
        username:"username",
        password:"password",
        maxrows:number,
        timeout:milliseconds
   })
```

There are actually two different ways you can express the `CF.query` and `CF.http` functions. Both are acceptable, and here's what the other method looks like:

```
CF.query(datasource, sql);
CF.query(datasource, sql, maxrows);
CF.query(datasource, sql, username, password);
CF.query(datasource, sql, username, password, maxrows);
```

◆ `CF.http`: `CF.http` is an ActionScript function that allows `HTTP POST` and `GET` methods to be executed from within a Flash movie. `CF.http` provides a gateway through which information can be passed back and forth to the ColdFusion MX server. The following syntax shows the arguments that `CF.http` supports in this version:

```
CF.http
    ({
        method:"get or post",
        url:"URL",
        username:"username",
        password:"password",
        resolveurl:"yes or no",
        params:arrayvar,
        path:"path",
        file:"filename"
    })
```

Within Dreamweaver MX, check out Using ColdFusion in Dreamweaver MX for a complete description of how to set up Macromedia Flash Remoting MX and invoking `CF.query` and `CF.http`. You can access Using ColdFusion by pressing Ctrl+F1.

Understanding the Macromedia Flash Communication Server MX

The Macromedia Flash Communication Server MX provides a similar functionality as Macromedia Flash Remoting MX; the primary difference between the two is in the design. In the Macromedia Flash Communication Server MX design, rather than talking directly to an application server, the Macromedia Flash MX client talks to the Macromedia Flash Communication Server MX, which in turn talks to the ColdFusion MX server. You can find out more about the Macromedia Flash Communication Server MX in Book V, Chapter 10.

If you're interested in learning more about how and when to use the Macromedia Flash Communication Server MX, you should check out "Macromedia Flash Communication Server MX: Use Cases and Feature Overview for RichMedia, Messaging, and Collaboration," a white paper written by Jonathan Gay and Sarah Allen, the engineers who built the product. You can find this paper in the ColdFusion MX support documentation area of the Macromedia Web site at `www.macromedia.com/desdev/mx/flashcom`.

Charting

The other integration point between ColdFusion MX and Macromedia Flash MX is in ColdFusion MX's charting tools. `.fla` is the default file type for charts generated using the `<CFCHART>` tag. You can also choose to have the files generated as JPEG and PNG files. At present, if you select Macromedia Flash MX as the format, ColdFusion MX does not animate or otherwise take advantage of Flash animation in the generated chart.

Book VII

Bringing It All Together

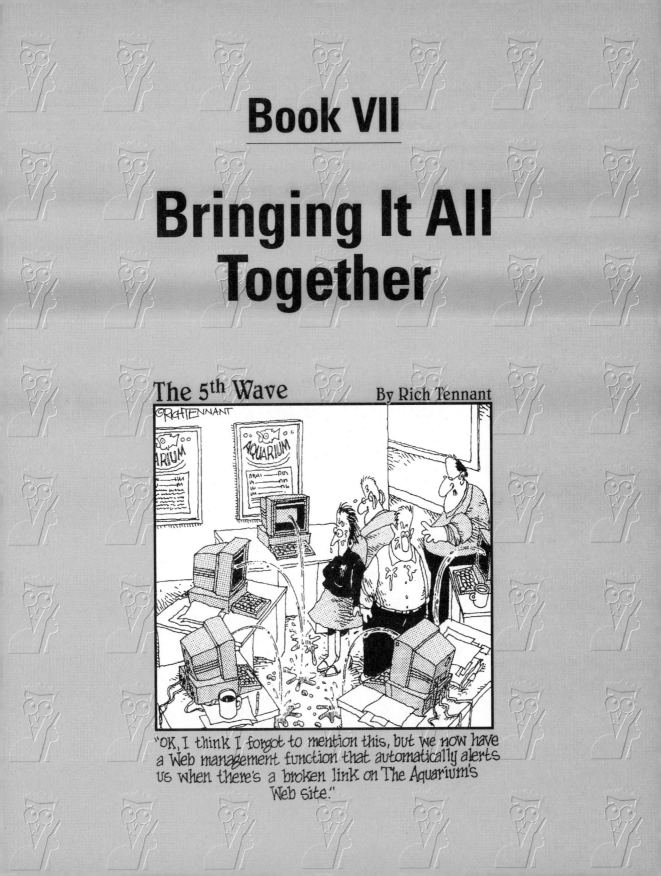

The 5th Wave   By Rich Tennant

"OK, I think I forgot to mention this, but we now have a Web management function that automatically alerts us when there's a broken link on The Aquarium's Web site."

Contents at a Glance

Chapter 1: Organizing Your Site

*B*ook VII is designed to be a mini-project of sorts, a hands-on example of how to use the Macromedia Studio MX tools in combination with one another to produce a Web site. This chapter is both an introduction to a test case (a Web site for the imaginary emporium, Earl's Bowlateria), as well as a checklist on preparing yourself to build a site. Some of this preparation requires the Macromedia Studio MX tools, and some doesn't, but all of it is required if you're going to bring a site to life!

Getting to Know Earl

Earl is the owner of a medium-size bowling products store in Anywhere, USA. After a few years of fiddling with the Internet, and even putting up a "brochure-ware site" (the equivalent of a printed brochure), Earl has decided to expand his Web presence in order to attract new customers and begin selling some of his products online. For the sake of this test case, we assume that Earl has already done the following:

✦ Purchased and installed a copy of Macromedia Studio MX on his machine at his store

✦ Found an Internet Service Provider that supports both ColdFusion MX Server and Microsoft Access and/or SQL Server

✦ Has a Windows machine that has all the Internet services, specifically Internet Information Server (IIS), already configured

✦ Has decided to build his site locally, and post live content to a remote server

You might carry out the operations described in Book VII in any number of different ways. We have chosen what we feel is the most common path to building a Web site. Whether you're publishing your site to your corporate network, hosting the site on your own internal server, or working with a model more like Earl's, you'll find plenty of pertinent information in this chapter.

Choosing Content

You may have many goals for your site, but you should spend some time setting priorities. What is your *primary* goal in building, posting, and maintaining a Web site? What are your other goals?

Here are some possible objectives you may have for your site:

✦ Sell products and/or services

✦ Provide widespread access to information

✦ Provide special access to privileged information

✦ Supplement or duplicate existing materials, like course catalogs

✦ Entice users to a physical destination, such as a hotel or spa

✦ Solicit information

✦ Provide a forum for discussion

For Earl, the primary goal is to sell products. Almost everything on his site is a product for sale or leads somehow to a product. For example, Earl's Bowling Tip of the Day always includes a link to a product mentioned in the tip. That's no accident: The tips are written with sales in mind.

If you already have printed materials, it's tempting to imagine that all you need to do is put them online and — voila! — you'll have a Web site. However, if you approach your site that way, you may miss the opportunity to utilize the Web's unique advantages over printed materials — interactivity, animation, video, audio, and of course, instantaneous publishing.

If your primary goal is to provide widespread access to archival materials, your main task will be to figure out the best way to organize the materials so that users can find what they want easily, not to decide what to post and what not to post. Otherwise, you may be tempted to make your site so complete that it's unwieldy.

Instead of having everything available all the time, you may want to consider rotating information. This keeps the site fresh, so users want to revisit your site regularly, and it avoids overwhelming users with too many choices.

Earl has done an analysis of his current customers, online competitors, and potential audience. He's an ambitious guy, so he wants the following on his new site:

✦ Detailed specification and price information for all the products he sells, which includes

   • Bowling balls

   • Shoes

   • Clothes

   • Accessories

✦ Online purchasing and the ability to track orders

✦ A search tool that enables users to find products quickly

✦ Information on his store, such as its history and location

✦ Information on upcoming tournaments and teams that Earl's Bowlateria sponsors

✦ Flashy promotions to get people excited to be on his site

✦ A good help section to guide customers through the site

Adding product purchasing to a site is a big step, one that requires you to consider issues like security, messaging, and even inventory, all of which are outside the scope of this demo. As a primer, consider picking up a copy of Greg Holden's *Starting an Online Business For Dummies,* 3rd Edition (published by Wiley Publishing, Inc.).

Getting Organized

When you know basically what you'd like to accomplish, you need to get your content organized. This usually involves both the creation and collection of a variety of elements:

✦ **Graphics:** We worked with Earl to collect and create graphics for all the products and services for the Bowlateria, using Fireworks MX to make or modify the images.

✦ **Product information:** We collaborated with Earl to gather the pricing and descriptive information about all the products and add them either to a spreadsheet or to a database such as Microsoft Access.

✦ **Other content:** We asked Earl to generate the content for the other areas of the site (tournaments, help, privacy policy, and so on), usually using a product like Microsoft Word.

✦ **Categories:** We worked with Earl to create meaningful categories to apply to the various types of content. The goal in doing this kind of categorization is to provide relationships between content elements so that they can be displayed in multiple locations on the site. Table 1-1 provides a brief example of what this could look like for Earl's products.

Table 1-1	Categorization Sample for Earl's Content		
Item	*Primary Category*	*Secondary Category*	*Tertiary Category*
AMF Bowling Ball	Products	Balls	AMF
Dexter Bowling Shoes	Products	Shoes	Dexter
Earl's Store	About	History	Location
Tournament Information	Tournaments	About	Sponsorships
AMF Bowling Ball on Sale	Products	Balls	Sale Items

Table 1-1 shows a linear progression of content items down through a logic tree. To be able to show related products, for example, it's also good to include additional categories for things like product relationship.

Looking Toward the Future: Maintenance

Part of the strength of the Web is that information can be accurate up to the minute. Users now expect sites to have accurate, timely information. Additionally, you want visitors to return to your site, and one way to entice them is to include new material regularly. When you set out to build a site, be sure to consider the following questions:

✦ How often will the site (or parts of the site) be updated?

✦ Who will do the updating? Somebody who knows HTML? Somebody who has a strong grasp of Dreamweaver MX but doesn't know HTML? Somebody who knows how to use a word processing application but not Dreamweaver MX or HTML?

✦ What kind of content (copy, images, animations) will need to be updated on a regular basis? On a semi-regular basis? Once in a blue moon?

Your maintenance needs can have a decisive impact on the way you build your site. If you have lots of content that needs to be updated continually, you'll want to take advantage of ColdFusion MX's dynamic nature. (See Book VI.) If you have a weekly newsletter that will be maintained by an untrained member of your staff, ColdFusion MX may be overkill; instead, you probably want to employ Dreamweaver MX templates.

If the person doing site maintenance only needs to update text on a few pages, you can set up Dreamweaver MX templates and have the person update the site with Macromedia Contribute. (See `www.macromedia.com/ contribute` for details about that easy-to-use site maintenance application.) If the person maintaining the site is comfortable with Dreamweaver MX, you probably don't need to do anything special to prepare the site for them, no matter what the update requirements are.

Establishing Your Site in Dreamweaver MX

Before you start building your site, getting your workspace set up the way you find most efficient is a good move. Earl is going to be working locally on his desktop and posting his content to a remote server (a common working method), so the instructions that we provide here reflect that fact.

To get your workspace configured, follow these basic steps:

1. **Open Dreamweaver MX by choosing Programs⇨Macromedia⇨ Dreamweaver MX from the Windows Start menu.**

2. **In Dreamweaver MX, choose Site⇨New Site.**

    The Site Definition window appears.

3. **Fill in the Local Info.**

    The Local Info includes the site name, local root folder, default images folder, and URL.

4. **Add the remote information by selecting Remote Info from the Category area.**

    Earl is going to use FTP to connect to his ISP. Figure 1-1 shows how this would look for Earl.

5. **Click OK.**

    Your site definition is complete. You're now ready to start adding files to the local version of your site.

For more information on this process, see Book II, Chapter 3.

**Book VII
Chapter 1**

Organizing Your Site

After you have established your site in Dreamweaver MX, you may want to consider creating a folder structure for your site. Your folder structure should be based on your content organization scheme — you can create a folder for each primary category, for example. That way, when you create a site map in Dreamweaver MX, the linkages in the ColdFusion MX files from folder to folder will already be in place.

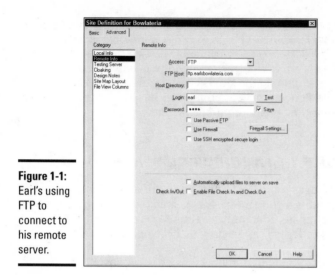

Figure 1-1:
Earl's using
FTP to
connect to
his remote
server.

Modeling Your Web Site

Before you start designing a site, you should always have at least an idea of how the site will be structured (that is, how the content will be divided into pages), and how users will navigate from page to page within the site.

Understanding the role of a site map

A *site map* is a diagram you create to map out the structure of your site. The site map displays the following:

✦ The width of the navigation scheme, which specifies how many top-level sections the site will have. (The top-level sections correspond to your primary categories.)

✦ The depth of the navigation scheme, which specifies how many levels of content the site will have in its hierarchy of information. For example, you could have five top-level sections, each of which has two or three sub-pages or sub-sections. Each of the sub-sections could then be further divided into sections, in which case you have three levels of content.

✦ Which pages will have static HTML content, maintainable via Dreamweaver MX, and which will have dynamic content, enabled by ColdFusion MX and maintained via a database or spreadsheet.

✦ Which pages will be linked to which other pages.

Building a site map from the ground up in Dreamweaver MX is a bit cumbersome. However, you can create a site map in Fireworks MX, like the one shown in Figure 1-2, that should serve your purposes.

Figure 1-2: A simple 3-level site map, created in Fireworks MX.

You may want to institute a "three-clicks" rule: A user should never have to click more than three times to get from any page on your site to any other page on your site. If you decide to implement this rule, creating a site map and User Interface document can help you visualize your site and make sure the final site meets this requirement.

Creating a User Interface document

A User Interface (UI) document is a guide to various aspects of how a user navigates through and experiences your Web site. The process of creating a UI document is known as User Interface design. A UI document can include information such as the following:

✦ Diagrams of pages that show what kinds of content is going to be displayed on each page and roughly where the different kinds of content should go.

✦ What the primary, secondary, and tertiary navigation for the site is going to be, where on the page each might sit, and which navigation needs to appear on which pages.

 • **Primary navigation** is the means by which users get to the top-level pages on your site.

- **Secondary navigation** provides a way to move from page to page *within* a section.

- **Tertiary navigation** allows the user to hop from page to page within subsections of the sections.

  You might also specify which navigation should be graphic (buttons) and which should be HTML text links.

✦ How technological solutions like ColdFusion MX fit into the structure of the site, which entails detailing which pages will include dynamic content and which will be static HTML.

✦ What other kinds of multimedia content are used on the site (Flash animations, audio, video), and what browser plug-ins are required to access the content.

✦ Guidelines for acceptable page download speeds, image file sizes, and accessibility requirements.

The following section explains how Macromedia Studio MX can help you with some of this work. You can use many other applications — or even pencil and paper! — to accomplish the tasks of creating site maps and UI documents. When you create a site map in Dreamweaver MX, though, you end up with a sort of clickable model of your site structure, which is a nice benefit.

As the technological complexity of your site increases, something interesting happens. Site maps become harder to create, because they usually involve fewer pages and more templates. When we say *templates* here, we're referring to pages in which the content is inserted dynamically by the server rather than hard-coded in Dreamweaver MX (not to be confused with *Dreamweaver MX templates,* which are HTML documents in which some code is locked and some code is editable). Concurrently, User Interface documents become more important, because the variability from page to page and section to section increases. So if you're working on a simpler site, focus more on the site map. As the complexity of your site increases, consider spending more time on the User Interface documents.

Generating User Interface diagrams for typical pages

The second step to consider before diving into building a site is the creation of some sample diagram pages that show the functionality of the site. This process of describing the functionality of the site by creating User Interface (UI) diagrams is called *User Interface (UI) design,* and it's a growing discipline in Web development. When you create a UI diagram, your goal is to clarify the following:

✦ How all the features of a site will work

✦ The interrelation of various content types in a site

✦ How a user can navigate through the entire site

Many times, the outcome of the UI design process is a set of "pages" that show the functionality of a site from one end to the other: In effect, what you create is a working version of the site on paper. In general, the greater the complexity of the site, the more UI diagrams you need to build to show the extent of a site's functionality.

No Macromedia tool is designed specifically to do User Interface design, but using Fireworks MX for this process is not uncommon. Figure 1-3 shows how we used Fireworks MX to generate a User Interface diagram for the Bowlateria.

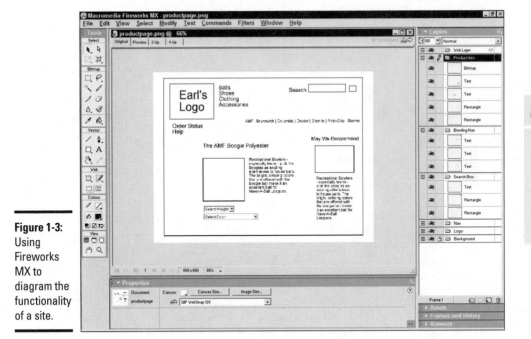

Figure 1-3:
Using
Fireworks
MX to
diagram the
functionality
of a site.

Chapter 2: Designing the Look of Your Site

In This Chapter

✔ Planning the Web site's design

✔ Laying out the pages in Fireworks MX

✔ Adding basic interactivity in Fireworks MX

✔ Designing animations with Macromedia Flash MX

✔ Moving beyond designing

*Y*ou have assembled your team, created, gathered, and organized your content, and finalized your site map and User Interface design. The next step is to work on your site's *look* — its visual appearance.

Planning Your Design

You should pay attention to things like navigation, color scheme, and how graphics and text will be used on your site as you design the different pages of your site. These details affect how users interact with your site and contribute to a user's overall impression of you, your business, and your site.

Designing navigation

The navigation on the various pages should be intuitive and consistent. Generally, main site navigation should be either at the left or top of the page, so that it's visible when the page loads regardless of the size of the user's browser window. Navigation should be in a consistent place from page to page to ensure that the user never has to go looking for it.

Also, if you have graphic buttons for your main navigation, you may want to consider having redundant links in the form of HTML text at the bottom of the page.

Choosing colors

Limit your palette to Web safe colors if a significant portion of your user base will be using monitors set to 8-bit color. (This is pretty rare these days, but still possible. Unless your audience is likely to be using 15-year-old computers, you don't need to worry about 8-bit color.)

In general, keeping page background colors consistent, at least by section if not site-wide, is one of the best ways to give your Web site a strong, unified identity.

If you are using color to impart information (to distinguish text on a button from the button's background color, for example), make sure to use significantly contrasting tones, such as dark text on a light background or vice versa. You can also include ALT or LONDESC attributes in your HTML <IMG> tags to make the button information available as text to color-blind users.

Including graphics

Avoiding overly-large images is a good idea, especially images with gradients, unless your user base has fast Internet connections. What constitutes an "overly-large" image varies, depending on your audience's Internet connection speeds. If your audience is likely to be viewing the site over a 56k modem, a good guideline is that your page should be able to load in a browser in less than ten seconds over a 56 Kbps modem (a page weight of 50K for HTML *and* images). If you've got a couple of 30K JPEGs on a single page, you've already surpassed the limit! On the other hand, if you're catering to a broadband crowd (college students in wired dorms or business users at large corporate offices), you may be able to get away with having page weights of 120K or higher.

Often, you can use page, table, or cell background colors to add visual interest to your page without adding significant download time. You can also limit buttons to two states (normal and rollover), in which case you can have the rollover double as the on state for the page that the button represents. (See Book III, Chapter 5 for instructions on using Fireworks MX to create button rollovers.)

You may find that you need only Fireworks MX to create your page designs. However, suppose that you're building a site for your new company, and you need to create a logo that you can use in printed material and on your Web site. In this case, you choose FreeHand 10 so you can take advantage of the application's superior drawing capabilities and adaptability for print repurposing.

Print design versus Web design

If you're creating a site for a company that has existing print materials (brochures and magazine advertisements, for example), how much the Web design should mimic the printed materials is a decision the client will need to make. Web design has rules and conventions that differ from the rules and conventions of print design, of course, so typically you don't want to simply put an HTML version of a print piece online. In general, you need to be more conservative with your use of graphics on the Web,

because each image has to be downloaded. When designing for print, you don't have to worry about optimizing a graphic for quick download or concern yourself with the possibility that a reader will change your text size or resize the printed page. In fact, if you want to put a brochure or other print materials online, often you're better off making PDFs or word processing documents and posting them for people to download.

Vector graphics can have much smaller file sizes than bitmap graphics, as we discuss in Book III, Chapter 3, but vector graphics won't necessarily be smaller in your final optimized Web images. This is because GIFs and JPEGs are bitmaps. In a Flash SWF, on the other hand, vector graphics download as vector graphics, so you can use vectors graphics instead of bitmaps to minimize download times of Flash animations.

Using HTML text

Where necessary, leave room for HTML text to be resized by users without breaking the design. That's not to say that you need to leave blank spaces wherever there's text; it means that when you build your tables in Dreamweaver MX, you need to use a `COLSPANS` attribute and/or nest tables in cells with a `VALIGN="top"` attribute wherever there's text in adjacent cells. Also, be aware that text appears smaller on a Macintosh computer than on a PC. That means if you're designing on a Mac but most of your audience uses PCs, you need to allow enough space for PC-sized HTML text, regardless of whether or not some users increase the text size in their browsers.

Be sure to test your HTML in the browsers and platforms you expect your users to have, and check if the table holds together the way you want it to when you increase the text size in each browser/platform.

If you're designing a ColdFusion MX template (see Book II, Chapter 6), it's even more important that you create a design that is flexible enough to allow for different amounts of text where the text is going to be variable.

Laying Out the Pages in Fireworks MX

When you define your site requirements, you need to decide on an ideal screen resolution. That is, based on your knowledge of the kinds of people likely to browse to your site, you need to establish guidelines for the width of your page designs, particularly if you want to use a fixed-width design.

Nowadays, you can assume that most users have at least a 15-inch monitor, set to a resolution of 800 x 600 or higher. If you're planning to design for a resolution of 800 x 600, remember that the browser window takes up some of the width, especially with the vertical scroll bar on the right. If you want people to be able to print out the pages from their browser, you should make sure all the key information is within 650 pixels from the left edge of the design. If you're designing variable-width pages, just make sure no graphics are keeping the table wider than 650 pixels in its smallest state.

You need to set limits on page width, but what about page height? Sometimes you hear Web designers talk about making sure key information is "above the fold." (The *fold* is the bottom of the browser window.) Although scrollbars make information below the fold pretty easy to get to, you never know if a user will bother to scroll. So loading all the important information in the part of the page that you know users are guaranteed to see when they browse to the page is best. Primary and secondary navigation, for example, ought to be above the fold, as should page headers and at least one paragraph of text (if you have text on the page).

Designing the home page

No law says that your home page has to be a different design from the rest of your site, but it's common practice for Web designers to make home pages a little fancier than sub-pages. This is because your home page is usually the place people get their first impression of your site, and you want to make a good first impression.

Remember not to overdo it with the fancy, hi-res graphics, though — you don't want a user's first impression to be that your site takes forever to load! We designed the Earl's Bowlateria home page, shown in Figure 2-1, to download at a decent rate on a 56 Kbps modem, so we avoided putting in large 400 x 300 pixel, 60K JPEGs or complex GIFs.

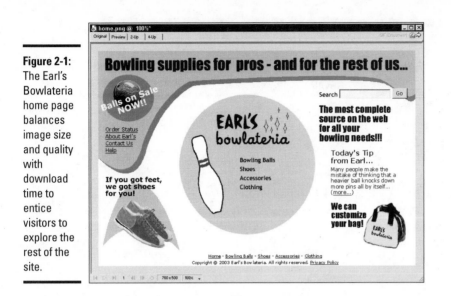

Figure 2-1:
The Earl's Bowlateria home page balances image size and quality with download time to entice visitors to explore the rest of the site.

Also, keep in mind that while your home page can look different from the rest of your site, the home page shouldn't look like it's from a different site altogether. In fact, you may want to use the same navigation buttons or other graphics on the home page as you do on the rest of the pages in your site. That way, the graphics will already be cached (saved to a temporary space on the user's hard drive, so the browser can grab them from there instead of downloading them repeatedly) when users go deeper into the site, reducing download times for the rest of your pages.

Laying out the section landing pages

The *section landing pages* are the pages you go to when you click the main navigation buttons. In the case of Earl's Bowlateria, which is first and foremost an online storefront, the sections are divided based on the type of product.

Design-wise, section landing pages often occupy a middle ground between the showier attractiveness of the home page and the plainer aesthetics of lower-level pages. For an online store, a section landing page might show a cross-section of models of a particular kind of item. When users click on an item, they might be taken to a detail page for that item (Figure 2-2 shows a detail page for a particular make and model of bowling ball).

**Book VII
Chapter 2**

Designing the Look
of Your Site

Figure 2-2:
All products use the Product Detail template; the overall design remains the same regardless of the type of product shown.

Although Earl always has bowling balls on the Bowling Balls landing page, new models are added and old ones are dropped, not only to reflect changing stock, but also to keep the page fresh for return visitors. The overall design remains the same, but the text and images are updated regularly. As we mention in Book VII, Chapter 1, to a certain extent, maintenance requirements drive design and technology choices. In the case of a page like this, the design must be flexible enough in certain places to fit different amounts of content at different times.

Organizing lower-level pages

Your site can have as many levels of navigation as you see necessary, but you should try to make sure that no page on your site is more than a few clicks from any other page: If people get lost or confused trying to get to a page they visited previously, they're likely not only to leave your site but also to avoid your site in the future.

Earl's site has only two levels of navigation:

✦ **The section landing pages:** The user lands on these pages by clicking one of the primary navigation buttons.

✦ **The product details pages:** The user gets to these pages from the section landing pages, and product details pages include secondary navigation that enables users to go directly from one product details page to another.

On the Bowlateria site, the product pages are dynamically generated. Rather than make a page for each of the hundreds of items the Earl's Bowlateria site sells, Earl made a product detail template and used ColdFusion MX to populate the template based on the user's choices.

Designing a template is not much different than designing any other kind of page, except that you need to make sure that your design is flexible enough to accommodate the dynamic content. The product name can extend farther to the right, or go to two lines if necessary. The product description has enough room to be as long as it needs to be (though it's unlikely to get much longer than the dummy text used for design purposes).

This page also leaves room for tertiary navigation at the left, should Earl ever decide to include deeper content levels on his site. While you can't anticipate every possible change a client may want to make to a Web site, as you design, you should consider what options for growth you're closing off and what options you're leaving open with your layout.

You can see in Figure 2-2 that the main content of the page is divided into three columns:

✦ **The left column:** This column holds navigation and an illustration. If Earl ever needs to add more navigation items, the illustration can be pushed down, changed, or eliminated.

✦ **The middle column:** This column contains the meat of the page: a description of a product, a price listing, a couple of drop-down menus with product options, and, of course, a button that allows the user to add the item to a virtual shopping cart.

✦ **The right-hand column:** This column includes text links to other models of bowling balls made by the same manufacturer, as well as a link to a complementary product.

We designed each of the columns to be independent of the others: One can grow longer without squashing the contents of the other two. We used Dreamweaver MX to nest a table in each column and added a `VALIGN="top"` attribute to each of the three cells in the row to make that work.

Adding Basic Interactivity in Fireworks MX

Whether you add rollovers and links in Fireworks MX or Dreamweaver MX doesn't matter to users, but it makes a big difference to you. (There's no point adding links and behaviors to all your images in Fireworks MX if you're not going to export the HTML code that includes them.) If you want to create your HTML code exclusively in Dreamweaver MX, you will only need to use Fireworks MX to design, optimize, and export your images.

We recommend that you leave the HTML part of site creation to Dreamweaver MX, which gives you much more control over the code. If you don't want to look at, think about, or alter code, however, Fireworks MX can indeed generate functioning HTML pages.

If you prefer to use Fireworks MX to generate your HTML code, you'll want to take a few extra steps when you create any slices for navigation buttons:

+ **Prepare a site map and name your HTML pages ahead of time.** This process is described in Book II, Chapter 3. You want to do this before you start working with Dreamweaver MX in any case, of course.

+ **Select each image and type a URL in the text field in the Property inspector.** If you don't type in a URL, Fireworks MX won't include a link in the HTML. Of course, adding a link to an image in Dreamweaver MX is a snap (see Book II, Chapter 2), so you don't have to add URLs for slices unless you want to avoid Dreamweaver MX altogether.

+ **Add a frame (with a button graphic) for each button state.** If the button graphic is the same for both the rollover state and the on state (that is, the graphic for the button when you're on the page the button represents), you only need two frames. (See Book III, Chapter 5.)

+ **Add a rollover behavior to each linked navigation button slice.** If you design each page separately, that can be a lot of work. Sometimes it's more efficient to create a master navigation bar, save it as a Fireworks MX file, and then copy and paste or import the generated code into each HTML page. Then you can use Dreamweaver MX to replace images and remove behaviors as appropriate. (See Book III, Chapter 5.)

+ **Export HTML when you export images.** If you're designing each page separately in Fireworks MX, and you don't have any dynamic content or Flash movies, you're finished! Well, not quite. You still need to test your site to make sure all the images show up and all the links work. And you may need to do some tweaking in Dreamweaver MX (or Fireworks MX) when you preview your site in a few different browsers and on a Mac and PC. (See Book III, Chapter 7.)

+ **Upload the files to a remote server.** Unless you're hosting the site on your local computer, you need to upload the files to a remote server, from which users can access it. (See Book II, Chapter 3 for instructions on how to use Dreamweaver MX's built-in FTP capabilities, or use your favorite FTP application.)

Designing Animations with Macromedia Flash MX

Macromedia Flash MX is a powerful and versatile application. You can build a whole site using nothing but Macromedia Flash MX, or you can use it to enhance an HTML-based site.

Browse to `www.macromedia.com/showcase` and select Flash from the Browse Showcase By list at the right to see how other developers have used Macromedia Flash MX to build or enhance their Web sites.

Using Macromedia Flash MX as a design tool

Given the widespread use of the Macromedia Flash Player and the richness of experience you can give a user with Flash animation and interactivity, why shouldn't you build your whole site in Macromedia Flash MX? Here are a few reasons why creating an entire site in Macromedia Flash MX may not be the best approach:

✦ **Lack of universality:** Some users are bound not to have the Macromedia Flash Player, or maybe they just don't have one up-to-date enough to view your content. (Macromedia Flash MX can export SWFs that require the Flash 6 plug-in, but as of this writing many users haven't upgraded from the Flash 5 plug-in.) You can develop a parallel HTML-only version of your site, but this can be costly and time-consuming. You can also try to force those Flash-deprived users to get the latest version of the plug-in (which they can download for free from `www.macromedia.com`), but you have to accept that not all your users will go to that trouble just to see your site.

✦ **Lack of accessibility:** Unless you have a voice-over soundtrack, vision-impaired users won't get much information from your SWF. If you do have a voice-over that includes information not available visually in your SWF, deaf users won't get that information. HTML text, on the other hand, is available to hearing-impaired people visually and to blind people via browsers that "read" the text aloud.

Macromedia Flash MX has added new accessibility features that allow text-reading software to access the content of an SWF, but you need to save your movie as a Flash 6 SWF to get that benefit, and you need to do a little extra prep work. We recommend that you also test the movie to make sure the text-reader says what you want it to say.

✦ **Flash detection is never foolproof:** If you have a non-Flash version of your content, you can redirect users without the plug-in to your alternative display of HTML. Unfortunately, there's no way to detect the plug-in for Internet Explorer on the Macintosh, and Flash-based and JavaScript-based detection for other browsers is not 100 percent effective. As a result, some users may never see your Flash content, even if they have the Macromedia Flash Player plug-in. Others may be told they don't have the plug-in, even if they do.

✦ **Difficulty of maintenance:** If you're a Macromedia Flash MX whiz, and you're planning to maintain the site yourself, the complexity of Macromedia Flash MX won't be an issue for you. Otherwise, the number of acceptable ways to accomplish many of the tasks of building a site in Macromedia Flash MX can make the job of updating the source file a frustrating experience for somebody who didn't create the source file in the first place.

If you are very comfortable with Macromedia Flash MX and are sure that your audience has the version of the plug-in necessary to view your content (or that your content is so compelling, people will take the time to upgrade their plug-in), you should feel free to build your site for the latest version of the Macromedia Flash Player plug-in. Generally, however, Macromedia Flash MX is best used as a spice rather than as a main ingredient of a site.

Examining Earl's Flash content

For Earl's Bowlateria, we used Macromedia Flash MX to add a little visual interest to the home page and other pages throughout the site. Nothing draws visual attention like motion, which is a good reason to use animation, but it's also a good reason to use motion sparingly. You know how annoying it can be to have a banner add flashing at the top of a Web page when you're trying to read the text below. (See Book V, Chapter 5 for details on creating Flash animation.)

The bottom left graphic with the shoes (shown in Figure 2-3) on Earl's home page is a Flash animation. The highlighted slice in the Fireworks MX file shows the dimensions and basic look and feel of the SWF that will occupy the lower left spot in the Earl's Bowlateria home page. The images and text in the animation rotate every 45 seconds to showcase a different product. We have taken advantage of Macromedia Flash MX's vector animation capabilities to make each product's moment in the spotlight unique. Users who don't have the Macromedia Flash Player will see a static GIF much like the one being used as a placeholder in the Fireworks MX design file. Users who have the plug-in will see an animation that highlights various items for sale on the site, along with links to the detail pages for those items.

We used Fireworks MX to prepare the product images and background shapes to be imported into Macromedia Flash MX, but we could also have used FreeHand 10 for this process.

Book VII
Chapter 2

Designing the Look
of Your Site

Figure 2-3:
A slice
in the
Fireworks
MX file is
where the
SWF will go.

Using a ColdFusion MX database to drive a Flash animation

If a movie on a Web page is going to change regularly, and the person maintaining the Web site is not familiar with Macromedia Flash MX, you can use a technically tricky implementation: You can leverage the connection between Macromedia Flash MX and ColdFusion MX to use a regularly-updated database to control which images and text appear in the animation. Instead of including the tagline text and corresponding bitmap images in the Flash file, you include variables.

If you choose to go this route, you would never have to update the FLA file itself. Instead, you would just prep the images, place them in a particular folder, add the text teaser and image name to a database, and set a field of the database to On or Off. That enables anyone with even marginal computer savvy to change the SWF on the home page, without even having to open Macromedia Flash MX!

The details of this technique are a bit advanced for this book, though. See Book V for general information about how you, as a beginner, can use Macromedia Flash MX to add motion and interactivity to your site.

Looking Beyond the Design Phase

After you've completed the design phase, you're ready for the integration phase, in which you integrate the images, text, and extras, such as SWFs, into HTML pages using Dreamweaver MX (see Book II). If you have dynamic content, use Dreamweaver MX to add ColdFusion MX code to the HTML to make CFM pages, as we describe in Book II, Chapter 6.

Depending on the size of your team and the structure of the site and deadlines, the design phase and integration phase may overlap. The content creation phase may be concurrent with the design phase, or various other phases may have to happen at the same time. Ideally, each phase would be complete before the next begins. Alas, Web development doesn't always proceed in an ideal manner.

Changes in content can dictate changes in design and user interface, which can be unfortunate if you receive those content changes when you're in the integration phase. Roundtrip HTML between Fireworks MX and Dreamweaver MX can sometimes ease the pain created by that kind of problem. (See Book II, Chapter 8 and Book III, Chapter 8 for information about Roundtrip HTML.)

Sometimes it doesn't matter in what order you complete particular tasks. For example, if you have set aside a place in your design for a Flash movie, as long as the SWF fits the assigned dimensions and you decide ahead of time what to name the file, you don't need the final SWF in order to integrate the page. You can put the name of the movie in and then just drop the SWF file in the correct folder, or you can use a placeholder name or movie and change the name later in Dreamweaver MX.

Designing a logo in FreeHand 10

Your first step in creating a logo is to choose the font family for spelling out the name of your company or group (or perhaps your own name). Of course, you could design a custom font to use in the logo (using FreeHand 10 in conjunction with Macromedia's Fontographer, for example), but that's beyond the scope of this book.

In general, it's better for graphic text on your site to use a typeface other than the one in the company logo. Many branding experts argue that if you use the logo font anywhere on the site besides the logo (on navigation, for example) you dilute the logo's impact.

We used different typefaces for the first and second words of our demo company's name, Earl's Bowlateria. Both fonts have a '50s retro look intended to establish a warm, nostalgic feeling. The words are left-aligned, and a pattern floating next to the words adds a little whimsy, as you can see in the figure.

One thing to keep in mind as you select colors for your logo is that there is likely to be some color shift when you go from the RGB settings (for the Web) to CMYK (for print), or vice versa. You can minimize the amount of shift by choosing a color that has a close equivalent in the other format. FreeHand 10 displays both CMYK and RGB colors, so you can get some idea how close the colors are, at least on-screen. (If you're designing only for display on computer monitors, whether as GIFs, JPEGs, or for Flash movies, you don't need to worry about CMYK.)

Chapter 3: Adding Flash Movies to Your Site

In This Chapter

✔ **Creating efficient Macromedia Flash MX files**

✔ **Importing files into Macromedia Flash MX**

✔ **Making a movie**

Macromedia Flash MX is more than just a cool animation tool: It's a deep and powerful application that you can use to create vibrant, complex, interactive movies. Among many other things you can do with Macromedia Flash MX, you can perform the following tasks:

✦ Combine bitmap and vector images in a single animation

✦ Create animated masks

✦ Run digital video from within a Flash SWF animation

✦ Use Server-Side ActionScript to connect to ColdFusion Components or create SQL queries

Maximizing Efficiency

Keep in mind that some features of Macromedia Flash MX are more bandwidth-efficient than others. (Merely importing a video or bitmap image into Macromedia Flash MX does not make the imported file any faster to download.) You should also remember that having too much going on at once in a Flash movie, especially at a high frame rate, can tax a user's CPU, causing the SWF to *chunk* (play erratically).

Ensuring efficiency for the user

Just like when you design the pages where you place your Flash movies, you should always be thinking about your audience as you conceive and develop your Macromedia Flash MX project. You should ask yourself the following questions:

✦ How fast will your average user's connection be?

✦ How fast will your average user's CPU be?

✦ How long will a user wait for a movie to download?

✦ What version of the Macromedia Flash Player plug-in do you want to require users to have?

✦ What accessibility accommodations do you want to make for vision-impaired or hearing-impaired users?

Given at least provisional answers to these questions, you can start to establish the structure of your movie and choose the content and methods best suited to command the attention of your users. For example, if your users are likely to be viewing your site with 56 Kbps modems, you'll want to avoid packing your movie with heavy bitmaps. However, if your users are avid gamers with fast processors and the latest video cards, you can get away with using higher frame rates.

Streaming

You can stream SWFs of course, so they can begin playing before they download, but you have to decide how much of the animation to preload (send to the user's computer before the animation starts, so the animation can play back smoothly, even if the user's Internet connection is not consistent). How much effort you need to put into deciding how — and how much — to pre-load depends on how graphics- and sound-heavy your main SWF is and the expected speed of your users' connections.

One trick to make the wait seem less like a wait is to load a simple animation that plays while your heavier animation loads, the most basic version of which is to animate the word "loading."

Be sure to take advantage of the Generate Size Report option in the Publish Settings dialog box when you publish your movie. This report provides information about the way your SWF will download to the user's computer by showing how much data needs to be downloaded for each frame. You can use the information to decide how long to make your preload and to see where your animation might chunk because too many new symbols have to be downloaded at once.

If you want to stream high-quality audio in your movie, keep in mind that the audio's continuity takes precedence over the animation, so keep the animation simple if you don't want the movie to skip frames. (The movie appears to stop for a moment and then suddenly leap forward, trying to keep up with the sound.)

Addressing accessibility

If you want to take advantage of the new accessibility features of Macromedia Flash MX, you need to publish your SWF at the Flash Player 6 setting. This means that your users need to have (or download from Macromedia's Web site) the Flash 6 plug-in. If you don't need to take advantage of the capabilities of the latest Flash plug-in, publish your movie at a Flash Player 5 or Flash Player 4 setting to guarantee the widest possible audience for your SWF.

Using best practices

We offer the following as general best practices; some may apply more to one kind of project than another. All the same, when you make a Flash movie, you'll best take advantage of Macromedia Flash MX's efficiency if you do the following:

+ **Use vector graphics:** Use bandwidth-hogging high-resolution bitmaps sparingly and use vector graphics wherever possible.

+ **Avoid resizing bitmaps:** If you use large bitmaps, avoid moving or resizing them too much, especially in movies with high frame rates.

+ **Use symbols:** Use symbols as much as possible, and reuse them where possible.

+ **Use low frame rates:** Use as low a frame rate as possible to achieve the desired smoothness of animation.

+ **Give users something to look at:** If your SWF requires a long preload, put up some kind of low-bandwidth loading movie or scene.

+ **Compress audio:** Compress audio as much as possible without totally compromising quality. Use stereo audio files only when necessary.

+ **Let users control the sound:** If your movie has audio, make a volume control or at least on-off button for the sound.

+ **Split your movie up:** If you have lots of high-bandwidth content, split your movie into several movie clips so some can load in the background while others play.

All these practices are geared toward the user. These steps ensure that the user will be able to enjoy your Flash movie without getting impatient for it to load, and that the movie plays smoothly and seamlessly.

Ensuring efficiency for you

When you think efficiency, you can think about the end result, but you also need to consider how to take advantage of the streamlined production environment that Macromedia Flash MX provides to make your process efficient. The following features in Macromedia Flash MX can enhance production efficiency:

✦ **Motion tweening:** Macromedia Flash MX fills in the middle if you make the beginning and ending frame of an animation. (See Book V, Chapter 5 for more on motion tweening.)

✦ **Components:** You can drop customizable, precoded elements, such as buttons and text input fields, into your movies instead of having to build them from scratch. (See Book V, Chapter 9 for more on using components.)

✦ **Grid and guides:** You can adjust the grid size and use Snap to Grid or move guides and use Snap to Guide to line up items on the stage quickly. (See Book V, Chapter 4 for more on guides.)

✦ **Starter templates:** You can use a pre-existing template or create and use your own custom templates to eliminate several steps from the beginning of making a Flash movie.

Importing Files into Macromedia Flash MX

Macromedia Flash MX can import many file formats, including GIF, JPEG, PNG, FH10, WAV, and even SWF. If you have QuickTime 4 or later installed on your PC, you can also import PSD (Photoshop files), PICT, and TIFF files. For the lowdown on importing audio and video into Macromedia Flash MX, see Book V, Chapter 6.

When it comes to importing files from other Macromedia Studio MX applications, you want to think ahead and prep your files for the import process. Organize your objects by layer or frame depending on how you want to use the layers or frames in Macromedia Flash MX. (See Book III, Chapter 5 for information about how to use layers and frames in Fireworks MX.)

Importing files from Fireworks MX

When you import a file from Fireworks MX to Macromedia Flash MX, you need to choose some settings. Choose File⇨Import or use the keyboard shortcut Ctrl+R, and select a Fireworks PNG from the Import dialog box. The Fireworks PNG Import Settings dialog box (shown in Figure 3-1) appears, offering the following choices:

✦ **File Structure:** Select either the Import as Movie Clip and Retain Layers option, which leaves not only layers but also frames as discrete elements of the movie clip, or select the Import into New Layer in Current Scene option, which flattens the layers of the PNG and puts the flattened image in a new layer in the Flash movie, leaving the frames intact.

✦ **Objects:** Select either the Rasterize if Necessary to Maintain Appearance option, which maintains appearance but sacrifices editability, or the Keep All Paths Editable option, which keeps editability but sacrifices some Fireworks MX patterns, textures, and other treatments that Macromedia Flash MX can't do.

✦ **Text:** Select either the Rasterize if Necessary to Maintain Appearance option to preserve the appearance of the text but lose editability, or the Keep All Text Editable option to keep the text editable but possibly lose some aspects of the text's appearance.

✦ **Import as a Single Flattened Bitmap:** Select this check box if you want to flatten the file into a single bitmap for import into Macromedia Flash MX. (*Note:* If you select this check box, the rest of the options become unavailable.)

Figure 3-1:
Choose how to import your file in the Fireworks PNG Import Settings dialog box.

Importing files from FreeHand 10

Importing FreeHand 10 files is roughly the same as importing Fireworks MX PNGs. The first steps in importing a FreeHand 10 file into Macromedia Flash MX actually take place in FreeHand 10. (See Book IV, Chapter 2 for information about organizing objects in layers in FreeHand 10.) How you want the elements of the imported file to work in Macromedia Flash MX determines how you organize the objects into layers in Freehand 10 and which options you choose when you import the file into Flash MX.

Choose File⇨Import or use the keyboard shortcut Ctrl+R, and select a FreeHand 10 document from the Import dialog box. The FreeHand Import dialog box (shown in Figure 3-2) appears, offering the following choices:

✦ **Mapping Pages:** Select the Scenes option if you want each page of your document to be imported as a separate scene, and select the Key Frames option if you prefer each page to be imported as a keyframe, with all keyframes in a single scene.

✦ **Mapping Layers:** Select the Layers option if you want each FreeHand 10 layer to be a Macromedia Flash MX layer. Select the Key Frames option if you want each FreeHand 10 layer to be a keyframe in Macromedia Flash MX. Select the Flatten option if you want the imported FreeHand document to be flattened to a single layer.

✦ **Pages:** Select the All option or select a page range by typing in the numbers of the first and last pages of the range you want to import.

✦ **Options:** Select the Include Invisible Layers check box if you want to import all layers, even ones that are turned off in your FreeHand document. Select the Include Background Layer check box if you want the background layer to be imported into Macromedia Flash MX. Select the Maintain Text Blocks check box if you want to be able to edit the imported text.

Importing flattened bitmaps is a much simpler operation, of course, but it does mean that you can't edit any of the elements that make up the PNG or FreeHand 10 file after the file has been imported into Macromedia Flash MX.

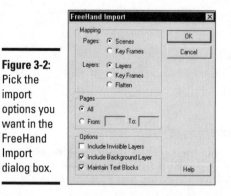

Figure 3-2: Pick the import options you want in the FreeHand Import dialog box.

FreeHand 10 offers more control over certain properties of individual graphical and text elements than Macromedia Flash MX, so Macromedia Flash MX sometimes has to approximate a FreeHand 10 effect when importing a FreeHand 10 file. For example, a gradient fill in Macromedia Flash MX cannot contain more than eight colors, while a gradient fill in FreeHand 10 can contain a lot more than eight colors. If you try to import a gradient fill with more than eight colors into Macromedia Flash MX, Macromedia Flash MX changes the gradient fill into clipping paths (vector-outlined masks). Unfortunately, that change increases the file size and complicates editing.

Several other restrictions apply when you import FreeHand 10 files into Macromedia Flash MX. See the online help files in Macromedia Flash MX for more details.

Making a Movie

The number of ways you can make a movie is nearly infinite. Some operations must be carried out in a strict order, and others can be done in any order. For example, you have to make objects you draw on the stage into symbols before you can use them as buttons or movie clips. On the other hand, it makes no difference whether you create layers one at a time as you go or create a bunch of empty layers before you start placing objects on the stage.

You can read more details about these operations in Book V. Macromedia Flash MX can be a bit daunting at first, but if you stick to it, you'll be able to make everything from simple animations with synchronized audio tracks to full-fledged interactive multimedia presentations.

For the Earl's Bowlateria home page, we created an SWF for the home page that shows a series of products. Each product has an individualized text tagline and accompanying vector shape in the background, and each product is linked to a page showcasing that product. In the original PNG, we put each object in its own layer, and then named each layer.

If you imported a multi-layered PNG as a movie clip, retaining the layers (see the section "Importing Files from Fireworks MX") as we did when creating the SWF for the Earl's Bowlateria home page, and you want to separate the elements for use in a Flash animation, follow these steps:

1. **When you import the PNG, Macromedia Flash MX automatically duplicates and places each bitmap as a discrete symbol into the library.**

   The bitmaps exist twice in the Library (as individual bitmap symbols and as layers of a movie clip).

2. **Rename all the bitmaps from their default names of Bitmap 1, Bitmap 2, and so on.**

   You don't have to rename them, of course, but they're much easier to work with if they have meaningful names that makes sense in the context of the Flash file.

3. **Double-click the movie clip symbol in the Library to edit it.**

   The movie clip opens for editing. Each layer of the PNG file is a layer in the symbol.

4. **Click an object on the stage, and choose Edit⇨Cut or use the keyboard shortcut Ctrl+X.**

5. **Create a new symbol by choosing Insert⇨New Symbol or using the keyboard shortcut Ctrl+F8.**

   The Create New Symbol dialog box opens. Enter a name for the symbol, and select the Movie Clip radio button. For more details on this part of the process, see Book V, Chapter 3.

6. **Choose Edit⇨Paste or use the keyboard shortcut Ctrl+V to paste the object into the open symbol.**

   When the imported movie clip is left with nothing but the bitmaps that already exist as discrete symbols, you can safely delete the movie clip. You can also delete the duplicated bitmaps from the movie clip as you go and then delete the empty movie clip when you're finished.

If you are making a movie that shows several animated movie clips with added button behaviors, you can continue as follows:

1. **Make a movie clip for each of your animations.**

   See Book V, Chapter 3 for details on making movie clips.

   If the movie clips all have the same basic layout (text at the top, vector shape with bitmap overlay below the text, for example), you may find it helpful after you have created the first clip to duplicate it and then swap elements, varying the way vector shapes, bitmaps, and text appear and change on the stage.

2. **Create a button with a link to a page on your site and put the corresponding movie clip in the button by dragging the movie clip from the Library onto the Stage in the button's Up instance.**

   You can leave the Over, Down, and Hit states of the button blank. Do that for each of your movie clips. Be sure to use an absolute URL for your link, such as `http://www.earlsbowlateria.com/bowling-balls.htm`, (rather than just `/bowling balls.htm`).

3. **Place each button on its own layer in the main movie timeline and add frames to each layer to set the order in which you want the buttons to appear.**

   See Book V, Chapter 4 for details on how to use the timeline. If you want a pause at the end of each movie clip before the next one starts, add a `stop` action to the end of each clip and leave enough frames in the main movie timeline for each clip to stay on the stage after it stops.

4. **Test the movie several times by pressing Ctrl+Enter (see Figure 3-3), and save the movie repeatedly along the way.**

We typically use the Save As command and rename the file each time. (Filenames like `home01.fla`, `home02.fla`, `home03.fla`, and so on, work well for this purpose.)

Figure 3-3: Press Ctrl+Enter to test your movie in the Macromedia Flash Player.

5. **Save the completed file and export the SWF by choosing File⇨Export or using the keyboard shortcut Ctrl+Alt+Shift+S.**

You can specify the version of Flash that your file will be exported as in the Export Flash Player dialog box, shown in Figure 3-4. If you're not using any new MX advanced features for your movie, you should consider exporting it as a Flash 5 or Flash 4 SWF. Exporting for an earlier version of the Macromedia Flash Player plug-in instead of Flash 6 guarantees you a wider audience, because people are more likely to have the earlier version of the plug-in. People with more up-to-date plug-ins will still be able to see your movie. If your movie requires a later version of the plug-in than the user has, a prompt to upgrade the plug-in may appear on the user's screen.

See Book V, Chapter 7 for more on exporting SWFs from Macromedia Flash MX.

Figure 3-4: The Export Flash Player dialog box.

Integrating an SWF into a Dreamweaver Document

As with Fireworks MX, you can export HTML from Macromedia Flash MX. If you're generating a page that will hold only the Flash movie, that's a perfectly acceptable way to go. However, if you plan to integrate your SWF into an HTML page with other elements, Dreamweaver MX makes that process a snap.

Export the SWF to a folder in the local copy of your site and then follow these steps to insert a movie into an existing Dreamweaver document, as we did with the product movie on the Earl's Bowlateria home page:

1. **Place your cursor in the table cell where you want your SWF to go by clicking where you want to insert the animation.**

2. **Click the Macromedia Flash MX icon in the Common tab of the Dreamweaver MX Insert panel.**

   The Select File dialog box appears.

3. **Navigate to the SWF file and double-click it, or click it once and then click OK in the Select File dialog box.**

   The Select File dialog box closes, and your SWF appears in the Dreamweaver MX window as a gray box with an F in it.

4. **If you want to adjust any of the movie's parameters, click on the gray box representing the movie and make adjustments to the Property inspector, which is shown in Figure 3-5.**

   If you click the Play button at the bottom of the Property inspector, your SWF will play in Dreamweaver MX. If the Loop check box at the left is selected, the movie repeats until you click the button again. Otherwise, to see your movie in the more realistic context of a browser window, press F12.

Figure 3-5:
Click Play
to test your
Flash movie.

Chapter 4: Building Your Site with Fireworks MX, Dreamweaver MX, and ColdFusion MX

In This Chapter

✔ Slicing the layout in Fireworks MX

✔ Building static pages in Dreamweaver MX

✔ Building dynamic pages using ColdFusion MX

✔ Posting and testing

✔ Going live

*W*hether you're collaborating on a large project with other people or building a site by yourself, you may want to begin the integration process (the process of building your HTML, CFML, or XHTML pages in Dreamweaver MX) before you have all the final content in hand and the design completed.

Nevertheless, before you start integrating a page, you need to have at least a few things ready. For example, you should have a solid site map and finalized user interface. Most importantly, you need a Fireworks MX PNG with a page layout. Slicing the PNG and exporting the images is either the final stage of design or the first stage of integration, but you need to decide how you're going to build the page before or as you slice the PNG. The slicing stage can be a chance to play with different structural possibilities.

Slicing the Layout in Fireworks MX

When you design a page, you should always be mindful of how the layout will be recreated with HTML. You need to position your text, graphics, and other elements on the Web page. Unless you use CSS positioning (Cascading Style Sheets positioning), which still has only partial support from current browsers and no support at all from browsers before version 4.0 on Netscape and Internet Explorer, your sliced PNG needs to be reassembled in Dreamweaver MX as an HTML table. The table is a rectangular grid made up of cells, divided into rows and columns. The simpler the table, the faster a page downloads and renders in a browser window. (See Book II, Chapter 5 or check out "Defining CSS Style Positioning properties" in your Dreamweaver MX Help files for more information on CSS positioning.)

Line up design elements into rows and columns. If you want a less grid-like, more organic look for your design, you may still be able to slice the design in such a way as to minimize irregularities in the grid. Remember, all your slices will be rectangles, regardless of the shapes of the images within those rectangles. So if you have an image shaped like a circle (like the bowling ball containing the Earl's Bowlateria logo), you can make one slice that contains the whole circle, or you can divide the circle into pieces in countless ways. How you slice that circle may end up being dictated by how you want pieces of the circle lined up with other slices on the page.

Remember also that you can use HTML tricks, such as image alignment, `VSPACE`, `HSPACE`, and `CELLSPACING` or `CELLPADDING` to position elements in table cells, which allows you to minimize slice dimensions and image sizes. (Refer to Book III, Chapter 6 for the specifics of how to slice up content destined for the Web. If you're not familiar with the HTML attributes above, you may want to pick up *HTML 4 For Dummies Quick Reference,* 2nd Edition, by Deborah S. Ray and Eric J. Ray, published by Wiley Publishing, Inc.)

You can legitimately cut up a layout in many different ways, but a couple choices usually rise above the others as the most viable options. How you slice things depends on several considerations besides the design itself:

✦ Which slices will have rollover behaviors

✦ Which parts of the table will have HMTL text

✦ How often the various parts of the table will be updated and who will be doing the updates

You need separate slices for each button that has a rollover behavior, for example. You should also make sure that any cell that contains HTML text (especially if that text is going to be updated) won't drag other cells open and destroy their alignment if the amount or size of the text increases. The underlying principle is always the same, though: Make the grid as simple as possible given the factors that you must take into account.

Figure 4-1 shows the above-the-fold part of the sliced file for the About Earl's Bowlateria page. (The term *above the fold* refers to the portion of the page that is initially displayed in a browser.) The slices in this PNG hold all the images needed in order to reproduce the page with HTML, except for the page background image (the wavy design element at the top, which has to be exported separately). A couple of things in this image are especially noteworthy:

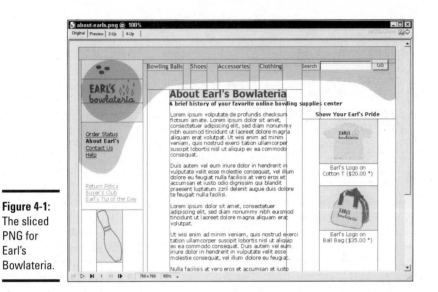

Figure 4-1:
The sliced
PNG for
Earl's
Bowlateria.

✦ The Earl's Bowlateria logo on the bowling ball at the top left is sliced independently of the top and bottom of the ball. That's because we want only the logo itself to be a link to the home page.

If we had wanted the whole ball to link to the home page, we could have made it a single slice. Or we could have made it all one slice but made an image map that linked only the logo part of the image to the home page (see Book II, Chapter 6, or Book III, Chapter 7), which is a different way to accomplish what we did by slicing the ball into three pieces. Either of the alternatives would have been perfectly acceptable.

✦ You can see also that the slice of the bowling pin drawing at the bottom left is only big enough to hold the image. We center align that image in its cell by adding the attribute `VALIGN=center`, which we can do in Dreamweaver MX by selecting the cell and selecting Center from the Horz drop-down list in the Property inspector. (By default, the cell width is the same as the width of the bowling ball slices above.)

✦ We didn't need to slice any areas that will hold HTML text or worry about "empty" areas, because we're exporting only images from Fireworks MX, not HTML and images. We build the HTML from scratch in Dreamweaver MX.

If you choose to export HTML from Fireworks MX and take advantage of Roundtrip HTML, the extent of the changes you can make to overall table structure is very limited.

If all this slicing business still seems a little abstract, read on to see how slicing strategies play out as we integrate the page in Dreamweaver MX.

Building Static Pages in Dreamweaver MX

Until CSS-Positioning (a way of placing elements like text and graphics on a page by using coordinates instead of tables) gets full support from both Netscape and Internet Explorer, people building Web sites will continue to use tables to position elements on pages. As we noted earlier, simpler tables are better.

Sometimes, instead of making your page by using a single complicated table, which can be a confusing tangle of COLSPANS and ROWSPANS, when you want to change things, you can make a simple table, each cell of which contains a nested table or tables. Creating a nested table in Dreamweaver MX is easy: just insert a table in an existing table cell. For each cell with a nested table (or each cell adjacent to a cell with a nested table), it's a good idea to set the alignment by selecting the cell and choosing, say, Left from the Horz drop-down list and Top from the Vert drop-down list in the Property inspector. That way, no matter how big your nested table gets, elements in adjacent cells won't drift apart when the cell holding them gets bigger.

You can nest tables within tables within tables, but the deeper you nest tables, the longer it will take for a browser to render your page. It's best to avoid nesting tables more than three deep.

A word about "empty" cells

By default, Dreamweaver MX puts a non-breaking space ( ) in every cell when you insert a table into a page. Putting a space in the cell holds it open when text or images are placed into other cells in the same row, allowing you to select the open cell in Design View.

If you're trying to create a spacer row with a height of less than 12 pixels, you need to replace all non-breaking spaces — which show up in the Code view as   — with spacer GIFs (1 x 1 pixel transparent GIFs, which can be stretched to any width or height to hold a cell open horizontally or vertically). If you don't need the spacer row to hold the table open horizontally, you can leave cells empty. The HTML code for an empty cell looks like this:

```
<td></td>
```

There is one catch: Netscape will not show a table's background color in an empty cell if the table's background color is different from the page's specified background color. So if you have specified a page background color and your table's background color is different, be sure to put a non-breaking space or a spacer GIF in any cell for which you don't have content.

A row will always be at least as wide as the widest element in it, and a column will always be at least as tall as the tallest element in it. If you double the amount of text in a cell, the text pushes the bottom of the cell down. As a result, the other cells in that row are also stretched. If you set the Vert of a cell to Top (in HTML terms, setting the VALIGN attribute equal to top), no matter how tall the cell gets stretched, the elements in it, be they text, graphics, or a nested table, stick to the top.

You can even stack simple tables one on top of the other. (See Figure 4-2 for an example of these techniques.) We prefer to stack or nest tables because we find it easier both in building and maintenance, but to a certain extent, it's a matter of personal preference.

Here's a high-level view of the process of building a page:

1. **Choose File⇨New in Dreamweaver MX or create a new page by using the keyboard shortcut Ctrl-N.**

2. **Choose Modify⇨Page Properties and set the page properties, including background image, marginheight, marginwidth, leftmargin, and topmargin.**

   See Book II, Chapter 2 for details on setting page properties.

Figure 4-2:
About.htm is made up of simple stacked tables, nested in a larger 2-column, 3-row table.

3. **Insert a table.**

   For the Earl's Bowlateria About Us page, we created the simple 2-column, 3-row, 760-pixel-wide table to hold the nested tables.

   See Book II, Chapter 2 for details on inserting a table.

4. **Create each nested table in turn, by inserting tables in the cells of the main table.**

5. **Fill the nested tables with content and check your work against the source PNG file by previewing in Internet Explorer and Netscape.**

   See Book II, Chapter 2 for information about previewing your page in a browser.

6. **Add rollovers to the main navigation items using the Behaviors panel.**

   See Book II, Chapter 2 for information about how to add Behaviors to graphics.

How often you save as you work is also up to you, but we'll repeat the mantra: Save early, save often. We recommend saving your work after each step in the preceding list.

Because all the pages on the site (except the home page) have the same basic structure, we can copy and paste much of the code from this page into the pages we subsequently build. In fact, we could copy and paste all the code from this page into the rest and just replace the text and images as needed. Of course, cutting and pasting isn't very efficient. That's where ColdFusion MX and dynamic sites come into play. As you see in the subsequent section, we can also turn this structure into a template that gets used with every page.

Building Dynamic Pages Using ColdFusion MX

This section is designed to give you a taste of how you can use ColdFusion MX to bring your site to life. As with most complex tools, it's better to crawl before you walk. So, in the case of your (and Earl's) nascent Web site, it's probably best to just focus on two things:

✦ Using templates to build the structure of the site

✦ Generating the product pages from a database

Together, these two simple things can become a springboard for building a much more robust and dynamic site in future iterations.

Making templates for a site

Take a look at Figure 4-3, which shows one of the product pages for the Earl's Bowlateria site, divided into its major component parts:

✦ The top navigation

✦ The left side navigation

✦ The footer

✦ The main content

The way that Earl's page is divided is typical of many Web sites. A traditional HTML site would require cutting and pasting most of the first three items across a whole series of pages. With ColdFusion MX, you can create four distinct templates — one for each of the listed elements — and then dynamically change the data in each element, depending on its location in the site.

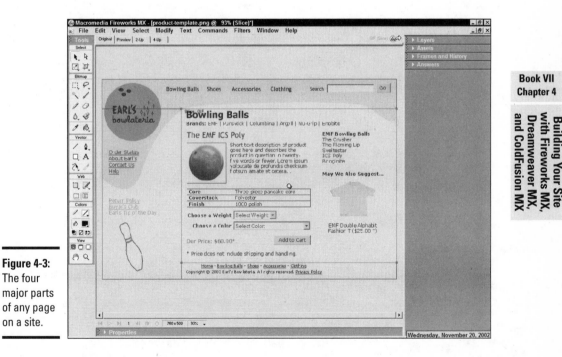

Figure 4-3: The four major parts of any page on a site.

Book VII
Chapter 4

Building Your Site
with Fireworks MX,
Dreamweaver MX,
and ColdFusion MX

To set this kind of structure up for all the pages in a site (except the home page), follow these steps:

1. Break up the HTML into its four distinct parts.

As a starting point, this process really just involves cutting and pasting the HTML into four new ColdFusion MX files, which we call leftnav.cfm, topnav.cfm, content.cfm, and footer.cfm.

Begin with the leftnav.cfm file, because in most cases, the left side of the page represents the first lines in the HTML. If you refer to Figure 4-3, not including the JavaScript code for the rollovers, here's the HTML that would make up the leftnav.cfm file:

```
<HTML>
<HEAD>
<TITLE>Earl's Bowlateria </TITLE>
<META http-equiv="Content-Type" content="text/html;
    charset=iso-8859-1">
<LINK href="csstyles.css" rel="stylesheet"
    type="text/css">
</HEAD>

<BODY background="images/bg.gif" leftmargin="0"
    topmargin="0" marginwidth="0" marginheight="0"
    onLoad="MM_preloadImages('images/t-bowling-
    balls_f2.gif','images/t-shoes_f2.gif','images/t-
    accessories_f2.gif','images/t-clothing_f2.gif')">
<TABLE width="760" border="0" cellspacing="0"
    cellpadding="0">
  <TR>
    <TD><IMG src="images/spacer.gif" width="164"
    height="29"></TD>
    <TD><IMG src="images/spacer.gif" width="596"
    height="2"></TD>
  </TR>
  <TR>
    <TD align="left" valign="top"><table width="100%"
    border="0" cellspacing="0" cellpadding="0">
      <TR>
        <TD><IMG src="images/spacer.gif" width="6"
    height="6"></TD>
        <TD align="center" valign="top"><IMG
    src="images/ball-top.gif" width="145"
    height="45"><BR>
          <A href="index.cfm"><IMG
    src="images/logo.gif" alt="EARL'S Bowlateria"
    width="145" height="56" border="0"></A><BR>
          <IMG src="images/ball-bottom.gif"
    width="145" height="44"><BR> <TABLE width="100%"
    border="0" cellspacing="0" cellpadding="2">
            <TR>
```

```
            <TD><IMG src="images/spacer.gif"
width="2" height="16"></TD>
            <TD><IMG src="images/spacer.gif"
width="135" height="2"></TD>
        </TR>
        <TR>
            <TD></TD>
            <TD valign="top"><FONT size="2"
face="Verdana, Arial, Helvetica, sans-serif">
                <A href="#" class="lnav1">Order
Status</A><BR>
                <A href="#" class="lnav1">About
Earl's</A><BR>
                <A href="#" class="lnav1">Contact
Us</A><BR>
                <A href="#"
class="lnav1">Help</A><BR>
                <IMG src="images/spacer.gif"
width="2" height="50"><BR>
                <A href="#" class="lnav2">Return
Policy</A><BR>
                <A href="#" class="lnav2">Buyer's
Club</A><BR>
                <A href="#" class="lnav2">Earl's Tip
of the Day</A></FONT></TD>
        </TR>
        <TR>
            <TD><IMG src="images/spacer.gif"
width="2" height="16"></TD>
            <TD><IMG src="images/spacer.gif"
width="135" height="2"></TD>
        </TR>
        </TABLE>
        <IMG src="images/icon-pin.gif" width="62"
height="122"> </TD>
    <TD><IMG src="images/spacer.gif" width="13"
height="6"></TD>
    </TR>
  </TABLE></TD>
```

A few things within this code are especially notable:

- **It includes only part of the** `<HTML>` **and** `<BODY>` **tags.** The close tags for these elements will be included in the footer and, as you see in Step 3, we're going to include in the index page all these templates to create a whole page.

- **The table is incomplete.** Like the `<HTML>` and `<BODY>` tags, we're going to composite the final table, so only parts of it are here in this particular file.

**Book VII
Chapter 4**

**Building Your Site
with Fireworks MX,
Dreamweaver MX,
and ColdFusion MX**

TIP

Remembering where all your table elements are located is often the trickiest part of working with templates. The best remedy: Comment your code! (Code commenting is discussed in more detail in Book I, Chapter 4.)

- **The links to URLs only include the pound (#) sign.** The reason for this is that later in the process, we're going to use ColdFusion MX to determine the locations for these URLs. Some will be static, others will be dynamic.

You follow the same basic procedure for the other three sections. Copy the remaining HTML, paste it into the new files (`topnav.cfm`, `content.cfm`, and `footer.cfm`), and then save those files.

2. **Create a ColdFusion MX page called** `index.cfm` **for each major area in the site.**

For the Earl's Bowlateria site, there can be as few as 6 of these, and as many as 12, depending on the weight given those topics along the left hand side. For ease of development, we choose six:

- Bowling Balls
- Shoes
- Accessories
- Clothing
- Search
- Miscellaneous

Each of these `index.cfm` files should be saved in a directory for that major area.

3. **Within each of the** `index.cfm` **files, you now want to call each of the templates using** `<CFINCLUDE>`.

For this part of the example, the following is the only code you need in the `index.cfm` file. The code for the products index page looks as follows:

```
<CFINCLUDE template="../templates/leftnav.cfm">
<CFINCLUDE template="../templates/topnav.cfm">
<CFINCLUDE template="../templates/content.cfm">
<CFINCLUDE template="../templates/footer.cfm">
```

4. **To preview your new template architecture, press F12 from within Dreamweaver MX.**

Figure 4-4 shows what the composited page should look like after you press F12.

Figure 4-4:
Using
CFINCLUDE,
you can
composite
your pages.

Book VII
Chapter 4

Building Your Site
with Fireworks MX,
Dreamweaver MX,
and ColdFusion MX

Making your templates dynamic

After you have your templates set up, you can begin to work within them to add additional dynamic functionality. Suppose that within each of the major sections of your Web site, you want to include a header that is appropriate to that section. In addition, when you are in a given section, you want the rollovers in the top navigation for the current section to be static in their rollover state. This is a common, simple example of an opportunity to add dynamic functionality.

You can approach this situation in a number of ways. As your site grows, or as the complexity of it grows, you may find new approaches that are more appropriate. The beauty of ColdFusion MX is that you can always accomplish the same task in more than one correct way.

The method we propose is simple and straightforward and uses the same products page from earlier in this chapter as the test case:

1. **In the products** index.cfm **page, create a variable called** section **and give it a value of** BowlingBalls.

The code for assigning the value to the variable looks as follows, and the variable should be above your include files in the `index.cfm` page (the ones from the previous section):

```
<CFSET section = "BowlingBalls">
```

This variable is going to be used to let ColdFusion MX and the templates know that they're now working in the products section of the site. Setting variables and their values is covered in Book VI, Chapter 5.

2. **In** `topnav.cfm`, **use** `<CFIF>` **and** `<CFELSE>` **to swap images, depending on your location in the site.**

   Here's the HTML that's used to represent the bowling ball rollover in `topnav.cfm`:

```
                <TD align="left" valign="middle">
<A href="../bowling-balls.cfm"
onMouseOver="MM_swapImage('bowlingballs','','../
images/t-bowling-balls_f2.gif',1)"
onMouseOut="MM_swapImgRestore()">
<IMG src="../images/t-bowling-balls.gif"
alt="Bowling Balls" name="bowlingballs" width="86"
height="16" border="0" id="bowlingballs"></A></TD>
```

   We want this content, which includes a call to the rollovers that are managed with JavaScript, to appear only when the user is *not* in the Bowling Balls section of the site. When the user is in the Bowling Balls section, we want to just show the rollover state for the current section. This can be achieved using a `<CFIF>` and a `<CFELSE>` tag to evaluate whether or not the current section is defined as `BowlingBalls`. If it is, the static image will be displayed, and if not, the image with the rollover will appear. Here's how the code looks:

```
<CFIF section is "BowlingBalls">
<IMG src="../images/t-bowling-balls_f2.gif"
    alt="bowlingballs" width="86" height="16"
    border="0">
<CFELSE>
<A href="../bowling-balls.cfm"
    onMouseOver="MM_swapImage('bowlingballs','','../
    images/t-bowling-balls_f2.gif',1)"
    onMouseOut="MM_swapImgRestore()">
<IMG src="../images/t-bowling-balls.gif"
    alt="Bowling Balls" name="bowlingballs" width="86"
    height="16" border="0" id="bowlingballs"></A>
</CFIF>
```

   If we do this for the other navigational items in the `topnav.cfm` file, when users move from section to section on the site, the proper image for that section will be static.

Creating image rollovers using Dreamweaver MX is covered in more detail in Book II, Chapter 7.

3. **Add a dynamic section heading using** `<CFSWITCH>`.

   The following code provides you with the four basic cases for each of the sections in `topnav.cfm`:

```
<CFSWITCH expression = "#section#">
<CFCASE value="BowlingBalls">
    <CFSET SectionHeader = "Bowling Balls">
</CFCASE>
<CFCASE value="Shoes">
    <CFSET SectionHeader = "Shoes">
</CFCASE>
<CFCASE value="Accessories">
    <CFSET SectionHeader = "Accessories">
</CFCASE>
<CFCASE value="Clothing">
    <CFSET SectionHeader = "Clothing">
</CFCASE>
</CFSWITCH>
```

   In this code, the `<CFSWITCH>` tag tells ColdFusion MX that it's going to evaluate the variable called `#section#` (which was defined in the index page). Then, each of the `<CFCASE>` tags evaluates the variable. Finally, if the value of the variable `#section#` equals the value in the `<CFCASE>` tag, whatever is in between that specific `<CFCASE>` `</CFCASE>` is what is passed to ColdFusion MX. In this case, a new variable called `SectionHeader` is set to a string that represents the name of each section.

   The `<CFSWITCH>` and `<CFCASE>` tags offer an alternative to using `<CFIF>` and `<CFELSE>`. Although you can use `<CFIF>` and `<CFELSE>` to perform this kind of operation, the `<CFIF>` and `<CFELSE>` tags are more server intensive. As your site begins to grow, this means that the `<CFIF>` and `<CFELSE>` tags take longer to process and can slow down your site. So, as a matter of good development, you're better off using `<CFSWITCH>` and `<CFCASE>`.

4. **In your content page, output the value for** `SectionHeader`.

   In the case of Earl's product page, that value would be "Bowling Balls." The code to get the output of `SectionHeader` looks like this:

```
<P class="sectionhead">
<CFOUTPUT>#SectionHeader#</CFOUTPUT></P>
```

   Put this code in your HTML where the Product Section name goes (right above the product information in the main content area).

5. Press F12 to preview your page.

You need to do this same customization for all the elements on your site that are section-specific but are not selected from a database.

You can add all your page-specific variables within the same switch, keeping all your work in a contained space that's easy to find and update.

When you've gotten the hang of this methodology, you'll be getting all your templates up and running in no time.

Generating product pages from a database

Check out Figure 4-5. It shows a basic product database being designed for Earl's Bowlateria. Table 4-1 lists the final fields and what data they contain. With this information, we can build the product page that you see in the content area of Figure 4-4.

Figure 4-5: Building Earl's product database.

Table 4-1	Columns in Earl's Bowling Balls Table
Column	*Description*
Name	Name of the product
Company	Company that makes the product
Image	Name of the image file
Price	Regular price for the product
Salesprice	Sales price for the product
Desc	Text description of the product
Core	Type of bowling ball core
Coverstock	Coverstock type
Finish	Type of finish
CategoryID	ID that will be used in the categories table to associate the product with other products
ProductID	A unique identifier for this product

Here's a simple way to generate the content dynamically using a database. Again, you can approach this in many ways, but we chose this one because of it's ease:

1. **Create three SQL queries using** `<CFQUERY>`, **one for the listing of products, one for the specific product being displayed, and one to capture the related product IDs.**

   The query for the product information may look something like this:

   ```
   <CFQUERY datasource="Products" name="ProductQuery">
   SELECT name, company, image, price, desc, core,
       coverstock, finish
   FROM Bowling_Balls WHERE productID = "#ProductID#"
   </CFQUERY>
   ```

   In this case, the variable *#ProductID#* determines which product to display. Ideally, you pass that variable in the URL string, as follows:

   ```
   http://www.loungeboy.com/products/index.cfm?productid=
       SomeString
   ```

2. **Create the outputs in the content template.**

   You need to do this for all elements on the page. We only need one `<CFOUTPUT>` tag for all of the product information:

   ```
   <CFOUTPUT query="ProductQuery">
   ```

Book VII
Chapter 4

Building Your Site
with Fireworks MX,
Dreamweaver MX,
and ColdFusion MX

That tag surrounds all the HTML for the product information, and within it, we include the output variables from the query, such as #desc# for the product description.

3. **Press F12 to preview your pages as you're building them.**

When you have your product pages displaying the way you want, you should take both the queries and the HTML and put them in a separate file. Then, as part of your <CFSWITCH>, you can use a <CFINCLUDE> to show that file for the Bowling Ball products. This will help you to distinguish these product pages from other products which may have different page designs, such as clothing or accessories.

Posting and Testing

You should use the Dreamweaver MX Preview in Browser command often as you build pages. Remember, you can edit the browser list to include all the browsers you have on your computer. (You should have Internet Explorer and at least one version of Netscape Navigator.) This will allow you to have a pretty good idea of how your pages look in at least two browsers before you upload them to your remote server.

Test your site locally, so if you need to make tweaks, you don't need to keep uploading revised pages. There may be certain functionality you can't test locally or that is easier to test on a remote server, but you should be able to test most of the site on your local server. When you're sure the site is good to go, use Dreamweaver MX or an FTP client to upload your site to your remote server. The process of using Dreamweaver MX to upload your site is described in detail in Book II, Chapter 3.

If you have an existing site already, you may want to create a "staging environment" on your remote server. That can be as simple as creating a folder for all the new material. Name the folder test or some such thing, and browse to it by using your current URL plus a slash and the folder name (for example, http://www.earlsbowlateria.com/test).

If you don't have an existing site, but have your URL set, you can upload your site to the main directory where it will reside, but temporarily rename your home page file to something like index2.htm (or index2.cfm), leaving your "Coming Soon" page, if you have one, as index.htm. That way, users won't accidentally stumble across your site before you're ready to go live.

When your site is up, check it out on a few different computers. View the site using the major browsers on the Mac as well as on a couple of versions of the major browsers on Windows machines if you can. Before you go live, you should test your site and ensure that you have addressed the following issues:

✦ Make sure that all the links work.

✦ Check to see that all the text is correct, up-to-date, and free of typos.

✦ Ensure that all the images are in place and properly sized.

✦ Verify that all the multimedia components function properly.

Going Live

Going live is the culmination of the process of building a site. Whether you go live by changing the name of a file to `index.htm` or by updating a DNS entry, when you go live, your site is available to anybody with a Web browser. If you're building the site for yourself or your business, getting the site built and on the Web is not the end, but the beginning.

Just because your site is online doesn't mean people can find it. Publicizing your site, getting high rankings on search engines, and so on, is beyond the scope of this book. (See *Creating Web Pages All-in-One Desk Reference For Dummies,* by Emily Vander Veer, for great information on publicizing your site.)

Don't forget to maintain your site. Whether your site is static or dynamic, chances are you want to keep people coming back. So keep the content on your site fresh. Macromedia Studio MX is there to help, whether you're adding new pages or replacing content on old ones.

Macromedia Studio MX gives you all the power you need to create a rich, compelling Web site. What you do with that power is up to you. So get some compelling content together and get to work!

**Book VII
Chapter 4**

**Building Your Site
with Fireworks MX,
Dreamweaver MX,
and ColdFusion MX**

Index

Numerical

A

S

T

W

FOR DUMMIES®

A world of resources to help you grow

TRAVEL

0-7645-5453-0

0-7645-5438-7

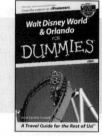

0-7645-5444-1

Also available:

America's National Parks For Dummies
(0-7645-6204-5)
Caribbean For Dummies
(0-7645-5445-X)
Cruise Vacations For Dummies 2003
(0-7645-5459-X)
Europe For Dummies
(0-7645-5456-5)
Ireland For Dummies
(0-7645-6199-5)

France For Dummies
(0-7645-6292-4)
Las Vegas For Dummies
(0-7645-5448-4)
London For Dummies
(0-7645-5416-6)
Mexico's Beach Resorts For Dummies
(0-7645-6262-2)
Paris For Dummies
(0-7645-5494-8)
RV Vacations For Dummies
(0-7645-5443-3)

EDUCATION & TEST PREPARATION

0-7645-5194-9

0-7645-5325-9

0-7645-5249-X

Also available:

The ACT For Dummies
(0-7645-5210-4)
Chemistry For Dummies
(0-7645-5430-1)
English Grammar For Dummies
(0-7645-5322-4)
French For Dummies
(0-7645-5193-0)
GMAT For Dummies
(0-7645-5251-1)
Inglés Para Dummies
(0-7645-5427-1)

Italian For Dummies
(0-7645-5196-5)
Research Papers For Dummies
(0-7645-5426-3)
SAT I For Dummies
(0-7645-5472-7)
U.S. History For Dummies
(0-7645-5249-X)
World History For Dummies
(0-7645-5242-2)

HEALTH, SELF-HELP & SPIRITUALITY

0-7645-5154-X

0-7645-5302-X

0-7645-5418-2

Also available:

The Bible For Dummies
(0-7645-5296-1)
Controlling Cholesterol For Dummies
(0-7645-5440-9)
Dating For Dummies
(0-7645-5072-1)
Dieting For Dummies
(0-7645-5126-4)
High Blood Pressure For Dummies
(0-7645-5424-7)
Judaism For Dummies
(0-7645-5299-6)

Menopause For Dummies
(0-7645-5458-1)
Nutrition For Dummies
(0-7645-5180-9)
Potty Training For Dummies
(0-7645-5417-4)
Pregnancy For Dummies
(0-7645-5074-8)
Rekindling Romance For Dummies
(0-7645-5303-8)
Religion For Dummies
(0-7645-5264-3)

Available wherever books are sold. Go to www.dummies.com or call 1-877-762-2974 to order direct

Macromedia® Studio MX All-in-One Desk Reference For Dummies®

Cheat Sheet

Keyboard shortcuts for opening and closing panels in Fireworks MX

Panel	Keyboard Shortcut
Tools	Ctrl+F2
Properties	Ctrl+F3
Answers	Alt+ F1
Optimize	F6
Layers	F2
Frames	Shift+F2
History	Shift+F10
Styles	Shift+F11
Library	F11
URL	Alt+Shift+F10
Color Mixer	Shift+F9
Swatches	Ctrl+ F9
Info	Alt+ Shift+F12
Behaviors	Shift+F3

For Dummies: Bestselling Book Series for Beginners

Macromedia® Studio MX All-in-One
Desk Reference For Dummies®

Cheat Sheet

Document-related view buttons in Dreamweaver MX

Button/Tool	Name	What You Can Do
	Show Code View button	Enables you to view the HTML page code full screen
	Show Code and Design View button	Allows you to view the HTML page code and the Document window at the same time
	Show Design View button	Enables you to view the Document window full screen
	Server Debug	Runs the page through the server in the work-space window rather than in the browser
	Live Data View	Allows you to test your dynamic content in the workspace window rather than in the browser
	File Management button	Click and then select Get to retrieve files from the Web site host or select Put to send files to the host
	Preview/Debug in Browser button	Click and select to preview or debug in IE or Navigator
	Refresh	Reloads your page
	Reference button	Click to open the Reference panel for CSS, HTML, and JavaScript assistance
	Code Navigation	Allows you to set breakpoints in your code to stop the program from executing its code. Used for debugging applications
	View Options button	Click to select tools (such as Visual Aids and the Ruler) to assist you in viewing your site